The Making of Saint Louis

THE MAKING OF
SAINT LOUIS

Kingship, Sanctity, and Crusade
in the Later Middle Ages

M. Cecilia Gaposchkin

Cornell University Press

ITHACA AND LONDON

Publication of this book has been aided by a grant from the Medieval Academy of America.

First published 2008 by Cornell University Press

Printed in the United States of America

Library of Congress Cataloging-in-Publication Data
Gaposchkin, M. Cecilia (Marianne Cecilia), 1970–
  The making of Saint Louis : kingship, sanctity, and crusade in the later Middle Ages /
M. Cecilia Gaposchkin.
     p. cm.
  Includes bibliographical references and index.
  ISBN 978-0-8014-4550-7 (cloth : alk. paper)
    1. Louis IX, King of France, 1214–1270—Cult.   2. Canonization—Political aspects—
France—History—To 1500.   3. Church and state—France—History—To 1500.   4. France—
Kings and rulers—Religious aspects.   5. France—Church history—987–1515.   I. Title.
  DC91.5.G37 2008
  944'.023—dc22   2007052329

Cornell University Press strives to use environmentally responsible suppliers
and materials to the fullest extent possible in the publishing of its books. Such
materials include vegetable-based, low-VOC inks and acid-free papers that are
recycled, totally chlorine-free, or partly composed of nonwood fibers. For further
information, visit our website at www.cornellpress.cornell.edu.

Cloth printing   10 9 8 7 6 5 4 3 2 1

FOR CHRIS, IN MEMORIAM

Contents

Illustrations

Maps, Diagram, and Tables

Acknowledgments

I thank first Geoffrey Koziol, my doctoral advisor, and now friend. He remains the best reader I know, and his willingness to continue reading for me, long after I finished my degree, is an act of considerable generosity.

The debt I owe to Elizabeth A. R. Brown is immense. Her influence is evident on every page, her shared interest in the topic and her challenges to my conclusions have led repeatedly to reassessment and further discoveries. Anyone who knows her work and her generosity will recognize how much poorer my own work would be without her input, both published and personal.

Sean Field, whose work on and interest in Louis' sister Isabelle shares so many questions with mine on Louis, has read every chapter, often multiple times, has become my "Capetian confidant," an able critic, and a generous friend.

Christopher MacEvitt and Walter Simons, have both, over the years, read and commented on the entire manuscript, and I have been uncommonly fortunate to have two such good friends in colleagues at my own institution. Phyllis Katz has been of tremendous support, not least for her help with difficult Latin. I owe much to William Chester Jordan for his quiet interest in my work. Caroline Smith, Daisy Delogu, Andrew Hughes, Father Chrysogonus Waddell, and John Coakley commented on individual chapters. David D'Avray, whom I have never met in person, graciously volunteered to go over sermon transcriptions. Samantha Kelly's response to my treatment of sermons at the Davis Seminar was invaluable.

Harvey Stahl (†2002), Robert Brentano (†2003), and Charles Wood (†2004) are no longer here for me to thank, though I wish to acknowledge their deep generosity to me as scholars and mentors while I was in graduate school and immediately after finishing.

Early versions of chapters 2 and 4 previously appeared in the *Journal for Medieval History* (2003) and in *Majestas* (2002). Invitations to present various elements of my work at earlier stages came from William Jordan (the Davis Center), Susan Boynton (New York Liturgy Society), Larissa Taylor (Renaissance Society of America), Tom Madden (Conference on the Crusades), and Meredith Fluke (Branner Forum). At Dartmouth, the John Sloan Dickey Center included me in their manuscript review program, and I extend my gratitude to Walter Simons, Carl Estabrook, Sean Field, Jane Carroll, Phyllis Katz, Roberta Stewart, Andrea Tarnowski, Bill Summers, Christianne Hardy-Wohlforth, and especially to Sharon Farmer and Kay Brainerd Slocum for reading the manuscript and participating in the review seminar. The manuscript was substantively changed at this stage, and I am deeply indebted to everyone's feedback. All errors are, of course, my own.

I also thank Allen Hockley, Kevin Reinhart, Jane Carroll, and Lauren Clarke, who, at Dartmouth, have enriched my life as a medievalist and as a teacher. My work would have been impossible without the help of the Dartmouth Library and the Interlibrary Loan staff. I owe John Ackerman at Cornell University Press great thanks for all his work and patience in seeing me through this process. I am greatly indebted to the office of the Dean of Faculty at Dartmouth College for financial support, and to the Medieval Academy for enabling publication as part of their subvention program. I want also to recognize the aid and influences of Tom Brady, Elizabeth Theta Brown, Heather Burrows, Daniel Cravens, Emily Dalgarno, Consuelo Dutschke, Daniel Gaposchkin, Alyce Jordan, Gàbor Klaniczay, Laura Lovett, Thomas Madden, Stephen Murray, Patrick Nold, Monika Otter, Dana Polanichka, Alexa Sand, Jill Savage, Patricia Stirnemann, and John Zaleski.

My parents, Anne and Mike, have always managed to be interested in the obscure details of my arcane work. It is a great and unbounded sadness that my eldest brother, Christopher Geoffrey, whose unending confidence in me always made me into a better and more able version of myself, did not live to see me complete this project. The book is dedicated to his memory. To Paul I owe far too much to be able to express here. To Michael I owe unexpected joy.

Abbreviations

Bibliographic

AASS
: *Acta sanctorum.* Edited by Jean Bolland, Jean Carnandet et al. 70 vols. Paris: Victorem Palme, 1863. Reprint, Brussels: Cultures et Civilizations, 1965.

AH
: Blume, Clemens, and Guido Maria Dreves, eds. *Analecta hymnica medii aevi.* 55 vols. Leipzig: Reisland, 1886. Reprint, 1961.

BHL
: *Bibliotheca hagiographica latina antiquæa et mediæa æatatis.* Brussels, 1898.

B.VIII
: Boniface VIII, "Sermones et bulla de canonisatione sancti Ludovici, regis Francorum," in Bouquet, Martin, ed. *Recueil des historiens des Gaules et de la France.* Paris, 1738. Reprint, Farnborough, UK 1967. Vol. 23, 148–160.

BLQRF
: "Beati Ludovici vita: et veteri lectionario extracta," in Bouquet, Martin, ed. *Recueil des historiens des Gaules et de la France.* Paris, 1738. Reprint, Farnborough, UK 1967. Vol. 23, 160–167.

Bréviaires
: Leroquais, Victor. *Les bréviaires manuscrits de bibliothèques publiques de France.* 5 vols. Paris: Macon Protat Frères, 1934.

GB *vita*
: Geoffrey of Beaulieu, "Vita ludovici noni," in Bouquet, Martin, ed. *Recueil des historiens des Gaules et de la France.* Paris, 1738. Reprint, Farnborough, UK 1967. Vol. 20, 1–27.

Glor. reg.
: *Gloriosissimi regis,* unedited vita of Saint Louis. BHL nos. 5047 (fourteenth-century version) 5042 (fifteenth-century version).

HLF
: *Histoire littéraire de la France.* 41 vols. Paris: Imprimerie Nationale, 1832–1974.

Jackson *Ordines*
: Richard A. Jackson, ed., *Ordines Coronationis Franciae: Texts and Ordines for the Coronation of Frankish and French Kings and Queens in the Middle Ages.* 2 vols. Philadelphia: University of Pennsylvania Press, 1995–2000.

Joinville	Jean de Joinville, *Vie de Saint Louis*. Edited by Jacques Monfrin. Paris: Garnier, 1995. Cited by paragraph markers (§).
	Unless noted, translations have been taken from: *The Life of St. Louis*. Translated by René Hague from the text edited by Natalis de Wailly. New York: Sheed and Ward, 1955.
LCB *procès*	Louis Carolus-Barré, *Le procès de canonisation de Saint Louis (1272–1297): Essai de reconstitution*. Edited by Henri Platelle. Collection de l'École Française de Rome 195. Rome: l'École Française de Rome, 1994.
LMLO	Hughes, Andrew. *Late Medieval Liturgical Offices: Texts*. Edited by the Pontifical Institute for Mediaeval Studies. *Subsidia Mediaevali* 23. Toronto, 1994.
MOPH	*Monumenta Ordinis fratrum praedicatorum historica*. 27 vols. Rome: 1896–.
PL	Migne, J.-P., ed. *Patrologia cursus completus, Series latina*. Paris, 1844–1891.
RHF	Bouquet, Martin, ed. *Recueil des historiens des Gaules et de la France*. 24 vols. Paris, 1738. Reprint, Farnborough, UK 1967.
Sacramentaires	Leroquais, Victor. *Les sacramentaires et les missels manuscrits des bibliothèques publiques de France*. 3 vols. Paris, 1924.
Schneyer	Schneyer, Jean-Baptist. *Repertorium der lateinischen Sermones des Mittelalters für die Zeit von 1150–1350*. 11 vols. Münster, 1969–1973.
Schneyer CD	Schneyer, Jean-Baptist. *Repertorium der lateinischen Sermones des Mittelalters für die Zeit von 1350–1500*. Electronic resource, CD-ROM. Münster, 2001.
WC *vita et actibus*	William of Chartres, "De vita et actibus inclytae recordationis regis francorum ludovici et de miraculis," in Bouquet, Martin, ed. *Recueil des historiens des Gaules et de la France*. Paris, 1738. Reprint, Farnborough, UK 1967. Vol. 20, 28–44.
WSP *sermo*	H.-François Delaborde, "Une oeuvre nouvelle de Guillaume de Saint-Pathus," *Bibliothèque de l'École des Chartes* 63 (1902): 261–88.
WSP *vie*	Guillaume of Saint-Pathus. *Vie de Saint Louis*. Edited by H. François Delaborde. *Collection de textes pour servir à l'étude et à l'enseignement de l'histoire* 27. Paris: A. Picard, 1899.
YSD *gesta*	Yves of St.-Denis, "Gesta Sancti Ludovici Noni, Francorum Regis, auctore monacho sancti dionysii anonymo," in Bouquet, Martin, ed. *Recueil des historiens des Gaules et de la France*. Paris, 1738. Reprint, Farnborough, UK 1967. Vol. 20, 45–57.

SHELF-MARKS

Arsenal	Paris, Bibliothèque de l'Arsenal
BL	London, British Library
BM	Bibliothèque Municipale
BNF	Paris, Bibliothèque Nationale de France
Mazarine	Paris, Bibliothèque de la Mazarine
Vat	Bibliotheca Apostolica Vaticana

<small>LITURGICAL OFFICES</small>

Ben	Benedictus antiphon
CA	Compline antiphon
Cap	Chapter reading
EO	*Exultemus omnes* (Office for the Translation of Relics)
FR	*Francorum rex* (Franciscan Office)
Invit	Invitatory antiphon
LA (1–5)	Lauds antiphons
LC1	*Lauda celestis* 1 (Cistercian office)
LC2	*Lauda celestis* 2 (Secular office)
LC3	*Lauda celestis* 3 (Saint-Denis, Saint-Germain-des-Prés office)
LDR	*Ludovicus decus regnantium* (Secular/Dominican Office)
LH (1–5)	Lauds hymn (five strophes)
MA (1–9/12)	Matins antiphon
Mag	Magnificat antiphon
MH (1–5)	Matins hymn (five strophes)
MRV (1–9/12)	Matins responsory
MR (1–9/12)	Matins response
MV (1–9/12)	Matins verses
NL	*Nunc laudare* (Dominican Office)
OA	Octave antiphons
Oct	Octave
V	First Vespers
VA (1–5)	Vespers antiphons
VH (1–5)	Vespers hymn (five strophes)
W	Second Vespers

Unless noted, nonbiblical translations are my own, and biblical translations are taken from the Douay-Rheims Bible.

The Making of Saint Louis

Introduction

On August 11, 1297, at the papal palace in Orvieto, Pope Boniface VIII canonized Louis IX of France as a confessor of the church. This finished a week of elaborate papal ceremonial celebrating Louis' inscription in the catalogue of saints. In a sermon preached on the same day he issued the bull of canonization, the pope took as his theme the opening antiphon for the Christmas office, *Rex pacificus magnificatus est*—the pacific king is exalted. The language drew on passages from the Old Testament praising Solomon, but here the pacific king referred directly to Christ.[1] Boniface thus made implicit reference to two of the great legitimizing tropes of medieval kingship—comparison with Old Testament kings and reference to Christic kingship. But Boniface also insisted that King Louis, so glorified, exalted not the French monarchy, but rather God and the glory of the church. This touched on the critical tension in the very notion of a royal saint—saintliness is essentially otherworldly, whereas kingship is rooted in the exercise of temporal power. Boniface's sermon thus raises a number of issues: What role did kingship play in the conceptualization of Louis' sanctity? To what extent did this reflect on the institution of the monarchy? To what ends was the sanctified figure of Saint Louis directed once canonized? Why exactly did people think Louis was a saint?

Louis had died twenty-seven years earlier, in 1270, while besieging the Muslim city of Tunis on his second crusade. As king, between 1226 and 1270, he had accrued the reputation for piety, justice, and good rule and had mounted two crusades. From the very moment of his death, moves were made to begin

1. RHF. vol. 23, 152; René Jean Hesbert and Renatus Prévost, *Corpus Antiphonalium Officii* (Rome, 1963), vol. 3, 446, no. 4657 (Vigilia Nat. Domini). Cf. 1 Kgs. 10:23, 2 Chr. 9:22. LCB *procès*, 291–292, n. 29.

the canonization process by which his sanctity would be officially confirmed. Canonization was pushed by the Capetian and Angevin royal houses, the papacy, and elite churchmen of the realm, and dozens of men and women testified to miracles that he effected as a saint. But even with such strong support, the canonization took more than a quarter-century to accomplish, and when finally promulgated it was of great note for a number of reasons.

The first is that Louis' canonization confirmed Capetian claims of holy lineage and saintly authority. Louis' successors, Philip III (1270–1285) and Philip IV ("the Fair," 1285–1314), had lobbied hard for the canonization in order to secure the prestige and legitimacy that a dynastic and royal saint would convey to the monarchy. The English crown had Edward the Confessor (can. 1161). The Germanic realms had Henry II (can. 1152) and Charlemagne (canonized by an antipope in 1165). But for all their claims to sacral authority the Capetians had yet lacked this most potent marker of spiritual legitimacy—a royal saint. Philip the Fair lost no time in evoking his grandfather, once canonized, as a sanctifying legitimator of royal policy, and for a long time thereafter Saint Louis served as the touchstone for Capetian, and later Valois, authority.

And so, the canonization was a coup for the French monarchy, especially because, in 1297, Louis was the first king canonized in more than a century.[2] Before the development of formal canonization processes the early Middle Ages had seen a number of kings as saints, confirmed not by the papacy but by the local episcopacy.[3] However, by the time the papacy had cleaved to itself the exclusive authority to make saints and had overseen the formalization and institutionalization of canonization, the age of the king-saint was waning. This was in part because the process of canonization itself was becoming more cumbersome and, perhaps, because a post-Gregorian papacy was increasingly cautious about offering spiritual sanction to lay, especially royal, authority. Though popes did canonize a number of royal figures in the twelfth century, they were rarer than in an earlier age, and none, save Louis, were confirmed in the thirteenth. Louis was also the last king of the Middle Ages to be canonized. He thus represented the end of an age, the last truly medieval king, the last king who embodied the ideals of virtue articulated and, by this time, vetted by the church.

Moreover, given the centralized institutionalization of canonization and the politics of papal and royal power, papal authorization of royal sanctity necessarily had political dimensions. This was never quite so true as in 1297, when

---

2. Robert Folz, *Études sur le culte liturgique de Charlemagne dans les églises de l'Empire* (Paris, 1951); Bernhard Scholz, "The Canonization of Edward the Confessor," *Speculum* 36 (1961): 38–60; Robert Folz, "La chancellerie de Frédéric Ier et la canonisation de Charlemagne," *Le Moyen Âge* 70 (1964): 13–31.

3. Robert Folz, *Les saints rois du Moyen Âge en occident (VIe–XIIIe siècles)* (Brussels, 1984); Gábor Klaniczay, *Holy Rulers and Blessed Princesses: Dynastic Cults in Medieval Central Europe*, ed. Lyndal Roper and Chris Wickham (Cambridge, 2002).

Louis was canonized as a direct result of an attempt to resolve the escalating dispute between Philip the Fair and Boniface VIII in the great "church-state" conflict of the period. Despite sincere conviction in Louis' sanctity, even contemporaries recognized the political nature of the canonization, and it is likely that without the immediate political pressures in which Louis' canonization was a bargaining motivator, his canonization might well never have gone through. This underscores the important point that, while the notion of sanctity may speak to a culture's ideals and spiritual aspirations, the institutional pressures and imperatives that produced saints included vested secular interests that cannot be fully disentangled from religious motivations.

One of the ironies of 1297 is that the papacy gave the French monarchy this symbol of spiritual legitimacy at precisely the point when it may have needed it least. The thirteenth century had witnessed the waning of papal authority as a kind of inverse reflection of the ascendant power of the European monarchies. With the addition of Normandy and Provence in the first half of the thirteenth century, France emerged as preeminent in Europe. Louis IX himself was pivotal in the consolidation of Capetian power. Louis' son, Philip III, and his grandson, Philip IV, continued this centralization and institutionalization of royal authority. As part of this process the crown asserted its independence from the papacy and its sovereignty over the church in France, and no king was more adamant about this than Philip the Fair. Indeed, this conviction is what led to the conflict between the king and the pope that resulted in Louis' canonization, because Philip had pushed what he claimed as his sovereign right to tax the French clergy over the pope's objections. To many, the canonization seemed like a political sop by a weakened pope to an increasingly assertive monarch.

At the same time, kingship was becoming increasingly inimical to sainthood. The tension between the spiritual ideals of sanctity and the actual realities of secular rule had always animated the formulation of royal sainthood. But at no time was the tension greater than at the end of the thirteenth century, when kings were claiming sovereignty and saints were espousing poverty. Earlier kings could be revered as saints because they died ("martyrdom"), because they played an important role as apostles of the faith in the Christianization of their kingdom, or because they had led chaste and pure lives. But the paradigms of sanctification that had allowed men like Edmund Martyr of East Anglia (d. 978) or Canut of Denmark (d. 1086) to be revered as saints, or even Wenceslaus of Bohemia (d. 935), Ladislas of Hungary (d. 1095), and Edward the Confessor (d. 1066), were inapplicable once Saint Francis (d. 1226) and the religiosity he has come to embody had infused sanctity with the virtue of ascetic suffering and poverty. It was also inapplicable in a context where France itself had been long Christian and where the monarchy was considered the most powerful in Europe. The question, then, is what exactly was it that constituted Louis' sanctity, and what place was carved out for it among the competing paradigms of virtue at the turn of the fourteenth century?

Areas of Inquiry

This book traces the process by which Louis was turned from a king into a saint, looks at how contemporaries understood his saintly kingship and his royal sanctity, and traces the shape of his cult in the two generations following his death. These are issues that have received sporadic and often focused but rarely sustained attention, despite the fact that Louis remains the most emblematic, if also the least representative and the most paradoxical, of saint-kings. Yet the question of Louis' sanctity is of undeniable importance, given Louis' high profile as a saint both in the Middle Ages and in our own interpretations of late medieval sanctity and of monarchy, for the role Saint Louis continues to play in French national memory, and for how a saint of the universal church became a symbol of monarchy. The issues raised by Louis' sanctity and his cult therefore illuminate a number of broader spheres of historical inquiry: the construction of the memory of Louis, the nature of sanctity in the later Middle Ages, and the evolution of Capetian kingship.

Constructing Louis

The sanctification of Louis IX constituted the early stage in the process by which Saint Louis became one of the canonical figures of French identity, a repository of communal, national, and historical identity—one of Pierre Nora's *Lieux de mémoire* (though not one that received an essay in the collection).[4] My story here focuses on the period not only during which the identity of *Saint* Louis took shape, but which also constituted a moment of transition for the Middle Ages itself, as the papacy and the Christian universalism its claims represented seemed to recede, as the elements within the church took on national characteristics and loyalties, as kingdoms became countries and kings became sovereign, as the institutions and ideologies of monarchies changed, as the Levantine crusades folded in on themselves, and as the sociology of sainthood shifted increasingly away from a model that could accommodate a king.[5]

Colette Beaune and Jacques LeGoff have both discussed the construction and memorialization of Louis during this formative period. Beaune first raised the issue in her influential study *Birth of an Ideology* (original publication 1985, translated 1991) as part of a series of icons that fed developing ideals of

---

4. Pierre Nora, ed., *Realms of Memory*, 3 vols. (New York, 1996–1998). Louis plays an important role in Alain Boureau's article on "the king"; Alain Boureau, "Le roi," in *Lieux de mémoire*, ed. Pierre Nora (Paris, 1986), vol. 3, part 3, 785–817 (translated as Alain Boureau, "The King," in *Rethinking France; Les lieux de mémoire*, ed. Pierre Nora [Chicago, 2001–], vol. 1, 181–191).

5. Joseph R. Strayer, *On the Medieval Origins of the Modern State* (Princeton, N.J., 1970); Francis Oakley, *The Western Church in the Later Middle Ages* (Ithaca, N.Y., 1979); Norman Housley, *The Later Crusades, 1274–1580: From Lyons to Alcazar* (Oxford, 1992); André Vauchez, *Sainthood in the Later Middle Ages*, trans. Jean Birrell (Cambridge, 1997); William C. Jordan, *Unceasing Strife, Unending Fear: Jacques de Thérines and the Freedom of the Church in the Age of the Last Capetians* (Princeton, N.J., 2005); Alain Boureau, *La religion de l'état: La construction de la République étatique dans le discours théologique de l'Occident médiéval (1250–1350)* (Paris, 2006).

French identity and nationhood in the fourteenth and fifteenth centuries.[6] Her third chapter dealt with the role that the figure of Saint Louis came to play in the development of national consciousness as a symbol of Frenchness, on one hand, and in particular ways for particular groups and constituencies, on the other. She discussed in broad terms how Louis came to represent justice and crusading in a portrait largely advanced by mendicant biographers, then showed how to special interest groups he could symbolize, for instance, "fiscal freedoms" and "sound coinage" (to the nobility), or "gallican liberties" (for the monarchy). Beaune argued for the importance of these symbols in constructing notions of Frenchness and for the flexibility of these symbols—the ability for these inclusive and unifying symbols, in their specifics, to mean different things to different people. This flexibility in turn explained both their power and their importance in constructing (and for historians, reconstructing) ideology. Beaune recognized how deeply Louis' valorizing impact depended on his sanctity. More recently Jacques LeGoff, in his 1996 biography of Louis, asked whether we as historians could even get at who Louis IX was.[7] LeGoff began with a historical and chronological discussion of Louis' life and reign (part 1), and then discussed, source by source, the different ways in which Louis was represented, a process LeGoff usefully termed "the production of royal memory" (part 2).[8] LeGoff explored how different people, drawing on personal identities and competing historical frameworks, represented Louis in diverse ways. He drew mainly on the principal hagiographic sources that have long been at the root of our understanding of the period's interpretation of Louis' sanctity. LeGoff's interest was aimed at deconstructing the source tradition to get at the "real Saint Louis," but he ends, finally, by questioning whether this is possible. Like Beaune, LeGoff argued that Louis' sainthood was an integral aspect of what he came to represent for contemporaries and near contemporaries writing about him.[9]

Royal Sanctity

As a saint-king Louis was not unique in the Middle Ages, and the issue of his identity as a saint feeds into the larger issue of the "royal saint" and developing notions of sanctity generally in the Middle Ages. The work on the phenomenon of royal sanctity and its inverse corollary, sacral royalty, had largely

6. Colette Beaune, *Naissance de la nation France* (Paris, 1985), 126–164; Beaune, *The Birth of an Ideology: Myths and Symbols of Nation in Late-Medieval France*, trans. Susan Ross Huston (Los Angeles, 1991), 90–125, 327–330. I hereafter cite the English translation.

7. Jacques LeGoff, *Saint Louis* (Paris, 1996).

8. In a sense, LeGoff "constructed" Louis in the first part and then "deconstructed" him in the second. His third and final part consisted of a series of discrete essays dealing with various aspects of Louis in history—Louis as a suffering saint, Louis as a feudal king, Louis and sacral kingship, and so forth.

9. In a slightly earlier article (1991) LeGoff addressed the question of Louis' sanctity. See Jacques LeGoff, "La sainteté de Saint Louis: Sa place dans la typologie et l'évolution chronologique des roi saints," in *Fonctions de saints dans le monde occidental (IIIe–XIIIe siècle): actes du colloques* (Rome, 1991), 285–293.

focused on the many king-saints of early medieval history.[10] These kings were characterized by their weak Christianity, often achieved sanctity through martyrdom or death, and came from newly Christianized lands.[11] Explanations of this have ranged from the argument (no longer in favor) that royal sanctity in the early medieval period was a Christianized transmutation of an earlier, non-Christian, sacral kingship, to the idea that the church sought to bolster struggling Christian governments by giving spiritual sanction to Christian rulers in newly Christianized areas. Both explanations were rooted in the recognition that royal sanctity emerged first not in France or Italy but on the periphery of Christian Europe—Anglo-Saxon England and Eastern Europe.[12]

Louis IX—a strong king from the heartland of medieval Christianity—fits unevenly into most of these schemes, and only two authors have explicitly incorporated discussion of Saint Louis in comprehensive assessments of royal sanctity. The first, Robert Folz, in *Les saint rois du Moyen Âge en occidents* (1984), identified the thirty-four kings that were regarded as saints in the Middle Ages and laid out a chronological typology for the evolution of the royal saint. He observed that in the early Middle Ages saint-kings were usually men who had renounced their kingship either through martyrdom or death. Only later did the model of the just king, where kingship was an element of the saintly portrait, emerge. A few years later (1992) Folz took the same approach to saintly queens.[13] Together, his works highlighted the chronology and variability of the

10. Karl Hauck, " 'Geblütsheiligkeit'," in *Liber Floridus. Mittellateinische Studien. Paul Lehmann zum 65. Geburtstag gewidmet*, ed. Bernard Bischoff and Suso Brechter (St. Ottilien, 1950), 187–240; Frantisek Graus, *Volk, Herrscher und Heiliger im Reich der Merowinger* (Prague, 1965), 303–389; Karol Górski, "La naissance des états et le 'roi-saint'," in *L'Europe au IXe au XIe siècles*, ed. Tadeusz Manteuffel and Aleksander Gieysztor (Warsaw, 1968), 425–432; Górski, "Le roi-saint: un problème d'idéologie féodale," *Annales ESC* 24 (1969): 370–376; Janet Nelson, "Royal Saints and Early Medieval Kingship," in *Sanctity and Secularity: The Church and the World*, ed. Derek Baker (New York, 1973; repr., *Politics and Ritual in Early Medieval Europe*, London, 1986, 69–74), 39–44; Graus, "La sanctification du souverain dans l'Europe centrale des Xe et XIe siècles," in *Hagiographie, cultures et sociétés, IXe–XIIe siècles* (Paris, 1981), 559–572; D. W. Rollason, "The Cult of Murdered Royal Saints in Anglo-Saxon England," *Anglo-Saxon England* 11 (1983): 1–22; Patrick Corbet, *Les saints ottoniens: Sainteté dynastique, sainteté royale et sainteté féminine autour de l'an Mil* (Sigmaringen, 1986); Susan J. Ridyard, *The Royal Saints of Anglo-Saxon England: A Study of West Saxon and East Anglian Cults* (Cambridge, 1988), 39–44. For a broad historiographical view, see Klaniczay, *Holy Rulers*, 232–18.

11. Gábor Klaniczay, *The Uses of Supernatural Power: The Transformation of Popular Religion in Medieval and Early-Modern Europe*, ed. Karen Margolis, trans. Susan Singerman (Princeton, N.J., 1990), 79–94; Klaniczay, "The Paradoxes of Royal Sainthood as Illustrated by Central European Examples," in *Kings and Kingship in Medieval Europe* (London, 1993), 356–358, Klaniczay discusses what he calls the "mitigated form" of royal sainthood that emerged in the early Middle Ages; See also Klaniczay, *Holy Rulers*, 62–113.

12. Continuity theory: Hauck, " 'Geblütsheiligkeit' "; William A. Chaney, *The Cult of Kingship in Anglo-Saxon England: The Transition from Paganism to Christianity* (Berkeley, Calif., 1970). Royal-authority-bolstering theory: Górski, "La naissance des états et le 'roi-saint' "; Górski, "Le Roi-saint." Periphery theory: Klaniczay, *Uses of Supernatural Power*; Gábor Klaniczay, "Le culte des saints dynastiques en Europe Centrale (Angevins et Luxembourg au XIVe siècle)," in *L'église et le peuple chrétien dans les pays de l'Europe du centre-est et du nord (XIVe–XVe siècles)* (Rome, 1990), 91–93; Klaniczay, "The Paradoxes of Royal Sainthood"; Klaniczay, *Holy Rulers*.

13. Robert Folz, *Les saintes reines du Moyen Âge en Occident: VIe–XIIIe siècles* (Brussels, 1992).

phenomenon of royal sanctity along with many insights about the cults and nature of individual saints. Folz understood Louis within this scheme as an example of the confessor, the just king, and emphasized the influence of Louis' own writings on later ideals of kingship.[14] More recently, Gábor Klaniczay has revisited the issue of the development of the royal or dynastic saint (original publication 1998, translated 2002).[15] Drawing on a deep historiography of kingship and holiness, Klaniczay traced the evolution of royal sanctity through the histories and representations of royal saints from Constantine onward, following figures from Hungary and Kiev to France and England. Casting his net more broadly than Folz, Klaniczay looked not only at crowned kings and emperors but at queens and princesses and other ancillary figures attached to royal houses. This range allowed him great nuance and enabled him to fill in the gap created by Folz's analytical division between saint-kings and saint-queens. This was the gap of the missing saints-kings of the thirteenth century. What Klaniczay found was that the royal saints of this century were by and large princesses, not kings. This was because the new requirements of sanctity necessitated a humility, poverty, and asceticism that were difficult to square with the requirements of successful kingship but needed not compromise the expectations of queenship.[16] While as a chivalric crusader and ascetic prince, Louis echoed models of royal sanctity in favor in the twelfth century, at the end of the thirteenth century he found a place in this new Franciscanized scheme as the "compassionate face of royal power."[17] And yet, it was precisely because, as Klaniczay has shown, royal power and active charity no longer fit together evenly that Louis stands out as the paradox.

Another aspect of Klaniczay's broad view was the extent to which royal sanctity in the later Middle Ages increasingly reflected a wider dynastic sanctity that has been labeled the *beata stirps*—the holy lineage. Klaniczay's framework outlines why, as Sean Field has recently shown, someone like Louis' sister, Isabelle of France (d. 1270), was widely considered a saint by contemporaries. She refused marriage, took a vow of virginity, became a patron of Franciscan women, and thus fulfilled the patterns and expectations of saintly humility, although in this way she accrued to herself esteem and authority.[18] Louis' sanctity can thus no longer be understood exclusively in terms of his special character or charisma but rather requires an understanding of the larger context of piety and religiosity at the French court that allowed Louis to be considered a saint.

---

14. Folz, *Saints rois*, 107–113, 144–146, 168–172.

15. Klaniczay calls royal sanctity the "medieval variant of sacral kingship" (*Holy Rulers*, 4). Klaniczay's subtitle, "Dynastic Cults in Medieval Central Europe," is misleading and suggests a much narrower focus than he in fact treats.

16. Klaniczay, *Holy Rulers*, 196.

17. Ibid., 296.

18. Sean L. Field, "New Evidence for the Life of Isabelle of France," *Revue Mabillon* n.s. 13 (2002): 117–131; Field, *The Writings of Agnes of Harcourt: The Life of Isabelle of France and the Letter on Louis IX and Longchamp* (Notre Dame, Ind., 2003); Field, *Isabelle of France: Capetian Sanctity and Franciscan Identity in the Thirteenth Century* (Notre Dame, Ind., 2006).

This focus on the shape that the royal saint took in the thirteenth century specifically highlights the extent to which Louis' role as a king-saint is deeply entwined with the larger arc in the development of sanctity in the later medieval period—an arc that was deeply influenced by Saint Francis and the spirituality that he represented.[19] André Vauchez, whose *Sainthood in the Later Middle Ages* (original publication 1981, translated 1997) remains the touchstone, outlined a series of trends, including the effects of the institutionalization of canonization on sanctity; the tension between local, popular sainthood and papally recognized sainthood; and the various forms sanctity took. Vauchez traced the development of lay sanctity throughout Europe and outlined the typology of sanctity—lay and clerical, male and female, episcopal and mendicant—that was increasingly predicated on humility and penitence. Underlying these larger conclusions was the necessarily political aspects of canonization.[20]

The emergence of lay sanctity in this period was one of the most important trends in the evolving definition of religious ideals in the later Middle Ages.[21] This was rooted in the revalorization of the active life "influenced by the new spirituality based on humility, active charity toward the outcasts of fortune, and the spirit of poverty."[22] No longer was absolute chastity or virginity required of sanctity. Women were increasingly able to achieve the status of saint, as were, in some areas, men of a social class beneath the high aristocracy. No longer did one have to cloister oneself from the world to achieve saintliness. Sanctity was increasingly predicated on compassion and charity—that is, on suffering with (*compassio*) and on love (*caritas*) that was rooted in humility (*humilitas*) before God. Sanctity could be achieved by laymen and women acting in this world. And so, if as a king Louis represented a disappearing form of royal sanctity, as a layman he fit a newly emerging model of sanctity that was predicated on ascetic piety, charity, and love of the poor. The key question here is how that model of lay sanctity was reconciled with the kingship of the

19. Herbert Grundmann, *Religious Movements in the Middle Ages: The Historical Links between Heresy, the Mendicant Orders, and the Women's Religious Movement in the Twelfth and Thirteenth Century, with the Historical Foundations of German Mysticism*, trans. Steven Rowan (Notre Dame, Ind., 1995); Vauchez, *Sainthood*. For other treatments, see Pierre Delooz, *Sociologie et canonisations* (Liège, 1969); Michael Goodich, "A Profile of Thirteenth-Century Sainthood," *Comparative Studies in Society and History* 18 (1976): 429–437; Goodich, *Vita Perfecta: The Ideal of Sainthood in the Thirteenth Century* (Stuttgart, 1982); and Donald Weinstein and Rudolph Bell, *Saints and Society: The Two Worlds of Western Christendom, 1100–1700* (Chicago, 1982). For an explicit discussion of the shift in royal sanctity in this period, see Jean-Guy Gouttebroze, "Deux modèles de sainteté royale. Édouard le Confesseur et saint Louis," *Cahiers de civilisation médiévale* 42 (1999): 243–258.

20. On this issue explicitly, see also Pierre Delooz, "Politiques et canonisations," in *Les églises comme institutions politiques / Churches as Political Institutions* (1970), 203–213; and Michael Goodich, "The Politics of Canonization in the Thirteenth Century: Lay and Mendicant Saints," *Church History* 44 (1975): 294–307.

21. Grundmann, *Religious Movements*; Vauchez, *Sainthood*, 249–284, 354–386.

22. André Vauchez, "Lay People's Sanctity in Western Europe: Evolution of a Pattern (Twelfth and Thirteenth Centuries)," in *Images of Sainthood in Medieval Europe*, ed. Renate Blumenfeld-Kosinski and Timea Szell (Ithaca, N.Y., 1991), 30.

new monarchies of the later Middle Ages; how, in Louis, the paradox of saintly and royal identity was reconciled.

Capetian Kingship

If Louis' sanctity and canonization bear on the larger issue of the evolution and definition of religious and saintly ideals in the later Middle Ages, they also bear on the history of the French monarchy and Capetian kingship. Louis has always been a pivotal figure in the classic focus on kings in the practice of medieval history.[23] For the same reason that contemporaries were convinced of his sanctity, historians have long found him an attractive subject of biography, many examples of which blur the distinction between history and modern hagiography. As a king and saint, Louis IX has become one of the canonical figures of French history, revered by historians of France as the fulcrum in the auspicious development of Capetian monarchy. Among a litany of biography-hagiographies that date back to the moment of Louis' death are a small number that stand out for their enduring historical value. It was Sébastien le Nain de Tillemont who, writing in the 1680s, first pioneered scientific study of Louis IX, reconstructing Louis' life (and some aspects of his cult) directly from the documentary record; historians still rely on his hefty six-volume *Vie de Saint Louis, roi de France* for its narrative and analysis.[24] The biographies have appeared in a near continuous stream, but an expanded approach to Louis emerged only in the second half of the twentieth century, and in the last generation a number of new ones have offered modern interpretations of Louis' reign.[25] Reexamination proper began with the work of Louis Carolus-Barré, who, in a number of articles, asked new questions and pushed new perspectives; he was also interested in the cult of Louis and the canonization proceedings, and his contributions in this area—a book on which was published posthumously in 1994—were the first substantial ones since Tillemont.[26] But it was William Chester Jordan's treatment in *Louis IX and the Challenge of the Crusade* (1979) that began the process of disentangling the reign of Louis from the hagiographical patina that had so often colored it. The irony was that this approach did not distance our interpretation of Louis from the saintly and pious hue that had long informed our understanding of his person, but rather

23. See for example Robert Fawtier, *Les Capétiens et la France; leur rôle dans sa construction* (Paris, 1942).

24. Sébastien Le Nain de Tillemont, *Vie de Saint Louis, roi de France*, 6 vols. (Paris, 1847–1851). On Tillemont's method, see Sean L. Field, "The Missing Sister: Sébastien Le Nain de Tillemont's Life of Isabelle of France," *Revue Mabillon* n.s. 19 (2008): forthcoming.

25. Margaret Wade Labarge, *Saint Louis: Louis IX, Most Christian King of France* (Boston, 1968); Gérard Sivéry, *Saint Louis et son siècle* (Paris, 1983); Jean de Beer, *Saint Louis: Louis IX, un roi de justice* (Paris, 1984); Jean Richard, *Saint Louis: Crusader King of France*, ed. Simon Lloyd, trans. Jean Birrell (Cambridge, 1992), French unabridged original in 1983; Gérard Sivéry, *Louis IX: le roi saint* (Paris, 2002); Georges Bordonove, *Saint Louis* (Paris, 2006).

26. Much of Carolus-Barré's work had been published in earlier articles. For a full bibliography of Carolus-Barré's scholarship on Louis, see LCB *procès*, 11–12. In a personal communication to me in 2007, Elizabeth A. R. Brown referred to Carolus-Barré as the "godfather of modern Louis studies."

highlighted the ways in which Louis had understood his own kingship as imbued with the imperatives of Christian governance. When, after numerous articles, Jacques LeGoff published his massive biography of Louis in 1996, the
approach was different, but he also stressed the fundamental importance of the
role that the idea of Christian kingship played in shaping Louis' reign.[27]

Louis himself, although he built on ideological foundations long established,
played a pivotal role as king in the development of the ideological framework
of kingship that was part and parcel of the growth and institutionalization of
monarchy in this period.[28] Capetian kingship was deeply indebted to Carolingian and Ottonian models, although it was Suger's (d. 1151) biography of Louis
VI, "the Fat" (r. 1108–1137) in the middle of the twelfth century that marked
the renewal of an explicit construction of the symbols and attributes of French
royal authority.[29] Under Philip Augustus (1180–1223) the articulations of a
royal ideology were manifest in literature and art, drawing on a classicizing tradition, with references to the Trojan origins of the French and comparison to
Alexander the Great, as well as an emphasis on the sacralizing implications of
the coronation rites.[30] These claims grew in lockstep with royal authority, accel-
erating steadily over the course of the thirteenth century, and under Louis took
on a decidedly religious, biblical framework.[31] Notions of kingship increasingly
articulated a lineage of virtue extending back to Old Testament kings, and a

27. LeGoff, *Saint Louis*. Among the preceding articles were LeGoff, "Saint de l'église et saint
du peuple: les miracles officiels de saint Louis entre sa mort et sa canonisation (1270–1297)," in
Histoire sociale, sensibilités collectives et mentalités: Mélanges Robert Mandrou (Paris, 1985),
169–180; Jacques LeGoff, "Portrait du roi idéal," *L'histoire* 81 (1985): 71–76; Jacques LeGoff,
"Royauté biblique et idéal monarchique médiéval: Saint Louis et Josias," in *Les Juifs au Regard
de l'Histoire: Mélanges en l'honneur de Bernhard Blumenkranz*, ed. Gilbert Dahan (Paris, 1985),
157–167; LeGoff, "La sainteté de Saint Louis," 285–293.

28. This issue of the symbols, representations, and claims that went into the construction of po-
litical ideology in the Middle Ages goes back to the work of Percy Schramm and Ernst Kantorow-
icz, who traced the symbolic constructions of political authority back to the classical period. See
Ernst H. Kantorowicz, *Laudes Regiae: A Study in Liturgical Acclamations and Mediaeval Ruler
Worship*, ed. G. H. Guttridge, R. J. Kerner, and F. L. Paxson (Berkeley, Calif., 1946); Kantorowicz,
The King's Two Bodies: A Study in Mediaeval Political Theology (Princeton, N.J., 1957); and Percy
Ernst Schramm, *Der König von Frankreich: das Wesen der Monarchie vom 9. zum 16. Jahrhundert,
ein Kapitel aus der Geschichte des abendländischen Staates*, 2 vols. (Weimar, 1960). On Louis IX
specifically, William Chester Jordan, *Louis IX and the Challenge of the Crusade: A Study in Ruler-
ship* (Princeton, N.J., 1979), 182–213; and Andrew Lewis, *Royal Succession in Capetian France:
Studies on Familial Order and the State* (Cambridge, Mass., 1981), 104–133.

29. Andrew Lewis, "Suger's Views on Kingship," in *Abbot Suger and Saint-Denis: A Symposium*, ed. Paula Lieber Gerson (New York, 1986), 49–54; Suger, *The Deeds of Louis the Fat*, ed.
Richard Cusimano and John Moorhead (Washington, D.C., 1992).

30. Elizabeth A. R. Brown, "La notion de la légitimité et la prophétie à la cour de Philippe Auguste," in *La France de Philippe Auguste: le temps de mutations. Actes du Colloque international
organisé par le C.N.R.S. (Paris, 29 septembre–4 octobre 1980)*, ed. Robert-Henri Bautier (Paris,
1982), 77–111; John W. Baldwin, *The Government of Philip Augustus: Foundations of French
Royal Power in the Middle Ages* (Berkeley, Calif., 1986), 355–393.

31. Marc Bloch, *The Royal Touch*, trans. J. E. Anderson (New York, 1989), 14–18; LeGoff,
Saint Louis, 826–857; Alyce Jordan, *Visualizing Kingship in the Windows of the Ste.-Chapelle*
(Turnhout, Belgium, 2002). For recent problematization of the relationship between the development of sovereign power and its religious sanctification, see Alain Boureau, "How Christian was
the Sacralization of Monarchy in Western Europe (Twelfth–Fifteenth Centuries)?" in *Mystifying*

sacral kingship based on Christ's royalty. These ideas were bolstered by the coronation ritual and royal unction (on the model of the Old Testament kings), which provided for a sacrality manifest in the royal touch. During Louis' reign these claims were given their most sublime visual form in gorgeous iconographic programs such as those of the Ste.-Chapelle and the many illuminated manuscripts produced at the court.[32] The Ste.-Chapelle was built for the Crown of Thorns, which Louis purchased in 1238 and which was surely the most potent symbol of Christian kingship in an age attuned to passion and humility.[33]

But if Louis promoted the cult of kingship, it was his canonization and the symbol of the Capetian king-saint created by it that came to represent the core ideals of French kingship—saintly lineage, Christian virtue, sacral authority, and royal dignity. Because of this, as Elizabeth A. R. Brown in particular has shown, the monarchy, having secured Louis' canonization, was eager to foster his cult.[34] Philip the Fair, during whose reign Louis was canonized, was the first, but not the last, to promote and patronize the cult of the saint-king, both out of sincere devotion and as part of the "cult of kingship" that was becoming increasingly pronounced in this period. Louis' successors promoted Louis' cult in a way tightly linked to the cult of kingship and the development of royal authority and dynasticism in general.[35] Louis' cult was popular in

the Monarchy: Studies on Discourse, Power, and History, ed. Jeroen Deploige and Gita Deneckere (Amsterdam, 2006), 25–34.

32. Daniel Weiss, *Art and Crusade in the Age of Saint Louis* (Cambridge, 1998); Jordan, *Visualizing Kingship*; William Noel and Daniel Weiss, eds., *The Book of Kings: Art, War, and the Morgan Library's Medieval Picture Bible* (London, 2002). Harvey Stahl's long-awaited and posthumously published book must surely also be consulted: *Picturing Kingship: History and Painting in the Psalter of Saint Louis* (University Park, Penn., 2008).

33. See the works of Chiara Mercuri: "Stat inter spinas lilium: le lys de France et la couronne d'épines," *Moyen Âge* 110 (2004): 497–512; *Corona di Cristo corona di re: la monarchia francese e la corona di spine nel Medioevo* (Rome, 2004); and "Les reflets sur l'iconographie de la translation de la couronne d'épines en France," in *Reliques et sainteté dans l'espace médiéval*, ed. Jean-Luc Deuffic (Saint-Denis, 2006), 117–126. See also Meredith Cohen, "An Indulgence for the Visitor: The Public at the Sainte-Chapelle of Paris," *Speculum* 83 (2008), forthcoming.

34. Elizabeth A. R. Brown has written a series of articles on the shape that the cult of Saint Louis took, particularly during Philip the Fair's reign: "The Chapel of St. Louis at Saint-Denis," *Gesta* 17 (1978): 76; "Philippe le Bel and the Remains of Saint Louis," *Gazette des Beaux-Arts* 97 (1980): 175–182; "The Chapels and Cult of Saint Louis at Saint-Denis," *Mediaevalia* 10 (1984): 278–331; "The Prince Is the Father of the King: The Character and Childhood of Philip the Fair of France," *Mediaeval Studies* 49 (1987): 310–314; "Persona et Gesta: The Images and Deeds of the Thirteenth-Century Capetians. The Case of Philip the Fair," *Viator* 19 (1988): 225–227; and "La généalogie capétienne dans l'historiographie du Moyen Âge: Philippe le Bel, le reniement du *reditus* et la création d'une ascendance carolingienne pour Hugues Capet," in *Religion et culture autour de l'an Mil: royaume capétien et Lotharingie. Actes du colloque Hugues Capet 987–1987. La France de l'an Mil. Auxerre, 26 et 27 juin 1987–Metz, 11 et 23 septembre 1987*, ed. Dominique Iogna-Prat and Jean-Charles Picard (Paris, 1990), 199–214.

35. Elizabeth M. Hallam, "Philip the Fair and the Cult of Saint Louis," in *Studies in Church History 18 (Religion and National Identity)* (Oxford, 1982), 201–214; Anne D. Hedeman, *The Royal Image: Illustrations of the Grandes Chroniques de France, 1274–1422* (Berkeley, Calif., 1991), 63–68, 98, and throughout; Joan Holladay, "The Education of Jeanne d'Evreux: Personal Piety and Dynastic Salvation in Her Book of Hours at the Cloisters," *Art History* 17 (1994): 69–100; Gerald Guest, "A Discourse on the Poor: the Hours of Jeanne d'Evreux," *Viator* 26 (1995): 153–180.

particular among his descendants and was heavily cultivated in and around Paris.

Yet, as this book suggests, there were different loci for the promotion of Louis' sanctity and his cult, and each different locus—whether an institution or an individual—memorialized Louis in a different way, understood him to be a saint for different reasons, and conceptualized his sanctity around different, sometimes competing, notions of sanctity. Louis was a saint to the crown, and he was a saint to the Cistercians, and he was a saint to the Franciscans, but he was not necessarily the same saint to each of these groups. This speaks to the multifaceted—what Sharon Farmer calls polysemic—nature of Louis' appeal to his contemporaries.[36] This multivalent appeal points to why so many different constituencies advocated for Louis' canonization following his death. But this complex picture of competing notions of sainthood and sanctity also speaks more broadly to a vibrant, if contested, culture in which the nature of devotion, religious perfection, political ideals, and, indeed, Christian virtue were matters of dispute.

Sources

We are rarely better informed about a medieval saint than we are for Saint Louis of France. As king during the increasingly literate and prolific thirteenth century, there survives a myriad of historical sources of every genre through which to study Louis: not only his own writings and letters, acts and actions, diplomas, legal decisions, and coins but the many chronicles, poetry, and images that took him and his court as their subject. These have been plumbed since his death in writing the history of his reign and the biography of his personality.

Another type of source exists that speaks to Louis IX and the ways in which Louis appealed as a symbol of virtue to his contemporaries and near contemporaries. These are the hagiographical sources that grew out of his cult and constitute the principal source base of this study. Hippolyte Delehaye in his influential *Les légendes hagiographiques* defined hagiographical sources as not limited strictly to hagiographical lives (*vitas*) but to anything that served to describe and define the sanctity of an individual for the religious edification of the faithful.[37] These include not only the most obviously hagiographical *vitas*—such as Geoffrey of Beaulieu's *Vita et sancta conversatio* and William of Saint-Pathus' *Vie et miracles* (entitled the *Vie monseigneur saint Loys*)—but canonization documents, liturgical texts and music, feast-day sermons, image cycles in glass, manuscripts and frescoes, and miracle stories. That is, hagiography comprises all the ways in which saints were commemorated and their special virtue made evident through representation, usually though not always within a religious context and often within an ecclesiastical sphere.

36. Sharon Farmer, *Communities of Saint Martin* (Ithaca, N.Y., 1991), 2.
37. Hippolyte Delehaye, *The Legends of the Saints*, trans. V. M. Crawford (Notre Dame, Ind., 1961), 2.

I make use of some of these sources—in particular, the liturgical and sermon sources that are less well known to us and thus in the modern tradition of writing about Louis. This has the advantage not only of enriching the source base by which we understand who Saint Louis was thought to be and how his cult grew and interacted in society, but also of getting at the saint as he was lived on a daily basis, within the institutions of the court, the cloister, or the church. The hagiographical texts through which historians like Vauchez and LeGoff have parsed Louis' sanctity are rich and deep, and they are used here heavily as well. But these vitas were just one means by which Louis as a saint was manifest in the medieval world, and perhaps not the one with the greatest influence on how he was most frequently or forcefully experienced by men and women participating in devotional and ritual life. Indeed, for modern historians, the reified printed text—so easily accessible in libraries—may well distort the extent to which these very texts were known in the Middle Ages. We, as teachers and historians, know Joinville as the predominant—vibrant—view of Louis, but his text survives in a single manuscript from the fourteenth century and was discovered by a larger reading audience only in the sixteenth. Some version of this is true, too, for the other principal texts gathered and printed in the twentieth and twenty-third volumes of the *Recueil des historiens de Gaul et de la France*. In this respect, the texture, nuance, and force of representation found in these lesser-known, sometimes tricky to use, sources such as liturgical offices, hours, and sermons may offer a view into the Louis who was known, experienced, and venerated in the years around the turn of the fourteenth century. The irony is that, while today these are sources that historians are *less* familiar with, they were the more commonly known, broadly distributed, and widely available texts at the time. I want to briefly discuss the importance of liturgies and sermons and how I have approached these as sources for my construction of the cult.

Liturgy and Liturgical Sources

There were, depending on how we categorize and count them, six different liturgical offices written for Saint Louis as well as the "Hours of Louis" found in devotional books of hours.[38] They present, in a number of ways, ideal sources for examining the evolution and competing interpretations of Louis' sanctity. Andrew Hughes has heralded the potential of the liturgical office in the history of sanctity and saints' cults,[39] and interdisciplinary work by musicologists and

---

38. Texts and bibliography are found in appendices 1 and 2. See also Andrew Hughes, "The Monarch as the Object of Liturgical Veneration," in *Kings and Kingship in Medieval Europe*, ed. Anne. J. Duggan (London, 1993), 413–418; Andrew Hughes, "Late Medieval Plainchant for the Divine Office," in *Music as Concept and Practice in the Late Middle Ages*, ed. Reinhard Strohm and Bonnie Blackburn (Oxford, 2001), 79–81.

39. Andrew Hughes, "Rhymed Offices," in *Dictionary of the Middle Ages*, ed. Joseph R. Strayer (New York, 1988), vol. 10, 366–377; Hughes, *LMO: texts*; Hughes, *LMO: sources*; Hughes, "*Rex sub deo et lege: Sanctus sub ecclesia*," in *Political Plainchant? Music, Text and Historical Context of Medieval Saints' Offices*, ed. Roman Hankeln (Ottawa, forthcoming 2008).

historians has demonstrated the versatile ways in which these sources can be put to use.[40] Liturgical offices constitute a trove of source material concerning late medieval sanctity that allows us to trace the pace of a cult and the constructions of sanctity, particularly after ca. 1150, when production of these offices exploded. The new liturgical texts for Louis form part of a dynamic history of canon formation at the end of the Middle Ages, a canon that was central to the articulation of ideology and identity. Known in the Middle Ages as *historia*—the saint's story—a liturgical office advanced a focused interpretation of a saint's life.[41] As Hughes has written, "In the texts of these musical genres the essence of the liturgical celebration is crystallized and often, it seems, the most distinctive characteristics of the saint are emphasized."[42] Because multiple offices were often written for an individual saint, because it is possible to identify individual liturgies with particular institutions, and because it is possible to some extent to trace the transmission and influence of different traditions as they moved from place to place or from order to order, liturgical offices can offer evidence of varying or competing interpretations of a single saint, evolution of interpretation, or institutional values in memorialization and devotion.

In this respect, one of the advantages of liturgical sources—though one that often presents interpretive complications—is that the "use" of any particular tradition was often local and specific. There was no such thing as prescriptive use or a normative text, even among the ecclesiastical orders that strove for standardization, such as the Cistercians and the Dominicans. An office might be modified through additions, subtractions, or alterations to fit local need. Thus we can talk about the Franciscan office for Louis, but most Franciscans did not avail themselves of this rite and resorted to the common (i.e., generic) office for a confessor. Cistercians wrote an office, but it was not widely disseminated. The secular office used at the Ste.-Chapelle was embellished with an octave service, but the breviaries of most secular churches did not adopt this. When this office was adopted by Dominicans, the number of antiphons recited during first vespers was reduced from four to one. The version of the office used at St.-Denis and St.-Germain-des-Prés varied with respect to its distribution of antiphons throughout the day, and so forth.

These liturgical offices were tied up with memory and memorialization in a number of ways.[43] First, the offices themselves were produced to memorialize

40. Michael McGrade, "*O Rex Mundi Triumphator*: Hohenstaufen Politics in a Sequence for Saint Charlemagne," *Early Music History* 17 (1998): 183–219; Margot Elsbeth Fassler and Rebecca A. Baltzer, eds., *The Divine Office in the Latin Middle Ages: Methodology and Source Studies, Regional Developments, Hagiography: Written in Honor of Professor Ruth Steiner* (Oxford, 2000); J.-F. Goudesenne, *Les offices historiques ou "historiae" composés pour les fêtes des saints dans la province ecclésiastique de Reims (775–1030)* (Turnhout, Belgium, 2002); Kay Brainerd Slocum, *Liturgies in Honour of Thomas Becket* (Toronto, 2004).
41. Ritva Jonsson, *Historia. Études sur la genèse des offices versifiés* (Stockholm, 1968).
42. Hughes, "The Monarch as the Object of Liturgical Veneration," 375.
43. Virginia Reinburg, "Remembering the Saints," in *Memory and the Middle Ages*, ed. Nancy Netzer and Virginia Reinburg (Boston, 1995), 17–33.

a particular figure. This was true in the sense that all liturgy was explicitly commemorative, and the essential role of saints' liturgies was the saint's remembrance. A saint would be honored within the liturgical cycle at one or more points during the year to recall his or her virtue and sanctity to the worshipping community. After the fervor of popular devotion had died down, many saints were remembered only in the liturgical cycles by which commemoration was institutionalized. By the later Middle Ages, the term *memoria* had come to refer to the commemoration of any saint in the ecclesiastical office and to the most modest liturgical honor, indicating a reading of a mere few prayers that would not interrupt the normal liturgical cycle but would ensure that a saint would not be wholly forgotten.[44]

Second, in the aggregate, liturgical offices also formed the canonical and communal memory of a religious community or institution, defining and ultimately institutionalizing interpretations of sacred history and particular saints.[45] It was in these texts—these canonical and authoritative texts which together constituted the work of God (*opus dei*)—that values, ideals, and valorizing histories were constructed, articulated, and then rehearsed, ritually and annually. In a sense, liturgical traditions of this sort represent one of the most potent forms of Brian Stock's textual communities, serving both to define and to bound the ideals of a particular group.[46] Thus the offices for Louis demonstrate how Louis himself was remembered and sanctified in different and competing ways, and in turn they contributed to the history of institutional values and social memory. Offices are evidence both of the interpretation of that saint at a particular moment in time, often at a particular place, and, because of the cyclical and institutional nature of liturgical performance, of the solidification of memory ritually. Once incorporated into the corpus of the *opus dei* any individual liturgical rite became part of the defining canon. That is, liturgical memorialization reflected interpretation and served to create identity.

Last, the meaning evoked by the recitation of an office was inflected by associations fostered by the medieval arts of memory.[47] Churchmen drew on

44. Charles Du Fresne Du Cange, *Glossarium ad scriptores mediae et infimae latinitatis*, 7 vols. (Basel, 1762), vol. 5, 336; John Harper, *The Forms and Orders of Western Liturgy from the Tenth to the Eighteenth Century: A Historical Introduction and Guide for Students and Musicians* (Oxford, 1991), 130–131.

45. Thomas J. Heffernan, *Sacred Biography: Saints and Their Biographers in the Middle Ages* (New York, 1988); James Fentress and Chris Wickham, *Social Memory* (Oxford, 1992).

46. Brian Stock, *The Implications of Literacy: Written Language and Models of Interpretation in the Eleventh and Twelfth Centuries* (Princeton, N.J., 1983).

47. Leo Treitler, "Oral, Written, and Literate Process in the Transmission of Medieval Music," *Speculum* 56 (1981): 471–491; Andrew Hughes, "Memory and the Composition of Late Medieval Office Chant: Antiphons," in *L'Enseignement de la musique au Moyen Âge et à la Renaissance*. Colloque organize par la Fondation Royaumont en coproduction avec l'A.R.I.M.M. (Asnières-sur-Oiuse, 1987), 53–72; Mary Carruthers, *The Book of Memory: A Study of Memory in Medieval Culture* (Cambridge, 1990); Gabrielle Spiegel, "Memory and History: Liturgical Time and Historical Time," *History and Theory* 41 (2002): 149–162; Anna Maria Busse Berger, *Medieval Music and the Art of Memory* (Berkeley, Calif., 2005). The issue is treated among offices for saint-kings in Hughes, "Rex sub deo."

banks of scriptural and liturgical images, texts, and vocabulary, deeply en-
grained in memory and whose recitation and recall was fostered by the musical and scriptural associations. This meant that a single text—an evocation,
for instance, of a phrase from the Psalms—would evoke the entirety of that
Psalm and the other liturgical texts and songs thereby associated with it. The
linear narrative embedded in (most) saints' offices further fostered memorialization.[48] The same was true for the musical element, the evocation of which
might recall a whole corpus.[49] Thus, when Franciscan friars recited an antiphon in the office of Saint Louis that used vocabulary from the office of Saint
Francis (see chapter 6), the entire complex of ideas, images, and meanings associated with Francis was in turn associated with and mapped onto the figure
of Louis.

Far from representing an ossified, conservative media, the liturgical form
proved a dynamic mechanism of devotional practice, informed by changing
spirituality in a changing world. Liturgical sources not only articulated (for
them) and illuminate (for us) contemporaries' view of Louis' sainthood and
virtue, but they also contributed to the construction of identity and ideology in
the later medieval period.

Sermons and Sanctity

Once placed in the catalogue of saints and adopted in the sanctorale, Louis
became an exemplar that could be used for preaching the virtues of the Christian life.[50] If the liturgy was performed in Latin by and to members of the
clergy, sermons (though recorded in Latin) were the principal mechanism
through which the moral teachings exemplified in the lives of the saints were
conveyed, in the vernacular, to the broader audience of medieval Christian society.[51] Taken in the aggregate, sermons represent the clerical interpretation of

48. For example, Catherine Cubitt, "Memory and Narrative in the Cult of Early Anglo-Saxon
Saints," in *The Uses of the Past in the Early Middle Ages*, ed. Yitzhak Hen and Matthew Innes
(Cambridge, 2000), 503–519.

49. On chant transference, Owain Tudor Edwards, "Chant Transference in Rhymed Offices,"
in *Cantus Planus: Papers Read at the Fourth Meetings, Pecs, Hungary, September 1990* (Budapest,
1992), 503–519.

50. No exhaustive study of sermons dedicated to Louis yet exists; for existing bibliography, see
appendix 3. Studies of *exempla* based on Louis are treated in Albert Lecoy de la Marche, "Saint
Louis, sa famille et sa cour d'après les anecdotes contemporaines," *Revue des questions historiques* 22 (1877): 465–484; and LeGoff, *Saint Louis*, 363–377. Nicole Bériou discusses the mention of Louis in sermons at the French court of Philip III and IV: *L'avènement des maîtres de la
Parole: la prédication à Paris au XIIIe siècle*, 2 vols. (Paris, 1998), 306–307. For themes of royalty
in general, see Albert Lecoy de la Marche, *La chaire française au Moyen Âge: Spécialement au XI-
IIe siècle d'après les manuscrits contemporains* (Paris, 1886; reprint, Geneva, 1974), 376–403,
part of which comprises his article of 1877; and David L. D'Avray, *Death and the Prince: Memorial Preaching before 1350* (Oxford, 1994), 117–158.

51. On the cult of saints as represented in the sermon genre, see George Ferzoco, "Sermon Literature concerning Late Medieval Saints," in *Models of Holiness in Medieval Sermons* (Louvain-
la-Neuve, 1996), 103–125; and Ferzoco, "The Context of Medieval Sermons Collections on
Saints," in *Preacher, Sermon, and Audience in the Middle Ages*, ed. Carolyn Muessig (Leiden,
2002), 279–291. On sermons as a mechanism of dissemination, see Beverly Mayne Kienzle, "Introduction," in *The Sermons*, ed. Kienzle (Turnhout, Belgium, 2000), 147–159.

Louis' sanctity and, ultimately, a kind of created social and dilated memory of Louis IX. Because the sermon form constituted a mechanism for the dissemination of knowledge of Louis in the later Middle Ages,[52] and because, as recent work has demonstrated, sermons were often targeted specifically to context and audience,[53] sermons allow us a measure of the ways in which Louis, and stories about him, survived and varied in a more popular form.[54] They also allow us to trace how, and the extent to which, some of the themes elucidated in the hagiographical and liturgical texts were then taken up by later interpreters and disseminated in print, and then in word, to a broader society.

Most sermons treated here were written to be preached on Louis' feast day, August 25, and were included in volumes of *sermones de sanctis.*[55] (See appendix 3.) Generally, these sermons were intended for preaching by a priest to a congregation of clerics or laymen in the broad context of the daily mass, though evidence is often thin for exactly the context or audience for the performance of preaching. I know of fifty-one sermons written for Louis before ca. 1500, though there are no doubt more which are as yet undiscovered and uncatalogued. Some belonged to model sermon collections, and the influence of a sermon might be gleaned from the manuscript(s) in which it survives—number, type, usage—although this is indirect evidence at best. The texts are treated here as texts, and thus as only cues about the images of Louis that were disseminated, since generally little is knowable about the "if," "what," "when," and "where" of these texts as actually translated or transmitted in preaching.[56]

With sermons, we have (as with any other text) individuals, often with multivalent loyalties and particular interests, representing a view of Louis. As texts, hagiographical, liturgical, and preaching sources may reflect a broader institutional ideology or the condition or context of an individual author. The categories chosen throughout this book—"Franciscan," "Dominican," "Angevin," "royal," and so forth—are in some measure specious, designed to

---

52. On model sermon collections, see David L. D'Avray, *The Preaching of the Friars: Sermons Diffused from Paris before 1300* (Oxford, 1985).

53. Bériou, *L'avènement des maîtres*, 293–383; Jacqueline Hamesses et al., eds., *Medieval Sermons and Society: Cloister, City, University (Proceedings of International Symposia at Kalamazoo and New York)* (Louvain-la-Neuve, 1998); Carolyn Muessig, ed., *Preacher, Sermon, and Audience in the Middle Ages* (Leiden, 2002).

54. The literature on preaching in the later Middle Ages is vast and growing. The best reference is now Beverly Mayne Kienzle, ed., *The Sermon* (Turnhout, Belgium, 2000). See in particular Nicole Bériou's contribution ("Les sermons latins après 1200," 363–448) in this volume; and her *L'avènement des maîtres*. See also Lecoy de la Marche, *La chaire française*; Jean Longère, *La Prédication Médiévale* (Paris, 1983); D'Avray, *Preaching of the Friars*; and Hervé Martin, *Le métier de prédicateur à la fin du Moyen Âge 1350–1520* (Paris, 1988).

55. On the relationship between the liturgy and sermons in this period, see Maura O'Carroll, "The Friars and the Liturgy in the Thirteenth Century," in *La predicazione dei frati dalla metà del '200 alla fine del '300* (Spoleto, 1995), 201–207; Bériou, "Les sermons latins après 1200," 386–394, 412.

56. On these tensions, see Bériou, "Les sermons latins," 423–430; and Kienzle, "Introduction," 168–174.

offer different ways of understanding individual texts as contextualized in certain ways by institutional or political identity. For example, two of the Franciscan Bertrand of Tours' sermons represent themes evinced in other Franciscan sources and are discussed in chapter 6, but Bertrand wrote another sermon that, strongly dynastic, speaks more to Capetian royal ideology and should be seen in the context of his support of the monarchy. It should, thus, surely be noted that these categories of identity are not hard and fast; they are used here as "ways into" these texts, not answers to them.

The sermons represent, in my own mind, the link both actually and symbolically to the unrecoverable Saint Louis. The texts we have were not the texts that were preached, and certainly not the texts that audiences "heard" or themselves interpreted or the message that was taken away by a member of a listening audience. So the sermon form represents, in a sense, the process by which the official, controlled interpretation of Louis was let loose. The texts are (yet another) individualized interpretation of a received tradition, but one that was written down with the intention of being disseminated and perhaps being used by other preachers or clerics in their construction and then their preaching of sermons. They indicate the further fragmentation of the interpretation of Louis and the subsequent release of the image and understanding of Louis into the ether of what has been lost to history.

Plan of Inquiry

In this book I look at these sources in relationship to one another in an effort to understand why and how Louis was thought to be a saint by his near contemporaries, how he was memorialized, and how, at certain times, his image or memory was marshaled to other immediate ends. My aim has been above all to see how the story of Louis as a saint unfolded in the sources that spoke of him specifically and explicitly as a saint, tracing the idea of Louis' sanctity from his death in 1270s through his canonization in 1297 and into the first decades of the fourteenth century. This is a book, thus, about the posthumous Louis. It divides into two parts of unequal length. The first, comprising the first three chapters, is structured chronologically. These chapters follow the process by which Louis was canonized, the different constituencies that advocated for his canonization, and the process—political, interpretive, devotional, institutional—by which the king was transformed into a saint. Chapter 1 looks at the texts that were written and the arguments that were made in advance of Louis' canonization, explores the way individual memories of Louis were reconciled to tropes of late medieval sanctity, and discusses the kind of consensus that emerged about why Louis was a saint. The second chapter stops in 1297 to examine the canonization itself, weighted down as it was by the political events that surrounded and largely explain it. The third chapter traces the early establishment of the official cult. Here Philip the Fair was the central personality, as he worked to establish cult centers for Louis in and around Paris. However, Philip did not have a monopoly on Louis, and other agents took ownership of Louis and established patterns of veneration in France and elsewhere.

It is at this point that the official institutional centers of the monarchy and the papacy lost control of the representation of the Capetian saint-king. Once Boniface had given the official stamp of sanctity in 1297, the identity of Saint Louis—so carefully constructed between Louis' death and his canonization around a consensus that sought to meld the special character of the individual to the expectations of saintliness—refracted. This refraction—the multiplicity of Saint Louis (plural) that was produced from the complex interplay among memory, ideals, and loyalty—is the subject of the five chapters that constitute the second part of the book. These chapters take up again the hagiographical sources but also look in detail at liturgy and sermons. In advance of these chapters I offer a short excursus on liturgical offices, intended to clarify some of the basic terminology ("antiphons," "matins") that recur in following chapters. The fourth chapter looks at the way in which Louis was used at and by the court as a mechanism of constructing sacral kingship. The principal argument here is that Louis' sanctity was defined in terms of his rulership in a way that sanctified in general the work and the business of the king and reflected on Capetians in general. The force of this interpretation is brought to light, I hope, by comparison with the material discussed in the fifth chapter, which looks at how Louis was understood as a saint in the cloister—first among Cistercians, who played a larger role in defining Louis as a saint than we have understood, and then among the Benedictines of Paris (St.-Germain-des-Prés and St.-Denis). The sixth chapter examines the evidence for the memorialization of Louis among the Franciscans, who shied away from Louis as the king and focused on Louis the crusader. The shadow of Saint Francis himself casts a pall over the Franciscan interpretation of Louis, and the crusades highlighted virtues of renunciation and *imitatio Christi* that were at the very heart of the Franciscan worldview. The seventh chapter takes up the well-known text of Jean de Joinville. I take the view that Joinville wrote the completed text in two phases—one dating to the 1270s or 1280s, and one after 1297, probably in the first decade of the fourteenth century during which a number of stakeholders were laying claim to Louis' memory and contesting the nature of his sanctity. Joinville's text thus represents not merely Jacques LeGoff's "true Louis"[57] but one of the many refractions of the saint around 1300, at once an aristocratic view of the ideal king and the symbol by which the nobleman could resist the monarchy's claim of sanctity and sacrality for the entire lineage. The eighth chapter then returns to images of Louis associated with the court but looks at a different strand in which Louis, as a devotional focus, was model and intercessor, a symbol of dynastic lineage. This chapter begins with the liturgical office for the Translation of Louis' head, written in 1306, but looks forward, past 1328 when the Capetian dynasty died with the last son of Philip the Fair,

---

57. LeGoff, *Saint Louis*, 473–498. LeGoff's chapter on Joinville is entitled, "Le 'vrai' Louis IX de Joinville."

to the Valois dynasty, which often found cause to root its legitimacy in descent from Saint Louis. The predominant theme of this chapter is the relationship between lineage and virtue.

Throughout, I hope I have avoided the mistake of wanting to see everything as solely motivated by political self-interest, though I have often tried to understand the way in which representations of Louis reflect individualized concerns. The interpretations of Louis' sanctity and kingship were rooted in piety, and in a sincere desire to exalt him as a saint and to request his intercession. This does not mean that these presentations and interpretations were not to a large extent animated by broadly defined values and outlooks, political (or politicized) predispositions, or inherited vocabularies and rhetorical frameworks. Nor does it mean that political concerns did not sometimes motivate a particular use of Louis' sanctity. But to his devotees Louis was, above all, a saint—a figure of admiration, veneration, and intercession.

We may, by looking at the hagiographical sources in this way, be able to peel back part of the veneer of the saint that has sometimes clouded the king. A reconstruction of these sources offers, for all intents and purposes, a reconstruction of the cult of Louis in the decades immediately following his death. And it provides a great deal more texture to what historians have long understood as politicized aspects of Louis' sainthood for the French crown. I hope it also demonstrates the extent to which the veneration of Louis was not merely an act of political expediency but rather the result of intermingled devotional and ideological impulses. As such, a central claim of this book is simply that there was no single Saint Louis. He represented different things to different constituencies, institutions, or individuals in ways that on one hand, were motivated by both politics and devotion and, on the other, reveal broader ideological fissures in the religious and spiritual ideals of the later Middle Ages. As a legitimizing symbol of political authority and religious virtue, ideals of sanctity and royalty, piety and virtue, were contested in competing articulations of why Louis was a friend of God. The case of Louis thus demonstrates how the discourse of sanctity was itself a locus of politicized articulation of values and ideologies.

1
The Making of a Saint, 1270–1297

There may very well have been a sense of inevitability to Louis' canonization. Even in his lifetime, Louis IX had been considered an exemplary Christian and a saintly man. Writing before 1259, the gossipy English Benedictine Matthew Paris spoke with admiration of Louis as *pius rex* and *rex magnanimus*, calling him the pinnacle of kings.[1] The Dominican Stephen (Étienne) Bourbon (d. 1261) used Louis as a model of virtue in his *exempla* collection and praised him for taking up the cross.[2] Salimbene of Adam, recalling events he witnessed in 1248, called Louis *sanctus*, although certainly not in any technical or canonical sense.[3] Between 1256 and 1263, another Dominican, Thomas of Cantimpré, singled Louis out among all kings, of whom he was generally critical, thanking God for the gift of this great king who provided an example to all of peace, charity, and humility.[4] Even men who derided Louis, such as the poet Rutebeuf, did so for being too much of a friar and not enough of a king.[5] In the letter that Philip III wrote from Carthage announcing Louis' death less than three weeks after its occurrence, he spoke of

1. Matthew Paris, ed., *Matthæi Parisiensis, monachi Sancti Albani, Chronica majora*, 7 vols. (London, 1872), vol. 5, 442, 481. On Matthew's representation of Louis, see LCB *procès*, 296–298, and LeGoff, *Saint Louis*, 433–450.

2. Étienne de Bourbon (Stephanus de Borbone), *Anecdotes historiques, légendes et apologues, tirés du recueil inédit d'Étienne de Bourbon, Dominicain de XIIIe siècle*, ed. Albert Lecoy de La Marche (Paris, 1877), 89–90, 337–338.

3. Jordan, *Louis IX*, 182, citing fifteen different instances where Salimbene attaches the word to Louis IX.

4. LCB *procès*, 298–299. Thomas de Cantimpré, *Les exemples du "Livre des abeilles": une vision médiévale*, ed. Henri Platelle (Paris, 1997), 266–268, nos. 234–236.

5. Lester K. Little, "Saint Louis' Involvement with the Friars," *Church History* 33 (1963): 125–147; Arié Serper, "Le Roi Saint Louis et le poete Rutebeuf," *Romance Notes* 9 (1967): 134–140; J. Dufournet, "Rutebeuf et les moines mendiants," *Neuphilologische Mitteilungen* 85 (1984): 152–168.

Louis' life and acts as *sanctissimos*.[6] Soon after, the regents for the kingdom, Matthew of Vendôme and Simon of Nesle, wrote to Philip recalling Louis for his "admirable grace, which shone out like the light of the sun in the midst of the planets."[7] Troubadours from the south lamented Louis' death, one saying that the church had "never had a more loyal servant,"[8] and a northern poet spoke of God's holding the doors of paradise open for him.[9] Gregory X's first act upon his election to the papacy was to request from Louis' confessor an accounting of Louis' life in view of, in Gregory's opinion, certain canonization. Even before his canonization in 1297, some began to refer to Louis with laudatory epithets: *christianissimus* (as were all French kings), *Ludovicus Justus,*[10] and *servus Dei rex Francie benedictus*.[11] William Maire, the bishop of Angers, called Louis *sanctissimus* and, elsewhere, *très saint prince Loys,* as early as 1294.[12] Four years prior to his canonization, a redaction of the *Historia regum* said of Louis that "people say he is a saint."[13] Nuns at Longchamp, the Franciscan convent founded by Louis' sister Isabelle, had dreams of Louis' intercessions before his canonization, and pilgrims to his tomb at St.-Denis after 1271 experienced miraculous cures that they credited to his intercession.[14] But because canonizations in the late thirteenth century were rare, they were never inevitable.

The canonization process of Louis IX followed the basic norm for canonization in the second half of the thirteenth century. Saintliness in a canonical sense had become, in the course of the thirteenth century, something that the papacy determined. Proof had to be offered, testimony given, and miracles confirmed before the papacy would pledge to someone's sainthood. Between the mid-eleventh and the mid-twelfth centuries, the papacy successfully asserted its right to determine the legitimacy of a claim of sainthood.[15] The papacies of Alexander III (1159–1181) and Innocent III (1198–1216) witnessed the establishment of a process whereby the pope would institute an inquiry to be held, usually at the place of burial of the rumored saint, presumably because

6. Benjamin Guérard, ed., *Cartulaire de l'église Notre-Dame de Paris,* 4 vols. (Paris, 1850), vol. 1, 189–190.

7. Richard, *Saint Louis,* 330. The quote is from Richard, not the original source.

8. Paul Meyer, "Notice: Daspol (Vers 1270)," *Bibliothèque de l'École des Chartes* 30 (1869): 281.

9. "Et Diex li a la porte de paradis ouverte," Marquis de Villeneuve, *Histoire de saint Louis, roi de France,* 3 vols. (Paris, 1839), vol. 3, 674.

10. Jordan, *Louis IX,* 182.

11. William of Puy-Laurent, RHF, vol. 20, 775.

12. *Livre de Guillaume le Maire,* ed. Cèlestin Port (Paris, 1877), 132, 134.

13. "On dist on que il est sainz" (RHF, vol. 23, 146). Cited by Lewis, *Royal Succession,* 147 and 288, n. 210.

14. Field, *Writings,* 84–87; Percival B. Fay, ed., *Guillaume de Saint-Pathus: Les miracles de saint Louis* (Paris, 1932); Sharon Farmer, *Surviving Poverty in Medieval Paris: Gender, Ideology, and the Daily Lives of the Poor* (Ithaca, N.Y., 2002).

15. Margaret Toynbee, *Saint Louis of Toulouse and the Process of Canonisation in the Fourteenth Century* (Manchester, 1929); Eric Waldram Kemp, *Canonization and Authority in the Western Church* (London, 1948; repr., New York, 1980), 56–106; Goodich, *Vita Perfecta,* 20–47; Vauchez, *Sainthood,* 33–84.

that was the locale of the majority of miracles. The pope was generally responding to a request made by the local bishop attesting to the developing *fama* of the saint's miracles, and an inquiry would be held to determine both the quality of the saint's life and the truthfulness of his or her reported miracles. Testimony about the life of the would-be saint became increasingly important in canonization inquiries because the devil, like God, could perform wonders through his minions. Once the inquest was completed, the report (along with a summary, as the proceedings became increasingly voluminous with time) was dispatched to the curia for consideration and, after deliberation and perhaps consultation with the cardinals, a decision was made.[16] The pope would announce a successful canonization with one or more bulls, which would enjoin liturgical celebration within the diocese or region, sometimes providing the liturgical elements for the mass—the *collecta*, the *secreta*, and the *postcommunio*. Sometimes, as was the case with the canonization of Saint Louis, the pope would preach a canonization sermon to commemorate the event.[17]

After 1260 the papacy's effective control over the canonization of new saints had lengthened and regularized the increasingly legalistic process for the confirmation of new saints. The mounting cost of a successful petition often restricted new saints to those who had a powerful lobby with deep pockets—a religious order or a royal dynasty—to advocate his or her cause.[18] Under these circumstances, canonization became necessarily political. Those with interests and enough money to pursue canonization invariably constituted political forces of their own, and their stakes in the canonization of a particular saint were often as much political as they were pious. This goes far in explaining the disproportionate number of nonordained (that is, lay) saints belonging to royal families.[19] The canonizations of royal saints in the twelfth century—Edward the Confessor, Charlemagne, Ladislas of Hungary—were always championed by their dynastic successors.[20] Between 1150 and 1400 the Andechs of central Europe could boast over thirty *sancti* or *beati* from their family.[21] The canonization of Louis of Toulouse began with a request by his father, King Charles

---

16. Peter Linehan and Francisco J. Hernández, " 'Animadverto': A Recently Discovered *Consilium* concerning the Sanctity of King Louis IX," *Revue Mabillon* 66 (1994): 83–105; Michael Goodich, "The Judicial Foundations of Hagiography in the Central Middle Ages," in *"Scribere sanctorum gesta": Recueil d'études d'hagiographie médiévale offert à Guy Philippart* (Turnhout, Belgium, 2006), 627–644.

17. Theodor Klauser, "Die Liturgie der Heiligsprechung," in *Heilige Uberlieferung, Festschrift I. Herwegen* (Münster, 1938), 212–238; Stephen Kuttner, "La reserve papale du droit de canonisation," *Revue historique du droit français et étranger* 4th ser., 17 (1938): 172–228; Vauchez, *Sainthood*, 55–57.

18. Goodich, "Politics of Canonization"; Vauchez, *Sainthood*, 64–65.

19. Vauchez, *Sainthood*, 226.

20. On Edward, see Scholz, "The Canonization of Edward the Confessor." On Charlemagne, see Folz, "Chancellerie": 13–31; Robert Folz, *Le souvenir et la légende de Charlemagne dans l'Empire germanique médiéval* (Geneva, 1973). Note that it was the antipope Pascal III who canonized Charlemagne in 1165, making his saintly designation less secure. On Ladislas, see Klaniczay, *Holy Rulers*, 174–175. Their cults are all treated in Folz, *Saints rois*, 69–115.

21. Goodich, "Politics of Canonization," 295; Klaniczay, *Uses of Supernatural Power*, 111–128.

II of Anjou, to the pope.[22] After 1260 canonized lay persons came almost exclusively from "royal families politically allied to the papacy."[23] Laymen without such ties effectively had no chance of official canonization.[24] The canonization process was equally political among potential saints from the religious orders. Saint Gilbert of Sempringham's and Thomas of Cantilupe's successful canonizations were in no small part aided by the support of kings of England.[25] In Italy, an association with the Guelfs or the Ghibellines might determine whether a pious figure would be considered a saint or a heretic, and the second half of the thirteenth century witnessed the papacy's concerted promotion of anti-Ghibelline saints.[26] Likewise, candidates with pro-Spiritualist leanings were denied sainthood in the later thirteenth century.[27] The canonization of Thomas Aquinas in 1323 was pressed in part to keep the saintly power of the Franciscans and the Dominicans in balance after the canonization of the Franciscan Louis of Toulouse in 1317, though, because of Angevin support, it also provides another example of the importance of political advocacy.[28] In the first three-quarters of the fourteenth century, almost all successful claimants, lay or religious, were supported by what Vauchez termed the Franco-Angevin lobby.[29]

In this sense, Louis IX fit the profile of persons effectively canonizable in the thirteenth century, particularly in the north, where saints were culled from aristocratic and elite circles.[30] A solid reputation for piety and devotion to the church, and the backing of Philip III and Philip IV, his son and grandson, and his brother Charles of Anjou, king of Sicily, gave Louis' cause the necessary advantage. This chapter discusses the process of Louis' canonization as well as the texts written between his death in 1270 and the conclusion of the process in 1297 that sought to promote and define his sanctity. It looks at the making of a saint—at the transformation of King Louis IX of France into Saint Louis. This transformation revolved on three pivots—piety, crusades, and kingship.

This chapter makes four points. First, the efforts of the men who first described Louis' saintliness were aimed primarily at getting Louis canonized, and their texts sought largely to conform Louis to traditional tropes of sanctity revolving around piety, active charity, and love of Christ. That is, the early image of Louis as a saint was driven by an effort to have him accord with standards of sanctity that shaped his representation in certain directions, away from kingship

22. Goodich, "Politics of Canonization," 296–297; Julian Gardner, "The Cult of a Fourteenth-Century Saint: The Iconography for Louis of Toulouse," in *I francescani nel Trecento: Atti del XIV convegno internazionale, Assisi, 16–17–18 ottobre 1986* (Perugia, 1988), 182.
23. Goodich, *Vita Perfecta*, 43.
24. Goodich, "Politics of Canonization," 298; Goodich, *Vita Perfecta*, 191.
25. Vauchez, *Sainthood*, 38.
26. Goodich, "Politics of Canonization," 306; Goodich, *Vita Perfecta*, 41–42, 76, 194–195.
27. Vauchez, *Sainthood*, 76.
28. Gardner, "The Cult," 184–185.
29. Vauchez, *Sainthood*, 79–81.
30. Ibid., 173–177 and passim.

and toward piety. Second, the depiction of piety that was advanced was itself shaped by a trajectory of sanctification in the thirteenth century that emphasized active Christian work, charity, and humility—the apostolic model. Third, Louis' crusades were not valorized so much as crusades—that is, as military ventures—but rather as a mechanism of a devotional narrative of suffering and passion, which is what allowed some to argue that he was a martyr. And last, Louis' kingship was a subsidiary concern. Where kingship did emerge as an attribute of sanctity, it drew on a tradition of kingship writing that was concerned with the personal virtue of the king that was easily adaptable to a discourse of sanctity. "Rulership" is distinguished from "kingship"—that is, good kingship is predicated on piety, whereas modes of rulership are determined by effective actions of power and governing, which include the exercise of justice, the administration of peace, and waging war. Where Louis' rulership, per se, was at issue, Louis was praised for equity in judgments and an absence of favoritism that struck the lay elite, in particular, as extraordinary.

1270: The Death of Louis IX and the Rhetoric of Saintliness

Within three weeks of Louis' death, on September 12, Philip III (not yet crowned, but described as *Dei gratia Francorum rex*) wrote to French ecclesiastical institutions to announce Louis' death and to ask that prayers be said for his soul, "even if, as many believe, he may not need the intercession of another."[31] The letter's ostensible aim was to ask for prayers, but it also praised Louis for his saintly behavior, his Christian kingship, his efforts against the infidel, and the manner of his death. This deliberate characterization suggests that a plan was in place within the royal entourage from the moment of the king's death to make the case for canonization.

The letter, replete with expressions of sadness and grief, recounted the missionizing goals of the crusade to Tunis and spoke of Louis' desire to spread the Christian faith, and of his plans to capture Carthage and to obliterate the authority of the evil, barbarian, and savage Saracen race.[32] But it was mainly concerned with a description of Louis' death, a description that was decidedly hagiographical in tone. Louis was referred to conventionally as "most illustrious king of France, of pious and noble memory,"[33] but also as "esteemed by

---

31. "Licet, ut a multis creditur, aliena intercessione non egeat." For the letter, see Guérard, ed., *Cartulaire*, vol. 1, 189–190, see 191 for quotation. The letter is also printed in Duchesne, *Historiae Francorum scriptores coetanei* (Paris, 1636–1649) vol. 5, 440–441; and Gérard DuBois, *Historia Ecclesiae Parisiensis* (Paris, 1690), vol. 2, 467. The only discussion of the letter that I know of is Villeneuve, *Saint Louis*, vol. 3, 420–421. At least one contemporary writer thought Louis would need to be pardoned for his sins; Meyer, "Daspol," 283, where the troubadour Daspol, shortly after Louis' death, hopes that God will pardon the good king's sins.

32. Guérard, ed., *Cartulaire*, vol. 1, 190: "expulsa barbarie ac nephanda Sarracenice gentis eliminata spurcicia."

33. Ibid.: "pie ac preclare recordationis Ludovicus, Francie rex illustrissimus, precarissimus dominus ac genitor noster quondam."

God" and "beloved by men," with a will that was "always directed toward salvation" and a life that was "deemed to be fruitful for the entire church."[34]
Louis was "the pious king, the pacific king, the father of the poor, the refuge
of the wretched, the solace of the oppressed, an especial advocate of all religion and innocence, the zealot of justice, the defense of faith and the
church."[35] Philip hoped that he, who would next hold his father's station on
earth, might "follow in the footsteps of such and so laudable a progenitor,
imitate his examples, fulfill his counsels, [and] follow his sacred works and his
salutary writings, the merits and virtuous acts of whose life we should justly
glorify rather than mourn his death, if the force of grief permits reason."[36]
Philip spoke of "all who recognize that [Louis'] life and his acts were *most
saintly*," and explained that he was transferred from the cares of the temporal
kingdom to the glories of the eternal kingdom without end.[37] Pronouncements of a saintly life and a rapid journey to the eternal kingdom accorded
with the claim that Louis was in no need of intercessory prayers, for, as
Thomas Head has put it, "saints were people who had entered heaven—for
that is the simplest definition of sanctity—through the exercise of spiritual
power in their lives."[38]

The letter ends with a description of Louis' death, called an "inestimable in-
jury and lamentable loss to all of Christianity,"[39] that lays down basic elements that would be repeated in subsequent hagiographical accounts and that
strongly accorded with the common tropes of saints' deaths in hagiography.
Louis reached perfection after having completed labors and struggles. Weighed
down by bodily infirmity, he lay down on his bed. He received the sacraments
with great devotion, and "on Monday, on the day after that of Blessed
Bartholomew the apostle, at the same hour at which the Lord Jesus Christ son
of God, dying for the life of the world, expired on the cross, Louis, arriving at
his last hours and lying on a hair shirt and ashes, rendered his happy spirit to
the highest creator."[40] The mindfulness of this description may well represent a

34. Ibid.: "Deo dilectus, ab hominibus gratiosus," "semper dirigit ad salutem," and "cujus
vita toti ecclesie fructuosa fuisse dinoscitur."
35. Ibid., vol. 1, 190–191: "Lugent pariter universi regem pium, regem pacificum, patrem
pauperum, miserorum refugium, solatium oppressorum, totius religionis et innocentie auctorem
precipuum, zelatorem justitie, fidei et Ecclesie defensorem."
36. Ibid., vol. 1, 191: "O quis nobis daret, tenentibus locum ejus in terris, talis ac tam laud-
abilis progenitoris sequi vestigia, et imitari exempla, implere consilia, sacra ejus exequi merita et
salubria documenta, de cujus vite meritis et actibus virtuosis nobis esset non immerito gloriandum
potiusquam de morte dolendum, si rationem admitteret vis doloris!"
37. Ibid.: "Dolor quidem hic inconsolabilis censeretur, nisi de ipso certa spes ab omnibus vitam ejus ac actus sanctissimos agnoscentibus haberetur, quod jam de regni temporalis sollicitudine
sit translatus ad eternum regnum et gloriam sine fine."
38. Thomas Head, *Hagiography and the Cult of Saints: The Diocese of Orléans, 800–1200*
(Cambridge, 1990), 10.
39. Guérard, ed., *Cartulaire*, vol. 1, 190: "sed et totius christianitatis inestimabile dampnum
et lamentabile detrimentum."
40. Ibid., vol. 1, 190: "feria secunda in crastino beati Barthlomei apostoli, hora illa qua dominus Jhesus Christus Dei filius in cruce pro mundi vita moriens expiravit, ad extremam horam ve-
niens et super sacum et cinerem recubans, felicem spiritum reddidit altissimo Creatori."

deliberate modeling of Louis as a saint.[41] By dying (or, by being described as dying) wearing a hair shirt, on a bed of ashes, Louis conformed to one of the most common hagiographical tropes of western sanctity, one established in the fifth century by Sulpicius Severus' description of Saint Martin at his death, lying on a bed of ashes and uttering the words *Abrahae me sinus recepit.*[42] Suger's account of Louis the Fat (VI)'s death told of how the king wanted a cross of ashes placed on the carpet on which he lay down during his last hours.[43] The hair shirt and ashes became commonplace, almost ubiquitous, in the hagiographical deaths of eleventh- and twelfth-century monk-saints, representing the penitential aspect of sanctity.[44]

   We come here to the troublesome issue of reliability. Discussions of hagiographical texts have long been marked by the question of where truthful rendition of the subject leaves off and fictitious modeling begins, in order to reconcile the saintly subject to the trope of sainthood.[45] In other words, did Philip III say that Louis died wearing a hair shirt and lying on a bed of ashes in order to make Louis conform to what might have been thought to be a requirement of sanctity, or was Louis lying on a bed of ashes because, as a man devoted to the lives of the saints, he wanted to prepare for death as they had done?[46] Gábor Klaniczay has argued that in a number of cases saints or would-be-saints can be seen to be imitating a template of behavior and actions provided by hagiographical accounts of related or relevant saintly figures.[47] Applied here, one might suppose that Louis, because he aimed at either piety or sanctity (or both), imitated the model provided by hagiographical lives of earlier saints (or pious kings) as a guide to sanctity and piety. We know that the death of Saint Martin was on Louis' mind before his death because he referred to Martin and his death as an example in the *Enseignements* he wrote for Philip at about that time.[48] Both possibilities could, in fact, be true. That is, Philip may have included this truthful detail precisely *because* he understood that this aspect of Louis' death revealed his sanctity. Indeed, the idea that

41. An extended description of pious death, often characterized by suffering and devout evocation of God or his saints, was one of the essential characteristics of the lives of the saints, and often a substantial portion of a vita—as much as a quarter—might be devoted to its description. See Patrick Henriet, " 'Silentium usque ad mortem servaret': La scène de la mort chez les ermites italiens du XIe siècle," *Mélanges d'archéologie et d'histoire publiés par l'École française de Rome: Moyen Age* 105 (1993): 265–298; and Henriet, "Les paroles de la mort dans l'hagiographie monastique des XIème et XIIème siècles," *Histoire médiévale et archéologie* 6 (1993): 75–86.

42. PL, vol. 20, cols. 181–183.

43. Suger, *The Deeds of Louis the Fat*, 158.

44. Henriet, "Les paroles de la mort," 76–77.

45. On these issues, see Jennifer R. Bray, "Concepts of Sainthood in Fourteenth-Century England," *Bulletin of the John Rylands University Library of Manchester* 66 (1984): 40–77; and Heffernan, *Sacred Biography*, 3–37.

46. Geoffrey of Beaulieu wrote that he often read the lives of saints approved by the church (GB *vita*, 15 [ch. 23]).

47. Klaniczay, *Uses of Supernatural Power*, 95–110.

48. David O'Connell, *The Teachings of Saint Louis: A Critical Text* (Chapel Hill, N.C., 1972), 59, ch. 25. On the dating of the composition, see O'Connell, 46–49, where he suggests 1267 as the probable date of composition.

Louis may have intended the form of his death to be meaningful may be discerned from Joinville's report that Louis' son Pierre d'Alençon had told him that his father, nearing the end, had evoked Sainte Geneviève, after which "the holy king had himself laid on a bed covered with ashes."[49]

The point is that Philip immediately and deliberately made an argument for his father's sanctity. He was not the only one to move in this direction—to use the language and effect the rituals and gestures of sainthood for the now dead king. Charles of Anjou (Philip's uncle, Louis' brother, and the reigning king of Sicily) was not at the camp when Louis died, but he arrived shortly thereafter and immediately took things in hand. Geoffrey of Beaulieu said that Charles' arrival revived the flagging spirits of the army and put fear into the hearts of the enemy,[50] and it seems clear that, as the elder statesman, it was he who took over settlement negotiations with the emir, al-Mustansir, prepared the exit of the army, and laid further groundwork for Louis' sainthood. Louis' remains were boiled down (so as to separate the flesh from the body) in preparation for their return to France. Geoffrey of Beaulieu, writing well before Louis' canonization, referred to these as holy relics.[51] Charles asked Philip for the heart and the intestines, and these he had buried in the abbatial cathedral in Monreale, near Palermo.[52] Miracles were attested at this point.[53] Drawing on rituals of relic translations, the remainder was carried in a processional cortège from Tunis, to Sicily (Trapani) and then Calabria by sea, then onto to Rome, Viterbo, and Orvieto, through Tuscany and Lombardy, across the Alps, and onward to France.[54] The relics were wrapped in rich folds of silk embalmed with spices, and they ceremoniously entered Paris.[55] In the process "many miracles" were effected.[56] Philip accompanied the cortège first to Notre-Dame, and the following day, to St.-Denis, where, on May 22, 1271, the king's remains were solemnly buried in the Abbey Church of St.-Denis.[57]

Indeed, Charles was instrumental in the initial translation of Louis' relics

49. Joinville, §757.

50. GB *vita*, 24 (chs. 46–47).

51. Ibid. (chs. 46–48): "ossa sacra corporis," "sacras reliquias," "sanctas reliquias," "ipsius reliquiae," "ossium sacrorum reliquiae," "ossibus sanctis," "sacrae reliquiae."

52. There is some dispute over where Louis' heart was finally buried. See LeGoff, *Saint Louis*, 309.

53. RHF, vol. 23, 68–73; Salimbene, *The Chronicle of Salimbene de Adam* (Binghamton, N.Y., 1986), 495. Lettrone, "Sur l'authenticité d'une lettre de Thibaud, roi de Navarre, relative à la mort de saint Louis," *Bibliothèque de l'École des Chartes* 5 (1843–1844): 112.

54. RHF, vol. 20, 482–487. William of Nangis lists the following route: Tunis, Trapani, Palermo, Messina (Sicily), Calabria, Rome, Viterbo, Montefrascone, Orvieto, Florence, Bologne, Modena, Parma, Cremona, Milan, Verceil, Suse, Mont Cenis, Lyons, Mâcon, Cluny, Châlons, Troyes, Paris.

55. RHF, vol. 20, 468–469.

56. GB *vita*, 24 (ch. 47): "multa miracula ibidem cooperante Domino acciderunt." On the miracles, see Sharah Chennaf and Odile Redon, "Les Miracles de Saint Louis," in *Les Miracles Miroirs des Corps* (Paris, 1983), 53–85; LeGoff, "les miracles officiels," 169–180; and Nicole Chareyron, "Représentation du corps souffrant dans la Vie et les Miracles de Saint Louis" *Cahiers de recherches médiévales (XIIe–XVe s.)* 4 (1997): 175–187.

57. RHF, vol. 20, 468–469.

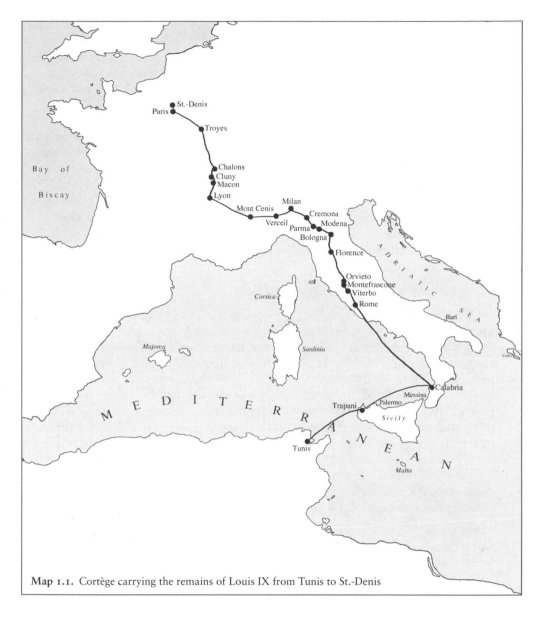

Map 1.1. Cortège carrying the remains of Louis IX from Tunis to St.-Denis

to Paris, and he would ultimately offer testimony as part of the canonization proceedings. More than anyone, Charles was interested in promoting Louis' sanctity—not in and of itself, but as part of an argument of dynastic virtue in general.[58] It was Charles' cadet line, the Angevins of Sicily, that most pushed and perfected the notion of the *beata stirps*, pulling in saintly ancestors from multiple ancestral lines and making the argument that sanctity

58. On Charles of Anjou's role in Louis' sanctification, see Jean-Paul Boyer, "La 'foi monarchique': royaume de Sicile et Provence (mi-XIIe–mi-XIVe siècle)," in *Le forme della propaganda politica nel Due e nel Trecento: relazioni tenute al convegno internazionale organizzato dal Comitato di studi storici di Trieste, dall'École française de Rome, e dal Dipartimento di storia dell'Università degli studi di Trieste (Trieste, 2–5 marzo 1993)* (Rome, 1994), 95–96.

was being funneled to, and thus concentrated in, the Angevin dynasty.[59] And so, Charles promoted not just Louis', but rather his family's sanctity in general. In the early 1280s he commissioned, for instance, a life of his (and Louis') sister, Isabelle, to lay the groundwork for possible canonization.[60] When in 1282 he testified at the proceedings into Louis' sanctity, he did not just advocate for Louis' saintliness but talked about the death of his mother, Blanche of Castile, in terms of her saintliness, and spoke of the entire family as belonging to a saintly lineage, including, he said, his two other brothers, whom he called respectively a glorious martyr (Robert of Artois) and a martyr through love (Alphonse of Poitiers). His testimony here is worth quoting: "[Blanche's] saintly soul is freed, whence the saintly root produced saintly branches, not only the saintly king [Louis] but also the count of Artois, a glorious martyr, and the count of Poitiers, [a martyr] by love."[61]

1275: Official Requests for Canonization

Upon his assumption of the papal throne in 1272, one of Pope Gregory X's first initiatives was to instigate an investigation into Louis' sanctity in view of canonization. On March 4, Gregory, who had known Louis, wrote to Louis' confessor, Geoffrey of Beaulieu, OP, to ask him to compose a vita. In this letter Gregory recalled Louis' "high merit," the "blessedness of his life," and how he should be held up "as an example of blessed living to other orthodox princes." Gregory asked Geoffrey to write about "each and every act of Louis of blessed memory" and send it as soon as possible, secretly and under cover of seal, to the curia.[62] Despite the quiet nature of Gregory's initial steps, there were broader expectations of Louis' canonization in France. In 1275 Gregory received letters from leading prelates requesting immediate consideration of the matter of Louis' canonization. The letters represent the stage in the canonization process where local ecclesiastical authorities make a request for formal

---

59. André Vauchez, "*Beata stirps:* sainteté et lignage en occident aux XIIIe et XIVe siècles," in *Famille et parenté l'Occident médiéval* (Rome, 1977), 397–496; Klaniczay, *Holy Rulers*, 298–331; Samantha Kelly, *The New Solomon: Robert of Naples (1309–1343) and Fourteenth-Century Kingship* (Leiden, 2003), 119–29.

60. Field, *Writings*, 52–53; Field, *Isabelle*, 147–148.

61. Paul Edouard Didier Riant, "Déposition de Charles d'Anjou pour la canonisation de saint Louis," in *Notices et documents publiés pour la Société de l'histoire de France à l'occasion du cinquantième anniversaire de sa foundation* (Paris, 1884), 175: "sancta illa anima soluta est, unde sancta radix sanctos ramos protulit, non solum regem sanctum, sed et comitem Atrabatensem, martirem gloriosum, et comitem Pictavensem, affectu." The fragment ends, but Riant assumed that Alphonse was a martyr by *affectu*. He is, in any event, later called "martir voluntate."

62. LCB *procès*, 17–18; Thomás Ripoll, Brémond, Antonin, *Bullarium Ordinis FF. [i.e. Fratrum] Prædicatorum: sub auspiciis SS. D.N.D. Benedicti XIII, pontificis maximi, ejusdem Ordinis* (Rome, 1729), vol. 1, no. 1, p. 503: "precelsa merita," "beatitudine vite sue, que ceteris principibus orthodoxis beate vivendi prebebat exemplum"; Augustus Potthast, ed., *Regesta Pontificum Romanorum inde ab a. Post Christum natum MCXCVIII ad A. MCCCIV*, 2 vols. (London, 1875), vol. 2, 1652, no. 20511. The letter is also printed in Marie-Dominique Chapotin, *Histoire des Dominicains de la Province de France. Le siècle des fondations* (Rouen, 1898), 648, n. 1.

consideration of a person's sainthood based on local *fama,* and they all spoke of Louis' widening reputation for sanctity. Gregory X seems at this point to have asked his legate in France, the Franciscan Simon of Brie, to begin inquiries into Louis' holiness.[63] The first letter came in June from the archbishop of Reims, who wrote on behalf of his suffragans, the bishops of Soissons, Beauvais, Noyon, Tournai, Châlons-sur-Marne, Amiens, Arras, and Senlis. Not long after, in July, the archbishop of Sens, representing his suffragans—the bishops of Chartres, Paris, Orléans, Autun, Trier, Nevers, and Meaux—did the same.[64] There were also letters (not extant) from the archbishop of Tours and "other prelates from the kingdom of France," delivered to the curia by the bishops of Chartres and Amiens.[65] By September 1275, the Dominican prior for the province of France), Jean of Châtillon, writing on behalf of all Dominicans under him, followed suit.[66] The content of the letters from Sens and Reims were essentially identical, and the Dominican letter, though using its own language, expressed tone and content so close as to suggest that its author had consulted one of the letters sent earlier that summer. This, and the fact that the letters were all dispatched in such close proximity, points to a singular and concerted effort among northern French ecclesiastics to canonize Louis.

The letters from Reims and Sens began by evoking the immense goodness of God who continuously assists the weak "in these most recent times." To this end, He arranged to "illuminate our land with new splendor." Louis was the bright light whose rays were diffused everywhere. Such a light, said the prelates, must not be concealed. Louis was called the "sun of kings, lamp of princes" whose saintly memory and celebrated fame shone throughout the world, not only in the French lands but "also in remote and foreign nations." Louis, the letters argued, showed himself to be a saint not only by the "admirable course of his life" but also by his "commendable death." He complied with the heavens and was devoted to God, and the people subject to him were faithful and pious. It ought be remembered (and not only by the people of his own kingdom) how very peacefully and with what honor he ruled such a kingdom with God's authority, and how under Louis France flourished above all other kingdoms.[67]

63. LCB *procès,* 18–19; J.-H. Sbaralea, ed., *Bullarium Franciscanum,* 4 vols. (Rome, 1759–1768; reprint, 1983), vol. 3, 241. André Callebaut, "Les provinciaux de la province de France au XIIIe siècle," *Archivum Franciscanum Historicum* 10 (1917): 338, believed that in 1273 Eudes of Rigaud, OFM, was one of three prelates directed to undertake the inquiry. There is no evidence for this that I know of, and Callebaut may have assumed that the "Archbishop of Rouen" charged by Martin IV (Simon of Brie) along with the bishops of Auxerre and Spoleto to run the canonization inquiry was Archbishop Eudes of Châteauroux. It was, in fact, William of Flavacourt (LCB *procès,* 20).

64. *Gallia Christiana,* vol. 12, "Instrumenta" cols. 78–79, no. CII (102); Guillaume Marlot, *Histoire de la ville, cité et université de Reims, Métropolitaine de la Gaule Belgique,* 4 vols. (Reims, 1843–1846), vol. 3, 815, no. 173, and discussed at 639.

65. Sbaralea, ed., *Bullarium Franciscanum,* vol. 3, 474.

66. Chapotin, *Histoire des Dominicains,* 648–649, n. 1.

67. Ibid., 648–649, n. 2.

Then the prelates came to the crux of their argument—that Louis' great virtue lay in his impulse to crusade and especially in his christomimetic death in Tunis. Louis was a zealot for the propagation of the faith. He abandoned his own inheritance and his fatherland not once but twice, "so that he might extend the name of Christ among the infidels and barbarians." He was not afraid to risk his brothers and sons and the nobles of his kingdom for the faith. Finally—the trump card—Louis "offered himself in sacrifice [*sacrificium*], so the king himself could offer repayment to the Highest King, who sacrificed himself up to God for our salvation as the acceptable victim [*hostia*] on the altar of the cross."[68] The use of the word *sacrificium* with regard to Louis, when juxtaposed to the word *hostiam*—that is, Christ, described as the King of Kings—linked Louis' death to that of Christ. By 1275 the word *hostia* referred to the bodily reenactment of Christ's original sacrifice, and the use of this language here suggests that Louis' death was such a reenactment. Thus it was that Louis died as a martyr for the Christian faith. The letter continued, calling him a glorious athlete of Christ and a faithful contestant of the cross who accepted death for the cause, and said that Louis "is not believed to have lost the palm of martyrdom, whose cause he did not abandon."[69] The archiepiscopal letter then reported miracles that had occurred at Louis' tomb and urged apostolic consideration, since it would be against the interests of the faith to hide such a light. The authors hoped for Louis' canonization for the purposes of "an increase of divine praise and glory, the laying bare of worldly pride, an edification for kings and princes, and the fruit of common devotion, and for the new grace of spiritual joys."[70]

Jean of Châtillon's letter proceeded in much the same way, saying that Louis left his homeland twice on the pilgrim's long journey, abandoned his inheritance, and—as a pilgrim and foreigner, sparing neither labor nor expense, neither himself nor his family—went with his brothers overseas in order to pursue the cause of Christ, so that he might pay back the payment to He "who worked for our salvation on the altar of the cross."[71] "From this," echoed the Dominican letter, "it is easy to believe that, even if the sword of the persecutor did not take his saintly soul, he did not lose the palm of martyrdom."[72] The argument for Louis' martyrdom in all three letters was truly extraordinary. A martyr

68. Marlot, *Histoire* vol. 3, 815–816; *Gallia Christiana*, "Instrumenta," 78.

69. Marlot, *Histoire*, vol. 3; *Gallia Christiana*, "Instrumenta," 78: "Seipsum tandem in sacrificium offerens, ut rex ipse vicem redderet summo regi, qui pro nostra salute semetipsum hostiam acceptabilem in ara crucis obtulit Deo Patri; sicque gloriosus hic athleta Christi, et crucis agonista fidelis, in agone prosecutionis dicti negotii mortem suscipiens gloriose, palmam martyrii, cujus causa non defuit, sicut pia corde sentiunt, non creditur amisisse."

70. Marlot, *Histoire*, vol. 3, 816; *Gallia Christiana*, "Instrumenta," 78–79: "speratur ad augmentum divinae laudis et gloriae, ad mundanae detectionem superbiae, ad aedificationem regum et principum, ad communis devotionis fructum, et ad novam spiritualium gratiam gaudiorum."

71. Chapotin, *Histoire des Dominicains*, 648–649, n. 2: "qui pro nostrae salutis negotio semetipsum in ara crucis."

72. Ibid.: "Ex quo facile potest credi quod etsi sanctam ejus animam gladius persecutoris non abstulit, palmam tamen martyrii non amisit."

was technically someone who had voluntarily endured persecution to the point of death. Thomas Aquinas, at about this time, had defined martyrdom as the right endurance of suffering (*passionum*) unjustly afflicted and the voluntary adherence to truth and justice to the point of death against the assaults of persecution.[73] Although popular conceptions of the crusader martyr, propounded by the *chansons des gestes,* may have called figures like Roland, dying on the battlefield, martyrs, Louis had died of illness while himself besieging the enemy. In no way could he be canonically accorded the martyr's status. The high-level ecclesiastics must surely have understood this—as Jean of Châtillon's letter uneasily revealed when he insisted that Louis was a martyr "even if the sword of the persecutor did not take his saintly soul." But Louis' passion for crusading—or his crusading "passion" (i.e., sacrifice, suffering)—does seem to have been central to his aura of saintliness in the years following his death.

Hagiography: Geoffrey of Beaulieu and William of Chartres

The most important texts in the formulation of Louis' sanctity were the hagiographical vitas that were written in promotion and defense of his canonization. Two of the three principal hagiographic accounts of Louis were written before his canonization: Geoffrey of Beaulieu's *Vita et sancta conversatio* and William of Chartres' *De vita et actibus.*[74] As clerics at the court (Geoffrey was the king's confessor), these two men, both Dominicans, were ideal witnesses to his sanctity. Both men had known Louis since before 1248 and were with him on his first crusade in Egypt. And both men were mentioned in Philip's 1270 letter as having been with the king in Tunis at the time of his death. Both authored their works as personal testimonies of the king's sanctity during the earlier stages of the canonization inquiry, and both had as their aim the success of the process.[75] Colette Beaune and Jacques LeGoff have argued that Geoffrey and William presented an image of the king's sanctity that was largely rooted in mendicant ideals of humility, piety, and service to the poor.[76]

Geoffrey of Beaulieu began his *libellus* in 1272 at Gregory X's request.[77] Geoffrey's own death in 1275 provides the *terminus ante quem* for his work.

---

73. Thomas Aquinas, *Summa Theologiae. Latin text and English translation, introductions, notes, appendices, and glossaries,* 60 vols. (Cambridge, 1964–1976), vol. 40, 42, 55, 2a 2ae, qu. 124, parts 1 and 4. See also Caroline Smith, *Crusading in the Age of Joinville* (Burlington, Vt., 2006), 99.

74. Both works are found in RHF, vol. 20, 1–27 and 27–44; and in Duchesne, *Historiae Francorum scriptores,* vol. 5, 444–465 and 466–477.

75. Geoffrey's last chapter is a plea that Louis should be counted with glory and honor among the saints (GB *vie*, 26 [ch. 52]).

76. Beaune, *Birth,* 93–95; LeGoff, *Saint Louis,* 328–344.

77. In 1272 Pope Gregory X asked Geoffrey of Beaulieu to compose a vita of Louis and have it secretly delivered to the curia. See Ripoll, *Bullarium Ordinis FF. [i.e. Fratrum] Prædicatorum: sub auspiciis SS. D.N.D. Benedicti XIII, pontificis maximi, ejusdem Ordinis,* vol. 1, 503, no. 1.

His account was hugely influential, and verbatim passages from his vita were borrowed by every hagiographical author thereafter. Rather than presenting a strictly chronological narrative (though following some chronologically guided framework), Geoffrey structured his vita around Louis' virtues.[78] Geoffrey wrote chapters on Louis' humility (7, 9), his marital chastity (11), his devotion to the religious orders (12, 14), his religious instruction of his children (13, 14), his penances (16), his austerities (17) and abstinences (18), his works of mercy and alms (19), his devotion to the divine office and prayer (21), his devotion to sermons and scripture (23), his devotion to relics (24), and his hatred of blasphemy and oath swearers (32–33). Geoffrey devoted a chapter to how Louis washed the feet of the poor (9), another chapter to how he wished to abandon the throne and enter religion (12). Geoffrey detailed Louis' confessions and bodily penances (14), that he wore a hair shirt (17), how he fed the poor at his own table (11), and how he acquired the relics of the Passion and built the Ste.-Chapelle (24). In chapter 15, Geoffrey transcribed the *Enseignements*, the advice on rule and kingship that Louis wrote for his successor, Philip III, which revealed Louis to be deeply imbued with a desire to do right as king before God, to protect and care for the poor, to serve the interests of his subjects, and to promote peace within Christian society. Chapters 25–30 treat Louis' first crusade, including chapters on his years in the Holy Land (26), his pilgrimage to Nazareth (22), and his conversion efforts (27). Geoffrey ended with several chapters on Louis' decision to take the cross again, a defense of his choice to go to Tunis, his death in the field before Carthage, the return of his bones to France, and ultimately the record of some miracles.

Geoffrey was not terribly interested in issues of kingship, but he did transcribe two items in his vita that came to represent Louis' exemplary Christian rule. The first was the *Enseignements*.[79] The second was the Great Reform Ordinance of 1254, which showed the extent to which Louis was invested in ensuring just government throughout the realm by legislating the purity and probity of his agents.[80] The ordinance exemplified the prerogatives of saintly kingship (defined by our authors as an ability to render justice equitably without regard to favoritism or self-interest) extending to the administration of the realm.[81] Geoffrey's one short chapter (only six lines long) on Louis' rule made this point explicitly. Here Geoffrey explained that Louis was as responsible as were his provosts and bailiffs for injuries done to his subjects, and for that

---

78. The absence of a strict chronological order distinguishes these early vitas as a genre from the *gesta* written soon after at St.-Denis by William of Nangis, which gave a chronological account of the political deeds of the king.

79. The critical edition is O'Connell, *Teachings*.

80. Raymond Cazelles, "Une exigence de l'opinion depuis saint Louis: la réformation du royaume," *Annuaire bulletin de la société de l'histoire de France* (1962–1963): 91–99; Louis Carolus-Barré, "La Grande ordonnance de 1254 sur la réforme de l'administration et la police du Royaume," in *Septième centenaire de la mort de Saint Louis: actes des colloques de Royaumont et de Paris (21–27 mai 1970)* (Paris, 1976), 85–96.

81. For this understanding of justice, see WC *vita et actibus*, 34; GB *vie*, 5 (ch. 6); WSP *vie*, 141 (ch. 17); Joinville, §§66–67.

reason he sent out diligent and faithful inquisitors throughout the kingdom to uncover injuries and make restitution. Even within his own household, Louis punished those proven guilty accordingly.[82]

Geoffrey's overall treatment of rule was, despite this short chapter, minimal. Indeed, he paid it so little attention that William of Chartres wrote his vita, he explained, in part because he felt Geoffrey had neglected important aspects of Louis' life, including the "prosperity of his rule, the adversity of his incarceration, and his death."[83] William did not divide his vita into chapters. But, like Geoffrey, he treated the ethical and religious behavior of Louis that, as a cleric at the royal court, he had been in a position to observe. He listed the king's ritualistic devotions during the liturgical year: Louis mortified his flesh; he despised secular, profane music; and he dressed in simple clothing, went barefoot to church, and gave alms to the poor, even when traveling in new cities. William described the king's attendance at mass and his love of sermons. Louis built the Ste.-Chapelle for the relics of the Passion and established a number of new liturgical ceremonies in their honor. He had great compassion for the poor and sick. He gave alms and founded hospitals. He founded and encouraged the reform of new monasteries, including Cluniac priories, Marmoutier of Tours, St.-Denis, St.-Benoît of Fleury, and Cîteaux. William described Louis as endeavoring to help the religious poor, called him the *pater pauperum*, and described him as obedient and devout to the church. Louis provided funds for the building of the Dominican house of Compiègne and the Franciscan convent in Paris. He gave money to support the poor.

William also treated Louis' crusades. The cleric had accompanied Louis to Egypt and into captivity in 1250. Explaining the defeat, William said it was necessary that temptation should test Louis in order to show him worthy.[84] The cleric recounted the king's negotiations with the Saracens (who were themselves impressed with Louis' integrity and courage), how the Saracens killed their own sultan and threatened to renege on their deal, and how they threatened Louis with a bloody sword. Although William's vita was not terribly influential in later accounts, it did give rise to the celebrated "breviary miracle":[85] While imprisoned, Louis was unable to recite his prayers for having lost his breviary. In this early version, a Saracen brings the king the book, evidently captured along with the king, so that he might recite vespers. William's purpose in telling the story was to underscore Louis' steadfast devotion to the

82. GB *vita*, 5 (ch. 6).

83. WC *vita et actibus*, 28. William is thought to have died before 1282 because he did not appear among the witnesses who testified at St.-Denis in 1282–1283. On William, see Louis Carolus-Barré, "Guillaume de Chartres clerc du roi, frère prêcheur, ami et historien de saint Louis," *Collection de l'École Française de Rome* 204 (1995): 51–57. Carolus-Barré remarked that it could be no coincidence (p. 55) that William's *vita* began with the same phrase that Jacques of Châtillon OP's letter of 1275 to the curia opened with: "Mirabilis in altis Dominus." They both belonged to the Dominican convent of St.-Jacques.

84. WC *vita et actibus*, 30.

85. Larry S. Crist, "The Breviary of Saint Louis: The Development of a Legendary Miracle," *Journal of the Warburg and Courtauld Institutes* 28 (1965): 319–323.

ritual forms of religious life and his commitment to Christ. As the story developed, it was God (or an angel, or a dove), not a Saracen, who delivered Louis his breviary, and the story came to demonstrate not Louis' devotion, but rather God's miraculous protection and intervention. William of Chartres was also the one who recorded how Louis, after his release from captivity, labored to pick up the dead bones of crusaders who had died on the field at Sidon in order to give them a proper Christian burial.[86] No one else, said William, could bear the task because of the putrid, horrifying smell. In all, the Dominican sought to record the moral comportment of the king's personal and public life.

William treated aspects of Louis' rule more directly than Geoffrey.[87] He lauded Louis for curbing the power of "insolent nobles" who sought to despoil the poor and for settling disputes and forestalling unjust injuries to his subjects. William connected Louis' foundation of monasteries and reforms of religious virtues to his role as a "pacific king, an especial lover of peace and of religion."[88] Also an element of his good rule was his respect for the holy church, his support of the inquisitors of heretics, his desire to banish usury and his loathing of the Jews. Indeed, with regard to Louis' persecution of heretics and Jews, William wrote of the *enquêteurs*, of Louis' care in choosing his bailiffs and seneschals that met the requirements of honesty and justice,[89] and of the reforms he introduced in the municipal government of Paris. Louis outlawed the judicial duel, did not favor personal ties when rendering justice, and sought out faithful men for his government.[90]

St.-Denis and the Canonization Inquest

Gregory X's death in 1276 and the swift turnover of popes that followed effectively halted affairs at the curia and slowed Louis' canonization.[91] Nicolas III tried to restart the process in 1278 when he commissioned Simon of Brie to again undertake the inquiry.[92] But it was not until the election in 1281 of Simon of Brie himself as Pope Martin IV that Louis' cause was again taken up by a man who, as papal legate to France after 1261, had been a friend of the king. By now, Geoffrey of Beaulieu and probably William of Chartres had completed their vitas. An impressive delegation of ecclesiastics from France went to the curia to push the new pope for the king's inscription into the catalogue

---

86. WC *vita et actibus*, 31. Salimbene made reference to this between 1282 and 1287, Salimbene, *Chronicle*, 334. The story is not found in GB, but was picked up during the proceedings and is repeated in WSP *vie*, 99–100 (ch. 11); BLQRF, 162 (lection 5); YSD *gesta*, 55 (ch. 12); and the Dominican lections of 1306 (MOPH, vol. 4, 22, L6).

87. WC *vita et actibus*, 31–34, esp. 32–33.

88. Ibid., 33: "Rex ipse pacificus, tanquam pacis ac religionis amator praecipuus, paci ac reformationi, necnon et conservationi ecclesiarum et monasteriorum omnium regni sui."

89. Ibid., 32–33.

90. Ibid., 34.

91. The following is taken from LCB *procès*, 17–28.

92. Sbaralea, ed., *Bullarium Franciscanum*, vol. 3, 368–369, dated November 30, 1278.

of saints. In November 1281 the pope instructed the archbishop of Rouen (William de Flavacourt) and the bishops of Auxerre and Spoleto (William de Grez and Roland de Parma) to conduct an inquiry into the life and miracles of Louis IX.[93] Canonization was further pressed by Charles of Anjou (Louis' brother, the king of Sicily) who, among other things, had been instrumental in Simon of Brie's election. It was about this time (February 1282) that Charles of Anjou formally provided testimony for the cause.[94] The inquest was conducted during the period from May 1282 to March 1283 at St.-Denis, the abbey church where the king's remains were buried and where most of the miracles described had occurred. Over 330 witnesses were interviewed. The inquiry into Louis' life lasted about two months, while the inquiry into his miracles lasted almost a year (arguably, in the canonization proceedings, the more important consideration).[95] Among those interviewed were the reigning king (Philip III, Louis' son), Pierre d'Alençon (another of Louis' sons), Jean de Joinville (who said he testified for two days), Matthew of Vendôme (abbot of St.-Denis), Nicholas d'Auteuil (bishop of Evreux), and a series of other witnesses, including mendicant preachers, members of the king's household, bourgeois, and nuns.[96] Other documents in support of Louis' sanctity may have been furnished for the inquest at this time, including the letter on Louis' foundation of the Abbey of Longchamp, dated to December 1282, that describes how a dove appeared at the moment when Louis laid the first stone.[97] In March 1283 the contents of the inquisition were sent to the curia for consideration, and Boniface said of these reports that more was written than a single ass was able to carry.[98] We know that at some stage a written summary was made of the inquisition's findings and approval regarding Louis' life (as opposed to his miracles), since William of Saint-Pathus refers on a number of occasions in his sermon to a (lost) vita approved by the curia, the *vita curia approbata*.[99]

There is no way to overestimate the importance of the canonization inquisition and testimony. Dozens of anecdotes were provided, which filled in the dossier of Louis' sanctity. Unfortunately, of the two copies of the proceedings— one sent to the curia, the other remaining at the Franciscan convent in Paris— only the barest fragments survive. The results of the inquisition, however, constituted the basis for a number of subsequent texts that did survive, including Boniface's canonization bull and sermons of 1297, *Beatus Ludovicus quondam Rex Francorum* (written as lections for the liturgical office), the vita written by Yves of St.-Denis sometime in the early years of the fourteenth century, the

93. Ibid., vol. 3, 475–476, dated November 22, 1281.
94. Riant, "Déposition," 162–163.
95. WSP *vie*, 4 (prologue) tells us that the former lasted from June 12, 1282, to August 8, 1282, while the latter lasted from May 1282 to March 1283.
96. LCB *procès*, 141–264, gives biographies of all known witnesses. For Joinville's testimony, see Joinville, §760.
97. Field, *Writings*, 9, 46–49.
98. B.VIII, 151–152.
99. WSP *sermo*, 270–271.

works of William of Saint-Pathus written in 1302–1303, and probably the anonymous *Gloriosissimi Regis*.[100] William of Nangis—the Dionysian historiographer who wrote an early, largely political *gesta* of Louis in the years following the completion of the canonization process—drew heavily on the work of Geoffrey of Beaulieu,[101] and Joinville also garnered materials from the proceedings (in a roundabout way) when he was polishing his account of Louis' crusade.[102]

The most valuable text in reconstructing the testimony of 1282–1283 is William of Saint-Pathus' *Vie monseigneur saint Loys*. This is a tricky text to parse—at once both "royal" and "mendicant," both incorporating the testimony of 1282–1283 and reflecting a constructed vision of sanctity that William himself sought to elucidate. William was a member of the Franciscan community and was also the confessor to Louis' widow, Marguerite of Provence, and their daughter, Blanche.[103] In 1302 Blanche asked him to compose a vita based on the records compiled at the canonization proceedings held at St.-Denis in 1282–1283, a copy of which was by 1302 housed at the Couvent des Cordeliers.[104] Although it seems William originally wrote in Latin, we possess only the French translation done in the first half of the fourteenth century. William's vita did not appear until 1302–1303, though he saw his task precisely as a reworking of the material from the proceedings of 1282–1283. He explained that a copy of the proceedings came into his hands from John of Antioch and that the veracity of the events concerning the life of Louis contained in them had been examined and approved. When William described the nature of his task, he explained that Blanche, the "devoted daughter of this same glorious Saint Louis not only pushed me to this but constrained me to copy the inquest on the attested [*jurée*] life and on the miracles of this glorious saint Louis done by the authority of the court of Rome in the time of our very

---

100. BHL. *Gloriosissimi Regis* (hereafter cited as *Glor. Reg.*) exists in two forms: one dating to ca. 1300 (BHL 4057) and one dating to the second half of the fifteenth century (BHL 5042). The earliest extant exemplar I know of the vita (BHL no. 5047) is found in a collection of the Golden Legend, Vat. Reg. Lat. 534, 242v.–246r., at 243r. An expanded version (BHL 5042) is found in Vienna ÖBN 12807, fols. 141r.–146r.; Vienna ÖNB 12706, fols. 225r.–232v.; and Brussels 197, fols. 25r.–29v. My citations for the vita are taken from Vat. Reg. Lat. 534 (BHL 4057) except where I cite the fifteenth-century version. The version of ca. 1300 (BHL 5057) formed the basis of lections for the Franciscan office and the lections for one early version of the secular office. On this last, see Rebecca A. Baltzer, "A Royal French Breviary from the Reign of Saint Louis," in *The Varieties of Musicology: Essays in Honor of Murray Lefkowitz*, ed. John Daverior and John Ogasapian (Warren, Mich., 2000), 23–25.
   101. William of Nangis, RHF, vol. 23, 310–311.
   102. On William of Nangis, see Auguste Molinier, *Les sources de l'histoire de France des origines aux guerres d'Italie (1494), III. Les Capétiens, 1180–1328* (Paris, 1903), 102. On Joinville, see the discussion in chapter 7, 185.
   103. Paulin Paris, "Le Confesseur de la Reine Marguerite, auteur de la Vie et des Miracles de saint Louis," in HLF, vol. 25, 154–177; Louis Carolus-Barré, "Guillaume de Saint-Pathus, confesseur de la reine Marguerite et biographe de saint Louis," *Archivum Franciscanum Historicum* 79 (1986): 142–152; William Courtenay, "The Parisian Franciscan Community in 1303," *Franciscan Studies* 53 (1993): 164–167.
   104. William de Saint-Pathus' text is printed in RHF, 20: 58–121, and WSP *vie*. The Latin original is lost, though elements of it were copied in William's sermon, WSP *sermo*.

holy father of good memory."[105] He said that a copy of the proceedings had been deposited at the convent for anyone who wished to verify the accuracy of his account; and he added that he saw his task not to add or embellish but to record only those things that he had seen, as they had been attested to, written down, examined, and approved by the Roman curia. William, then, saw as his task to "copy" the events attested to during the inquest. He seems to have transcribed large portions from the canonization records verbatim.[106] Repeatedly, William attributed certain stories to particular people, cited specific depositions given at the inquest, and referred explicitly to the testimony of specific witnesses.[107] He clearly saw himself as but a redactor, and it is for this reason that his *Vie et miracles* is our best evidence for the contents of the otherwise lost canonization proceedings.[108]

That said, William of Saint-Pathus did seek to organize the material according to themes and topics. In his prologue he explained that, though he has remained scrupulously faithful to the content of the inquest's report, he has not always followed a chronological narrative but rather grouped items together that were similar in theme. (This method was taken from Bonaventure's *Legenda maior* of Saint Francis.) William's chapter organization rested on the notion that all the events could be categorized according to Louis' various saintly virtues. Thus, the twenty chapters of the *Vie et miracles* include a description of Louis' wonderful manner of living (2), his firm faith (3), his strong hope (4), and so on, including a long central chapter (11) on his works of compassion, and other chapters on love, devotion, study of scripture, humility, patience, penitence, conscience, continence, honesty, clemency, and perseverance. Only one chapter (18, on his "*haute justise*") treats events that allowed specifically for a discussion of the nature of his rule. William of Saint-Pathus, in this way, imposed a mendicant (or at least clerical) vision on the interpretation of Louis' sanctity by structuring the evidence according to categories consonant with his own (mendicant) religiosity. But behind—or *within*—this imposed structure is a wider, broader discourse about Louis' life and virtues as seen by people from different walks of life—kings, bishops, knights, nuns, members of the household, residents of the town of Saint-Denis, as well as mendicant preachers (and still others)—who had testified at the canonization proceedings. Between William of Saint-Pathus' list of virtues is a series of events.

Certain themes, such as Louis' humility, piety, and acts of charity, reflected the early hagiography, but, in, for instance, chapters on his love of neighbor

---

105. WSP *vie*, 3–4 (prologue): "devote fille de cel meesmes glorieus saint Loys, ne m'eust a ce semons et meemement m'eust contreint la copie de l'enquest sus la vie jurée et sus les miracles du glorieus saint Loys fete de l'autorité de la cort de Romme el tens de beneurée memoire de nostre tres saint pere."

106. Paris, "Confesseur de la Reine Marguerite," vol. 25, 154–177, esp. 155.

107. WSP *vie* (ch. 13), citing the deposition of Ysambert; ch. 15, citing the deposition of Nicolas, bishop of Evreux; ch. 16, citing the testimony of Charles of Anjou; and ch. 17, citing the testimony of Jean of Joinville. See also LCB *procès*, 24; and Farmer, *Surviving Poverty*, 9.

108. LCB *procès*. The study is based on this premise.

(9) and his works of compassion (11), William was able to multiply example upon example. These themes accorded in general terms with mendicant influences in the larger trend in sanctity in the period. But other stories may reflect the concerns of nonclerical witnesses in 1282–1283. The sheer number of stories treating Louis' commitment to equity and to the defense of the wretched against the powerful suggests how much these impressed those of privilege who testified. In chapter 10 William recounted how Louis, after the capture of his army in 1250, refused to allow the rich to ransom themselves and the poor to languish in captivity (a story we know originated with Charles of Anjou).[109] After quoting Louis' pronouncement that he would pay the ransoms with his own funds, and noting that he did so, William commented, "This came from his great courtliness (*courtoisie*), his great loyalty, his great largesse, and his great charity."[110] Another story about the integrity of Louis' language has him described as "greatly courteous" (*merveilleusement courtois*).[111] Louis was praised for the honor with which he negotiated his release and that of his army from the Saracens. The central segment of Joinville's text, written around the same time as the inquiry although with a different aim, also exuded chivalric and aristocratic concerns and expressed amazement at Louis' integrity and honor during his captivity. When the Franciscan Jean of Samois preached the sermon for the first translation of Louis' bones at St.-Denis in 1298, he praised Louis, whom he described as the "most loyal man of his time" for keeping his word and thus his honor.[112] The importance of honor, keeping one's word, and loyalty resonated with the values of the secular, chivalric world.

A pervasive theme throughout the proceedings—the crusades—is indicated by the number of men, now aged, who had gone to Egypt with Louis in 1248 and who testified at St.-Denis in 1282. Men like Joinville, Jean of Acre, Pierre of Laon, Gui Bras (probably), Roger of Soisy, William Breton, and Hugues Porte Chape, all of whom had joined the crusade of 1250, testified to the king's zeal for crusading, and especially to the dignity with which he submitted to his captivity.[113] In these discussions, crusading was understood primarily as an element of Christian identity, a reflection of an individual Christian's probity and virtue. The east provided the context for a description of Louis' many pious works, including the refortification of cities, the burial of dead Christians, and the purchase of captives. Someone at the proceedings testified to Louis' missionary work, saying that Louis baptized forty Saracens, had these men instructed by Dominicans, and then brought them back to France to be

109. WSP *vie*, 76 (ch. 10); Riant, "Déposition."
110. WSP *vie*, 76 (ch. 10): "la quell chose li vint de grant cortoisie, de grant loiauté, de grant largece et de grant charité." See also the details in chapter 11, and 132 (ch. 17, on his "honesté").
111. WSP *vie* 133 (ch. 16).
112. Joinville, §764: "le plus loiaus home qui onques feust en son temps."
113. Jean d'Acre did not technically accompany Louis on the crusade, but he was born in Acre and met Louis there (LCB *procès*, 164–165).

married to Christian women.[114] Underlying all these recollections was always
a notion that Louis' militancy was a virtue. Someone at the proceedings recalled Louis saying that "knights should never engage in discussion about the
faith, but, if they perchance know an unbeliever (*mescreant*) they should kill
them with their own sword."[115] Joinville later recalled Louis making a similar
statement in the context of a dispute set up by the Cluniacs with local Jews.[116]
And in his memoirs written about this time, Joinville recalled how in 1250
Louis, upon learning of a Frenchman from Provins who had remained in Egypt
after the fifth crusade and converted to Islam, ordered him out of his sight:
" 'Be off with you' said the king, 'I will not speak to you.' "[117] Exhibiting a different spirit, Joinville ran after the apostate to inquire of his story.

What witnesses remembered above all about the crusades was Louis'
staunch faith in the face of persecution. Someone at the inquest recounted how
Louis refused to take an oath to deny Christ if he failed to fill his terms of the
treaty, quoting him as saying in horror "never will these words come out of
my mouth."[118] Another witness remembered that a "pagan admiral"[119] said to
him: "You are our prisoner and our slave in our prison and you speak so
haughtily? Either you do what we want of you or else you will be crucified, you
and your men [or family]."[120] Witnesses also testified to Louis' integrity in
keeping his word during negotiations with his captors.[121] Joinville, who heard
about the events from the king himself on the boat to Acre, wrote of the negotiations with the sultan and his council, was particularly impressed with this,
and spoke of how Louis had even been threatened with torture.[122]

The (rare, surviving) testimony of Charles of Anjou, Louis' younger brother
who accompanied him to Egypt, may in this regard be exemplary.[123] The
fragment, which survives in a collection dealing with the history of Holy War,
centers on the events of the crusade of 1250, including the retreat from Damietta; the perpetual illness and debility that afflicted the army; Louis' captivity,

114. WSP *vie*, 20–21 (ch. 3. On the relationship between Louis' conversion efforts and his crusading, see Benjamin Z. Kedar, *Crusade and Mission: European Approaches towards the Muslims*
(Princeton, N.J., 1984), 161–165; and Michael Lower, "Conversion and Saint Louis's Last Crusade," *Journal of Ecclesiastical History* 58 (2007): 222. I extend my thanks to Sharon Farmer for
the line of analysis.
115. WSP *vie*, 25 (ch. 3).
116. Joinville, §53.
117. Joinville, §§394–396.
118. WSP *vie*, 23–24: "Certes ce n'istra ja de ma bouche!" This story was recorded in the liturgical vita, BLQRF 163 (lection 7); B.VIII, 156; YSD gesta 55. It was also incorporated into the
Franciscan office for Louis, FR MR5.
119. WSP *vie*, 24 (ch. 3): "un paien qui estoit amiral."
120. WSP *vie*, 24 (ch. 3): "Vos estes nostre chetiz et nostre esclave et en nostre charter, si par-
lez si hardimiement! Ou vos ferez ce que nos vodron, ou vos serez crucefiez vos et les voz." See also
account of WC *vita et actibus*, 31. William of Chartres was with Louis in captivity.
121. WSP *vie*, 23 (ch. 3); 27 (ch. 15).
122. Joinville, §340–342.
123. For the discussion that follows, see Riant, "Déposition," 154–176.

the coup in the Muslim camp that brought the Mamluks to power; and finally, the negotiations for the release of the king and his army. The testimony is extraordinary. Describing Louis' saintly character, Charles repeatedly focused on Louis' desire for self-sacrifice and devotion to his people. In discussing the retreat from Damietta, Charles recalled Louis' refusal to abandon his people. Charles rebuked him for thus endangering the entire army, and Louis replied irritably that it was he who was king and that he would never abandon his people: "Oh, Count of Anjou, Count of Anjou! If you are so burdened by me, then why don't you leave! Because I shall never leave my people."[124] After their capture, as Louis learned that some of his knights were negotiating on their own to buy their freedom, the king flew into a rage, forbidding anyone to make independent deals. He fumed that the rich would be freed and the poor would remain forever imprisoned. "I want alone to be burdened to pay the price of my ransom and that of everyone else too."[125] After the Egyptian coup, fearing massacre, Louis returned to his tent to recite the hours of the Holy Spirit, the Cross, and other prayers. Charles (like others) recalled Louis' refusal to take an oath to deny Christ should he renege on the treaty. During these negotiations, Louis wanted to be the one held hostage (ultimately, the honor went to Alphonse). The account was one of Louis' steadfast faith, his accountability to his army, and his desire to sacrifice himself first.[126] Joinville, when writing his prologue after 1297, picked up this same interpretation of the events of 1250, emphasizing Louis' willingness for self-sacrifice as the reason why the crusades exhibited his sanctity.[127]

The other theme in evidence at the canonization testimony and recorded in William of Saint-Pathus' long seventeenth chapter was Louis' equitable judgments. These anecdotes were originally related by members of the high aristocracy—men like Simon of Nesle—who had been called to testify about the nature of Louis' character at his canonization proceedings (1282–1283). They revealed a king who used his authority as arbiter of justice to settle matters raised in the baronial courts, to suppress the judicial duel and minimize private warfare, and to abrogate the right and responsibility of the business of justice to the crown (no evidence of *clementia* here).[128] The most famous was the anecdote of how Louis summoned Enguerrand de Coucy to the royal court to settle a dispute originating with the count's summary execution of three minor nobles.[129] Louis had the count imprisoned, then refused Enguerrand the right to settle the matter through trial by battle, and finally imposed a substantive penalty on him,

---

124. Ibid., 171: "Comes Andegavensis, comes Andegavensis! Si vos estis oneratus de me, dimittatis, quia ego populum meum non dimittam."

125. Ibid., 172: "Sed volo solus esse oneratus ad solvendum de meo pretium redemptionis omnium quorumcumque."

126. Ibid., 172–173.

127. Joinville, §§7–13.

128. WSP *vie,* 73–74, 132–152; WC *vita et actibus,* 3l; BLQRF, 164; Joinville, §§61–64, §§679–684; Dominican Lections of 1306 (MOPH, vol. 4, 23, L9.).

129. WSP *vie* 136–140 (ch. 17). Jordan, "Representation of Monastic-Lay Relations in the Canonization Records."

which included depriving the count of certain rights of *haute justise*.[130] Another story had Louis claiming authority over Charles' comital court.[131] Joinville also focused on Louis' admirable conduct as king-judge in hearing cases and issuing judgments.[132] These stories were designed to demonstrate Louis' exalted sense of justice, but they also revealed ways in which as king he exploited the dignity of his role as royal judge to augment the authority of the crown.[133] It may be the reality of an increasingly institutional administration of royal justice that prompted the popularity of the nostalgic image of Louis making himself personally available to hear cases, "especially from the poor and orphans," and settling disputes in the public gardens in Paris or in the Woods of Vincennes.[134]

Canonization and the Constraints of Interpretation

Louis IX had enjoyed a reputation as a good and just king during his lifetime, and this reputation may well have been at the root of the general expectation of saintliness at his death. But no king had gained official canonization for over a century, and the expectations of saintliness were exemplified instead by other saints canonized by the papacy in the second half of the thirteenth century—expectations that fit ill with the characteristics of power associated with a king. The three most recently canonized were Saints Hedwig (1267, royal princess), Richard of Chichester (1262, bishop), and Clare of Assisi (1255, female Franciscan), all of whom were lauded for their piety and service to Christ. By the end of the thirteenth century, hagiographical expectations had absorbed the priorities of mendicant ideals, and Louis' earliest biographers—all mendicants themselves—presented a portrait of Louis that conformed to the traditional tropes of saintly virtue that emphasized active Christian piety and humility. The expectations of the genre are important here because hagiographical accounts were designed to demonstrate how an individual fulfilled the patterned expectations of saintliness, and men were described as saints in ways that accorded with other, recognized saints. It is for this reason that stories of Louis' piety, humility, and charity featured so strongly in the vitas, since these provided the most straightforward evidence for his sanctity. All this was conventional, and it was the way in which Louis' devotion to Christ played out in his crusading ambitions (or suffering) that somehow made him stand out and gave him his particular appeal. Lastly, the advocates of his sanctity were also not unaware that his rightness of character was manifest as a ruler and judge. In this sense, he was seen as an ideal king,

130. Ibid., 140–142 (ch. 17).
131. Ibid., 143 (ch. 17).
132. Joinville, §§57–60.
133. See also GB *vita*, 5 (ch. 6); WC *vita et actibus*, 34; WSP *vie*, 143, 146–147 (ch. 17).
134. B.VIII, 249 (for the poor and orphans); BLQRF, 164 (lection 8); *Glor. Reg.* (ch. 8); Dominican lections of 1306 (MOPH, vol. 4, 23 (L9). The specificity of place is indicated only by Joinville, §59, but the image of personal justice came up repeatedly (as shown in several of the sermons discussed below). This is a point made by Beaune, *Birth*, 115.

but one whose ideal kingship was largely defined through his piety and devotion, and for which his commitment to justice before God resulted in justice to his people.

Piety and Devotion

Piety was the *sine qua non* of sanctity, and favored anecdotes included Louis' habits of prayers; devotion and asceticism; his austerities; his alms to and love for the poor; his ecclesiastical and charitable foundations; and, of course, his crusades. His humility, desire for ascetic renunciation, and penitential devotions were made more deeply impressive by the exalted condition of his royalty. But most impressive was Louis' love of the poor, his desire to serve lepers, and his deep humility in ministering personally to *infirmos et pauperes*,[135] and these stories were cited repeatedly and at length. Louis patronized and endowed churches and built monasteries, hospitals, and leper houses. Though Louis' love of prayer and of sermons was cited, his piety was primarily a kind of active piety, focused on charity, an emphatic love of the poor, and the humility that allowed for it.

These were the attributes of a lay sanctity defined within the context of the century of Francis of Assisi and Elizabeth of Hungary—a sanctity of active piety in which a love of Christ was manifest by actions of devotion and charity directed at the benefit of others, particularly the poor; in which men and women of power and wealth denied the pomp and pride of privilege and directed their energy, concerns, and resources to the *minores* and *miseratos* of society; and in which one served God by serving in the world rather than renouncing it.[136] William of Saint-Pathus' longest and richest chapter is the one entitled "on the works of compassion," which includes stories about washing the feet of the poor, feeding the poor at his own table, ministering to lepers, and so forth. William of Chartres' discussion of what made Louis a good king is similar and included Louis' concern for the religious poor, his willingness to wash the feet of the leprous monk at Royaumont, his alms to famine-ravaged Normandy, his aid to the Maison-Dieu in Paris, his many religious and charitable foundations, and so forth.[137] Louis' sanctity was above all rooted in his piety, and his piety was manifest in charity and service in the world.

Crusades and Martyrdom

The thing that spoke most clearly to contemporaries regarding Louis' virtue was his crusading. We saw that much of the testimony about Louis' life given in 1282 was about the crusades, and all the hagiographical treatments devoted long sections to it. Gonzalo Perez, the archbishop who wrote a memo for

---

135. A phrase used in WSP *sermo*, 282, and *Glor. Reg.* (ch. 7). The spirit is frequent: GB *vie*, 8 (ch. 15), 11 (ch. 19), 18 (ch. 31); WC *vita et actibus*, 35; YSD *gesta*, 52; B.VIII, 152; BLQRF, 162 (lection 6).

136. Goodich, *Vita Perfecta*, 186–205; Vauchez, "Lay People's Sanctity," 21–32; Vauchez, *Sainthood*, 354–369.

137. WC *vita et actibus*, 33–36.

Boniface VIII in support of Louis' canonization, cited the crusades (he con-flated the two) as a, or *the*, chief reason why canonization was justified.[138] Joinville, for one (though notably not Geoffrey of Beaulieu or William of Chartres), would later described Louis' sickbed vow in 1244 explicitly as a con-version moment, and the texts produced around this time tended to see it as a turning point in his reign and an indication of the intensity of his piety.[139] But the crusades themselves were a tricky issue, since both of Louis' crusades had ended badly, with the king imprisoned on the first and dying on the second. In the end, the crusades became a vehicle for showing Louis' steadfast faith, his enduring commitment to Christ, and ultimately, his martyr's virtue (if not, though some argued it, a martyr's death). Indeed, we have seen how elite churchmen in 1275 argued outright that he was a martyr. Geoffrey of Beaulieu early on described him as an indefatigable martyr and fighter for the Lord.[140] Joinville, by 1308, would rebuke the papacy for canonizing him merely as a confessor.[141] And although most people understood that Louis could not be given the status of a martyr, the crusades, through their failure, allowed his ha-giographers to laud Louis for his sacrifice in the name of the Lord and pro-vided the vehicle to model the king within the framework of a sainthood of suffering which so dominated late medieval trends in sanctity. This framework helps make sense of the function of the crusades more generally in the pre-canonization material in which, for instance, Louis' suffering and illness were highlighted, his refusal to take an oath to deny Christ before the Saracens was exalted, and his captors' threat of torture was elaborated. Indeed, Louis' re-peated refusals to abandon his men even to his own danger accorded further with the ideals of martyrdom and self-sacrifice. These all played into what—quietly folded into a larger treatment of Louis' life—was essentially a passion narrative. This was itself tied to the changing ideology and rhetoric of the cru-sades over the thirteenth century, one that appealed to and was advocated in particular by the Franciscans, and which increasingly was modeled as an *imi-tatio Christi* that sacralized the suffering and self-sacrifice inherent in the en-deavor.[142]

Kingship and Rule

Louis' piety and his crusades were far more important in the early modeling of Louis' sanctity than issues of rulership. Rulership was something different from kingship, and Louis was certainly understood and lauded as an ideal king. But this is because ideal kingship had long been predicated on precisely

138. Linehan and Hernández, " 'Animadverto'," 100.
139. On the vow, Jordan, *Louis IX*, 3–13.
140. GB *vie*, 4 (ch. 2): "tanquam martyr et pugil domini indefessus."
141. Joinville, §5.
142. Christoph T. Maier, "Mass, the Eucharist and the Cross: Innocent III and the Relocation of the Crusade," in *Pope Innocent III and His World*, ed. John Moore (Brookfield, Vt., 1999), 351–360; Maier, *Crusade Propaganda and Ideology: Model Sermons for the Preaching of the Cross* (Cambridge, 2000), 59–68.

the actions of piety and humility that were serving to define Louis' sanctity. A notion that secular power was a response to the Fall and thus a necessary concession in a necessarily imperfect society was rooted in scripture. A long tradition of writing about good kingship, a tradition begun by Saint Augustine and matured under the Carolingians, had made personal sanctity a necessary precondition of good kingship. In this view, the king himself needed to be right, and just, and good, in order to foster as much as possible good within the imperfect and alienated social order. For the Carolingians, just kingship was thus rooted in the personal virtues of the king—piety, humility, chastity, clemency, wisdom, and so forth—and was characterized by the king's temperate rule over himself.[143] Later medieval authors, many writing for the Capetians themselves, imbibed these basic precepts, allowing them to be adapted to the changing realities of the elaborated and increasingly institutionalized monarchies of the later Middle Ages.[144] It was easy enough to understand Louis, because of his notable humility, charity, and self-restraint, as fulfilling age-old requirements of the ideal king. Because of his charity and generosity, his hagiographers explained that Louis' rule effected peace and benefited the poor and the church.[145]

Rulership—the exercise of power in governance—was a different issue. Where rulership and sanctity did come together was in the virtue of justice, and it was in Louis' role as a just arbiter of justice that he demonstrated good rule and thus his sanctity. So, Geoffrey of Beaulieu noted that he sought to redress the wrongs of the crown through the *enquêteurs*. William of Chartres noted that Louis was "prompt and careful in rendering justice to everyone, by justly executing what was just to all who were affected, tempering the rigor of justice with the leniency of mercy."[146] Above all, for contemporaries, being a "just king" meant an ability to exercise power—particularly judicial power—without favoritism. At the canonization proceedings, members of the secular elite, deeply impressed with the impartial (if severe) nature of Louis' ability to render justice, discerned a sanctity in this aspect of his rule, and saw as a saint the king who judged and rendered true justice. The stories that emerged from the proceedings about Louis' exercise of justice at the royal court showed how mechanisms of centralization and institutionalization in the thirteenth century had been understood within the language of good kingship and sanctified in

143. Wilhelm Berges, *Die Fürstenspiegel des hohen und späten Mittelalters* (Leipzig, 1938; repr., Stuttgart, 1952); Hans H. Anton, *Fürstenspiegel und Herrscherethos in der Karolingerzeit* (Bonn, 1968).

144. Lester Kruger Born, "The Perfect Prince: A Study in Thirteenth- and Fourteenth-Century Ideals," *Speculum* 3 (1928): 470–471; Dora M. Bell, *L'idéal éthique de la royauté en France au Moyen Age, d'après quelques moralistes de ce temps* (Geneva, 1962); Jacques Krynen, *L'empire du roi: Idées et croyances politiques en France XIIIe–XVe siècles* (Paris, 1993), 32–64.

145. GB *vita*, 13, 15; B.VIII, 149, 152–153; YSD *gesta*, 54. BLQRF, 164; Joinville, §715–718; Vita from St.-Germain-des-Prés (RHF, vol. 23, 170).

146. WC *vita et actibus*, 34. "Licet autem in reddenda omnibus justitia promptus esset ac sollicitus, juste quod justum erat totis affectibus exequendo; rigorem tamen justitiae misericordiae lenitate temperans."

the person of Saint Louis. The stories demonstrated Louis' exalted sense of justice, and they revealed ways in which as king he exploited the dignity of his role as royal judge to augment the authority of the crown. A careful reading of the evidence for the canonization proceedings is suggestive of a close accord between the magnification of Capetian authority and the sanctification of the idea of the king in the person of Louis.

The early hagiography thus worked out the series of basic notions of Louis' sanctity—piety, crusades, kingship—on which the image of Saint Louis would repeatedly draw. They were largely indebted to evolving notions of sainthood in the later Middle Ages that were themselves intertwined with the ongoing evaluation of the crusades. But they also drew on a long tradition of thinking of good kingship as itself modeled on classic notions of sanctity, humility, and self-restraint that, since Augustine, had been seen as the only bulwark against the corruption of power necessary after the Fall. On these three pivots—piety, crusade, kingship—would rest the successive re-imagination of Louis as saint, as he was redefined and redeployed, thereafter, as a symbol of both saintly virtue and just kingship. It is to these successive, sometimes competing, images of Saint Louis that we now turn.

2
The Canonization of 1297

Pope Boniface VIII (r. 1294–1303) canonized King Louis IX of France on August 11, 1297. The canonization occurred as part of the rapprochement effected at the end of the first phase of the conflict waged between Boniface and Louis' grandson, Philip IV "the Fair" (r. 1285–1314), which had begun the previous year. It has generally been understood as a concession by Boniface to Philip, who had long desired official endorsement of Louis' sanctity and hence the special virtue of the French monarchy.[1] In the bull of canonization, Boniface emphasized Louis' good kingship as an element of his sanctity:

> Indeed, for a long time, he exercised the rule of this kingdom, and, with fore-sightful consideration, he guided a governance filled with cares. Harmful to no one, unjust to no one, and violent to no one, he preserved and nourished the boundaries of justice completely, not relinquishing the path of equity. He checked the evil deeds of perverse men with the sharp edge of due punishment, crushing the efforts of evil men, reining in the illicit daring of depraved men. He stood out as an extraordinary zealot of peace, an ardent lover of concord, a conscientious promoter of unity, fleeing quarrels, avoiding scandal, and abhorring dissension. On account of this, in the time of his happy reign, with a calm tide on all sides, with crime having been subdued, with all winds having been routed, the dawn of sweet flowing tranquillity shone upon, and the happy serenity of prayed-for prosperity smiled upon, the inhabitants of his kingdom.[2]

---

1. In 1286, less than a year after Philip's ascent to the throne, Philip requested the newly elected Honorius IV to expedite Louis' canonization (Lewis, *Royal Succession*, 133). Georges Alfred Laurent Digard, *Philippe le Bel et le Saint-siège de 1285 à 1304* (Paris, 1936), vol. 1, 26–27, suggests that the documents may have been prepared by the abbot of St.-Denis, Matthew Vendôme; for the documents, see vol. 2, 218.

2. B.VIII, 155: "Longi quippe temporis spatio praedicti regni regimini praefuit, ejusque gubernacula, plena curis, provida circumspectione, direxit. Nulli noxius, non injuriosus alicui,

Boniface's description of Louis' saintly virtue reflected classic formulations of good kingship in the Middle Ages. The pope described the saint-king's commitment to royal justice, his love of peace, and the happiness of his subjects, emphasizing that the king's justice included punishment of evildoers and the promotion of peace. These were tropes of good rule in the ideal kingship literature—the so called *Specula Principum* (Mirrors for Princes). Only a few decades earlier, for instance, a handbook on kingship written for Louis IX included chapters on how to exercise justice, how to balance justice with clemency, how to correct injuries, and how to establish peace.[3] And a treatise often attributed to Thomas Aquinas described the good king as one who "makes a whole province rejoice in peace, who restrains violence, preserves justice, and arranges by his laws and precepts what is to be done by men."[4] At his coronation, the French king promised to "preserve true peace . . . forbid all rapine and all iniquities . . . and enforce equity and mercy in all judgments."[5]

One reason for noting the emphasis that Boniface placed on Louis' just rule in 1297 is that he did so within the context of a dispute between the papacy and the French crown in which the nature of good kingship (and specifically whether or not Philip IV was a good king) was at issue. The two sermons and the long bull (*Gloria laus*) that Boniface issued for Louis' canonization all portrayed Louis as a good and just king, describing him according to longstanding tropes of ideal kingship.[6] Though unusual in the hagiographical tradition for Louis, Boniface's emphasis on kingship is better understood if viewed against the backdrop of the rhetoric of just authority and good rule that surrounded the conflict. Boniface's claim that Louis was a good king stood in critical juxtaposition to his insistence that Philip was a bad one.[7]

---

nemini violentus, justitiae limites summopere servavit et coluit aequitatis tramitem non relinquens. Perversorum conatus nefarios ponae debitae mucrone compescuit; malorum molimina conterens, pravorum illicitos ausus frenans. Pacis zelator eximius, fervidus amator concordice, promotor sollicitus extitit unitatis, dissidia fugiens, vitans scandala, dissensiones abhorrens. Propter quod sui felicis regiminis tempore, sedatis undique fluctibus, subductis noxiis, turbinibus profugatis, regni ejusdem incolis aurora dulcifluae tranquillitatis illuxit, laetaque serenitas votivae prosperitatis arrisit."

3. Guibert de Tournai, *Le traité Eruditio regum et principum de Guibert de Tournai, O. F. M. (étude et texte inédit)*, ed. Alphonse de Poorter (Louvain, 1914), 66–91. Seventeen different chapters (about half of the treatise) treat justice, equity, and peace. In language that strongly resembles Boniface's, Guibert speaks of *malum intuitu suo satagit dissipare*, at 21, and of the ideal of *unitas, pax et concordia*, at 88. See also Vincent of Beauvais, *De morali principis institutione*, ed. Robert J. Schneider (Turnhout, 1995), xxvii, 63, where Vincent discusses the king's obligation to render justice by discerning between good and evil.

4. The treatise, *De regimine principum, ad regem Cypri* has, in both medieval and modern times, sometimes been attributed to Thomas Aquinas, though there is a good deal of debate on this attribution. See the introduction in Bartholomew of Lucca and Thomas Aquinas, *On the Government of Rulers: De regimine principum*, ed. James M. Blythe (Philadelphia, 1997), 1–59. For translation of the portions putatively written by Aquinas, see Thomas Aquinas, *On Kingship, to the King of Cyprus*, ed. G. B. Phelan, 2d ed. (Toronto, 1982), 41.

5. Jackson, *Ordines*, vol. 2, 383–384.

6. The texts are collected in RHF, vol. 23, 148–160, and in Duchesne, *Historiae Francorum Scriptores*, vol. 5, 481–491.

7. Lewis notes that Louis was used as a rhetorical device by both sides of the debate (Lewis, *Royal Succession*, 135).

The Political Context: The First Phase of the Conflict
between Boniface VIII and Philip IV (1296–1297)

Boniface's representation of Louis as the ideal king bore particular force because of the contentious political context in which it was promulgated. The canonization came at the conclusion of the first battle of wills between Philip the Fair and Boniface VIII.[8] Boniface had inherited the matter of Louis' canonization when he became pope in 1295. As Benedict Gaetani, he had known Louis as a young man while living in Paris, and in 1282 he had personally taken Charles of Anjou's deposition as part of the inquiry into Louis' sanctity.[9] Boniface was well aware of how important the matter was to Philip IV of France; and for this reason, he realized how advantageous his authority to confer canonization might be in his relations with the French crown. In February 1297, six months before Louis' canonization, Boniface wrote to Philip urging marriage negotiations between one of Philip's sons and the daughter of the count of Burgundy. The pope asked Philip to act at once and held out the prospect of Louis' canonization as a reward, calling the unrelated marital matter an impediment to the "solemn canonization of Louis king of France, your grandfather" which, once disposed of, would allow for the solemn inscription of Louis into the catalogue of saints.[10]

Tension between Boniface and Philip had begun a year earlier when Boniface issued *Clericis laicos* (February 24, 1296), forbidding lay taxation of the clergy. 'Lay' of course meant 'royal,' and within six months Philip had responded by forbidding the export of gold and silver from France, to the detriment of papal income.[11] Boniface in turn issued a second bull, *Ineffabilis amoris* (September 21, 1296), which accused Philip of insensate tyranny with all the fiery rhetoric the pope could muster. Propaganda emerged from French circles that defended royal claims to clerical revenues, including a tract known today as the *Dispute between a Priest and a Knight*, which concluded, unsurpris-

---

8. Useful in this context are T. S. R. Boase, *Boniface VIII* (London, 1933); Digard, *Philippe le Bel*; Charles T. Wood, *Philip the Fair and Boniface VIII; State vs. Papacy*, 2d ed. (New York, 1971); John Marrone and Charles Zuckerman, "Cardinal Simon-of-Beaulieu and Relations between Philip-the-Fair and Boniface VIII," *Traditio* 31 (1975): 196–222; Joseph R. Strayer, *The Reign of Philip the Fair* (Princeton, N.J., 1980), 237–323; and Jean Favier, *Philippe le Bel*, Nouvelle éd. (Paris, 1998), 250–288.

9. Riant, "Déposition," 162–163; LCB *procès*, 22.

10. Georges Digard, Robert Fawtier, and Maurice Faucon, eds., *Les registres de Boniface VIII: recueil des bulles de ce pape publiées ou analysées d'après les manuscrits originaux des archives du Vatican* (Paris, 1884), vol. 1, 906–907, no. 2039: "quodque rationabiliter impedimento cessante sancta memoria Lodoyci regis Francorum avi tui canonizata sollempniter in sanctorum cathalogo sollempnius annotetur." See also Brown, "Philippe le Bel," 180, n. 2. In using the phrase *impedimento cessante*, Boniface echoes the principle of *cessante causa, cessare debet et effectus* that when a cause ceases, so will the effect cease, openly suggesting that Philip's conclusion of this marriage agreement would be the effective cause of Louis' canonization (Elizabeth A. R. Brown, "*Cessante Causa* and the Taxes of the Last Capetians: The Political Applications of a Philosophical Maxim," *Studia Gratiana* 15 [Post Scripta] [1972]: 567–587).

11. There is some dispute as to whether Philip's actions were in direct response to *Clericis laicos* or ought to be attributed to other causes as well (Strayer, *The Reign of Philip the Fair*, 251).

ingly, that the king had a right to tax the clergy,[12] and another, *Antequam essent clerici*, which amounted to a defense of Philip's actions up to that point.[13] Back in Rome, trouble in the form of an immediate challenge from Boniface's longtime rivals, the Colonna family, staged in May 1297, induced Boniface to palliate what he saw as less pressing problems, and he thus agreed to rescind the original decree, an act that took the form of a bull called *Etsi di statu* (July 31, 1297). One of Philip's ministers, Pierre Flote, arrived at the papal court in early June to negotiate a settlement with Boniface.[14] The official acts were announced at the papal palace in Orvieto, and the aggregate legislation that emerged from the settlement has generally been viewed as a complete and total capitulation to French interests. To ensure the king's appreciation of the pope's good will, Boniface also agreed to the long sought canonization of the king's grandfather (August 11, 1297). Promulgation was preceded by two lengthy sermons, which Boniface preached on August 6 and August 11.[15] That the canonization was politically motivated was not lost on contemporaries: fifteen years later Cardinal Peter Colonna bitterly charged that Boniface canonized Louis to gain an ally in his crusade against his principal enemy, the Colonna family.[16]

Boniface's Interpretation of Louis' Sanctity: The Texts

At the beginning of the thirteenth century, Innocent III had decreed that a person's life (*vita*) was as important as his miracles in determining his sanctity.[17] Thereafter, bulls of canonization became lengthier and more detailed as popes sought to explicate the life and special virtue of a new saint, and the bulls themselves became in essence short hagiographical pieces. The canonization bull for Louis IX, *Gloria laus*, amounted to a compact vita in which Boniface outlined the qualities and characteristics that justified Louis' canonization.[18] His presentation of Louis' sainthood was rooted in the records from the canonization proceedings that had been sent to the curia as early as

12. Norma Erickson, "A Dispute between a Priest and a Knight," *Proceedings of the American Philosophical Society* 111 (1967): 288–309; Thomas Renna, "Kingship in the *Disputatio Inter Clericum et Militem*," *Speculum* 48 (1973): 675–693.

13. Pierre Dupuy, *Histoire dv différend d'entre le pape Boniface VIII et Philippes le Bel, roy de France*, 2d ed. (Paris, 1655; reprint, Tuscon, 1963), preuves, 21–23.

14. On Flote's mission, see Digard, *Philippe le Bel*, vol. 1, 336–345.

15. B.VIII, 148–153.

16. Digard, *Philippe le Bel*, vol. 1, 340. For documentation, see Jean Coste, *Boniface VIII en procès: articles d'accusation et dépositions des témoins (1303–1311)* (Rome, 1995), 806–808, Z 48 and 49. Coste indicates (809, n. 4) that Peter Colonna distorted the timing of events in 1297 to suit his own purposes.

17. Kemp, *Canonization and Authority*, 104–105; Goodich, *Vita Perfecta*, 21–47; Vauchez, *Sainthood*, 36–40.

18. It was thus adopted in hagiographic collections. Bernard Gui used it in his entry on Louis in the *Speculum Sanctorum*. See BNF Lat 5406, 152r.–155r. Compare with Mombritius's entry for Louis in his *vitae sanctorum* of 1477 (Boninus Mombritius, *Sanctuarium seu Vitae Sanctorum* [Milan, 1477; repr., Paris, 1910], vol. 2, 117–122).

1283 and owed much to the hagiographical tradition begun by Geoffrey of Beaulieu.

Boniface began the bull by saying that Louis was a confessor who merited sanctity because of his "kind consideration" and "wondrous work."[19] The pope wrote of the "eminent proofs of Louis' sanctity" (by which he meant the sixty-three miracles that the papacy approved) and the "excellence of his multiple merits."[20] Louis' piety was expressed through his acts of charity and love for others, and through humility and self-discipline. Here Boniface took up many familiar themes: Louis' chastity, his justice, his humility, his piety, his crusades, his ecclesiastical foundations and alms. Louis visited the poor, fed lepers, gave to drought-ridden areas, was disciplined by his confessor, slept on a wooden camp bed, and so forth. Boniface devoted most of his bull to the events on the crusade—Louis as the "defender of the orthodox faith."[21] He emphasized the firmness of faith Louis displayed while being taunted by the Saracen infidel, thus reflecting both the testimony of the canonization proceedings as well as the papacy's increasing interest in promoting saints who actively defended the Christian faith.[22] He spoke of Louis' taking of the cross, his capture and the ransom negotiations (including his refusal to take an oath to deny Christ), and his decision, after his release, to fortify Christian cities and to seek the release of Christian prisoners. Boniface followed Louis' return home in 1254, recounting how he founded monasteries and hospitals, took the cross a second time, and died in Tunis. Miracles began to occur at his tomb and proved his sanctity. Boniface concluded by enjoining all churches to celebrate Louis' feast day on August 25, the anniversary of his death.

Boniface took up this material again in his two sermons. The first and longest, *Reddite quae sunt Caesaris*, was largely devoted to describing the history of the canonization process and lauding the sixty-three miracles that Boniface himself approved.[23] Drawing on his theme, "render unto Caesar," Boniface explained that Caesar represents Louis, to whom, as a saint, we now owe homage. "Of his works" the sermon explained, "his sanctity was made manifest especially in his alms for the poor, his construction of hospitals, his building of churches, and many other works of mercy which would take too long to enumerate."[24] Louis was a good king, listening to the causes of justice and bringing peace to the kingdom. Boniface returned to the theme of the crusade, stating that the king forsook riches and exposed his body and his life for Christ. He again described Louis' imprisonment and his refusal of the oath. And he embellished an episode about Louis' first day in captivity: wanting to

---

19. B.VIII, 154: "benigna consideratione" and "operaque mirifica."
20. Ibid.: "praecelsa sanctitatis insignia."
21. Ibid., 159: "tantique propugnatoris fidei orthodoxae."
22. Goodich, "Politics of Canonization," 305–307; Goodich, *Vita Perfecta*, 23, 30, 37, 209.
23. B.VIII, 151.
24. B.VIII, 149: "Quantum vero ad opera, fuit manifesta specialiter in eleemosynis pauperum, in fabricationibus hospitalium, in aedificiis ecclesiarum, et ceteris misericordiae operibus, que omnia enumerare longum est."

recite vespers but having lost his breviary, the volume appeared miraculously (*per miraculum*) before him.[25] After the king's return to France, he wore simple clothing, built churches, visited the sick and the blind, and fed the leprous monk at Royaumont. Before his death, Louis wrote saintly instructions for his son and his daughter (the so-called *Enseignements* and *Instructions*), and, on a second crusade, he died a good death.

The second, shorter sermon, *Rex pacificus magnificatus est*, treated the subject of the ideal king explicitly and was therefore less tied to the hagiographical tradition. The *Rex pacificus* theme allowed Boniface to make an explicit comparison between Louis and the biblical Solomon:

> [The church] adapts words which, although they were said literally of King Solomon in the Old Testament, nevertheless, because they were spoken in exaltation of the church, we are able to put these same words forth in the same spirit for the purpose of magnifying and exalting the most saintly king Louis, in which the saint king Louis is commended in three ways: first on account of his eminent status, because he was king; second, on account of his talents and virtues, because he was peace-giving; third, on account of his rewards and recompenses, because he is, of course, magnified in the church militant.[26]

The first two points of the sermon (those that deal with the points *rex* and *pacificus*) described Louis as the ideal king. Boniface's final point (glossing the word *magnificus*) presented a spiritual interpretation of how Louis was "distinguished" in four dimensions: long, large, deep, and high.[27] He was long (*longus*) in perseverance, wide (*latus*) in his charity, deep (*profundus*) in his humility, and high (*elevatus*) in his right intention toward God.

The focus on rulership in Boniface's rhetoric stands out. Departing from conventional descriptions of Louis' sanctity, Boniface borrowed a number of tropes from the tradition of the *specula principum* authors who discussed ideal kingship and for whom good rule lay in the defense of justice and the promotion of Christian virtue. Augustine had spoken of the good ruler as one who was slow to punish, granted pardons easily, exerted vengeance only in necessity, used coercion in the hope of correcting iniquity, and favored leniency and mercy over the severity of justice.[28] Augustine's vision of good kingship as the ordered exercise of justice through Christian virtue was immensely influential,

25. Ibid., 250. See also Crist, "Breviary of Saint Louis," 319–323.
26. B.VIII, 152: "et tamen mutat verba, quae licet ad litteram dicta sunt de rege Salomone in Veteri Testamento, tamen quia de exaltatione Ecclesiae loquitur, propter magnificationem et exaltationem sanctissimi regis Ludovici possumus eodem Spiritu de ipso verba proposita exponere, in quibus sanctus rex Ludovicus in tribus commendatur: primo ab excellenti statu, quia rex; secundo, a donis et virtutibus, quia pacificus; tertio a praemiis et remunerationibus, quia magnificatus in Ecclesia scilicet militanti."
27. Ibid., 153.
28. The critical passage is Augustine, *City of God*, book 5, ch. 24; PL, vol. 41, cols. 170–171. On this tradition, see Anton, *Fürstenspiegel*, 47–51; J. M. Wallace-Hadrill, *Early Germanic Kingship in England and on the Continent* (Oxford, 1971), 135–140; Berges, *Fürstenspiegel*; Bell, *L'idéal éthique*; and Krynen, *L'empire du roi*, 163–239.

and the notion of the king's obligation to ensure the peace of God's good order through the exercise of justice suffused early writings about kingship.[29] Augustine was primarily concerned with the Christian ruler's duty to ensure peace through the restraint of personal passions, and he therefore rooted good rule in humility.[30] Borrowing from Augustine, Isidore of Seville defined kingship etymologically from the Latin *regere* and argued that the king was obliged to rule through correction and punishment.[31] Carolingian authors in turn emphasized the relationship between personal virtue and the health of the kingdom. From restraint and virtue flowed the king's justice, his duty to protect the kingdom, to defend the church, and to ensure tranquillity for his subjects. The ideal of royal justice through virtue was something of a constant in kingship literature and was reflected in the coronation rites of French kings, including the *ordo* of 1250—the rite probably used in Philip's coronation in 1285, during which the king promised to preserve true peace, forbid iniquity to all people, enforce equity through mercy in judgments, and eradicate heretics from the land.[32]

It was not difficult for the personal virtues that marked good kingship to be incorporated into a formulation of Louis' sanctity. Implicit in themes of the canonization sermons, *Reddite quae sunt Caesaris Caesari, et quae sunt Dei Deo*, and *Rex pacificus magnificatus est*, was the notion of legitimate rule and glorified royalty,[33] and in *Reddite que sunt* Boniface explicitly praised Louis' justice as the source of the kingdom's tranquillity:

> The greatness of his justice appeared clearly not only by examples, but also by tangible evidence. Indeed, he sat almost continually, on a couch [*lectum*] on the ground so that he might hear cases, especially from the poor and orphans, and he made the fullness of justice shown to them. He rendered to each what was his. Thus it is possible to say of him what is said in Ecclesiasticus (16.22): *Who will declare his works of justice?* as if to say they could not be enumerated. And thus in great peace and quietude he held his kingdom. For peace and justice were in concord. And as he sat in justice in this way, so his kingdom rested in peace. And thus, what is said in Proverbs (20.28) is made true in him: *Mercy and truth guard the king and his throne will be confirmed by clemency.*[34]

29. Jonas of Orleans, "De Institutione regia," in PL, vol. 106, 304, ch. 17; Hincmar of Reims, "De regis persona et regio ministerio," PL, vol. 125, ch. 5, 839; *On Kingship to the King of Cyprus*, book 1, ch. 9.

30. Anton, *Fürstenspiegel*, 47–51.

31. Krynen, *L'empire du roi*, 168.

32. Versions of both these oaths appeared in rites dating from the eighth (for the first) and ninth (for the second) centuries (Jackson, *Ordines*, vol. 2, 368, 83–84). A version of this prayer (excluding the last line) appears in the ca. 980 Ratold Ordo (ibid., vol. 1, 179 [Ordo 15]).

33. The first sermon, *Reddite quae sunt Caesaris Caesari* (Matt. 22:21), was preached at the papal palace in Orvieto on August 6. The second sermon, *Rex pacificus*, was delivered August 11 at the Franciscan convent in Orvieto. See LCB *procès*, 267–268.

34. B.VIII, 149: "Item, quantae fuerit justitiae, apparuit evidenter non solum per exempla, imo etiam per tactum. Sedebat enim quasi continue in terra super lectum, ut audiret causas, maxime pauperum et orphanorum, et eis faciebat exhiberi justitiae complementum. Unicuique etiam reddebat quod suum est. Unde potest dici de ipso quod dicitur (Ecclesiastici XVI): 'Opera justitiae ejus quis enunciabit?' quasi dicat, enumerari non possent. Et ideo in pace et quiete magna tenuit

The core of good kingship was always justice, and Boniface drew on the traditional image of the king as the dispenser of justice in his description of Louis. The image of the king protecting the poor and orphans, for instance, was commonplace in the *speculum* literature. The image of Louis hearing cases while sitting on a *lit* (Latin *lectum*) echoed Joinville's later recollection of the same event,[35] but the language and sentiment also bore echoes of the ninth-century *specula*. Jonas of Orleans, for instance, had written "the duty (*ministerium*) of the king is especially to govern the people of God and to rule with equity and justice and to strive so that they have peace and concord."[36] The verse from Proverbs 20 about mercy and truth that Boniface cited was a favorite of these authors and of political exegetes writing about just power in the thirteenth century.[37]

The second sermon, *Rex pacificus magnificatus est,* described Louis' perseverance, charity, humility, and reverence for God—virtues often associated with the ideal king. Boniface then took up a notion that was a mainstay of medieval handbooks on rule—that the virtue of a king begins with temperate rule over himself.[38]

> On the first point, it ought to be noted that he who rules himself and his subjects well is truly king. But of him who does not know how to rule himself and his subjects, it must be boldly stated that he is a false king. This man [Louis] was a king in truth, because he governed himself as well as his subjects truly, justly, and in a holy manner. He governed himself because he subjected flesh to spirit and all impulses of sensuality to reason. And he ruled his subjects well, because he cared for them in all justice and equity. He also ruled churches, because he preserved unharmed the ecclesiastical rights and liberties of the church [*iura ecclesiastica et libertates ecclesiae*]. But those who in fact do not rule well, these are not kings.[39]

---

regnum suum. Concordes enim sunt pax et justitia. Et ideo sicut sedit in justitia, ita regnum ejus quievit in pace. Unde verificatum est de ipso quod dicitur (Prov. xx): 'Misericordia et veritas custodiunt regem, et roborabitur clementia thronus ejus.' "

35. Joinville, §§59–60.

36. Jonas of Orleans, "De institutione regia," PL, vol. 106, 290–291: "Regale ministerium specialiter est populum Dei gubernare et regere cum aequitate et justitia, et ut pacem et concordiam habeant studere."

37. Ibid., 287, 294. See also Smaragdus' "Via regia," PL, vol. 102, 950; and Sedulius Scotus, "De rectoribus Christianis," in PL, vol. 103, 306. Among thirteenth-century writers, see Guibert de Tournai, *Eruditio regum et principum,* 67; and Vincent of Beauvais, *De morali principis,* 59. For thirteenth-century exegetical use of the verse, see Philippe Buc, "Pouvoir royal et commentaires de la Bible (1150–1350)," *Annales ESC* (1989): 696–697.

38. Krynen, *L'empire du roi,* 168. For antecedents, see Sedulius Scotus's *De rectoribus christianis,* whose second chapter is entitled "How an Orthodox Ruler Should First Govern Himself." "A man may know that he is rightly addressed by the title of king if he does not fail to rule himself with reason," and later in the same chapter, "he who rules the passions of his will and subdues the dissolute lures of the flesh is rightly called a king." See Sedulius Scotus, *On Christian Rulers, and the Poems,* trans. Edward G. Doyle (Binghamton, N.Y., 1983), 54–55.

39. B.VIII, 152: "De primo notandum, quod qui bene regit seipsum et subditos suos, ipse vere rex est. Sed qui nescit regere se et subditos, audaciter dicendum est quod falsus rex est. Iste vero rex fuit in veritate, quia seipsum et subditos vere, juste, et sancte regebat. Seipsum enim rexit, quia carnem subjecit spiritui, et omnes motus sensualitatis rationi. Item subditos bene regebat, quia in omni justitia et aequitate ipsos custodiebat. Rexit etiam ecclesias, quia jura ecclesiastica et libertates Ecclesiae illaesas conservabat. Sed qui de facto bene non regunt, reges non sunt."

The precept of self-governance was a favorite of Carolingian authors and had been incorporated into coronation prayers that were retained in later rites.[40] Late medieval commentators on kingship always cautioned rule of self,[41] and biblical exegetes ruminating on the problem of royal power often pointed to the restraint of personal passions as one of the keystones of good kingship.[42] Rule of self was a prerequisite of rule of kingdom, and in Boniface's interpretation Louis' rule of his person through reason led to the reasoned rule of his subjects, and likewise his rule of the church. Boniface, however, understood the defense of the church in his own pressing terms, namely that Louis ruled [*rexit*] churches well because he ensured the unharmed preservation of "ecclesiastical rights and liberties."

Another classic ideal of good kingship was the relationship between the peace of the king's interior soul (or heart) and the peace of the kingdom.[43] The importance of the king's peaceful inner self was increasingly stressed in the later Middle Ages. Boniface expanded on the theme of peace and justice in precisely these terms:

> Secondly, [Louis] is commended by his talents and virtues, because he is called peace-giving [*pacificus*], that is to say, one who makes peace. By this talent and this virtue are understood all other talents and virtues. He was peace-giving in himself and to all, not only to his subjects but also to foreigners. He was peaceful in himself. For he had temporal peace, spiritual peace, and therefore he finally acquired the peace of eternity. How he held his kingdom peacefully, all his contemporaries knew well. This peace is not without justice, since it follows justice. And because he was just with respect to himself, to God, and to his neighbors, he had peace.[44]

Boniface's interpretation of Louis' sainthood was, in sum, modeled by classic attributes of the ideal king: royal virtue through the exercise of justice, the kingdom in peace and tranquillity, rule of self as the prerequisite for rule of

40. "Te ipsum bene regas." It was used as early as 877, and in subsequent rites. See Jackson, *Ordines*, 8B (121), 13A (149), 15 (187), 16A (210), and so forth.

41. For instance, Guibert of Tournai, writing for Louis IX in 1259, listed discipline of the self (*diligentia sui*) as one of the four virtues necessary in a king (*Eruditio regum et principum*, 3, 9). Vincent of Beauvais instructed the king to use wisdom to control himself and in his rule (*De morali principis*, 60–61). Giles of Rome, in writing the *De regimine principum* (Rome, 1482) for the young Philip IV just a few years earlier, had predicated the very structure of his tripartite work on the notion that the government of the kingdom began with government of the self, in which the first part treated the rule of self, the second the rule of family, and the third the rule of kingdom. See also LeGoff, "Portrait du roi idéal," 71–76.

42. Buc, "Pouvoir royal," 691–713.

43. For example, Sedulius Scotus, *On Christian Rulers*, 66–67; Buc, "Pouvoir royal," 694, 699–700; and James Michael Heinlen, "The Ideology of Reform in the French Moralized Bible" (Ph.D. diss., Northwestern University, 1991), 201–203.

44. B.VIII, 152–153: "Secundo, commendatur a donis et virtutibus, cum dicitur pacificus, id est pacem faciens. Per istud enim donum et per istam virtutem intelliguntur cetera dona et virtutes. Fuit autem pacificus in se et quoad omnes, non solum subditos, sed extraneos. In se fuit pacificus. Habuit enim pacem temporis, pacem pectoris, et idcirco tandem consecutus est pacem aeternitatis. Qualiter vero pacifice tenuit regnum suum, hoc sciunt omnes qui sunt illius temporis. Ista vero pax non est sine justitia; sequitur enim justitiam. Et quia iste justus fuit quoad se, quoad Deum et quoad proximum, ideo pacem habuit."

kingdom, the relationship between the tranquillity of the king's soul and the peace of his kingdom.

Politics, Sanctity, and the Interpretation of Virtue

Boniface praised Louis for precisely the things he had criticized Philip for failing to do a year earlier when he attacked Philip during their dispute over the king's right to extort money from the French clergy. In the bull *Ineffabilis amoris* (21 September 1296), which Boniface issued after learning that Philip had forbidden the export of specie from France, the pope warned Philip not to make enemies of his neighbors, provoke the holy church with injuries, or risk violating ecclesiastical liberty (*ecclesiasticae libertatis infractor*).[45] He suggested that Philip ought be more careful at a time when so many foes were against France, especially when he needed the church's support in his wars against England and Spain. In what read as an inversion of Boniface's praise of Louis' peaceful rule of both subject and neighbor, Boniface asked Philip what would happen if he offended the church and made enemies of his allies. Where Boniface praised Louis for the reason (*ratio*) that guided his rule, he railed at Philip for actions that were not only *improvidum* but *insanum*.[46] Where he spoke of the happy prosperity afforded to the inhabitants of Louis' kingdom, Boniface warned that Philip had lost the heart of his subjects. "The subjects of the king," wrote Boniface, "are so oppressed by diverse burdens, that their subjection to you and their usual devotion are believed to have been greatly hardened, and the more they are burdened, the more their devotion will grow cool in the future. Nor is he thought to have lost little, who loses the hearts of his subjects."[47]

At the core of the pope's objections was the issue of ecclesiastical rights and liberties—a duty that dated back to the Carolingian period and had become central in the rhetoric of the debate between Philip and Boniface.[48] Boniface thundered that Philip was in danger of abusing ecclesiastical liberty. The pope asked Philip "What shield of defense can protect one who violates ecclesiastical liberty against God?"[49] He counseled Philip, as "son,"

45. The bull is found in Dupuy, *Histoire dv différend*, preuves, 15–17; and in Digard, Fawtier, and Faucon, eds., *Registres*, vol. 1, col. 614–620, no. 1653. Discussions are found in Charles Victor Langlois, *Saint Louis—Philippe le Bel. Les derniers Capétiens directs (1226–1328)*, ed. Ernest Lavisse, vol. 3, pt. 2 (Paris, 1901), 132–133; Boase, *Boniface VIII*, 139–140; and Digard, *Philippe le Bel*, vol. 1, 273–280.

46. For Boniface's description of Louis' rule through reason, see RHF, vol. 23, 152. For the reference to Philip's improvident and insane actions, see Dupuy, *Histoire dv différend*, preuves, 17; and Digard, Fawtier, and Faucon, eds., *Registres*, no. 1653, vol. 1, col. 616.

47. Digard, Fawtier, and Faucon, eds., *Registres*, no. 1653, vol. 1, col. 616: "Ipsi quidem subditi adeo sunt diversis oneribus aggravati, quod eorum ad te subjectio et solita multum putatur refriguisse devotio, et quanto amplius agravantur, tanto potius in posterum refrigescet; nec parum amisisse censeatur, qui corda perdit subjectorum."

48. On the background to the obligation of the king to protect ecclesiastical rights and liberties, see H. E. J. Cowdrey, *The Cluniacs and the Gregorian Reform* (Oxford, 1970), 8–15.

49. Dupuy, *Histoire dv différend*, preuves, 15; Digard, Fawtier, and Faucon, eds., *Registres*, no. 1653, vol. 1, col. 614: "Quis ecclesiastice libertatis infractor contra Deum et Dominum, cujusvis defensionis clippeo protegatur."

not to turn away from the voice of fatherly concern, then explained that he was dismayed to learn that Philip had issued a new constitution which seemed to have had the intention of impinging on ecclesiastical liberty and subverting it in the kingdom where it had long flourished. Boniface added that this would result in great reproach to Philip and great harm and grievance to his subjects and others who lived in the kingdom of France.[50] Then, he asked rhetorically, "what would happen to you if, God forbid, you should deeply offend the holy see and establish it as the helper of your enemies? But rather you would make it the principal force against you, since, if God should concede it from on high, we and our brothers are prepared not only to endure persecution, ruin, and exile but even to sacrifice our lives for ecclesiastical liberty."[51] A few months later Boniface would praise Louis for his protection of the church, and Boniface's reference to Louis as a good king for having preserved unbroken (*illaesas*) ecclesiastical law and ecclesiastical liberty contrasted sharply with his claim in 1296 that Philip was a violator (*infractor*) of ecclesiastical liberty.

Boniface even went so far as to evoke Louis specifically, referring to the miracles attested at the canonization proceedings. He referred to the time "in the days around the discussion and examination of the miracles which are said to have occurred at the invocation of Louis your grandfather of shining memory." He asked why Philip, in spite of his youth, should be judged differently from his forebears, whose felicitous acts "nourished this See in pure faith and sincere devotion, with greatest diligence from antiquity, by joining themselves to those things pleasing to it."[52] In this way the pope obliquely reminded Philip that the power of canonization lay in his hands. And he used the very reason why Philip wanted his grandfather canonized in the first place to his own rhetorical advantage: the virtue of the grandfather was supposed to reflect upon the grandson. But here, Boniface accused Philip of not living up to his "ancestors"—among whom Louis was preeminent, and whose (potential) sanctity he had just mentioned. He then pleaded with Philip not to stain the brightness (*claritas*) of the virtue of his worthy ancestors. By deftly interweaving the essentially unrelated matters of Louis' pending canonization and the dispute over taxation, the pope may have been implicitly hinging the former

50. Dupuy, *Histoire dv différend*, preuves, 16; Digard, Fawtier, and Faucon, eds., *Registres*, no. 1653, vol. 1, col. 615–14.

51. Dupuy, *Histoire dv différend*, preuves, 19; Digard, Fawtier, and Faucon, eds., *Registres*, no. 1653, vol. 1, col. 619: "Quid ergo tibi accideret, si, quod absit, sedem ipsam offenderes graviter, eamque hostium tuorum constitueres adjutricem, quin potius contra te faceres principalem, cum nos et fratres nostri, si Deus ex alto concesserit, parati simus non solum persecutiones, damna rerum et exilia substinere, set et corporalem mortem subire pro ecclesiastica libertate?"

52. Dupuy, *Histoire dv différend*, preuves, 17–18; Digard, Fawtier, and Faucon, eds., *Registres*, no. 1653, vol. 1, c. 617–618: "dum diebus istis circa discussionem et examinationem miraculorum, que ad invocationem clare memorie Ludovici avi tui facta dicuntur. . . . Cur degenerat tuae clementia juventutis a felicibus actibus progenitorum tuorum, quibus dictam sedem fide pura et devotione sincera summis ab antiquo studiis coluerunt, se ipsius beneplacitis coaptando?"

on the resolution of the latter. He would do so explicitly the following February (1297), when he urged the king to conclude marriage negotiations with the count of Burgundy.

By associating Louis with an imagined golden age, Boniface sought to use Louis to erect a standard of royal behavior by which to upbraid Philip. He referred to a past when French kings, he said, defended the liberties of the church and were thus exemplars of good kingship, a past from which he claimed Philip had sadly departed. But Boniface was careful to explain that praise of Louis was not praise of monarchy. In the sermon that most explicitly dealt with Louis' kingship, *Reddite quae sunt Caesaris*, Boniface explained that Caesar represented Louis because homage is owed to Louis just as homage was owed to Caesar. But when, in quoting Psalm 67:36 (*Mirabilis Deus in sanctis suis*), the pope claimed that "the homage owed to the man is owed to God, who is praised in his saints," he was insisting this homage was owed to Louis as saint, not to Louis as king.[53] Elsewhere, Boniface explained that it was the militant church that was glorified in Louis' glorification and exaltation.[54] It was to the greater glory of God, not the greater glory of the Capetian monarchy, that praise of Louis fell. The pope also suggested that by Louis' example kings and princes would be incited to good.[55] The point was that, as king, Louis was not typical; he was extraordinary.

If Boniface had wanted to criticize Philip in this way, he must have had some expectation that his criticism would somehow reach the king's ears. Nicholas of Fréauville, the king's confessor, later recalled Philip's happy reaction when the news of Louis' canonization reached the French court two months after the event.[56] Copies of both the bull and the sermons reached France.[57] More important was the presence of no less a man than Pierre Flote at Orvieto in August 1297. Flote, Philip's one-eyed chancellor, had been one of the chief architects of Philip's papal policy in 1296–1297. It was he who headed the delegation to Orvieto in the spring of 1297 that produced the concessions that included both *Etsi di Statu* and Louis' canonization.[58] There is no mistaking Flote's strong-arm tactics, and however strongly Boniface felt he needed a reconciliation with the French Capetians to survive the Italian Colonnas, he surely resented the corner into which Flote pushed him. The political nature of the canonization and the context of the strained relations between the curia and the French crown offer a great deal of room for interpreting the canonization

53. B.VIII, 149.
54. Ibid., 152.
55. Ibid.
56. Coste, *Boniface VIII en procès*, 784–785.
57. William of Saint-Pathus cites Boniface in his *vie*, and phrases of the bull were also incorporated into the lections for *Exultemus Omnes*. Copies of Boniface's sermons were found in a fourteenth-century manuscript of sermons that included one by William of Saint-Pathus. WSP *sermo*, 265.
58. Digard, *Philippe le Bel*, vol. 1, 336–342.

texts to have a dual meaning, where praise of Louis' saintliness could also be read as a critique of Philip's kingship. If Boniface had to canonize Philip's grandfather, he might as well use the occasion as an opportunity to establish a standard of kingly conduct that gave Boniface, in his political weakness, the moral high ground.

James of Viterbo and the Duties of Kingship

The notion that there was a "papal" or "ecclesiastical" view of Louis' sanctity and that it reflected on the idea of monarchy is evident in the sermons of the Augustinian canon and theologian James of Viterbo. James is best known as the author of the *De regimine christiano* (On Christian rule), a tract written in 1301 or 1302 in the context of the simmering conflict between Boniface VIII and Philip the Fair in which James argued for the subordination of royal power to priestly authority. The theological equivalent of Boniface's brazen bull, *Unam sanctam* (1302), the treatise offered a cogent theological defense of papal supremacy targeted squarely at Philip.[59] James was living in Paris in 1297, the year of Louis' canonization; he was raised to the archepiscopacy of Beneveneto in 1302 by Boniface himself. Just three months later, on December 12, 1302, Charles II of Anjou (Charles I of Anjou's son, Louis' nephew, and king of Sicily, d. 1309) had James elevated to the archepiscopacy of Naples, a post he held until his death in 1308 and which put him for those years within the orbit of the royal court of the Kingdom of Sicily. James wrote a series of sermons on Saint Louis, preached between 1303 and 1308 within the earshot of, if not to, the Angevin royal court. To some extent, the sermons are evidence of how Louis was transmitted to the Kingdom of Sicily as part of the Angevin dynastic program. They also demonstrate how Louis could be marshaled to advocate for a limited view of kingship.[60]

It was the framework of James's thinking developed in *On Christian Rule* that governed his interpretation of Louis as an ideal king. Drawing directly from his argumentation there, James treated Louis as the exemplar of the ideal

---

59. James of Viterbo, *Le plus ancien traité de l'église: Jacques de Viterbe, De regimine christiano (1301–1302)*, ed. Henri Xavier Arquillière (Paris, 1926). For an English translation, see James of Viterbo, *On Christian Government = De regimine christiano*, trans. R. W. Dyson (Woodbridge, UK, 1995). On dating, see Dyson's introduction at xvi–xvii.

60. Jean-Paul Boyer, "Prédication et état napolitain dans la première moitié du XIVe siècle," in *L'état angevin: pouvoir, culture et société entre XIIIe et XIVe siècles: Actes du colloque international organisé par l'American Academy in Rome, l'École française de Rome, l'Istituto storico italiano per il Medio Evo, l'U.M.R. Telemme et l'Université de Provence, l'Università degli studi di Napli "Federico II"* (Rome-Naples, 7–11 november 1995) (Rome, 1998), 132–133, 149. Boyer, at 143, speaks of James (along with others) as "véritable orateur de la cour." On this autograph manuscript, see Giovanni Morello and Ambrogio Piazzoni, *Diventare Santo: Itinerari e riconoscimenti della santità tra libri, documenti e immagini* (Vatican City, 1998), 131, no. 20. On preachers preaching cautions to royal authority at the (French) royal court, see Bériou, *L'avènement des maîtres*, 306–313. On James's sermons to Louis, see appendix 3 below.

king, defining his kingship in terms of its limitations and obligations and measured by the yardstick of God's providence. James understood the ideal king to rule mercifully and justly on the model of God's rule, to be "the minister of God," and to rule as "the image of God on earth."[61] And yet James emphasized above all that kingship and kingdom were conditional upon God's favor, and he stressed the duties of the king, the fragile and dependent nature of the king's claim to the throne, and God's ultimate power over royal authority.[62] The mark of Louis as a good king was that he established just laws, adhered to scripture, and followed the cult of the Lord.[63]

These conditions—just laws, adherence to scripture, and following the cult of the Lord—had all been laid out as elements of good kingship in *On Christian Rule*. James's source for his view of kingship were the injunctions of Deuteronomy 17:15–20, which he referenced both in *On Christian Rule* when justifying the priority of priestly over royal power and then again in his sermons on Louis.[64] Deuteronomy 17 spoke of the king's duties to the people and to God, the limits of the king's authority, his obligation to divine laws, the injunction against pride, the duties of the king in the worship of the Lord, the attention to scripture, and his obligations toward his peoples. James's gloss on the scriptural passage emphasized cupidity and avarice as dangers to good kingship, and a respect for divine law as the basis for good kingship.[65]

In the sermon of 1305 James explained that Louis fulfilled these very prescriptions:

> Thus blessed Louis did what was ordered of kings in Deuteronomy 17. [Deuteronomy] ordered them how they ought behave with respect to themselves and with respect to others, because they ought not have multiple wives, nor amass immense wealth, the first of which pertains to the impurity of the flesh, and the other to avarice. For out of desire for these very things kings are accustomed to degenerate into tyranny. It is further ordered of them [kings] how they ought to hold themselves with respect to God. Because he ought always consider the law of God, so that he might always fear and obey the Lord, it is further ordered how he [*sic*] ought

---

61. James of Viterbo, 4, *Magnificans salutes regis eius*, Vat. Capit San Petri D 213, c. 380–381: "Unde de ipso potest exponi id Ps. *Deus iudicium regi da* [Ps 71:2] id est formam et modum iudicandi et regendi, ut scilicet iudicet cum iustitia et misericordia sicut deus ipse iudicat et sequitur alia faciat que ad regimen pertinent imitando formam divini regiminis ut possibile est, cum sicut quasi dei minister et sit qui ymago dei in terris."

62. Much of *Rex in eternum* repeats the argumentation of his *De regimine christiano*, book 8, in which the good king is understood as an agent of God, ruled by a rule other than his own will (i.e., Providence), and as such the king is a "saviour" to his people. See *Rex in eternum* (2), Vatican Capit San Petri D213, c. 116: "Deus enim est qui reges et regna instituit, Dan. 2: *Regna transfert adque constituit* [Dan 2.21] constituit de novo et transfert propter peccata; eccli x: *Regnum a gente in gentem transfertur propter iniustitias et iniurias et contumelias et diversos dolos* [Eccli. 10.8]." Jacob then follows with a long exposition from Gregory the Great's *Moralia in Job*, which takes up again the nature of God's ultimate authority over the kingdom. A king who abandons the interests of justice is an apostate.

63. James of Viterbo, 2, *Rex in eternum*. Vat. Capit San Petri D 213, c.116–117.

64. James of Viterbo, *De regimine christiano*, 66, 79, 110, 122.

65. James of Viterbo, *Plus ancien traité*, 259–260; James of Viterbo, *De regimine christiano*, 122.

to behave toward his subjects, namely that he not scorn them or oppress them pride-
fully. Nor should he turn away from justice. And blessed Louis did all these things.[66]

Having said that Louis met the requirements of Deuteronomy 17, James
then tied this scriptural formulation of the king's duties to the oath that the
French king takes at his coronation ceremony (the *promissio*).

> Thus blessed Louis did that which was promised by kings. When a Christian king
> is instituted and crowned and anointed, he makes his vow just as monks do. And
> thus they must keep and carry out that [vow]. For he said in his vow, *I declare
> and I promise before God and his angels to henceforth and thereafter preserve
> the law, justice, and peace for the holy church of God and for the people subject
> to me, to the best of our power and knowledge, with safe, considerate concern
> for mercy, as we are able to better discover, with the counsel of our faithful men;
> and to preserve inviolate those things that have been collected and rendered to
> churchmen by emperors and kings.* And the other things that follow [in the coro-
> nation ritual], all of which things Blessed Louis did. Indeed, Blessed Louis ac-
> complished that which is revealed to kings. For, that which was done by good
> early kings is revealed to kings as an example.[67]

James had earlier cited the coronation ceremony in *On Christian Rule* VIII,[68]
but there made use of the imperial rite (on which the Angevin rite was based),
quoting both the emperor's oath and the bishops' prayer that the king should
be the defender of God's holy church.[69] For his sermon on Louis, James dug up
the French rite and replaced the episcopal prayer and imperial oath with the

---

66. James of Viterbo, 3, *Fecit Ezechias*. Vat. Capit San Petri D213, c. 249: "Fecit enim beatus
ludovicus id quod regibus precipitur in libro qui dicitur Deuto. 17. Precepit enim eis qualiter se
habere debeant ad seipsos, quia non debent habere plurimas uxores, nec multiplicare immensas
opes, quorum unum ad carnis immundiciam, aliud ad avaritiam pertinet, ex istorum enim cupi-
dine solent reges degenerare in tirampnidem. Precipitur etiam eis qualiter debeant se habere ad
deum. Quia semper debet cogitare de lege dei ut semper sit in dei timore et obedentia. Precipitur
etiam eis qualiter debeat [*sic*] se habere ad subditos, ut scilicet non superbe eos contempnat aut op-
primat, neque etiam a iusticia declinet. Et hec omnia fecit beatus Ludovicus." Much of this sermon
is drawn from the argumentation of *De regimine christiano*, book 8.

67. James of Viterbo, 3, *Fecit Ezechias*, Vat. Capit San Petri D213, 249: "Fecit etiam beatus ludovicus id quod a regibus promittitur. Quando enim rex christianus instituitur et coronatur et un-
gitur facit professionem suam sicut religiosi suam, et ideo illam servare et facere debent. Dicit enim
in sua professione: *profiteor et promitto coram deo et angelis eius, amodo et deinceps legem [cor-
rected from pacem]et iustitiam pacemque sancte dei ecclesie populoque mihi subiecto pro posse et
nosse facere et conservare, salvo condigno misericordie respectu, sicut cum consilio fidelium nostrorum melius invenire poterimus, pontificibus quoque ecclesiarum dei condignum et canonicum
honorem exibere adque ea que ab imperatoribus et regibus ecclesiasticis eis collata et reddita sunt
inviolabiliter conservare*, et alia que secuntur: que omnia fecit beatus ludovicus. Fecit etiam beatus
ludovicus id quod regibus ostenditur. Regibus enim ostenditur ut exemplum id quod gestum est a
bonis regibus precedentibus." This version of the *promissio* best matches Jackson *Ordines*, vol. 1,
262, Ordo XIX, which dates to ca. 1200.

68. For the text, see PL, vol. 78, 1242 (Imperial Coronation Rite, XVB). This is the text on
which the Angevin rites of 1289 and 1309 were based. See Jean-Paul Boyer, "Sacre et théocratie:
le cas des rois de Sicile Charles II (1289) et Robert (1309)," *Revue des sciences philosophiques et
théologiques* 81 (1997): 561–607. The *promissio* cited by James is found only in the French rite.

69. James of Viterbo, *De regimine christiano*, 125.

king's *promissio*. In both versions, the *promissio* is the instance in ceremony
in which the king voluntarily admits to the limits of his authority, where his
kingship is defined by duties and obligations, not rights and status.[70] It is notable in this context because the king specifically vowed to uphold the canonical privileges of the church; to serve the interests of law, justice, and peace
for the holy church; and to preserve ecclesiastical rights inviolably. One
might well note that these were the same virtues that Boniface, a few years
earlier, had highlighted when canonizing Louis. For James, then, the coronation ceremony was not the emblem of sacral kingship but rather the moment
where the king bound himself and his office to duty before and to the church.
And the relationship between Louis' sainthood and the coronation oath allowed James to tie all kings, by their oath, to the standard of piety and conduct established by Louis himself.

Philip's Response

Philip himself did not recall Louis during the 1296–1297 spat that ended
with Louis' canonization. But once Louis had been canonized—despite any
implicit criticism that Boniface may have tried to impart to Philip in doing
so—Louis' royal sanctity and the symbol of his reign was to Philip's, not Boniface's, political advantage. This was, of course, why Philip wanted Louis canonized in the first place. Philip immediately began citing Saint Louis—and the
peace and glory that his saintly kingship had engendered—in his own legislation.[71] In 1299 he began an *ordonnance* by saying that he wished to "follow in
the footsteps of our ancestors and in particular of Blessed Louis our forebear,
in those things which they did to promote virtue, abolish vice, and assure the
tranquillity and peace of our subjects."[72] When Philip started proceedings
against the luckless Bernard Saisset in 1301, touching off the second phase of
the conflict with Boniface, he charged Bernard with saying that Louis ought
not to have been canonized because he was actually in hell,[73] and that Louis
himself predicted that the kingdom would be destroyed under the present king
(that is, Philip the Fair) and handed over to foreigners.[74] Louis' moral authority as a saint now had everything to do with his kingship. His virtue as a saint
was understood to reflect the virtue of the dynasty, and it was very much in
Philip's interest that Louis' sanctity be rooted in his royalty.

Thus, in 1301 at the start of the next, calamitous, phase of the conflict

70. On the *promissio*, see Marcel David, "Le Serment du Sacre du IXe au XVe siècle: contribution à l'étude des limites juridiques de la souveraineté," *Revue du Moyen Age Latin* 6 (1950):
5–272.
71. Folz, *Saints rois*, 170; Brown, "The Prince," 310; Beaune, *Birth*, 104–105.
72. *Ordonnances des roys de France de la troisième race, recueillies par ordre chronologique*,
ed. Eusèbe Laurière et al., 21 vols. (Paris, 1723), vol. 1, 333. Also cited in Folz, *Saints rois*, 170, at
n. 120.
73. Dupuy, *Histoire dv différend*, preuves, 628.
74. This was a charge repeated by almost every witness. See Langlois, *Saint Louis—Philippe le
Bel*, 142–245.

between Boniface and Philip (although the pope himself now limited his references to Philip's saintly grandfather), Philip began to allude with some frequency to Saint Louis to justify his own royal prerogatives.[75] Royalist propaganda cited Louis in defense of the French king's rights over the temporalities of the French church. One tract took up the argument made in Philip's response in 1296 to *Clericis laicos*, known as *Antequam essent clerici*, citing the antiquity of the king's right to ecclesiastical revenues.[76] It advanced the royalist position in the strongest possible terms, arguing for the absolute priority of royal over papal authority. Concluding one section of his argument, the author cited the canonization itself as evidence of the king's rights to the church's monies.

> If anyone should say that in temporal matters the king and the Kingdom of France are lawfully subject to the Roman Empire, and consequently to the pope, although in fact a different situation prevails, it can be argued that . . . it is clear that the kings of France were in good faith in that possession. For they were always faithful to Christ's church, and to the church in the prosecution of their rights, as many examples show. . . . For Louis [VIII], great-grandfather of the lord king who now reigns, died while campaigning against the Albigensians for the defense of the church. His father Philip [III] passed to God while pressing the cause of the church in Aragon. The Blessed Louis, Philip [the Fair]'s grandfather, paid the debt of all flesh at Carthage while spreading the Christian faith. And certainly, if he had not been in good faith in the aforesaid prescription of supremacy, he would never have been canonized by the church, nor would Jesus Christ, the Author of the faith, have proved his sanctity by so many and so great and so manifest miracles. Through this same reasoning it can be concluded that the king of France has the full right to take *regalia*—that is, episcopal revenues—when the offices of bishop are vacant in various churches in France, and to confer ecclesiastical benefices, whose collections belonged to those bishops when they were alive.[77]

To Boniface, if this ever crossed his desk, the claim must have seemed unbelievably impertinent—for royalist claims to ecclesiastical temporalities to be linked to the fact of the very canonization that Boniface had used to criticize Philip for making such claims in the first place. Philip's allusions to Saint Louis increased after 1302, particularly after 1303 when he began devaluing the currency.[78] In Philip's sweeping reform ordinance of 1303, which was itself

---

75. Boniface did cite Louis' canonization after 1297, mostly to emphasize the political credit he thought he was due by reminding Philip that he had done so, or, again, by making oblique references to the honor of Philip's predecessors. See, for instance, Dupuy, *Histoire dv différend*, preuves, 78, 80.

76. The author is unknown, though believed to have probably been on the faculty at the University of Paris. See Walter Ullmann, "A Medieval Document on Papal Theories of Government," *English Historical Review* 61 (1946): 182–183.

77. For the Latin, see Dupuy, *Histoire dv différend*, 675–676. This translation is taken from Ewart Lewis, *Medieval Political Ideas* (New York, 1954), 470.

78. *Ordonnances*, vol. 1, 389, 390, 402, 406–7, 429, 431, 432, 441, 444, 449, 452, 454, 477, 536. See also Justine Finhaber-Baker, "From God's Peace to the King's Order: Late Medieval Limitations on Non-Royal Warfare." *Essays in Medieval Studies* 23 (2006): 21–22.

modeled on Louis' reforms of the 1250s, the king evoked Louis specifically in
regard to ecclesiastical liberties and franchises in language that recalled the issues of 1296–1297: "We wish that the privileges, liberties, franchises, customs,
and immunities of the said churches, monasteries, and ecclesiastical persons
should be wholly and inviolately protected, held and preserved for them, just
as they were preserved inviolately in the times of Blessed Louis of happy memory, our grandfather."[79] In 1303, in a letter addressed to the curia, the king responded to charges made by Boniface about the king's right over the collation
of benefices and over *regalia*—two of the central issues in the debate over
libertas ecclesiae—by citing the time of Saint Louis.[80] Certainly Philip was prepared to celebrate Louis' saintly kingship as a mark of Capetian virtue
whether or not Boniface had done so first. Philip hesitated, however, to evoke
Louis in his campaign to impugn Boniface's legitimacy as pope; he was quiet
on the subject, perhaps lest Boniface's credibility as legitimate pope be linked
to Louis' credibility as legitimate saint.[81] Indeed, at the trial of Boniface's
memory in 1310, one witness defended Louis' canonization at one point by
saying that even such a tyrant as Boniface did some things right.[82] But in general, once canonized, Louis became one of Philip's most potent symbols for
defending royal prerogatives.

This strategy worked only because Louis' saintly virtue could be rooted in
the quality of his kingship, but it would be a mistake to think that the tight
association between sanctity and governance was a foregone conclusion. We
have seen that mendicant authors generally rooted Louis' sanctity in the depth
of his faith and his humility and that sanctity was by and large defined by inherited tropes of sanctity. But Boniface drew explicitly and intentionally on the
deep traditions of good kingship to define Louis as a saint, in part to create a
standard of kingship against which to measure future kings, and Philip
specifically. The link that was successfully forged between Louis' sanctity
and his kingship came about in large measure because the chief proponents
of Louis' cult were members of the French royal family and the abbey church
of St.-Denis, both institutions invested in sanctioning the monarchy's historical
virtue. And in the end, the regalization of Louis' sanctity had nothing to do
with the fact that Boniface was the first to exploit the symbol of Louis as a just
king; Philip was far too invested in the sacral dignity of his office not to

---

79. *Ordonnances*, vol. 1, 357 (March 23, 1302): "Volumus autem quod privilegia, libertates,
franchisie, consuetudines, seu immunitates dictarum Ecclesiarum, Monasteriorum, & personarum
Ecclesiarum integre, & illese serventur, teneantur, & custodiantur eisdem, sicut temporibus
felicis recordationis Beati Ludovici avi nostri inviolabiliter servate fuerunt." On Philip's use of
Louis' memory when devaluing the currency, see Brown, "Persona," 231.

80. Dupuy, *Histoire dv différend*, preuves, 93–94.

81. See the documents collected in Coste, *Boniface VIII en procès*. Also see the documents for
the general assemblies, first convened by Philip as he sought to try Boniface *in memoriam*, collected in Georges Picot, *Documents relatifs aux États généraux et Assemblée: réunis sous Philippe
le Bel* (Paris, 1901).

82. Boniface would be so defended (as recorded by Nogaret's paraphrase of the arguments
made by one of Boniface's defenders). See Brown, "The Prince," 310, n. 99; and Coste, *Boniface
VIII en procès*, 737, n. 2.

understand Louis' virtue in terms of his kingship or to recognize the symbolic import of emphasizing that association. But it is the very existence of multiple interpretations that is worth noting, because this observation suggests that the act of interpreting could be—was—politically charged. Both Boniface and Philip sought to sanctify Louis for the qualities of his life that served their own interests. For both, Louis' reign came to represent a golden age, the idealized reflection of which was intended to justify the political and ideological claims that both pope and king were making in the years around 1300. The process of sanctifying Louis thus became a vehicle of political posturing and ideological discourse.

3

Constructing the Cult

Bones, Altars, and Liturgical Offices

In the bull of August 11, 1297, pronouncing Louis a saint of the church, Boniface VIII enjoined that Louis' feast day be "devoutly and solemnly" celebrated "in a fitting manner" by "churches of all cities and dioceses" on the day following the feast of Saint Bartholomew, that is, on August 25, Louis' *dies natalis*.[1] Responding to the papal mandate, religious orders and individual ecclesiastical houses formally instituted the feast. The feast was probably adopted in Paris in 1298.[2] The general chapter of the Cistercian order in the same year decreed a feast of two masses and twelve lections to be established throughout the order, while in 1299 it added that special prayers (*propria ipse historia*—literally, prayers or lections that deal specifically with Louis) be sung, and the Cistercians composed a monastic office called *Lauda celestis*.[3] The Dominican order established "a simple feast on the octave kalends of September" for Louis in 1298, ordered that the feast be listed as a *simplex* feast in 1301, and published lections for the feast in 1306.[4] As early as 1272, Bonaventure secured from Gregory X permission to celebrate a solemn anniversary on August 25 within the Franciscan

1. B.VIII, 159.
2. Leroquais, *Bréviaires*, x. 1, cxiii, posits that the feast was adopted in Paris in 1298. Leroquais cited Arch. Nat. LL. 39, fol. 121 (actually 121v.). This is the cartulary copy of the letter Philip the Fair sent out that invited churchmen to participate in the translation at St.-Denis.
3. Joseph Canivez, *Statuta capitulorum generalium Ordinis Cisterciensis ab anno 1116 ad annum 1786*, 8 vols. (Louvain, 1935), vol. 3, 294, item 5, 298, item 2. AASS, V, Aug. 25, 532. M. Cecilia Gaposchkin, "The Monastic Office for Louis IX of France: *Lauda Celestis Regio*," *Revue Mabillon* (forthcoming). Note Troyes BM 2066 in the August calendar (9r.) where *Ludovici xii lections ii missa* is added in a later hand.
4. MOPH, vol. 3, 289 (for 1298), vol. 4, 21–23 (for 1306; AASS, V, Aug. 25, 532). In the general chapter of 1271, the Dominicans had instituted a yearly mass for Louis.

order.[5] The Franciscans then adopted the feast at the chapter held in Lyon in 1299, and because the papal calendar adopted Franciscan usage in the course of the thirteenth and fourteenth centuries, Louis' feast made its way into the curial calendar.[6] An ecclesiastical council held in Béziers in 1299 instituted the feast "in all churches in the province of Narbonne," to be celebrated with the common for confessors.[7] The Augustinians instituted the feast in 1300,[8] and the Cluniac general chapter of 1300 or 1301 included Louis in a flurry of new feasts, to be celebrated *in capis* (the choir wearing copes).[9] The Carmelites formally instituted the feast only in 1306.[10]

The news of the canonization had the greatest impact in Paris and the Île-de-France. Memory of Louis was concentrated there—in the people and institutions that remembered his reign, in his relics at St.-Denis and then at the Ste.-Chapelle, in the monarchy that promoted his sanctity—making the city the natural center of Louis' cult. The news of his canonization did not reach Paris in time to celebrate the new saint's feast in 1297, but preparations were in full swing the following year. The first feast day, August 25, 1298, occasioned the translation of Louis' relics—the transferral of his bones from his place of burial to a reliquary on an altar—at St.-Denis.

It was Philip IV, more than anyone, who mobilized to promote veneration of his grandfather. Philip, we saw, was the one principally responsible for pushing Louis' canonization in the first place. Within months of its promulgation, Philip began construction of a costly new religious foundation dedicated to Louis at Louis' place of birth, Poissy, which he made a Dominican foundation.[11] By June he had commissioned a liturgical office to be composed for

---

5. Franz Ehrle, "Die ältesten Redactionen der Generalconstitutionen des Franziskanerordens," *Archiv für Literatur- un Kirchen- Geschichte des Mittelalters* 6 (1892): 41.

6. Stephen Joseph Peter Van Dijk, *Sources of the Modern Roman Liturgy; the Ordinals by Haymo of Faversham and Related Documents (1243–1307)* (Leiden, 1963), vol. 1, 213 and 214, n. 2, vol. 2, 449 (item e).

7. AASS, V, Aug. 25, 533.

8. *Bréviaires, vol.* 1, cix; AASS August 25, 533. The general chapter was held in Naples.

9. The institution of the feast appears in the statutes of 1301: Celestin Douais, *Statuts de Cluny édictés par Bertrand, Abbé de Cluny, le 3 Avril 1301* (Paris, 1893), 10, no. 15; G. Charvin, ed., *Statuts, chapitre généraux et visites de l'ordre de Cluny*, 2 vols. (Paris, 1965–), 75, no. 40. A collection of Cluniac statutes copied in or around 1389 date the institution of the feast to 1300 throughout the order (BNF nal 2263, fol. 47; Leroquais, *Breviaires, vol.* 1, cv). The texts are not identical, though they match generally in content. On the dating of BNF nal 2263, see Léopold Delisle, *Inventaire des manuscripts de la Bibliothèque nationale fonds de Cluny* (Paris, 1884), 318.

10. *Bréviaires*, vol. 1, cxi. No known statutes of the Carthusian general chapters institute Louis' feast day (*Bréviaires*, vol. 1, ciii), though according to Leroquais' catalogue, at least two Carthusian breviaries included material for August 25 (Charleville BM ms 98 and Charleville BM 154, a Carthusian breviary/missal and a Carthusian missal).

11. Alain Erlande-Brandenburg, "La Priorale Saint-Louis de Poissy," *Bulletin Monumental* 129 (1971): 85–112. For evidence of Philip's emotional ties to Poissy, see Elizabeth A. R. Brown, "Royal Salvation and the Needs of State in Late Capetian France," in *Order and Innovation in the Middle Ages: Essays in Honor of Joseph R. Strayer*, ed. William C. Jordan, Bruce McNab, and Teofilo F. Ruiz (Princeton, N.J., 1976), 370–373; Hallam, "Philip the Fair," 201–214; and Brown, "The Prince," 311.

Louis.[12] The king's treasury furnished funds for the copying and illumination of a number of vitas of Saint Louis both for the court and for Poissy.[13] In 1299 the crown defrayed costs for an office at the church St.-Aniane in Orleans.[14] An account of 1299 also shows Philip paying for the "transport" of thirty-two codices *de sancto Ludovico*, an astonishing number that represents a kind of mass production of veneration.[15] In 1302 or 1303 the king also paid for a chalice to be repaired for the chapel to Saint Louis in Carcassone.[16] Accounts indicate that in 1304 he paid for an "image" of Louis made of silver and gold which was given with a relic to the King of Norway.[17] After 1303 he founded Val-des-Écoliers (Royallieu) in Louis' honor and then, after 1305, in memory of Jeanne of Navarre, his wife; and in 1308 Philip founded the Carthusian priory at Mont-Saint-Louis in Louis' name and later provided revenues for a number of other chapels dedicated to the saint-king.[18] It was his wife who asked Joinville to write his famous account of Louis' crusade.[19]

This chapter aims to tell the story of the early and various efforts at cult building that followed immediately upon Louis' canonization in 1297. These efforts were fostered largely by Philip the Fair, who promoted veneration throughout his realm, although the cult's greatest focus was always Paris. After receiving the news of Louis' canonization Philip began actively building Louis' cult in the area, focusing the task on three institutions closely associated with Louis and the crown: St.-Denis, where Louis was buried; the Ste.-Chapelle, which Louis had built; and St.-Jacques, the Dominican convent he had supported. But Philip was not the only one. Louis was also commemorated at princely courts, his cult spread to Angevin Italy, and ecclesiastical orders prepared to honor his feast. Various evidence—from the religious orders, noble households, and even the poor coming to seek Louis' miraculous intercession at St.-Denis—demonstrates how fervid were the early years of devotion to Louis.

Philip at St.-Denis

The first order of business after Louis' canonization was the translation of his relics. Translations involved the removal of a saint's relics from their place

---

12. Jules Marie Édouard Viard, *Les journaux du trésor de Philippe IV le Bel* (Paris, 1940), nos. 727, 799, 902, 928, 941, 1008. See also nos. 663, 680, 693, 812 918, 951, 994, 1014, 1015, 1028, 1047, 1051, 1063, 1098, 1292, 1300.

13. Ibid., no. 994; Robert Fawtier, *Comptes royaux (1285–1314)* (Paris, 1953), vol. 1, nos. 2589, 6685; vol. 2, 536, nos. 23914, 773, no. 27677. On the library at Poissy, see Joan M. Naughton, "Manuscripts from the Dominican Monastery of Saint-Louis de Poissy" (Ph.D. diss., University of Melbourne, 1995); and Naughton, "Books for a Dominican Nuns' Choir: Illustrated Liturgical Manuscripts at Saint-Louis de Poissy, c. 1330–1350," in *The Art of the Book: Its Place in Medieval Worship*, ed. Margaret M. Manion and Bernard J. Muir (Exeter, 1998), 67–110.

14. Fawtier, *Comptes royaux*, vol. 1, 120, no. 2589: "pro officio sancti ludovici."

15. Ibid., vol. 1, 166, no. 3490.

16. Ibid., vol. 1, 626, no. 12961.

17. Ibid., vol. 2, 535, no. 23914.

18. Hallam, "Philip the Fair," 207–208; Brown, "The Prince," 310.

19. Joinville, prologue §§1–6.

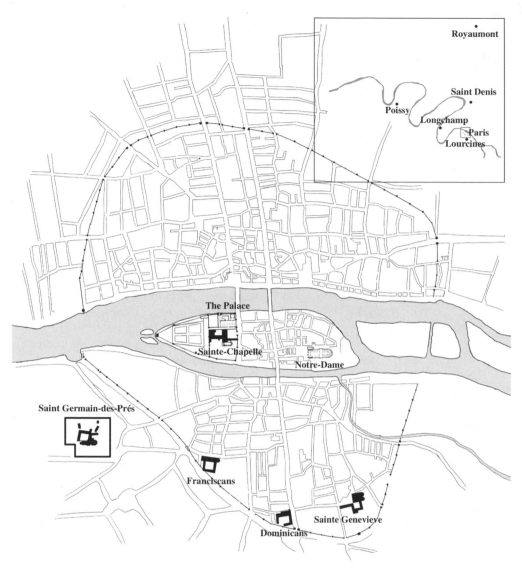

Map 3.1. Paris and Paris-area under Philip the Fair (adapted from Géraud, Hercule. Paris sous Philippe-le-Bel, d'après des documents originaux et notamment d'après un manuscrit contenant "le rôle de de taille" imposée sur les habitants de Paris en 1292. Paris, 1837.)

of burial to a reliquary and an altar and constituted the establishing act of an official cult. Louis' bones had been boiled down after his death to allow for their transport from Africa. His heart and entrails were buried at the request of his brother (Charles of Anjou, King of Sicily) in Monreale, and the remaining bones were transported to St.-Denis, where in 1271 they were formally interred, alongside many of his ancestors.[20] Because St.-Denis was the place of

20. On Louis' burial, see Elizabeth A. R. Brown, "Death and the Human Body in the Later Middle Ages: The Legislation of Boniface VIII on the Division of the Corpse," *Viator* 12 (1981): 231–235; and Brown, *Saint-Denis: La basilique* (Paris, 2001), 393–398. On his original tomb, see

his burial, it was also the *locus sanctus* where miracles were reported and thus credited to his intercession. Accordingly St.-Denis was the site where the formal inquiry into his sanctity was begun in 1282. The monks were surely delighted when in 1297 Louis was declared a saint and they found themselves suddenly in the possession of important relics. Because Louis was buried there, it was in their church that the formal elevation of relics occurred, and the monks promptly embarked upon a series of cult-building endeavors (including the construction of a glazed chapel, the composition of an hagiographical vita, and the adoption of a liturgical office) to honor the new saint and, no doubt, provide suitable support for the growing cult.

The monks of St.-Denis had their own reasons to promote Louis' sanctity, but the affair seems to have been co-opted by the king. Joinville claimed that the feast was Philip's (rather than Boniface's or the monks') decision. "After this good news had come from Rome," he wrote, "the king appointed a day, the day after Saint Bartholomew's, on which the body of the saint was exhumed."[21] And it was Philip who sent out invitations in early May 1298 requesting the attendance of the elite churchmen and magnates of the realm to St.-Denis—invitations in which Philip referred to Louis as "my dearest ancestor."[22] A series of payments in July and August 1298 show Philip making costly preparations for the first feast of Saint Louis ultimately held at St.-Denis.[23] In 1300 Philip was still settling his accounts for work done during the canonization "at the Roman curia and at Saint Denis."[24] The liturgical office he commissioned in June of that year may have been intended for the inaugural feast at St.-Denis.

This was all as might have been expected, especially since the abbey and the crown had a long relationship cemented by their mutual project of legitimizing Capetian history, for which there could be no more suitable symbol than a Capetian saint-king. But, as Elizabeth A. R. Brown has taught us, sometime in late May or June 1298 Philip resolved to translate Louis' remains to the Ste.-Chapelle, the chapel Louis himself had built at the palace in the heart of the city.[25] Philip must have envisioned the maiden celebration of Louis' feast day as a solemn but glorious event in which Louis' holy remains

Alain Erlande-Brandenburg, "Le tombeau de Saint Louis," *Bulletin Monumental* 126 (1968): 7–36; Wright, "The Tomb of Saint Louis," 65–82; and Erlande-Brandenburg, *Le roi est mort: étude sur les funérailles, les sépultures et les tombeaux des rois de France jusqu'à la fin du XIIIe siècle* (Geneva, 1975), 165–166.

   21. Joinville, §762.

   22. Different versions of Philip's invitation are printed in DuBois, *Historia ecclesiae Parisiensis*, 521 (to the abbot of St.-Magloire); and AASS Aug V 534–535 (to the Abbot of Moissac: "sanctus Ludovicus Rex Francorum carissimus avus noster").

   23. A. Vidier, *Le Trésor de La Sainte-Chapelle: Inventaires et Documents* (Paris, 1911), 305, and 308–309 (for reparations payments made by the treasury for property damaged or destroyed during the 1299 celebration of Louis' feast day).

   24. Viard, *Journaux (Philippe IV)*, no. 4542, March 16, 1300.

   25. Brown, "Philippe le Bel," 175–182; Brown, *Saint-Denis*, 402–403. Philip had sought to gain control of Louis' relics as early as 1294 (Brown, "The Prince," 310).

would be returned home to the palace, the center of the realm, its chapel the symbol of royal piety and sacrality. At the time, he wanted the entire cache of relics. On June 27 Boniface granted Philip the right to translate Louis' relics to the Ste.-Chapelle, and the following day saw the pope issue an indulgence for those visiting the relics at the royal chapel.[26] The monks must have objected, since on July 7 Boniface ordered them to comply with Philip's project for the translation and be content with a mere arm or a leg bone.[27] How exactly they thwarted these plans is unknown, but they did, and on the appointed day the king came to St.-Denis only to participate in the elevation of Louis' relics to an honored spot on an altar of the abbey church, where they remained.

We have several interdependent descriptions of the event. The sources all emphasize the royal presence at the ceremony. William of Nangis, in the *Chronicle*, describes the "incredible joy and exultation" felt by Philip and, indeed, the entire kingdom.[28] A fourteenth-century text recounted that Louis' "venerable body" was exhumed from the tomb that "befitted his regal magnificence" and placed into a silver reliquary near the tomb of Saint Denis.[29] Joinville, who was in attendance, added that the archbishops of Reims and Lyon were the first to carry the relics; that the relics were placed on a bier, or platform, that had been built (probably outside the church, since he later says they were borne back into the church to be placed behind the main altar); and that after the ceremony, the Franciscan friar Jean of Samois, who had been instrumental in lobbying for Louis' canonization, preached a sermon in which he recalled Louis' oath to the Saracens.[30] After the sermon, Philip and his brothers Charles of Valois and Louis d'Évreux carried the relics back into the church to an honored place behind the matutinal altar. Even the Dionysian sources emphasize the extent to which the translation was a Capetian affair.

Philip at the Ste.-Chapelle

Louis' earthly remains may have been buried at St.-Denis, but it must have been unimaginable to Philip that the center of Louis' cult should be anywhere but the Ste.-Chapelle, the exquisite palace chapel Louis IX had built in the 1240s to house the Crown of Thorns. The building represented Louis' acute devotion to the kingship and the Passion of Christ—both inherent in the symbol of the Crown of Thorns—and once Louis' obsession with taking back the Holy Land had taken hold, the chapel became increasingly associated with crusading aspirations. Designed above all to represent royal authority to a Parisian public audience, the chapel constituted the monumental representation

26. Vidier, *Le Trésor*, 269/302–270/303, no. 36.

27. Brown, "Philippe le Bel," 175. For Boniface's bull, see Vidier, *Le Trésor*, 303–304.

28. William of Nangis, *Chronicon*: "cum ingenti laetitia & exultatione." See also RHF, vol. 20, 579, for the canonization, and 580–81, for the elevation.

29. BNF Lat 14511, 180v.: "venerabile corpus . . . prout regalem magnificentiam decuit."

30. Joinville, §§ 763–764.

of Capetian sacral kingship, emphasizing both Old Testament kingship and the
kingship of Christ.[31] And as the chapel attached to the palace, the Ste.-Chapelle
was also associated with the crown—the royal administration, the courts of
justice, the center of the kingdom—what Philip would later call the head of the
whole kingdom of France.

After Louis' death the building was naturally associated with his memory,[32]
and it was only fitting that Louis, who in his sanctity had actualized and personified the monarchy's ideal of sacral kingship, should now be identified with
the Ste.-Chapelle, whose function and iconography aimed to do the same. In
the years following Louis' canonization, Philip refurbished the chapel's interior
decoration. In 1299 the first musical organ was installed, and at the king's
command, a considerable sum was spent to repaint the entire chapel, "both
upper and lower," including, it seems, with *ymaginibus*.[33] Draperies were repaired, new lamps were hung, altar cloths were painted.[34] Seven pounds were
paid for the "writing of some histories and legends of Saint Louis in books for
the chapel," and another 48 sous to bind these volumes.[35] A payment for the
correction of the chapel's gradual attests to other liturgical changes.[36] A slim,
elegant volume, BNF Lat 911, containing the relevant liturgical materials
for Louis' office and mass, was compiled around this time, probably for the
Ste.-Chapelle. This volume represents a late medieval example of the "shrine
book" and was perhaps an exemplar from which the liturgical texts and music
could be copied into other volumes.[37] It contains an early (though not the earliest) copy of the highly polished and widely used office *Ludovicus decus regnantium*.[38] By 1301 an altar in honor of Saints Louis and Nicolas had been founded

---

31. Jordan, *Visualizing Kingship*, 16–29, 58–69; Mercuri, "Stat inter spinas," 497–512;
Mercuri, *Corona*, 181–209; Mercuri, "Reflets," 117–126. For the sacralizing and public function of the architectural features of the Ste.-Chapelle, see Meredith Cohen, "The Sainte-
Chapelle of Paris: Image of Authority and Locus of Identity" (Ph.D. diss., Columbia University,
2004); and her important re-evaluation of the "private vs. public" nature of the building, "An
Indulgence for the Visitor: The Public at the Sainte-Chapelle of Paris," *Speculum* 83 (2008
forthcoming).

32. See, for instance, the poetic lament in Villeneuve, *Saint Louis*, vol. 3, 677: "Chapèle de
Paris! bien eres maintenue . . . De la mort sont plaintifs et grand gent et menue."

33. The August 25 feast was surely celebrated at the court as of 1298. See Michel Brenet, *Les
Musiciens de la Sainte-Chapelle du Palais* (Paris, 1910; repr., Geneva, 1973), 23. 1299 is the first
year for which we have records for the liturgical history of the chapel (ibid., 12). On the organ, see
ibid. On the painting, see Fawtier, *Comptes royaux*, vol. 1, 166, no. 3534; and Robert Branner,
"The Painted Medallions in the Sainte-Chapelle in Paris," *Transactions of the American Philosophical Society* ns. 58 (1968): 10. See also the entry in the anonymous Chronicle of Caen relating
to Philip's *renovatio Palatium Parisius* (RHF, vol. 22, 25).

34. Fawtier, *Comptes royaux*, vol. 1, 166, nos. 3505, 3506, 3509, 3512, 3516, 3521, 3522.

35. Ibid., vol. 1, 166, no. 3524, 3525; 165, no. 3490.

36. Brenet, *Les Musiciens*, 12; Fawtier, *Comptes royaux*, vol. 1, 166, no. 3523.

37. Epstein, "Perspectives," 287–288; Gaposchkin, "Philip the Fair," 45. The inventory of
1336 lists in the treasure a "liber de sancto Ludovico" (Vidier, *Le Trésor*, 310/335). It is not clear
to me whether this is a book of hagiography (more likely) or of liturgy (less likely), as the terminology is inconsistent.

38. The earliest copy that I know of is Washington D.C. LC 15, 554r.–558v. On this manuscript, see Baltzer, "A Royal French Breviary."

in the lower chapel of the Ste.-Chapelle and was served by its own chaplaincy.[39] An extant statuette of Louis dating to ca. 1300 and found today at the Museé Cluny is thought to have originally been part of a retable from the chapel.[40] Another altar, in honor of Saints Louis and Michael, was founded twelve years later.[41] It is perhaps one of these altars (maybe a retable or a predella) that was painted with four scenes from the life of Saint Louis: Louis feeding a leprous monk at Royaumont; Louis washing the feet of the poor; Louis being chastised by his confessor; and an angel bringing Louis a breviary while in captivity.[42] (See figures 16 and 17 in chapter 8.) The images reflected the developing iconography for Louis. Both the liturgical office and the mass prosa made reference to the increasingly popular breviary miracle.[43] As Louis had made the Ste.-Chapelle a monument to Christ's Passion, Philip was making it a monument to Louis.

But Philip lacked the most important commodity in a cult center: relics. Despite his efforts in 1298, Louis' relics still lay at St.-Denis. As Brown has argued, Philip never intended that situation to be permanent. A goldsmith was already at work for Philip on a head reliquary for Saint Louis in 1298, the year after the monks secured control of the bones, and the king got Boniface to reissue an indulgence bull for the transference on February 5, 1300 (an initiative that foundered on their increasing difficulties).[44] But it was not until the papacy of Clement V that the king finally succeeded in appropriating Louis' head (exempting the jawbone). As one of his first acts as pope, Clement approved the translation and issued an indulgence in February 1306.[45] On May 17 of that year, almost eight years after his first effort to secure Louis' bones, Philip went to St.-Denis to get the greater part of his grandfather's skull and install it in a lavish reliquary at the Ste.-Chapelle.[46] The elaborate gold and heavily bejeweled head reliquary, wearing the crown, underscored the regalization of the imagery

---

39. M. Sauveru-Jérôme Morand, *Histoire de la Sainte-Chapelle royale* (Paris, 1790), pièces justificative 23–24, 28–30. Two entries from the treasury accounts dated 22 October 1301 confirm the foundation (Viard, *Journaux (Philippe IV)*, 774, no. 5323, 825, no. 5706).

40. Musée du Louvre, *Le trésor de la Sainte-Chapelle* (Paris, 2001), 188, no. 44.

41. Morand, *Histoire*, pièces justificative, 27–28.

42. Auguste Longnon, *Documents Parisiens sur l'iconographie de S. Louis* (Paris, 1882), 3–7; Emile Mâle, "La vie de Saint Louis dans l'art français au commencement du XIVe siècle," in *Mélanges Bertaux: recueil de travaux, dédié a la Mémoire d'Émile Bertaux* (Paris, 1924), 198; Louvre, *Trésor*, 190–192, no. 45.

43. LDR MR5; Prosa: BNF Lat 911, 32r. For text, see AH, vol. 55, 255, no. 227. A sequence found in a sixteenth-century breviary for the Ste.-Chapelle (BNF Lat 8890, fols. 59v.–61v.) includes the reference as well; for text see AH, vol. 8, 171, 224.

44. On William Julian, Philip's goldsmith, and his head reliquary, see Direction des archives de France and Sainte-Chapelle (Paris, France), *Saint Louis: Sainte-Chapelle: mai–août 1960* (Paris, 1960), 88, no. 174; Brown, "Philippe le Bel," 75; and Louvre, *Trésor* 186, no. 43. For documents, see Vidier, *Le Trésor*, 310/276–315/281 (on William Julian), 316/282–317/283 (for indulgences of 1300); and Viard, *journaux (Philippe IV)*, nos. 918, 1047 (on William Julian).

45. Exactly one year after Boniface last issued such an indulgence, on February 5, 1306 (Vidier, *Le Trésor*, 317–318).

46. DuBois, *Historia ecclesiae Parisiensis*, 521–522; Brown, "Philippe le Bel," 175–176.

of Louis in this most royal context, centered on the imagery of Christ's crown and kingship.

A great many ecclesiastics attended the translation, including three archbishops and eighteen bishops; and as one chronicler recounted it, the citizens of Paris rejoiced.[47] Soon afterward, Philip wrote a letter to Clement V requesting indulgences for anyone who visited the Ste.-Chapelle, or anyone who should visit in the future, on the day of the translation and until the day of its octave, and for any other feast of Saint Louis. Philip's letter made clear that Louis was to be remembered for his devotion to the passion relics and that the Ste.-Chapelle was to be associated with Louis as much as with the Passion. Philip spoke of the "most blessed Louis, glorious confessor of Christ, formerly king of the French, our grandfather," who held dear the "sacrosanct insignia of the dominical Passion and other relics," which he bought for the palace chapel during his lifetime. And thus, he continued, it is deemed worthy "that the head of this most glorious confessor, who was in his own time laudably in charge of and of glorious benefit to the French, be solemnly transferred to that very same chapel, which we, by the judgment of rigorous examination, call the head of the whole kingdom of France."[48] The symbolism of the Ste.-Chapelle as the sacral head of the kingdom was underscored not only by the relic of Louis' own head but also by other head relics that Louis himself had acquired during his own reign that were part of the chapel's relic treasury—the heads of John the Baptist, Blaise, Clement, and Simeon.[49] Philip plumbed the image of the head as a symbol of the monarchy, which developed into a central motif in the propaganda of Louis' sanctity as it related to the crown.[50] Identical language is found in the original version of the liturgical office written for the event, where the final lection said that it was fitting for the head of the saint who had ruled France well to have been transferred to the "head" of the kingdom of France, the royal palace.[51] The antiquarian Gérard du Bois, in his *Historia ecclesiae Parisiensis*, cited a passage he claimed came from the *officio proprio sanctae capellae* that again associated Louis' head with the font of governance: "Near this place, where the kings' basilica was [i.e., the Ste.-Chapelle], Philip rendered royal justice; so

47. For the list of ecclesiastics, see DuBois, *Historia ecclesiae Parisiensis*, 521; and Morand, *Histoire*, 87. The *Grandes Chroniques* mentions that the translation was done "a grant joie et a grant feste de la gent de Paris" (Jules Marie Édouard Viard, *Les grandes chroniques de France*, 10 vols. [Paris, 1920], vol. 9, 249).

48. Etienne Baluze and Guillaume Mollat, eds., *Vitae paparum avenionensium; hoc est Historia pontificum romanorum qui in Gallia sederunt ab anno Christi MCCCV usque ad annum MCCCXCIV*, Nouv. éd. (Paris, 1914–1927), vol. 3, 63–64: "beatissimus Ludovicus, gloriosus Christi confessor, quondam rex Francorum, avus noster . . . dignum esse decrevimus ut ad capellam eamdem, quam caput totius regni Francie per stricti districtionem examinis appellamus, prefati caput gloriosissimi confessoris, qui Francis tum laudabiliter prefuit et profuit gloriose sollempniter transfer[r]ctur." For indulgences, see Vidier, *Le Trésor*, 317/282–320/286.

49. Louvre, *Trésor*, 20. My thanks to Sharon Farmer for this observation.

50. Brown, "Philippe le Bel," 176, 181, n. 20. Brown has suggested that, by this claim, Philip undermined St.-Denis' claim to being the *caput francie*.

51. BNF Lat 14511, fol. 180r.–v.

that the august head of the king, for whom the desire to render equity and justice was unassailable, after his death became the measure of behavior, the model of laws and judicial decisions, and the exemplar of judgments."[52]

A second feast day was established at the Ste.-Chapelle to commemorate the translation. Shortly after the event in 1306, Philip wrote a letter to Clement in which he indicated that he intended from the start to institute the new feast, and a new liturgical office was composed for the feast of the translation.[53] Its success was necessarily limited since there was no cause for its use much outside Paris. It was not adopted at Poissy and was ignored by the monks at St.-Denis. But it was an important addition to the calendar in Paris, and within a week of the transfer, Philip assigned the annual celebration of the new feast at the Ste.-Chapelle to the Augustinian friars of Paris.[54]

A few years later, in 1309, Philip asked the Franciscans and Dominicans to be responsible for the celebration of the August 25 feast. He requested that they come to the royal chapel to do the mass (*sollemnitas*) and the office of "Blessed Louis confessor, our grandfather, in our chapel in Paris," that is, to perform the August 25 office for Louis at the Ste.-Chapelle.[55] This was one way to increase the solemnity of the celebration, and it was quite possibly done in imitation of Louis himself, who, when instituting the ceremonies for the Crown of Thorns in the 1240s, established three new processions at the Ste.-Chapelle that were celebrated separately by Dominicans, Franciscans, and a third, unnamed, order.[56] The rubric for BNF Lat 13238, a fifteenth-century breviary for the Ste.-Chapelle, states explicitly that the office is to be conducted by the Preachers and Minors; and the Ste.-Chapelle Ordinary gives specific instructions for the use of the altar decorated with fleurs-de-lis.[57]

Philip managed to control further distribution of the stash, and he gave away Louis' relics as a way of promoting his cult.[58] As early as 1298 he furnished a hand reliquary with a relic of Louis to the fortifications of the Montjoie-Saint-Louis, also founded by Philip.[59] According to Tillemont, the emperor, the count of St.-Paul, the regular canons at the Val-des-Écoliers at Compiègne, and the abbess of Lys were each given a finger bone. The Dominican friars of Paris known as the *Jacobins* got another bone from Louis' hand. The abbey of Pon-

52. DuBois, *Historia ecclesiae Parisiensis*, vol. 2, 522. Cited also in AASS, Aug 25, V, 536. I have not been able to locate any contemporary manuscript sources to confirm the text.

53. The institution of the feast day was confirmed by a contemporary; see Baluze and Mollat, eds., *Vitae paparum*, vol. 1, 3–4; also noted in Vidier, *Le Trésor*, 285/319.

54. For the act itself, see Morand, *Histoire*, pièce justificative, 25. The act is dated to May 24, 1306 (Vidier, *Le Trésor*, 320/286, no. 54).

55. Morand, *Histoire*, piéce justificative, 26. The act is dated to October 1309.

56. WSP *vie*, 41–42.

57. BNF Lat 13238, 290v.; Arsenal 114, 162r. A lost miniature (which survives in a nineteenth-century copy) of the altar in the upper chapel shows the floor around the altar covered in fleur-de-lis (Louvre, *Trésor*, 127, no. 27). This miniature also shows a statuette of Louis.

58. Vidier, *Le Trésor*, 315/281–316/282, no. 50; Tillemont, *Vie vol.* 5, 223–225; LeGoff, *Saint Louis*, 305–310. For relic distribution after the period covered here, see AASS, Aug (V), 536.

59. Direction des archives de France and Sainte-Chapelle (Paris, France), *Saint Louis: Sainte-Chapelle*, 88, no. 171.

toise (Maubuisson) and Notre-Dame of Paris each received a rib. Philip also gave Notre-Dame a jewel-encrusted gold and silver reliquary.[60] Royaumont got part of the shoulder. In 1308 Philip gave a finger bone to the king of Norway. That with this last relic Philip also offered to the Norwegian king one of the thorns from the Crown of Thorns housed at the Ste.-Chapelle indicates that Philip was melding Louis' saintly-kingship with the kingship of Christ.[61]

Philip and the Dominicans

The Dominican convent at Paris constituted the third focus of Philip's active promotion of Louis' cult. In part, like the monks of St.-Denis, the Dominicans of the Rue-St.-Jacques had independent cause to commemorate and celebrate Louis' sanctity.[62] Louis had been an important and devoted patron of the friars, and he drew his confessors from among them—his mendicant hagiographers later claimed that Louis had said that he would have liked to divide himself in two and give half to the Dominicans and half to the Franciscans.[63] The ties were only strengthened under Philip the Fair. But unlike Louis, who split his devotions, it seems, evenly between Preachers and Minors, Philip seems to have had a marked preference for the Dominican order. (It was his wife who patronized the Franciscans.)[64] Many of the clerics at court were Dominicans, and Philip chose confessors from among the Dominicans, all but one of whom came from St.-Jacques.[65] In contrast to Franciscans, who were largely absent from court affairs during Philip's reign, Dominicans were rewarded with important posts, such as his confessor Nicolas of Fréauville who ultimately rose to be a papal legate. Philip wanted his heart to be buried with the Dominicans, at first choosing the Jacobins in Paris where he had had his father's heart buried, later deciding on Poissy.[66] As Philip came to rely more heavily on friars from St.-Jacques, the same friars became increasingly supportive of Philip's royalist causes, of which the promotion of Saint Louis was a centerpiece.

60. William Chester Jordan, "Liturgical and Ceremonial Cloths: Neglected Evidence of Medieval Political Theology," *Revue des archéologues et histoires d'art de Louvain* 12 (1979): 105. The gift to Notre-Dame was noted by John of Saint Victor; Baluze and Mollat, eds., *Vitae paparum*, vol. 1, 4.

61. In 1304 (Fawtier, *Comptes royaux*, vol. 2, 536, no. 23914). On subsequent dispersions of the relic collection of the Ste.-Chapelle, see Jean-Michel Leniaud and Françoise Perrot, *La Sainte Chapelle* (Paris, 1991), 54–55.

62. Little, "Saint Louis," 125–137. As early as 1271 the General Chapter instituted an annual commemoration for Louis.

63. For Louis' desire to split himself in two, see GB *vita* 7 (ch. 12). For patronage, see C. H. Lawrence, *The Friars: The Impact of the Early Mendicant Movement on Western Society* (London, 1994), 167.

64. Xavier de la Selle, *Le service des âmes à la cour: confesseurs et aumôniers des rois de France du XIIIe au XVe siècle* (Paris, 1995), 310–315.

65. Abbé Oroux, *Histoire ecclésiastique de la cour de France, Où l'on trouve tout ce qui concern l'histoire de la Chapelle & des principaux Officiers Ecclésiastiques de nos Rois* (Paris, 1776), 371, 381–82, 390; Georges Minois, *Le confesseur du roi: les directeurs de conscience sous la monarchie française* (Paris, 1988), 190–195; de la Selle, *Service des âmes*, 102, 262–267.

66. Brown, "The Prince," 300.

That Philip made St.-Louis of Poissy a Dominican foundation underscores the importance of the role the Dominicans played in Philip's efforts to establish a fitting veneration of his grandfather.[67] He began building the sumptuous church immediately upon getting the news of Louis' canonization, suggesting that the plans must have been long underway and just waiting for official go-ahead.[68] Philip spared no expense on the project. In July he was paying for the liturgical books for the new foundation;[69] and the following year the treasury financed a good portion of the priory's new library, including a number of vitas of its patron, Saint Louis.[70] The decoration at Poissy included sculptures of Louis and his family in the transepts—an indication of Capetian *beata stirps*. In his will, Philip provided enormous, almost crippling, sums for the convent's support after his death.[71]

The Dominicans of Paris were natural allies for Philip in promoting the cult. This explains some of the confusing evidence regarding the composition and dissemination of two liturgical offices that were associated with—and here is the point—both the court and the Dominicans, especially because their representation of Louis' sanctity was consonant with the ideological aims of the crown. The two offices were intimately related to one another: they shared a number of texts; the same hymns were associated with both; and both were based on the same principles of composition that reworked verses from the Psalms. Although the exact circumstance of their composition remains unclear, what is certain from the available evidence is that the two royalizing offices emerged out of the web of relationships that encompassed the court, the friars of St.-Jacques, and the Dominican nuns of Poissy.

Two sets of conflicting evidence exist concerning the authorship of these offices. The king's treasury accounts show him paying a considerable amount to four men, including a well-reputed liturgist named Pierre de la Croix, for an office for Louis in July and August 1298. Pierre was a secular cleric, probably from Amiens, who wrote a treatise on modes and was active in Paris in these years.[72] At the same time, though, Bernard Gui, the historian of the Dominican order, claims at two different instances that in 1297 Arnaud du Prat,

67. Erlande-Brandenburg, "La Priorale"; Alain Erlande-Brandenburg, "Art et politique sous Philippe le Bel. La priorale Saint-Louis de Poissy," *Comptes rendus de l'Académie des Inscriptions et Belles Lettres* (1987): 507–518.

68. Hallam, "Philip the Fair," 205.

69. Viard, *Journaux (Philippe IV)*, 158, no. 994, dated July 30, 1298.

70. Alexandre Vidier, *Extraits de Comptes Royaux concernant Paris: I. Journal du Tresor (1298–1301)* (Paris, 1912), 40–41. Between April 19, 1298, and December 15, 1301, Philip paid for the copying (*pro scriptura*) of multiple volumes for the priory on at least twelve different occasions. The volumes about Saint Louis are recorded in a payment of July 30, 1298. In all twelve instances the copyist is noted to be from the Order of Preachers. See also Naughton, "Manuscripts from Poissy."

71. Brown, "Royal Salvation," 365–379.

72. Amédée Gastoué, *Les primitifs de la musique française* (Paris, 1922); Glenn Pierr Johnson, "Aspects of Late Medieval Music at the Cathedral of Amiens" (Ph.D. diss., Yale University, 1991), 460–567.

OP[73] from the south of France, wrote a liturgical office for Louis that had been adopted at the royal court over other available offices.[74] Two authors. Two offices. Because the Ste.-Chapelle and the *Capella regis* (two different institutions) both used *Ludovicus decus*, this office is generally associated with the Dominican du Prat.[75]

The available manuscript evidence provides another view of the problem. The office *Nunc laudare* is extant in but three manuscripts, two of which belonged to the original commission of liturgical books made for Poissy and paid for by Philip the Fair.[76] The third volume, Mazarine 374, belonged to the friars of St.-Jacques. All three exemplars are in hands dating to about 1300. Philip also paid friars from the convent to copy the liturgical volumes for the nuns at Poissy in 1298, and the copy in Mazarine 374 probably served as an exemplar for the Poissy volumes.[77] The context here is squarely Dominican.

The two earliest known exemplars of *Ludovicus decus regnantium* are associated with the court. The first, Washington Library of Congress ms. 15, includes the office atypically paired with lections for *Gloriosissimi regis* (suggesting an early, provisional pairing). Rebecca Baltzer has argued that the manuscript belongs to a family of manuscripts produced for the court and suggested that it belonged to Robert of Claremont, Louis' youngest son.[78] The second, BNF Lat 911, the shrine book containing all the liturgical materials for Louis' feast day, is also not a Dominican volume.[79] Lat 911 bears instead all the indications of belonging to the Ste.-Chapelle or the *Capella regis*. It included the rare set of octave antiphons prescribed by the fifteenth-century Ordinary for the Ste.-Chapelle (Arsenal 114) found only in volumes from the Ste.-Chapelle and Notre-Dame.[80] Later in the fourteenth century, the manuscript was given

---

73. For Arnaud du Prat, see Jacques Quétif, Jacques Échard, and Remi Coulon, *Scriptores ordinis Praedicatorum* (Louvain, 1961); Thomas Kaeppeli and Emilio Panella, *Scriptores Ordinis Praedicatorum Medii Aevi*, 4 vols. (Rome, 1970–1993), vol. 1, 127; C. Douais, *Les frères prêcheurs en Gascogne au XIIIème et au XIVème siècle: chapitres, couvents et notices: documents inédits* (Paris, 1885), 365; and Félix Lajard, "Arnaud du Pré (Arnaldus de Prato)," in HLF, vol. 25, 240–244. Most of what we know of Arnaud du Prat comes from Bernard Gui (*De fundatione et prioribus conventuum provinciarum Tolosanae et provinciae ordinis praedicatorum*, ed. Paul A. Amargier, vol. 24 [Rome, 1961], 112).

74. Gaposchkin, "Philip the Fair," 39–40, n. 29.

75. Robert Branner, "The Sainte-Chapelle and the *Capella Regis* in the Thirteenth Century," *Gesta* 10 (1971): 19–22.

76. BL Add 30027, fols. 413v.–425r. (not BL Add 3072, as listed by Dreves in AH, vol. 13, no. 74) and Rouen Y 233, 273r.–277v. Both volumes include both *Nunc laudare* and the *Ludovicus decus*, the latter in a later hand. These are discussed and catalogued in Naughton, "Manuscripts from Poissy."

77. Vidier, *Extraits*, 40–41; Naughton, "Manuscripts from Poissy," ch. 2.

78. Baltzer, "A Royal French Breviary," 3–25.

79. The volume lacked the distinctive paleographic *custos*—the upward dash at the end of the line—prescribed by Dominican copyists of liturgical books. See Michel Huglo, "Notated Performance Practices in Parisian Chant Manuscripts of the Thirteenth Century," in *Plainsong in the Age of Polyphony*, ed. Thomas Forrest Kelley (Cambridge, 1992), 32–44.

80. Arsenal 114, fols. 163v.–164r. On this manuscript, see Barbara Haggh, "An Ordinal of Ockeghem's Time from the Sainte-Chapelle of Paris: Paris, Bibliothèque de l'Arsenal, ms 114," *Tijdschrift van de Koninklijke Vereniging voor Nederlandse Muziekgeschiedenis* (1997): 33–71.

to the College of Navarre, which Charles V had established as the center for commemoration of Louis' sanctity at the university a few years earlier.[81]

Internal evidence provides other clues. *Nunc laudare*, the office found in the Poissy and St.-Jacques manuscripts in about 1300, followed the Dominican format for the liturgical office, comprising only one antiphon (instead of five) for First Vespers. This fact is consistent with its use at the two Dominican houses. In contrast, *Ludovicus decus*, which Gui suggests was made for Dominican use, included five antiphons for First Vespers, which conformed to secular usage in place at the Ste.-Chapelle. In and of itself, this would suggest that *Nunc laudare* was written for a Dominican context, and *Ludovicus decus* for a secular one. Moreover, the heavy use, particularly in the hymns, in *Nunc laudare* of vocabulary insisting on the newness of the celebration—*nunc laudare, nove laudis, nove regis preconia, nova sollemnia*—belonged to a tradition within the poetic aesthetics of Dominican liturgical composition from the proceeding century, and its hymns borrowed their incipits from the office of Saint Dominic.[82] And, lastly, the modal order (a medieval categorization for chant that is determined by the reciting pitch of the final note of a chant line) of the offices suggests that *Nunc laudare* was quickly and provisionally compiled, awaiting the production of the elaborate, ordered, *Ludovicus decus*.[83]

Ludovicus decus was ultimately adopted at the two Dominican houses. Mazarine 374, the volume from St.-Jacques, which included *Nunc laudare* in an early hand, also included a copy of *Ludovicus decus* in a hand that dates to about 1330.[84] This section of the manuscript was clearly added later, and emendations to both the litany and the instructions for the Feast of the Assumption in the same hand indicate liturgical changes that involved Louis' feast day. The official examination copy for the Dominican order—BL Add 23935—also includes *Ludovicus decus* in a section of the manuscript added between 1358 and 1363.[85] Volumes from Poissy that date to mid-century also include *Ludovicus decus*, though here the office is altered to conform to Dominican usage with only one First Vespers antiphon.[86]

Taken by itself, the manuscript evidence indicates that *Nunc laudare* was written hastily for a Dominican context—either Poissy or St.-Jacques or both. (Official institution of a new feast took at least three years, and the friars of St.-Jacques may well have wanted to jumpstart their liturgical

81. Gaposchkin, "Philip the Fair," 44–45.

82. On the theme of "newness," see Josef Szövérffy, *Die Annalen der Lateinischen Hymnendichtung: Ein Handbuch*, 2 vols., vol. 2: *Die lateinischen Hymnen vom Ende des 11. Jahrhunderts bis zum Ausgang des Mittelalters* (Berlin, 1965), vol. 2, 233–235.

83. Andrew Hughes, "Modal Order and Disorder in the Rhymed Office," *Musica Disciplina* 37 (1983): 29–51; Gaposchkin, "Philip the Fair," 58–59.

84. Mazarine 374, fols. 308v.–314v.

85. BL Add 23935, 7r.–9r. (the office for Saint Louis), 14r. (the mass of Saint Louis), 20r.–21r. (the lections for Saint Louis). On the dating of the addition, see G. R. Galbraith, *The Constitution of the Dominican Order, 1216 to 1360* (Manchester, 1925), 197–198.

86. Arsenal 603, 317r.

honors.)[87] This would account for the jumbled modal order of the office, since the Dominicans may have quickly compiled an office for their saint early on, in 1297. The hymns associated with both offices all begin with phrases for the office of St.-Dominic, and Marcy Epstein has noted that some of the music used for *Nunc laudare* was derived from the Dominican office for the Crown of Thorns.[88] In contrast, *Ludovicus decus* appears to have been written at greater leisure for a secular and royal context, using *Nunc laudare* as a starting template, and adopting its hymns. Ultimately, the well-ordered, more polished secular office displaced *Nunc laudare* at St.-Jacques and Poissy, perhaps after 1309 when Philip brought the Dominicans in to celebrate *Ludovicus decus* on August 25. *Nunc laudare*, ultimately short-lived among Dominicans, had something of an afterlife at the court. The Translation Feast of 1306 adopted a number of its items, as did *Sanctus voluntatem*, the office that was included in books of hours made for members of the royal family.

The question of who wrote what still remains up in the air. Pierre de la Croix may have written *Nunc laudare* at Philip's request for Poissy in 1298. Or he may have written *Ludovicus decus*, and Bernard Gui was mistaken about Arnaud's office being used at court. Arnaud du Prat, a Dominican, may have written *Nunc laudare* as a provisional office in 1297 (as Gui said), or it is possible that he reworked *Nunc laudare* into *Ludovicus decus* at some later point (in which case, Gui would have gotten the date wrong). The idea that Arnaud, a Dominican, composed the Dominican *Nunc laudare,* and Pierre, a secular cleric, composed the secular *Ludovicus decus*, is an elegant and clean solution, but not definitively demonstrable. Either way, what is evident is that the composition and use of the two liturgical traditions were intertwined, and that the friars at St.-Jacques were heavily involved in constructing liturgical aspects of Louis' sanctity.

This point is cast into higher relief by looking at the role the Dominicans played at Philip's court. That the Dominican convent should be a center for the promotion of Louis' cult, and specifically for Philip's vision of Louis' sanctity, fits not only with the order's devotion to the king but also with their general interest in kingship and their support of Philip's royalist claims. By 1301, when things heated up again between Philip and Boniface VIII, the Dominicans of St.-Jacques

87. In the Dominican order, a new feast was required to be confirmed three times by the general chapter before it was officially instituted. For Louis, these occurred in 1298, 1300, and 1301 (since no chapter met in 1299). On this procedure, see Leonard Boyle, "Dominican Lectionaries and Leo of Ostia's *Translatio S. Clementis,*" *Archivum Fratrum Praedicatorum* 28 (1958): 362–394. For the process of codification and the early sources for the Dominican office, see essays in Leonard Boyle and Pierre-Marie Gy, eds., *Aux origines de la liturgie dominicaine: le manuscrit Santa Sabina XIV L 1* (Rome, 2004). See, in particular, the essay by Michel Huglo, "Comparaison de 'prototype' du couvent Saint-Jacques de Paris avec l'exemplaire personnel du Maître de l'ordre des prêcheurs (Londres, British Library, Add. ms 23935)," 197–214.

88. Epstein, "Perspectives," 298, 301, although she believed *Nunc laudare* to be derived from *Ludovicus decus*. On the Dominican office for the Crown of Thorns, see Judith Blezzard, Stephen Ryle, and Jonathan Alexander, "New Perspectives on the Feast of the Crown of Thorns," *Journal of the Plainsong and Medieval Music Society* 10 (1987); and Mercuri, "Stat inter spinas," 501.

were especially supportive of the king's controversial claims.[89] The king's confessor, Renaud d'Aubigny, preached a public sermon defending Philip against Boniface.[90] At the curia, Philip's other confessor, Nicholas of Fréauville, was accused of inciting the king's animosity toward the pope.[91] It was a Dominican, John of Paris, who wrote the most cogent theological and juridical justification of Philip's position against the papacy.[92] As we'll see, the Dominican office was strongly royalizing, and the Dominicans of Paris preached a number of sermons that exalted Louis in terms consonant with the ideals of Philip's court.

Other Princely Courts

Though Philip IV was most invested in constructing and promoting the cult of Louis, the new royal saint clearly appealed to the princely class with ties to the French court and an investment in Capetian identity. Joinville tells us that he erected an altar in his chapel at Chevillon in Louis' honor, in which mass would be sung in perpetuity.[93] Household accounts and other administrative records document the rapid incorporation of Louis into the devotional spheres of high aristocratic circles. In Artois, at the court of Robert II, a number of innovations were made to recognize Saint Louis. As early as December 13, 1298, payments were recorded for the copying of sixteen liturgical offices for Louis.[94] At least one of the two palace chapels attached to the castle at Hesdin was refurbished in 1299, perhaps in anticipation of Philip the Fair's visit to the court, and a statue of Saint Louis was installed in the countess's oratory. Mahaut of Artois, Robert's daughter, was also devoted to her sainted great-uncle. Jules Marie Richard's study of her household has documented a rich array of commissions in his honor.[95] Accounts a generation later from Hainault indicate that members of the court were continuing to request various items out of devotion to Louis.[96] In 1335 a certain *livre de saint Loys* was purchased by a noble member of the household. In 1332 Louis' *Enseignements,* the instructions for Christian rule written for Philip III, were copied

---

89. Minois, *Le confesseur du roi,* 193–194; de la Selle, *Service des âmes,* 103, 152, 251. For the reaction of the friars at St.-Jacques to the letters of adherence, see William J. Courtenay, "Between Pope and King: The Parisian Letters of Adhesions of 1303," *Speculum* 71 (1996): 596–599, who argues that there was in fact a dissenting voice among the Jacobins.

90. De la Selle, *Service des âmes,* 152.

91. Minois, *Le confesseur du roi,* 194.

92. John of Paris, *On Royal and Papal Power,* ed. John A. Watt (Toronto, 1971).

93. Joinville, §767.

94. Malcolm G. A. Vale, *The Princely Court: Medieval Courts and Culture in North-west Europe, 1270–1380* (Oxford, 2001), 228–229, ns. 298 and 299.

95. These commissions included several liturgical books with hours to Saint Louis, and a sculpted image and two silver images for an oratory and the chapel at Hesdin. See Jules-Marie Richard, *Une petite nièce de Saint Louis: Mahaut, comtesse d'Artois et de Bourgogne (1302–1329). Étude sur la vie privée, les arts et l'industrie, en Artois et à Paris au commencement du XIVe siècle* (Paris, 1887), 104, 248, 252, 307, 327, 339.

96. Vale, *Princely Court,* 273.

for the future count (William IV). The *Enseignements* became a devotional and exemplary model among princes. The "Petits Heurs" of Jean, duc de Berry, included a copy of the *Enseignements,* oddly, given the fact that the text was not liturgical.[97]

Other cadet branches valued Louis, probably as a prestigious symbol of their connection to the royal house. Female members of the Navarre line included the rare Hours of Louis in their books of hours, and Blanche of Navarre sponsored imagery to Louis in her funerary chapel of Saint Hippolyte at St.-Denis (ca. 1372).[98] A Burgundian tradition of commemorating Louis may also have been promoted primarily by the female line, whose descent from Louis was through Agnes of France, his youngest child. Agnes herself commissioned a chapel to Louis in Dijon, modeled on the Ste.-Chapelle, to which she donated one of his crowns, and another at her castle at Lantenay.[99] Her son Eudes confirmed her expenditures in his will, and it has been argued that her daughter Jeanne (Philip VI's wife) may have commissioned the illustrated *Vie* by Saint-Pathus.[100] Another of her daughters, Blanche of Savoy (or Burgundy), was the owner of the Savoy Hours, which included the rare cycle to Louis. As early as 1304 another granddaughter, married to Rodolf of Austria, founded a Franciscan church in Vienna dedicated to Louis.[101]

The cult of Louis was also promoted by men who wanted to flatter the crown. Enguerran de Marigny, Philip the Fair's ill-fated chamberlain and minister, had executed no less than three statues of Louis for chapels at Plessis and at Mainneville, and for the collegiate church of Notre-Dame of Ecouis that he founded.[102] In 1305 Pierre de Chambly, a chamberlain of Philip IV, patronized three chapels near Beaumont sur Oise, Gisors, and Louviers dedicated to Louis.[103] One of Philip's counselors founded a church in Montcabrier dedicated to Louis.[104] Philip Valois' procurer of Parliament endowed a chapel dedicated to Saint Louis in the parish church of Dormans.[105] Cultivation and commemoration of Louis' sanctity may also have

97. François Avril, Louisa Dunlop, and Brunsdon Yapp, *Les Petites Heures de Jean, duc de Berry: Introduction au manuscrits lat. 18014 de la Bibliothèque nationale, Paris* (Lucerne, 1989), 66–67, at fols. 14–20.

98. Keane, "Remembering Louis," 130.

99. Ibid., 66.

100. Proposed by Jane Geein Chung-Apley, "The Illustrated *Vie et Miracles de Saint Louis* of Guillaume de Saint-Pathus (Paris, B.N., ms. fr. 5716)" (Ph.D. diss., University of Michigan, 1998), 144–171.

101. Paul Deschamps, "À propos de la statue de Saint Louis à Mainneville," *Bulletin monumental* 127 (1969): 38.

102. Direction des archives de France and Sainte-Chapelle (Paris, France), *Saint Louis: Sainte-Chapelle*, 82, no. 158; *L'Art au temps des rois maudits: Philippe le Bel et ses fils, 1285–1328* (Paris, 1998), 101–102, no. 51.

103. Deschamps, "À propos," 38.

104. Hallam, "Philip the Fair," 208.

105. Carra Ferguson O'Meara, *Monarchy and Consent: The Coronation Book of Charles V of France, British Library MS Cotton Tiberius B. VIII* (London, 2001), 142.

had antimonarchical elements to it. Joinville's use of Saint Louis as a warning against the monarchical abuses of his descendants is well known, and Joinville participated in the Leagues of 1314 that formed to protest abuse and usurpation of governmental power where Louis was hailed as an exemplum of royal behavior against Philip the Fair, and then against Louis X.[106] Marie of Brabant's foundation in 1312 of a Parisian-style gothic chapel to Louis (and Saint Paul) at the collegiate church of Mantes may have been a strategy of legitimacy once she had been sidelined from the court.[107]

Though we know less about nonroyal, nonaristocratic devotion to Louis, piecemeal evidence exists for the years immediately after 1297. An inscribed enamel funerary plaque made for the otherwise unknown Guy de Meyos and dating to 1307 shows the cleric kneeling in prayer before the hallowed and crowned Louis IX.[108] Sharon Farmer and William Chester Jordan have focused attention on sources that indicate a level of devotion from less visible sectors of society. Farmer's study of the social networks of the poor evidenced in the miracle collections in Louis' canonization dossier—transcribed by William of Saint-Pathus—has focused inquiry on poor men and women otherwise lost to the historical record. These men and women, drawn to the Abbey of St.-Denis to request the intercession of Saint Louis prior to his canonization, testified at the hearings in 1282–1283; their testimony demonstrates veneration to the king-saint among the lower strata of society, including beggars and the working poor.[109] In turn, Jordan highlights two documents (from 1317 and 1320) recording the foundation of an endowment for three masses a week at an altar dedicated to Louis' honor at a parish church, St.-Martin, in the town of St.-Florentin, northeast of Paris, by the well-to-do townsman and prévôt Jean le Voyer. As a prévôt and thus an agent of the crown, Jean le Voyer may have identified with the royal identity of the saint, but the foundation is testament to veneration of Louis outside strictly aristocratic or royal circles, which may have been stronger than the record now allows us to suggest.[110] In both cases, what is noteworthy is the chance survival of sources that point to a wider veneration of Louis than is generally acknowledged.

106. Joinville, §42, 761. On the Leagues, see André Artonne, *Le mouvement de 1314 et les chartres provinciales de 1315* (Paris, 1912); and Elizabeth A. R. Brown, "Reform and Resistance to Royal Authority in Fourteenth-Century France: The Leagues of 1314–1315," *Parliaments, Estates, and Representation* 1 (1981): 109–137, repr., in Brown, *Politics and Institutions in Capetian France* (Hampshire, UK, 1991), V.

107. Philippe Plagnieux, "Une foundation de la reine Marie de Brabant: La chapelle Saint-Paul Saint-Louis," in *Mantes médiévale: La collégiale au coeur de la ville* (Paris, 2000), 110–116; Keane, "Remembering Louis," 135.

108. Reproduced in John Philip O'Neill, *Enamels of Limoges: 1100–1350*, trans. Joachim Neugroschel, Sophie Hawkes, and Patricia Stirneman (New York, 1996), 420–421; *L'Art au temps des rois maudits*, 219–220, no. 144.

109. Sharon Farmer, "Down and Out and Female in Thirteenth-Century Paris," *American Historical Review* 103 (1998): 345–372; Farmer, *Surviving Poverty*.

110. William Chester Jordan, "Honoring Saint Louis in a Small Town," *Journal of Medieval History* 30 (2004): 263–277.

Saint Louis in the Kingdom of Sicily

Dynastic and royal interests paved the way for Saint Louis of France to make his way southward to Italy and to the Kingdom of Sicily (Naples).[111] In 1265 Charles of Anjou had been invited to throw out the Hohenstaufen line and take over the Kingdom of Sicily as a fiefdom of the papacy. The newly established dynasty sought to confirm its authority and establish the legitimacy of its rule, and it did so in part by advancing a highly developed articulation of the *beata stirps,* the argument that the royal line itself was blessed and that this was manifest in members of the lineage who were now saints: Elizabeth of Hungary (can. 1235), Kings Stephen and Ladislas of Hungary (the latter can. 1192), and, most important, Louis of Toulouse (Charles II's son, Robert of Anjou's brother, can. 1317), and Louis IX, who was older brother to the dynasty's founder, Charles I. Charles himself, we saw, had been instrumental in the canonization effort for Louis and as early as 1282 had advanced the idea that not only Louis but the entire lineage was holy.[112] With the canonization of Charles' grandson (Louis' great-nephew), Louis of Toulouse, the *beata stirps* theme became predominant for the Angevins.[113]

It is within this context that the cult of Louis IX traveled to the Kingdom of Naples, piggybacking, as it were, on the shoulders of Louis of Toulouse. Mary of Hungary, the wife of Charles II, had a statuette of Saint Louis (IX) that she left to Franciscan nuns.[114] Her son Robert of Anjou (also king of Sicily) wrote two sermons for Louis IX, one of which he indicated could also be preached for his brother, Louis of Toulouse.[115] James of Viterbo, who preached no less than five sermons at (probably) the Angevin court, also wrote a sermon to Louis of Toulouse *before* his canonization.[116] The tombs for Charles of Calabria (d. 1328) and Robert of Anjou (d. 1343) bore images of both Louis of Toulouse and Louis of France.[117] On the Last Judgment Fresco in the Clarissan church

111. The standard work on this remains Émile Bertaux, "Les saints Louis dans l'art italien," *Revue des deux mondes* 158 (1900): 616–644. See also Gardner, "The Cult," 167–193; Alessandro Barbero, "La propaganda di Roberto d'Angiò re di Napoli (1309–1343)," in *Le forme della propaganda politica nel Due e nel Trecento: relazioni tenute al convegno internazionale organizzato dal Comitato di studi storici di Trieste, dall'École française de Rome, e dal Dipartimento di storia dell'Università degli studi di Trieste, Trieste, 2–5 marzo 1993* (Rome, 1994), 111–131; and Nancy Thompson, "Cooperation and Conflict: Stained Glass in the Bardi Chapel of Santa Croce," in *The Art of the Franciscan Order in Italy,* ed. William R. Cook (Leiden, 2005), 257–277.

112. Riant, "Déposition," 175.

113. Vauchez, *"Beata stirps,"* 397–406; Klaniczay, *Holy Rulers,* 295–394; Kelly, *The New Solomon,* 119–129.

114. Bertaux, "Les saints Louis," 629.

115. On Robert's preaching, see Jean-Paul Boyer, *"Ecce Rex Tuus:* Le roi et le royaume dans les sermons de Robert de Naples," *Revue Mabillon* ns 6 (= 67) (1995): 101–136; and Darleen N. Pryds, *The King Embodies the Word: Robert d'Anjou and the Politics of Preaching* (Leiden, 2000).

116. David Anderson, " 'Dominus Ludovicus' in the Sermons of Jacobus of Viterbo (Arch. S. Pietro D. 213)," in *Literature and Religion in the Later Middle Ages: Philological Studies in Honor of Siegfried Wenzel,* ed. Richard Newhauser and John Alford (Binghamton, N.Y., 1995), 275–295.

117. Kelly, *The New Solomon,* 123.

of Donna Maria Regina in Naples, built by Mary of Hungary in the early fourteenth century, Louis IX appeared alongside Louis of Toulouse among the
saints.[118] The Franciscans played a role in this context, particularly because
Louis of Toulouse was a Franciscan bishop and the court of Naples included
patrons of the Franciscans. From Naples, as Emile Bertaux showed, Louis' cult
moved into northern Italy.[119] Louis IX began appearing in image cycles that
included other members of the Angevin-Arpadian complex in Assisi and Florence as well as Naples.[120] Images of Louis IX venerating the passion relics began appearing on Tuscan earthenware, and Louis of France became the subject
of sermons preached by Italians such as John of San Gimigniano OP, Giovanni
Regina OP, Remegius of Florence OP, and Arnaud Royard OM.[121] Like James
of Viterbo, many of these preachers were tied up in the politics and rhetoric of
the Angevin court. A number of them preached funeral orations for members
of the Angevin royal family that never failed to make mention of the two Saint
Louis of their lineage.[122] Here Louis IX's royal identity was preeminent. Sermons for Louis did not usually draw on the narrative of his life but tended to
take as their focus the more general themes of "justice," or "kingship," indicating that, as memory of Louis was increasingly distanced from Paris, specific
knowledge about his life and the qualities that had made him saintly were replaced with the singular notion of his royalty. A sermon by John of San
Gimigniano—which troubles through the question of the power of the royal
touch as an attribute of sanctity—drew its information not from a life of Louis
but from a life of Saint Remegius, the early bishop whose baptism of Clovis
became the source for the legend of the miraculous consecration that came to
be understood as the source for the royal touch.

The Scope of Commemoration

If sermons and iconography are one way of tracing a cult, another measure
is the extent of liturgical honors.[123] The years immediately following Louis' canonization witnessed an energetic and fluid composition of liturgical and paraliturgical texts relating to his feast day. A number of surviving and interrelated

118. Samantha Kelly, "Religious Patronage and Royal Propaganda in Angevin Naples: Santa
Maria Donna Regina in Context," in *The Church of Santa Maria Donna Regina: Art, Iconography, and Patronage in Fourteenth-Century Naples*, ed. Janis Elliott and Cordelia Warr (Burlington, Vt., 2004), 39.

119. Bertaux, "Les saints Louis," 616–644, esp. 634.

120. Gardner, "The Cult"; Kelly, "Religious Patronage"; Thompson, "Cooperation and Conflict."

121. Erkinger Schwarzenberg, "Der Hl. Ludwig von Frankreich in Anbetung der Reliquien der
Sainte Chapelle auf einer toskanischen Schüssel des späten Trecento," *Mitteilungen des Kunsthistorischen Institutes in Florenz* (1985): 159–173. See Appendix 3 for sermons by these preachers.

122. D'Avray, *Death and the Prince*, 117–158; Boyer, "Prédication et état napolitain," 146.

123. Jean Fournée, "Le culte et l'iconographie de saint Louis en Normandi," *Art de Basse Nor-
mandi* 61 (1971): 35–46; Beaune, *Birth*, 327–330. On dedications (*vocables*), see Pierre Morel,
"La culte de Saint Louis," *Itineraires, documents* (1970): 127–151; Pierre Morel, *La culte de saint
Louis et les vocables paroissiaux* (Paris, n.d.).

texts emerged at this time that were probably associated with the liturgy, including two vitas in twelve chapters (which could suggest a monastic context), and another in nine chapters that was an edited version associated with the secular office.[124] Louis' name was added to the calendar of dozens of breviaries, missals, and psalters dating to the thirteenth century, and sometimes appeared in the margin of the August calendar or the Sanctorale of late August.[125] This simple addition did not necessarily, or even usually, mean the inclusion of a proper office; and many houses simply resorted to the Common for Confessors (among whom, the Carmelites, the Augustinians, and the Carthusians).[126] Dozens of late medieval breviaries in Italy, Germany, and Scandinavia included a version of the collect for the August 25 feast.[127]

For those communities with strong ties to Louis and a strong desire to commemorate Louis with special services, a proper liturgy was used. A number of proper masses were composed, as were elaborate liturgical offices.[128] We have already encountered two of these—*Nunc laudare* and *Ludovicus decus*. Several others were compiled for the feast of August 25, and another office was compiled for the feast of the translation of his relics to the Ste.-Chapelle, which occurred in 1306 and was scheduled for the first Tuesday following Ascension (or sometimes simply May 17).[129] Shortly thereafter, the "Hours of Louis" were compiled and incorporated in the private devotional books of hours executed at the royal court. The different liturgical offices were:

(1) *Nunc laudare.* *Nunc laudare* was the Dominican office written in the early flush of enthusiasm that came with Louis' canonization, by (probably) the Dominican lector Arnaud du Prat, either for St.-Jacques or Poissy. It was, however, never widely copied and may have been intended for provisional use only. It was replaced by *Ludovicus decus*. None of the extant liturgical volumes include

124. The two vitae in twelve chapters were *Gloriosissimi regis* and a longer version of a text that begins with *Beatus Ludovicus quondam rex Francorum*. The latter text was edited to nine chapters to produce the lections associated with *Ludovicus decus*.

125. Charleville 50, Premonstensian Breviary, in margin fol. 237; St.-Genevieve MS 2619 (Breviary from St.-Quentin-le-Beauvais), Provins BM ms 80 (Paris Breviary); Reims BM 316 (St.-Remi breviary, added at fol. 390v.); St.-Quentin ms 3 at 10v. (St.-Quentin breviary); Sens, trésor de la cathédrale, in margin at fol. 499; Soissons BM ms 120, Premonstensian Breviary; Charleville BM 154 (Carthusian missal); Le Mans BM 157, Soissons Psalter; Rouen BM 299 (Jumieges missal). Two prosa were added to Paris BNF Lat 15615, a Paris missal; BNF Lat 8884, fol. 277, a Dominican missal adapted to Paris usage; BNF Lat 750 (a breviary from Jouarre-en-Brie); Amiens BM 115, fol. 339r. (breviary from Corbie); Arras BM 465, a breviary of St.-Vaast d'Arras. Lections were added to Mazarine 396; BNF Lat 1043, fol. 387v.; BNF Lat 1280 (Franciscan Italian breviary, Louis added to calendar); BNF Lat 14810, a diurnal for St.-Victor's in Paris, where the collect for Louis has been added in the bottom margin in a fourteenth- or fifteenth-century hand (fol. 85r.); Laon, BM 13 (a thirteenth-century Cistercian Psalter, with "ludovici regis xii lc" added in August calendar); BNF Lat 9376 (breviary adapted to use at Longchamp, in calendar).

126. Mazarine 357 (for the Carmelites); Vat Ottob Lat 221, fols. 185va.–186ra. (for the Augustinians); BL Add 40154, fol. 167 (for the Carthusians).

127. Barth, "Kult," 159–169.

128. For texts of the masses for Saint Louis, see AH vol. 4, 189; vol. 40, 211–212, nos. 239–240; vol. 55, 255–257, nos. 227–228.

129. BNF Lat 1435, fol. 21v (Ordinary for the capella regis).

lections, though *Nunc laudare* may have been paired with the abbreviated lections the Dominican order published in 1306.[130]

(2) *Ludovicus decus regnantium. Ludovicus decus* is the most important of the offices in that it was by far the most widely disseminated and widely influential.[131] Probably commissioned by Philip the Fair for the Ste.-Chapelle, it was influenced by *Nunc laudare*, employing the same poetic logic for its antiphons and incorporating its hymns and a number of its prayers. *Ludovicus decus* was, however, far more polished, musically more elaborate, and internally consistent. Its use spread from Paris to a number of secular churches in the Île-de-France and northern France, and it ultimately displaced *Nunc laudare* at St.-Jacques and Poissy. The hagiographical lections associated with *Ludovicus decus* constituted a short vita in nine parts whose incipit is *Beatus Ludovicus quondam rex francorum* (hereafter *Beatus Ludovicus*) that was specifically compiled to accompany it.[132] At some later point, but probably by about 1310, when BNF Lat 911 was copied, eight antiphons were compiled for the Octave service, which adopted text items from the Franciscan office (*Francorum rex*), the Monastic office (*Lauda celestis 1 or 3*), and from the Dominican office (*Nunc laudare*).

(3:1–3) *Lauda celestis. Lauda celestis* survives in three forms.[133] The Cistercians first composed *Lauda celestis 1*, a liturgical office that followed the monastic cursus (including twelve, rather than nine, readings and responsories during Matins). It was limited in use, surviving in only two known manuscripts, but was incorporated into printed breviaries in 1630 and 1641. A secular version of this office was then composed (*Lauda celestis 2*), in which the antiphons and responsories were reduced in number. This office was then re-expanded for monastic use at Paris (*Lauda celestis 3*), in manuscripts associated with the Benedictine abbeys of St.-Germain-des-Prés and St.-Denis, both with close ties to the crown. The adaptation involved the incorporation of a number of chant items drawn from *Ludovicus decus regnantium.*

(4) *Francorum rex* was the office written by the Franciscan friars of Paris. *Francorum rex* adopted lections from the hagiographical life, *Gloriossisimi regis.*

(5) *Exultemus omnes* was the office for the Feast of the Translation of the Head of Louis established in 1306 and celebrated at the Ste.-Chapelle, Notre-Dame, and a few other secular houses in Paris. The feast was celebrated on the Tuesday following Ascension (variable because it falls in the Easter cycle), though some calendars list the feast for May 17.[134] The office is shorter than the other four, having only three instead of nine lections. It was composed in part by adapting a number of prayers from the defunct *Nunc laudare.*

---

130. The evidence for this is that these lections appear in Mazarine 374 in the same hand, though in a different location, as *Nunc laudare* (Paris Mazarine 374, fols. 402v.–403v.). For the text published by the Dominican general council of 1306, see MOPH, vol. 4, 21–23.
131. Gaposchkin, "Philip the Fair," 35–36.
132. The version of *Beatus Ludovicus* that survives widely (see RHF, vol. 23, 160–167) was an edited version of a vita that survives only (as far as I know) in Orleans BM 348, 1–18. 348 is a later witness, but represents an early *vie*. It seems to have been edited specifically for use with *Ludovicus decus*. The two earliest versions of the pairing of *Beatus Ludovicus* with *Ludovicus decus* are found in BNF Lat 911 and BNF Lat 1028.
133. The survival and transmission of the different versions of *Lauda Celestis* is treated in Gaposchkin, "Monastic Office," forthcoming.
134. BNF Lat 1435, fol. 21v.

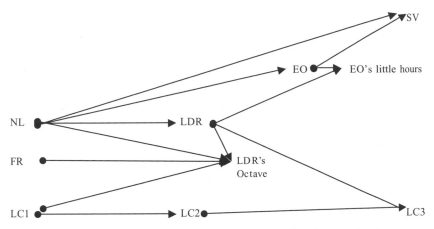

Diagram 3.1. Relational transmission of text items among offices for Saint Louis

(6) *Sanctus voluntatem*, or, "the Hours of Saint Louis," was produced sometime in the first quarter of the fourteenth century to be included in Books of Hours, including the Hours of Jeanne d'Evreux (Cloisters ms 54.1.2., ca. 1324). *Sanctus voluntatem* was composed drawing heavily on elements from *Nunc laudare* and *Exultemus omnes*. Because the office was produced for Books of Hours and did not constitute an office for communal service, its structure differed substantially. The texts for these offices are reproduced in Appendix 2.

In determining the ultimate scope of the celebration of Louis' feast day and the use of these various offices, we are dependent primarily on manuscript evidence, much of which has not survived, and there is no way of knowing what once existed. What does survive, however, points to Paris and the surrounding regions as the center of a limited cult. The crown's adoption of *Ludovicus decus regantium* was followed by its adoption in the secular churches in Paris. Notre-Dame, to whose parish Louis had belonged, adopted both the August 25 feast at the level of duplex and the Feast of the Translation, and liturgical volumes from St.-Magloire and St.-Eloi include proper items from *Ludovicus decus* for August 25.[135] This usage for Louis' principal feast day then spread to secular churches in northern France, and *Ludovicus decus* became the most widespread of the offices for Louis. Although it did not in fact "come into universal use in France,"[136] secular churches scattered from Troyes to Caen ultimately adopted *Ludovicus decus*, and it was incorporated into a number

135. St.-Magloire: Mazarine 344, 346; Arsenal 133. St.-Eloi: Mazarine 398 (lectionary). "Paris use": BNF Lat 1026, 1291, 10485; Arsenal 582; Mazarine 342, Chateauroux BM 2. On Louis' feast in the Paris liturgy, see Craig M. Wright, *Music and Ceremony at Notre Dame of Paris, 500–1550* (Cambridge, 1989), 73 and 80.
136. As per Archdale Arthur King, *Liturgies of the Religious Orders* (London, 1955), 328; Anne Walters Robertson, *The Service-Books of the Royal Abbey of Saint-Denis: Images of Ritual and Music in the Middle Ages* (Oxford, 1991), 77.

of printed breviaries in the fifteenth and sixteenth centuries.[137] Some changes were made to the edition of the breviary in 1580, and it was not until the Post-Tridentine edition of the breviary of 1640 published by Jean François Gondi that *Ludovicus decus* was abandoned in Paris for a new version.[138]

It is traditional to say that the cult was disseminated by the Franciscan and Dominican orders, though the manuscript evidence indicates that this is true only to a limited extent. Louis was added to the calendar of each order, but in almost all cases with a limited celebration. Though each order sought a standardization of liturgical celebration among their respective houses, neither *Francorum rex* or the Dominicanized version of *Ludovicus decus* was adopted universally within their orders. That the Dominicans in Paris—that is, those with ties to the crown—actively commemorated Louis' feast day is evident from the manuscripts cited earlier. *Ludovicus decus*, we saw, was copied into the Dominican liturgical exemplar in the mid-fourteenth century (BL Add 23935), but this does not appear to have translated into its use throughout the order. The injunctions published by the Dominicans in 1298, 1299, and 1300 (which have previously been interpreted as a commission of *Ludovicus decus regnantium* for use throughout the order) did not mandate the celebration of a proper office, and in 1306 only abbreviated lections were published.[139] In 1299 the Dominicans of Évreux were the first to dedicate a church to Louis, and presumably a proper office was used there.[140] We are somewhat hampered in this question by the limited survival of Dominican breviaries, especially from southern France. But it does seem that while Dominicans throughout France and Italy observed Louis' feast, the norm for celebration was a proper collect and proper readings paired with the Common for the Confessors.

The same thing can be said for the Franciscans. Veneration certainly occurred at Franciscan houses that had particular ties to Louis and the crown. At Longchamp, the Franciscan house that Louis' sister Isabelle had founded, for instance, a nun who was seeking Louis' intercession had an extraordinary dream in which Louis appeared in a procession of kings, and the nuns later claimed to possess relics of Louis.[141] Elsewhere, the order's devotion to Louis was manifest in piecemeal ways; by 1369, for instance, there was a chapel dedicated to Louis in a Franciscan church as far away as Bruges.[142] But it was really the Franciscans in the Paris area who were passionate about Louis. At

137. Gaposchkin, "Philip the Fair," 35–36, n. 8. For a list of select printed breviaries see AH, vol. 13, 188, no. 71.

138. AASS, August V 533–34. *Breviarium Parisiense: Ad Formam Sacrosancti Concilii Tridentini Restitutum. Illustrissimi et Reverendissimi In Christo Patris D.D. Ioannis Francisci de Gondy, Parisiensis Archiepiscopi auctoritate, ac eiusdem Ecclesia Capituli consensu editum.* (Paris, 1640), 1048–1053; Mazarine call number 1170[E]. The liturgy of 1640 owes much to the original *Ludovicus decus regnantium*. See Lajard, "Arnaud du Pré (Arnaldus de Prato)," 240–244.

139. MOPH, vol. 4, 21–23.

140. Tillemont, *Vie*, vol. 5, 221.

141. Field, *Writings*, 85, 87; Field, *Isabelle*, 233, n. 24.

142. Walter Simons, "Aantekeningen bij de XIVde-eeuwse geschiedenis van de timmerlieden-broederschap in de Brugse franciscanenkerk," *Het Brugs Ommeland* (1985): 155–160.

least one, and perhaps two, vitas for Louis and a proper liturgical office (*Francorum rex*) were composed by friars at the Couvent des Cordeliers. Yet the majority of Franciscan breviaries reduced the propers for Louis to what could fit on a single folio, either the collect only or the collect and simplified readings. While many portable Franciscan breviaries, which were more likely to have been used by the friars themselves, include lections for Louis, few include the long cycle of proper chant, since their portability necessitated abbreviation.

Among Benedictines, adoption of the feast seems to have been limited to a small number of individual houses. Though the Cistercians composed a proper office, *Lauda celestis,* following the general chapter of 1298, it too does not seem to have found universal use within the order. In Paris, monastic houses with links to the crown—St.-Germain-des-Pres and St.-Denis—adapted a secularized version of *Lauda celestis* to their own needs.[143] In later years the monastery at Fontevrault adopted a liturgy partially drawn from the secular office.[144] A volume from a parish church associated with Cluny gives proper lections only, which would have been paired with the Common for the Confessors, and the printed breviary of 1546 lists Louis in the August calendar but does not include him in the Sanctorale.[145] A fourteenth-century breviary from the Benedictine monastery of St.-Jouarre-en-Brie near Meaux gives short readings with incipits for the Common for the Confessor.[146] Surprisingly, Louis is not found in the liturgical books from the abbey at Fécamp, a Benedictine monastery that boasted the most extensive glass cycle to Saint Louis of the fourteenth century.[147] A breviary printed in 1586 for the Benedictines gives only the collect.[148]

More widely disseminated were proper lections (readings) for Louis that would accompany common chant, which spread beyond France.[149] Yet even in

143. Gaposchkin, "Monastic Office."

144. *Breviarium sancti dominici ad unque curatissime castigatum iuxta correctorium totius ordinis predicatorum quod in conventu Parisiensi habetur* (Paris, 1519) (Fontevrault). Mazarine in 8 = 23839.

145. St. Genevieve 2628, fols. 427v.–428r.; *Breviarium cluniacense* (Paris, 1546). Mazarine in 8 = Rés N. 23888.

146. BNF Lat 750, 257r.–257v.

147. Leroquais seems to have been surprised by this, since he explicitly notes this fact. Louis shares the glass cycle at Fécamp with Edward the Confessor. The volumes from Fécamp in which Louis does not figure in the calendar or the Sanctorale are Rouen BM 205, from the second half of the thirteenth century with fourteenth-century additions, see *Bréviaires,* vol. 4, 94–96 in which appears the feast for Edward the Confessor (Oct 13, fol 323); Rouen BM 206 from the beginning or the first half of the fourteenth century, see *Bréviaires,* vol. 4, 97; Rouen BM 251, from the fourteenth century, which includes at 194v. the feast for Edward, see *Bréviaires,* vol. 4, 117–118. Likewise, Louis does not appear in the missals from Fécamp, Rouen BM 292, *Sacramentaires,* vol. 2, 377; Rouen BM 295, *Sacramentaires, vol.* 2, 153; Rouen BM 293, *Sacramentaires,* vol. 3, 159; and Rouen BM 294, *Sacramentaires,* vol. 3, 258. On the Fécamp glass, see Jean LaFond, "Les vitraux de l'abbaye de la Trinité de Fécamp," in *L'Abbaye Bénédictine de Fécamp: ouvrage scientifique du XIIIe centenaire, 658–1958* (Fécamp, 1961), 103–107.

148. *Breviarii monastice congregationis casalis benedicti, pars estivalis* (Paris, 1586), fol 224v.; Mazarine 23832.

149. For example, Margarete Andersson-Schmitt and Monica Hedlund, *Mittelalterliche Handschriften der Universitätsbibliothek Uppsala: Katalog über die C-Sammlung* (Stockholm, 1988), vol. 5, 82.

France, many churches did not, in the end, adopt proper celebration for Louis, or if they did, they incorporated proper lections into the Common for the nonpontiff confessor. The Carmelites and the Premonstretensians also used the Common. A fourteenth-century breviary from the Victorines of Paris gives lections but no office, though another paraliturgical volume includes the translation office.[150] Ultimately, proper celebration for Louis withered. By the fifteenth century many breviaries just gave a proper collect and lections. The advent of print and printed breviaries witnessed the diminution of the celebration even further, with most offering only the collect. Only in Paris did elaborated proper celebration continue; after the Tridentine Reforms, a new office based loosely on *Ludovicus decus regnantium* was included in the breviary of 1640 issued by Bishop de Gondi.[151] A sixteenth-century breviary for Bourges that provided readings even got his number wrong, calling him *Ludovicus quintus, Galliae rex*.[152] It was not until Cardinal Richelieu's (prime minister, 1624–1642) absolutist promotion of the Louis symbol that Saint Louis' cult was revived.[153] Under Louis XIII and then Louis XIV, new churches were dedicated to Saint Louis, and a new, lengthy office was commissioned to honor the saint-king.[154]

150. BNF Lat 14811, 568r.–569r. The collect was added in a later hand in Mazarine 347, fol. 467. The translation office is found in BNF Lat 14511, 179v.–181v.

151. *Breviarium Parisiense*, 1640, 1048–1953; Mazarine 1170[E].

152. *Breviarium Bituricense* (Bourges, 1587), 657; Mazarine 23798.

153. Morel, "culte."

154. BNF Lat 8828, made for Versailles in 1686, includes a new mass for Saint Louis, 86–98; BNF Lat 8831, made for the Invalides in 1719, includes a new office for Saint Louis, 2r.

Excursus

A Short Primer on the Structure
of the Liturgical Office

The genre of the rhymed office was a product of the high and late Middle Ages.[1] Liturgical offices belong to the liturgical genre popular in the late Middle Ages of rhymed chant bearing poetically and metrically composed texts. They are best considered here as musical poetry and were generally intended for celebration by a choir of monks, canons, or friars (depending on the house). The term "office" is used to designate the entire round of noneucharistic prayer prescribed by the rule of St. Benedict and centered on the complete weekly recitation of all 150 psalms undertaken by monks, nuns, canons, and friars, as well as to designate an individual series of prayers for a single feast day, such as the Feast of the Assumption of the Virgin, Pentecost, or the feast day of Saint Margaret or Saint Louis.[2] When referring to the celebration of any given day, a distinction is made between proper offices or texts and common offices or texts: a proper office is unique to a given feast day and used only then. Alternatively, an office that was common could be used on several different occasions. Thus, the Common for Confessors was an office that might be used to celebrate the feast day of *any* nonpontiff confessor saint and was not, by definition, proper to any one saint. Feasts were given different rankings to indicate their level of solemnity, ranging from a *memoria* (that is, a minor celebration for lesser saints which would not interrupt or alter the general daily round of prayers) to *duplex* (a "double" feast for saints more important to the church, which would include a greater number of proper items) or a *totum duplex* (a "major double," a feast

1. Jonsson, *Historia*; Hughes, "Rhymed Offices," 366–377.
2. For an overview, see Willi Apel, *Gregorian Chant* (Bloomington, Ind., 1958); Harper, *The Forms and Orders*; and David Hiley, *Western Plainchant: A Handbook* (Oxford, 1993). A discussion relevant to this context is O'Carroll, "La predicazione."

day of great liturgical embellishment, such as Easter, which would have the largest number of rituals and texts proper to that day only). Many saints' days would be celebrated with only a proper (i.e., individual) collect with recourse to the Common of the Saints (i.e., generic), though many others were celebrated with elaborately composed proper offices.

The high and late Middle Ages witnessed a burgeoning of the Sanctorale, the portion of the ecclesiastical calendar devoted to the celebration of saints' feast days, and the many new feasts created in this period resulted in the production of an immense corpus of new liturgical writings. New offices were written for recently adopted saints—such as Francis (canonized 1228), Dominic (canonized 1234), and Louis (canonized 1297)—and for long-revered ones, like Augustine and Benedict (both revered since their deaths in the fifth and sixth centuries). Saints' offices are generally found in the Sanctorale portion of liturgical books devoted to the office, including antiphoners (liturgical books that include all the office chant for the feast days throughout the year), diurnals (liturgical books that include the chant and music for the daytime), and especially breviaries (liturgical books that include both the chant and the lections, and sometimes also music). The breviary—a book that contained "in brief" all the elements needed for the liturgical day—was itself a response to the growth in the complexity of the liturgy in this period and the need to coordinate the different types of chant and prayer texts in a single volume. The enormous production of the breviary in the late medieval period has made these volumes the chief source for this kind of work.[3]

Although offices vary in length and format, they all follow basic structural patterns based on the canonical hours long established by ecclesiastical custom. The individual liturgical day was divided up into the eight canonical hours (matins, lauds, prime, terce, sext, none, vespers, and compline), and the office comprised a series of chants, hymns, and readings that were said or sung over the course of that day. Celebration of major feasts (including in some churches the feast of Saint Louis) began on the eve of the actual feast day with first vespers and ended only the following evening with second vespers.

Each service (i.e., first vespers, matins, and so forth) comprised different types of chanted or recited texts.[4] These included antiphons, hymns, responsories (response-verse pairs), lections, and other chanted or sung texts. The service of matins, the nocturnal office, was the longest and, sheerly in terms of amount of material, the richest of the eight services. It was here that readings (lections) were recited relating to the lives of the saints, which were answered by the chanted reflections known as responsories (Latin: *responsorium*). These

3. Pierre Salmon, *L'Office divin au Moyen âge, histoire de la formation du bréviaire du IXe au XVIe siècle* (Paris, 1967); Eric Palazzo, *A History of Liturgical Books from the Beginning to the Thirteenth Century* (Collegeville, Minn., 1998), 169–172.

4. Apel, *Gregorian Chant*, 19–23; Harper, *The Forms and Orders*, 73–102; Hiley, *Western Plainchant*, 25–30.

readings were often culled from available hagiography and were just as likely to be the source for the office itself;[5] in some cases special texts were written specifically for the office. Matins itself is divided into three parts—first, second, and third nocturns—and the number of lections differs according to the rank of the feast and whether it was performed in a secular or a monastic house. The services of first vespers (for duplex feasts) and lauds also included a number of sung texts (antiphons) and recited texts (chapter reading, the collect). For the so-called little hours (prime, terce, sext, none), often a single proper item was prescribed.

The antiphon—used in vespers, matins, lauds, and elsewhere—was a chant text that was followed by the reading of a psalm or part of a psalm (which in the offices for Saint Louis, all follow the Common of the Confessor), or, sometimes a canticle (the singing of a short scriptural passage). Antiphons were sung by alternating halves of the choir—that is, sung antiphonally. The antiphon was sometimes repeated multiple times—depending on the use, usually at the end of the reading of the psalm. Many antiphons were newly composed and proper to a particular saint. Frequently an antiphon played with the words or the themes of the psalm with which it was paired. For example, the second matins antiphon in *Nunc laudare* is paired with Psalm 2, which begins

"Ego autem constitutus sum rex ab eo super Syon, montem sanctum eius predicans preceptum eius." (Ps. 2:1)

(But I am appointed king by him over Sion his holy mountain, preaching his commandment.)

The antiphon paired with this psalm ran:

A Deo constitutus	Appointed king by God,
rex custos innocencie	guardian of innocence,
cum eo consecutus	he attained with Him
est solium glorie.	the throne of glory.

In these offices, antiphons and responsories (and sometimes hymns) would usually rhyme in a regular scheme—in this example A-B-A-B. Antiphons also followed canticles (scriptural passages sung to music) or other passages—in particular, the Benedictus, the Invitatory, and the Magnificat. An antiphon, for example, followed the Invitatory, the recitation of Psalm 94 that marked the beginning of matins.

Another chief element of the office and a particular feature of the service of matins were the great responsories, the response-verse pairings that were sung by the choir following a reading. The responsories were set to music, and, sequenced from the start to the end of matins, they often (though not always)

5. Hughes, "Rhymed Offices," 366–377.

followed a narrative progression of a saint's life. This was the reason that the word *historia* sometimes referred to the service of matins in particular. A typical example is FR MRV6, the sixth responsory for matins from the Franciscan office, *Francorum rex*. Following the recitation of the sixth lection, the choir would sing the following:

[R] Regressus rex ad propria non destitit insistere operi virtuoso, se mactat penitentia, egenos levat munere ministrat leproso	[R] The king having returned to his own land did not stop insisting on virtuous works; he magnified himself in penance; he raised up the poor with gifts and ministered to lepers.
[v] Visitat monasteria domos Dei ex opere construxit sumptuoso	[v] He visited monasteries; he built the houses of God with lavish expenditure.

The choir (or a subset of singers) would sing the responsory and one (or perhaps two) soloists would recite the verse, and then repeat the second half of the responsory (in this instance, beginning at *egenos levat munere*—"he raised up the poor"). Here, the rhyme scheme was A-B-C-A-B-C-A-B-C.

Lections were the readings recited during matins and were each followed by the recitation of a responsory. The secular cursus (used, for instance, by canons of most cathedral chapters and adopted by the mendicant orders) included nine readings, which would be followed by nine responsories. The monastic cursus (used by Benedictine, Cistercians, and so forth) included twelve readings. In the case of the office for late medieval saints, the lections were usually hagiographical in nature and would often vary in length depending upon the importance of the saint and the proclivities of the office. In well-constructed offices, themes might be echoed between lections and responsories.

First vespers, matins, lauds (the three longest services), and compline each included a hymn. Hymns were metrical and stanzaic songs of praise, a kind of musical poetry, often quite complicated and evocative in their language and imagery.[6] They were considered distinct from the liturgical office in a proper sense, were sometimes composed separately or adopted from a separate tradition, but were absolutely integral to the recital of the office during the day. In breviaries they appear as part of the office for the day.

A feast might also have an octave, which was a set of items that were performed during the week and on the eighth day following the feast. This is the case for some uses of *Ludovicus decus* (at the Ste.-Chapelle and at Notre-Dame), where eight antiphons were listed for the octave, which would have

---

6. Szövérffy, *Die Annalen der Lateinischen Hymnendichtung*; Joseph Szövérffy, *Latin Hymns* (Turnhout, Belgium, 1989).

been recited (depending on local use) either daily from August 26 to September 1 or as another feast on September 1. There were other texts read. A chapter (*capitulum*) was a short text taken or adapted from the Bible. The collect (*oratio*) was a short prayer read by the officiating priest during both the office and the mass.

The great bulk of the divine office was set to music and sung, and although the musical aspect is not treated here, it should not be forgotten that most of the chant texts discussed in the following chapters would have been understood largely in musical terms. The musical element would have undoubtedly added to (or perhaps contested?) their meaning. So, for example, *Ludovicus decus*, a liturgy that emphasizes Louis' royalty, emphasizes words associated with kingship (*rex, regiminis*, and so forth), with elaborate melismas.[7] (A melisma is where a single syllable is sung with a series of notes, lengthening and emphasizing that syllable).

We must take care to distinguish between the sung texts and lections of the liturgical offices. Together, chanted material (antiphons, responsories, verses, hymns) and recited material (the lections, the collect) articulate clear and variant interpretations of Louis' sanctity. Matins, for instance, began with a hymn, and the chanted material was interspersed with lections. To treat them separately belies the fact that they were performed together. Yet, though mingled, chanted material might follow certain themes and narrative lines, while the lections followed other themes and lines, and so forth, often because each was composed separately.

I have here followed a simplified version of the system of notation to refer to various parts of the offices. The Excursus table lists the secular and monastic structure of an office of nine or twelve readings. In the event of a lesser office (such as the translation office with only three readings), the number of readings and responsories in matins is accordingly reduced. The elements that are most commonly referred to and that are not easily identifiable by their names (such as the invitatory antiphon, which is in fact an antiphon but whose place as the opening prayer for matins is unique within any single office) are identified, according to Hughes's system, by two letters and a number. The first letter—V, M, or L—refers to the service: either vespers, matins or lauds. W takes the place of second vespers in the rare instances where it differs from the first, and O stands in for the octave. The second letter of the sequence—A, H, L, R, V—stands for antiphon, hymn, lection, responsory, and verse. Thus the unit VA1 indicates the first antiphon of vespers, while ML3 indicates the third lection of matins.

The texts of the offices for Louis are listed in Appendix 2. They are cited in the footnotes according to the taxonomy given in the second part of the List of Abbreviations.

7. For music, see Epstein, "Perspectives."

Table Excursus 1. The basic structure of the secular and monastic office

	Secular		Monastic	
1 VESPERS	antiphon*	[=VA1]	antiphon*	[=VA1]
	antiphon	[=VA2]	antiphon	[=VA2]
	antiphon	[=VA3]	antiphon	[=VA3]
	antiphon	[=VA4]	antiphon	[=VA4]
	antiphon	[=VA5]	antiphon	[=VA5]
	chapter	[=VCap]	chapter	[=VCap]
	response	[=VCapR]	response	[=VCapR]
	verse	[=VCapV]	verse	[=VCapV]
	hymn	[=VH1–5]	hymn	[=VH1–5]
	Magnificat		Magnificat	
	antiphon	[MAG]	antiphon	[=MAG]
	collect (*oratio*)		collect (*oratio*)	
	*Number of antiphons may vary		*Number of antiphons may vary	
COMPLINE	antiphon	[=CA]	antiphon	[=CA]
MATINS	invitatory		invitatory	
	antiphon	[=Invit]	antiphon	[=Invit]
	hymn	[=MH1-5]	hymn	[=MH1-5]
1st Nocturn	antiphon	[=MA1]	antiphon*	[=MA1]
	antiphon	[=MA2]	antiphon	[=MA2]
	antiphon	[=MA3]	antiphon	[=MA3]
	lection	[=ML1]	antiphon	[=MA4]
	response	[=MR1]	antiphon	[=MA5]
	verse	[=MV1]	antiphon	[=MA6]
	lection	[=ML2]	lection	[=ML1]
	response	[=MR2]	response	[=MR1]
	verse	[=MV2]	verse	[=MV1]
	lection	[=ML3]	lection	[=ML2]
	response	[=MR3]	response	[=MR2]
	verse	[=MV3]	verse	[=MV2]
			lection	[=ML3]
			response	[=MR3]
			verse	[=MV3]
			lection	[=ML4]
			response	[=MR4]
			verse	[=MV4]
			*Number of antiphons can vary	
2nd Nocturn	antiphon	[=MA4]	antiphon	[=MA7]
	antiphon	[=MA5]	antiphon	[=MA8]
	antiphon	[=MA6]	antiphon	[=MA9]
	lection	[=ML4]	antiphon	[=MA10]
	response	[=MR4]	antiphon	[=MA11]
	verse	[=MV4]	antiphon	[=MA12]
	lection	[=ML5]	lection	[=ML5]
	response	[=MR5]	response	[=MR5]
	verse	[=MV5]	verse	[=MV5]

	Secular		Monastic	
2nd Nocturn (cont.)	lection	[=ML6]	response	[=MR6]
	response	[=MR6]	response	[=MR6]
	verse	[=MV6]	verse	[=MV6]
			lection	[=ML7]
			response	[=MR7]
			verse	[=MV7]
			lection	[=ML8]
			response	[=MR8]
			verse	[=MV8]
3rd Nocturn	antiphon	[=MA7]	lection	[=ML9]
	antiphon	[=MA8]	response	[=MR9]
	antiphon	[=MA9]	verse	[=MV9]
	lection	[=ML7]	lection	[=ML10]
	response	[=MR7]	response	[=MR10]
	verse	[=MV7]	verse	[=MV10]
	lection	[=ML8]	lection	[=ML11]
	response	[=MR8]	response	[=MR11]
	verse	[=MV8]	verse	[=MV11]
	lection	[=ML9]	lection	[=ML12]
	response	[=MR9]	response	[=MR12]
	verse	[=MV9]	verse	[=MV12]
			scriptural reading	
			collect	
Lauds	antiphon	[=LA1]	antiphon	[=LA1]
	antiphon	[=LA2]	antiphon	[=LA2]
	antiphon	[=LA3]	antiphon	[=LA3]
	antiphon	[=LA4]	antiphon	[=LA4]
	antiphon	[=LA5]	antiphon	[=LA5]
	chapter reading		chapter reading	
	hymn	[=LH1–5]	hymn	[=LH1–5]
	benedictus antiphon [=Ben]		benedictus antiphon [=Ben]	
			collect	
Little Hours				
Prime	chapter reading for each service		chapter reading for each service	
Terce	followed by a versicle and		followed by a versicle and	
	a response		a response	
Sext				
None				
2 VESPERS	Magnificat		Magnificat	
	antiphon [=Mag]		antiphon [=Mag]	
OCTAVE	antiphon(s) [=OA]		antiphons(s) [=OA]	

4
Royal Sanctity
and Sacral Kingship

The liturgical books of the Ste.-Chapelle and the breviaries associated with members of the royal family included the liturgical office *Ludovicus decus regnantium* for Louis' feast day.[1] *Ludovicus decus* emphasized, above all, themes of royalty, Christic kingship, and sanctity specific to kings, rooted in the language of the Psalms and exalting sacral kingship. The office articulated the fundamental claims of Capetian ideology around 1300: Louis had been chosen by God; he ruled with justice and mercy; he was necessarily humble; and he was the successor to Old Testament kings and rulers, in particular David and Solomon. At the heart of the office was the notion, embedded throughout scripture, and indeed throughout medieval ideas of political theory generally, that earthly kings are the instruments of God's will. At the same time, *Ludovicus decus* is also the office least specific to the person of Louis, least tied to the hagiographical tradition, and least explicitly representative of the sanctity that the canonization process had approved. A single responsory constituted the only specific reference to what was known of Louis' life.[2] Instead, *Ludovicus decus* formulated the king's virtue in the biblical language of kingship, and the result was, in effect, an articulation of a specifically royal sanctity—sanctity rooted in the quality of rule and its relationship to Christ; that is, a sanctity specific to kings.

This was probably the office that Philip the Fair paid for in 1298.[3] It was also the most widely distributed of the offices for Louis, ultimately adopted by

---

1. BNF Lat 911, 1r.–33r., BNF Lat 1023, 560r.–563r., BNF 1052, 468v.–476v., BNF Lat 13238, 290v.–300v., Chantilly, Musée Condé, ms. 1887, 335v.–343r. Washington LC 15, 554r.–560r. Indications exist for other volumes. For instance, Robert of Artois paid for the noting of sixteen offices for Louis on parchment; see Richard, *Petite nièce*, 99.
2. LDR MR5.
3. Gaposchkin, "Philip the Fair," 33–61.

many secular churches in Paris and northern France in the following century. In this sense, the liturgical texts constituted one mechanism of the court's production and propagation of royal ideology in these years and underscores the role that Saint Louis played in Philip's promotion of sacral kingship and sacred kingdom.[4] If what Philip wanted was to exalt Louis' kingship, he could hardly have done better than *Ludovicus decus regnantium,* which was, like Marigny, more royal than the king.

With *Ludovicus decus,* the crown fostered a royalized image of Louis' sanctity that merged sacral royalty with saintly kingship. Behind this royalizing strategy lurked the Dominicans of the Rue St.-Jacques in Paris, whose efforts both preceded and echoed the court's image of Louis. The Dominicans of Paris were closely tied first with Louis and then with Philip, had defended Philip's royalist policies, and showed interest in defining the ideal role of the king in God's greater plan. And so the story of the crown's royalizing of Louis' sanctity involved ties and kindred aims with the friars of St.-Jacques. This chapter uses *Ludovicus decus* to explore the way in which Louis was used as the source of sacralizing authority for the monarchy, and the way in which Louis' royal sanctity was marshaled to the crown's sacral royalty. These themes were echoed both in the short-lived Dominican office (*Nunc laudare*) on which *Ludovicus decus* was based, and in sermons written by Dominicans that propagated that message beyond the court and cloister. In many ways, then, this is the story of crown's imaging of Saint Louis, intertwined with Dominican influences and ideas.

The Dominican Contribution

Ludovicus decus was based on the provisional Dominican office *Nunc laudare.* The compositional strategies used in *Ludovicus decus* were first used in *Nunc laudare,* many of its texts and some of its music were taken from *Nunc laudare,* and the emphasis on royal glory was established there, pointing not only to Dominican interpretation of Louis' sanctity but also to their role in constructing the royalized saint-king of the court. A word, then, about this office.

Nunc laudare was conscious both of its own newness and the newness of the saint it was celebrating, with multiple references to the "new praise" and "new joy," and the celebration which is "now done."[5] The two principal themes of the office were, first, Louis as a *royal* saint and, second, Louis' transference from the earthly kingdom to the kingdom of heaven. A vespers antiphon spoke

---

4. Studies on *Ludovicus decus* include: Heysse, "Antiquissimum officium," 559–575; Szövérffy, *Die Annalen der Lateinischen Hymnendichtung,* vol. 2, 284–287; Folz, "Sainteté de Louis IX," 31–45; Epstein, "Perspectives," 283–334; Gaposchkin, "*Ludovicus Decus,*" 27–90; and Gaposchkin, "Philip the Fair."

5. NL VH1: "nove laudis." MH4: "iam coronatus." VMag: "nunc est honorata." Invit: "nova sollempnia." MH1: "Nova regis preconia." MR6: "iam ingressus." MA8: "nunc sanctorum agmini iunctus." LA21: "novum festum."

of how the "king reigns now in heaven," the vespers hymn of how Louis was conveyed from the terrestrial kingdom to the throne of the kingdom of heaven, a lauds antiphon of how he acquired the kingdom of the celestial homeland, and the Benedictus antiphon (which would be incorporated by *Ludovicus decus* as its opening line) of Louis, the glory of rulers, who, happy, crossed to the throne of the heavens.[6] Matins exclaimed that the Lord "exalted the king of the French, whose end is now in the kingdom of the blessed."[7] Other examples could be offered, since the themes of Louis' earthly and heavenly royalty permeated the entire office. This theme was also at the heart of the collect that, notably, was imported into all the other offices thereafter.

These ideas were transmitted to *Ludovicus decus* with the many texts it adopted, including *Nunc laudare*'s three hymns, five lauds antiphons, and numerous other antiphons and responsories. It is, furthermore, in *Nunc laudare* that we first find the strategy of choosing Psalm texts that drew on kingship as the basis for the antiphons, which is discussed at greater length below. The Dominican office thus provided both the formal framework and the interpretive scheme for the royalizing emphasis that would so dominate the popular *Ludovicus decus regnantium*, that presented Louis' sanctity in ways that emphasized Louis' royal identity and served to sacralize the crown.

Constituency

As reworked, however, *Ludovicus decus* emphasized that Louis was a saint for the French people. Newly composed for *Ludovicus decus* were four of the vespers antiphons (VA2–5) with which the office opened, which identified the specifically French nature of Louis' constituency.[8] It addressed the French people (*francigena*) and the kingdom of France (*regnum francie*), and distinguished the French from foreigners (*gens avena*).[9] The office relentlessly emphasized his kingship, calling him "Louis, glory of rulers" (*Ludovicus decus regnantium*) and comparing him to the highest King (*summi regis*).[10] Louis was the saintly advocate, protecting and defending the French as he had done when he was king. "Rejoice, O kingdom of France, to whom the King of glory gave such an excellent gift, because you have your own king to aid you, a patron [*patronum*] in the heavens."[11] Vespers compared his protective defense of his subjects as king to his spiritual protection of these same people as saint, explaining that as a king, when alive and ruling, he defended the French; and that now, in heaven, he intercedes for them.[12] French people

---

6. NL VA1, VH2, LA1, Ben (=LDR VA1).

7. NL MA4.

8. Noted by Szövérffy, *Die Annalen der Lateinischen Hymnendichtung*, 285.

9. LDR VA4. Bernard Guenée, "État et nation en France au moyen âge," *Revue historique* 237 (1967): 25.

10. LDR VA1, 2 and 4.

11. LDR VA2.

12. LDR VA3

ought "rejoice under the patronage of your former king."[13] And then, "You [the French] were protected by his rule on earth and under his name; may he now seek grace and favor for you in the sight of Christ."[14] Elsewhere Louis beseeched the Lord on behalf of his subjects who comprised a "devout France," which should rejoice especially at the "saint-king of France."[15]

The office was explicit that as a saint, Louis protects in heaven those whom as king he ruled and defended on earth. It was the normal course of things that saints should intercede on behalf of those who beseeched them, but here the devotees were envisioned specifically as Louis' former subjects, and his spiritual constituency was defined by the political community of his earthly reign. First vespers thus expressed the logical extension of the theology of intercession to a king-saint whose duty in heaven was understood as the transmuted extension of his office on earth, a protector and defender of his people.[16] Such mutation was possible within a politico-religious climate that had long envisioned the king as the principal and intimate supplicant to God on behalf of his subjects, who in turn beseeched the king.[17] And the mutation from earthly to heavenly protector was especially intelligible to an age that witnessed the beginnings of a sentiment of a collective identity based on the notion of a France made up of the French at whose head was the person of the king; it was also an odd but bold twist on the general efforts, traced by Ernst Kantorowicz, of political entities to transfer to themselves the symbols of religious authority in the promotion of a political theology.[18] If the French were the most Christian people, it made sense that their most Christian king in heaven advocate especially for the French.

Modes of Composition: Mapping Louis onto Scripture

One of the chief mechanisms of sacralization was the use of biblical language that evoked scriptural prescriptions on kingship—a technique that had already been used for *Nunc laudare*. The chant texts were rooted in the language of the Bible, and the meaning of each prayer was dependent upon its scriptural source and the wider liturgical tradition that used it. In both *Ludovicus decus* and *Nunc laudare*, the matins antiphons were based on the Psalms. The antiphons—musical responses sung by one-half of the choir in response to individual verses from the Psalms sung by the other half—juxtaposed in sung dialogue scriptural prescriptions on rule with Louis' fulfillment of those prescriptions. The psalmody drew

---

13. LDR VA4.
14. LDR VA5.
15. LDR MR8, MH1, LH1.
16. On this theme, see Folz, *Saints rois*, 215–220. On royal saints as mediators, see Vauchez, *Sainthood*, 162.
17. For hints of this in an earlier tradition, see Geoffrey Koziol, *Begging Pardon and Favor: Ritual and Political Order in Early Medieval France* (Ithaca, N.Y., 1992), 77–103.
18. Kantorowicz, *King's Two Bodies*, 193–272.

from the Common for Confessors, whereby the first antiphon of nocturns was followed by Psalm 1:1, *Beatus vir qui non abiit in consilio impiorum*, the second antiphon was answered with Psalm 2:1, *Quare fremuerunt gentes et populi*, and so forth. The antiphons themselves were modeled on other verses from the same psalm that touched on kingship and thus provided the central image for the antiphon.[19] So, for example, the fifth matins antiphon, which read, "Led in justice [*deductus in iustitia*], he ruled his subjects clemently and he wisely instituted laws, punishments, and rewards," echoed Psalm 5:9: "Lead me, o Lord, in thy justice [*Domine, deduc me in iustitia tua*];[20] because of my enemies direct my way in thy sight." Here Louis (who is led in justice) is likened to King David (who, as the author of the Psalms, beseeches God to lead him in justice). This method was used for both offices.[21] The eighth matins antiphon—"The king of virtue shall rejoice in divine virtue [*rex virtutis in virtute divina letatur*], because firm hope was given to him concerning salvation"—drew from Psalm 20:2: "In thy strength, O Lord, thy king shall joy [*Domine, in virtute tua letabitur rex*], and in thy salvation he shall rejoice exceedingly." Psalm 23:4, "The innocent in hands and clean of heart" (*Innocens manibus et mundo corde*) provided the image of the ninth antiphon "The innocent hand gave cleanliness of heart to Louis," (*Innocens manus prebuit cordis quoque mundicia Ludovico*), and so forth.

Through the repeated use of the images and vocabulary of kingship from the Psalms—images and vocabulary that would have been second nature to those in the Middle Ages who lived and breathed the Scriptures—Louis was linked to David's virtue as God's king and servant. In lauds (identical in *Nunc laudare* and *Ludovicus decus*) each Psalm verse was retooled in such a way as to make Louis conform to biblical prescription. For example, Psalm 92:1 used in the first lauds antiphon, "And the Lord hath reigned, he is clothed with splendor,"[22] was reworked so that "Louis today is dressed in splendor, having acquired the kingdom of the celestial fatherland." As Louis praised the Lord on the model of King David, so the choir now praises Louis.[23] In response to Psalm 62:2, David's praise, "O God, my God, thee do I watch [*vigilo*]," the third antiphon replied "[Louis] always watched [*vigilavit*] you, my Lord." The antiphons further made clear that Louis followed the prescriptions of scripture. Psalm 102:22 commanded to "bless the Lord in all his works," and the fourth antiphon responded that "Louis blessed the creator in his works."[24] Psalm 148:1 commanded to "praise ye the Lord from the heavens" and the fifth antiphon responded that indeed "Louis praised the Lord from the heavens."[25] Louis, as David, fulfilled the exhortations of the Lord and, as his faithful servant, is now in heaven.

---

19. Szövérffy, *Die Annalen der Lateinischen Hymnendichtung*, 285; Epstein, "Perspectives," 289–291. Epstein was also interested in the exegetical influences from the *Glossa Ordinaria*.

20. Douay-Rheims renders *deduc me* as "conduct me."

21. Gaposchkin, "*Ludovicus Decus*," 76–81.

22. Douay-Rheims renders *decorum* as "beauty."

23. NL and LDR LA2.

24. NL and LDR LA4.

25. NL and LDR LA5.

A similar approach was used in matins but drew on biblical language broadly. A responsory found in both the Dominican (*Nunc laudare*) and the secular (*Ludovicus decus*) offices ran:

> MRVı: The King of kings, laying out a kingly wedding feast for the king's son, offers him, after the race in the stadium, the delights of heaven in glorious exchange. [v] In exchange for the kingdom of earthly things, Louis has the celestial kingdom as reward.[26]

The theme of royalty—Christ's royalty, Louis' royalty—is emphasized with the opening words (*rex regum regis filio regales*), but the meaning of the text is oblique without recourse to the scriptural context from which the language was drawn. The image of the wedding feast evoked the Song of Songs and the marriage at Cana, although more relevant here was Matthew 22:2 and 1 Corinthians 9:24. Matthew 22:2 begins the parable of the wedding banquet: "The kingdom of heaven is likened to a king, who made a marriage for his son [*fecit nuptias filio suo*]. And he sent his servants, to call them that were invited to the marriage; and they would not come" (Matt. 22:2). The king is the King of heaven (God), and the royal banquet for his son (Christ) is salvation. The parable concerns those who pay no attention to God's wedding banquet and are subsequently excluded from it (salvation).[27] But here the image of the King's royal banquet was meant to evoke the glory which Louis gains for successfully running the race. The image of the race (*certamen*) in the stadium (*stadio*) in turn derives from 1 Corinthians 9:24: "Know you not that they that run in the race [*in stadio currunt*], all run indeed, but one receiveth the prize? So run that you may obtain." The athlete is the earthly Christian and the prize is heaven. Only the combination of these scriptural allusions makes MRVı sensible. Louis has won the race, and God rewards him with salvation. MRVı exclaims that Louis exchanged the lesser for the greater kingdom, and that he earned "the delights of heaven in a glorious exchange." Divinity and humanity are opposed just as are the temporal and the heavenly kingdom. Then later: "Happy race [*cursus*] of the one living, happy end of the one running [*currentis*] thus, always serving God."[28]

In this way, Louis' reign was worked into a discourse on kingship rooted in scriptural allusions and language by constructing a series of compact, bunched references to biblical pronouncements touching on, or interpreted in the light of, kingship. In this way, Louis was implicitly compared to King David, and his kingship modeled on Christ's. The cumulative effect of the office amounted to a liturgical gloss on good kingship, and by using the language of scripture, a sacralization of the profession and duties of kingship.

---

26. NL and LDR MRVı.

27. See the entry on this verse in *The New Interpreter's Bible: General Articles and Introduction, Commentary, and Reflections for Each Book of the Bible, including the Apocryphal Deuterocanonical Books*, ed. Abingdon Press (Nashville, 1994), vol. 8, 417.

28. NL and LDR MV8.

The Precepts of Good Kingship: Humility and Justice

Two central themes in the discourse on kingship—humility and justice—
were embedded in the office. These were long recognized as classic virtues of
the good king.[29] With first nocturn, the antiphons began with Louis' rejection
of the throne and temporal delights, his surrender to humility, and his exchange of the temporal kingdom with the celestial kingdom.[30] Louis' good
rule and thus his sanctity were defined by his humility, and in second nocturn
he is explicitly compared in this to King David. A responsory originating with
Nunc laudare claimed, by comparing Louis to David, that Louis' glory (i.e.,
his sainthood) was *not* rooted in the authority he garnered as temporal king
but rather in a humility individual to him. "He appeared glorious [*gloriosus*],
not because of the adornment [*cultu*] of a ruler, but because he excelled unadorned [*incultus*], in the manner of David playing [*ludentis*]. And the authority of a ruler was not lacking in him because of this."[31] Louis excelled in
humility and is like David who, undressed, played instruments and danced
before the ark of the Lord. *Incultus*, applied to Louis, meant at once "undressed," like David who danced naked before the Lord, and "unadorned" or
"inelegant" in a way that evoked Louis' humility. The accompanying lection
emphasized the simplicity of Louis' appearance and his simple clothes.[32] The
biblical story that the responsory evoked described David, who stripped and
played music (*ludebant*) before the Lord: "But David and all Israel played
before the Lord [*ludebant coram Deo*] on all manner of instruments"
(2 Sam. 6:5). Michol, his wife, watching him from the window, mocks him:
"How glorious [*gloriosus*—as Louis is at MR4] was the king of Israel today,
uncovering himself before the handmaids of his servants, and was naked, as if
one of the buffoons should be naked" (2 Sam. 6:20). David's reply provides
the key: "I will both play [*ludam*] and make myself meaner [*vilior*] than I have
done: and I will be little [*humilis*] in my own eyes: and with the handmaids of
whom thou speakest, I shall appear more glorious [*gloriosior*]." Davidic humility was also echoed in the associated lection. "Humility, the glory of all
virtues, shone to such a degree in him that the greater [*maior*] he was, just like
another David, the more he bore himself with humility, and appeared before
God meaner in his own eyes."[33] The lection then described Louis humbling
himself through acts of charity, serving the poor at his own dinner table, and
washing and kissing the feet of the poor.[34] The importance of the comparison,
then, was not that Louis, like David, was chosen by God, but that Louis, like

---

29. Berges, *Fürstenspiegel*, particularly 47–51.

30. LDR MA1–3.

31. NL MR2 = LDR MR4. The responsory is discussed by Epstein, "Perspectives," 291. The
Glossa ordinaria's commentary understood David's nakedness as humility.

32. BLQRF L4.

33. BLQRF L4: "Omnium virtutum decor humilitas adeo refulgebat in eo ut quanto major
erat, velut alter David tanto humilius se gerebat et coram deo in oculis suis vilior apparebat."

34. The divisions of the liturgical office vary from manuscript to manuscript. I use here divisions as they appear in BNF Lat 911.

David, was saintly because, having been chosen, he humbled himself before the Lord.

Humility was necessary because it allowed for justice, the necessary core of good rule. *Ludovicus decus* praised Louis for being a good king in terms classically established in kingship literature: good kingship proceeds from the king's personal virtues and the exercise of self-restraint, the good king exercises a justice tempered by mercy, protects peace, and scatters the wicked; the king who rules his subjects well wins heaven. Matins spoke of how, led by justice, Louis governed his subjects with clemency, and wisely instituted laws, punishments, and rewards.[35] He is compared to David and Solomon for the strength and justice of his rule.[36] Images of the good and godly king were painted in Old Testament language. One description of Louis' rule drew on the image of the *rex sapiens* from Proverbs and Psalms:

> Happy is the land whose king is wise, just, clement, modest, patient, whose countenance strikes evil men, and entices good men. [v] Louis thus ruled the earth because he merited the heavens by his ruling.[37]

Proverbs had said "a wise king scattereth the wicked. . . . Mercy and truth preserve the king and his throne is strengthened by clemency," and "take away wickedness from the face of the king, and his throne shall be established with justice" (Prov. 25:5). Wisdom held that "a wise king is the upholding of the people" (Wis. 6:26). The idea that good rule began with the king's personal virtues went back to the Carolingian authors on kingship and had become commonplace by the thirteenth century. The virtue of self-discipline was echoed in a responsory that understood Louis' good rule to proceed from the serene quality of his inner peace. "When the king of inner sweetness was at his repose, hindering the plagues of the flesh and blood with a powerful spirit, guarded by the encirclement of good things, he shone with the ruler's scepter."[38] Louis restrained evil but all the while remained within the standard of the clement One (God).[39]

Sacral Kingship

It was the ability to secularize the meaning of religious language that allowed for multivalent interpretations.[40] This was true of the image of the king crowned by God. For instance, in *Ludovicus decus*, the sixth antiphon said that the saint was "crowned with glory and honor" (*coronatur gloria sanctus*

---

35. LDR MA5.
36. LDR MV6.
37. LDR MRV2. For *rex sapiens*, see Prov. 20:26 and 28, 25:5, Wis. 6:26, and Jer. 23:5.
38. LDR MR6 = NL MRV7: Cf Cant 1.1. Epstein, "Perspectives," 291, says that the *Glossa ordinaria* equates *nardus* with the virtue of *caritas*.
39. NL MRV2 = LDR MV4. Cf: LC1–3 MV1.
40. On the interplay between the sacred and the secular, and the musical (rather than textual) borrowing from coronation liturgies and other royal celebrations, see Leo Schrade, "Political Compositions in French Music of the 12th and 13th Centuries," *Annales musicologiques* 1 (1953):

et honore).[41] The image was reworked from *Nunc laudare*'s sixth antiphon, which said, "with glory and honor the crowned king reigned," (*gloria et honore regnat rex coronatus*).[42] The language came from the Psalms (8:6: *Gloria et honore coronasti eum*), which was in turn borrowed by Paul in Romans 16:27 (*cui est honor et gloria in secula seculorum*), and it resonated in the discourse of medieval kingship. The Carolingian *Laudes regiae* had praised the king or emperor as *a deo coronatus*.[43] The prayer written for the moment of crowning in the ninth-century Ordo of Judith began with *Gloria et honore coronet te Dominus, et ponat super caput tuum coronam de spirituali lapide pretioso* and ended by quoting Romans 16:27.[44] The Last Capetian Ordo (probably used for Philip IV's coronation) included this prayer: *Coronet te Deus corona glorie atque iusticie, honore et opere fortitudinis*.[45] Crown wearing had nothing to do with kingmaking in the biblical context (the crucial bit was unction), and most crowns (*corona*) and diadems (*diadema*) of scripture referred not to temporal rule but to salvation. Use of the crown image, then, in the coronation liturgies demonstrates how easily the crown of heaven, intended metaphorically to signify the glory of salvation, could be transposed to the secular sphere and understood in terms of earthly royalty. The language of the actual coronation melded spiritual and secular imagery, and it was this capacity to secularize and make temporal biblical language that could give *Ludovicus decus* a particular meaning in court circles.

The office emphasized, as the coronation liturgies long had, the essential element of sacral kingship—that the king was appointed by (*constitutus*) and his authority came directly from God.[46] The ritual of unction that bore the legitimacy of its Old Testament models gave this claim ritual and constitutive form. As part of the ecclesio-political theology that developed under the Carolingians, one of the ninth-century coronation rites included this blessing for the moment of unction: "As Samuel anointed David as king, so might you be blessed and constituted king [*constitutus rex*] in this kingdom, which your Lord God gave to you for ruling or governing, over this people."[47] Although

---

9–63; Andrew Hughes, "Antiphons and acclamations: The Politics of Music in the Coronation Service of Edward II, 1308," *Journal of Musicology* 6 (1988): 150–168; and Hughes, "Rex sub deo," section IV.4, where he cites LDR.

41. LDR MA6.

42. NL MA6.

43. H. E. J. Cowdrey, "Anglo-Norman Laudes Regiae," *Viator* 12 (1981): 48.

44. Jackson *Ordines,* Ordo V, 79.

45. Jackson *Ordines,* Ordo XIIA, 401.

46. The verb *constituere* was used repeatedly throughout the commentary of the moralized bibles to indicate that the authority of Old Testament rulers came from God. See Gerald Guest, "Queens, Kings, and Clergy: Figures of Authority in the 13th-Century Moralized Bibles" (Ph.D., New York University, 1998), 239–240.

47. "Sicut unxit Samuhel David in regem, ut sis benedictus et constitutus rex in regno isto, quod dedit tibi dominus Deus tuus super populum hunc ad regendum vel gubernandum." For text, see Jackson *Ordines,* Ordo IV, 70. On Carolingian roots, see Cornelius A. Bouman, *Sacring and Crowning: The Development of the Latin Ritual for the Anointing of Kings and the Coronation of an Emperor before the Eleventh Century* (Groningen, 1957), 107–108 and 124.

absent in the intervening years, the formula was adopted verbatim by the so-called Ordo of 1200, and from there was transmitted to the later rites used by the Capetians.[48] Likewise, the second antiphon for matins spoke of Louis as being king appointed over Sion: "Having obtained the throne of the kingdom, [Louis] showed himself humble, and, appointed in Sion [*Syon constitutus*], he distinguished himself in the worship of the Lord."[49] The text was itself a reworking from *Nunc laudare*, which said that Louis was "appointed by God" (*a deo constitutus rex*),[50] and it drew on Psalm 2:6, whose early history may itself have originated in a coronation prayer for the kings of Israel.[51] Psalm 2 tells of the obligation of the earthly king to the subjects over whom he rules and to the God who instituted (*constitutus*) his kingship. God speaks, commanding His king to rule "with a rod of iron," to "receive instruction, you that judge the earth," and to "serve ye the Lord with fear: and rejoice unto him with trembling." Sion is Jerusalem, kingdom of God. Kings are chosen and instituted by God. "But I am appointed king by him over Sion [*Ego autem constitutus sum rex ab eo super Syon*], his holy mountain, preaching his commandments" (Ps. 2:6).[52] Sion (Jerusalem) is thus associated with France. The second matins antiphon also evoked language from the Psalms, Kings, and Chronicles that refers to the *thronum regni, cultu Domini* and the *cultu domus Domini*,[53] but perhaps especially 1 Maccabees 2:57: *David in sua misericordia consecutus est sedem regni in secula* (David by his mercy obtained the throne of an everlasting kingdom).

Several other instances of biblical vocabulary in Louis' office echoed its use in the coronation liturgies. The scriptural image of the *virgam virtutis*, beloved by the coronation liturgists, was adopted in the fourth matins verse. "He held the scepter [*or*, rod] of power [*or*, of virtue], through which he curbed evil, but did so according to the norm of the clement One."[54] The image of the *virgam virtutis* came from Psalm 109:2: "The Lord will send forth the scepter of thy power [*virgam virtutis*] out of Sion: rule thou in the midst of thy enemies." Like Psalm 2, Psalm 109 is considered one of a handful of royal psalms that treated earthly rule, and it emphasizes that God stands behind the king's authority.[55] Psalm 109, which calls the king "a priest for ever according to the order of Melchisedech" (verse 4), may have been a battle prayer or

---

48. Jackson *Ordines*, Ordo IV, 70 (Benedictional of Freising); Ordo XIX, 256 (the Ordo of 1200); Ordo XXI, 354 (the Ordo of 1250); Ordo XXIII, 491 (the Ordo of Charles V).

49. LDR MA2.

50. NL MA2.

51. *The New Interpreter's Bible*, vol. 4, 689. On the so-called royal psalms, see Scott R. A. Starbuck, *Court Oracles in the Psalms: The So-Called Royal Psalms in Their Ancient Near Eastern Context* (Atlanta, Ga., 1999).

52. Psalm 2:6. In the Vulgate translation the speaker was instituted (*constitutus*) by God (*ab eo*). Recent translation has understood this to constitute God's command: "I have set my king on Zion, my holy hill" (NRSV). *The New Interpreter's Bible*, vol. 4, 689.

53. For *thronum regni* see 2 Sam. 7:13, 1 Kings 9:5, 2 Chr. 7:18; for *cultu domini* or variations see, Exod. 10:26, 1 Chr. 23:28, 2 Chr. 29:35.

54. NL MRV2 = LDR MV4.

55. *The New Interpreter's Bible*, vol. 4, 1128–1131.

a liturgy to celebrate success after battle. The *virgam virtutis* verse shows God giving the authority and power of kingship to the earthly king, so that he may be victorious over his enemies. This militant image was employed consistently in the coronation rites from Hincmar of Reims' the Ordo of Louis the Stammerer onward, and its use in the Last Capetian Ordo was entirely conventional.[56] The bishop enjoined the king to "take the scepter, the emblem of royal power, the lawful rod [*virgam rectam*] of the kingdom, the rod of virtue,"[57] and equated the *virgam virtutis* with the power with which the king should defend the holy church and Christian people, guide the wicked, correct the corrupt, and bring peace to the righteous. In the thirteenth century, the scepter was a potent symbol of royal authority. Louis was himself given both a rod and a scepter at his coronation, and the bestowal of the *virgam virtutis* (the rod) was part of his investment with the symbols of authority.[58] In the moralized Bibles it was the rod, not the crown, that signified monarchical authority. *Ludovicus decus* also spoke of the "scepter of rule,"[59] and the image of the *virgam* was again used in the Translation liturgy of 1306, where it was linked to Louis' equity.[60] *Ludovicus decus* thus echoes the tone and content of the coronation rite in its injunction to restrain evil and maintain justice with clemency.

Because the office conceptualized Louis' sanctity as rooted in the quality of his rule, the notion that a king could win heaven by effective and just rule was embedded in the idea of his sanctification. This idea was regularly articulated in the coronation rites and by late medieval *Specula principum* authors.[61] It was also expressed throughout *Ludovicus decus*: The king exchanges the earthly kingdom for the celestial kingdom;[62] "Louis rules the lands because he earned the heavens by his ruling";[63] "Louis exchanged the crown of justice for the crown of glory."[64] Third nocturn said that Louis was rewarded in heaven for his just earthly rule. Because he lived graciously among men, he will live on the summit of the Lord with confidence.[65] For his innocent hands and clean heart he merited the rewards of the celestial heavens.[66] In Louis, the *rex*

56. Jackson *Ordines*, 121, 149 (Ordo XIIIA), 162 (Ordo XIV), 187 (twice, Ordo XV), 210 (twice, Ordo XVIA), 245 (Ordo XVIII), 260 (Ordo XIX), 358 (Ordo XXI), 399 (Ordo XXIIA). For later Ordos, see 496, 543, 602.

57. Jackson *Ordines*, 399.

58. Herve Pinoteau, "La tenue de sacre de Saint Louis IX roi de France son arrière-plan symbolique de la 'renovatio regni juda,'" in *Vingt-cinq ans d'études dynastiques* (Paris, 1982), 156; Hervé Pinoteau, "La main de justice des rois de France: Essai d'explication," *Bulletin de la Société Nationale des Antiquaires de France* (1982): 262–264; Hervé Pinoteau, *La symbolique royale française: Ve–XVIIIe siècles* (La Roche-Rigault, 2003), 304–318.

59. LDR MR6.

60. EO VA3.

61. Born, "Perfect Prince," 474, 477, 484.

62. LDR MR1.

63. LDR MV2.

64. LDR VH5.

65. LDR MA7.

66. LDR MA9.

virtutis took the form of a *rex sanctus*. By means of Louis' achieved status of saint, the logic of a king's heavenly merits could be pushed to its useful extreme since not only heaven but sanctity was the characteristic and reward of good governance and just rule. This was where sacral royalty and saintly kingship met. Royalty was sacral not only because, like the priesthood, the king was a mediator of God's rule, but also because the king was chosen by God to effect His reign on earth.

Typology

The royalist emphasis of *Ludovicus decus regnantium* was further evoked through its use of biblical typology.[67] These texts, not found in *Nunc laudare,* were newly composed at this stage. The antiphon for the Magnificat (second vespers) evoked the four great kings of the Old Testament—David, Solomon, Ezechias, and Josiah.

> The Divinity magnifies with miracles Louis, in whom David's humility, Solomon's serenity, and Ezechias' truth shone forth to all eyes, and whom a benevolence for his people equal to that of Josiah made solemn with signs of grace.[68]

David, Ezechias, and Josiah were grouped together by the biblical author Ecclesiasticus as the only kings who had not "sinned greatly," for the others "forsook the law of the Most High; the kings of Judah came to an end" (Eccli. 49:4–6). The proper sequence for the mass of Saint Louis used at the court compared Louis to the countenance (*vultum*) of King David, with Ezechias for his zeal for law, and Josiah for his devotion.[69] Solomon embodied royal justice. These four Old Testament kings had long been evoked as exemplars of good kingship.[70] The tenth-century pontifical of Mainz had included a prayer that was much the same (though it replaced Josiah with Moses): "Trusting in Moses' gentleness, strengthened by Joshua's fortitude, exalted by David's humility, and honored with Solomon's wisdom, may he be pleasing to you in all things and may he always walk on the path of justice, his advance unhindered."[71] The coronation liturgies routinely spoke of

67. On the use of typology with respect to Louis, see LeGoff, *Saint Louis,* 388–401. LeGoff, "Royauté biblique."

68. LDR WMag. This text is found in an exemplar of *Nunc laudare,* Rouen Y233, 278r., though in a different—assumed later—hand.

69. BNF Lat 911, fol. 32r.; Mazarine 413, 229r.; Washington D.C. LC 15, 558v.: "Vultum habens david regis ezechie zelum legis et iosie stadium."

70. J. M. Wallace-Hadrill, "The *Via Regia* of the Carolingian Age," in *Trends in Medieval Political Thought,* ed. Beryl Smalley (Oxford, 1965), 26. For example, Smardagus cites David, Ezechias, Solomon, and Josiah, as well as Joshua, as examples for the prince; cited in LeGoff, *Saint Louis,* 390.

71. Cyrille Vogel and Reinhard Elze, eds., *Le Pontifical romano-germanique du dixième siècle,* 2 vols. (Rome: Vatican City, 1963), vol. 1, 251: "Moysi mansuetudine fretus, Iosue fortitudine munitus, David humilitate exaltatus, Salomonis sapientia decoratus, tibi in omnibus placeat et per tramitem iustitiae inoffenso gressu semper incedat."

David's humility and Solomon's wisdom.[72] In 1259 Guibert of Tournai, writing his *Eruditio regum et principum* for Louis, listed David, Ezechias, Josiah, and Solomon as the kings from the camp of Israel (*castris Israel*) to whom a king ought conform.[73] In *Ludovicus decus* David, Solomon, Ezechias, and Josiah were the Old Testament kings presented as types for Louis, who encompassed in himself their different virtues—humility, serenity, veracity, and kindness.

Of these, the most frequently evoked was David. Articulations of sacral kingship had always invoked David, the model for royal elevation and anointing at the hand of God, and for the same reasons he was the biblical predecessor to whom saint-kings were most often compared in their hagiography.[74] As a sinful king, David functioned also as the *topos* for the king who, corrected by a prelate, is redeemed. And because Christ was of David's house, David's kingship was directly Christic, a point made consistently in the thirteenth century by the increasingly popular iconography of the Tree of Jesse.[75] As both saintly king and sacral king, David was evoked consistently in the coronation rites that linked Carolingian and Capetian ideology. Solomon, the *rex pacificus*, was a close second. Solomon, too, was a standard in the *Ordines* and was associated especially with images of the just and pacific king. Yet, Andrew Hughes has recently shown that evocation of David and Solomon as types was *not* a common feature in liturgical offices for royal saints in general, underscoring its intentionality here.[76] In *Ludovicus decus*, David was evoked no less than five times in the office (six, counting the reference in the fourth lection), Solomon twice (three times, counting the lections). At MV6 Louis is compared to both: "MV6: He sits on the throne of King David, doing the justice of Solomon."[77] The Benedictus antiphon, which echoed the language of Luke 1:69, spoke of how the Lord loved Louis little less than he loved David, and called Louis David's twin in virtue.[78]

It would be a mistake to think these typologies worked on a mechanical one-to-one basis. But the ubiquity of the borrowed language (scripture) and borrowed images (kings) provides the key to the overall scheme of the office, which is at root both biblical and royal and is wholly grounded in its biblical/royal referent. The chapter reading for first vespers played with the association between France and Jerusalem. God is praised for giving the heart of the earthly king the will "to glorify His house, which is Jerusalem."

---

72. Jackson, *Ordines,* 159 (Ordo XIV), 181 (XV), 207 (XVIA), 258–259 (XIX), 356 (Ordo XXI), 394 (XXII-A).

73. Guibert de Tournai, *Eruditio regum et principum,* 21. A few sentences later, Guibert offers Solomon up as a model for a king's wisdom. For the image of the *castris Israhel*, see 2 Sam. 1:3.

74. Folz, *Saints rois,* 19, and for specific examples, 56–58, 209, 212–213.

75. James R. Johnson, "The Tree of Jesse Window of Chartres: 'Laudes regiae,'" *Speculum* 36 (1961): 1–22; Jordan, *Visualizing Kingship,* 18; Klaniczay, *Holy Rulers,* 43–45.

76. Hughes, "Rex sub deo," section IV.2a.

77. LDR VCapV and MV6.

78. LDR Ben.

Blessed be the Lord, God of our Fathers, who gave this desire in the king's heart, to exalt His house, which is in Jerusalem.[79]

The prayer was adapted from 1 Ezra 7:27:

Blessed be the Lord, God of our fathers, who gave this in the king's heart, so that he might glorify the house of the Lord, which is in Jerusalem.[80]

Louis is thus implicitly compared to the Old Testament king whose heart the Lord made sure would honor Jerusalem. Placed within the context of Louis' sanctity, Jerusalem was implicitly identified with France, at the same time that royal propagandists were linking the two in sermons.[81] When Louis translated the Crown of Thorns to Paris, Gautier Cornut, the archbishop of Sens, could speak of how France had succeeded the Holy Land for the veneration of the Passion.[82] A Parisian preacher of the fourteenth century made the link explicit when, in a sermon in honor of Louis, he wrote that "the house of Israel, seeing God through true faith, is the house of France."[83] And Jacob of Lausanne OP wrote that God chose Louis to reign over the people of France as he had chosen kings, out of love, to reign over Israel and to render judgment and justice.[84] If Louis was the new chosen king, so France was the new Israel, the chosen kingdom, the chosen people.

The chapter readings at terce, sext, and none—all rooted in scripture—make God's directorship of kingship even more explicit:

Terce: Among many nations there was not a king like him, and he was beloved of his God, and God made him king over all Israel.[85]

Sext: And in chains God left him not, till He brought him the scepter of the kingdom, and power against those that oppressed him.[86]

None: And the Lord magnified him over all Israel: and gave him the glory of a reign such as no king had before him.[87]

Louis' name is never mentioned here; the texts are each based on ones for Solomon and for Joseph, but the comparisons are unmistakable. Terce made

79. LDR VCap.
80. Ezr. 7:27: "Benedictus Dominus Deus patrum nostrorum qui dedit hoc in corde regis ut glorificaret domum domini quae est in Hierusalem."
81. Joseph R. Strayer, "France: The Holy Land, the Chosen People, and the Most Christian King," in *Action and Conviction in Early Modern Europe: Essays in Memory of E. H. Harbison*, ed. Theodore K. Rabb and Jerrold E. Seigel (Princeton, N.J., 1969), 9–10; repr., *Medieval Statecraft and the Perspectives of History* (Princeton, N.J., 1971), 300–315.
82. Paul Edouard Didier Riant, *Exuviae sacrae constantinopolitanae fasciculus documentorum minorum, ad exuvias sacras constantinopolitanas in occidentem saeculo XIII translatas, spectantium, & historiam quarti belli sacri imperijo: gallo-graeci illustrantium* (Geneva, 1876; repr., Paris, 2004), vol. 1, 47.
83. Anon 3, OFM, *Misericordia et veritas*, BNF Lat 3303, 187v.
84. Jacob of Lausanne 3, *Rex sapiens*, BNF Lat 14799, 191v.
85. LDR Terce. Cf. 2 Ez. 13:26.
86. LDR Sext: Cf. Wis. 10:14. = NL None.
87. LDR None: Cf. Chr. 29:25.

use of a line from Ezra that, although chastising Solomon for idolatry, spoke of Solomon (and thus Louis) as unequaled among kings and emphasized that God had made Solomon (Louis) ruler over all of Israel (France). God chose Louis, as he chose Solomon, to rule over the entire kingdom, and as he had for Joseph, he raised Louis to power for his virtue. France is Israel. It is more glorified under Louis than ever before.

The verse for Sext (Wis. 10:14) evoked Louis' captivity in Egypt during his first crusade; in the original passage from the Book of Wisdom the actor is *not* the Lord, but the personification of Wisdom, and the object of her benefaction is Joseph. The use of the Joseph typology linked the reading for Sext back to the fifth responsory and lection, which also compared Louis to Joseph for their Egyptian captivities, but here the Joseph to whom Louis is typed was not only the Joseph who escaped captivity but also the Joseph who rose to the heights of political power after his escape: "God did not leave him in his chains, so long as he could convey to him the scepter and the power of the kingdom against those who oppressed him."[88] Notably, the phrase was reworked with the inclusion of *Dominus* in the place of the implied *Sophia*, and it is thus the Lord, not Wisdom, who saves the king and gives the king his authority. The office in this way emphasizes God's will in Louis' kingship.

The same strategy drove the choice of 1 Chronicles 29:25 for the None hour. The scriptural passage told of David's death and Solomon's elevation to the throne: "And the Lord magnified Solomon over all Israel: and gave him the glory of a reign such as no king of Israel had before him." As reworked for Louis' office, the text simply dropped "Solomon," making Louis "magnified" by the Lord to rule over all Israel (France). The sleight of hand was purposeful. Louis at once both *is* Solomon and is his successor as the Lord's anointed, chosen one.

The office celebrating Louis' sanctity fell within a longer trajectory in the Capetians' construction of their own special identity. Many of the themes that *Ludovicus decus* evoked could be traced back to the Carolingian period and beyond. But the office was perfectly in line with strategies of sacralization that the Capetians had been following throughout the thirteenth century. In this regard it may be worth emphasizing the affinity between the themes and approaches of the office and the narrative glass cycle that dominated the interior space of the Ste.-Chapelle (consecrated 1248), for which *Ludovicus decus* was written and where it was performed.[89] *Ludovicus decus*' use and choice of biblical types for Louis specifically, and kings of the Capetian lineage generally, as well as its expression of the importance of coronation and justice in the definition of kingship, echo the iconographic program of the royal chapel and the broader ideological program it reflected. As Meredith Cohen has shown, the chapel itself was designed to promote the cult of kingship.[90] The glass cycle

---

88. LDR Sext. Cf. Wis. 10:14.

89. Jordan, "Stained Glass and the Liturgy," 247–297. On royalizing liturgical texts at the Ste.-Chapelle, see also Mercuri, "reflets," 117–126.

90. Cohen, "An indulgence for the visitor."

illustrated the continuity of kingship from the Old Testament period through to the Capetian (and projected forward to the End of Time). Louis had himself depicted within, and as part of, the framework of biblical-royal history. This lineage of Old Testament kingship was solidified by a Tree of Jesse in the apse (including David and Christ), and ultimately linked to the Capetians themselves. The Ste.-Chapelle had conceived of kingship in Christic terms, extending backward to Old Testament kings and forward to the Capetians and ultimately, in teleological terms, to the kingdom of Heaven. Daniel Weiss has argued that Louis himself built the upper chapel to evoke the Throne of Solomon.[91] Alyce Jordan has demonstrated how important the typological models of Joseph, David, and Solomon were to the glazing cycle and to notions of Christian kingship in Capetian circles in mid-century.[92] Chiari Mercuri has shown how the liturgy and iconography of the Crown of Thorns served to link French kingship to Christ's kingship.[93] Themes of justice and coronation were preeminent in the cycle. And these were the very themes used to laud Louis as a saint. That this mechanism of sacralizing royalty around 1240 was in turn used to regalize sanctity about 1300 demonstrates the extent to which these two ideological programs had become a single discourse.

The Liturgical Readings: *Beatus Ludovicus quondam Rex Francorum* (BLQRF)

A liturgical vita, *Beatus Ludovicus quondam Rex Francorum*, ultimately supplied the lections for *Ludovicus decus*.[94] *Beatus Ludovicus*—an edited version of a slightly earlier text that survives in a single manuscript—has been largely overlooked even though it was the most frequently copied hagiographical treatment of Louis in the fourteenth and fifteenth centuries, was included in collections of saints' lives, was used in the composition of sermons, and became a source for a number of other histories.[95] *Beatus Ludovicus* echoed the

---

91. Weiss, *Art and Crusade*, 56–74. Note that Gautier Cornut implicitly compares Louis and Blanche to Solomon and his mother, Riant, *Exuviae sacrae*, vol. 1, 47.

92. Jordan, *Visualizing Kingship*. Jordan, "Stained Glass and the Liturgy," 274–297.

93. Mercuri, "Stat inter spinas lilium"; *Corona di Cristo*; "reflets sur l'iconographie."

94. An early exemplar of *Ludovicus decus*, Washington Library of Congress ms 15, 554r.–560r., had paired the office with lections taken from *Gloriosissimi regis* suggesting a stage of provisional usage before the order of the celebration was fixed. On this manuscript, see Baltzer, "A Royal French Breviary," 3–25. All other manuscripts paired the office consistently with some form of *Beatus Ludovicus*.

95. The earlier redaction of the text is found only in Orleans BM 348, 1r.–18r. The second redaction was included in collections of saints' lives: BNF Lat 14652, BNF nal 1755. It was also included in expanded versions of Jacob of Voraignes' *Legenda aurea* (originally written before Louis' canonization). By 1483 an English translation was included in the first volume of Caxton's translation of the *Golden Legend*: Jacob of Voragine, *The Golden Legend, or, Lives of the Saints, as Englished by William Caxton* (London, 1900). An anonymous chronicler lifted most of his material directly from the text; see "E chronico anonymi cadomensis ad annum M.CCC. xliii perducto" in *RHF*, vol. 22, 21–26. Bernard Gui used it in the composition of his life of Louis in the *Speculum sanctorum*, BNF Lat 5406, 152r.–155r. The text can also be seen reflected in sermons on Louis; see Anon 3, *Misericorida et veritas*, and Jacob of Lausanne 1, *Videte Regem*.

major themes of humility, just and clement rule, and typology embedded in
Ludovicus decus. The lections recounted episodes of Louis' life, upbringing,
fatherhood, patronage of religious houses and institutions, love and charity of
the poor, crusades, good and just rule, and death. As originally conceived, the
text was elegantly structured. It was organized around the fifth, central, and
longest lection, which treated the crusades. The first four lections treated the
personal and private aspects of Louis' sanctity and were substantially shorter
than the sixth, seventh, eighth, and ninth lections, which discussed the public
character of Louis' sanctity and his Christian kingship. The text presented
Louis' life and sanctity as follows:

  (1) Parents' example and advice to Louis
    (2) His "rule" of his family
      (3) Piety in a personal setting
        (4) Alms for individual poor
          (5) Crusades
        (6) Alms for communities of poor
      (7) Piety in a public setting
    (8) His "rule" of his kingdom
  (9) Parents' example and advice to Louis

The first and the last lections both considered the Capetians' worthy lineage:
parents advising and directing the successor to the crown. The second and
eighth both dealt with the way in which Louis' personal piety led him to treat
others (his children, monks) and guided his rule. The third and seventh both
dealt with other aspects of his personal piety (personal, then public), while the
fourth and sixth both took up the issue of his generosity, alms, and compassion for the poor (the feeding of individual paupers and the foundation monasteries for the blind and beguines). The lections interpreted the 1248–1254
crusade as the central turning point in Louis' life. The four lections preceding
the discussion of the crusades thus treated Louis' private behavior and personal habits, whereas the four lections following the crusade bore witness to
virtues that have a social and civic character, touching on public aspects of his
rule. Where the third lection treated individual, private charity (feeding the
poor at his own table, compassionately ministering to the sick and elderly with
his own hands and without disgust), the corresponding seventh lection treated
his public, institutional charity (founding hospitals, funding monasteries).
Even the last lection, which considered advice given to his eldest son and heir,
dealt primarily with how a king ought to rule the kingdom in accordance with
God. Because the lections also followed a temporal progression and conveyed
a sequential narrative, the structure in this regard presented the first half of
his life as characterized by the exercise of private virtue, and the second half
of his life as defined by his exemplification of public virtue. The structure suggests that the text was originally written for a liturgical celebration of nine
readings.

The text's themes were integrated with the office. The opening antiphon for matins spoke of Louis' virtue *ab infancia* and the first lection elaborated on his virtuous upbringing. We saw that the fourth lection echoed the chant's typological comparisons between Louis and David. Solomon was evoked in both the chant texts and the lections; and as Epstein noticed, the fifth lection, which treated Louis' captivity during the crusades and in which Louis was described as *Eductus itaque velud Joseph de carcere Egyptico,* was paired with a responsory that spoke of Louis' incarceration and miraculous release and compared it to Joseph, having been detained, later being freed.[96] The eighth responsory and the eighth lection both spoke to the rightness of Louis' reign, and the ninth responsory and ninth lection both treated his good death.

Echoing central themes of the chant, the liturgical vita emphasized that humility, the root of good kingship, shone in Louis. The third lection spoke of his humility, sobriety, and mercy, praising Louis for guarding himself against the treacheries of the world, the flesh, and the devil.[97] The fourth lection, as we have seen, compared Louis to David for the quality of his humble kingship. The sixth lection spoke of how he served friars, beguines, the blind, and the ill, for whom he built monasteries, convents, and hospitals "with humility and charity," and so forth.

The liturgical vita was also careful to connect Louis to his Capetian lineage and the virtue of the dynasty. The text emphasized the continuity of Capetian virtue, a continuity in which Louis was the strongest link. The first lection established Louis VIII, referred to as *christianissimus rex*, as the defender of the Christian faith in his battle against the Albigensian heretics, just as Louis IX would make war against the Saracen infidel. Blanche, his mother, was the one to instruct Louis in Christian morality. Blanche arranged Louis' marriage so that the noble kingdom might not lack in royal succession, a marriage that resulted in offspring whom Louis in turn took care to raise in the love of God and contempt for the world.[98] The virtues for which Louis IX's parents were praised (defense of the faith, edifying instruction of children, most Christian kingship) were then melded in the person of Louis himself. The second lection made clear that Louis instructed his own children in virtue as well, and the fifth lection showed how Louis battled the Saracens. The ninth lection functioned to demonstrate the continued lineage of instruction, sanctity, and virtue: Louis brought his three sons with him on his second crusade to defend the Holy Land from imminent dangers; as Louis prepared to *migravit a Christum* (Louis VIII was also described as having *migravit a Christum*), he instructed the future Philip III that to rule well was to "spare nothing for Christ and the church"[99]; lastly, the ninth lection made reference to the *Enseignments*

---

96. LDR MV5.
97. BLQRF L3: "Et quia sciebat quod in deliciis sobrietas, et in honoribus humilitas periclitari solent, ideo sobrietati, humilitati et misericordiae animum dedit, ab insidiis mundi, carnis et diaboli sollicite custodians semetipsum."
98. BLQRF L2.
99. BLQRF L9.

that Louis wrote for Philip, in order that he might fittingly rule the realm. This was the ultimate example, in a royal context, of the instruction of Christian virtue to one's children: the instruction in Christian kingship.

The liturgical text also echoed the office's theme of justice balanced with clemency. The eighth lection spoke of how he ruled himself and his subjects with rectitude, saying that Louis governed himself and the kingdom, rendered judgment and justice in all cases, was feared by counselors and magnates, made himself available to the poor each week to render justice so that their cases might not be overlooked, expedited justice, prohibited the judicial duel, abolished usury, labored for peace, and gave tranquillity to the realm. The responsory that followed claimed that Louis had prayed to God for himself and his subjects, taking the "right path with virtue."[100] The ninth lection ended by quoting the king's own advice on good rule and kingship to his son, which involved sparing nothing—not wife, family, or kingdom—for Christ and the faith.[101]

Composed within the orbit of the royal court of Philip the Fair, *Ludovicus decus regnantium* was unremittingly royalizing, drawing on themes integral to the discourse of royal legitimacy and royal identity fostered by the Capetians: the notional relationship between new France and the Israel of old, Old Testament models of kingship, the central role of justice and humility for kings, the implicit claims of family descent and shared virtue, and the importance of a king's rule of self in his rule of the kingdom. Its sacralizing language was borrowed from biblical prescriptions on kings, kingship, and rule. The language of scripture, and specifically the language associated in the Bible with David, linked Louis in turn with these biblical types, sacralizing Louis with biblical models of kingship. The office thus employed a complex of biblical-royal language into which the Capetian Louis was drawn, for the purposes of, as Gabrielle Spiegel has argued for another venue, "legitimizing present political life."[102] Such biblical-royal typing, a mainstay of royal ideology in any event, was more explicitly expressed at other parts of the liturgy when Louis was directly compared to worthy Old Testament kings. Moreover, by rooting Louis' sanctity in the quality of his kingship—that is, by identifying his sanctity specifically with his rule and not as in other schemes with his piety, alms, or crusades—*Ludovicus decus* sacralized French kingship, and thus, potentially all French kings.[103] Because *Ludovicus decus* was disseminated beyond the Ste.-Chapelle, the court, and Paris specifically, the office served as one of the mechanisms in the dissemination of royal ideology.

---

100. NL MRV8 = LDR MR8.

101. This is taken from *Glor. Reg.*, whence it originated.

102. Gabrielle Spiegel, "Political Utility in Medieval Historiography: A Sketch," *History and Theory* 14 (1975): 322.

103. Within two decades, a royalist preacher would go so far as to talk about the "saintly kings" (*sancti reges*) of France. Jean Leclercq, "Un sermon prononcé pendant la guerre de Flandre sous Philippe le Bel," *Revue du moyen âge latin* 1 (1945): 169. On the date of this sermon, see Elizabeth A. R. Brown, "Kings Like Semi-Gods: The Case of Louis X of France," *Majestas* 1 (1993): 10, n. 15.

Dominicans Redux

The fact that a number of these strategies and themes were first worked out in the short-lived Dominican *Nunc laudare* highlights the Paris Dominicans' role in the formulation of a specifically royal sanctity. We have already noted the close relationship shared between the Paris Dominicans and the court. But the Dominicans of the Rue St.-Jacques had shown a particular interest in defining good kingship in other contexts as well. In the half-century or so preceding Louis' canonization, the Dominicans had written a number of *Specula principum* for members of the Capetian court: Vincent of Beauvais' *De eruditione filiorum regalium* and his *De moralis principis instructione*, Bartholomew Vincent's lost *Liber Tertius de informatione regiae prolis,* and the Pseudo-Thomas's (William Perrault's) *De eruditione principum*. At about this time, Thomas Aquinas (probably) wrote the *De regno ad regem Cipri* for (probably) the Lusignan court in Cyprus. A bit later, a Dominican of St.-Jacques wrote the *Liber de informatione principum* for Louis X. These were works of ethical pedagogy designed to instruct kings on how to live up to ideals of kingship. Increasingly influenced by Aristotelian ethics and ideas of authority, they were all predicated on the notion of an institution of kingship that fell within the framework of God's divine plan, and the idea that the earthly king was an element of God's transcendental reign.[104]

William of Sauqueville (d. post 1330) and Jacob of Lausanne (d. 1333) both wrote sermons on Louis for his feast day that offer examples of how two Parisian Dominicans interpreted Louis' sanctity in ways consonant with the court's ideological agenda for Louis.[105] These sermons focus as much on abstractions of kingship as on Louis himself, and they worked toward a definition of Louis' sanctity that was rooted in and in turn exalted rulership: the king is just in his execution of justice; the virtue of the king represents the virtue of the kingdom; the good king is wise, just, and prudent; the king is comparable to David and Solomon.

In two sermons, both structured on Wisdom 6:26—*Rex sapiens stabilimentum populi* (the wise king is the foundation of his people)—Jacob and William

104. Born, "Perfect Prince," 470–505; Bell, *L'idéal éthique,* 1–70; Jean-Philippe Genet, ed., *Four English Political Tracts of the Late Middle Ages* (London, 1977), xi–xiv; Krynen, *L'empire du roi,* 163–239.

105. William probably arrived in Paris around 1316, after Philip's death and the accession of Louis X, and was at the university through about 1322, but had left by 1330. On William of Sauqueville, see Kaeppeli and Panella, *Scriptores,* vol. 2, 162; *HLF,* vol. 34 (1924) 298–307; Schneyer, c. 2, 593, no. 70; Coester, "Der Königskult in Frankreich um 1300"; and Christine Chevalier Boyer, "Les sermons de Guillaume de Sauqueville: l'activité d'un prédicateur dominain à la find du règne de Philippe le Bel" (Ph.D. Thesis, Université Lumière Lyon 2, 2007). Jacob was a member of the community at St.-Jacques, and he signed the letter of adhesion in support of Philip in 1303 during the second phase of the conflict with the papacy. Courtenay, "Between Pope and King," 599. On Jacob of Lausanne, see *HLF,* vol. 33 (1906), 459–479; Beryl Smalley, *English Friars and Antiquity in the Early Fourteenth Century* (New York, 1960), 248–251; and Kaeppeli and Panella, *Scriptores,* vol. 2, 323–329. For sermons, see Schneyer, vol. 2, 55–157.

each developed the notion of Louis' wise kingship.[106] Wisdom, a classic attribute of good kingship, was increasingly emphasized in the fourteenth century.[107] William's sermon explored how Louis fulfilled the ideal of the wise king (a characterization not rooted in the hagiographical tradition).[108] A kingdom is made stable when it is ruled by a wise king. A wise king, he explained, is one who is not deceived by the falsehoods or appearances of this world. And thus was Louis, who was not deceived by riches, delights, or honors.[109] Louis was a wise king because he did not go after useless ("sophist") wisdom but rather pursued virtue. Louis ruled his soul as he ruled his kingdom, through reason, which orders everything else, and through the light of wisdom, which is juxtaposed to "inferior reason." Here Louis is compared to Solomon, "who did not seek delights or riches but rather wisdom, and pleased the Lord exceedingly."[110] But unlike Solomon, Louis was not elevated through pride. Likewise, in his *Rex sapiens*, Jacob explained that a ruler, or a leader, requires the light of wisdom. Just as there is light of fire and light from stars, so there are two types of wisdom, terrestrial and divine. God bestowed on Louis divine wisdom, which results in devotion to God and compassion for people, and directs one both spiritually and temporally.

Jacob's sermon identified Louis' royal and saintly virtue with the virtue of the French people, saying that a worthy king was a gift by God to a virtuous people. This was a strategy in harmony with the crown's own desire to equate Louis' sanctity with the legitimacy of the dynasty and in turn the virtue of the most Christian king with that of the French people—the chosen people. Jacob built on the "head and body" model of society (*congregatio* or *communitas*, depending on the manuscript), in which "the body" is the "body of Christ" and the "head" is referred to as the *rector*, which could be either secular or ecclesiastic. This represented a conflation of the two corporate metaphors in use at the time—Christ as the head of the body-church, and the king as the head of the body-kingdom—which was in sympathy with the transcendentalizing metaphor of the *corpus reipublicae mysticum* that had been developed at the French court by two Dominican tracts on kingship written for Louis in mid-century.[111] Jacob continued: when the head is healthy, the entire body and its

---

106. Jacob of Lausanne 3, *Rex sapiens*; William of Sauqueville 1, *Rex sapiens*.

107. Brown, *"Rex ioians, ionnes, iolis:* Louis X, Philip V and the Livres de Fauvel," esp. 60–61; Philippe Buc, *L'ambiguïté du livre: Prince, pouvoir, et peuple dans les commentaires de la Bible au Moyen Âge* (Paris, 1994), 195–205; Kelly, *The New Solomon*, 259–269.

108. The only place I know of its explicit use elsewhere is WSP *sermo*, where William of Saint-Pathus described the four qualities of the king as "splendor sapiencie, dulcor compassionis, nitor continenciae, fervor devotionis" (WSP *vie*, 278). Jean of Samois, OFM, preached *to* Louis IX at the Ste.-Chapelle on the importance of wisdom for good kingship (Bériou, *L'avènement des maîtres*, 311).

109. Chevalier Boyer, "Les sermons de Guillaume de Sauqueville," 577.

110. Ibid., 587: "Set ipse habuit regere populum multum. Ergo indiguit multa sapientia et eam habuit. Figuram de Salomone 3 Reg . . . , qui non petiuit delicias uel diuicias set sapientiam et multum placuit Domino."

111. Kantorowicz, *King's Two Bodies*, 208. On these, see Krynen, *L'empire du roi*, 170–179. The head and body metaphor was found earlier in John of Salisbury's *Politicratus*, V.2.

members are ruled well. If a single member deviates, no great harm is done, but a prince's errors will injure many. If the head is healthy and without corruption, then all the members will be secure. Louis, Jacob said, was a "golden head." Moreover, the head is God's choice, and a bad ruler signifies God's hostility toward the community. But a good ruler is the sign that God loves the community, and a good ruler is the minister and friend of God, for which the community must give thanks to God. Such was Louis, a "friend of God."[112] Jacob established a feedback loop of sanctity between the king and his community of subjects. As Joseph Strayer famously formulated it, if the king was the most Christian king, the French were the most Christian people.[113]

The royal virtue most closely associated with Louis was justice. Jacob of Lausanne wrote that,

> Judgment ought rightly be done by punishing, and justice in executing. For the judge ought to be like a pair of scales, in which things are weighed, which, with equity, shows the weight of all things to be precious or cheap, gold or lead, silver or a mere alloy. Thus the prince, in judging, ought to weigh equitably the rights of the poor without favoritism to anyone. Deuteronomy 1: *You shall hear the little as well as the great; neither shall you respect any man's person because judgment is of God.* That is what Saint Louis did. Indeed, once or more each week he would make himself publicly available so that the poor could have access to him. Thus he punished the great just as the small. . . . The cause of the poor, however right it may be, may appear in a twisted form thanks to false advocates or false counselors. . . . Justice is like a strong torrent, which if it meets a strong tower, does not sweep it along with it but drags away little things. For, nowadays, the execution of justice does not drag away great and powerful lords, but only the small and the poor. This was not the case with blessed Louis. Concerning which we can say 2 Kings 8 [15]: *And he did judgment and justice to all people.*[114]

---

112. Jacob Lausanne 3, *Rex sapiens*. BNF Lat 14799, f. 191va. "Osee 13: *dabo vobis regem in furore meo* [sic, for *dabo tibi regem in furore meo*, Hos. 13:11]. Sed rector bonus est minister dei et amicus et ideo communitas commissa tali rectori commissa est amico quod est signum dilectionis de qua dilectione est deo valde regratiandum. Talis fuit beatus ludovicus. Unde fertur dixisse quod prius vellet quod omnes filii essent mortui quam quod deum offenderent per peccatum mortale. Unde fuit amicus dei. In manu huius regis amici sui posuit deus populum francie. Unde signum est spiritualis amoris." The text in Vat Lat Reg 1259 differs slightly in order and text: *congregatio* appears in place of *communitas*.

113. Strayer, "France: The Holy Land," 3–16.

114. Jacob Lausanne 3, *Rex sapiens*. BNF Lat 14799, fol. 193ra: "Iudicium recte sentenciando, et iusticiam in exequendo. Iudex enim debet esse sicut libra in qua res ponderantur que equaliter demonstrat pondus omnium rerum preciosarum et vilium, auri et plumbi, argenti et stannic: sic princeps in iudicando debet ponderare iura pauperum sine acceptione personarum. Deut 1: *ita parvum audietis sicut magnum, et non accipietis personam cuiusquam, domini enim iudicium est* [Deut 1:17]. Sic fecit beatus ludovicus unde semel vel pluries in septimana sedebat in loco communi ut pauperes possent habere accessum ad eum. Ita puniebat magnos sicut parvos. . . . Sic causa pauperum quantumcumque recta sit apparet tortuosa per falsos advocatos et falsos consiliarios. . . . Iustitia est quasi turrens fortis, quod si obviet turri forti, non trahit eam secum sed res minutas trahit: sic exequtio [executio] iusticie nunc non trahit magnos dominos potentes, sed parvos et pauperes. Non sic fecit beatus ludovicus, de quo potest dici illud 2 Reg. 8: *quod faciebat iudicium et iusticiam omni populo.*

Louis' ability to judge well, honestly, and in the interest of the poor had been an important aspect of defining the saintliness of his kingship in the hagiographical tradition. Jacob evoked this image again in another sermon dealing with the execution of justice (*Bene omnia fecit*), saying that a prince carries a sword for the "punishment of evildoers," and that a prince must weigh the scales of justice carefully so that he can protect the interests of the poor.[115] In this trope, the image of Louis hearing the cause of the poor was preeminent.

William of Sauqueville drew on the same trope in his discussion of royal wisdom. A kingdom, he said, is made firm by wise kings through established and created laws, and in this way was Blessed Louis truly a wise king.[116] People are ruled poorly (as with Saul) when the poor cannot gain admittance to the king. In contrast (as with David), people are ruled well if "anyone can gain approach to him." "Concerning Blessed Louis," William continued, "we can read that each week he sat in a public place so that anyone who wished could approach him"[117] (itself an interesting reference to the hagiography).

In general, the tone of the sermons emphasized authority and strength in relationship to rule. Elsewhere Jacob developed comparisons between Louis and Solomon. In *Videte regem*, he talked about how difficult it was for a man of wealth and status to accede to heaven. Jacob emphasized the strength of the king and his militant status as a fighter on the crusade, speaking of "the fortitude of his power," and saying that "the strength of power is required in every warrior and especially in a leader or a king," before discussing Louis' taking of the cross, the capture of Damietta, and the subduing of the surrounding regions.[118] Louis was praiseworthy because he "fought strongly against the enemy," "exposed himself to danger," and "chose a just cause."[119] He called Louis a *pugnator prudens*, and said that to fight well against the world required being armed with humility.[120] Thus did the sermon shift from earthly crusade to metaphysical battles (against haughtiness, against the flesh, and

115. The phrase is taken from 1 Pet. 2:14. Jacob of Lausanne 4, *Bene omnia fecit*, BNF Lat 1475, fols. 158vb.: "princeps portat gladium ad vindictam malefactorum."
116. Chevalier Boyer, "Les sermons de Guillaume de Sauqueville," 577: "Regnum stabilitur legibus per sapientes conditis et inuentis. Unde dicitur de sapientia Prov. 9 (8.15): *per me reges regnant*, et loquitur sapienter: beatus Ludouicus fuit rex valde sapiens, quod sic patet."
117. Ibid., 578: "Unde bene rexit Dauid, Saul male? Quare Saul eminebat super populum ab humero et supra, Dauid autem fuit paruus, ruffus, etc. Sic aliquando rex est *ita eleuatus per superbiam*, quod nullus pauper potest habere accessum ad ipsum et propter hoc populus male regitur. Econtra Dauid fuit *in medio populi* et paruus et quilibet poterat accedere. De beato Ludouico etiam legitur, quod in singulis septimanis sedit in communi loco, ut omnes qui uellent accederent, set Saul habet multos successores."
118. Jacob of Lausanne 1, *Videte regem*, BNF Lat 15962, 26r.: "fortitudo sue potentie." "Licet vigor potentie requiratur in omni bellatore magis tamen in duce vel rege."
119. Jacob of Lausanne 1, *Videte regem*, BNF Lat 15962, 26r.: "Et tangit auctoritas tria puncta fortitudinis quam habuit ludovicus propter quam laudandus: primus est pugnare fortiter contra hostem; *pugnauit*. Secundum est exponere se periculo; *dedit animam periculis*. Trium est iustam causam eligere; *ut eruerem vos de manu madian*." Cf. Jgs 9:17.
120. Jacob of Lausanne 1, *Videte regem*, BNF Lat 15962, 26r.: "Bene pugnans contra mundum debet esse armatus virtute humilitatis."

against pride, which he fought through penitence), and then returned to the theme of Solomonic wisdom. "In a prince, wisdom is more necessary than fortitude. Thus did Solomon say that wisdom was better than fortitude."[121]

Jacob ended *Videte regem* by returning to the image of Louis hearing the cases of the poor. "But note," he enjoined "that [Louis] sat in a public place to hear the plaints of the poor. *Thus say to Wisdom, my sister, though art prudence.*"[122] For William, in turn, this was the episode that demonstrated the link between justice and regal humility. Praising Louis and comparing him to King David, William contrasted him with rulers who, elevated by pride, would allow no pauper to gain admittance to them, on account of which people are ruled badly.[123] Jacob, in *Bene omnia fecit*, broached this idea of personal rule when he exhorted the good king to be active, arguing that it does not suffice to send out men on behalf of the king, but that the king must himself travel around the lands entrusted to him so that he might guard the acts and mores of his subjects.[124] Here the king is made responsible for the virtue of his subjects.

In any event, these two Parisian Dominicans constructed Louis in terms of the ideals of rulership, doing things critical to rule (justice) with exceeding perfection and so bolstering the authority of the king. The yardstick of Louis' sanctity was the nature of his rulership and his relationship to his subjects (rather than his charity, humility, or obedience). This strategy exalted the idea and the image of the king through Louis not by emphasizing that which made him saintly, but by emphasizing that which made him kingly. This emphasis on the royal aspects of Louis' saintly authority may have been natural within a Parisian context in the years immediately following Louis' canonization, where the Dominican friars were among the most ardent supporters of Philip the Fair and his monarchy. And, as with the liturgical office, the texts regalized Louis' sanctity, celebrating Louis as a saint for precisely the qualities normally linked to good kingship.

The Sanctity of Kingship

To identify Louis' sanctity with the language of kingship was to sacralize the office of the king. The vision thus articulated first by the Dominicans and then transmitted to and found in *Ludovicus decus* abandoned the notion that Louis somehow found sanctity in spite of his kingship, or that his saintly character was highlighted all the more because it stood in such awesome contrast to the necessities or presumptions of kingship. Indeed, the idea that a king's sanctity

---

121. Jacob of Lausanne 1, *Videte regem*, BNF Lat 15962, 26v.: "In principe sapientia plus est necessaria quam fortitudo. Unde Sapiens dicit sapientiam esse meliorem fortitudine" [cf. Eccl. 9:16].

122. Jacob of Lausanne 1, *Videte regem*, BNF Lat 15962 26v.: "Sed nota quod ipse sedebat in communi loco ad audiendas causas pauperum; ergo dicit Sapientia, *soror mea es et prudenciam* [Prov. 7:4].

123. Chevalier Boyer, "Les sermons de Guillaume de Sauqueville," 587.

124. Jacob of Lausanne 4, *Bene omnia fecit*, BNF Lat 1475, fols. 159v.–160.

was necessarily at cross-purposes with the requirements of kingship, that a king was a saint against all odds and despite his royal office, was the presumption among king-saints of an earlier era.[125] Janet Nelson has said of early medieval kings that "they were not saints in virtue of their royalty, but in spite of it. They qualified for sainthood either through the act of renouncing the world, most spectacular in their case because they had most to lose, or through self-subjection to defeat and death."[126] This interpretive impulse was arguably at root in the works of Louis' earliest hagiographers. In contrast, the royalist interpretation of Louis' sanctity as expressed in *Ludovicus decus* identified his saintly characteristics with the qualities of rule and kingship attributed to French kings in the normal language of political theology found in traditional sources for French kingship—that is the coronation *Ordines* and the *Specula principum*. To be a good king of France in traditional Christian terms was to be holy. Or put another way, *Ludovicus decus* mapped back onto Louis the qualities of good kingship that the crown was in 1300 claiming as characteristic of its own virtue and identity, and his sanctity was made to conform to and thus legitimize the ideals of the crown. It is precisely for the legitimacy that Louis, as an officially recognized saint, could offer the Capetian line that his canonization was so ardently sought by Philip IV. And it was Philip's great and sad irony that his royal line came so abruptly to an end with the reigns of his ill-fated, some said damned, sons.

125. Graus, *Volk, Herrscher und Heiliger im Reich der Merowinger*, 390–437; Nelson, "Royal Saints"; Folz, *Saints rois*; Ridyard, *Royal Saints of Anglo-Saxon England*; Klaniczay, *Holy Rulers*, 62–113, and, on how Louis specifically fits into this scheme, 295–298.
126. Nelson, "Royal Saints," 40–41.

5
The Monastic Louis
Cistercians and Dionysians

Although the central and guiding impetus for Louis' cult was the crown, veneration spread beyond Paris, and he was incorporated into the Sanctorale of monastic and secular churches in France. This may have involved merely his addition to the calendar, the celebration of a memoria, or the recital at matins of proper lections drawn from the liturgical vita for Louis in conjunction with the Common for Confessors. But Louis himself had been deeply devoted to aspects of the monastic lifestyle and was a patron of monastic institutions, and certain houses made special cultic arrangements in his honor following his canonization. The Cistercians composed a proper office for Louis, and an altered version of the office was adopted at the Benedictine houses in or near Paris, St.-Germain-des-Prés and St.-Denis. A chapel at the Cistercian foundation of Royaumont was named after him. Cistercian institutions collected his relics. A chapel with eight stained glass windows was erected at St.-Denis for Louis.

Saint Louis was thus specially honored by monastic houses that he had himself, as Louis IX, honored and patronized. This chapter traces how Louis' cult was adopted at these institutions and how the monastic image of Louis was produced, adopted, and then adapted differently at each house. Unsurprisingly, the Louis revered in these institutions took on a saintly hue colored by the culture and history of the institution. Just as Louis was painted as a sacral king at the court, he was painted as an ascetic and contemplative Christian and king by the Cistercians who emphasized themes of bodily exile and spiritual union with God. The Cistercians thus constructed a Louis according to a conservative spiritual ideal, and one that portrayed an image of a saint-king more in line with those of an earlier age. Among Benedictines in Paris this image of Saint Louis was complemented by a further emphasis on royalty. St.-Denis, in particular, capitalized on a portrait of Louis that evoked the essential identity and special history of that institution, with close ties to the Capetians and as the principal promoters of their sacred royal history. The monks there emphasized Louis' own particular devotion to their patron, Saint Denis, and were conscious of promoting a cult center and pilgrimage site.

Cistercian Liturgical Commemoration and the Capetians

Close ties between the Cistercians and the Capetians had predated Louis' reign and were only solidified during his lifetime by his patronage. The most famous example of these ties was Blanche's and Louis' foundation of Royaumont, a Cistercian house to which Louis often retired for prayer and respite, and where he buried two of his children. He loved Châalis as well and held Cistercians in general in high esteem.[1] This patronage was recognized by Cistercians liturgically. The white monks had regularly acknowledged the Capetian royal family in their prayers. As early as 1228 and 1229 the general chapter prescribed prayers on behalf of Louis and Blanche.[2] In 1240 this decree was renewed, and all priests were prescribed to say the mass of the Holy Spirit for the king, the queen mother Blanche, the queen Marguerite, and their daughter.[3] In 1244 and again in 1245, the General Chapter instituted special masses for the royal family.[4] In 1254, when Louis returned from overseas, the order prescribed that every Cistercian priest should celebrate the mass for the Holy Spirit, the mass for the Blessed Virgin, and the mass for the Holy Cross, in honor of Louis and his family.[5] Each year Louis would write to the order specifically requesting these exact provisions.[6] This custom of liturgical honors for the Capetians generally and Louis specifically is in evidence in a number of Cistercian manuscripts. After Louis' death, the order sought special commemoration for Louis even before his canonization. The General Chapter of 1271 ordered a double service for Louis be celebrated throughout the order for two years, after which a mass would be sung yearly on August 25.[7] The abbot of Royaumont wrote specifically to the General Chapter of 1271 for permission to establish an anniversary for Louis at the monastery (the request was granted).[8] A number of Cistercians testified in 1282–1283 at Louis' canonization proceedings.[9] A thirteenth-century manuscript listed the feast day of

1. Anselme Dimier, O.C.R., *Saint Louis et Cîteaux* (Paris, 1954), 109–112; Jordan, *Unceasing Strife*, 38–39, where Jordan says the monks considered Louis as a kind of "second founder."
2. Henri Louis Duclos, *Histoire de Royaumont, sa foundation par saint Louis et son influence sur la France*, 2 vols. (Paris, 1867), 323, citing Martene, Anecdot., vol. 4, 1349.
3. Ibid., 323, citing Martene, Anecdot., vol. 4, 1373.
4. Canivez, *Statuta, vol.* 2, 276, 292.
5. Ibid., vol. 2, 400–401.
6. WSP *vie,* 56.
7. Canivez, *Statuta, vol.* 3, 103, item 72, for 1271; Dimier, *Saint Louis et Cîteaux,* 139.
8. Duclos, *Histoire de Royaumont,* 324, citing Martene, Anecdot., vol. 4, 1436. The grant comes in article 8.
9. LCB *procès,* 121–128, 236–238.

Louis among those saints' days in the order for which special indulgences were afforded.[10]

Those Cistercian foundations that boasted particular ties to Louis himself or members of his family—Royaumont, Châalis, Maubuisson, Lys—were particularly committed to his sanctity. At the canonization proceedings in 1282–1283, both the abbot of Royaumont, Adam of Saint-Leu, and Brother Girard, a monk from the abbey, testified about Louis' role in the construction of the abbey, his frequent visits there, his participation in the liturgy, and, most famously, his loving charity to the leprous monk, Légier.[11] The chapel of Saint Agnes, one of the two chapels at the convent that Louis had favored for prayer during his lifetime, came afterwards to be known as the Chapel of Saint Louis,[12] and on the walls of this chapel a short account of Louis' life was inscribed. The inscriptions spoke of how Louis' father died in 1226; how in his testament Louis VIII ordered his son to build the abbey; how Louis himself was crowned and anointed at Reims when he was twelve; how Louis ordered the building of Royaumont and ministered there personally; how he confessed each Friday and received the discipline from his confessor; how he first went overseas to fight the infidel; that he purchased the Crown of Thorns and other relics, which he placed in the Ste.-Chapelle; that the pope persuaded him to take the cross a second time; and how, at Carthage, he gave his soul up to God.[13] Given how many of these themes were represented in the iconography developing around Louis, it may well be that this chapel was decorated with images as well. At the canonization proceedings the prior from Châalis testified that Louis would come to the abbey to listen to sermons and eat with the monks in the refectory and to a dramatic healing miracle, and the Abbey treasured one of Louis' cloaks as a relic.[14] The abbess at Lys was given a finger relic, and Notre-Dame de Maubuisson had several of Louis' relics—including a rib which was encased in a fancy gilded reliquary that included an image of Louis with his two sons, a finger, and part of an arm.[15] An inventory of 1464 of the abbey's manuscript holdings attests to liturgical books containing the office for Louis, including two antiphonaries and a breviary.[16]

10. Jordan, *Louis IX*, 91, n. 185.

11. LCB *procès*, 121–128, 236–238.

12. Duclos, *Histoire de Royaumont*, 289. It does not appear that the chapel was ever formally rededicated to Saint Louis.

13. Ibid., 325, citing Archives de Seine-et-Oise, liasse cotée R.

14. Dimier, *Saint Louis et Cîteaux*, 131–134; Jordan, *Unceasing Strife*, 38. LCB *procès*, 127–128, 237–238.

15. Tillemont, *Vie*, vol. 5, 223–225; *Recueil d'anciens inventaires imprimés sous les auspices du Comité des travaux historiques et scientifiques: Section d'archéologie*, vol. 1: *Inventaires de l'abbaye de Notre-Dame la Royale dite Maubuisson de Pontoise* (Paris, 1896), 4, no. 6, 18, no. 6, 21, no. 21, 22, no. 25; *Enamels of Limgoes*, 361–363.

16. *Recueil d'anciens inventaires*, 37–38, no. 204–205, 40, no. 220.

Lauda Celestis 1: The Cistercian Office

Thus, following Boniface VIII's canonization of Louis in August 1297, the order naturally established regular liturgical celebration for the new saint. At the meeting of their General Chapter in 1298, Cistercians decreed that Louis' feast day be observed throughout the entire order with two masses and twelve lessons, just as is done for the feast day of Saint Anthony.[17] The following year the General Chapter further stipulated that *historia* (that is, a liturgical office) be sung throughout the order. The Cistercians duly composed an office, *Lauda celestis*, which survives in a Cistercian breviary dating from about 1300, Troyes BM 1973, fols. 224va.–226vb. Troyes BM 1973 may have belonged to Clairvaux, where the monks had honored Louis prior to his canonization and later dedicated an altar to him.[18] The office follows a Benedictine format, with twelve antiphons and responsories for matins.[19]

Of the five offices for Louis, *Lauda celestis* adopted the most clearly hagiographical and narrative approach, drawing on themes and stories that had been established in the hagiographical tradition. The office followed Louis' saintly progression from boyhood to death, beginning with his virtuous upbringing and outlining his saintly virtues, his austerities, his obedience, his hatred of oaths and blasphemy, his comportment on crusades, his instruction of his children, and his saintly death. The vespers service spoke of Louis' father who fought heresy, and of his saintly boyhood and upbringing, a theme that carried over into the narrative in matins. Louis' father was a powerful knight; he was educated by the sage judgment (*sensu*) of his illustrious mother,[20] and as a boy he honored his parents and "proceeded into happiness."[21] His spirit was renewed by doctrine, and he founded churches and aided the poor.[22] After his father's death, he acceded to the throne, and the kingdom was guarded by his mother.[23] He hated and punished blasphemy and he deemed oaths bad.[24] Second nocturn treated the crusade. The king "crossed the sea, upheld by his firm faith, and suffered many grave insults from unworthy people. Under the sign of the cross, by a secret judgment [of God], captured by misfortune, he was freed by a miracle. . . . He deemed it a glory to suffer outrage in the name of Christ, in every peril."[25] He zealously sought to promote the catholic faith.[26] The office then turned to Louis' pious habits. He fasted, wore a hair shirt, and

---

17. Canivez, *Statuta*, vol. 3, 294, item 5, for 1298. For an overview on Cistercian liturgy, see King, *Liturgies of the Religious Orders*, 62–156; and Louis J. Lekai, *The Cistercians: Ideals and Reality* (Kent, Ohio, 1977), 248–260.

18. On the altar, see Dimier, *Saint Louis et Cîteaux*, 138.

19. Proper celebration of *Lauda celestis*, however, did not spread throughout the order. Gaposchkin, "Monastic Office."

20. LC1 MA1–2.

21. LC1 MA2, MR2, MA4.

22. LC1 MA5, MRV3.

23. LC1 MRV4.

24. LC1 MA7, MRV7, MRV8.

25. LC1 MA9–11.

26. LC1 MR5.

had himself disciplined with five little iron chains.[27] He labored for works of mercy during the day and prayed in church in song at night.[28] Matins ended where hagiography generally did: with the saint's death. Before dying, Louis composed his final testament, bequeathed the "treasure of learning" (*thesaurum doctrine*) to his children, and entered the Kingdom of Heaven.[29] Lauds described Louis' rule in heaven, calling him the "flower of regal dignity," who now belonged to the choir of heaven. Louis had joined the Father in the sky, blessed the creator, and sung praise to God.[30]

The chant text was resonant with scriptural references that injected them with greater meaning.[31] Thus when the third matins antiphon spoke of Louis, entering adulthood and shedding the preoccupations of childhood (*Ab amore seculi iuvenis abstratus ea que sunt parvuli vacuat vir factus*), the celebrant was reminded of 1 Corinthians 13:11: "When I was a child, I spoke as a child, I understood as a child, I thought as a child. But, when I became a man, I put away the things of a child" (*cum essem parvulus loquebar ut parvulus*). The antiphon for terce—"*Luce vigil ad dominum*"—drew on Psalm 62:2—"*ad te de luce vigilo.*" A reference to Louis' refusal to take the oath—*est est, non non, dicens amplius malum indicavit*[32]—evoked Matthew 5:37—*sit autem sermo vester est est non non quod autem his abundantius est a malo est.*[33] Examples can be multiplied, and some are discussed below. The office thus drew on biblical language in the same way that *Ludovicus decus* did, but unlike *Ludovicus decus*, the scriptural allusions mostly were focused not on kingship but rather on devotion, piety, and asceticism. Biblical evocation of this sort infused the office, weaving the narrative of Louis' hagiographic vita into apostolic and evangelical history.

The Image of Kingship in the Cistercian Office

The Cistercian liturgical office also drew on images of kingship from the Old Testament, incorporating the theme of kingship into the hagiographical narrative. The office spoke of Louis' transferral from the earthly to the heavenly kingdom. It spoke of the "earthly king" who is worthy of the heavenly kingdom and referred to Louis as "king of France."[34] Certain chants commemorated Louis in a language that echoed the discourse of kingship. MA5—"truth and mercy have seized the house of the heart, and peace and justice have come together in a kiss"[35]—drew directly on Psalm 84:11 "mercy and

---

27. LC1 MRV9–10.
28. LC1, "*ad cantica antiphona.*"
29. LC1 MRV11–12.
30. LC1 LA1–5.
31. My thanks to Father Chrysogonus Waddell for help in identifying many of these.
32. LC1 MV7.
33. The reference to Cor. 13:11 also recalled a passage from Geoffrey of Beaulieu's vita in which Geoffrey said that, in regard to oath taking, Louis followed these words of the Evangelist. GB *vita* 25 (ch. 7).
34. LC1 VA1, VA2, see also Mag, MH2, LA1.
35. LC1 MA5.

truth have met each other; justice and peace have kissed," which had done long service in kingship literature and which recalled the classic virtues of good rule. The first matins verse also modeled Louis according to another classic ideal: "The king, sitting on the throne, discerned justice, [and] having beheld the reward, destroyed wickedness."[36] The lauds hymn spoke of the "pacific state of the realm," and of Louis as a "zealot of justice."[37]

But the clearest royalizing strategy—its royal typologies—governed the office's interpretation of saintly kingship. The Old Testament typological models the office drew upon—Josiah, Solomon, David, Manasseh, Jacob, and Ahasuerus—were mostly royal. (Jacob was the only one among them who was not a king, but he was an ancestor of the Twelve Tribes and a model of the exiled leader.) Excepting Ahasuerus, the typological motifs appeared in verse responses of matins and thus echoed the central image of the responsory. The second matins verse spoke of Louis explicitly as a type of Josiah—specifically, it said that Louis is figured (*figuratur*) in Josiah, when he attended to laws, which here referred to divine law and scripture.[38] Josiah (2 Kings 22 and 23) was a king of Judah remembered as a good soldier, a builder of temples, and above all a restorer of the law.[39] In the office, the evocation of Josiah, though, highlighted Louis' piety and zealous attention to matters of devotion—a theme that was emphasized by the office. Louis is compared to Solomon for the way in which he honored his mother, saying that he had put her on the throne.[40] The fourth matins verse drew upon 1[3] Kings 2:19, "and the king arose to meet her, and bowed to her, and sat down upon his throne: and a throne was set for the king's mother, and she sat on his right hand," and blended its royal typology with the theme of parental honor and respect elicited elsewhere in the office. David was evoked in a verse that dealt with Louis' dangerous ocean crossing, comparing Louis, "secure in God," to David, "a man stable in faith."[41] The reference was to 2 Samuel 24:15–25, where David's firm faith and obedience to the Lord resulted in the Lord lifting a plague and becoming "merciful to the land." The ninth verse called upon Manasseh as a model for royal imprisonment, exile, and penance.[42] This comparison was not typical, but was relevant because of its royal type and meaningful because of the endurance, trial, and piety Manasseh evoked. Jacob was evoked in the eleventh responsory, which treated Louis' death: lying on his cot, overwhelmed by illness, he composed his final testament. "Like Jacob to his children at the end [of his life], he [Louis] bequeathed a treasure of doctrine as a benefit to his descendants."[43] The verse referred to

36. LC1 MV1.
37. LC1 LH3–4.
38. LC1 MV2.
39. Geoffrey of Beaulieu and William of Chartres both used this Josiah typology: GB *vita*, 3–4 (ch. 1 and 2), 9 (ch. 16), 25 (ch. 51); WC *vita et actibus*, 29. See also LeGoff, "Royauté biblique," 157–167.
40. LC1 MV4. The biblical reference is 1 Kings 2:19.
41. LC1 MV5.
42. LC1 MV9.
43. LC1 MV11.

Genesis 49, in which Jacob addressed his sons on his deathbed with blessings and prophecies, which was likened to Louis' final salutary instructions to his son, the *Enseignements*. And last, in the final matins responsory Louis is compared to Ahasuerus, the king from the Book of Esther, as sincere in the worship of God (*sincerus . . . cultor dei*).

The point to be made about these typologies is not only that they were royalizing, but that they understood virtuous royalty in terms of humility, service, suffering, penance, devotion, and obedience before God. This definition of royal sanctity was essentially the traditional one, and represented a different royal typology from, for instance, that adopted by the court, with its strong undertones of divine election and sacral royalty. Where the secular office modeled Solomon as the just king whom God chose to rule over all Israel, the Cistercian office modeled Solomonic kingship as obedience. Likewise, the secular office, in drawing on Joseph's captivity, described how God raised him over his oppressors in triumph. Manessah's emphasized trial, endurance, and suffering. The Cistercian version of saintly kingship was rooted in the traditional virtues of monastic culture—honor, obedience, devotion, asceticism, learning, exile, and worship—at the heart of the monastic life. In this it was thus sympathetic to an older instinct of praising saint-kings, in figures like Edward Confessor or Henry II, in which it was their piety, devotion, chastity, and ascetic impulses that made them saints.

Monastic Spirituality and the Liturgy

This image of saintly kingship was rooted in a conservative complex of monastic ideals that underpinned Cistercian identity. Resonant throughout the office were a number of classic themes in monastic spirituality—earthly exile from God, the imprisonment of the body, chastisement of the flesh, obedience to authority, the virtue of sacred learning—which distinguished its general tenor from its secular and mendicant counterparts. In many ways, the imagery of the Cistercian office hearkened back to a vocabulary of asceticism found with the desert fathers and throughout the monasticism of the central Middle Ages. But in applying these ideals to the secular, lay king, the office also presented an image of the converted knight-aristocrat that spoke to root ideals of the Cistercian order itself.[44]

The office celebrated Louis' obedience and humility, both toward his parents and toward God. Vespers spoke of the "humble, modest, pious king of France."[45] Louis followed in the footsteps of Christ, and he is called a prudent

---

44. On monastic spirituality, see Jean Leclercq, *The Love of Learning and the Desire for God: A Study of Monastic Culture*, 3d ed. (New York, 1982). On Cistercians specifically, see Simone Roisin, *L'hagiographie cistercienne dans le diocèse de Liège au XIIIe siècle* (Louvain, 1947); and Lekai, *The Cistercians*, 227–247. I have found particularly helpful Martha Newman, *The Boundaries of Charity: Cistercian Culture and Ecclesiastical Reform, 1098–1180* (Stanford, Calif., 1996), especially at 25–27. For a case study of a contemporary Cistercian defending the order's traditional prerogatives, see Jordan, *Unceasing Strife*, 37–55.

45. LC1 VA2.

and faithful servant.[46] Louis obeyed the greatest instructor [*summum precep-torem*], protected the honor of his parents with humility,[47] and honored his mother with wondrous reverence.[48] Churches were enjoined to praise the "humble, modest, pious king of France, Saint Louis."[49]

The *laus perennis*, that perpetual, unceasing celebration of the divine office that lay at the heart of the Cistercian vocation, structured the hymns. "Sing the praise of Louis," began the hymn for vespers. The matins hymn (sung in the middle of the night) recognized the often demanding nature of the *opus dei*: "In the time of the nightly office let the devout mind stay awake, let the unwearied voice rejoice, brought forth by a chaste body."[50] And the relief, at lauds (sung af-ter sunrise), was evident in the opening strophe of that hymn: "Let the morning prayers awaken the sleeping to song; let the voice of psalmody recite the mag-nificent deeds of the king."[51] In turn, Louis was remembered for his own habit of contemplative prayer and devotion. The office recalled how his father instructed him in the worship of God from childhood, praised him for his worship of the Lord, and commemorated him for his praying in church throughout the night.[52] He is described at different junctures as "the watchman in divine worship," as a "true worshipper of God," and as "seized in mind toward the divine."[53]

The monastic life and the *opus dei* sought to lessen the gap brought about by man's exile. Themes of exile were deeply rooted in the monastic spirituality of the West, and these included exile from God, brought about by the Fall and in-herent in the human condition, and in turn the exile from worldly, secular life that the monastery represented.[54] The Cistercian office thus drew on the lan-guage of exile. It praised Louis as a young man for having been, like the clois-tered monk, "separated from love of the world,"[55] and spoke of Louis, in heaven, having overcome his exile on earth: "He sings praises to God, having left his exile; having been translated into joy, he was not mindful of his afflic-tions."[56] To combat exile, Louis was eager to follow in the footsteps of Christ (*sollicitus Christi sequi vestigia*),[57] a line that drew on another image that Jean Leclercq called "dear to the Cistercian school of thought from its inceptions."[58]

46. LC1 MR1, Terce.
47. LC1 MA4.
48. LC1 MR4.
49. LC1 VA2.
50. LC1 MH1. On the weariness of the liturgical rite among Cistercians, see Lekai, *The Cis-tercians*, 249.
51. LC1 LH1.
52. LC1 VA4, MA8, VCapA, "*ad cantica antiphona*."
53. LC1 MA8, MR12, MA12.
54. Hans von Campehausen, "The Ascetic Idea of Exile in Ancient and Early Medieval Monasticism," in *Tradition and Life in the Early Church: Essays and Lectures in Church History* (Philadelphia, 1968), 231–251.
55. LC1 MA3.
56. LC1 None.
57. LC1 MR1.
58. Jean Leclercq, "Lettres de vocation à la vie monastique," *Analecta monastica* 3 (Studia Anselmiana, 37: Rome (1955), 174, n. 11: "Ce theme avait été cher à l'école cistercienne dès ses

One of the many attributes of man's exile was his corporality. The monastic sanctorale often commemorated saints for being released from the prison of the body on the day of their death,[59] and Bernard of Clairvaux himself had spoken of how man's body exiled him from God: "And for each one of us who desire His coming he also stands behind the wall as long as this body of ours, which is certainly sinful, hides His face from us and shuts out His presence. For 'so long as we are in this body we are exiles from the Lord.' [cf. 2 Cor. 5:6]."[60] In the office for Louis, the matins hymn extolled the effort required to overcome this bodily and spiritual exile: "After the labors of exile, after the accumulation of virtues, running the road of salvation toward the repose of the blessed. What he saw darkly [*vidit enigmatice*], enclosed in the prison of the flesh [*carnis clausus ergastulo*], he sees, this obstacle having been endured [or, perhaps, overcome—the word is *sublato*], in the mirror of eternal light [*lucis eterne speculo*]."[61] The phrase *vidit enigmatice . . . lucis eterne speculo* drew on 1 Corinthians 13:12 (*videmus nunc per speculum in enigmate tunc autem facie ad faciem nunc cognosco ex parte tunc autem cognoscam sicut et cognitus sum*—which the American Standard version translates "For now we see in a mirror [*speculum*], darkly; but then face to face"). 1 Corinthians 13:12 had a long pedigree in monastic writings associated with contemplative and mystical writings, and Bernard himself made recourse to it with some frequency.[62] Other images in the hymn further reveal its monastic roots: the notion of exile; the monk as an athlete of Christ, "running the road" toward Heaven; explicit reference to the "prison of the flesh"; the labors involved in overcoming the alienation of exile. Later, the Benedictus antiphon celebrated the spirit of the saint-king who rises to the sublime hemisphere in the stars and enjoys the rewards of the fatherland only after having been separated from his body.[63]

The whole weight of monastic asceticism grew out of the premise that the corrupting body impeded reunion with God. "Man's wretchedness," wrote

---

débuts." See 176 for use in the thirteenth-century Cistercian letter Leclercq discussed. On this theme, see also Giles Constable, "Nudus Nudum Christum Sequi and Parallel Formulas in the Twelfth Century," in *Continuity and Discontinuity in Church History: Essays Presented to George Hunston Williams* (Leiden, 1979), 83–91; and Giles Constable, "The Ideal of the Imitation of Christ," in *Three Studies in Medieval Religious and Social Thought* (Cambridge, 1995), 143–248.

59. Gregorio Penco, "Monasterium—Carcer," *Studia monastica* 8 (1966): 138–139; Jean Leclercq, "Le cloître est-il une prison?" *Revue d'ascétique et de mystique* 47 (1971): 409–410, esp. his n. 9 for the liturgy of Saint Benedict; Paul Meyvaert, "The Medieval Monastic Claustrum," *Gesta* 12 (1973): 53–39; Leclercq, *Love of Learning*, 37–38; Ludovicus Milis, *Angelic Monks and Earthly Men: Monasticism and Its Meaning to Medieval Society* (Woodbridge, UK, 1992), 143–147.

60. Bernard of Clairvaux, *On the Song of Songs*, trans. Kilian Walsh, 4 vols. (Spencer, Mass., 1971–1980), vol. 3, 90, Sermon 56.3.

61. LC1 MH3–4. For the "road of salvation": in the original, *compendii*, meaning "gain" or "profit," here spiritual profit or salvation.

62. Bernard McGinn, *The Presence of God: a History of Western Christian Mysticism*. 3 vols. *The Growth of Mysticism*, vol. 2 (New York, 1991–), 71, 76 (Gregory the Great), 209 (Bernard of Clairvaux), 228, 256 (William of St.-Thierry), 279 (Guerric of Igny), 379 (Hugh of St.-Victor).

63. LC1 Ben.

Leclercq, "comes from his physical nature, from original sin. . . . It must be put to rout constantly: not only at the outset of our actions, by purifying our intentions, but also during our actions, and again at the end, for it is always a menace to us."[64] *Lauda celestis* therefore displayed a particular concern for Louis' chastisement of the flesh and bodily austerities. The ninth matins responsory commemorated his "many fasts, the tears of his vigils and disciplines, his pallor, the bluish aspect of a dead man, his hair shirt, the hardness of his bed, [which] all revealed a body consumed by meagerness, subjugated to the spirit," and then compared Louis, who chose punishing and harsh conditions, to Manasseh for conquering himself inwardly.[65] The next responsory spoke of his chastisement of the flesh, how he happily bore the lashes from the iron chain of his confessor while remembering the wounds of Christ, and how, scourged by punishment, Louis was "freed from prison, freed from his chains," and entered the kingdom.[66] The very notion of conquering oneself inwardly was monastic in impulse, and the verse interpreted the body as a prison from which one must escape to enter heaven, understanding escape from the "chains" of the flesh as the subjugation of the flesh to the spirit. The matins hymn (we saw) had also spoken about how Louis sought to escape the prison of the flesh.[67] The body as a prison and the cloister as a prison were both images that structured much monastic thought and contemplative practice, for the aim was to release one's soul from the exile of bodily flesh through celibacy, meditation, and the rule of the flesh.

The uncommon comparison with Manasseh (cf. 2 Chr. 33; 2 Kings 21) is revealing for how it linked a model of rulership with the ideals of exile, imprisonment, and harsh asceticism. Manasseh was an Old Testament king who came to the throne at twelve (Louis was fourteen) and ruled for fifty-five years (Louis ruled for forty-six).[68] Manasseh was remembered for an episode of his own capture and cruel imprisonment at the hands of the Assyrian monarch, which led to his repentance of idolatry and penitence. He is said (like David) to have humbled himself before the Lord (2 Chr. 33:23), and the Lord restored him to his kingdom and his court abandoned idolatry. The evocation of Manasseh thus drew on themes of royal capture and exile, penance, strict austerity, and the spiritual benefits of the physical trials of captivity, interweaving references to Louis' Egyptian captivity and images of bodily exile.

The images of exile and imprisonment in the hymns may have been designed as an interpretive gloss on the narrative of Louis' tribulations in Egypt, when captured and incarcerated by the infidel. The office recalled Louis' captivity at

---

64. Leclercq, *Love of Learning*, 37.
65. LC1 MRV9.
66. LC1 MRV10. For the tradition of the five iron chains, see GB *vita*, 10 (ch. 16), WSP *sermo*, 28 (part 25), though it is omitted from the *vie*; *Glor. Reg.* 5. The theme of Louis' asceticism is also taken up by YSD *gesta*, 53 (ch. 7).
67. LC1 MH4.
68. 2 Chr. 33:1–3; 2 Kings 21:1.

several points in its narrative treatment of the crusade.[69] One antiphon spoke of Louis "having been captured by misfortune, [and] saved by a miracle."[70] The hymns served to spiritualize the idea of the crusades, understanding the physical journey as a metaphor for the soul's struggle against alienation from God. This may offer the key to understanding a strophe in the vespers hymn. Having spoken of how Louis had freed himself from desires for secular merit and was increasing in the exercise of virtues, and how, now in heaven, he was freed from performing works of charity, the fourth strophe spoke metaphorically of the cleansing of Louis' soul: "His pious tears, and his sea crossing, cleansed every guilt of his soul, which by his human nature he contracted [*contraxit humanitus*]."[71] The strophe construed his sea journey more as a spiritual crusade of penance and contrition (the "pious tears" for the sins he contracted *humanitus*, that is, for original sin) than as the physical journey of a missionizing, militant crusader. And indeed, the crusades, as representative of the active, militant life, were not in general central to the monastic ideal of *contemptus mundi*.[72] Unlike the mendicant ideal, monastic culture was not missionizing in inspiration but rather valorized the stationary, solitary, contemplative life. This explains why the Cistercian's treatment of Louis' first crusade focused more on the king's own spiritual response to the crisis and his imprisonment and alienation than it did on aims to spread the faith, reported so openly by his mendicant biographers. The spiritualized imagery of crusading also fed into the Cistercian move to understand the monastic vocation as spiritualized warfare. Cistercian literature often favored military themes and images, drawing on the idea of the monk as *miles Christi*, a soldier fighting for God through the *opus dei*, themes that were particularly applicable to Cistercian culture, which valorized the adult knight who converted to the monastic life.[73] As an image of the saint-king-crusader Louis served these interests, presenting an actualized model of the knight-monk. At one point, Louis is addressed as "Soldier of Christ, glorious and very holy Saint Louis," who is then asked to intercede with "pious intervention."[74]

This monastic sensibility was further evoked through themes of learning and contemplation, other strongly Cistercian values.[75] One of the ways in which monks sought to escape the prison of the flesh was through learning, study of

---

69. LCI MA9, MA10, MA11.

70. LCI MA10. The notion of the hidden judgment of God and of Louis' capture can be found in the hagiographical record. See WSP *vie* 23, BLQRF 162 (lection 5), and *Glor. Reg.* ch. 10.

71. LCI VH4.

72. On the relationship between monasticism and the crusades, see Etienne Delaruelle, "The Crusading Idea in Cluniac Literature of the Eleventh Century," in *Cluniac Monasticism in the Central Middle Ages*, ed. Noreen Hunt (Hamden, Ct., 1971), 191–216; Milis, *Angelic Monks*, 115–119; and Giles Constable, "Cluny and the First Crusade," *Collection de l'École française de Rome* 236 (1997): 179–193.

73. Newman, *Boundaries of Charity*, 29–37.

74. LCI VCapR.

75. Newman, *Boundaries of Charity*, 37–41.

sacred letters, and contemplation,[76] an ideal at the heart of the sixth matins antiphon: "Avoiding the din of the world, sitting in the bastion (i.e., refuge) of his house, he was restoring his spirit with the nourishment of sacred doctrine."[77] Perhaps nowhere did the office more clearly attribute to Louis the virtues valued within the monastic sphere, as a monk having escaped the distractions of secular life by entering the contemplative haven of the monastery. This antiphon described Louis, out of his contempt for the noise of the secular life, seeking to restore his soul through spiritual renovation found in the study of sacred doctrine. His dedication to *doctrine* (doctrine, learning, instruction) was emphasized again near the end of Matins: "In the manner of Jacob, at the end [Louis] left the treasury of learning [*doctrine*] to his children who would come after him."[78] This verse followed the responsory that described how at the moment of death, Louis "composed his final testament."[79] The reference to bequeathing the treasure of learning was thus a reference to the *Enseignements* that had become so important in his memorialization. The prayer may also have drawn on passages from Geoffrey of Beaulieu that spoke of how Louis took care to instruct his children. But in his vita, Geoffrey specified that Louis sought to teach his children to go to mass, listen to sermons, say the canonical hours, learn to read, and know how to recite the hours of the Blessed Virgin[80]—that is, Louis sought to instruct his children in the devotional practices of the literate layman. Study of sacred doctrine was different.

Louis was not in general remembered for his love of doctrine or theological knowledge. The weight of the hagiographical tradition placed the emphasis of his Christian perfection on the active (not the contemplative) life, demonstrating the nature of his commitment to Christ primarily through his charitable activities and crusades. Charitable activities were barely mentioned in the office.[81] Geoffrey of Beaulieu and William of Saint-Pathus included discussions of Louis' love of learning in short chapters on his devotion to sermons, the Bible, and sacred literature.[82] As evidence for his devotion to scripture, Geoffrey recalled Louis' interest in gathering the writings of patristic theologians, including Augustine, Ambrose, Jerome, and Gregory the Great.[83] The reason Geoffrey gave, however, was that the king had learned that a Saracen sultan was researching Muslim philosophy and religion to disprove the Christians and wanted to marshal Christian theologians to refute the Sultan. In Geoffrey's version, then, Louis' impulse to gather together and have copied the writings of the Christian fathers came from a (typically mendicant) missionary impulse, not from his own love of study and contemplation. Devotion to learning, "dogma," and

---

76. Leclercq, *Love of Learning*, 76–93; McGinn, *The Growth of Mysticism*, 119–146.
77. LC1 MA6.
78. LC1 MV11.
79. LC1 MR11.
80. GB *vie*, 7 (ch. 13).
81. LC1 MR3 includes a single reference to his church foundations and aid of the poor.
82. GB *vie*, 14–15 (ch. 23). WSP *vie*, 52–54 (ch. 7).
83. GB *vie*, 15 (ch. 23).

"sacred doctrine," belonged rather to the "love of learning" that Leclercq, for one, pointed to as one of the foundations of the monastic vocation. Reading and study, and the subsequent writing based on the fruits of that study, were what monks did.

The last theme in *Lauda celestis* that echoed traditional concerns of the monastic life was Louis' entrance to the heavenly kingdom. To be sure, the translation from earthly kingdom to heavenly kingdom and Louis' heavenly reward were present in all five offices.[84] The monastic liturgy, however, emphasized his ascent into the heavens and Louis' present life among the saints with discernible force. The Magnificat spoke of Louis, "whose saintly soul ascends the sublime, with the saints of the fatherland, under the happy end of the perpetual kingdom,"[85] and lauds emphasized Louis, having left the exile of earthly life, in the joys of heaven with the "Father of Light." Hope of a future heaven was the aim of all Christian vocations, but as a devotional trope the theme was of particular importance to monastic communities.[86] The monastery itself was an attempt to recreate a corner of heaven in the earthly sphere, and the ideology of devotional prayer underscored the ultimate goal, which was the attainment of glory in heaven.

Lauda Celestis 3 in Paris

A modified version of *Lauda celestis* was ultimately adopted at the Benedictine abbeys of St.-Germain-des-Prés and St.-Denis. Both were long-venerated monastic establishments in or near Paris with long-standing ties to the kings of France. St.-Germain was the burial site of Clovis and Clotilde, the founders of Frankish Christian kingship, and the abbey maintained good relations with the crown, whose palace was just across the Seine.[87] St.-Denis's history was deeply entwined with that of the monarchy and of Louis' sanctity. Both would have naturally augmented their sanctorale with a proper office for Louis after his canonization. The earliest exemplar of this version of *Lauda celestis* is an early fourteenth-century breviary belonging to St.-Germain (BNF 13239), though a diurnal from the abbey dating to the end of the century suggests that the office was no longer in use there by 1400.[88] Our earliest evidence for Dionysian usage of any kind regarding Louis' office is a breviary that dates to about 1350 (Oxford Bodleian Canon Liturg 192), though it is entirely possible the office was adopted sometime earlier.[89] The adaptation did not depend directly on the

---

84. This was the central theme of the collect, which is identical in all five versions of the office.
85. LC1 VMag.
86. Leclercq, *Love of Learning*, 57–75.
87. François Ribadeau-Dumas, *Histoire de St. Germain des Prés, abbaye royale* (Paris, 1958), 46–85. See 62 for relations with Louis IX, which were minimal.
88. BNF Lat 12043, 96v., offers only the proper collect for Louis. His feast is listed in the calendar as "xii lectiones." See also BNF Lat 12085, fols. 146r.–147r., a benedictional, for further evidence of Louis' cult at St.-Germain.
89. This office as it appears in Bodleian Canon Liturg 192 also appears in a printed breviary of 1550, attesting to use over time at St.-Denis. See appendix 1 for citation. On the volume, see Léon Levillain, "L'office divin dans l'abbaye de Saint-Denis," *Revue Mabillon* 1 (1905): 54–72.

Cistercian office but rather on a secular (and thus shorter) version of the office that survives in Orleans BM ms 348. The revamped version of the office replaced the items that had been suppressed in the secularized version of the office (MA4, MA8, MA12, MRV4, MRV8, and MRV12) with a series of chant texts taken from *Ludovicus decus* (MA9, MA10, MA11, MRV7, and MRV8 [repeated also in first vespers]), and then added one newly composed antiphon (MA9). The St.-Germain exemplar also incorporated the *postcommunio* and the *secreta* from the mass.[90] The use of texts from *Ludovicus decus* may have been a mere expedient since the office was obviously available, but the texts appropriated from *Ludovicus decus* all emphasized royalty and thus lent to the new office an emphasis on kingship that was appropriate for the Parisian context. The remodeled version of the monastic office was paired with readings taken from *Beatus Ludovicus* (the hagiographical lections associated with *Ludovicus decus*) though, at St.-Denis, was further adapted to accommodate the new context by eliding direct references to Franciscans and Dominicans and calling those involved in Louis' education simply "religious men."[91] It is worth noting that the full text of *Beatus Ludovicus* was also included in the *Sanctilogium* of Gui of Chartres, the abbot of St.-Denis (1326–1342), a collection of saints' lives compiled ca. 1320.[92] We do not know for which of the two houses—St.-Germain or St.-Denis—the office was initially adapted. In any event, its royalizing themes would have been appropriate to both venues.

The revamped office retained elements from the Cistercian version that were explicit about Louis' kingship—including most of the royal typologies, and other chant items that modeled Louis as a saint-king. Thus, the opening vespers antiphons spoke of the "king of earthly things . . . the king of France" who was now in the Kingdom of Heaven,[93] and the office retained responsories that described Louis as the "illustrious king, glory of the French kings," and as sitting on the throne, doing justice, and destroying wickedness.[94] Beyond this, though, the monks embellished their office with texts taken from the royalizing *Ludovicus decus*, including ones that spoke of Louis, ruled by justice, clement with his

90. For a fuller discussion, see M. Cecilia Gaposchkin, "The Monastic Office for Louis IX of France: *Lauda Celestis Regio*," *Revue Mabillon* (forthcoming).

91. The original text of the first lection reads "sub cura specialis magistri et consilio religiosum, maxime ordinis fratrum predicatorum et minorum, in moribus et scientia tradidit imbundeum" (as in BNF Lat 911, 7v.–8r.). Dominican volumes read simply "fratrum predicatorum in moribus," thus eliding Franciscan recognition (BL 23935, 20r.; Mazarine 374, 309r.; Arsenal 603, 313v.–314r.). BNF Lat 13239, at 384v. (from Saint Germain) includes the lines "fratrum predicatorum et minorum," but Oxford Canon Liturgy 192, 422v., and the printed edition of 1550 (both associated with St.-Denis) read simply "sub cura specialis magistri et consilio religiosorum in moribus." This last formulation was taken up in the hagiographical version of the text found in the *Sanctilogium*.

92. Mazarine 1732, 347r.–349r. In the prologue Gui of Chatres indicates that he conceived of the collection before becoming abbot, which occurred in 1326. On the *Sanctilogium*, see Henri Omont, "Le *Sanctilogium* de Gui de Chârtres, Abbé de Saint-Denys," *Bibliothèque de l'École des Chartes* 86 (1925): 407–410; and Omont, "Gui de Chârtres, Abbé de Saint-Denys, auteur d'un Sanctilogium," in *HLF* (1927), vol. 36, 627–630.

93. LC2 = LC3 VA1–2.

94. LC2 = LC3 MRV1.

subjects in respect to laws and punishment, wisely instituting rewards, and crowned in glory and honor.[95] The office now said that Louis "shone with the scepter of rule," and compared him to David for his rule and Solomon for his judgment.[96] A (uniquely) newly composed text spoke of how, after his return to France he loved the church and favored good men.[97] And last, the office adopted the responsory from *Ludovicus decus* that made reference to the miracle of the breviary that occurred while Louis was in Egyptian captivity.[98]

Saint Louis at St.-Denis

The chant texts that incorporated images of kingship into the office evoked long-standing ideas about ideal Christian kingship that permeated the secular/royal office, and their adoption here was in a sense representative of the "shared history" of the abbey and the crown which was rooted in the sacralization of French kingship and thus the regalization of Louis as saint. The abbey was an object of Merovingian patronage, and as early as the eighth century, the monks of St.-Denis began to court the Carolingian monarchs. The ties between the two institutions tightened with the rise of the Capetian dynasty.[99] With rare exceptions, the Capetians were buried in the abbatial church.[100] The first half of the twelfth century witnessed a solidification of the alliance between the abbey (and her protector Denis) and the Capetian kings. In the twelfth century the Capetians began the practice of retrieving from St.-Denis their war banner, which came to be identified as the oriflamme of Charlemagne.[101] Louis VI augmented the abbey's many privileges, including giving it rights over the profitable Lendit Fair in 1124.[102] The twelfth and thirteenth centuries witnessed the confirmation of the abbey's claim to store the increasingly numerous regalia.[103] Philip Augustus and then later Louis IX fulfilled a

95. LC3 MA10 = LDR MA5; LDR MA6 = LC3 MA11.
96. LC3 MR8 = LDR VCapR, MR6 and NL MR7; LC3 MV8 = LDR VCapV, MV6 = NL MV7.
97. LC3 MA9.
98. LC2 MRV7 = LDR MRV5.
99. The early relationship is discussed in Gabrielle Spiegel, *The Chronicle Tradition of Saint-Denis: A Survey* (Brookline, Mass., 1978), 17–18; Geoffrey Koziol, "Is Robert I in Hell? The Diploma for Saint-Denis and the Mind of a Rebel King (Jan. 25, 923)," *Early Medieval Europe* 14 (2006): 233–267. On the relationship with the Capetians, see Gabrielle Spiegel, "The Cult of Saint Denis and Capetian Kingship," *Journal of Medieval History* 1 (1975): 43–69. The apt characterization "shared-history" comes from Hedeman, *Royal Image*, 28.
100. The exceptions were Philip I, who chose St.-Benoît-sur-Loire (Fleury) at his death in 1108, and Louis VII, who was buried at the Cistercian Abbey of Barbaux. See Erlande-Brandenburg, *Le roi est mort*, 75–76; and Elizabeth A. R. Brown, "Burying and Unburying the Kings of France," in *Persons in Groups: Social Behavior as Identity Formation in Medieval and Renaissance Europe: Papers of the Sixteenth Annual Conference of the Center for Medieval and Early Renaissance Studies*, ed. Richard Trexler (Binghamton, N.Y., 1985), 242–244.
101. Philip Contamine, "L'oriflamme de Saint-Denis au XIVe et XVe siècles," *Annales de l'Est* 25 (1973); Anne Lombard-Jourdan, *Fleur de lis et oriflamme: Signes célestes du royaume de France* (Paris, 1991).
102. Spiegel, *Chronicle Tradition*, 29.
103. Ibid., 31–33.

legendary tradition by offering four bezants to Saint Denis in recognition of the saint's role as spiritual protector of the king and the realm.[104]

The monks actively fostered the myth that Saint Denis himself was a patron of the kings and kingdom.[105] Through their writings, the monks of St.-Denis sought to promote not only the cult of Saint Denis, but also the rising cult of kingship. In this context of mutual self-interest the monks became the official historians of the Capetian kings. They undertook the writing of a comprehensive history of France for the first time sometime between 1120 and 1131, beginning a tradition of historiography that culminated at the end of the thirteenth century with the vernacular *Grandes chroniques de France*, a work designed to legitimize Capetian dynastic history.[106] In the twelfth century this included Suger's *Gesta Ludovici Grossi*, a work that inaugurated the modeling of a specifically Capetian kingship.[107] At the monastery, works of hagiography, such as the *Vita et actus beati Dionysii* (1223) and Yves of St.-Denis' *Vita et passio sancti Dionysii* (1317), also promoted the notion of Saint Denis actively participating in French history. Both in their historiographical and their hagiographical works, the monks highlighted the rise and authority of the French kings as much as they emphasized the role that Denis played in that story, and the cult of French kingship became central to the identity of the abbey itself. Dionysian authors were thus delighted to report that Louis had invoked Saint Denis at the time of his death.[108]

Indeed, the notion of a saintly king, buried in the abbey itself, played into multiple strands critical to the identity of the abbey, and the early history of Louis' sanctity was closely linked to St.-Denis. The texts associated with St.-Denis also reveal a particular interest in the abbey as a cult and pilgrimage center. As recounted in Dionysian texts, after Louis IX's death in Tunis on August 25, 1270, his remains were boiled down so that his bones could make their way back to the traditional burial place of the French kings.[109] The remains were brought back to Paris, interred at St.-Denis, and, because of the miracles reported along the journey home, and again at the abbey, the canonization inquest instigated by Martin IV was held, in 1282 and 1283, at St.-Denis itself. Matthew of Vendôme, the abbot of St.-Denis, was among those who testified.[110]

Thus, when in August 1297 Boniface VIII finally canonized Louis IX, the monks had, in an instant, become the possessors of relics of singular importance. A Capetian king as a saint, resting in their own church, represented the ideal amalgam of royalty and sanctity for the abbey. This was, of course, why Philip the Fair wanted to appropriate Louis' relics for the Ste.-Chapelle—because

104. Spiegel, "The Cult," 60–61.
105. Ibid., 53.
106. Spiegel, *Chronicle Tradition*, 11, 40–44; Hedeman, *Royal Image*.
107. See Suger, *The Deeds of Louis the Fat*, 48, 62, 128–132, 153 for Saint Denis' relationship to Louis VI.
108. YSD *gesta*, 52 (ch. 5), 56 (ch. 12); William of Nangis, RHF vol. 20, 460.
109. William of Nangis, *Gesta Philippi Tertii Francorum Regis*, RHF, vol. 20, 466–468.
110. LCB *procès*, 118–121, 223–236.

Louis' relics embodied the unity of royalty and sanctity. The monks lost little
time in promoting Louis' cult, beginning preparations for what would undoubtedly be one of the more important feasts celebrated in their church. They began
to refer to Louis as *sanctus* in their documents that year (1297),[111] and the elevation of Louis' relics, attended by Philip and other of the kingdom's elite, was
made to coincide with his first feast day in 1298. As the keeper of Louis' relics,
St.-Denis would profit in finances and prestige from any cult that centered on the
saint-king's grave. By 1299 plans were already underway for the construction of
a magnificent new chapel dedicated to Louis in the southeast corner of the
chevet.[112] The chapel, completed by 1304, included a stained-glass cycle depict-
ing eight events from Louis' life (figs. 1–4).[113] The cycle followed the early hagiographic tradition with images of Louis chastised by his confessor, instructing
his children, in prison in Egypt, at sea in prayer, gathering the bones of dead
Christians at Sidon, feeding lepers at a monastery in France, his death, and then
his veneration at St.-Denis. Each window included a Latin inscription identifying the episode. The last window tied Louis' story to the abbey itself, since it
showed four devout Christians praying at his tomb, before a standing statue of
Louis as king. Within two decades, another chapel was erected on the other side
of the church. And, of course, Louis was added to the sanctorale.[114]

The revamped version of the Cistercian office was thus appropriate for St.-
Denis. Like *Ludovicus decus*, from which it adopted chant texts, so the office
used at St.-Denis conceived of Saint Louis as a saint specifically for the people of
France, and his role as king as the heavenly, eternal equivalent of his royal office
on earth. Elsewhere the liturgy specified Louis' French constituency: the hymn
for matins from *Lauda celestis* 3 enjoined: "The joy of new glory arises for the
race of the French [*genti francorum*]; Louis attained the kingly throne in
heaven."[115] The first line of the prosa for the proper mass for Louis used at
St.-Denis enjoined *Gaude, prole, Francia*, and included prayers that referred to
Louis as the special protector of the French people—"protect the king, rule the
kingdom, you who are reigning with the King of Heaven, through whom so
many miracles are effected throughout the ages."[116] The monks of St.-Denis, and
in particular Primat in the *Grandes chroniques*, were among those who were at
this time articulating a notion of a single, unified, French nation.[117] For these

111. Robertson, *Service-Books*, 77–78, esp. n. 142. She notes that in the records of the
Comptes de la Commanderie, there are records for payments "pro pitancia ludovici regis" in the
year 1296, and in 1297 the words read "pro pitancia sancti ludovici." She further notes that "this
designation continues in all subsequent references."

112. Brown, "Chapels," 280–283.

113. Ibid., 284–289; Bernard de Montfaucon, *Les Monuments de la Monarchie Françoise, qui
comprennent l'Histoire de France*, 5 vols. (Paris, 1729–1733), vol. 2, 156–159, with plates 22–25.

114. Note that this was part of a larger expansion of the sanctorale; see Robertson, *Service-
Books*, 72–83, particularly at 77–78.

115. LC1–3 MH2.

116. *AH* vol. 40, 213, no. 240; the manuscript is BNF Lat 1107. On this missal, see Robertson, *Service-Books*, 355, 381–383. "Regem serva, regnum rege, tu, qui cum celorum rege regnans,
per quem per secula tot fiunt miracula."

117. Guenée, "État et nation," 26.

Figure 1. Louis at sea; Louis in prison with miraculous delivery of the breviary. From the glazing from the glass cycle in the chapel of Saint Louis at St.-Denis (nonextant). After Bernard de Montfaucon, *Les monuments de la monarchie françoise, qui comprennent l'histoire de France*, 5 vols. (Paris, 1729–1733), v. 2, pl. 22.

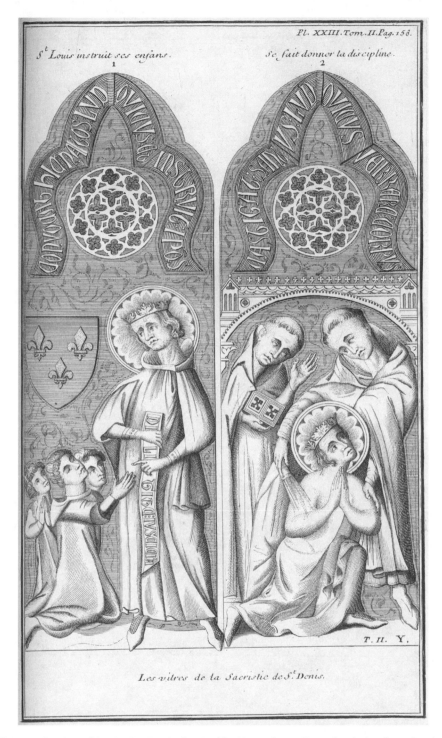

Figure 2. Louis teaching justice; Louis chastised by his confessor. From the glazing from the glass cycle in the chapel of Saint Louis at St.-Denis (nonextant). After Bernard de Montfaucon, *Les monuments de la monarchie françoise, qui comprennent l'histoire de France*, 5 vols. (Paris, 1729–1733), v. 2, pl. 23.

Figure 3. Louis gathering bones; Louis feeding a leper in bed. From the glazing from the glass cycle in the chapel of Saint Louis at St.-Denis (nonextant). After Bernard de Montfaucon, *Les monuments de la monarchie françoise, qui comprennent l'histoire de France*, 5 vols. (Paris, 1729–1733), v. 2, pl. 24.

Figure 4. Louis' death; veneration of Louis at St.-Denis by pilgrims. From the glazing from the glass cycle in the chapel of Saint Louis at St.-Denis (nonextant). After Bernard de Montfaucon, *Les monuments de la monarchie françoise, qui comprennent l'histoire de France*, 5 vols. (Paris, 1729–1733), v. 2, pl. 25.

reasons St.-Denis, the monastery that considered itself the *caput regni nostri*, promoted the notion that Louis' constituency was the *gentes francorum*.[118]

The prosa finished with reference to Louis restoring sight to the blind, straightening the backs of the hunched, and calming the crazed—that is, to miracles effected by Louis at his tomb in the abbey church.[119] This sequence united Louis' protective function as the now heavenly and eternal protector with the miracles he performed as a saint when invoked by his French constituency at his tomb. This wedded the two functions that Saint Louis now played within the Dionysian framework—the king whose image represented France as a whole and the saint whose relics served (the monks hoped) as a pilgrimage site for the French people. As the burial place of almost all these kings, St.-Denis displayed in the many effigies that lay in the crossing the memorialized image of all past kings. The fact that William of Nangis said he wrote the *Chroniques abregées* as a guide to the royal tombs for abbey visitors suggests how consciously the monks understood their public image to be associated with the kings of France.[120] At Louis' tomb, the link was thus made between kingship and sanctity, and both William of Nangis and Yves of St.-Denis finished their vitas of Louis by speaking of the miracles that occurred there.[121] The chapel to Louis included an image of patrons venerating at his tomb.

The office's inclusion (from *Ludovicus decus*) of a reference to the "breviary miracle" also had a particular resonance at St.-Denis. We saw in chapter 1 that the episode itself—or rather, its interpretation as a miracle—was absent in the earliest hagiographical accounts. Larry Crist has traced the development of this story, which William told in order to highlight the constancy of Louis' faith, into a miracle whereby the king's breviary was miraculously delivered to him by an angel. The story was borrowed by William of Nangis sometime around 1280, but it was only with changes made to the translated version of William's Latin life as it was inserted into the *Grandes chroniques de France* around 1286, that the appearance of the breviary was described as somehow extraordinary. In this version, the breviary was both lost, and then brought to Louis in such a way that everyone around him was astounded (*merveillierent mout*).[122] Saracen agency was elided. That is, it was Dionysian authors who turned the episode into a wondrous event. By 1297 Boniface VIII turned the episode into an outright miracle, saying that the breviary was brought to Louis *per miraculum*.[123] And from here it was incorporated into the liturgical tradition, first in *Ludovicus decus*, and then in *Lauda celestis 3*: "The book lost in

118. Spiegel, "The Cult," 60.

119. AH vol. 40, 213, no. 240: "Cecis visum reddidisti, curvos sursum erexisti, furiosis prestitisti, sensum prece sedula."

120. Spiegel, *Chronicle Tradition*, 103.

121. William of Nangis, RHF, vol. 20, 462–464; YSD *gesta*, 57 (ch. 12).

122. Crist, "Breviary of Saint Louis," 320–321. According to Crist, it is only in Boniface's first canonization sermon in 1297 that the event is described as a *miraculum*.

123. B.VIII, 150.

the plunder appeared [*conspicitur*] before the king; the king handed over to the Saracens and exposed to the enemy was miraculously freed."[124] The chant text conveyed the principal elements of the story as it would have been known at St.-Denis by 1286. We know it was meant to be interpreted as a miracle because a glazed image in Louis' chapel dating to about 1303 depicted the event by showing an angel bringing the volume to Louis through the grilles of the prison.[125] (See figure 1.)

In addition, two works produced at the abbey before 1297 tied St.-Denis' royalizing, historiographical tradition to the memorialization of Louis IX and his sanctity: the *Grandes chroniques de France* and the *Vita sancti Ludovici regis Franciae*. The monk Primat compiled and translated the *Grandes chroniques de France* (quite possibly commissioned by Louis IX himself) and presented it to Philip III in 1274.[126] Although Primat's original version ended with the reign of Philip Augustus (d. 1223), later additions included an account of Louis' reign, which was closely related to the works of another Dionysian historian, William of Nangis. William wrote a number of Latin histories in the 1280s or 1290s, including the *Chronique universelle* and the *Vita Sancti Ludovici*, the latter heavily reliant on Geoffrey of Beaulieu's vita.[127] LeGoff has argued that William's *Chronique* modeled Louis as "ever more royal," and as the "king of a preeminent France, plunged into universal history."[128] Much of the material on Louis in the *Chronique* had been taken up from his own earlier *Vita*, and in his preface William listed his sources, saying that he drew from the work of Geoffrey of Beaulieu, as well as the work of his *commonachus*, Gilon of Reims, a monk of St.-Denis who had composed an account of Louis' reign through 1250 (unfinished at his death and now lost).[129] It is clear from William's work that the first half, dealing with the political events of Louis' early reign, was taken from Gilon, and portions from the second—those chapters detailing Louis' saintly virtue—from Geoffrey. Since William transcribed portions of Geoffrey of Beaulieu's detailed descriptions of Louis' personal acts of piety and religiosity, we assume that he also copied much of the earlier (political) material from Gilon. William criticized Geoffrey of Beaulieu for limiting himself to "those things that pertain to his morals" (*ad*

124. LC3 MR7.

125. Although it was Louis' release that was described as miraculous, the placement of the phrase *"miraculose solvitur"*—the central element in the five-phrase response—was probably also meant to lend some of its weight to the *"liber in preda perditus"* indicating the not-quite-ordinary nature of the breviary's deliverance.

126. For overviews, see Spiegel, *Chronicle Tradition*, 72–92, and 88–89 for patronage; and Hedeman, *Royal Image*, 1–6.

127. William of Nangis, RHF, vol. 20, 309–465. Primarily, Geoffrey of Beaulieu and the lost life of Gilon of Reims, a Dionysian monk who had written a lost life of Louis IX through the year 1248. See Spiegel, *Chronicle Tradition*, 101–103. On William's role in shaping Louis' sanctity, see Chris Jones, "The Role of Frederick II in the Works of Guillaume de Nangis," in *Representations of Power in Medieval Germany, 800–1500*, ed. Björn Weiler and Simon MacLean (Turnhout, Belgium, 2006), 273–294.

128. LeGoff, *Saint Louis*, 351, 357.

129. William of Nangis, RHF, vol. 20, 310.

mores) and not including the important military and political events—"the deeds of battles or of secular affairs," for which he evidently turned to Gilon.[130] William was more interested in narrating political developments of the realm than, like Louis' hagiographers, the personal development of Louis' character, mores, and saintly disposition. And thus William treated myriad events of Louis' reign—not all of which were necessarily focused on Louis specifically—such as the dispute between Innocent IV and Frederick II, the Barons' Crusade of 1239, Charles of Anjou's accession to the crown of Sicily, and so forth.

William of Nangis' account of Louis thus traced the major developments of his reign, but he was mindful to record Louis' devotion to Saint Denis and his benefaction and involvement with the abbey in particular, and in turn Denis' benefaction of the realm. Following a discussion of the founding of Royaumont, William recounted the refurbishment of St.-Denis at Louis' advice, and his extreme distress at the abbey's loss of one of the holy nails.[131] He told of how the king went to Saint Denis before setting off for his second crusade and of how he took the Vexin, which the kings of France held in fidelity from the church of St.-Denis.[132] The most notable example of this theme of obeisance and devotion is set during Louis' illness at Pontoise. Notably, William does not include Louis' crusading vow, which is recorded by other authors as having taken place then. Instead, the story revolves around Saint Denis' role in the young king's recovery. With Louis ill, his mother asked the Abbot of St.-Denis to elevate the "bodies" of Denis and his companions Rusticus and Eleutherius, "in whose protection the entire realm rejoices, and the power of the kingdom remains firm."[133] (This last is liturgical, from the prosa for the mass of Saint Denis.)[134] Excepting the Blessed Virgin, the king was devoted above all other saints to Denis and his companions, "as those who are advocates and protectors of both his own affairs and those of the kingdom."[135] The news spread that the saintly relics would be elevated and processed "not only for the health of the French king, but indeed because of the peril to his kingdom."[136] The relics were then carried by the monks, barefoot, through the cloister. The king was cured following the prayers of Denis and his companions.[137] A typical healing miracle, but one that associated Louis' devotion to Denis with the protection and the health of the kingdom. This was the general theme of Louis'

---

130. Ibid.
131. Ibid., 320. The episode is discussed in Edina Bozóky, *La politique des reliques de Constantine à Saint Louis* (Paris, 2006), 41–42.
132. William of Nangis, RHF, vol. 20, 440.
133. Ibid., 344: "quorum patrocinio tota gaudet regio, regni stat potentia"
134. *RHF*, vol. 20, 344, n. 4.
135. William of Nangis, RHF, vol. 20, 344: "utpote in suis et regni sui advocatis et protectoribus."
136. William of Nangis, RHF, vol. 20, 344: "nisi solummodo pro salute regis Franciae, vel regni sui periculo."
137. William of Nangis, RHF, vol. 20, 346.

relationship to the abbey. Later, William recounted how Louis invoked Denis, "the special patron of the French kingdom," on his deathbed, his burial in the abbey, and then the miracles that occurred "*ad tumulum sancti regis in ecclesia S. Dionysii.*"[138]

Unlike William of Nangis' political narrative, the work of Yves of St.-Denis followed traditional hagiographic organization. Written sometime between 1313 and 1317, the treatment of Louis' life was part of the third section of Yves' ambitious treatment in his *Vita et Passio Sancti Dionysii*, a sweeping account of Saint Denis' role in French history. The third and last section of this work, which was ultimately presented to Philip V, dealt with individual kings, highlighting ways in which Denis intervened in the history of French kings and showcasing that the kings' individual devotion to Saint Denis and patronage of his monastery resulted in the prosperity and strength of the kingdom. The segment dealing with Louis amounted to what Auguste Moliner described as a "purely hagiographic text," which is to say that it was organized according to Louis' virtues in a way designed to showcase his Christian virtue and that it made little attempt to narrate the political or military events of Louis' reign.[139] Much of the material was drawn from the canonization proceedings, and as a result he repeated much of what was already known from Geoffrey of Beaulieu and William of Saint-Pathus. It was divided into twelve chapters, including discussion of the innocence of Louis' youth, his pious activities, his devotion to saying the canonical hours, hearing the mass, and prayer, his deep veneration for relics (and particularly the True Cross and the Crown of Thorns), his bodily austerities, his deep humility, the crusades, and his death. A chapter on Louis' devotion to the study of sacred literature (chapter 2) valorized this traditionally monastic concern. Like Geoffrey of Beaulieu and William of Nangis, Yves also transcribed Louis' *Enseignements* to his son (chapter 3), the evidence of the king's exalted vision of Christian kingship. Yves' ninth chapter was dedicated to Louis' "very great justice" in which he described how Louis "walked the royal road of equity" and judged both great and small according to the merits

---

138. Ibid., 460, 462.

139. Molinier, *Les sources*, 118, no. 2545, "texte purement hagiographique." The text is printed in RHF, vol. 20, 45–57, under the title *Gesta sancti Ludovici noni, francorum Regis, auctore monacho sancti dionysii anonymo*, and in André Duchesne, *Historiae Francorum scriptores coaetanei . . . Quorum plurimi nunc primum ex variis codicibus mss. in lucem prodeunt: alij vero auctiores & emendatiores. Cvm epistolis regvm, reginarvm, pontificvm . . . et aliis veteribus rerum francicarum monumentis*, 5 vols. (Paris, 1636–1649), vol. 5, 395–406 under the title *Gesta alia S. lvdovici noni francorum regis avthore monacho sancti dionysii anonimo*. Duchesne published excerpts of Yves' work as separate chapters devoted to individual kings. See vol. 5, 257–261 for Philip Augustus, 288–289 for Louis VIII, and 395–406 for Louis IX. Spiegel, *Chronicle Tradition*, 112–113, discussed the segment on Louis IX without realizing that it was part of Yves of St.-Denis' larger work, which she then treated at 113–115. There is no evidence suggesting that the author was anyone other than Yves of St.-Denis, in whose work, the *Vita et Passio Sancti Dionysii*, the text appears. I am deeply indebted for my understanding of these issues to Elizabeth A. R. Brown, who is working on a study of Yves and his opus, and who generously shared both her insights and materials with me.

of the cases, showing no favoritism, even to the point of rendering judgment against his brother.[140] Here, he repeated material collected in William of Saint-Pathus' chapter on justice. Yves' twelfth chapter treated Louis' two crusades together and did not make them the central organizing element of the progression in his life and sanctity; it retold the story of his crusades, emphasizing, as in the earlier tradition, his captivity, his refusal to take an oath to deny Christ, his loyalty to his men, and his steadfast faith in Christ. The vita thus balanced the marks of piety, humility, and charity that were the essential hallmarks of the early hagiography with a portrait of Louis as a just king (here, king as judge) and a suffering but faithful crusader.

But elsewhere Yves betrayed the larger aim of a work designed to celebrate not Louis but Saint Denis. Yves' fifth chapter was largely devoted to Louis' special love for the monastery's patron—entitled "On the reverence that he held for the name of God, for the saints, for the saintly relics of God, especially for the vexillum of the Lord's cross, and for the patron of the realm, Saint Denis."[141] Every year, on the feast of Saint-Denis, the saint-king (if he was in the area) came to the abbey of St.-Denis and celebrated matins with the monks. He entered the monastery, proceeded barefoot to the saint's altar, and offered four gold byzants to Saint Denis. During his seven-year absence in the Holy Land, the king made sure the offering was maintained. Like William of Nangis, who, in the *Chronique universelle,* stressed the fact that Louis confirmed the rights held by the abbey, Yves recounted other ways in which Louis favored the institution. "He confirmed certain charters for the honor of St.-Denis, regardless of contrary use found in the royal registers, and he desired them to have the strength of firmness."[142] Louis also reconfirmed certain ancient privileges conceded to Denis by Charlemagne in spite of the opposition of certain nobles of the realm, and he conferred many liberties and privileges on Saint Denis, whom "he always revered as his especial patron."[143] Yves repeated a story originally told by Geoffrey of Beaulieu: when the king was at the abbey for Denis' feast day, he declared that he would be willing to spend the rest of his life in Saracen prison if the king of Tunis and his people would convert to Christianity.[144] At his death, as a sign of his particular confidence in Denis, Louis commended himself to his patron, Denis, and said that he desired to be buried at the monastery of St.-Denis.[145] The author wrote that "his glorious bones, along with his most holy heart . . . were transferred to the monastery of St.-Denis and were buried there, following the command of that

---

140. YSD *gesta*, 53–54 (ch. 9); Louis "aequitatis via regia incedens," 54.

141. YSD *gesta*, 51–52 (ch. 5).

142. YSD *gesta*, 52 (ch. 5): "Ad honorem etiam sancti Dionysii cartas aliquas, non obstante usu contrario in registris regalibus invento, approbavit et robur habere voluit firmitatis."

143. Ibid.: "quem semper ut patronum praecipuum veneratur."

144. GB *vita*, 22 (ch. 41); YSD *gesta*, 56 (ch. 12).

145. YSD *gesta*, 52 (ch. 5), and the stories are repeated at 57 (ch. 12).

saint-king [made] when he was still burdened with mortal care."[146] Louis' explicit desire to be buried at St.-Denis confirmed the monastery's continuing claim to be the burial place of the kings of France. Geoffrey of Beaulieu had mentioned that he had personally brought Louis' "holy bones" back from Tunis to St.-Denis, where "he had elected to be buried."[147] The detail (which Yves repeated twice) may have been deployed to rebut Philip the Fair's claims to Louis' remains—relics—by now partly housed in the Ste.-Chapelle. Yves praised Louis' devotion to Saint Denis and his support of the institution rather than Saint Denis' support of Louis. Even William of Nangis had emphasized that Saint Denis had been called upon to heal Louis from illness and that he was cured. But here, Saint Louis valorizes Saint Denis and his institution through Louis' devotion and Louis' patronage, not the other way around.

At St.-Denis, then, Louis' kingship was consciously tied to the abbey's prestige, and in turn Louis' advocacy and intercession was tied to the notion of his French constituency and potential devotees. The monks further fostered St.-Denis as the center of a cult and pilgrimage site. We know by the miracle testimony that ordinary people from the town of St.-Denis prayed to Louis at his tomb. In the year following his canonization, as the monks sought to promote his cult, the abbey collected the substantial amount of 50 *l. par.* in offerings to Louis—offerings that Elizabeth A. R. Brown calculated as "increasing spectacularly in later years." The chapel in Louis' honor, built at great expense, was underway by 1299 and finished by 1304. The last of the eight glazed windows depicted four people in prayer before Louis' shrine at St.-Denis, complete with the image of the saint-king, which stood atop the shrine, and the lost altar retable in the chapel commemorated the king's interventions with a series of images of Louis' miracles. (See figures 1–4.) If St.-Denis was the *caput regni*, the monks saw Louis as the protector of the French, who might seek out his intercession at the abbey.

Liturgy and Institutional Identity

The interplay between the sanctifying and liturgical traditions used by the Cistercians (*Lauda celestis* 1), at the royal court (*Ludovicus decus*), and then at the abbeys of St.-Germain-des-Prés and St.-Denis (*Lauda celestis* 3) demonstrates how powerful liturgy could be in creating, defining, and reinforcing local ideological priorities. The process of *Lauda celestis*'s transmission to Paris is murky, and the intentionality of the re-expansion to its form at St.-Germain-des-Prés and St.-Denis may have been in part a convenience (in drawing on the available secular office for texts) and in part ideological. One way or another, the transmission and transmutation demonstrates the importance of local practice, history, and identity in making sense of the meaning of liturgical texts, and of, as best we can, localizing the manuscripts in use at a particular house and insisting on locating the historical context in which they originated.

The liturgical office written by the Cistercians was tied to the hagiographic tradition established in the years between Louis' death and his canonization, but it modeled the information provided by that hagiography in a way suited to monastic and spiritual ideals. In fact, the Cistercian office represented a pointed interpretation of the hagiographical tradition that drew explicitly on a tradition of monastic virtue. The office thus included multiple references to the king's exile and his bodily asceticism, but only one reference to his charity (MR3) and did not, for instance, celebrate his love of the poor, desire to help lepers, many alms, and so forth. The office's emphasis on humility, obedience, bodily asceticism, and exile represented a spirituality of an early age, more appropriate, perhaps, to the praises of Gerbert of Aurillac or even Bernard of Clairvaux. At a time when spiritual ideals had so changed, an age that had imbibed the mendicant ideals of apostolic poverty and spirituality through active compassion, where the traditional orders such as the Cistercians were losing prestige and alms to new orders and the newer religiosity they represented, the modeling of Louis according to the older, contemplative ideals represented a conservative impulse suited to sacralize the values of the institution itself in the face of a broader social challenge. In a sense, it represented a reaffirmation of the root values of monasticism in a period when those values were out of style.

The serpentine transmission of this tradition to the monasteries in Paris, then, demonstrates the interplay and influence that liturgy could have among religious houses and institutions. At St.-Germain and St.-Denis the reworked office offered a somewhat different view of Louis—one that appropriated themes of monastic spirituality but emphasized royalizing attributes. In other texts, St.-Denis emphasized the special ties between Saint Louis, whose relics they now owned, and their own patron, Saint Denis, as well as the ties between the Capetian kings (whom Louis represented) and the abbey (whom Denis represented). The monks evinced awareness of the miracles Louis performed in their church, and thus consciousness of St.-Denis as a cult site of pilgrimage and veneration.

These different institutions—the crown, the Cistercians, St.-Germain, St.-Denis—may have all shared in their devotion to Saint Louis, but their interpretation of his sainthood was modeled by competing values which colored the glass through which Louis, and the rest of the world, was understood. The devotion to Saint Louis on the part of, say, the monks at Royaumont or at St.-Denis was a testament to the personal connection felt with the now sanctified ruler. No doubt there may have been an interest in celebrating the virtues of a patron, perhaps to encourage such royal favor and saintly munificence. But the evidence of the liturgical and hagiographical texts suggests a devotional connection rooted in the perception of shared values and the notion that the now sanctified ruler valorized the essential values at the heart of the institutional and communal identity. Sanctifying Louis according to ideals that reflected and defined the monastic community itself in turn served to sanctify those values and that community. For the Cistercians, whose ideals were rooted in an ascetic and contemplative spirituality celebrated by Saint Bernard that must have seemed old-fashioned at the end of the thirteenth century, a definition of Louis' sanctity that reflected on their own institutional identity in turn sanctified and in a sense modernized those values. Likewise (though perhaps less so) in Paris, the notion of Louis' particular relationship to St.-Denis as a king only served to reinforce the sanctity of the relationship between the monarchy and the monastery. This, in turn, was at the heart of Dionysian identity.

6

The Franciscans' Saint Louis
and the Specter of Saint Francis

The reign of Louis IX coincided with the establishment and institutionalization of the Franciscan order in Paris, and his death and canonization with a period of the order's internal fracture and debate. The history of the Franciscan order in the thirteenth century was, between the death of Saint Francis (1226) and the death of Saint Louis (1270), the story of the evolving self-definition of its root values and essential mission.[1] Over the course of the thirteenth century, with the support of the papacy, the Franciscans were transformed from the itinerant group of penitent preachers into a firmly institutionalized religious order. Its members were with increasing frequency ordained as priests, were increasingly educated and immersed in the university, increasingly infiltrated the traditional episcopacy, and became, in short, increasingly empowered members of the larger religious establishment. The shift in the institutional definition of the order went by no means unchallenged. The ideological precepts at stake were debated openly, as with the propaganda surrounding the conflict between the seculars and the mendicant masters at the University of Paris in the 1250s and 60s; and with the tracts surrounding the issue of the *Usus pauper* at the end of the century.[2] The battle was also waged

1. A. Van den Wyngaert, "Querelles du clergé séculier et des ordres mendiants à Paris au XIIIe siècle," *France Franciscaine* 5 and 6 (1922–1923): 5, 257–281; 6, 46–70; Yves Congar, "Aspects ecclésiologiques de la querelle entre mendiants et séculiers dans la seconde moitié du XIIIe siècle et le début du XIVe," *Archives d'histoire doctrinale et littéraire du Moyen Âge* 28 (1961): 35–61; André Vauchez, "The Stigmata of St. Francis and Its Medieval Detractors," *Greyfriars Review* 13 (1999): 61–87; David Burr, *The Spiritual Franciscans: From Protest to Persecution in the Century after Saint Francis* (University Park, Pa., 2001). Note that a great majority of these tensions played themselves out among the communities in Paris. On Bonaventure's position in the nascent debate, see Burr, 24–27.

2. Michel-Marie Dufeil, "Le roi Louis dans la querelle des mendiants et des séculiers," in *Septième centenaire de la mort de Saint-Louis: Actes des colloques de Royaumont et de Paris* (21–27

over the interpretation of the past, particularly through the symbols of the order's identity. The preeminent symbol in this regard was Saint Francis himself,
and historians have looked to literary and artistic portraits of the founder as
mechanisms of definition or legitimation for certain ideological claims, and to
changes in those representations as signaling shifts within the order. Key elements of the legend of Saint Francis (renunciation; the stigmata) were reinter-
preted to accommodate the order's evolving requirements and aspirations.[3]
The early history of the order was thus reimagined in such a way as to conse-
crate what some now claimed had been its perennial ideals. Other saints were
also adapted to reflect Franciscan ideals through literary and artistic mediums.
The depiction of Saint Martin's investiture in the Church of San Francesco in
Assisi was influenced by evolving interpretations of Francis within a courtly,
aristocratic discourse, and artists increasingly opted to highlight Louis of
Toulouse's royal and episcopal identity over his mendicant and ascetic one.[4]

The Franciscan memorialization of Louis IX represents another instance of
such reimagination. Louis had been strongly attracted to the mendicants—
both Franciscans and Dominicans—and he was often associated with the friars, even though during his lifetime he was never really more than their
patron.[5] As king he had been influential in the order's settlement in Paris, se-
curing lodging for the group when they first arrived around 1220, and dis-
creetly siding with the friars during a blowout with secular university teachers
in the 1250s.[6] He had known Bonaventure, the minister general of the order
who resided in Paris and often preached before the king in the Ste.-Chapelle.[7]
Louis was also close to the only Franciscan bishop in France, Eudes Rigaud,
who also preached at the court.[8] Louis funded at his own personal expense the
enormous Franciscan convent after 1254, and after 1297 a statue of him stood
as the trumeau of the entrance.[9] Other members of the Capetian family were

---

mai 1970) (Paris, 1976), 281–289; David Burr, *Olivi and Franciscan Poverty: The Origins of Usus Pauper Controversy* (Philadelphia, 1989); Malcolm Lambert, *Franciscan Poverty: The Doctrine of the Absolute Poverty of Christ and the Apostles in the Franciscan Order, 1210–1323*, Rev. and ex-panded (original 1961) ed. (St. Bonaventure, N.Y., 1998).

3. Richard Trexler, *Naked before the Father: The Renunciation of Francis of Assisi*, ed. Peter Lang (New York, 1989); Chiara Frugoni, *Francesco e l'invenzione delle stimmate: una storia per parole e immagini fino a Bonaventura e Giotto* (Turin, 1993); Vauchez, "Stigmata"; Jacques Dalarun, *The Misadventure of Francis of Assisi: Towards a Historical Use of the Franciscan Leg-ends* (St. Bonaventure, N.Y., 2002).

4. Adrian Hoch, "St. Martin of Tours: His Transformation into a Chivalric Hero and Fran-ciscan Ideal," *Zeitschrift für Kunstgeschichte* 50 (1987): 471–482.

5. Little, "Saint Louis." In 1547 Louis was enlisted into the Third Order, and a sixteenth-century Franciscan office also suggested that he belonged to it (AASS, Aug. 25, V. 447).

6. Little, "Saint Louis."

7. Jacques-Guy Bougerol, "Saint Bonaventure et le roi saint Louis," in *Sanctus Bonaventura 1274–1974* (Rome, 1973), 469–493.

8. Adam Davis, *The Holy Bureaucrat: Eudes Rigaud and Religious Reform in Thirteenth-Century Normandy* (Ithaca, N.Y., 2006), 157–173. Williell Thomson, *Friars in the Cathedral: The First Franciscan Bishops, 1226–1261* (Toronto, 1975), 77–91.

9. Laure Beaumont-Maillet, *Le grand couvent des Cordeliers de Paris: Étude historique et archéologique du XIIIe siècle à nos jours* (Paris, 1975), 250–255, 262.

also generous patrons, and a number of Franciscan foundations had close royal ties. Louis' sister Isabelle founded Longchamp in 1255, and in later years the nuns venerated the sainthood of their founder's brother.[10] Louis' widow, Marguerite, founded the Clarissan convent, St. Marcel (Lourcines); and their daughter, Blanche, who retired to Lourcines, commissioned William of Saint-Pathus' *vie* of Louis and probably the fresco cycle there that Peiresc described in 1621. William of Saint-Pathus was himself a member of the *Cordeliers* of Paris. After Louis' death the Franciscans were instrumental in his canonization. As early as 1272, Bonaventure secured permission from Gregory X to celebrate a solemn anniversary for Louis in the order.[11] Jean of Samois, OFM, who had preached before Louis in the Ste.-Chapelle, spent almost twenty years—a number of them in Rome—working on Louis' canonization, and he was ultimately asked to deliver the sermon on Saint Louis on the inaugural feast day at St.-Denis in 1298.[12] It was natural that Paris-area Franciscans would honor Louis liturgically and hagiographically after his canonization.

But they did so in a peculiarly Franciscan way. Louis, as *princeps*, in some sense represented precisely the opposite of the ideal of abnegation and disempowerment that Francis himself had espoused, the ideal of poverty and humility which Francis had sought to emphasize by naming his fraternity the *fratres minores*. The ways in which the Franciscans saw fit to memorialize Louis thus speaks to the strategies Franciscans used for interpreting the past in ways that valorized the present. The Parisian *Cordeliers* presented Louis not only as a patron but also, through the pattern of his life and the quality of his faith, as a type of Francis, as a king living up to the Franciscan ideal. Rulership played little role in how he was envisioned as a saint, and if anything the mark of sanctity was his desire to renounce the powers and glory of being king. Instead of kingship, the Franciscans were interested in his active devotion, and particularly in his crusades as an emblem of devotion to Christ and saintly suffering. In this, the figure of Saint Francis himself, particularly the Francis of 1300, was deeply influential, and he cast a long shadow over the Franciscan memorialization of Louis.[13]

William of Saint-Pathus, Redux

This is true even of one of our most "royal" texts—the vita written by Marguerite of Provence's confessor, William of Saint-Pathus. We saw in the first

---

10. Gertrud Mlynarcyk, *Ein Franziskanerinnenkloster im 15. Jahrhundert* (Bonn, 1987), 84–88; Field, *Isabelle*, 63–66.

11. Ehrle, "Ältesten Redactionen," 41.

12. Louis Carolus-Barré, "Les franciscains et le procès de canonisation de saint Louis," *Les amis de St. François* ns 12 (1971): 3–6. Jean of Samois preached a sermon on the feast day of the Crown of Thorns at the Ste.-Chapelle before Louis.

13. Note that the Franciscan sources for the memorialization of Louis were probably all written in Paris, also the center of the disputes among Franciscans that produced so much of their self-defining polemic.

chapter how William reconciled the evidence from the canonization proceedings to a Franciscanized scheme of saintly virtue. William, faithful to the materials gathered during the canonization proceedings and writing for a royal (if Franciscan) patron, drew on the model of Saint Francis, particularly the Bonaventuran Francis deployed in the *Legenda maior*. The *Legenda maior* was commissioned in 1260 and finished by 1263. By 1300 every Franciscan convent owned a copy. If nothing else, William explicitly and formally followed Bonaventure's hagiographic method. Bonaventure, at the end of the prologue, after discussing whence he got his material and right before listing his chapter titles, explained how he organized his material thematically more than chronologically.

> I have not always structured the story according to the order of time, to avoid confusion, but rather I have aimed to preserve an order of things more suitably joined together, following different matters [*materiis*] done at the same time or those things done at different times that seem suitable to the same matters [*materiae*].
>
> Nec semper historiam secundum ordinem temporis texui, propter confusionem vitandam, sed potius ordinem servare studui magis aptae iuncturae, secundum quod eodem peracta tempore diversis materiis, vel diversis patrata temporibus eidem materiae congruere videbantur.[14]

William of Saint-Pathus, also at the end of his prologue, also following his discussion of his sources and right before his listing of his chapter headings, wrote:

> I have not always ordered the work according to the order of time, to avoid confusion, I have instead aimed to keep an order of those things more fittingly joined together; such that those things done at the same time seemed to be appropriate to different matters [*matires*], or such that those things done at different times seemed to belong to the same matter [*matire*].
>
> Ne je n'ai pas ceste oevre toz jors ordie selon l'ordenance du tens pour eschiver confusion, ainçois ai plus estudié a garder ordenance de plus convenable jointure, selon ce que les choses fetes en un meemes tens sembloient estre convenables a diverses matires, ou selon ce que les choses fetes en divers tens sembloient convenire a une meesme matire.[15]

If, as Paulin Paris argued, William did in fact write in Latin originally,[16] it seems likely that he simply lifted the language from the *Legenda maior*. William also constructed the *vie* by following the structure and method of Bonaventure's *Legenda maior* of Francis. Each author divided his vita into chapters on various virtues, with headings like "his zeal for prayer and the power of his prayer" (Francis, chapter 10), and "his humility and obedience and God's condescension

---

14. Enrico Menestò and Stefano Brufani, ed., *Fontes Franciscani* (Assisi, 1995), 780.
15. WSP *vie*, 6–7.
16. Paris, "Confesseur de la Reine Marguerite," 155–157.

to his slightest wish" (Francis, chapter 6), or "on his profound humility" (Louis, chapter 12), and "On his firm belief" (Louis, chapter 3). Both wrote vitas that began with their saint's youth and upbringing and ended with their death (though Bonaventure included the canonization story itself in the last chapter and William did not). Both wrote what was for all intents and purposes an addendum, a separate book on their saint's miracles.[17]

These similarities invite comparison of the texts not only structurally and formally but also thematically. In texts as long as each of these, it is easy enough to pick out similarities—both received communion frequently, both fasted, both had devout habits of prayer, both offered money and food to the poor, both personally ministered to the sick, and so forth. Chiara Frugoni has drawn attention to a number of parallels in Bonaventure's and William's portraits.[18] She compared the young Louis' building of Royaumont to Francis' building of the three little churches early in his saintly career. She noted that both sought to eat in humility, on the floor, and with the poor, and that both gave service and love to lepers. William further insisted on Louis' patronage of religious orders, his endowments of religious communities, his building of churches, and his service to the poor. The central and single longest chapter of his *vie* (chapter 11) was collected under the chapter heading *oevres de pité*, and described at length Louis' alms and patronage. And, though William felt himself duty bound to reproduce the material collected during the canonization inquest, it was Francis that was the measure and model of saintliness.

The Franciscan Liturgical Office for Louis

This same relationship between Francis as a model, or type, of saint to which Louis conformed is even more evident in the way that the Franciscans modeled their liturgical office for Louis after that of Francis. The Franciscan office for Louis, *Francorum rex,* was probably composed after the Franciscan General Chapter held at Lyon in 1299 instituted the celebration of his feast day. The office is found in a number of Franciscan breviaries of the fourteenth and fifteenth centuries, the production of most of which can be associated with the Paris region, and it was probably composed at the Franciscan convent,[19] although, because the Cordeliers' library was decimated in a fire in 1580, few "working" volumes survive. Most of the extant volumes containing the office are luxury breviaries that appear to have been produced for women—in particular, a group of Franciscan breviaries made around 1330 in the style and from the workshops of Jean Pucelle, the Master Honoré, and Mahiet.[20] This fact

17. For Francis, see Regis J. Armstrong, J.A. Wayne Hellmann, and William J. Short, eds., *Francis of Assisi: Early Documents*, 3 vols. (New York, 1999–2001), vol. 2, 650–683; and Menestò, ed., *Fontes*, 912–961. For Louis, see Fay, ed., *Miracles*.
18. Chiara Frugoni, "Saint Louis et Saint François," *Medievales* 34 (1998): 35–38.
19. Beaumont-Maillet, *Couvent des Cordeliers*, 255–257, 199–205.
20. Cambridge Dd V5, Cividale Museo Archeologico Nazionale ms CXL, Pierpont Morgan Library ms M149, Pierpont Morgan Library ms M75. In his entry on Cambridge DdV5, Nigel

points to another of the constellations of partnership and influence in the construction of Saint Louis, this one between the crown and the Franciscans. Not withstanding the irony of "luxury Franciscan" breviaries, the surviving evidence is also consonant with the penchant of wealthy women for entering Franciscan convents, for choosing Franciscans as their confessors and spiritual advisers in the early fourteenth century, and for the ties between Franciscans and royal foundations. An analogy here might be made to the survival of William of Saint-Pathus' *vie*, written in 1302–1303 at the convent and based on sources in its library but known to us only through the famous royal copy dating to the 1330s, also illustrated by Mahiet (BNF Fr 5716). Dissemination outside of Paris can be traced to personal ties by elite women attached to the Franciscans. Blanche of France, a daughter of Philip V who entered Longchamp in 1315, may have owned a breviary containing the office, presumably the office in use at the convent.[21] From Longchamp, the office was found in Marie de Saint-Pol's breviary;[22] Marie also founded a Franciscan convent for women in England, Denney, which adopted the rule from Longchamp. Yet, the absence of *Francorum rex* in many volumes that bear the characteristics of books actually used by the friars suggests a limited role for the office within the order more generally. It seems that for all intents and purposes proper celebration for Saint Louis among the Franciscans was local to Paris-area Franciscans and the women whose personal devotions were associated with them.[23]

The office's narrative content was drawn from the hagiographical tradition, and in particular from the anonymous (probably Franciscan) *Gloriosissimi regis*, whence the office took its lections. But the office was structurally and thematically (and probably musically) modeled on the office of Saint Francis, *Franciscus vir catholicus*.[24] *Franciscus vir* dated to 1232 and was composed by

---

Morgan includes a sixth in this grouping, the Hours of Jeanne d'Evreux, but this last contains the Hours for Louis (SV), not the Franciscan office (FR). See Paul Binski and Stella Panayotova, eds., *The Cambridge Illuminations: Ten Centuries of Book Production in the Medieval West* (London, 2005), no. 49, at 134. On Mahiet, see Richard Rouse, "Mahiet, the Illuminator of Cambridge University Library, MS Dd.5.5," in *The Cambridge Illuminations: The Conference Papers,* ed. Stella Panayotova (London, 2007), 173–186. See appendix 1 for other known manuscripts, and note that the office appears in two volumes that are not associated with the Franciscans: Evreux BM ms 12, and Tours BM ms 143.

21. New York Pierpont Morgan ms M. 149 On Blanche, see Elizabeth A. R. Brown, "The Ceremonial of Royal Succession in Capetian France: The Funeral of Philip V," *Speculum* 55 (1980): 271, nn. 16–17; and Mlynarcyk, *Franziskanerinnenkloster*, 193–194.

22. Cambridge Dd V5, 294r.–298v. Richard and Marie Rouse, "Marie de St-Pol and Cambridge University Library Ms Dd 5.5," in *The Cambridge Illuminations: The Conference* Papers (London, 2007), 187–191.

23. BL Harley 2864, 368v.–370v., a breviary that dates from the second half of the fifteenth century and includes the office, may be an exception. However, most Franciscan volumes include only a collect or proper lections intended to accompany the Common for Confessors.

24. For the Latin text, see AH 5, 175–179, no. 61; LMLO FR21; *Analecta Franciscana* 10 (1895–1946): 375–405; and Menestò, ed., *Fontes*, 1105–1121. For an English translation, see Armstrong et al., vol. 1, 327–345. For music, see Hilaren Felder, *Die liturgischen Reimofficien auf die heiligen Franciscus und Antonius gedichtet und componiert durch Fr. Julian von Speier (+1250)* (Freiburg, Schweiz, 1901), xv–xl.

Julian of Speyer, a young convert to the order. Julian belonged to the incipient Franciscan community that established itself in Paris during (coincidentally) Louis' youth and participated in the formulation of the mendicant ideal that so influenced the young king.[25] Before entering the Franciscan order, Julian had been a "master of song" at the court, during Louis IX's early years.[26] He also wrote a vita of Saint Francis (in 1234/35), shortly after Thomas of Celano had finished the better-known *Vita prima* (1228–1230), and later the office for Saint Anthony of Padua (canonized 1232). Julian himself had not known Francis, and both his office and his early vita are in content faithful to his principal source, the *Vita prima* of Thomas of Celano. *Franciscus vir* was paired with hagiographical lections, *Legendum ad usum chori*, also by Thomas of Celano.[27] A few additions were later made, such as the hymn for first vespers composed by Gregory IX and antiphons for the octave written by Cardinal Thomas of Capua before 1243.[28]

Julian's office, *Franciscus vir*, placed Francis within the tradition of orthodoxy and obedience to the hierarchical church.[29] The office opens by saying "Francis, the catholic and wholly apostolic man [*Franciscus vir catholicus, et totus apostolicus*] taught [us] to maintain faith in the Roman church and advised us to revere [her] priests above all," and much of the office is devoted to Francis as the founder, leader, and teacher of his order. He is called *Pater Francisce*, although he never took higher clerical orders. Lauds praises him for the three new orders he founded. Yet the greatest concern of the office are virtues that characterized Francis' sanctity and which would be interpreted in the light of Franciscan spirituality: Francis' devotion to the gospel, his humility, and above all his desire for poverty. The stigmata are commemorated in the Invitatory and the Benedictus antiphons. The narrative portion of the liturgy, matins, is focused on the defining event of Francis' life, his renunciation of wealth and adoption of poverty. In comparison to the hagiographical tradition, which dispensed with Francis' conversion and renunciation quickly within the early chapters, Julian devoted a great deal of space, even within the compressed form typical of liturgical chant, to the emotional and physical struggle between Francis and his father. The episode of the talking crucifix at Damiano is absent from *Franciscus vir* since Julian wrote the office before the Three Companions first introduced the story, and the explanation given for

25. Felder, *Liturgischen Reimofficien*, 140–141; Eliseus Bruning, "Giuliano da Spira e l'Officio ritmico di S. Francesco: osservazioni critico-estetiche sulla musica et sulla sua restaurazione attuale," *Note d'Archivio per la Storia Musicale* ser. 1 (1927): 131–139; Jason M. Miskuly, "Julian of Speyer: Life of St. Francis (*Vita Sancti Francisci*)," *Franciscan Studies* 49 (1989): 93–97; Giuseppe Cremascoli, "Iuliani de Spira: Vita Sancti Francisci. Introduzione," in *Fontes Franciscani*, ed. Enrico Menestò and Stefano Brufani (Assisi, 1995), 1017.

26. Miskuly, "Julian of Speyer," 94.

27. Menestò, ed., *Fontes*, 427–439; Armstrong, ed., *Francis*, vol. 1, 319–326.

28. Tiziana Scandaletti, "Una ricognizione sull'ufficio ritmico per S. Francesco," *Musica et storia* 4 (1996): 67–101; Armstrong, ed., *Francis*, vol. 1, 311.

29. Armstrong, ed., *Francis*, vol. 1, 313.

Francis' dramatic conversion was simply that God's great mercy desired it.[30] Absent also from the office is Francis' preaching to the sultan during the fifth crusade. In 1232 it was primarily renunciation and poverty that was the focus of Francis' liturgy. That is, the office memorialized Francis for things the Franciscans were particularly preoccupied with around 1230.

The legend of Francis evolved, however, between 1230 and 1297. In 1263 Bonaventure published the *Legenda maior*, the official life of Saint Francis, which was intended to supersede all previous accounts. Bonaventure gave to Francis' life the markings of a metaphysical identification with Christ. Self-identification with and devotion to the incarnate Christ, what John Moorman called "the most characteristic feature of the mysticism which stems from Saint Francis," took the form of, again in Moorman's words, "Francis' own life— renunciation and poverty, humility and self-abasement, the complete conquest of self-love and self-interest."[31] This tradition would come to emphasize the idea of the *imitatio Christi*. Following Bonaventure's lead, fourteenth-century Franciscans had increasingly understood Francis' life in term of typology and fulfillment. Driven by the increasing interest in the stigmata, image would make the subtle turn into identity, and Francis would ultimately come to be known as the *alter Christus*.[32] Though not fully articulated until 1385 when Bartholomew of Pisa wrote his *De conformitate vitae beati Francisci ad vitam Domini Jesu*, in Franciscan writing and representation the language of imitation and fulfillment begins to appear around 1300. The *Fioretti*, the dating of which is vexed but which seems to be early fourteenth century, began, "We must consider first how Saint Francis, in all the acts of his life, conformed to the blessed Christ."[33]

And so, in 1300 it was the notion of imitation—not in the reductive sense of copying but in the greater sense of fulfillment—that was at work in the liturgical office for Louis. In *Francorum rex*, the Franciscans interpreted Louis' sanctity as fulfilling the model provided by Francis. The contemporary term used for the liturgical office of a saint, and often specifically for the long, narrative portion recited at the nighttime service of matins, was *historia*. Like a hagiographical vita, the liturgical *historia* recounted the life—the story—of that saint.[34] In

30. Trexler, *Naked before the Father*, 74. On the place of the office within the ideological transformations in the order, see Scandaletti, "Una ricognizione," 97–100.

31. John Moorman, *A History of the Franciscan Order from Its Origins to the Year 1517* (Chicago, 1968; repr., 1988), 256.

32. The early biographies of Francis are treated in Moorman, *A History of the Franciscan Order*. At 256–277, Moorman discussed the integration of mystical themes. See also John Fleming, *An Introduction to the Franciscan Literature of the Middle Ages* (Chicago, 1977), 32–72. Dalarun, *Misadventure of Francis*, makes sense of the progression of themes. Recently the official image by Bonaventure has been discussed by Rosalind B. Brooke, *The Image of St. Francis: Responses to Sainthood in the Thirteenth Century* (Cambridge, 2006), 252–268. On the chronology of the development of the theme of *alter Christus*, see H. W. Van Os, "St. Francis of Assisi as a Second Christ in Early Italian Painting," *Simiolus* 7 (1974): 115–116, 123; and Jaroslav Pelikan, "Christ—and the Second Christ," *The Yale Review* 74 (1985): 321–345. Bartholomew of Pisa, in the *De conformitate vita beati Francisci ad vitam Domini Jesus*, ca. 1385, was the first to use the term "alter Christus."

33. Quoted in Fleming, *Franciscan Literature*, 66.

34. Du Cange, *Glossarium*, vol. 4, 209–210; Jonsson, *Historia*; Hughes, "Rhymed Offices."

Francorum rex, the narrative progression of Louis' *historia* was modeled on, and thus fulfilled the saintly type furnished by, the office of Saint Francis. The narrative in *Franciscus vir* was principally about Francis' adoption of poverty. In *Francorum rex* the narrative focused on Louis' crusade. Both were understood as kinds of renunciation.

Imitation was accomplished through meter, language, and structure (see table 6.1). Language was directly adapted. For example, the fifth antiphon for matins in *Francorum rex* describes Louis' steadfastness before the Saracens when in captivity: *Populi princeps furie non cedit effrenati monstrans se voluntarie pro Christo mala pati*. The antiphon was drawn directly from the fifth matins antiphon in the Office of Saint Francis, which described Francis' confrontation with his father: *Iam liber patris furie non cedit effrenati clamans se voluntarie pro Christo mala pati*. This adaptation of language identifying Louis directly with Francis would have served to recall Francis' life and virtues to the friars as they sung Louis' office. Each case of borrowed language was also an instance of borrowed structure; that is, language lifted from the second responsory from matins in Francis' liturgy was reworked for the second responsory from matins in Louis' liturgy, and so forth.[35] Not only were individual prayers adapted, but the basic structure of the matins *historiae* was adopted to mold the narrative progression of Louis' life. In some instances this required the narrative of the office to place events in a different order from that of the hagiographical tradition. But within the narrative structure dictated by matins, *Francorum rex* highlighted, or even invented, narrative parallels between the lives (*historiae*) of the two saints. In this way the very pattern of Louis' life (*historia*) was dictated by Francis' story (*historia*).

This imitative approach was not uncommon in the Middle Ages, particularly among the mendicant orders. In 1927 Eliseus Bruning noted the importance of the musical order of Francis' liturgy on subsequent Franciscan offices, establishing at least thirty-two offices that owed their poetic meter to Julian's compositions, and the importance of Francis' liturgy for later offices is well known.[36] There is also some evidence that the text of *Franciscus vir* played a role in modeling other Franciscan offices prior to the composition of Louis' office:[37] the language of the office for Saint Clare echoed Francis' office in parts, and the practice became fairly standard for Franciscan saints by the

---

35. A single instance shows that the author of *Francorum rex* also knew the liturgy of the only other male member of the Franciscan order to have been canonized by the early fourteenth century, Saint Anthony of Padua. Julian of Speyer was also the author of the Office of Anthony. Cf. Louis: [FR LA4]: Patris natum unicum *benedicant dominum cuncte creature qui tot per* ludovicum *signis auget hominum vite spem future*; and Anthony: [LMLO AO51 LA4] Celi terre marium *benedicant dominum cuncte creature qui tot per* antonium *signis auget hominum vite spem future*.

36. Bruning, "Giuliano da Spira"; Hughes, "Rhymed Offices"; Judy Taylor, "Rhymed Offices at the Sainte-Chapelle in the Thirteenth Century: Historical, Political, and Liturgical Contexts" (Ph.D. diss., University of Texas at Austin, 1994), 65–68; Hughes, "Late Medieval Plainchant," 55–58, 66–74.

37. Bruning, "Giuliano da Spira," 172–176, which includes on 174 a list of all the offices that include any amount of textual borrowing from *Franciscus vir*.

Table 6.1. Comparison of the matins service for the Offices of Saint Francis (*Franciscus vir*) and of Saint Louis (*Francorum rex*)

	Franciscus vir catholicus		Francorum rex magnificus		Notes
MA1	Hic vir in vanitatibus	8	Puer hic defuncto patre	8	Both raised (worthily
	nutritus indecenter	7	**nutritus est decenter**	7	or unworthily) by
	divinis charismatibus	8	a religiosa matre	8	parents
	preventus est clem**enter.**	7	cui paru**it** lib**enter.**	8	
	Replaced in 1260 with:				
	Hic vir in vanitatibus	8			
	nutritus indecenter	7			
	plus suis nutritoribus	8			
	se gessit insol**enter.**	7			
MA2	Excelsi dextre gra**tia**	8	Languoris vehemen**tia**	9	Both saints touched
	mirifice mu**tatus**	7	a Deo visi**tatus**	7	by God. Blessed
	dat lapsis spem de venia	8	est in convalescencia	8	and/or signed by
	cum **Christo** iam be**atus.**	8	cruce **Christi** sig**natus.**	7	Christ/Christ's cross. (Louis becomes crusader)
MA3	Mansuescit sed non	9	Tres fratres suos comites	8	Moral transformation
	penitus	8	secum cruce signavit	7	
	in primis per languores	8	et regni sui divites	8	
	qui captis armis celitus	7	ad idem animavit.	7	
	ad plenum mutat mores.				
MR1	**Franc**iscus ut in	8	**Franc**orum iam exercitu	8	Saints prepare
	publicum	7	sub rege Ludovico	7	themselves for
	cessat negociari	8	preparato pro transitu	8	subsequent
	in agrum mox dominicum	7	in conductu nautico	7	confrontation
	secedit meditari	8	legato ab ecclesia	8	
	inventum evangelicum	7	dato cum indulgencia.	8	
	thesaurum vult mercari.				
MV1	Deum quid agat unicum	8	In passagio signato	8	God invoked in both
	consultans audit celicum	8	Deo primum invocato	8	("consulted" /
	insigne sibi dari.	7	transivit princeps maria.	8	"invoked")
MR2	**In Dei fervens opere**	8	**In Dei fervens opere**	8	Both saints fulfilling
	statim ut sua vendit	7	**statim ut** transfretavit	7	the mission of the
	pauperibus impend**ere**	8	infideles laccess**ere**	8	active life. Francis
	pecuniam inten**dit**	7	gravi bello tempta**vit**	7	gives money to the
	que gravi suo pond**ere**	8	et Damiatam prop**ere**	8	poor. Louis attacks
	cor liberum offen**dit.**	7	vi captam occupa**vit.**	7	the Saracens.
MV2	**Quam** formid**ante** paupere	8	**Quam** desert**ere** turpiter	8	Francis throws away
	presbyt**ero** recip**ere**	8	popul**o** degen**ere**	7	the money.
	abiectam vilipen**dit.**	7	ipse potenter intra**vit.**	8	Saracens abandon the city
MR3	**Dum pater** hunc	8	**Dum pater**	8	Both saints meet their
	prosequitur	7	clementissimus	8	persecutors. (Francis
	latens dat locum ire	8	suum verberat populum	8	confronts his father;
	constanter post aggreditur	7	vir iste devotissimus	8	Louis confronts the
	in publicum prodire	8	ad deum levat oculum	8	Saracens)
	squalenti vultu cernitur	7	ut erat ferventissimus	8	
	putatur insanire.		obsequium dans sedulum.		

(continued)

Table 6.1.—*cont.*

	Franciscus vir catholicus		Francorum rex magnificus		Notes
MV3	Luto saxis impetitur sed paciens vir nititur ut surdus pertransire.	8 8 7	Hic Tobias notissimus qui mortuos humilimus portavit ad tumulum.	8 8 7	Humility, endurance
MA4	Pertractum domi verberat plus cunctis furens pater obiurgans vincit carcerat quem furtim solvit mater.	8 7 8 7	Lassato iam exercitu diuturno langore infideles cum fremitu accurrunt et furore.	8 7 8 7	Both men suffer at the hands of persecutors. (Francis's father = Louis' Saracens)
MA5	Iam liber patris **furie** **non cedit effrenati** clam**ans se voluntarie** **pro Christo mala pati.**	8 7 8 7	Populi princeps **furie** **non cedit effrenati** monstra**ns se voluntarie** **pro Christo mala pati.**	8 7 8 7	Both men refuse to give way before the fury of their persecutors; both men willing to suffer evils for Christ
MA6	**Ductus ad loci** presulem sua patri resignat nudusque manens exulem in mundo se designat.	8 7 8 7	**Ductus ad locum** carceris mire fert ad tentorium sollicito pro vesperis paganus breviarium.	8 8 8 8	Francis "led" before the bishop juxtaposed to Louis "led" to jail.
MR4	Dum seminudo corpore laudes decantat gallice zelator nove legis latronibus in nemore respondit sic prophetice preco sum magni regis.	8 8 7 8 8 7	Laus tibi per secula patri nato paraclito quod rex sine macula per te liberatur dum in soldani subito illa gens incredula tuo beneplacito morte effrenatur.	7 8 7 6 8 7 7 6	Narrative buildup
MV4	Audit in nivis frigore proiectus iace rustice futurus pastor gregis.	8 8 7	En Dei virtus sedula pro suis que tam cito pellendo pericula mira operatur.	8 7 7 6	
MR5	Amicum querit pristinum qui spretum in cenobio tunicula contexit contemptu gaudens hominum leprosis fit obsequio quos antea despexit.	8 8 7 8 8 7	Bissenis cum baronibus firmus rex in fide vera de pactis iuraturus saracenis furentibus respondet voce libera nunquam sum hoc facturus.	8 8 7 8 8 7	Louis' direct quotation: "I will never do this"; Francis ministers to lepers
MV5	Sub typo trium ordinum tres nutu dei previo ecclesias erexit.	8 8 7	Si non stas hiis sermonibus ait illi gens effera Christum es negaturus.	8 7 7	Francis "builds" the three orders
MR6	Audit in evangelio que suis Christus loquitur ad predicandum missis hoc inquit est quod cupio letanter his innititur memorie commissis.	8 8 7 8 8 7	Regressus rex ad propria non destitit insistere operi virtuoso, se mactat penitentia, egenos levat munere ministrat leproso.	8 8 7 8 8 6	Louis ministers to lepers; Francis's direct quotation: "this is what I desire"
MV6	Non utens virga calcio nec pera fune cingitur duplicibus dimissis.	8 8 7	Visitat monasteria domos Dei ex opere construxit sumptuoso.	8 8 7	Louis "builds" churches

Table 6.1.—*cont.*

	Franciscus vir catholicus		Francorum rex magnificus		Notes
MA7	**Cor verbis** nove **gracie** **sollicitus apponit** verbum**que** penitencie simpliciter **proponit.**	8 7 8 7	**Cor verbis** sacre **scripture** **sollicitus apponit** omnique regali curie verbum Dei **proponit.**	8 7 8 7	Both anxious to fulfill God's mission
MA8	Pacem salutem nunciat in spiritus virtute vereque paci sociat longinquos a salute.	8 7 8 7	Bonis semper operibus sanctus rex intendebat simile facientibus devotus inherebat.	8 7 8 7	Good works
MA9	Ut novis **sancti merita** **remunerantur natis** his nova **tradit monita** viam simpli**citatis.**	8 7 8 7	Ut regis **sancti merita** **remunerantur natis** his pia **tradit monita** semitas equi**tatis.**	8 7 8 7	Both "teach" their children
MR7	Carnis spicam contemptus ar**ea** Franciscus frangens terens terr**ea** granum purum excussa pal**ea** summi regis intrat in horr**ea.**	1 0 1 0 1 0 1 0	Toto corde cum rege Iosia quesivit Deum ab infancia David alter misericordia et Salomon est sapien**cia.**	1 0 1 0 1 0	
MV7	Vivo pani morte iunctus vita vivit vita functus.	8 8	Joseph est providentia et Gedeon constancia.	8 8	
MR8	**De pauper**tatis horreo** sanctus Franciscus saciat turbam Christi famelicam in via ne deficiat iter pandit ad gloriam et vite viam ampliat.	8 8 8 8 8 8	**De largitatis horreo** rex misericors tribuit plena manu pauperibus quos visitando circuit cibos ori intromittit et pedes supplex abluit.	8 8 8 8 8 8	Generosity and compassion
MV8	Pro paupertatis copia regnat dives in patria reges sibi substituens quo hic ditat inopia.	8 8 8 8	O quantus et qualis fuit qui tam pium cor habuit quod egenis compatiens servicium hoc prebuit.	8 8 8 8	Compassion for the poor
MR9	Euntes inquit in eum qui nutriat vos dominum iactate cogitatum sic fratribus erroneum precludit et interminum callem cupiditatum.	8 8 7 8 8 7	No MRV9 in original composition.	8 8 8 8 9 7	
MV9	Sit curis cor extraneum non providet in crastinum in zonis es ligatum sic previdet novis.	8 8 7 6		8 4 8 4	

fifteenth century.[38] The office for Saint Elizabeth of Hungary (d. 1231, can. 1235), another "royal saint" who became the patron of the Franciscan Tertiaries, constitutes another example of this kind of modeling since the early office *Gaudeat hungaria* owes some of its poetic features of rhyme and order (though not language) to the offices of Saints Francis and Anthony.[39] Nonetheless, these influences were far less direct than in *Francorum rex*, and the two early Franciscan saints for whom this sort of tight textual identification would have seemed most appropriate—Saint Anthony of Padua (canonized 1232) and Saint Louis of Toulouse (canonized 1317)—did *not* have offices whose texts dovetailed with *Franciscus vir*. In the years around 1300 when *Francorum rex* was composed, this type of liturgical modeling was therefore something of an innovation.

It was an innovation based on the idea of *imitatio*. Francis had "imitated" Christ.[40] His *imitatio* had taken the form of poverty, humility, preaching, and ultimately, a kind of martyrdom. Louis "imitated" Francis and, in so doing, participated in Christ's Passion. In turn, Louis' imitation of Francis took the form of avowal, renunciation, and faith. If Francis had been a type of Christ, Louis was a type of Francis. Thus the overall structure of Francis' and Louis' *historiae* follow the same basic trajectory. In both, matins is roughly divided into three parts. The first part deals with conversion or transformation; for Francis this is his adoption of poverty [MA1–MV2], while for Louis it is becoming a crusader [MA1–MV2]. The middle section speaks of confrontation with a spiritual enemy. For Francis, the spiritual impediment is his father and his father's wealth. For Louis, the spiritual enemy is the Saracen infidel. The narrative in this section builds, climaxing with a dramatic confrontation in which the saint makes a strong, public declaration of faith. The third part then shows the subject's sanctity manifest, describing virtuous actions and deeds, the daily behavior of piety and compassion exercised by both saints.

The *imitatio* is established at the outset of the office in first vespers where Louis' "Francorum rex magnificus, Ludovicus vir celicus" echoes the cadence and rhythm of Francis' "Franciscus vir catholicus, et totus apostolicus."[41] The

38. Cf. Office of Saint Bernhardis (d. 1444, can. 1450), Saint Bonaventure (can. 1482), Saint Achasius, and the Franciscan office for the *Sepulchre Domini* (ibid.).

39. Barbara Haggh, *Two Offices for St. Elizabeth of Hungary: Gaudeat Hungaria and Letare Germania. Introduction and Edition*, ed. László Dobszay, Barbara Haggh, and Ruth Steiner (Ottowa, 1995), xvii–xviii. The office dates to 1270–1280.

40. On the medieval tradition of *imitatio Christi*, see Constable, "The Ideal of the Imitation of Christ," 143–248, especially 92–93; Jan Ziolkowski, "The Highest Form of Compliment: *Imitatio* in Medieval Latin Culture," in *Poetry and Philosophy in the Middle Ages: A Festschrift for Peter Dronke*, ed. John Marenbon (Leiden, 2001), 293–305.

41. Compare these openings with those of other contemporary offices. The office of Saint Dominic began "gaude felix, parans hispania" [LMLO DO21], the office for Peter Martyr (died 1252, canonized 1253) began "colletetur, turba fidelium" [LMLO PT51]. The office for the Franciscan Louis of Toulouse (d. 1297, can. 1317) began "Ludovicus filius, regis sempiterni" (LMLO LV13). Language was also adopted from the office of Francis for the hymns. For instance, the matins hymns for both Francis' and Louis' office begin with "In celesti collegio." The final stanza for the lauds hymn for Francis is "Patri, nato, paraclito, decus, honor et gloria; sancti sint huius merito, nobis eterna gaudia." For Louis the same stanza reads, "Patri, nato, paraclito, decus, honor et gloria, qui Ludovici merito tanta fecit magnalia."

opening phrase of matins (the *historia*) both begin with the way in which the saint was raised (*nutritus*) by his parents—Louis is raised *decenter* where Francis was raised *indecenter* (MA2). From here, both offices move on quickly to the crucial turning point in their subjects' lives. For Francis, this is envisioned as his conversion to poverty and his renunciation of wealth. The event is juxtaposed in *Francorum rex* to Louis' taking the cross for his first crusade. Louis' office thus rejected the scheme generally adopted by the hagiographical authors who spoke at length of Louis' upbringing, his mores, his education, and his early alms before discussing his assumption of the cross. *Francorum rex* devotes only this one antiphon to the early stage of Louis' spiritual development. In Louis' office, at MA2, Louis when ill at Pontoise is visited by God (*a deo visitatus est*) and is marked by the sign of the cross (*cruce Christi signatus*, itself a Franciscan image), indicating the moment he became a crusader. In Francis' office at MA2, Francis, too, had been converted by the heavenly hand of God (*Excelsi dextre gratia mirifice mutatus*). At MR1 of both offices, each saint prepares himself for the subsequent dramatic confrontation: Louis prepares for the sea journey to battle the infidel, and Francis retreats to meditate before facing his father. In both liturgies God is invoked at MV1. And at MR2 both saints are *In dei fervens opere*, actively fulfilling their mission: Francis tries to give his money to the poor, while Louis attacks the Saracens.

The third responsory for matins marks the beginning of the middle section, in which both offices turn to themes of persecution, suffering, and confrontation. Both offices begin at MR3 with the words *Dum pater*, when both men meet their persecutors: Francis confronts his father, where Louis faces the Saracens (MR3). The verse then praises the humility of the saint in each case (MV3). At MA4 both men suffer at the hands of their persecutor. In Francis' liturgy, second nocturn retold the story of Francis' rebellion when the young Francis throws off his clothes and renounces his hereditable wealth. Francis is beaten by his father, whereas Louis' army is charged by the infidel. Francis' maligned father is recast in the analogous antiphon in Louis' office as the raging Saracens; that is, both are the spiritual enemy against which the saint reacts to prove his sanctity (MA5). At MA5 (quoted in full above) both men refuse to give way before the fury of their persecutors (*furie non cedit effrenati*, in both cases) and both declare themselves willing to suffer evils for Christ (*clamans* or *monstrans se voluntarie pro Christo mala pati*, in both cases). At MA6 Louis is led to jail (*Ductus ad locum carceris*) in the same way that Francis is brought before the bishop (*Ductus ad loci presulem*).[42] *Franciscus vir* and *Francorum rex* each include an episode in which their saint makes a famous and strong public declaration of faith. In Francis' story, the young saint declares his vow of poverty: "He heard in the Gospel that Christ had said to his

---

42. The parallelism in structure gets derailed at one point in second nocturn. Francis feeds and cares for lepers at MR5 and makes a public declaration of faith in MR6, where Louis makes his public declaration of faith at MR5 and feeds and cares for lepers at MR6. Francis builds churches (i.e., the three Franciscan orders) at MR6, and Louis builds and visits churches at MV6.

disciples to go out and preach: 'This,' [Francis] said, 'is what I desire,' and he happily remained, having committed these words to memory" [MR6]. In Julian of Speyer's construction this declaration, and not the talking crucifix of San Damiano, was the significant moment of Francis' conversion, the dramatic moment at which his sanctity was established. Likewise, *Francorum rex* quotes Louis' own avowal of faith—"I will never do this"—before the Saracens in response to the proposal that he take an oath to deny Christ if he failed to fulfill the terms of their peace [MR5].[43] These are the only two instances of direct quotation (at MR6 for Francis, MR5 for Louis). Both offices thus narrate the progression of a kind of conversion, a spiritual development, and then a fraught but decisive moment of public avowal of faith.

Then the narrative shifts in both cases to an explication of the saints' piety, mercy, and alms. Francis' office in MR5 remembers him for serving lepers (*leprosos fit obsequio*) whom he once despised. MR6 remembers Louis for ministering to lepers (*ministrat leprosos*). Both saints are remembered for "building" churches, although in different ways. Louis in MV6 is remembered for constructing (*construxit*) monasteries and houses of God, and Francis is remembered in MV5 for building (*erexit*) the churches of his three orders (the Franciscans, the Poor Clares, and the Tertiaries). In MA7, beginning in both cases with the words *cor verbis*, both saints are described as *sollicitus* to act according to God's precepts. The language is again identical in the ninth matins antiphon, where both are said to teach their "children": *ut regis/novis sancti merita remunerantur natis his pia/nova tradit monitas semitas/viam equitatis/simplicitatis* (Louis/Francis). In Francis' office the "children" (*natis*) referred to Francis' spiritual children, the early Franciscans. This line was easily adapted to Louis' *historia,* since the king's teaching of his (actual) children had been recorded in the first round of his hagiography.[44] The eighth responsory for both offices treated the saints' poverty and their generosity and compassion, where the text used the same vocabulary to describe how the saints fed the poor. *Franciscus vir* further commemorated Francis for instructing his brothers and writing the rule (MRV9). *Francorum rex* commemorated Louis for instructing his heir and for writing his famous testament (Benedictus antiphon). Neither office, notably, dealt with their saint's death.

By mapping Louis' liturgical *historia* onto that of Saint Francis, Louis fulfilled the model presented by Saint Francis. We do not possess the music for *Francorum rex,* but there is every possibility that it was either rooted in and evocative of the music for *Franciscus vir,* or—even more powerfully—that *Francorum rex* simply used the music for *Franciscus vir.* The ability to recall and anticipate the rhythms of melodies and poetry must certainly have deepened resonances for the meaning of Louis' life by its very association with Saint Francis.

---

43. The quotation "nunquam sum hoc facturus" was taken from *Gloriossisimi regis* and is found in WSP *sermo,* although no equivalent is found in the *Vie française* (WSP *vie*). Note that all are Franciscan sources.

44. GB *vie* 7 (ch. 13).

Imitatio Christi, Renunciation, Stigmata, and the Crusades

This fulfillment was accomplished in part because Louis' devotion to the cross was identified with Francis' renunciation. First vespers, the opening prayers recited on the eve of a feast, usually introduced and summarized the key themes of a liturgical office. In *Francorum rex*, first vespers located Louis' sanctity in the crusades, and in particular his rejection of wealth, family, and the trappings of royalty when he left on crusade. The three central stanzas read:

> He took up the sign of Christ's cross against non-Christian peoples first when a young man, and then, later in life, to the accumulation of merit.
>
> He left behind his kingdom, his mother, his infant children, still tender, and his sister, but afterwards, his sons having come of age, adhering to the councils of Christ, he sent away even his wife.
>
> This saint despised anything and everything transitory for the sake of the Kingdom of Heaven, as much carnal delights as deceptive riches, as well as the arrogance of the proud.[45]

This theme was repeated in the hymn that accompanied the opening antiphons, the third and fourth strophes of which linked crusading and renunciation:

> He spurned his kingdom and all things, following in the footsteps of Christ, he did not spare riches, nor his wife, nor his sons.
>
> From the ship onto which he had climbed, so that he might cross the sea, he urged his three sons, to do the very same, [his sons] whom he had brought with him.[46]

The vespers texts, like the matins narrative, highlighted Louis' crusade as the most distinctive feature of his saintly life, emblematic of Louis' renunciation of worldly things and his sacrifice of family. Renouncing wealth for poverty was the very basis of the mendicant ideal, and royal glories easily came to represent all that was moneyed, worldly, and secular. Thus did the Franciscan liturgical office for Louis of Toulouse (canonized 1317), who had actually renounced his claim to the throne of his father, Charles II of Anjou, to join the Franciscan order, also emphasize that Louis of Toulouse's virtue lay in his rejection of royal wealth: "He renounced the riches and all the honors of the tottering world, propelling himself forth to the fatherland."[47] Louis IX was described in first vespers as "despising deceptive riches" and in the accompanying hymn as "spurning his kingdom" and "not sparing riches."

Worldly things referred as much to family as it did to wealth, and as first vespers proclaimed, Louis abandoned (*reliquit*) not just his mother but his wife, his

---

45. FR VA2–4.
46. FR VH3–4.
47. AH, vol. 26, 265, no. 92, LMLO LV12 MR2: "labilis orbis opes, et honores abdicat omnes, ad patriam properans."

sister, his grown sons, his children, even babies. This is worth emphasizing because renouncing wealth and family was precisely what Francis had done.[48] In a sermon delivered in Paris on the feast day of Saint Francis, October 4, 1255, Bonaventure stressed just how central renunciation of family was to the Franciscan mission:

> It is essential for true discipleship to free oneself from useless cares in the affairs of life. . . . Saint Luke records [Jesus saying]: *If anyone comes to me and does not hate his own father and mother and wife and brothers and sisters, yes, and even his own life, he cannot be my disciple.* The Lord does not forbid us to love our father and mother, for the Decalogue commands that we honor them; what he does forbid us to be is inordinately attached to our parents, because inordinate attachment rejects the teachings of Christ. Understand this, Saint Francis hated his father and mother, and having broken the ties of natural attachment, he abandoned them completely. Anyone who desires to attain perfect discipleship of Christ must *forget his father's house* and hate *his own life,* that is, his natural affections, to imitate Christ who gave *his dear soul into the hands of her enemies.* . . . Saint Francis, then, can rightly say: *Learn from me,* that is, take me as your model of discipleship, for I am a true disciple of Christ.[49]

This sermon belonged to Bonaventure's rearticulation of the life and sanctity of Saint Francis, a rearticulation designed to make Francis conform to the necessary ideals of the now established, institutionalized, Franciscan order. And it was this vision of Franciscan renunciation—detachment from worldly ties for the sake of Christ—that molded the Franciscan view of Louis and his crusades.

The notion of crusade as renunciation was imbedded throughout the Franciscan view. The hymn also drew on another Franciscan image—following in Christ's footsteps (middle stanza again: *Christi sequens vestigia*). Derived from 1 Peter, and enjoying a long tradition in medieval religious thought, the image conveyed the very essence of Franciscan virtue and the ideology of *imitatio Christi.*[50] We saw earlier that the image of the *vestigia Christi* had been used by the Cistercians as part of a complex of imagery of ascetic spirituality. Among Franciscans the image had taken on a somewhat different flavor. For Francis it was associated with the adoption of poverty and the renunciation of family.[51] But for later Franciscans, particularly those who were enjoined to preach the crusades, the notion of following in Christ's footsteps was tied to passion, sometimes unto death, and the spiritual union that going on crusades made possible.[52] A favored line of scripture that was recalled frequently as a call of

---

48. See his own remarks in the first, "unapproved," rule: Armstrong, ed., *Francis,* vol. 1, 64. This is the thesis advanced in Trexler, *Naked before the Father.*

49. Armstrong, ed., *Francis,* vol. 2, 509–511, my ellipses. The sermons and its themes are discussed by Brooke, *Image of St. Francis,* 231–234.

50. Constable, "Nudus Nudum Christum Sequi and Parallel Formulas in the Twelfth Century," 83–91.

51. Cf. the opening of the *Regula non bullata* (Menestò, ed., *Fontes,* 185–186; Armstrong, ed., *Francis,* vol. 1, 63–64, 79).

52. Maier, *Crusade Propaganda,* 59–61; Smith, *Crusading,* 103–108.

imitatio Christi and served as the rallying cry for the crusades was Christ's own words, recalled by Matthew (10:38), "If any man would come after me, let him deny himself, pick up his cross, and follow me." This rhetorical context allowed for Louis' crusade to be understood as a renunciation and a passion, in line with Francis', and thus in imitation of Christ. These same values were all tied up in a story recounted in *Gloriosissimi regis*. In a passage that ultimately constituted the fourth lection for the office, Louis, boarding his ship and about to leave on his second crusade for Tunis, directs a moralizing speech to his successor, Philip III, on the obligations of kingship. Louis instructs his heir to spare nothing and to renounce all for Christ:

> "See that for faith in Christ and the church I neither spare my old age, nor do I take pity on your lonely mother. I relinquish wealth and honors and I abandon wealth for Christ. I take you who are about to rule, and I would even have taken your brothers and eldest sister with me (I would have brought even the fourth son had he been of age; thus I wish you to hear and to pay heed to within yourselves) so that after my death, when you attain the kingdom [i.e., when you become king], you should spare nothing for the sustenance and the defense of the church of God and his faith; neither you, nor your men, nor your kingdom, nor your wife, nor children. To you and your brothers I give this example, so that you may do the same." O blessed disciple, imitating the perfect teacher who teaches you this with words and fulfills it with works.[53]

Here was Louis speaking the Franciscan view of kingship, rooted in renunciation and service for Christ through crusade and a love of the church.[54] This view is echoed by *Gloriosissimi regis* as a whole, which dealt with Louis' royalty only in the context of its renunciation for, on one hand, crusade and, on the other, a religious vocation. The Franciscans, then, saw much of Louis' saintly virtue to be exemplified in his crusading. And crusade, which the Franciscans had been preaching throughout the thirteenth century, was in a sense the defining event of Louis' life that, through the suffering brought on by its failure, identified Louis with Christ.

So Louis' crusade was the equivalent of Francis' vow of poverty. But it also served on a metaphysical level the same representative function as did the stigmata for Francis—as the moment, through passion, in which Louis was united with Christ. The Franciscan liturgy for Louis ended with a prayer that treated

53. *Glor. reg.*: "Vide igitur quod pro fide christi et eius ecclesia nec mee parco senectuti, nec matri tue desolate misereor, delicias honores relinquo. Expono pro christo divitias, te quoque qui regnaturus es et fratres tuos ac sororem [primogenitam] mecum duco etiam quartum adduxissem filium si pubertaris annos plenius actigisset. Que idcirco te audire volui [velui] et animadvertere in te ipso ut post obitum meum cum ad regnum perveneris, pro ecclesia dei et eius fide sustinenda ac defendenda nulli rei parcas nec tibi nec tuis seu regno vel uxori aut liberis Tibi enim et fratribus tuis do exemplum ut et vos similiter faciatis. O beatus discipulus perfectum imitatus magistrum, qui quod verbo docuit opere adimplevit." This transcription is taken from Cambridge D.d.V, 297r.–v. (lection 7).
54. Note the adoption of Franciscan language. In Boniface's sermon quoted above, he repeatedly spoke of Francis as the "true disciple of Christ" and as "an excellent teacher" [of men] (Armstrong, ed., *Francis*, vol. 2, 508–516).

the crusades and began with the words *O martyr desiderio*. In ca. 1300 the only other use of those words in rhymed offices was the Benedictus for *Franciscus vir* and the office for the stigmata based on it.[55] Both interpreted the physical manifestations of the saint's suffering for Christ as the unitive element of the Christian life.[56] The liturgy of Saint Francis reads:

> O Francis, martyr by desire [*martyr desiderio*], suffering with such zeal, you followed Him, whom suffering you found in the book that you opened.
> You, peering into the sky, at the Seraph placed upon the cross, thereafter on your hands and your side and on your feet, you bore the likeness [*effigiem*] of the wounds of Christ.
> You, watch over your flock; you who, after your happy crossing showed the appearance of your glorified flesh, previously hard and greyish.[57]

By 1300 the reception of the stigmata had become the most emblematic episode in Francis' life. Following Thomas of Celano's version for both his vita and office, Julian of Speyer had the stigmata follow Francis' vision of the crucified man-seraph.[58] As Frugoni has shown, Bonaventure, melding the two events in later years, took this episode to be the most representative moment of Francis' sanctity, seeing the wounds as the most evident example of the identification of Francis' person with the body of Christ.[59] Bonaventure recounted Francis' reception of the stigmata as the metaphysical union with God which was rooted in suffering and passion. Bonaventure stressed the "*desire* for martyrdom" as the keystone of the Franciscan calling and the reception of the stigmata as Francis' ultimate reward for imitating the Christ and cross.[60] By the stigmata,

55. This is according to LMLO and to the index for the AH. See Max Lütolf, *Analecta hymnica medii aevi: Register* (Bern, 1978), vol. 1(b), nos. 18894–18896. The entire antiphon was adopted for the proper octave of *Ludovicus Decus Regnantium*. The only other saint for whom this phrase is used in Hughes's liturgical repertory is Augustine of Hippo, in a fifteenth-century office which postdates both *Franciscus vir* and *Francorum rex*; at MR6. LMLO AU11 (Augustine of Hippo). Or see AH, vol. 5, 138, no. 46.

56. Fleming, *Franciscan Literature*, 46.

57. Menestò, ed., *Fontes*, 1117: "O martyr desiderio, Francisce, quanto studio, compatiens hunc sequeris, quem passum libro reperis, quem aperuisti. ¶ Tu contuens in aere, Seraph in cruce positum, ex tunc in palmis, latere, et pedibus effigiem, fers plagarum Christi. ¶ Tu gregi tuo provide, qui post felicem transitum, durae prius et lividae, glorificatae speciem, carnis pretendisti."

58. Miskuly, "Julian of Speyer," 162–163.

59. On the development of the stigmata from spiritual to physical and metaphysical wounds, see Frugoni, *Francesco e l'invenzione delle stimmate*; Chiara Frugoni, "Saint Francis, a Saint in Progress," in *Saints: Studies in Hagiography*, ed. Sandro Sticca (Binghamton, N.Y., 1996), 161–190; Vauchez, "Stigmata."

60. On the desire for martyrdom and the Franciscans, E. Randolf Daniel, "The Desire for Martyrdom: A *Leitmotiv* of St. Bonaventure," *Franciscan Studies* 32 (1972): 74–87; E. Randolph Daniel, *The Franciscan Concept of Mission in the High Middle Ages* (Lexington, Ky., 1975), 40–49; Miri Rubin, "Choosing Death? Experiences of Martydom in Late Medieval Europe," in *Martyrs and Martyrologies. Papers read at the 1992 Summer Meeting and the 1993 Winter Meeting of the Ecclesiastical History Society* (Oxford, 1993), 153–183. On martyrdom and crusading, see Caroline Smith, "Martyrdom and Crusading in the Thirteenth Century: Remembering the Dead of Louis IX's Crusades," *Al-Masaq: Islam and the Medieval Mediterranean* 15 (2003): 189–196; Smith, *Crusading*, 98–103, 139–149. These themes intersect with Kedar, *Crusade and Mission*, 97–158.

Francis took upon his body the very sacrifice of the human Christ, and the penitential course of Francis' life became the compassionate (in the sense of the meaning of the Latin *compassio*—a suffering with) reenactment of Christ's own penitential redemption. Ultimately, Francis' preaching on the fifth crusade was folded into these complex of values; the ninth chapter of the *Legenda Maior* recounted Francis' trip to Damietta during the fifth crusade as rooted in his burning desire for martyrdom, which, when not achieved while in Egypt before the sultan, was later achieved through the unique privilege of the reception of the stigmata. Bonaventure's title for this chapter was *De fervore caritatis et desiderio martyrii*.[61] The desire for martyrdom on crusade, the eventual reception of the stigmata, and a spiritualized, metaphysical union with God were all tied together.

It was precisely *this* basically Franciscan interpretation of physical, worldly sacrifice that was at work in the Ludovican antiphon for the Magnificat. The text, too, began with the words, "o martyr desiderio":[62]

O martyr by desire, how you suffer with the Crucified One by the zeal of your pious mind, whose cross you twice took upon your shoulders [*crucem in humeris tuis bis affixisti*] (or, whose cross you were twice afflicted by [*afflixisti*]), the passion weakened you, but the fervor and zeal for Christ has made you a martyr.[63]

At the heart of both *O martyr desiderio* antiphons was the image of the cross. Both spoke of the saint's physical suffering and its relationship to the cross, and both emphasized in particular the saints' *desire* for martyrdom: both antiphons spoke of the *studium* and *desiderium* with which Francis and Louis yearned for martyrdom. Spiritual fervor engendered suffering for Christ, which took on a physical and metaphysical aspect. Both used versions of the word *compatior* to emphasize the idea of suffering for and with Christ and versions of the related word *passio*. *Francorum rex* employed the image of the cross—hung on the cross, taking up the cross, crucifixion, the crusades—to link Louis' crusading journeys to Christ's suffering and thus his salvation. This image of crucifixion was associated in *Franciscus vir* with the stigmata, Francis' own marks of the cross, when the second strophe spoke of the "Seraph on the cross," and the "wounds of Christ" borne on Francis' hands and feet. In some versions of *Francorum rex* Louis is described as having twice (making clear that the antiphon is referring to the king's *two* crusades) "affixed" (*affixisti*) the cross to his shoulders—"affix" being the word frequently employed in describing Christ on the cross. Other versions spoke of him being afflicted (*afflixisti*, that is *destroyed, crushed,* or *humbled*) twice by the cross. Both versions offered powerful images of Louis' passion. It did not hurt that Louis had in fact *died* on his

---

61. Armstrong, ed., *Francis*, vol. 2, 596–604; Menestò, ed., *Fontes,* 853–862. This was ultimately an elaboration of the event in Celano I and Julian of Speyer, both of whom spoke of Francis' desire for martyrdom.
62. A verse from the Mass of Saint Louis calls Louis *martyr desiderii* (BNF Lat 911, fol. 31r.).
63. FR WMag.

second attempt to crusade—making the suffering and the martyrdom of his cross—read: crusade—into Christ's own. Louis had "suffered with" Christ in the torments of his crusades just as Francis had "suffered with" Christ in receiving the stigmata. Both were seen as types of martyrs—willing martyrs who suffered "by desire." Louis' crusades, then, were his victory *precisely because* his suffering, brought about by its failure, identified him with Christ's own sacrifice. From a liturgical standpoint, it was appropriate that this was the antiphon for the Magnificat, which itself celebrated inversion—greatness in humility, eternal life in mortal death and so forth.[64] A hymn for the Mass for Saint Louis that appears in an early fourteenth century Franciscan breviary from Paris also spoke of Louis as *martir desiderio*.[65]

As early as the pontificate of Innocent III (1198–1216) the notion of imitating Christ by crusading had been increasingly associated with crusade suffering and passion.[66] Crucifixion and passion were preeminent within this typology of crusade—taking the cross and dying by taking the cross were imitating Christ through crucifixion. The second half of the thirteenth century found mendicants preaching this penitential and spiritual value of crusade, with Francis' own story becoming increasingly associated with a crusading mission and suffering that had inherent spiritual value. The crusading sermons of Franciscans such as Odo of Chateauroux and Guibert of Tournai repeatedly called upon images of imitation and Christ's footsteps in preaching the spiritual value of the crusades.[67] Bonaventure, we saw, stressed Francis' desire for martyrdom not only in his treatment of Francis' reception of the stigmata, but also of Francis' own pseudocrusade in preaching to the sultan. Preeminent in Franciscan preaching was the line from Matthew—"take up your cross and follow me" (Matt. 16:24)—that had been at the heart of crusading from its beginnings. At work in *Francorum rex* was a series of interlocking images and ideas—renunciation, taking the cross, following in Christ's footsteps, the crusades, suffering with Christ—which were both associated with crusading and lay at the heart of Franciscan articulations of virtue and spirituality.

And so, the Franciscan Bertrand of Tours, OM (ca. 1265/70–1333), in two of his sermons, drew on the theme of desired martyrdom and placed Louis squarely in the framework of martyr saints.[68] Bertrand was provincial minister for Aquitaine, then papal legate, cardinal, and ultimately vicar minister-general

64. Harper, *The Forms and Orders*, 272–273; Elizabeth A. Johnson, *Truly Our Sister: a Theology of Mary in the Communion of Saints* (New York, 2003), 266–267.

65. BNF Lat 1332, fol. 400v. See *Sacramentaires*, vol. 2, 218–219. The mass is not as clearly identified with a single order as the offices are, and this text is found in manuscripts associated with different orders.

66. Maier, "Mass, the Eucharist and the Cross: Innocent III and the Relocation of the Crusade," 351–360.

67. On Francis, see Kedar, *Crusade and Mission*, 116–131. On Franciscan preaching, see Penny Cole, *The Preaching of the Crusades to the Holy Land, 1095–1270* (Cambridge, Mass., 1991), 142–176, 182, 199; Maier, *Crusade Propaganda*, 56–68. Both Odo and Guibert quoted Luke 9:23 in associating the cross with penitence and martyrdom.

68. Bertrand of Tours 2 (*Beatus dives*) and 4 (*Probatus est in illo*).

of his order.[69] The rubric for *Probatus est in illo* said that the sermon could be used for the sermon of blessed Louis and for "the feast of any martyr."[70] Drawing on Ecclesiasticus 31:10—"Who has been tested thereby and made perfect, he shall have glory everlasting"—Bertrand associated the trial of crusade with suffering which, if overcome, warranted the glory of heaven. Louis was not fettered by temptation but rather conquered it. Early in the sermon Bertrand wrote: "Blessed Louis, who conquered many temptations, even if he was not a martyr by deed, he was made one by will and desire. Twice, indeed, he crossed the ocean for the spreading of the catholic faith, was captured by the Sarracens and surrendered to prison and, finally, ended his life in those parts in peace."[71] Bertrand explained that Louis, tested in the struggle of war (*in certamine belli*) and found perfect, was thus, like any martyr would be, crowned in the procession of saints (*in sanctorum agmine*). The saint was humbled through tribulations, sometimes "all the way to chains and lashes, sometimes all the way to prison, the cross, and death."[72] He was tested in these fires, like gold, and proven to warrant the glory of God. The remainder of the sermon develops the notion of the saint tested through trial and to perfection. In another sermon, *Dico vobis*, Bertrand spoke of Louis "reddening through the wish of martyrdom and the ardor of desire."[73] Bertrand may have been drawing on the liturgical text. Certainly, here, he advanced the interpretation of Louis' sanctity as rooted in an interpretation of crusade as passion.

Alms, Charity, and Religious Patronage

There were other themes encoded into the liturgical office for Louis, including religious patronage and compassion for the poor. The Franciscan office praised Louis because he built (*construxit*) houses of God and monasteries (MV6). (The recalling of Louis' construction of churches may reflect a change in the legend of Saint Francis that emphasized Francis' actual building of churches that bolstered conventualist claims to be able to own their own physical building and facilities.)[74] The matins hymn praised Louis as "the reviver of the poor, through the collection of alms." MR6 spoke of how Louis, upon his

69. On Bertrand, see *HLF*, vol. 36, 190–203; Smalley, *English Friars*, 242–245; Nold, "Bertrand de la Tour: Life and Works," 274–323; Patrick Nold, *Pope John XXII and his Franciscan Cardinal: Bertrand de la Tour and the Apostolic Poverty Controversy* (Oxford, 2003).

70. Bertrand of Tours 2, *Beatus dives*. Toulouse BM 325, 253r.: "Sermo in festo beati Ludovici quondam regis francorum et in festo cuilibet martyris."

71. Bertrand of Tours, 4, *Probatus est in illo*, Toulouse BM 325, 253r.: "Tunc enim proprie non solum probatus est. Sed est invenitur perfectus. Unde de beato Ludovico qui multas temptationes vicit, qui et si non fuit martir facto fuit tamen voluntate et desiderio. Bis enim mare transivit propter dilatationem catholicie fidei captus fuit per sarracenos et mancipatus carceri. Et tandem in illius partibus vitam in pace finivit."

72. Ibid.: "Interdum usque ad vincula et flagella. Interdum usque ad carcerem, crucem et mortem."

73. Bertrand of Tours 1, *Dico vobis*, Linz Stud B 71, 120r.: "rubens per voluntatem martirii et desideri flammam."

74. Trexler, *Naked before the Father*, 31–59; Dalarun, *Misadventure of Francis*, 251.

return from the Holy Land, raised up the poor with gifts; and in the verse that followed Louis was praised for visiting monasteries and building the houses of God with lavish expenditures. It was already noted that Louis was praised for ministering to lepers and for his distribution of alms to the poor. The same themes of patronage and alms were also emphasized in both William of Saint-Pathus' *vie* and *Gloriosissimi regis*.

These were not only themes found in the legend of Francis but also wholly consonant with the larger spiritual mission and ideals of the Franciscans. A number of these themes—piety, charity, and renunciation—were taken up in preaching texts in ways that minimized the image of rulership and power and emphasized tropes of piety. The overwhelming theme of an anonymous Franciscan sermon, *Misericordia et veritas,*[75] was Louis' alms and patronage. Its rubric claimed that the sermon could be used for Louis' feast but could also be applied to "any king or eminent prince,"[76] indicating that, despite its rich details relating to Louis specifically, its principal message regarded the virtues of the good monarch or the good leader in the abstract. The sermon drew on Proverbs 20:28—"Mercy and truth preserve the king and his throne is strengthened by clemency." In the first part of his life Louis was merciful and truthful in four ways, corresponding to the four elements of the first phrase: "king," "mercy," "truth," and "guard." First (king), he was born of "saintly parents" and raised his children in a saintly manner; second (mercy), Louis demonstrated the perfection of these virtues through the provisions he made for the poor and his compassion for monks and others; third (truth), the king demonstrated his profound (*infima*) humility and devotion to the catholic faith; and fourth (guard), God protected the king through many dangers while overseas.[77] The virtue of mercy is repeatedly characterized by his gifts to the poor, done with "mercy in his heart and compassion in his works."[78] The gloss on a passage from *Beatus Ludovicus* that detailed how Louis fed the poor and gave them alms exalted his "deep humility," spoke of his simple dress, his "devotion to the catholic faith," and his taking the cross (all Franciscan themes). The sermon then praised Louis' religious and charitable foundations, and great willingness to give alms.

Perfectus inventus,[79] another Franciscan sermon, included patronage and almsgiving as part of a wider complex of virtues that emphasized spiritual, ascetic, and pious ideals for a king. The rambling sermon drew verbatim from *Gloriosissimi regis*, the vita from which the lections of the office were taken.

---

75. Anon 3, OFM, *Misericordia et veritas.*

76. Anon 3, OFM, *Misericordia et veritas.*, BNF Lat 3303, fol. 183rb: "Thema de eodem in eodem festo sancti Ludovici regis francie, et potest applicari pro informacione cuiuslibet regis vel eminentis principis." The manuscript dates to the first third of the fourteenth century.

77. On the structuring of sermons in this way, see Bériou, "Les sermons latins," 370–382.

78. Anon 3, OFM, *Misericordia et veritas*, BNF Lat 3303, fol. 185 rb: "Dicit misericordias in plurali propter misericordiam quam habuit ad pauperes, quibus fuit misericors in corde, et miserator in opere, et quibus dedit escam et alia neccessaria pro corpore."

79. Anon 4 OFM, *Perfectus inventus*, BNF Lat 16512, 52r.–57r. The manuscript probably dates to the last half of the fourteenth century.

The sermon began by saying that Louis was victorious over spiritual enemies (carnal delights, secular honors, and worldly riches), which he subdued through the rigor of austerity, humility, and the love of generosity.[80] The sermon furnished a series of examples: he castigated his body with a hair shirt; he made gifts of generosity and works of mercy to the poor, churches, monks, religious, hospitals, and so forth. Louis wore simple clothing after his return from overseas, washed the hands and feet of the poor himself, kissing them humbly and devotedly. He would even eat food that the poor at his table had touched. He was devoted to the sacred relics of Christ, and, truly longing to extend the faith, he twice assumed the cross and left the kingdom. He frequented sacramental confession, he practiced the continence of conjugal chastity, and so on.

In the one place in *Misericordia et veritas* which explicitly treats Louis' kingship, the author defined good kingship in terms of his alms, charities, and endowments:

> For these works of mercy, the name of clemency is fitting to him. I Kings 20. *And we heard that the kings of the house of Israel are clement.* The house of Israel, seeing God through true faith, is the house of France, the house whose kings have always been clement. As a sign of their clemency. They have as their insignia the lily flower. And indeed, even among these clement kings, he was the most clement, which is evident since, after his return from overseas, *as gold and silver purified by fire*, he built hospitals, he founded innumerable houses for religious, and bestowed land and rents for the blind and other poor and sick people. He dispersed as much as he could to religious and other poor men, with great cheerfulness; he fed a horribly leprous monk with his own hands, whose abbot was not able to watch without weeping and tears. And it thus can indeed be said of him what is written in Proverbs 16: "In the cheerfulness of the king's countenance is life; and his clemency is like the late rain" [Prov. 16:15]. And thus, in the cheerfulness of the king's face there is life, because he always did works of piety with a cheerful face. Because he had learned that God loves a cheerful giver.[81]

The passage thus borrowed from a typological, dynastic, and lineal model of kingship that was the purview of dynastic and royal ideology (his virtue relates

---

80. Ibid., 52vb.: "Sequitur *vir*: ecce quod fuit vigorosus in certamine, tres siquidem hostes fortissimos. Fortissime debellavit: ¶ Carnales delicias per rigorem austeritatis. ¶Seculares excellencias per tenorem humilitatis. ¶ Mundiales divicias per amorem largitatis."

81. Anon 3, OFM, *Misericordia et veritas*, BNF Lat 3303, fol. 187va.–b.: "Ex hiis operibus misericordie convenit sibi nomen clemencie. I Reg xx. *Audivimus quod reges domus israhel clementes sunt.* Domus israhel videns deum per veram fidem est domus francie, cuius domus semper reges fuerunt clementes in signum clemencie: habunt flores liliorum pro insigniis. Inter autem clementes reges iste fuit clementissimus, quod apparet, quia post reversionem de ultra mare, quasi aurum et argentum igne examinatum, hospitalia hedificavit, innumeras domos religiosorum fundavit, cecis et aliis impotentibus et invalidis loca et redditus assignavit. Quam plures etiam religiosis et aliis pauperibus dispersit cum magna ylaritate; monachum horribiliter leprosum manu propria pavit quod abbas eius sine fletu et lacrimis videre non potuit: ut possit dici de eo illud proverb. xvi. *In ylaritate vultus regis vita clemencia eius quasi umber serotinus* [Prov. 16:15]. ¶ Et dicitur In ylaritate vultus regis vita. quia adhuc opera pietatis ylari vultu faciebat. Didiscerat enim quod ylarem datorem diliget deus." For *aurum et argentum igne examinatum* see Proverbs 17:3 or Ecclesiasticus 2:5.

to the other kings of France and to those of the kings of Israel), but it did so in a way that above all prized almsgiving and patronage as the principal signature of royal virtue. *Perfectus inventus* went further and quoted the very speech preserved in *Gloriosissimi regis* and used in the liturgical lections (quoted above) in which Louis exalted renunciation of wealth and honor and family to serve the church and God on crusade.[82] Elsewhere, in the context of a discussion of the saint's desire for chastity, the author relayed that Louis had hoped that when his eldest son had grown up he would, with his wife's consent, enter the religious life (also from *Gloriosissimi regis*).[83]

Bertrand of Tours, in another sermon entitled *Beatus dives*, praised a disregard for the temptations of wealth as a saintly characteristic. *Beatus dives* explained that Louis was the richest of men *temporaliter*, abounding in temporal riches even among kings, but was however not stained by the vice of extravagance, and, contrary to expectation, was chaste, beneficent, and humble. Picking up themes established by mendicant authors in the thirteenth century, Bertrand argued that "not even the substance of wealth is the cause of sin, since it may be well and truly produced and acquired, and since it is possible to hold in possession lawfully and without sin, as is evident in Abraham, Isaac, Jacob, and other saintly men of the Old Testament."[84] A rich man is not sinful if he uses his riches well, shuns the stain of extravagance, the inordinate love of opulence, and the arrogance of pride (as did Louis). "Louis was not an inordinate lover of temporal wealth, but rather was most generous and very poor of spirit. He even disdained all wealth and distributed his goods to the poor, for the building and upkeep of holy places, and for Christianity, for the love of which he twice crossed the sea at very great expense to fight the enemies of Christ; for he was not haughty or inflated with the wind of pride, but was very humble inwardly in mind and outwardly in deed."[85] Herein lay one resolution of the essential paradox of the saint-king—the king is only a good king if he is willing to renounce his kingship and power and wealth, or at least devote it entirely to the service of the church (or her members) and to God. For the Fran-

82. The quotation in *Perfectus inventus* is found at BNF Lat 16512, 54vb.–55ra. A part of this chapter was also taken up in BLQRF L9, *RHF* vol. 23, 164, and by Bernard Gui in his *Speculum sanctorale*, BNF Lat. 5406, fol. 154v. The version in *Perfectus inventus* conforms to the text of *Gloriosissimi regis*. I have had trouble rendering "quod non fuit qui ganniret."

83. Anon 4 OFM, *Perfectus inventus*, BNF Lat 16512, 55vb: "corde devoto firmiter proposuit quod adulto filio suo primogenito uxoris habito consensu religionem intraret." The passage derives ultimately from GB *vie*, 7 (ch. 12) but was incorporated into *Glor. reg.*, ch. 2, whence the sermon got this story.

84. Bertrand of Tours, 2, *Beatus Dives*, Toulouse BM 325, 249v.: "Non enim substantia diviciarum est causa peccati, cum sit bona et adeo effecta, et collate, unde potest licite et absque omni peccato possideri sicut apparuit in habraam, ysaae et jacob et aliis sanctis veteris testamenti." On the question of mendicant representations of money, see D'Avray, *Preaching of the Friars*, 204–216.

85. Bertrand of Tours, 2, *Beatus Dives*, Toulouse BM 325, 249v.: "Nec fuit amator inordinatus temporalis substantie, sed fuit largissimus et spiritu pauperrimus. Contempsit enim omnia, divisit bona sua pauperibus, locis piis edificandis et sustentandis, et christianitati pro cuius amore transivit bis mare cum maximis sumptibus contra Christi inimicos pugantus, nec fuit elatus, nec inflatus vento superbi sed fuit humillimus interius in mente et exteriori gestu."

ciscans, Louis' saintliness was at any rate not defined by the exercise of royal power.

Authority and Crusade among the Franciscans

The virtues of humility, almsgiving, patronage, renunciation, crusade, and almost-martyrdom were thus the principal themes in the Franciscan memorialization of Louis. Saint Francis always remained the root referent for these attributes, but after 1317 the Franciscans had an even more potent exemplar than Louis in Louis IX's grand-nephew, Louis of Toulouse, who actually (and dramatically) renounced his claim to the Angevin throne to join the Franciscan order. Louis IX did not go nearly this far, and this might explain why after 1317 Louis of Toulouse eclipsed Louis of France among Franciscans and in most Franciscan sermon collections.[86] But his desire to renounce his throne out of love of God, whether or not he did so, allowed the Franciscans to reconcile the notion of the good king with the good saint. This all spoke to the issue of how the Franciscans were at the end of the century negotiating their own evolving ideals—ideals that in Paris and elsewhere, were moving toward a more institutionalized, mainstream ideology, in which friars owned their own buildings and books, became bishops and cardinals, and frequented the court and served in royal administration. The Franciscans' memorialization of Louis thus was rooted in (and elucidates) several trends: the increasing institutionalization of the order, the proximity of its members to nodes of political power, the evolution of religious ideals among Franciscans, and, more broadly, Franciscan influences on the ideals and meaning of crusading.

In the second half of the thirteenth century the *Sacred Exchange between Saint Francis and Lady Poverty* (*Sacrum commercium*) offered a sharp criticism of the wealth and luxe associated with royal courts and the religious men who enjoyed it: "they [religious] sold their words to the rich, their greetings to matrons, and frequented courts of kings and princes with all-out zeal. . . . Now they are magnificent and rich, the powerful of the earth, because *they have gone from evil to evil, and have not known the Lord.*"[87] The sentiment reflected the early ideals of the order (and its self-definition against the older religious orders), ideals that had continued in certain (increasingly marginalized) quarters of the order well into the fourteenth century. It was in large part because Louis, as a king, had himself eschewed the trappings of luxury and wealth that he could be adopted among Franciscans and understood to live up to the ideal of Saint Francis himself in the essentials of his character and life. But the order itself was increasingly moving away from its strictest ideal, as an

---

86. The sermons discussed here are in a sense the exceptions. One indication of this is the distribution of sermons among Franciscan sermon collections. Schneyer gave as a designation "S62" for Saint Louis IX, but miscategorized many that were actually to Louis of Toulouse. Many collections of Franciscan sermons include sermons to Louis of Toulouse but not to Louis IX.

87. Menestò, ed., *Fontes,* 1724; Armstrong, ed., *Francis,* vol. 1, 547.

institution in which its members advised kings, visited court, and served in administrations. Louis' own court was perhaps the principal example of this trend, but it was reflected also at the courts of contemporary German and English rulers.[88] The appropriation of Louis as a Franciscan figure reflected the evolving institutional identity of the order itself and the role of friars within the political establishment.

The modeling of Saint Louis in the language of Saint Francis also represented a softening and shifting of the religious ideals that formed the foundation of the Franciscan movement. Louis was praised for his simplicity in dress, for his desire to relinquish his wealth, for his desire to go on crusade. The Franciscan interpretation of Louis made this revered king into a saint of compassion, abnegation, renunciation, charity, and patronage. His patronage of alms (on which the order depended) further made sense within a context of defining lay sanctity. The stress lay always on Louis' active piety and strength of faith in a way that was entirely consonant with the sanctification of lay life popularized by the mendicants in the thirteenth century, devoting well over two-thirds of the nighttime office (matins) to Louis' crusade.

This was one take on Louis' sanctity. If Louis, as king, were to fulfill the ideal set forth by Francis through the quality of his faith, then the Franciscan ideal was attainable even by those in positions of wealth and power. Passion and compassion, alms and patronage were the earmarks of sanctity, earmarks that a king could achieve and remain king. The same softening was seen in representations of Louis of Toulouse, quickly modeled as a royal and a bishop rather than an ascetic (spiritualist) friar.[89] The Franciscan interpretation of Louis (IX) also reflected evolving notions of crusade ideology and spirituality, an evolution in which the Franciscans themselves had played no small part. The crusades were central to the Franciscan memorialization of the king, and the liturgical office in particular interpreted Louis' crusade in the language of passion and martyrdom, as an *imitatio Christi* that was modeled on Francis' own *imitatio,* manifest in the stigmata. This reflected a language of crusading ideology that has been propagated during the preceding century by, among others, Franciscans preaching the crusade. It reflected both the Franciscan influence in the religious sphere more widely and in particular within the spiritual and religious aspects of crusading. Certainly, the sanctification of Louis along these lines (not only among Franciscans) sanctified the increasingly disastrous project of crusade in general around 1300. It also furnished a way of understanding the lay vocation of crusading in a Franciscan vein.

88. Lawrence, *The Friars*, 166–180.
89. Thompson, "Cooperation and Conflict," 266–269.

7
Joinville

The best known of the texts written to celebrate Louis' sanctity is Jean de Joinville's *vie* (which is what he himself calls it at §19, the *vie nostre saint roy Looÿs*).[1] Jean was the seigneur of Joinville, a lordship in Champagne, which during Louis' life was not yet under the direct suzerainty of the French crown (though it would be during Philip IV's reign). Born around 1225, Joinville was educated at the court of Thibaut of Champagne and inherited both the lordship of Joinville and the title of seneschal of Champagne at his father's death in 1239.[2] He was part of the large contingent of French knights that Louis, his elder by about a decade, corralled into his first crusading expedition in 1248, and as Joinville himself recounted it, the two young men became close friends in the course of their shared years in the Levant. Joinville's own genuine piety is clear from not only the evidence of the *vie* but also the Credo he wrote while in the East.[3] Joinville was enormously fond of the king. He looked up to him, was flattered to have been befriended by him, and was frequently impressed by him, but was also capable of disapproving of and disagreeing with Louis or his decisions (classically at §§168, 593, 604). Joinville stayed with Louis throughout his years in the East but

1. Translations are taken from Hague's edition of Joinville, *The Life of St. Louis*. The French is taken from Monfrin's edition: Joinville, *Vie de Saint Louis*. I cite the text by the paragraph divisions that have become standard and were established by Natalis de Wailly, *Histoire de Saint Louis, par Jean sire de Joinville, suivie du Credo et de la letter à Louis X* (Paris, 1868).

2. On Joinville's life, the classic work is Henri-François Delaborde, *Jean de Joinville et les seigneurs de Joinville, suivi d'un catalogue de leurs actes* (Paris, 1894). More recently, see Jacques Monfrin, "Introduction," in *Vie de Saint Louis* (Paris, 1995), 11–32.

3. A translation can be found in Hague's 1955 translation of Joinville, §§770–852. For the original, see Lionel J. Friedman, "Text and Iconography for Joinville's *Credo*" (Cambridge, Mass., 1958), 29–51. See also Charles Langlois, *La vie au moyen âge*, vol. 4 (Paris, 1928), 1–22; and Monfrin, "Introduction," 27–30. What survives is a later reworking of the text written during the crusade.

famously refused to participate in Louis' second crusade.[4] And he outlived the king by almost forty-seven years, dying in 1317 in his early nineties. He was called to St.-Denis in 1282 or 1283 to testify at the canonization proceedings and was apparently questioned for more than two days (§760).

In the dedicatory preface, Joinville explained that he was asked by Jeanne de Navarre (d. 1305), the wife of Philip the Fair, to write "a book of the holy sayings and good deeds of our King Saint Louis" (*un livre des saintes paroles et des bons faiz nostre roy saint Looÿs*). The result is the text that more than any other has shaped how the modern era knows Louis IX.[5] Yet it is not a simple text, because, as I understand it (though the point is arguable), it was written during at least two different stages between ca. 1270 and 1309 with different purposes in mind.[6] This chapter discusses the principal threads in interpretation of Louis as Joinville recorded them at each stage, asking what role kingship, piety, and crusading played in Joinville's representation of Louis. The core crusading narrative, probably written sometime after Louis' death in 1270 as a chronicle or personal memoir, was not designed to showcase Louis as a saint, but rather remembered him chiefly as a (fallible) man, a chivalric crusader, a feudal king, and a friend, as dictated by Joinville's own experiences with Louis. The frame, written shortly after Louis' canonization to record his words and deeds as saint, was influenced by the process of sanctification that had occurred in the intervening years, and presented Louis as an (infallible) saint, defined in terms of ideal kingship (characterized by justice) and the deep piety on which Louis' justice depended. It had as one of its overarching purposes the articulation of a model of just and saintly kingship directed toward Philip the Fair, in whom Joinville was disappointed, and his heirs, whom he hoped to influence with the positive model of Louis. The shift in representation may have accompanied Joinville's own evolving understanding of Louis, as his memories were influenced by the discourse of sanctity that had emerged during the canonization process, and it may also reflect his different goals in writing each section. But in its final form, his *vie* evinces his resistance to the royal presentation of Louis as the sacral sanctifier of the crown and lineage, the marshaling of the image of the good king, now officially sanctified, against Philip the Fair's claims of inherent legitimacy and virtue.

Chronology and Composition

Jeanne de Navarre died in 1305. The last line of the earliest surviving and most authoritative manuscript of the *vie* (the "Brussels manuscript," now BNF

---

4. On his reasons, which were as much circumstantial as ideological, see Smith, *Crusading*, 177–183.

5. Note that the text was not particularly well known until the sixteenth century; Alain Boureau, "Les Enseignements absolutistes de Saint Louis 1610–1630," in *La monarchie absolutiste et l'histoire en France: Théories du pouvoir, propagandes monarchiques et mythologies nationales* (Paris, 1987), 88.

6. Gaston Paris opened the debate with his "La composition du livre de Joinville sur saint Louis," *Romania* 23 (1894): 508–524. See also Paris, "Jean, sire de Joinville," in HLF, vol. 32, 291–451.

Fr. 13568) indicates that the text was written in October 1309, though this may refer to the copying of the presentation manuscript and the actual text as we have it may have been completed by the end of 1305.[7] With these as the parameters for interpreting the rationale and chronology of Joinville's surviving text, two schools of thought have emerged regarding its composition. One school, advocated most recently by Jacques Monfrin, has argued that Joinville composed his entire text in one go, sometime between 1305 and 1309, in response to Jeanne's request and explicitly as a hagiographical account of Louis' life and sainthood.[8] The second school, first advanced by Gaston Paris in 1894 and accepted here, holds that the text was composed or dictated at different stages. This view maintains that the core narrative, which treats the crusade of 1248–1254, was composed sometime in the 1270s or 1280s, when Joinville was in his fifties. This text was intended as a kind of memoir or chronicle of the crusades and centered on Joinville and his own experiences. Only after 1297, in response to the queen's request, did Joinville write the opening and closing portions that frame it. Here Joinville sought to accommodate his central crusading narrative to the expectations of hagiography and drew explicitly on models and examples of the genre. In stitching together his larger work he may have had occasion to edit or rework portions of the core narrative, but, as he himself said in the dedication, the work comprises two distinct sections.[9] He explained that he "divided [the book] into two parts"— the first being properly hagiographic and dealing with "how he ordered himself at all times by the will of God and of the Church, and for the well-being of his Kingdom," and the second being "the great things he did as a knight and a soldier" (§2)—virtues not classically hagiographic but necessary to incorporate the preexisting narrative and surely consonant with Joinville's own aristocratic perspective.[10] This explains in part the varying texture and mood of the *vie*'s different sections, and indeed, the best argument for a more complex history of the text's composition remains, as Gaston Paris originally noted, the text itself: the starkly different tone of the narration, compositional strategies, and narrative focus in each section; the discontinuous use of the term *saint*; and the shifting attitude toward knightly values.[11]

The central crusading section is not so much focused on Louis as it is on Joinville's own experiences, although Louis, as king and leader of the expedition,

7. This is the *terminus a quo* established by the death of Jeanne de Navarre. The postscript appears in only the fourteenth-century BNF Fr. 13568, and not in the two other surviving manuscripts, BNF Fr. 6273 and BNF Fr. 10148, both of which date to the sixteenth century.

8. Monfrin, "Introduction," 69–79. This view takes up earlier argumentation, for which see Alfred Foulet, "When Did Joinville Write His 'Vie de saint Louis'?," *Romanic Review* 32 (1941): 233–243, who sees Joinville's deposition in 1283 to the canonization commission as part of his "first redaction." In response, see Smith, *Crusading*, 58.

9. Paris believed the core narrative ran from §§110 to 666, but this may reflect parameters drawn too rigidly. I tend to see the core narrative ending around §609, when the king decides to return home. See Paris, "La composition du livre," 513.

10. Paul Archambault, "Joinville: History as Chivalric Code," in *Seven French Chroniclers: Witnesses to History* (Syracuse, 1974), 41–57. The argument is also found in Archambault, "The Silences of Joinville," *Papers on Language and Literature* 7 (1971): 115–132.

11. In addition to Paris, see also Smith, *Crusading*, 52–58, 61–62.

naturally played an integral role.[12] Joinville referred to Louis consistently as the king, but only three rare times as saint or saintly (and these may be interpolations).[13] In a telling line in the middle of the original crusade narrative, as he recounted the court's move to Acre after Louis' release in 1250, Joinville explicitly proclaimed his intent in composing the central account: "Now I must tell you of the many hardships and tribulations I suffered at Acre, from which God, in whom I trusted as I trust in Him now, delivered me. I shall have these written down that those who hear them may also put their trust in God when they suffer hardship and sorrow, and so God will help them as He helped me" (§406). Duly pious, this is standard crusading fare, and it is notable for its lack of reference to Louis. Joinville's model for this central narrative may have been the genre of the crusade chronicle, with which we know he was familiar because he referred to a *livre de la Terre sainte* (perhaps the *Chronique d'Ernoul*) at §77.[14] But Joinville's text fits into no genre exactly, and he seems to have been influenced by geographic entries in encyclopedias, collections of exempla, romance literature, and crusading epics.[15] Though literate and probably familiar with a number of different types of writing, at this stage Joinville himself may not have been explicitly and self-consciously writing in an attempt to effect a single type. In any event, a hagiographical account of Louis was, at this stage, not his aim.

The frame, on the other hand, follows different principles and had different aims.[16] The focus of the text is squarely Louis himself, and the organizational model was more thematic than chronological, where the chronology of events was sacrificed to the virtues they exhibited (a characteristic of hagiography).[17]

12. Michèle Perret, "A la fin de sa vie ne fuz je mie," *Revue des sciences humaines* (1981–1983): 17–37; Smith, *Crusading*, 52–53. The personal and vivid quality of the narrative is emphasized by Michel Zink, *The Invention of Literary Subjectivity*, trans. David Sices (Baltimore, 1999), 199–218.

13. Paris, "La composition du livre," 510. The instances appear at §§120, 207, 385. The term *saint roy* is also used twice at §565–566, but here as part of direct quotation, which functions differently. See also Elisabeth Gaucher, "Joinville et l'écriture biographique," in *Le prince et son historien: la vie de Saint Louis de Joinville* (Paris, 1997), 116, n. 26.

14. Delaborde, *Jean de Joinville*, 170–171.

15. On genre, see Marcus K. Billson III, "Joinville's Histoire de Saint Louis: Hagiography, History and Memoir," *The American Benedictine Review* 31 (1980): 418–442; Karl Uitti, "Novelle et structure hagiographique: Le recit historiographique nouveau de Jean de Joinville," in *Mittelalterbilder aus neuer Perspektive* (1985), 380–391; Christine Ferlampin-Acher, "Joinville, de l'hagiographe à l'autobiographe: approche de *La Vie de saint Louis*," in *Jean de Joinville: de la Champagne aux royaumes d'outre-mer*, ed. Danielle Quéruel (Langres, 1998), 73–91; de Combarieu du Gres, "La chanson du roi Louis (de Joinville et de la chanson de geste)," in *Jean de Joinville*, 109–129; Smith, *Crusading*, 61–64.

16. Billson, "Joinville's Histoire"; Uitti, "Novelle et structure."; Françoise Laurent, "La Vie de saint Louis ou le miroir des saints," in *Le prince et son historien: la vie de Saint Louis de Joinville* (Paris, 1997), 149–182; Jean-Pierre Perrot, "Le 'péché' de Joinville: Écriture du souvenir et imaginaire hagiographique," in *Le prince et son historien*, 183–207; Ferlampin-Acher, "Joinville, de l'hagiographe à l'autobiographe," 73–91; Dominique Boutet, "Hagiographie et historiographie: la Vie de saint Thomas Becket de Guernes de Pont-Sainte-Maxence et la Vie de saint Louis de Joinville," *Le moyen âge* 106 (2000): 277–293.

17. Jeanette M. A. Beer, "The Notion of Temporality in Early Vernacular History," *New Zealand Journal of French Studies* 8 (1987), 5–15; Laurent, "Vie de saint Louis," 156–172, and see 159 for thematic approach.

To gather materials to round out his work he consulted a French translation of William of Nangis' *Vie de Saint Louis* that had been seamlessly incorporated into a copy of the *Grandes chroniques* held at St.-Denis (BNF Lat 5925 or a lost prototype). At the end (§768), when reviewing his sources, Joinville refers to this as a *roman* (that is, a book in the French language). William of Nangis' Latin *vita* had itself drawn material from Geoffrey of Beaulieu's *vita* (written in 1272–1273). And so, it is from this *roman*—this copy of the *Grandes chroniques*—that Joinville got the descriptions of Louis' hatred of blasphemy (§685), his bestowal of benefices (§691), his charity to the poor (§§720–726), the account of the Prevoté of Paris (§§715–718), his religious foundations (§§727–729), and the *Enseignements* Louis wrote for his son (§§740–754).[18] In this way Joinville's text is injected with stories derived from a more formally hagiographic model, and they sit discordantly within even Joinville's ostensibly hagiographical frame.

The Portrait of Louis in the Crusading Narrative

For Jacques LeGoff, Joinville offered the most immediate, the most true, portrait of Louis, the one least suffused by the hues of sanctity that characterize the works of Geoffrey of Beaulieu, William of Chartres, and others.[19] The central narrative is imbued with secular, chivalric, and aristocratic values that Joinville would have personified and espoused as a member of the high aristocracy, a knight, a crusader himself, a descendant of a long noble lineage, and a member of the royal entourage.[20] Instead of a hagiographical model, it betrays the influence of the epic tradition that appealed to Joinville's lay, noble milieu.[21] Echoing the imagery of the *chansons de geste*, for example, the description of the Franks landing at Damietta glories in the imagery of the sultan's forces ashore (§148), furnishing images of coats of arms and pennons beating in the winds, and evokes the sounds of kettledrums and the Saracens' horns ("the noise was like lightening crashing from the heavens" [§§158, 159]). Throughout the central narrative Joinville is acutely aware of social hierarchy and feudal relations, and Louis is depicted as a military commander, crusading hero, and feudal overlord. In the early stages, describing the successful military operations in Egypt, Louis is described as dressed in full armor, sitting on a chair and surrounded by knights (§172). Landing at Damietta, Louis leaps into the water,

---

18. Paul Viollet, "Les Enseignements de saint Louis à son fils," *Bibliothéque de l'École des Chartes* 35 (1874); Natalis de Wailly, "Mémoire sur le 'roman' ou chronique en langue vulgaire dont Joinville a reproduit plusieurs passages," *Bibliotheque de l'École des Chartes* 35 (1874).
19. LeGoff, *Saint Louis*, 473–498. Lucken argues for a more stylized representation of Louis; see Christopher Lucken, "L'èvangile du Roi: Joinville, témoin et auteur de la *Vie de Saint Louis*," *Annales: histoire, sciences sociales* 56 (2001): 445–467. For LeGoff's response, see Jacques LeGoff, "Mon ami le saint roi: Joinville et Saint Louis (réponse)," *Annales: histoire, sciences sociales* 56 (2001): 469–477.
20. Archambault, "Seven French Chroniclers," 41–57.
21. Uitti, "Novelle et structure"; Ferlampin-Acher, "Joinville, de l'hagiographe à l'autobiographe," 85; Gres, "La chanson du roi Louis"; Smith, *Crusading*, 58–74.

"his shield round his neck, his helmet on his head, lance in hand," and must be dissuaded by three of his wiser companions (*preudeshomes*) not to fling himself upon the Saracens (§162). Shortly after the landing at Damietta, Joinville describes Louis in the battle outside Mansurah following the deaths of Robert of Artois and the Templars.

> While I was on foot with my knights, wounded, as I have already told you, up came the King with his own division; there was a great shouting and a tremendous noise of trumpets and kettledrums; he halted on a raised roadway. Never have I seen so fine a man in arms; he towered head and shoulders over his people, a gilded helmet on his head, and in his hand a sword of German steel. When he had halted there, the good knights of his household of whom I spoke before, with some of the brave knights of the King's division, hurled themselves into the midst of the Turks. You must know that this was a great feat of arms; for there was no shooting of arrows nor bolts; on both sides it was a fight with mace and sword, in a mixed mass of our men and the Turks (§§228–229).

Then, a bit later,

> It was said that this day we should all have been lost had it not been for the King in person; for the Lord of Courtenay and my Lord John of Saillenay told me that six Turks laid hands on the King's bridle and were dragging him off prisoner. He saved himself alone by great blows of his sword; and when his people saw how the King defended himself they took heart, and many gave up their attempt to cross the river and came back to his assistance. (§236)

Joinville repeatedly portrayed Louis as heroic, brave, and decisive and credits Louis' personal acts of bravery. Upon hearing that Muslim troops had boxed in Charles of Anjou "in the same way as a game of chess is played," Louis personally led the rescue charge. "When [Louis] heard how things were, he spurred, sword in hand, through his brother's division and flung himself so far into the Turkish ranks that his horse's crupper was caught by the Greek fire. This charge of the King's relieved the King of Sicily and his men, and they drove the Turks out of their part of the camp" (§267). Louis is also shown directing operations, as when he coordinated the construction of movable towers, ordered the construction of eighteen ballistic machines (§§192–194), determined that the covered causeway should be pushed forward (§212), or decided who of the high nobility would guard the camp (§216).

Insofar as Louis is represented as a king, it is primarily as feudal lord and military chief.[22] Early on, Louis summoned his barons to Paris to take an oath of fidelity to his children should he not return from the East—Joinville refused because he was not yet Louis' vassal (§114). Joinville described instances of Louis gathering his council together for advice, asking their opinion, and then

---

22. The issue of Louis' kingship while on crusade is discussed by Marie-Geneviève Grossel, "La sainteté à l'épreuve de la croisade: *La Vie de saint Louis* de Jehan de Joinville," *Cahiers de Recherches Médiévales (XIIe–XVe s.)* 1 (1996): 136–142.

determining the course of action regardless of the consensus; this happened on the shores outside Damietta (§149), after its capture to discuss the division of the spoils (§§167–168), during the decision whether to march on Cairo ("Babylon") or Alexandria (§183), and famously in the war council at Acre after which Louis decided to remain in the East (§§422–437). This representation of Louis as a benevolent, generous overlord (§§136, 440–441, 468) coincides primarily with Joinville's actual and practical interaction with him during their years in Egypt and the Levant and is more accidental than deliberate, a product of a recounting of his responsibilities and actions as military commander and king in these years. It does not reverence the quality of the ideal, just king of the kingship literature that is at work in the image of Louis as king in the framing, hagiographical sections.

The one place where Louis is shown as king in this traditional sense is in Joinville's discussion of "some of the sentences and judgments I heard pronounced during the king's stay at Caesarea" (§505). Joinville recounted four instances of the exercise of justice, in three of which Joinville was himself an interested party or observer. Louis, in turn, was involved in only three of these—the fourth being a matter among the Hospitallers that was adjudicated by the Master and in which Louis was uninvolved. The point was not to discuss Louis' exercise of justice per se but rather—as Joinville did so frequently throughout the core narrative—to record his acute observations on how things were and how things were done. Where Louis is involved, the aim is not really, as in the frame, to show Louis as an ideal king, and in two instances Joinville conveys clear disapproval of the way in which Louis resolved matters. In the first, Joinville requests that Louis give a confiscated horse to a poor gentleman, but Louis refuses and Joinville's comment betrays a disappointment; in the second Louis exiles the Marshal of the Temple from the Kingdom of Jerusalem (Acre), and Joinville makes it clear that everyone considered this unreasonable. Joinville is not outraged since the matter is of passing interest—but one does conclude that he would have resolved things differently if it had been up to him. To anticipate, this is wholly different from the strategy of the frame.

Likewise, the representation of Louis' piety is more complex than its pat representation in the frame. In discussing Greek fire, Joinville recalled how Louis, awakened by its assaults, would rise from bed, holding up his hands in prayer, weeping and asking God, "Dear Lord God, hold my people safe" (§207). Joinville added that he believed these prayers to have been of great help. (Given how out of place it is in what is otherwise a discussion of military operations, the fact that Joinville used the term *saint*, that he was evoking an obvious model of saintly intercession, and that this was one of the approved living miracles of Louis, one might wonder whether this episode was an editorial addition made after 1297 as Joinville was stitching together his new text.) But these explicit recollections of Louis' devotions are generally muted in the early narrative, and the portrait of his piety builds only with his captivity. This may well have to do with Joinville's own growing proximity to the king from this point onward and thus his closer appreciation of Louis' personal character. He spoke of Louis' (and his own) hardships and suffering (§397) and recounted in detail the events of the king's captivity and Louis' negotiations for his release. Joinville was struck by the humility and steadfast faith that Louis exhibited during this period, though we might note that Joinville was not actually with Louis at this time—an exception to the premise that the author recorded only things he witnessed (§768). But stories clearly swirled in the French camp about the king's ordeal afterwards (§339), and on the boat to Acre, as the two became friends, the king recounted his experience of captivity and ransom to the seneschal (§404). Joinville's depiction of Louis during this period intimates that the king was deeply demoralized, exhibiting a fatalistic attitude in the face of his captors, taking refuge in his deep faith in God (§§341, 362–363).

It is only after this point that Joinville took up Louis' habits of piety and Christian charity—his burying the bodies of dead Christians at Sidon (§582), his negotiation of the return from Egypt of the heads of Christians killed during the Egyptian campaign to be buried in consecrated ground, and the return of Christian children taken in infancy (§469).[23] Louis certainly brought with him to the Levant a desire to serve God and the Holy Land during his time there (§437), and he clearly enjoyed a reputation for his Christian charity during this period (§565–566). But stories of Louis' piety are not the priority in Joinville's narrative, and at one point Joinville even made light of the moral prestige the king had accrued. A group of Armenian pilgrims came through Acre and requested to meet the "saint-king" (*saint roy*). "Sir," said Joinville to Louis, "there is a crowd of people outside from Greater Armenia, who are on their way to Jerusalem. They are asking me, sir, to let them see the holy king; but I do not want to kiss your bones just yet" (§566).[24] Joinville's intent here was affectionate and playful, and he added that the king burst into laughter, telling Joinville to invite the group in. Here we are far from the aims and expectations of formal hagiography.

The Hagiographic Frame: Louis as Secular Saint

If in the central crusading narrative Joinville was interested in crusading and not kingship, the reverse is true of the frame. If the description of Louis' virtue is incidental in the core narrative, it is the pivot on which the frame, explicitly concerned with why Louis was a saint, turns. Here, Louis is explicitly modeled as a saint, and that sanctity is defined though his ideal, just, and Christian kingship.

In the frame, Joinville sought to fulfill the basic requirements of the hagiographical portrait, and he thus spoke of Louis' birth and upbringing, and recounted habits of piety and devotion that were part and parcel of his official sanctity. He drew on standard tropes of hagiography, such as the importance

---

23. This must have been related at the canonization proceedings because the episode made its way into the postcanonization hagiography (WSP *vie*, 100). WSP also relates in the same chapter (11: on Louis' works of pity) that he bought back Christian captives.

24. Hague translates this as "holy king." The term *saint roy* appears twice in this passage.

of holy speech and the saint's good death. He recounted Louis' miracles, the inquiry at St.-Denis (at which he testified), the canonization itself, and the invention and translation of the king's relics (§§740–759). He ended by describing how he himself built a chapel and endowed an altar with masses in honor of Louis and by piously requesting some of Louis' relics (§767).

The frame itself can be separated into the opening and the closing sections. Both are organized around short, moralizing anecdotes typical of the hagiographic genre that distinguish its tone from the core narrative. Those materials in the opening drew largely from Joinville's own experiences and memories with the king, while those in the closing section were largely drawn from and thus influenced by the hagiographic materials found in the *Grandes chroniques*, which, as Dominique Boutet has shown, Joinville accessed only later.[25] The result is that the stories at the end—where Louis is described as a patron of religious orders, sustainer of the poor, and so forth—convey him conventionally, drawing from a tradition established by and familiar from Geoffrey of Beaulieu and vetted by the canonization proceedings. He dressed modestly after his return from crusade (§667), was generous in his alms (§690), fed the poor (§§720–721), built monasteries, churches, and hospitals (§§691, 723–725, 758), patronized religious orders (§§726–729), washed the feet of the poor on Maundy Thursday (§29, §688), abhorred blasphemy and never took the name of God in vain (§§685–687). It is interesting that Joinville repeated these stories, though they tell us less about what Joinville himself thought of why Louis was a saint and perhaps more about Joinville's self-consciousness in trying to fulfill the expectations of *saintes paroles et bons faiz* (§2).

For what Joinville himself thought, it is more fruitful to look at the passages that were rooted in Joinville's own experience, the events that, in retrospect, Joinville believed revealed Louis' particular virtue.[26] In the opening frame, as Joinville worked toward the expectations of hagiography, he culled examples of Louis' sobriety (when he adds water to his wine, §22) and his love of honesty (since he refused to lie to the Saracens, §21), and his attendance at the office and the mass (§54), and practices of *imitatio Christi* (such as his washing of the feet of the poor on Maundy Thursday).[27] A series of anecdotes about the king's temperate habits (§§22–23), unflinching faith (§43), proper speech (§24), proper dress (§25), the comparative virtue of *un beguin* and *un prud'homme* (§32), status and seating arrangements (§35), and the relationship between status and dress (§36) betray Joinville's own preoccupation with status and courtly culture and seem designed to showcase a kind of human and personable yet exemplary humility that characterized Louis' relationship with the aristocrats of his court.

25. Dominique Boutet, "La méthode historique de Joinville et la réécriture des *Grandes chroniques de France*," in *Jean de Joinville: de la Champagne aux Royaumes d'outre-mer* (Langres, 1998).

26. Billson, "Joinville's Histoire."

27. For examples of Christomimetic piety, see §5, 20, 29, 39, 367, 622, 688, 757. See also Grossel, "La sainteté à l'épreuve de la croisade," 131.

Joinville included a number of stories that reveal a secular, and perhaps a layman's, perspective on Louis' sanctity. Nowhere in the hagiographical sources do we find the Louis who would reward a cleric who had murdered three of his own (miscreant) sergeants by engaging the cleric in royal service in order, Louis explained, that his officials would know that he would not shield their misdeeds (§§114–118). Elsewhere, Joinville praised Louis for abrogating to the crown certain ecclesiastical prerogatives and refusing to enforce excommunication on the basis of the bishop's authority alone (§§61–64, §§671–677). Though pious, Joinville himself did not seem to have had a cleric's knee-jerk respect for ecclesiastical authority and was reluctant to portray Louis as a servant of the church. Elsewhere Joinville recalled the king's militant approach toward the defense of the faith that may have resonated within a knightly and secular milieu. Louis told his friend of a dispute at Cluny between a knight and a Jew, which ended with the knight hitting the Jew and upbraiding the abbot for even allowing intellectual interchange with the unfaithful. Louis wasn't there, but he commented to Joinville on it: "I agree myself that no one who is not a very learned clerk should argue with them. A layman, as soon as he hears the Christian faith maligned, should defend it only by the sword, with a good thrust in the belly, as far as the sword will go" (§53).[28] Joinville included this in a series of stories about Louis' saintly sayings, but it is a striking formulation, and one perhaps indicative of a lay noble and crusader talking about the saintly virtue of another layman, crusader, and king.

Joinville's own recollections suggest that he was more impressed, not with ritual actions exemplified by Louis' devotional and ascetical practices or his dissemination of alms, but rather with Louis' deep consciousness of the state of his soul, of doing right before God, heeding the messages God sent forth to direct him, and of being conscious at all times of his relationship with God. It is in this vein that Joinville recounted Louis' famous query asking whether Joinville would rather be a leper or in a state of mortal sin (§§27–28). Twice Joinville described another event that highlighted the spirit of Louis' faith. Following the danger of possible shipwreck, Louis expressed his belief that God sends warning to men that they can heed and make amends (§§40–41, 635–637). To God Louis says "Your [that is, God's] warning, then, is not for Your profit but for our benefit, if we can turn it to good use." And then he explained to Joinville, "We should apply the warning that God has given us in such a way that if we feel that there is anything in our hearts, anything in our being, which is displeasing to God we should be quick to be rid of it; and if we think there is anything that will give Him pleasure we must hasten to set our hands to it" (§§40–41; then see also §637).

The passage may have revealed something important about Louis' spirituality, but Joinville specifically included it to set up his criticism of Philip the Fair.

---

28. This is echoed in WSP *vie*, 25 (ch. 3). LCB *procès* 97, believes WSP got the item from Joinville's testimony.

He continued: "Our present king, then, should be careful, for he has survived danger as great as that we were in, or greater. Let him mend his evil ways, that God's hand may not strike cruelly on him or on his possessions" (§42, see also §§25). By "possessions" Joinville meant the kingdom, which he warned just a few paragraphs later, through Hugh of Digne's sermon to Louis, could be lost to a king if he failed in justice.

> "To point a lesson to the King," recalled Joinville, "he [Hugh] said in a sermon that he had read both the Bible and the books which speak of infidel princes; he had never found, he said, either in Christian or infidel countries, that any Kingdom had been lost or had changed its ruler except through some offence against justice. 'The King,' he said, 'is going to France. Let him take care to give his people true and prompt justice, that Our Lord may allow him to hold his Kingdom in peace all the days of his life. . . .' The King never forgot this lesson, but governed his country in accordance with the laws and the will of God, as I shall tell you later" (§§55, 57).

The idea that possession of the kingdom is dependent on justice, which is in turn dependent on true piety, is central to Joinville's argument about Louis' saintly kingship. His very first anecdote (following the prologue) dealt with the just possession of the kingdom: the king admonished his son that he would rather the kingdom be ruled by a good and fair Scot rather than that his heir, the younger Louis (d. 1260), "should be seen by the world to govern it ill" (§21).

These are just two of several points in the frame where Joinville linked Louis' true piety directly to his just exercise of power and good rule (see also §§657–659, 689, 693). Joinville followed with a series of anecdotes about Louis' administration of justice that included the famous image of Louis dispensing justice beneath the oak at Vincennes and in the public gardens in Paris (§§57–60). In each case, the hallmark of Louis' true justice was his desire to do right and to not profit by its exercise. In the closing frame Joinville returned to this critical theme. He retold the story of Hugh of Digne's sermon at §§657–659, and then had Louis himself give his children the same lesson at §§689–693, where Louis recounted stories of good kings and good emperors whom they should take as examples, and of "wicked men of high estate, who, by their licentiousness and robberies and avarice, had lost their kingdoms" (§689). Notably, these were all Joinville's own materials and were not taken from the *Grandes chroniques*.

Indeed, the single overriding concern of the hagiographic frame is the portrayal of Louis as a just king along the lines of the theoretical literature on kingship that showed the king as the just judge, correcting evils, ensuring peace. Dominique Boutet has argued that Joinville saw Louis as fulfilling the essential elements of Augustinian kingship. To exemplify Louis' good kingship, Joinville drew on a variety of classic virtues of ideal rule: just distribution of wealth; peace, order, and prosperity in the kingdom; care and justice for the poor as well as well as for magnates; and the capacity to render judgment against one's own interest.[29] Justice itself was classically defined as giving each his due, and Louis is shown repeatedly making a just distribution of wealth and property (§§33, 34), personally administering justice and instructing his officials on how to do so properly (§§57–60), and rendering justice truly, even when directly against his own interest (§§66–67). He exhibited a deep concern for the poor and unrepresented in matters of justice. His reform of the Parisian office of provost was discussed in these terms: Louis "labored for the protection of the poor"; he sought to redress the situation whereby humbler people who were downtrodden were unable to assert their rights against the rich (§§715–718). Among kings and magnates, Louis played the role of peacemaker (§680). He ceded territory to Henry III against his own interests and the advice of his council in order to stabilize good terms (§§65–66, 679); and he negotiated peace among the magnates of his realm and among foreigners, even at his own expense (§679–684).

These themes—justice, distribution of wealth, peace and prosperity, the ability to render justice against one's own interests, concern for the poor—are all evinced in two of Louis' own works: the Great Reform Ordinance of 1254, and the *Enseignements* written to instruct his son and heir on Christian kingship.[30] With the Ordinance of 1254 Louis had sought to reform the process of justice in the kingdom and make royal officials more accountable to the ideals of good justice. The document reflected Louis' own desire to effect just kingship and establish an ideal Christian society in his own kingdom, an ideal expressed at the opening of the Ordinance, which said that royal officers "shall do justice to all men, without exception of person, to poor as well as to rich, to strangers as well as to natives, and shall keep the usages and customs that are good and proved" (§694). The other was the *Enseignements*—reflecting Louis' own ideals and evincing his deep concern for the poor, desire for peace and justice, caution against corruption, and (notably, because it is otherwise absent from Joinville's conception of kingship) respect for the church. Both had been preserved in the *Grandes chroniques,* and Joinville copied both of them out in the closing frame (§§694–714, 740–754). As evidence of Louis' desire to fulfill the precepts of Christian kingship, Joinville could do no better.

Piety, Kingship, Crusading, and Sanctity

Broadly speaking, the core of the *vie* portrays Louis' virtue in his crusades and the frame focuses on his virtuous kingship, though it would be wrong to distinguish too sharply between Louis the chivalric hero, memorialized in the 1270s or 1280s, and Louis the saintly king, set down about a decade after his canonization. Thus the saintly king of the frame exhibits some of the chivalric qualities of the *prud'homme*,[31] and the crusade leader of the central

29. Dominique Boutet, "Y a-t-il une idéologie royale dans la Vie de saint Louis de Joinville?" in *Le prince et son historien: la vie de Saint Louis de Joinville* (Paris, 1997), 71–99, esp. 75.

30. On the *Enseignements*, see O'Connell, *Teachings*; Krynen, *L'empire du roi*, 225–228.

31. As in the description of Louis at the Battle of Taillebourg of 1242 at §§98–102. Gres, "La chanson du roi Louis," 115.

narrative is described—particularly at Caesarea when he was the de facto secular authority—as king, doing justice and ensuring order. Yet there are important distinctions to be made between the overall priorities of the two different parts of the text, distinctions that relate to the difference in the purpose of each segment: feudal king vs. ideal, just king; crusader vs. peacemaker; and ultimately, man vs. saint.

First, the issue of Louis' piety and humility is treated differently in both halves. Its portrayal in the core narrative reflects Joinville's own experiences, and thus Louis' piety is mostly emphasized during his captivity in Egypt. In comparison, Joinville clearly sets out in the frame to paint a portrait of Louis as a pious layman—the *prud'homme,* an example, he says, of a layman who lived in a saintly manner (§4). The passages in the ending frame regarding his alms, his prayers, and his humility were rote, acquired from the *Grandes chroniques* and not really all that indicative of what it was that so impressed Joinville. But we have seen from passages in which Joinville drew on his own memories and impressions of Louis that what struck him most was what he understood to be Louis' sincere reverence for the awesomeness of God and his essential humility in the context of his exalted status.

Second, as discussed above, Louis as king is understood in different terms in the frame than in the core narrative. The core narrative showed Louis' kingship mostly in the way that Joinville experienced him as a king: feudal overlord and patron, leader of the crusade.[32] The frame depicted Louis as a king fulfilling the tropes laid out in a tradition of writing on ideal kingship: justice, a concern for the poor, peace. This was dealt with earlier, but the comparison is instructive because it highlights again the extent to which the core narrative constitutes Joinville's representation of the particular, the actual, the specific Louis, while the frame represents an ideal fulfilled. Put another way, the core represents the human Louis, the frame the saintly Louis.

Crusading is also valued differently in each section, if nothing else because it is essentially absent from the frame. It appears explicitly only at §§736–738 by way of setting up Louis' death, and the bulk of Joinville's treatment of Louis' second crusade constituted his transcription of his lessons to his son (the *Enseignements*), which served more as evidence of Louis' pious kingship than the crusade. Joinville's famous refusal to join Louis on the crusade of Tunis, and his harsh criticism of those who encouraged the venture, suggests a deep ambivalence for the enterprise, at least in 1269–1270 (§§736–737). Indicatively, he spoke of Louis' last crusade as a failure of kingship: "I thought that all who advised him to go," wrote Joinville, "committed a mortal sin, for while he was still in France the whole Kingdom enjoyed peace at home and with all its neighbors, but after his departure its condition grew constantly worse" (§736). The one place where Louis' sanctity is explicitly formulated in terms of his crusading is in

32. For a different conclusion on the representation of kingship in the central narrative, see Maureen Slattery, *Myth, Man and Sovereign Saint: King Louis IX in Jean de Joinville's Sources* (New York, 1985), 39–60.

the prologue, written last of all, after Joinville had stitched together the core and frame into a single work.[33] This seems to be a retrofitting of the central narrative to hagiographic ends and a reinterpretation of the crusades within the context of saintly portraiture. Joinville made two arguments here. First, he suggested that Louis suffered and died on crusade as did Christ and should thus have been canonized a martyr.[34] The argument was striking and accorded with the priorities of hagiography and sanctity as they had developed over the course of the thirteenth century. It also functioned to place the existing narrative and the failure of Louis' two crusades within a book designed to showcase his sanctity. It was, however, a thorny formulation, since it suggested that those who died on crusade were martyrs and thus saints, threatening to dilute the particular value of the extraordinary personal virtue of someone like Louis. One way or another, it is also worth noting that there is no hint of this interpretation in the narrative itself.[35]

In another way, too, the prologue introduced an interpretation of Louis' crusading that the narrative itself addressed in different terms. In the prologue Joinville argued that while on the crusade Louis repeatedly risked his own life for the sake of his people. In this way Joinville justified incorporating the account of Louis' "great deeds of knighthood and of his high courage" with instances from the crusade in which he "risked death that he might save his people from harm" (§5). He picked out four events from the central narrative—(1) jumping into the sea fully armed outside Damietta, (2) refusing to take a ship back to Damietta during the retreat from Mansourah, (3) the four years in which he left himself exposed to attack while in Acre, and finally, (4) remaining on board the ship outside Cyprus after it had hit ground. Christopher Lucken makes the apt point that each episode is an instance in which Louis refuses the counsel of his advisors out of concern for his people.[36] It might also be noted that in the first and third incidents, the narrative itself does not accord with the interpretation proffered in the prologue—an episode in which Louis risked his life for his people—suggesting that these episodes were originally written with different aims in mind.[37] The conceptualization of self-sacrifice in the prologue,

33. On the prologue, see Dominique Boutet, "Ordre, désordre et paradoxe dans le prologue et l'épilogue de la *Vie de Saint Louis* de Joinville [Essay]," in *"Si a parlé par moult ruiste vertu": mélanges de littérature médiévale offerts à Jean Subrenat* (Paris, 2000), 73–81.

34. Although note that in §760, Joinville says that pope and the cardinals "did him justice and numbered [Louis] among the confessors." On this question, see Smith, "Martyrdom"; Smith, *Crusading*, 144; and Grossel, "La sainteté à l'épreuve de la croisade," 142–146. I discuss it also in M. Cecilia Gaposchkin, "The Role of the Crusades in the Sanctification of Louis IX of France," in *Crusades: Medieval Worlds in Conflict* (Burlington, Vt., forthcoming).

35. Perrot has argued that the ransom negotiations (§§334–385) exhibit the tropes of passion literature ("Le 'péché' de Joinville," 196–198). Because I interpret this section differently, I am inclined to see echoes of the passion themes as the influence of popular hagiography generally on the interpretation of experience rather than as an explicit hagiographical device.

36. Lucken, "L'èvangile du Roi," 445–467.

37. For the first episode, see §§7–8, then §149; for the second episode, see §§9–10, then §306; for the third episode, see §§11–12, then (for the entire stay in the Levant) §§406–692. Only the fourth episode accords with its presentation in the prologue (§§13–15, 628–629).

it seems to me, was part of Joinville's efforts to make his heroic crusader chronicle into a saint's life, of Joinville's thinking about how Louis' chivalric behavior on crusade provided evidence of his saintly character, of working his preexisting crusade narrative into his hagiographic frame. In so doing, Joinville emphasized above all Louis' self-sacrificing devotion to his subjects. That is, even here the crusades are modeled in terms of the obligations of kingship.

The shift in the representation of Louis may have less to do with an evolution in Joinville's own memories than it does with his differing intent in writing each section and the expectations and priorities of the hagiographical genre that he was striving toward in ca. 1305. It certainly reflects his attempt to incorporate the ideals of sanctity and the priorities of hagiography that had been modeled by a process of official sanctification that had (in its written form) been shaped by clerical authorship. And yet, as I argue in the first chapter, we can discern in that process the interpretation of sanctity by a secular elite that participated (along with Joinville) in the canonization proceedings. That interpretation drew heavily on the memory of Louis as the just king who was, in judging and ruling, able to separate his own interests from those of true justice. Joinville's frame represents this view directly articulated. He may have written of Louis attending mass and building churches, but, like the other nobility who testified with him in 1282 and whose stories were recapped in William of Saint-Pathus' seventeenth chapter on justice, what impressed Joinville more was Louis' conduct as king, his immunity to the influence of status or family, and his ability to serve an overarching ideal of divine justice through the guidance of true piety.

This view may reflect the perspective developed during the early years of the fourteenth century in a political landscape increasingly dominated by Capetian authority and the person of Philip the Fair. In this work commissioned by Philip's wife and dedicated to his son, Joinville explained explicitly that his book ought be used as an exemplum for the future Louis X and his brothers (§18). Joinville claimed, famously, that Louis' descendants needed to work to live up to the model of Louis' kingship. Commenting on the event of Louis' canonization, Joinville wrote,

> For this there was, and should still be, great rejoicing throughout the Kingdom of France; great will be the honour to all those of his house who strive to resemble him in well doing, and great the reproach to all those who refused to imitate him in good works; great reproach, I say, to those of his house who seek to do ill, for fingers will be pointed at them and it will be said that the holy king from whom they are sprung would have scorned to do such wrong (§761).

In the first decade of the fourteenth century, as Joinville penned this stinging rebuke, the import and interpretation of Louis' sanctity was by no means a settled issue. Though Joinville sought to produce a reliable hagiography by drawing on the canonization materials, he was also, in the frame, staking out a particular interpretation of Louis, an interpretation that was part of an ongoing dynamic in these years among those who would appropriate Louis' sanctity to devotional and political ends. Joinville understood that sanctity to be

rooted in Louis' kingship and the qualities of justice and piety that underpinned his governance and his relations with his subjects. On one hand, then,
the *vie* represented an essential (and perhaps classically aristocratic) devotion
to the ideal of monarchy and the expectations of a *rex christianisissimus*. But
on the other, it arrogated that image to Joinville's own concerns, defining it in
terms of justice and its obligations to the noble class. In any event Joinville
flatly rejected Philip the Fair's claim that Louis' sanctity confirmed the inherent
and inherited sanctity of the Capetian line.

Saint Louis thus emerged into the political sphere as part of the vocabulary
of kingship. The potency of the symbol of Louis was tested only a few years
later, when leagues of noblemen formed throughout France to protest Philip
the Fair's levy for his war with Flanders. Joinville had warned, in the *vie*, that
the king risked losing his kingdom if he offended justice through avarice and
failed the laws of the country and the will of God. When, in November 1314,
Champenois noblemen, among whom Joinville, now aged, was an elder statesman, gathered, they hailed Saint Louis as their standard of conduct and rule.
The Leagues repeatedly made recourse to Louis, articulating their demands in
terms of a return to the good customs, moneys, and laws of Saint Louis.[38]
They deployed the symbol of Saint Louis in much the same way Joinville had
in the *vie*, and with Joinville, they flipped the notion of lineage around to challenge the crown's prerogatives. Philip, nearing his death, yielded later that
year. He rescinded the levy and promised to return the specie to its value during the time of his saintly grandfather. And when, in May of the following
year, Philip's son and successor, Louis X—the selfsame Louis to whom
Joinville had finally dedicated the *vie*—sought accommodation with the nobility, he renewed, en masse, the ordinances issued by Saint Louis, pledged a return to the specie of Saint Louis, consulted the registers of Saint Louis for
precedent, and, as king, promised to honor the customs of the "temps le saint
roy Loys."[39] He, too, had been reminded of the obligations of his descent from
Saint Louis, and in the ordinance of 1315, Louis X acknowledged both this
descent and this new standard, and recalled the time of "St Louis, nostre
bisayeul."[40] At this moment, it was Joinville's Saint Louis that prevailed.

---

38. For Joinville's participation, see Delaborde, *Jean de Joinville*, 159–161. The standard account of the Leagues is Artonne, *Le mouvement de 1314 et les chartres provinciales de 1315*,
51–52. For the League's many references to the time of Saint Louis, see 51–52, 65, 68, 87–88,
103–107, 113, 116, 141, 167, 171–172, 174, 176, 183, 186–187, 199–202, 206, 214; and
Brown, "Reform," 109–137.
39. Artonne, *Le mouvement de 1314*, 104–107, 172.
40. *Ordonnances*, 1, 574.

8

Private Devotion, Saintly Lineage, and Dynastic Sanctity

Though Joinville may have marshaled Saint Louis to his criticism of Philip the Fair, Louis' canonization gave Philip and his successors a preeminent symbol of Capetian sacral authority and historical prestige. Scions of Louis were often mindful of their descent from the saint-king and exhibited particular devotion to him. Louis X (d. 1316) owned four *cahiers* of Saint Louis. Mahaut of Artois (d. 1329) purchased an "Hours of Saint Louis." When Charles V (d. 1380), during the first century of Valois rule, established the royal library in 1371, his collection included seven copies of either Louis' *vita, vita et miracula*, or simply his *miracula* (all probably those of William of St.-Pathus), several stand-alone copies of the office (*service saint Loys, roy de France, noté*), and he kept both a copy of the Hours of Louis and a prose Life of Louis with him at all times.[1] The *Petites Heures* of his brother, Jean, Duc de Berry (d. 1416), opened with a copy of the *Enseignements*, Louis' instructions on Christian kingship written for his son.[2] Within this dynastic and devotional context, Louis represented the duties and obligations of kingship as much as an exaltation of the royal status.

Because of this emphasis on the ethical demands of Christian kingship the memory of Louis thus served to remind, or even instruct, the kings of France in royal virtue. Louis was imagined as a compassionate king, who loved the poor and the sick, did good works, gave alms, and ultimately served Christendom

---

1. On these examples, see Joan Holladay, "Fourteenth-Century French Queens as Collectors and Readers of Books: Jeanne d'Evreux and Her Contemporaries," *Journal of Medieval History* 32 (2006): 92–96. Léopold Delisle, *Recherches sur la librarie de Charles V*, 2 and Atlas vols. (Paris, 1907), 49–50, nos. 278–279, 153–155, nos. 935–943 and 947. For reference to the king's habits, see Delisle, vol. 2, 154, no. 936, "Le Roy l'a devers soy." See also 57, no. 325 and 59, no. 335 for the *Enseignements*.

2. Avril, Dunlop, and Yapp, *Petites Heures*, 66–67.

through crusade. In this tradition, the mendicant strand of charity and devotion that operated in the early vitas reemerged within the context of saintly royal behavior, and Louis became the model for saintly kingship, and ultimately, queenship as well. Gábor Klaniczay has argued that the religious virtues of the thirteenth century exemplified by the mendicants influenced the typology of royal sanctity.[3] This ability to model Louis according to virtues of humility and compassionate kingship offered one solution to the tension between saintly piety and glorious rule, and it showed how the changes in sanctity that had occurred over the course of the thirteenth century and had allowed both women and laymen increased access to the ranks of the saints, allowed Louis the king to be modeled within the context of a sanctity heavily influenced by the spirituality exemplified in Saint Francis. Prizing charity over justice, it also allowed Louis' sanctity to take on the hue of virtues associated with royal women.

Louis' fulfillment of the requirements of Christian kingship had a legitimizing edge as well. The relationship between Louis' virtue and the virtue of his descendants underscored the role he came to play in the dynastic context, which, in the two generations following Philip the Fair's death, was increasingly an issue of concern and anxiety. When the Capetian line died out with the last of Philip's sons in 1328, it was direct descent from Louis that paved the way for Philip VI, "Valois," to take the throne. The memory of Louis was thus used in negotiating the politics of dynastic rupture, whereby Louis was recalled both as the model of French kingship and as the proof of its virtue, and Louis became a sanctifier of the Capetian, Angevin, and Valois lineage. Louis thus often served as the anchor in a discussion of legitimacy which melded descent, virtue, sanctity, and royal authority for the Angevins and then, after 1328, the Valois.

The Translation Office (*Exultemus Omnes*)

In 1306, when Philip finally succeeded, after almost a decade, in translating the head relic of his sainted grandfather to the royal chapel, a new feast was instituted which was entrusted to the Augustinians. At some point—maybe in 1306, maybe somewhat later—a new liturgical office was composed. This office, *Exultemus omnes*, addressed Louis' descendants directly, and its principal themes were threefold: Louis as an example for his royal descendants, charitable kingship, and the crusades. The memory of the translation was centered on the Ste.-Chapelle, built by Louis himself and associated with his memory, which now housed the new relics (in a luxurious golden reliquary Philip had had fashioned). The office was confected for the Ste.-Chapelle,[4] and the manuscripts suggest an otherwise limited dissemination (Notre Dame of Paris,[5] and perhaps some of the parish churches right near the palace—all we know is that they are

---

3. Klaniczay, *Holy Rulers*, 195–294.
4. BNF Lat 911, fols. 35v.–37v. See also Arsenal 114, 142r.–v., for the instructions for the feast in the only surviving ordinary of the chapel, which indicate that the feast will be celebrated by the Augustinians.
5. Arsenal 660, Mazarine 345, BNF Lat 746a. See Leroquais, *Bréviaires*, vol. 2, 353, 367, 426.

"Paris usage"),[6] but the office is also preserved in at least two breviaries made for members of the royal court.[7] A shorter ritual (as a simplex feast), the office included only three responsories and lections. It was composed by using matins responsories taken from *Nunc laudare*, and composing a number of new hymns, antiphons, and lections. It makes several direct references to the translation and the specifically royal locale, including what seems to be a singular dig at St.-Denis. "By the body of whom Denis is amply enriched, his head now joyously graces Paris."[8] In some ways the office echoed the sacralizing *Ludovicus decus*, adopting royalizing items from it and its predecessor *Nunc laudare* and including chant items such as one which spoke of Louis "sitting in the judge's seat, driving away wickedness."[9] Yet the office and the feast contained an intimate and familiar tone and message that negotiated the tension between Louis' saintly glory and the model of good kingship that he came to represent.

The opening prayers of first vespers were newly composed for the Translation office, and addressed Louis' *successores,* the *reges francie.*[10] The chant texts spoke of how he gloriously ruled the earthly kingdom, serving Christ and the poor, striving to be a servant of God; how he never abandoned equity and truth, sought to have an "upright character," and "directed his successors toward God." The last antiphon for vespers exclaimed that "Saint Louis guided [*direxit*] the kings of France with the splendor of his conscience; having become a friend of God, the kingdom of glory is now his home."[11] The link between Louis and his royal successors was reinforced by the notion, predating the reign of Louis IX, that virtue begat virtue among the kings of France, that the sanctity of the Capetians "pertained to birth, not to office," and "that virtue was inherited."[12] A poem written shortly after 1270 lamenting the death of Louis IX and celebrating his piety, charity, love of the poor, humility, and simplicity exclaimed that since the trunk (*cime*) is now dead, the branch will now have to reign,[13] and by 1300 an anonymous vita was able to speak of Louis as the *rex christianissimus* who was "linearly descended from the royal *stirps* of the French," and that "since the good tree bears good fruit," Saint Louis inherited his father's "knowledge of truth, right justice of severity, and abundance of piety,"[14] the very virtues celebrated in the vespers hymn. Ecclesiasticus 8:10 had warned that "a kingdom is translated from one people to another, because of injustices, and wrongs, and injuries, and diverse deceits," and, as in the case of Joinville to Philip the Fair,

6. Mazarine 342, BNF Lat 911, BNF Lat 1024, BNF Lat 1291, BNF Lat 14511. See Leroquais, *Bréviaires*, vol. 2, 363, 476; vol. 3, 136–137.

7. BNF Lat 1052, BNF Lat 13233. See Leroquais, *Bréviaires*, vol. 3, 49. 235. Note that none of these manuscripts dates to before the second half of the fourteenth century. It is therefore possible that the office was not composed in 1306 but rather at a later date.

8. EO MA1.

9. EO LH2.

10. EO VA4–5.

11. EO VA5.

12. Lewis, *Royal Succession*, 122–133, quote at 123. Lewis argues that this strand of thought is augmented under Louis. See also Baldwin, *Philip Augustus*, 355–393.

13. Villeneuve, *Saint Louis*, vol. 3, 676.

14. RHF, vol. 23, 167–176.

Capetians were reminded that bad kings (or their descendants) might lose their kingdoms.[15] It is in this sense that the translation liturgy was admonitory, instructive, and prescriptive of virtuous kingship, calling Louis the model (*norma*) of sanctity for kings.[16]

The office thus emphasized the actions and obligations of Christian kingship. A pervading theme of the translation chant was Louis' care and protection of the infirm and weak. The office adopted those items from *Nunc laudare* that emphasized the king's compassionate service. His "lavish relief of the poor," "his equal judgment of truth," and the "quiet protection of the king" were the "evidence of the pious king's sanctity."[17] He scattered riches to the poor, despised luxury, cared for many sick, and championed the poor with singular zeal.[18] The hymns for matins made reference to Louis' "indulgence to the infirm and feeble, not denying favor to those needy people."[19] The central of the three lections was devoted to Louis' acts of compassionate patronage, including his building of monasteries and hospitals, his personal ministration of the sick, and his care of lepers. "He constructed many monasteries and hospitals for the poor; personally visiting in those places the infirm and those in bed, and he ministered food to them with his own hands, on bended knee. Further, he is known to have devoutly served certain lepers in the service of his great humility."[20] The August 25 octave, written at about the same time for the Ste.-Chapelle, included an antiphon that praised Louis as "the founder of pious alms by caring for the poor."[21] A prayer for Louis borrowed from the Franciscans praised him for exulting the spirits of the poor and the rich alike.[22] Another new text praised Louis by referring to the miracles Louis performed after his death, tying his aid of the oppressed to miracles that aided the sick and wearied: "eyes of the blind, walking staff of the feeble, shield of the oppressed, hammer of the perverse, nourisher of the lesser people [*minorum*], have pity on the people eager to praise you."[23] This last indicates an attempt to make the Ste.-Chapelle into a cult center, evidenced by the fact that Philip secured indulgences for anyone who came to the Ste.-Chapelle on Louis' feast day.[24]

15. Eccli. 10:8. The passage was quoted by John of Salisbury at IV.12: John of Salisbury, *Policraticus*, trans. Cary J. Nederman (Cambridge, 1990), 61. See also Vincent of Beauvais, *De morali principis*, xxv–xxvi, 229–29, and my thanks to Elizabeth A. R. Brown for this reference; Joinville §55 and §659; and Lewis, *Royal Succession*, 131, and 280, no. 128, where he notes other Capetian sources.

16. EO MA2.

17. EO MRV2.

18. EO MRV3, also used at VCapRV, EO VA2.

19. EO MH4.

20. The full lections can be found in the editions for the books of hours that adopted these lections. See appendix 1. BNF Lat 911, 36v.: "Plura monasteria et pauperum hospitalia construxit, infirmos et decumbentes inibi visitando personaliter, et manibus propriis ac flexo genu eis cibaria ministrando. Post autem humilitatis immense ministerium, leprosis quibusdam legitur impendisse."

21. LDR OA8.

22. LDR OA2 = FR VMag.

23. LDR OA5.

24. Vidier, *Le Trésor*, 302–303 (no. 35), 316–320 (nos. 51–53).

The Translation office thus presented Louis as a king, but one whose *behavior* as king qualified him as a saint. In this, it echoed the kind of didactic kingship literature that emanated from the court, commissioned for the edification of kings, which aimed at fostering good rule through a rigorous training of Christian education. The emphasis placed on Louis' care and protection of the weak highlighted the importance of moral guardianship in the medieval vision of rulership.[25] This was the principal message of a number of the Specula Principum ("mirrors for princes") written for the Capetians in this period. One of the most important was that by Guibert of Tournai, a Franciscan master at the University of Paris, who completed the *Eruditio regum et principum* for Louis IX in 1259.[26] The tract took the form of three letters written to Louis and presented the four qualities "necessary in a ruler": reverence in the face of God (in the first letter), discipline of the self and discipline of officers of the kingdom (in the second), and affection and protection for his subjects (in the third). Of the four imperatives (the second letter listed two), all but the third (discipline of officers) were echoed in the Translation office. Guibert's third letter on love and protection of subjects was described in terms of the justice of the king, the essential element of which was the protection of the poor. The opening of the letter also spoke of the king both as the avenger of iniquity (*ultor iniquitatis*—the translation liturgy called Louis the *ultor malorum* and says that he never abandoned the good of *equitatis*)—and the father of the poor (quoting Job, *pater eram pauperum*).[27] Guibert quoted St. Gregory, "In the exercise of charity, the pursuit of mercy becomes a faculty of nature, so that one might look upon those people with love, as if like sons, over whom, like a father, he was placed for their protection."[28]

The image of the pious and charitable Louis constituted one strand of memorialization at the court. Phillip III's death announcement of 1270 had spoken of Louis as the father of the poor, the refuge of the wretched, and the solace of the oppressed.[29] These themes were echoed in associated imagery. Two of the four images on the lost altar retable in the lower chapel of the Ste.-Chapelle depicted Louis washing the feet of the poor and feeding the leprous monk at Royaumont—two of the most emblematic images in the iconographic corpus.[30] (See figure 16 for the latter.) The only two references to Louis in a Dominican *Speculum principis* written for Louis X entitled the *Liber de informacione principum* made reference to Louis' ministration to the poor as an example of a *rex magnificus*, and to Louis' love of and support of churches, monasteries, temples,

25. A theme emphasized in John Dickinson, "The Medieval Conception of Kingship and Some of Its Limitations, as Developed in the *Policraticus* of John of Salisbury," *Speculum* 1 (1926): 320–321. See also overviews of authors' positions in Born, "Perfect Prince."

26. Guibert de Tournai, *Eruditio regum et principum*; Krynen, *L'empire du roi*, 170.

27. EO Mag; EO VA3. For VA3, the manuscripts read variously "limina equitatis"(BNF Lat 14511), "limam equitatis" (BNF Lat 746A, Arsenal 660), or "bonam equitatis" (BNF Lat 911, BNF Lat 1024). For Guibert de Tournai, see *Eruditio regum et principum*, 83.

28. Gregory I, *Moralia in Job*, ch. 24, vol. 16; *PL* vol. 76, p. 124.

29. Guérard, ed., *Cartulaire*, vol. 1, 190–191.

30. Louvre, *Trésor* 190–192, no. 45, with color plates.

Figure 5. Louis ministers to the sick. Manuscript, Jean Pucelle, French, active in Paris, ca. 1320–1334. The Hours of Jeanne d'Evreux, New York, Metropolitan Museum of Art, The Cloisters Collection (54.1.2), fol. 142v. (By permission of the New York Metropolitan Museum of Art.)

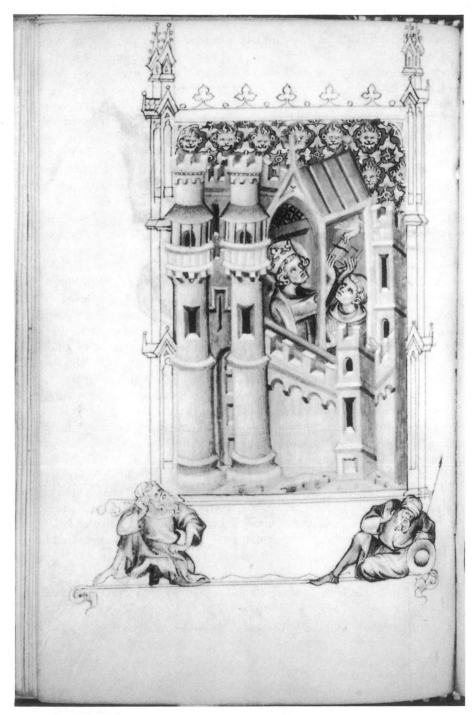

Figure 6. Breviary miracle. Manuscript, Jean Pucelle, French, active in Paris, ca. 1320–1334. The Hours of Jeanne d'Evreux, New York, Metropolitan Museum of Art, The Cloisters Collection (54.1.2), fol. 155. (By permission of the New York Metropolitan Museum of Art.)

and hospitals. It spoke of how Louis sent in secret many alms to "impoverished knights, shield-bearers, ladies, widows, and all other sorts of modest poor" in order to both protect their modesty and alleviate their needs. Louis wandered through monasteries of the religious poor and visited hospitals, and he would give alms according to need. He clothed the naked, fed the hungry, supported young men's studies, and found husbands for poor girls.[31] In this sense, Louis was not just a symbol of Capetian sacral authority but a model to Capetian kings of Capetian virtue and a reminder about their obligations of compassion and care.

Another theme was Louis' crusading. The crusades as the sacral duty to do the work of Christendom and the church in this context represented a preeminent obligation of kingship and emblematic of the duty of a most Christian king (*rex christianissimus*). It made sense to celebrate Louis for his crusades at the Ste.-Chapelle, which, more than any other place in Philip's France, envisualized Louis' crusading aspiration and commitment to the Holy Land.[32] The vespers hymn spoke of how "twice for the Christian faith he crossed the sea, he whom the impious people led to grave captivity, which he endured with humility."[33] The hymn for lauds made reference to his taking the cross, his capture by the infidel, and the miracle of the dashed ship, where Louis' prayers were widely believed to have saved the vessel from sinking. The lauds hymn spoke further of his faithfulness on crusade "After having taken up the cross, captured by infidels, he worshiped God with devout attention to his words and deeds."[34] The office also adopted *Ludovicus decus'* oblique reference to the king's captivity.[35]

The crusading theme was also emphasized in the lections written for the Translation office, which began with the first crusade, the capture of Damietta, and Louis' capture by the enemy. With God's permission, the lection explained, the sultan was killed by his own men, and the king liberated, "but not without the help of a divine miracle."[36] The lections continued the crusading narrative, recounting the agonies Louis endured for Christ, and the virtuous deeds he performed overseas. A short description of Louis' deeds of charity and faith in France was followed by the tale of his saintly death, set against the backdrop of the crusade to Tunis. At the hour of Louis' death, he repeated the words that Christ is known to have uttered at His death: "Lord, into thy hand I commend my spirit,"[37] and Louis rendered his spirit unto his creator. In 1306 this

31. BNF Lat 16622, fol 34r., and 41r. Chapter 26 of the Speculum is entitled "Rex debet esse magnificus (33v.). See also Léopold Delisle, "Anonyme: Auteur du *Liber de informatione principium*," in HLF, vol. 31, 35–47; and Krynen, *L'empire du roi*, 188–191.

32. Daniel Weiss, "Architectural Symbolism and the Decoration of the Ste.-Chapelle," *Art Bulletin* 77 (1995): 308–320; Weiss, *Art and Crusade*, 11–77.

33. EO VH3–4.

34. EO LH4.

35. LDR Sext = EO Sext.

36. BNF Lat 911, 36v.: "Cumque ad partes ultramarinas venisset, post damiete captionem ab exercitu christiano, subsecuta ipsius exercitus generali egritudine. In manu soldani et sarracenorum incidit, illo permittente qui de malis bona novit elicere et facere cum temptatione proventum. Nam soldano ipso cito post a suis interempto predictus rex fuit non sine divini ut pie creditur operatione miraculi, liberatus."

37. BNF Lat 911, 37r.: "In manus tuas domine commendo spiritum meum."

emphasis may have reflected the renewed enthusiasm for crusading at the royal court, during which Philip entertained the idea of abdicating the throne for his eldest son and leading a united effort to recapture the Holy Land.[38] Although Philip's personal commitment to crusading may be questioned, his interest in guaranteeing the close association between the French crown, leadership of crusade, and the defense of Christendom as part of the obligations and prestige of the most Christian kings cannot. In this climate, Philip's already considerable devotion to Louis was filtered through crusader-colored glasses, and alongside Louis the "king-saint" appeared Louis the "crusader saint." Louis' crusades, even in their failure, were celebrated as part of the obligations and prestige of Capetian kingship.

The version of the lections that survive in most copies of the office is actually an abbreviated form of the original text that was composed ca. 1306.[39] In the text's original form, the lections tied together Louis' crusading, his miracles, his canonization, Philip's original elevation of the relics at St.-Denis, his translation of the head relic to the Ste.-Chapelle, and finally the symbolism of the head of the saint-king at the palace chapel. In other words, the text couched Louis' sanctity and sanctification squarely in terms of the history of Philip's reign. Following the discussion of Louis' crusades, life, and death, the second lection covered the canonization (accorded by Boniface VIII, whose name is elided in one version of the text) and the authenticity of the miracles. The original second lection took pains to talk about the role the cardinals played in determining the validity of Louis' miracles and sanctity—perhaps reflecting discomfiture felt in 1306 at the fact that the canonization had been effected by the court's now principal enemy, Boniface VIII. The final lection commemorated important miracles (including resuscitating two from the dead, and one in Philip's own presence), and Philip's own role in the translation, referring to his present reign and explicitly recalling his descent from Louis. Finally, the lection tied Louis' own reverence for the Dominical signs of the passion and his building of the Ste.-Chapelle with the translation of his own head back to the palace chapel. It read:

> However, when he was leading his mortal life, this saint always held particular and zealous devotion for the sacrosanct symbols of the Lord's Passion and other relics, which he collected together in the palace chapel in Paris with great reverence. On account of this and so that the devotion of the faithful should be increased toward Him, the Lord sent into the heart of the king that the venerable head of the saint should be transferred to the same chapel with all due solemnity by an assembly of prelates and princes brought together for this purpose. Upon

38. This observation about the lections was made by Elizabeth A. R. Brown in a paper given at the Metropolitan Museum of Art in 1999 on the event of the exposition of the *Hours of Jeanne d'Evreux*. On the later crusades, see Joseph R. Strayer, "The Crusade against Aragon," *Speculum* 28 (1953): 102–113; Sylvia Schein, "Philip IV and the Crusade: A Reconsideration," in *Crusade and Settlement*, ed. Peter W. Edbury (Cardiff, 1985), 122; and Brown, "The Prince," 296.

39. BNF Lat 14511, fols. 179r.–182r.; the lections are found on 180r.–v. This text was incorporated into *Glor. reg.* at Rooklooster in the fifteenth century and thus must have been somewhat more broadly distributed than this single manuscript suggests.

consideration, he further deemed it fitting that, where the head of the entire king-dom of France is, there the head of the one who was gloriously in charge of and of benefit to the French shall forever be worshipped with great reverence and continual veneration.[40]

An edited version of this formulation was incorporated as the final lection into some versions of the shortened lections.[41] The text emphasized Philip's own role in the veneration of Louis and the translation, as well as the importance of the lineage. But most of all, the imagery of Louis' head resting in the palace, which was the head of the kingdom, echoed language Philip had used in corre-spondence with the pope in 1306, and it reflected the bold propaganda of the palace as the sacralized "head" of the kingdom that the court was formulating at the time.

Books of Hours and the "Hours of Louis" (*Sanctus Voluntatem*)

The importance of Louis in defining the virtues and qualities of the royal lineage, and the attraction he held as a devotional focus, can be seen in the Books of Hours that include the rare liturgical Hours of Louis, *Sanctus voluntatem*. The Louis-Hours must have been originally produced at the royal court of the future Charles IV (r. 1322–1328). Elizabeth A. R. Brown has ar-gued that the earliest surviving exemplar of the office—New York Public Li-brary Spencer 56 (not the earliest copy)—was probably given to Blanche of Burgundy for her prayers by either her mother (Mahaut of Artois) or her then husband (Charles IV). Charles was therefore at the center, in the 1310s and 1320s, of the production of this text, since soon after he gave to his next and last wife, Jeanne d'Evreux, the volume that includes the most famous exem-plar of the office.

Sanctus voluntatem survives in only six known volumes, all but one associ-ated with women related to Louis. That said, the Hours of Louis were doubt-less more common than the volumes that survive would indicate. An item in the royal accounts of 1313 referred, for instance, to a series of "Hours for Saint Louis" that were acquired for Louis of Navarre (future Louis X) by his confessor, Imbert of Louvel OP.[42] We know that among Mahaut of Artois'

---

40. BNF Lat 14511, fol. 180r.–v.: "Sanctus autem iste dum vitam in humanis ageret ad sacro-sancta dominice passionis insignia ceterasque reliquias, quas parisius in capellam palacii, cum summa reverencia collocaverat, sedulam semper et specialem devotionem habebat. Ob hoc igitur et ut fidelium augereter ad eum devotio in cor regis misit dominus ut ad capellam ipsam veneran-dum dicti sancti caput cum omni solempnitate quam fieri debet merito in talibus convocatione generali prelatorum & principum ob hoc facta specialiter transferretur. Decens siquidem esse con-siderate conspexit, ut ubi caput est tocius regni francie, ibi caput illius qui francis tam gloriose pre-fuit & profuit, cum ingenti reverencia, iugi veneratione in perpetuum colleretur."

41. BNF Lat 746A, 297r., and BNF Lat 1291, 113r. Both are fifteenth-century breviaries rep-resenting the Parisian sanctorale.

42. Fawtier, *Comptes royaux*, vol. 2, 773, no. 27677. The confessor was Imbert (Wybert) of Louvel, on whom see de la Selle, *Service des âmes*, 266–267.

books was an *"heures de Saint-Loys"*[43] and that Charles V also owned several *"heures saint Loys."*[44] In any event, four of the six known volumes contain some of the finest examples of late Gothic miniature painting from this period, and four of them were produced for descendants of Louis IX. This testifies to the central role played by the Capetian family as the locus and driving force behind much of Louis' cult. The rubric with which the Savoy hours introduced the cycle underscored the importance of Louis in valorizing the piety and sanctity of members of the Capetian line: "Here begin the Hours of Sir Saint Louis, king of France, suitable for being recited each day by those who bear especial devotion to him, particularly by persons who are of such a saintly and very noble line as that of France."[45]

These volumes belonged to the new and increasingly popular genre of private devotional books known as books of hours, which allowed elite laymen and women to engage in cycles of sacralizing daily prayer in imitation of the clergy. Having grown out of a secondary service in the monastic hours (the Little Office of the Blessed Virgin), the services found in books of hours used by the laity were structured differently from their ecclesiastical counterparts. By the later Middle Ages, this cycle of prayer constituted the heart of books of hours, and as new cycles were added to the new genre (for instance, the Hours of Louis), these adopted the format of the Little Hours.[46] Consequently, although many of the texts of the Louis-Hours (*Sanctus voluntatem*) derived from earlier sources, the requirements of the office's structure were different, needing, for instance, seven instead of three hymns, eight instead of one oration, and so forth. What this meant in practice was that the organizer adopted or incorporated the chants, hymns, and texts from earlier offices but reorganized them substantially and composed a litany of new items. The texts of the office were largely derived from the Translation office and the early Dominican *Nunc laudare*. The three (shorter) lections of the Translation office, with its related responsories (and its emphasis on the crusades and on charity), were adopted directly. Its three hymns were also incorporated, and nine antiphons for matins were adopted from *Nunc laudare* that lent the Hours strongly regal flavor. Then a series of entirely new texts were composed, principally the eight entreaties (*orationes*) of the new office, and a number of new hymns. The reading for none included a reference to "Louis' justice [which] was always linked with virtue and mercy."[47] Terce spoke of how Louis, "while still a

43. Richard, *Petite nièce*, 104.
44. Delisle, *Recherches*, vol. 2, 43, no. 247, 50, nos. 280–282.
45. Ibid., vol. 1, 210; Paul Durrieu, "Notice d'un des plus importants livres de prières du roi Charles V, Les Heures de Savoie ou 'Très belles grandes heures' du roi," *Bibliothèque de l'École des Chartes* 72 (1911): 510: "Ci commencent les heures Monseigneur saint Loys, roy de France, convenable à dire tous les jours à ceulz qui ont especial devotion à lui, mesmement à personnes qui sont de si sainte et de si très noble lignié comme est celle de France."
46. Roger S. Wieck, *Time Sanctified: The Book of Hours in Medieval Art and Life* (New York, 1988); Wieck, *Painted Prayers: The Book of Hours in Medieval and Renaissance Art* (New York, 1997).
47. SV None.

youth, attended to his conscience. Always growing in virtue, he became king of France."[48] Compline, the last service of the day, praised Louis for confessing humbly and sacramentally to the Lord, then performing many miracles. New hymns for none and compline spoke of the breviary miracle, Louis' hatred of dicing, his refusal to knight a Saracen, and his *Enseignements*. The reference to Louis' outlawing of gaming is interesting since the line itself—*ludos vincens Ludovicus*, Louis, conquering play—did a play-on-words of Louis' own name.[49]

The Hours adopted the standard collect that spoke of Louis' transfer from the earthly to the heavenly kingdom and the hope for his successful intercession on the supplicant's behalf. New orations were included that reformulated these two basic ideas, underscoring Louis' especial relationship to God at the same time it affirmed his special relationship to the governance of the French kingdom. Drawing on the incipits of the standard sequences in the Roman office, the oration for none ran, "We beg, o Lord, may the prayers of your blessed confessor Louis, for us, come to our aid, Louis whom you conducted from the concerns (*cura*) of the terrestrial kingdom to the court (*curia*) of the heavenly kingdom."[50] This theme of Louis' transference from the temporal to the celestial kingdom pervaded many of the prayers and reinforced the royalist theme of the office. The oration for terce emphasized that God ruled through kings.[51] These prayers also emphasized the personal and devotional relationship linking the owner of the book, the Lord, and Louis himself, whose saintly merits illustrated elsewhere are being asked to aid in the owner's own process of salvation.

The books of hours that survive share a number of characteristics that raise a number of questions—they are all made for women, mostly descendants of Louis himself, and are the highest end of luxury items, a number illustrated with gorgeous illuminations. Among these are the famous Hours of Jeanne d'Evreux and the Hours of Jeanne de Navarre but also the (lost) Savoy Hours, the Hours of Marie de Navarre, and two other lesser-known volumes, Spencer 56 and BNF nal 592. In the illuminated versions, the office was also paired with a cycle of eight or nine illuminations that presented Louis as a model for queenly behavior. The visual programs allow us to examine both the developing iconography of Louis and the way in which Louis' sanctity could be modeled for a royal and female audience.[52] They must be examined both in the context of the books of hours themselves and in the other (now mostly lost)

---

48. SV Terce.
49. This represents additions to the liturgical material from the hagiographic dossier. See Anonymous, *RHF*, vol. 20, 46: "vitabat ludos illicitos," and 49: "ludum taxillorum." Louis had outlawed the manufacture of dice in his reform legislation of 1254 (Carolus-Barré, "La Grande ordonnance de 1254 sur la réforme de l'administration et la police du Royaume," 87).
50. SV None.
51. SV Terce.
52. Madeleine Caviness, "Patron or Matron? A Capetian Bride and a Vade Mecum for Her Marriage Bed," *Speculum* 68 (1993): 333–362.

iconographic programs celebrating Louis' sanctity in the opening decades of the fourteenth century. Visually, this Louis tended to prize themes of devotional humility, compassion, and service, and in this the illuminations in the hours were broadly representative. This spoke in part to a trend in sanctity that had occurred over the course of the thirteenth century that lent itself to discussions of virtues associated with women, and thus to the way in which Louis might appeal, or come to be meaningful, to a female audience in the context of a history of sanctity in which women might claim authority through (mendicant) virtue.

The illuminated books of hours are closely connected. The earliest extant exemplar—New York Public Library Spencer 56, dating to ca. 1315—was probably made for Blanche of Burgundy, the daughter-in-law of Philip the Fair and wife of the future Charles IV who was disgraced and imprisoned after the discovery of an adulterous affair that disrupted the court.[53] The Hours of Jeanne d'Evreux (Met 54.1.2) were produced between 1324 and 1328 by Charles IV for his third wife, his last best hope for producing an heir and insuring the continuation of the Capetian dynasty.[54] The fame of this tiny volume is in part due to the fact that it is the great masterpiece of the Parisian painter, Jean Pucelle.[55] A third exemplar, the Hours of Jeanne (II) de Navarre (BNF nal 3145), is dated to after 1329, when she was crowned as queen of Navarre, and before Jeanne's death in 1343. Jeanne de Navarre was the daughter of Louis X (d. 1316) and the great-great-granddaughter of Saint Louis. Born in 1311, she was married in 1318 to Philippe of Evreux (also a direct descendant of Louis IX).[56] The (lost) Savoy Hours (Turin ms. E. V. 49), our fourth volume, was made for Blanche of Savoy (d. 1348) around 1335–1340. Blanche, through her mother, Agnes of France (1260–1325), was Louis IX's granddaughter. Despite a fire of 1904, we know a fair amount about this manuscript from the work of Paul Durrieu, conducted before the fire, and from portions of the manuscript acquired by Henry Yates Thompson that ultimately made their way to Yale's

53. Léopold Delisle, "Les Heures de Blanche de France, duchesse d'Orléans," *Bibliothèque de l'École des Chartes* 66 (1905): 489–539. Delisle also associated the volume with Blanche, on the basis of artistic style and two references to a "Blanche" and a "Philippe." More recently, these are the conclusions of Elizabeth A. R. Brown.

54. For the text of Jeanne d'Evreux's will, see Kathleen Morand, *Jean Pucelle* (Oxford, 1962), 30, no. 2. For studies that treat the iconography of the Louis cycle specifically, see James Hoffeld, "An Image of Saint Louis and the Structuring of Devotion," *Bulletin of the Metropolitan Museum of Art* 29 (1971): 216–266; Caviness, "Patron or Matron?" 333–362; Holladay, "Education of Jeanne d'Evreux," 585–611; Guest, "Discourse on the Poor," 153–180; Elina Gertsman, "Vir Iustus Atque Perfectus: St. Louis as Noah in the Miraculous Recovery of the Breviary Miniature from the Hours of Jeanne d'Evreux," *Source: Notes in the History of Art* 23 (2003): 1–8; Carns, *The Cult of Saint Louis and Capetian Interests*; and Holladay, "Fourteenth-Century French Queens," 69–100.

55. On the place of the Hours in Pucelle's oeuvres, see Morand, *Jean Pucelle*, 13–16, catalogue no. 6, 41–42; François Avril, *Manuscript Painting at the Court of France: The Fourteenth Century, 1310–1380* (New York, 1978), 44–59, pls. 3–10; and Charles Sterling, *La peinture médiévale à Paris: 1300–1500*, 2 vols. (Paris, 1987), 88–99.

56. Sterling, *La peinture médiévale*, 104–107; Avril, *Manuscript Painting*, 68–73.

Beinecke collections (Beinecke Ms 390).[57] Yet another volume containing the
Hours of Louis is the Hours of Marie de Navarre (daughter of Jeanne II de
Navarre and the great-great-great-granddaughter of Louis IX) (Venice Marciana Lat 1.104), illuminated by Ferrer Bassa after her marriage in 1338, perhaps in 1340 when Bassa was paid for a retable and a set of hours, and
certainly before 1342 when the king requested that Marie send him the book
illustrated by Bassa.[58] It is considered a masterpiece of the Spanish Gothic
style.[59] One last version of the Louis-Hours (BNF nal 592) dates to the mid-
fourteenth century.[60] This volume is unilluminated and cannot be associated
with a particular patron, though it, too, was made for an elite or even royal
woman. One prayer speaks of the owner as a woman of high station, another
of the people committed to her for governance, and another of the Archangel
Michael who is the especial protector of princes.[61] Several of the newly com-

57. Durrieu, "Notice," 500–555; Paul Durrieu, "Les aventures de deux splendides livres
d'heures ayant appartenu au duc Jean de Berry," *Revue de l'art ancien et moderne* 30 (1911):
5–16; Christopher de Hamel, "Les Heures de Blanche de Bourgogne, comtesse de Savoie," in
Le manuscrits enluminés des comtes et ducs de Savoie, ed. Agostino Paravicini Bagliani and Enrico
Castelnuovo (Turin, 1990), 89–91; Roger S. Wieck, "Savoy Hours and Its Impact on Jean, Duc de
Berry," *Yale University Library Gazette* 66 (1991): 159–180; Margaret M. Manion, "Women, Art
and Devotion: Three French Fourteenth-Century Royal Prayer Books," in *The Art of the Book: Its
Place in Medieval Worship*, ed. Margaret M. Manion and Bernard J. Muir (Exeter, 1998), 21–66,
particularly 41–44. For extant folios, see P. Blanchard, *Les Heures de Savoie: Facsimiles of Fifty-
Two Pages from the Hours Executed for Blanche of Burgundy, Being All That Is Known to Survive of a Famous Fourteenth-Century Ms, Which Was Burnt at Turin in 1904* (London, 1910).
Judging from one known miniature, the iconography was directly related to the Hours of Jeanne
de Navarre.
58. Alix Saulnier-Pinsard, "Une nouvelle oeuvre du Maitre de San Marcos: le Livre
d'Heures de Marie de Navarre," in *La Miniatura Italiana tra Gotico e Rinascimento. I: Atti del
II Congresso di Storia della Minatura Italiana, Cortona 24–26 Settembre 1982*, ed. Emanuela
Sesti (Florence, 1985), 35–50; Joaquin Yarza, "Ferrer Bassa revisado," in *Arte d'Occidente:
temi e metodi: studi in onore di Angiola Maria Romanini* (Rome, 1999), 716–719. Yarza posits
the existence of a lost Aragonese model for the volume, because documents refer to hours commissioned during the reign of Jaime II.
59. The volume exists in facsimile, *Libro de Horas de la reina Maria de Navarra: cuyo original se conserva en la Biblioteca Nazionale Marciana, Venecia, bajo la referencia Lat. I, 104
(=12640): Officium*, 1 + commentary vols. (Barcelona, 1996). SV is found at fols. 178v.–198.
See commentary, 348–362, for a transcription of the office for Saint Louis as it appears in this
volume.
60. Victor Leroquais, *Les livres d'heures manuscrits de la Bibliothèque nationale* (Paris,
1927), vol. 2, 260–266. The office appears on fols 161r.–187, and a memoria for Louis is found at
63v.–64. The purple filigree suggests a southern or southwestern French origin. The volume was
originally compiled in the first third of the fourteenth century, though the Hours of Louis were
added at the end of the volume mid-century or thereafter. I extend my thanks to François Avril
and Alison Stones for their opinions on the dating and provenance of this volume.
61. BNF nal 592, 30r. "Dame quar dex en cest munde vous ha mise en grant estat raison est
que vous de cuer et de corps vous humiliez devant soi." BNF nal 592, 45r.–v. "Per la quelle ie
puisse auximent governer le pueple que vous mavez commis: sanz moi meffaire vous vous ne vers
autrui. Per la quele i ie saiche norrir les enfanz que vous mavez donez en vostre servise. Ne ia ne les
amore damor contraire a la vostre." Note that prayer coincides with the ethic of compassionate
governance in evidence throughout the office. BNF nal 592, 58v.: "Faites auximant commemora-
cion en loneur de lange qui vous garde & de saint michie larchange. Car li archange hont espe-
cialment cure des princes. & dou commun bien qu'il hont a gouverner." Ibid., vol. 2, 266. suggests
it was made for a "princess or even a queen."

Table 8.1. Iconography in the Books of Hours

	Jeanne d'Evreux	Jeanne de Navarre	Savoy Hours (pace Durrieu)	Marie de Navarre
Opening of office	Jeanne at Louis' tomb, kneeling in prayer before a standing statue of the saint (102v.)		Blanche kneels before Louis, bearded, enthroned, with rod and scepter (3v.)	Breviary miracle (full page) (178r.) Figure 12
Matins	Louis submitting to chastisement from his confessor (103)	Louis learns to read, with Blanche (at left) and confessor with scourge (at right) (85v.) Figure 8	Louis enthroned in glory with 4 angels, his anointing depicted in margin (263v.)	Christ speaks to Louis, who is on his knees before an altar (179)
Lauds	Louis feeds a leprous monk (123v.)	Louis as child, attending mass (91v.)	Louis receives discipline ("barbu et grisonnat" (297r.)	Louis feeds a monk (Royaumont) (186) Figure 15
Prime	Louis administers to the sick (142v.) Figure 5	Louis en route to Reims for anointing (97)	Louis processing the Crown of Thorns ("barbu et grisonnant") (279r.) Figure 11	Louis feeding lepers or the poor (188v.) Figure 13
Terce	Louis washes the feet of the poor (148v.)	Louis receives unction, in prayer (99)	Louis while ill, takes the cross ("barbu et grisonnant") (281r.)	Louis and three others carry a sick person on a stretcher (190) Figure 14
Sext	Breviary miracle (155) Figure 6	Coronation of Louis (100v) Figure 9	Louis on the seas in crusading armour (284r.)	Louis caring for a sick person who lies in bed (191v.) Figure 15
None	Louis buries bones of Christians at Sidon (159v.) Figure 7	Louis processing the Crown of Thorns (102) Figure 10	Breviary miracle (286r.) Durrieu describes this scene as "Saint Louis en armure recevant un messager du ciel." This almost certainly	Death of Louis; his soul being carried up in the presences of Dominicans and Franciscans (194)

Table 8.1.—*cont.*

	Jeanne d'Evreux	Jeanne de Navarre	Savoy Hours (pace Durrieu)	Marie de Navarre
			represents the breviary miracle, which depicts an angel ("messenger") coming down from heaven. Durrieu, "Notice," 542.	
Vespers	Louis' death (165v.)	Louis ill in bed, vows the cross (104)	Louis buries bones of Christians at Sidon (288r.)	Pilgrims and venerators at tomb of Saint Louis (196v.)
Compline	Procession at/from Saint Denis (173)	Preaching the crusades (106v.)	Louis serves leper at table (291r.)	Marie in prayer before Saint Louis (198v.)

posed hymns were also incorporated into a hybrid office that was added to BNF Lat 13233 (673r.–678r.), a volume that was probably owned by Charles V, pointing again to its royal context.[62]

The iconography in these volumes is also interconnected. Spencer 56 has only a single historiated initial, and BNF nal 592 is unilluminated. The Evreux Hours, Savoy Hours, Hours of Jeanne de Navarre, and Hours of Marie de Navarre are all richly decorated. Portions of the Hours of Jeanne de Navarre were illuminated by Pucelle's follower, Jean le Noir. The Savoy Hours was illuminated by other followers of Pucelle and some of its iconography may have been related to the Hours of Jeanne de Navarre (see figures 10 and 11). Joachim Yarza has argued that Ferrer Bassa relied heavily on Parisian (Pucellian) iconography.[63] Although no single iconographic canon existed for Louis, thematically the images share a great deal. With the exception of the Hours of Jeanne de Navarre, the images downplayed Louis' kingship and highlighted themes of humility, piety, and charity appropriate to the devotional genre of books of hours, themes that echoed the basic representational priorities of the office, and were, in this context, appropriate to an audience of royal women. Table 8.1 presents

    62. *Breviaires*, vol. 3, 235–239. My thanks to Elizabeth A. R. Brown for pointing me to this reference.
    63. Yarza, "Ferrer Bassa," 716–719. For the one preserved illumination from the Louis Hours, see Francesco Carta, Carlo Cipolla, and Carlo Frati, *Monumenta palaeographica sacra. Atlante paleografico-artistico compilato sui manoscritti esposti in Torino alla Mostra d'arte sacra nel 1898, e pubbl. dalla R. Deputazione di storia patria delle antiche provincie e della Lombardia* (Turin, 1899).

the iconographic cycles contained in the four illuminated Hours (Savoy Hours as described by Paul Durrieu)[64] schematically.

Louis' charity, alms, and concern for the sick and poor are the pervading theme of the iconographic schemes. This has been noted in particular in the Hours of Jeanne d'Evreux. Madeleine Caviness described the image of Louis in the Hours as providing the young queen with a "gender-exchanged role model for a woman's acts of charity and humility and for a chaste progenitor," and has argued that the sexually provocative marginalia were designed to instruct Jeanne in the virtues of marital chastity, a queenly virtue for which Louis was also prized.[65] Joan Holladay and Gerald Guest have both argued that the Hours concentrate largely on service and charity and have related this emphasis to the expectations of French queenship in this period.[66] The tiny volume includes images of Louis feeding the leprous monk of Royaumont, Louis caring for a sick man who lies in bed (fig. 5). Louis washing the feet of the poor, and Louis gathering the bones of dead crusaders in the East in order to give them a proper burial (fig. 7). Holladay argued that these represented the seven orders of charity. These basic sensibilities were incorporated into the other volumes. The Savoy Hours also included images of the king's charity, including serving a leper at table and his burial of Christians. But the volume that most emphasized Louis' acts of charity is the Hours of Marie of Navarre, which included representations of Louis feeding the leprous monk, Louis feeding the poor at his own table, Louis caring for a sick man in bed, and Louis bearing another sick man to the hospital on a stretcher, this last an image otherwise unknown in the Louis iconography.[67] (See figures 13, 14, and 15.)

The Royaumont episode, in which Louis feeds a monk disfigured by leprosy while the repulsed abbot stands by was frequently depicted in the iconography of Saint Louis. The episode was first introduced during the canonization hearings of 1282–1283 and was incorporated into the hagiographic and the iconographic tradition.[68] The second lection, adopted from the Translation office, made reference to it. All but the Hours of Jeanne de Navarre included it, and it was also the singular image used in the Hours of Jeanne of Naples.[69] The Royaumont episode represented at once Louis' charity, his compassion, and his humility and obedience. It had obvious Franciscan overtones—Francis'

64. Durrieu, "Notice," 541–542.

65. Caviness, "Patron or Matron?" 344–345.

66. Holladay, "Education of Jeanne d'Evreux"; Guest, "Discourse on the Poor."

67. A story circulated of Louis and Thibaut de Navarre carrying the first poor man who arrived in the hospital at Compiegne (Brown, "Chapels," 290, 315–316, n. 36).

68. The story did not appear in GB *vita* or WC *vita et actibus*. It was recounted by Boniface VIII (B.VIII 150, 157), WSP *vie* (ch. 11), YSD *gesta*, 52, BLQRF 163, and in the Dominican lections of 1306 (*MOPH*).

69. Vienna ÖNB 1921, fol. 219. The volume does not include the full Hours of Louis. It is the only illumination of Louis, and it accompanies a commemorative prayer on 219v. which includes the Magnificat antiphon (*Magnificat gesta clarissima*) and the *Oratio* derived from LDR. The iconography reflects closely the Evreux Hours. See Saulnier-Pinsard, "le Livre d'Heures de Marie de Navarre," 47, 48 n. 14; and Martin Kauffmann, "The Image of Saint Louis," in *Kings and Kingship in Medieval Europe*, ed. Janet Bately (London, 1993), 282.

Figure 7. Louis buries bones of Christians at Sidon. Manuscript, Jean Pucelle, French, active in Paris, ca. 1320–1334. The Hours of Jeanne d'Evreux, New York, Metropolitan Museum of Art, The Cloisters Collection (54.1.2), fol. 159v. (By permission of the New York Metropolitan Museum of Art.)

Figure 8. Education of Louis. Manuscript. The Hours of Jeanne de Navarre, BNF nal 3145, fol. 85v. (By permission of the Bibliothèque nationale de France.)

Figure 9. Coronation of Louis IX. Manuscript. The Hours of Jeanne de Navarre, BNF nal 3145, fol. 100v. (By permission of the Bibliothèque nationale de France.)

Figure 10. Louis IX carrying the Crown of Thorns. Manuscript. The Hours of Jeanne de Navarre, BNF nal 3145, fol. 102. (By permission of the Bibliothèque nationale de France.)

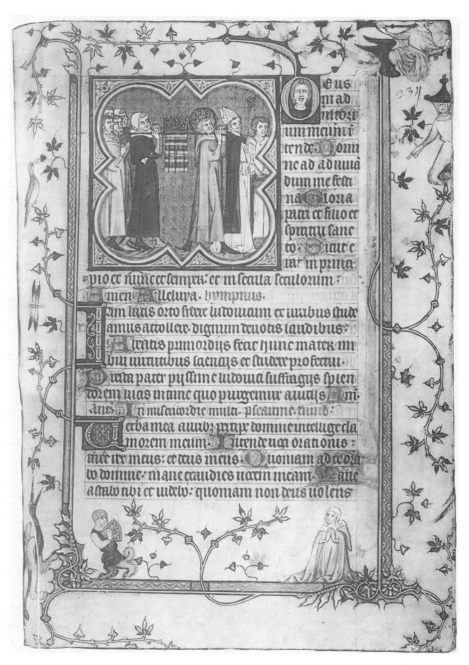

Figure 11. Louis carrying the Crown of Thorns. From the lost Savoy Hours (Hours of Blanche of Savoie). Turin ms. E. V. 49, fol. 279r. Lost in fire of 1904 but reproduced from Francesco Carta, Carlo Cipolla, Carlo Frati, *Monumenta palaeographica sacra*. (Turin, Fratelli Bocca, 1899).

Figure 12. Breviary miracle. Manuscript. Ferrer Bassa. Hours of Marie de Navarre, Venice, Bibl. Naz. Marc. Ms. Lat I 104/12640, fol. 179r. (By permission of the Bibliotheca Nazionale Marciana, Venice.)

Figure 13. Louis feeding lepers or the poor. Manuscript. Ferrer Bassa. Hours of Marie de Navarre, Venice, Bibl. Naz. Marc. Ms. Lat I 104/12640 fol. 186. (By permission of the Bibliotheca Nazionale Marciana, Venice.)

Figure 14. Louis and three others carry a sick person on a stretcher. Manuscript. Ferrer Bassa. Hours of Marie de Navarre, Venice, Bibl. Naz. Marc. Ms. Lat I 104/12640, fol. 190. (By permission of the Bibliotheca Nazionale Marciana, Venice.)

Figure 15. Louis caring for a sick person in bed. Manuscript. Ferrer Bassa. Hours of Marie de Navarre, Venice, Bibl. Naz. Marc. Ms. Lat I 104/12640, fol. 191v. (By permission of the Bibliotheca Nazionale Marciana, Venice.)

Figure 16. Louis feeds the poor. From the Ste.-Chapelle retable (after Peiresc), Manuscript. Bibliothèque inguibertine, Carpentras, ms. 1779, fol. 81r. (By permission of the Bibliothèque Inguibertine, Carpentras.)

Figure 17. Breviary miracle. From the Ste.-Chapelle retable (after Peiresc), Manuscript. Bibliothèque inguibertine, Carpentras, ms. 1779, fol. 76v. (By permission of the Bibliothèque Inguibertine, Carpentras.)

Figure 18. Louis taking Damietta, from the earliest surviving manuscript, Joinville, BNF Lat 13568, fol. 83. (By permission of the Bibliothèque nationale de France.)

love of lepers was one of the keystones of the love of the ill and disenfranchised that had so defined his sanctity.

The theme of obedience underlay the appeal of another favored theme of the hours and the iconography generally—Louis receiving discipline from his confessor, which was represented in the Savoy Hours, the Hours of Jeanne d'Evreux, and the Hours of Jeanne de Navarre. (See figure 8.) The image of a king submitting to clerical punishment and rebuke may have been remarkable and discordant. But it underscored the idea of obedience to clerical (and within a female audience, male) authority. In the Hours of Jeanne de Navarre the image is paired with Louis being instructed by a clergy member, under the supervision of his mother, reinforcing different themes of obedience (to parent and to cleric). (See figure 8.) On another level the iconography drew on the appeal of mortification and asceticism particularly prevalent in female spirituality in the period. Here, the figure of Elizabeth of Hungary was exemplary.[70]

The crusades—which we saw figured in the liturgical hours—were also represented in the image cycles in interpretations that highlighted trial, devotion, and faith. The Savoy Hours favored the subject of the crusade, with four of the eight narrative episodes devoted to it, including Louis' taking of the cross, Louis on sea in crusading armor, Louis in prison, and Louis gathering the bones of crusaders at Sidon (cf. Evreux, figure 7, as above). The emphasis in the imagery was not so much on battle or on passion but as an emblem of devotion and closeness to God. Comparison to the single narrative illumination in the only surviving fourteenth-century manuscript of Joinville is instructive, since this shows Louis as a military leader attacking Damietta.[71] (See figure 18.) Here, Louis, crowned and haloed, is shown triumphally on horseback, clad in fleur-de-lis emblazoned amour and chain mail, bearing a javelin and shield, leading a charge against the walls of the city. This was indeed a separate tradition. In the books of hours, the emblem of Louis' devotion and particular favor from God during the crusades was the so-called breviary miracle—the miraculous delivery of Louis' breviary from heaven, which was illustrated in the Hours of Jeanne d'Evreux, the lost Savoy Hours, and in the Hours of Marie de Navarre, where it was given pride of size and place in introducing the entire office. (See figures 6 and 12.) By this point, the story of the miraculous delivery of the breviary, where an angel or a dove brought Louis his breviary while the king was in a Saracen prison, was fully developed.[72] The newly composed vespers hymn made reference to the episode.[73] The image took on a particular and deep significance within the context of books of

70. Compare the iconography in the Louis Hours to the fresco image of the Flagellation of Saint Elizabeth (ca. 1320) in the Nuns' choir at Santa Maria Donna Regina in Naples. See Adrian Hoch, "Pictures of Penitence from a Trecento Neapolitan Nunnery," *Zeitschrift fur Kunstgeschichte* 61 (1998): 217 (fig. 8).

71. BNF Lat. 13568, fol. 83r. The only other illumination in the manuscript is the dedication miniature, showing Joinville presenting the volume to Louis of Navarre.

72. Crist, "Breviary of Saint Louis," 321–323.

73. SV VH3.

hours designed to be used eight times daily for prayer, since the story cele-brated the king for his devout commitment to daily prayer with precisely such a devotional volume and the miraculous attention paid to that devotion by God.

The iconographic evidence of the Hours of Jeanne d'Evreux, Blanche of Savoy, and Marie de Navarre interwove, then, themes of royal integrity, saintly virtue, and devotional sincerity. Ironically, the representation of this important king bears on the history of late medieval queenship. In many ways, the characteristic qualities of good queenship and of female sanctity converge in this period, as advisers would preach to queens precisely the qual-ities that were deemed pious and saintly. The confluence between queenship and female sanctity is best illustrated in the person of Elizabeth of Hungary, the young consort of Ludwig IV of Thuringia, who, after being widowed in 1227 at the age of twenty, adopted a life of renunciation, piety, and service. She died in 1231 and was quickly canonized. The hallmark of her sanctity was the extent to which she was associated with the early Franciscan move-ment and incorporated into her own behavior and queenly station the Fran-ciscan ideal of service to the poor.[74] The imagery that sprung up around Elizabeth's memorialization emphasized the same qualities. Images contem-porary with her initial sanctification, and with the sanctification of Louis, showed her distributing alms, feeding the hungry, washing the feet of the poor, caring for the sick, and being disciplined by her confessor. That Eliza-beth became the model for this kind of lay-royal-female sanctity is clear in the example of Hedwig of Silesia (can. 1267), the last saint officially canonized preceding Louis, whose vita and canonization bull lauded her for precisely the same qualities Louis was also remembered for: marital chastity, washing the feet of lepers, frequent and regular devotions and prayers, fasting, and wear-ing simple clothes.[75] Another example of the hagiographical priorities for royal women is provided by a vita of Louis' own sister, Isabelle (d. 1270), also closely tied to the Franciscans. Although she was never canonized (a potential probably sacrificed to her brother's canonization), her vernacular life offers a portrait of Isabelle's sanctity that closely resembles that of Louis as re-counted by Geoffrey of Beaulieu (writing in the 1270s).[76] Her sanctity is summarized by innocence, penance, patience, chastity (she took a vow of vir-ginity), and mercy, and she is described as being guided by sacred scripture, rejecting marriage, engaging in daily prayer, giving many alms to the poor and to hospitals, visiting the sick, and founding Longchamp, a monastery for Franciscan women (though she debated between this and a hospital).

That charity and service were the hallmarks of female virtue is attested not only by descriptions of female saints but also by prescriptions for female queens. We have a number of contemporary prescriptions specifically on the

---

74. On the sanctity of Elizabeth and its sources, see Folz, *Saintes reines*, 105–129.
75. Ibid., 129–144. Klaniczay, *Holy Rulers*, 220–224, 251–255.
76. Field, *Writings*; Field, *Isabelle*, 41–42.

subject of good queenship.[77] Louis himself wrote to his daughter, Isabelle of Navarre, urging her to love the poor and give alms.[78] A few years later, the Franciscan Durand of Champagne wrote for the queen of Philip the Fair (also called Jeanne de Navarre, d. 1305, but not the owner of our volume here) a *Speculum dominarum*, sometime before 1300.[79] Entitled a "Mirror for Women," the tract assumed a royal station and was really a handbook for good queenship. Part 1, section 2, discussed how the queen ought to comport herself[80] and included chapters on how she ought to be preeminent in the sanctity of her life (part 2, chapter 4),[81] how she should be most lavish in giving out money (part 2, chapter 8), how she should be the *consolatrix* of the oppressed (part 2, chapter 9), how she should abject herself toward humility (part 2, chapter 12), and so forth.[82] She ought to exercise her power to constrain the bad, promote the good, reproach the delinquent, punish the iniquitous, and defend the poor and wretched.[83] As she travels throughout the kingdom, as both rich and poor come to greet her pleading causes,[84] she should expend great alms to the poor and needy and bear herself with a heart of piety. She should visit churches and monasteries wherever she goes, seeking their aid. She should search out the humble huts of lepers and the poor to console them.[85] All people should be able to go to her to attain justice, and she ought to hear the cries of the innocent, the complaints of the oppressed, the causes of the poor, the afflictions of people. She ought to inquire into the truth, correct injuries, and punish the iniquitous. By her, the injured shall be consoled and rejoice, injustices rectified, and peace, justice, joy, and security secured.[86] Chapter 22 explained that among the virtues to which she ought to aspire the queen should pay out alms to the poor, institute chapels, build monasteries and hospitals, alleviate the needs of poor monks, and give liturgical instruments for altars; in addition she ought to alleviate injustices and secure peace and justice.[87] Above all she must remember to remain humble before God, resisting the temptations of luxury and the exaltation of the people afforded to her by her status.

77. This paragraph is indebted to Holladay, "Education of Jeanne d'Evreux," 599–604.

78. David O'Connell, *The Instructions of Saint Louis: A Critical Text* (Chapel Hill, N.C., 1979), 80, nos. 13, 14, 18.

79. BNF Lat 6784. Delisle assumes a date of before 1297 because he thinks it is inconceivable that, in this Capetian context, such an author would have not furnished Saint Louis as an example had he already been canonized (Delisle, "Durand de Champagne," in *HLF*, vol. 30, 318). The treatise is also discussed by Born, "Perfect Prince," 493–494.

80. BNF Lat 6784, 12v.–26v. This section is discussed in Delisle, "Durand de Champagne," 322–323.

81. BNF Lat 6874, 13v.–14r.: "Sit eciam excellentissima sanctitate vite. Sicut nempe preminet et precunctis excellit magnificencia dignitatis sic debet omnes precellere preminencia sanctitatis."

82. BNF Lat 6874. These are taken from chapter headings, summarized on 12v.–13r.: "quod debet esse largissima ad erogandum," "quod debet esse piissima consolatrix oppressorum," "inclinat eam ad humiliacionem."

83. BNF Lat 6784, 15r.

84. Ibid.

85. Ibid., 15v., part 2, ch. 8.

86. Ibid., 15v.–16r.

87. Ibid., 25v.

Gábor Klaniczay has argued that royal sainthood became associated with female members of royal families in the thirteenth century, in part because the influence of mendicant—and in particular Franciscan—forms of piety that privileged renunciation and disempowerment was incompatible with most kings.[88] Shifts in the larger patterns of sanctity after 1200 allowed for women, who had always had a tougher time gaining the canonical recognition of sanctity, to get the proportionally larger share of lay and royal sainthood. Male saints achieved sainthood through the total renunciation of worldly power. But women, because of the social requirements of their gender—and queens in particular, because these requirements were highlighted by their exalted social status—could participate in the activity of humbling charity without giving up the institutional status of their queenship. Louis IX has always been something of a paradox in this scheme since he managed to proffer the effect of pious and humble charity at the same time as he retained and augmented his actual, worldly, and royal authority. The enormous gap between his actual power and his seeming desire for humility and self-humiliation made the quality of his saintly spirit appear even more exalted.

The image of Louis in this context—private, instructive, devotional, royal—suggests a number of interrelated points. The first is that Louis provided the royal model for active and compassionate piety that characterized so much of thirteenth-century sanctity. As already suggested, Saint Francis is a good marker (probably more exemplary than causal, but useful nonetheless) for the growing prestige of the active life, its impact on notions of sanctity, and its effect of bringing more laymen into the saintly fold. But the qualities of personal devotion, compassion, service, and protection of the poor drew also on a tradition of writing on kingship. In this sense, the images (both textual and visual) of Louis found in the Translation office and books of hours reflected a type of hortatory literature written by clerics and produced for kings—instructions on good royal behavior found, for instance, in the moralized bibles produced for the Capetians in the first half of the thirteenth century or the *specula* written by Guibert of Tournai or Vincent of Beauvais. It should not be surprising that two different ways of articulating ideals ("sanctity" and "ideal kingship") should draw on the same overarching set of socially valued virtues, but it is notable that they should be brought together in this way and appropriate that Louis should represent this junction of ideals. The third point, which relates to the applicability of these ideals to royal women, also emerges from this confluence of influences. That Francis' active life of charity and compassion for the poor and sick reflects on the articulation of the ideals of queenship is testament to its broad appeal and reach. But this in turn allowed Louis to represent virtue to royal women, who were elsewhere being encouraged to effect the behavior of charity and compassion.

Another frame against which to measure the devotional formulation of Louis in these books of hours is the developing iconography for Louis more generally. A number of visual cycles for Louis were created in the first decades

---

88. Klaniczay, *Holy Rulers*, 195–294.

of the fourteenth century—many of which are unfortunately lost.[89] At St.-Denis the glazing cycle was installed in the chapel by 1303.[90] (See figures 1–4.) At the Benedictine Abbey of La Trinité at Fécamp a chapel included a vast cycle to Louis of twenty-one episodes and dated to about 1310.[91] From the work of Nicolas-Claude Fabri de Peiresc (1580–1637), we know of frescoes at the Franciscan Convent of Saint Marcel (Lourcines, founded by Marguerite of Provence in 1289 and thus directly tied to royal patronage), dating probably to about 1320, and of the four episodes that appeared on the lost retable or altar frontal in the lower chapel at the Ste.-Chapelle, also dated to about 1320.[92] We still possess the gorgeously illuminated copy of William of Saint-Pathus' French *vie*, produced, probably, around 1330–1340.[93] At Royaumont, a document attests to a chapel with eight inscriptions detailing episodes from Louis' life—and given the monumental nature of the context we might well entertain the idea that these accompanied images on the chapel wall.[94]

Martin Kaufmann has discussed how two competing tensions—on one hand, royal leadership and, on the other, mendicant virtue—emerged within the corpus of the iconography for Louis. Collating this evidence indicates that the strand of memorialization that prized humility and charitable devotion had a wider appeal than just the books of hours attesting to the influence of this interpretation of Louis' sanctity. That appeal can often be located within a context of mendicant piety or patronage. It also shows that the iconography through the 1320s and 1330s was fluid and—like the offices and other texts examined throughout this book—responded to particular contexts and modeled Louis in particular ways. The image of Louis' discipline was found at Lourcines, on the Ste.-Chapelle retable, and at St.-Denis. The breviary miracle and Louis' ministration to a leper at Royaumont appeared in these venues and Fécamp as well. Lourcines and St.-Denis both showed the king at sea saving his ship through intercessory prayer. Inscriptions commemorated these three events at Royaumont. But the cycles could be quirky. The illustrations in the Saint-Pathus manuscript, each introducing a chapter, followed many of the author's themes and showed the king overwhelmingly involved in devotional and charitable activities. But schemes that took their information from William of Saint-Pathus' text often found different ways of picturing Louis. The monumental representations at Fécamp focused primarily on Louis' time in the East, showing him at sea, taking Damietta, being thrown in prison with hands tied

89. Longnon, *Documents parisiens*; Mâle, "La vie de Saint Louis dans l'art français," 193–204. The best overall treatment of the iconography is Kauffmann, "The Image." Glass cycles at St.-Denis and Poissy, for instance, are no longer extant.

90. Montfaucon, *Monuments*, vol. 2, 159–159, plus 22–25; Louis Grodecki, "Saint Louis et le vitrail," *Les monuments historiques de la France*, s. 16 (1970): 14–18; Brown, "Chapels," 283.

91. LaFond, "vitraux," 103–107.

92. M.-Cl. Leonelli, "Mémoires pour la vie de saint Louis. Rheims. La Pucelle d'Orléans. Les énergumènes et la sorcellerie," in *L'universel épistolier. Nicolas-Claude Fabri de Peiresc (1580–1637)* (Carpentras, 1998); Louvre, *Trésor*, 190 192, no. 45.

93. Chung-Apley, "The Illustrated *Vie et Miracles*."

94. Duclos, *Histoire de Royaumont*, 325.

behind his back, in negotiation with his captors, picking up bones in Sidon, returning to France, and so forth. (Oddly, there is no evidence of liturgical commemoration of Louis at Fécamp—a true puzzle given the glazing cycle.) Peiresc's description indicates that the Franciscan convent at Lourcines prized images of Louis' humility, piety, and almsgiving, including images of his foundation of churches at the Maison Dieu, his care for a nun at Vernon, his prayer, confession, and discipline, and the king feeding the leper at Royaumont, washing the feet of the poor, serving poor people at his own table, and giving alms. The cycle also included several images relating to the crusade of 1250, including the breviary miracle, and (in Peiresc's description) "how he gave faith to the infidel." Royaumont's description of Louis concentrated far more on his role as king, in France and particularly with reference to the convent itself—including references to Louis VIII's testament instructing his son to build the abbey, how Louis himself was crowned and anointed at twelve, how he ordered the building of Royaumont, and so forth. The iconography may have been interdependent, but it was never determinative. Quite the contrary. As with the many texts that envisioned Louis' sanctity, so the iconography was malleable to shape a Saint Louis appropriate to particular venues and values.

Dynasticism, Crusade, and Legitimacy

The extent to which Louis was modeled according to the themes of active piety and devotion is underscored by the iconographic priorities found in the anomalous Hours of Jeanne de Navarre, which constitutes in a sense the exception that proves the rule.[95] Jeanne was the daughter of Louis X, whose claim to the Capetian crown was passed over in favor of her uncle Philip V. During the debate over succession, descent from Saint Louis was used both in her favor and in Philip's favor.[96] Her hours made the same point. The visual cycle of her hours emphasized, instead of humility, devotion, and piety, Louis' sacral royalty. It concentrated on the period of Louis' reign preceding his departure on crusade, and the sacralizing unction that legitimized Louis' institutional authority: Louis and his mother en route to Reims for his coronation; the young Louis receiving the all-important sacral anointing; Louis' coronation by the peers of France; and Louis carrying the Crown of Thorns.[97] (See figures 9 and 10.) The last two miniatures showed Louis taking up the cross and the preaching of the crusade. The iconography of the anointing and coronation images echoed the standard iconography of coronations as found, for instance, in BNF Lat 1246, the illuminated *ordo* made during Louis' own

---

95. Thomas, "L'iconographie"; Keane, "Remembering Louis." The standard work on the dynastic succession of 1328 remains Raymond Cazelles, *La société politique et la crise de la royauté sous Philippe de Valois* (Paris, 1958).

96. Anne-Hélène Allirot, "*Filiae regis Francorum*: princesses royales, mémoire de saint Louis et conscience dynastique (de 1270 à la fin du XIVe siècle)" (Ph.D. thesis, Université Paris X-Nanterre, 2007), 38–40.

97. On the sacralizing elements of Louis' cycle, see Keane, "Remembering Louis," ch. 3.

reign.[98] The procession scene of fol. 102, with its elaborate emphasis on the similarity between Louis' (royal) crown and Christ's (thorny) crown show-cased the link between Christ's royalty and Louis' sacral royalty.

This emphasis on Louis' royalty may well be related to the peculiar circumstances of Jeanne de Navarre's reign. Jeanne's exclusion from the throne is the event that prompted the rediscovery and redeployment of what would come to be known as the Salic Law, which, reinvented by the Valois, stated that the French throne could not go to a woman and, ultimately, could not pass through a woman. In 1328, when Jeanne was again passed over, and Jeanne's cousin (and Louis' great-grandson) Philip VI Valois ascended the throne, he ceded his claims to the Kingdom of Navarre to Jeanne and her husband who were, as if in recompense, then crowned as king and queen of that realm. This context argues for the heightened importance of the constitutional issues at stake in her status and thus for the appeal of the political implications of coronation imagery to dynastic claims. The cycle challenged doubts about Jeanne's own legitimacy (her mother's fidelity had been impugned) and her exclusion from the Capetian throne. It highlighted that Jeanne was a direct descendant of Louis IX and had a legitimate claim to the lineage of succession and sanctity.[99]

Louis' importance within the context of the legitimacy of the royal lineage was exemplified in a sermon written soon after Philip Valois' accession to the throne.[100] Written by Bertrand of Tours, OFM, between 1328 and his death in 1333, the sermon placed Louis within a historical and lineal framework that sanctified the dynasty as a whole. Bertrand was the Franciscan Minister General whose sermons on Louis were discussed earlier although these were enormously different in tone. He was also a friend to both the Capetian and the Angevin dynasties.[101] A reference in *Dico vobis* to the gospel reading for Louis' feast in the Church of Paris suggests a Parisian localization for this sermon.[102] The sermon was as much about the glories of the French royal houses

98. LeGoff et al., *Le sacre royal*, plates IX and XIV.

99. Tania Mertzman, "An Examination of Miniatures of the Office of St. Louis in Jeanne de Navarre's Book of Hours," *Athanor* 12 (1994). Marcel Thomas has argued further that the focus on the period prior to Louis' departure on crusade, may relate to her husband's own crusading ambitions. Thomas, "L'iconographie."

100. Bertrand of Tours 1, *Dico vobis*. Transcriptions are taken from Linz Stud. B 71, though they have been checked against the other exemplars. The sermon can be dated by its reference to the accession of Philip VI in France (king as of 1328) and Bertrand's own death in 1332 or 1333.

101. Bertrand wrote a number of sermons in Angevin interests: D'Avray, *Death and the Prince*, 152–156, 191–192, including a sermon on the death of Robert's son, Charles of Calabria. See Kelly, *The New Solomon*, 41 (on his relationship to the Angevins), and 311–312 (for his dynastic sermons). Bertrand probably met Robert of Anjou during his years as cardinal, since the two overlapped in Avignon for a time. Robert's queen, Sancia, mentions Bertrand in a letter (Nold, "Bertrand de la Tour: Life and Works," n. 34). Bertrand mentions Robert of Anjou himself, who was then on the throne, and a number of other Angevin rulers, in the sermon discussed here.

102. Bertrand of Tours 1, *Dico vobis*, Linz Stud 71 118v.: "Dico vobis quod nec Salomon in omni gloria sua fuit coopertus sicut unus ex istis Matt 6 [29]. Istud verbum sumptum est de quodam evangelio quod appropriavit parisiensis ecclesia festo gloriosi confessoris beati ludovici condam francorum regis." On model sermons, see D'Avray, *Preaching of the Friars*. Note that the sermon discussed here, *Dico vobis*, was elided from a number of the manuscripts.

(Merovingian, Carolingian, Capetian, Angevin, and Valois) as it was about Louis IX specifically, and it included elements of purely royalist propaganda, such as the Trojan origins of the French people, the *beata stirps*, and the comparison to Old Testament kings (and in particular Solomon, whom Louis exceeded in glory). Above all, the sermon represented the claim of sanctified lineage which was the singular hallmark of late Capetian, Valois, and Angevin royalist propaganda.[103] Its focus on lineage and dynasty was underscored by its rubric, which indicated that the sermon could be "used on the feast of the blessed Louis, once bishop of Toulouse, who was the nephew of the just-mentioned saint-king and son of Charles II, king of Sicily."[104] The entire sermon hammered home the idea that Louis was just one of many saintly kings of the line.

Bertrand's sermon took as its theme Matthew 6:29: "But I say to you (*Dico vobis*) that not even Solomon in all his glory was arrayed as one of these."[105] Drawing on the theme of the gospel for Louis' feast day, "Consider the lilies of the field" (Matt. 6:28), Bertrand interpreted the field as the House of France "which bore as many lilies as had most noble and most Christian kings." Bertrand played with the image of the lilies throughout the sermon, both as the insignia of the House of France and as tied to the idea of religious and moral purity.[106] If the field was the French royal house, the lilies were its individual worthy kings. The long sermon is divided into four parts. In the first, Bertrand spoke of the many lilies that have grown from the field (the House of France), returning frequently to the cultivation metaphor. He recounted the mythic origins of the French people from the Trojans—a royalist motif that went back to the seventh century and was revived during the reign of Philip Augustus.[107] Bertrand then ran through the legendary lineage of French royalty from Pharamund, through Clovis, "first among the kings of the French, baptized by Saint Remigius and consecrated with the sacramental chrism sent from the heavens,"

103. Among Capetians, see Gabrielle Spiegel, "The reditus regni ad stirpem Karoli Magni: a new look," *French Historical Studies* 7 (1971); Brown, "Généalogie capétienne," 199–214; and Brown, "La notion," 77–111.

104. Bertrand of Tours 1, *Dico vobis*, Linz Stud B 71, 118v.: "Sermo in festo beati ludovici confessoris quondam francorum regis, potest etiam esse sermo in festo beati ludovici quondam episcopi tholosani qui fuit nepos predicti regis filiusque karoli secundi Sicilie regis." The rubric also appears in Graz UB 717, 118r., and Vat Burgh 31, 143r. This "dual purpose" sermon was not uncommon. See the sermons of Arnaud Royard (*Rex iustus erigit terram* and *Benedictio domini super capud iusti*), which indicated that they could be used for the feast of either [Saint] Jacob or "Saint Louis Bishop" (Padua Anton 208, 336v.). Other examples are listed by Kelly, *The New Solomon*, 121, n. 172, 125–125.

105. Bertrand of Tours 1, *Dico vobis*, Linz Stud B 71, 118v. For manuscript sources, see Schneyer, vol. 1, 558, no. 711. I have consulted Vat. Burgh. 31, 143r.–145v., Linz Stud. B71, 188v.–120r., and Graz UB 717, 188r.–190v. The texts are fairly consistent.

106. For the background, see Beaune, *Birth*, 201–225; William Hinkle, *The Fleurs de Lis of the Kings of France, 1285–1488* (Carbondale, 1991.

107. Baldwin, *Philip Augustus*, 372–374; Elizabeth A. R. Brown, "The Trojan Origins of the French and the Brothers Jean du Tillet," in *After Rome's Fall: Narrators and Sources of Early Medieval History. Essays Presented to Walter Goffart*, ed. Alexander Calladar Murray (Toronto, 1998); Alexander Calladar Murray, "*Post vocantur Merohingii*: Fredegar, Merovech, and 'Sacral Kingship,'" in *After Rome's Fall*; Spiegel, "reditus regni ad stirpem."

Charlemagne "who was emperor," Hugh "count of Paris" (who, Bertrand takes care to tell us, was descended from royal blood), all the way to "Philip (VI, "Valois") who is reigning now,"[108] and then unself-consciously interwove the cadet Angevin branch of the French royal house into the lineage. Obsession with lineage was a hallmark of sanctified dynasticism in France and Sicily, but here the emphasis was clearly on the continuity of sanctity, and on a single "house of France," despite multiple dynasties. This theme allowed a legitimizing bridge to the Valois kings.

> The third point indeed is that this land produced other lilies, of which the first was that very same Hugh, the second was Robert, named the Pious, and many others, all the way to this Philip [VI] who is reigning now. Although he was not the son of the king [Charles VI], [Philip VI] was, nevertheless, descended from royal blood following a straight line. Indeed, his father, Lord Charles, count of Valois, was the son of King Philip [III], the son of blessed Louis. From among the number of these last lilies, however, came the glorious king, blessed Louis, whose feast is celebrated today.[109]

Bertrand passed over the dynastic breaks, including that recent break in 1328, speaking of the Capetians obliquely only as "these last lilies." Bertrand here reflected Philip Valois' own strategies in using descent from Louis to legitimize his claim. Philip VI recalled this descent in his legislation, minted coins like Saint Louis, and even, despite the failure of the crusade of Saint Louis, used these as a model for his own projected crusade.[110] But for Bertrand, the House of France extended to the Angevins as well, and the sermon echoed memorial sermons he wrote for dead princes in which he hailed Saint Louis—along with Clovis, Charlemagne, and Charles of Anjou—as leaders of the "Christian people against evil men," all from the House of France.[111]

In the second part of the sermon Bertrand explored the virtues of the French royal house by way of the nine characteristics of the lily, the insignia of the arms of France.[112] This was done through an extended discussion of the image

---

108. Bertrand of Tours 1, *Dico vobis*, Linz Stud B 71, 118v: "qui inter francorum reges primus fuit christianus baptizatus a sancto Remigio et sacramento chrismate misso celitus consecratus." "Hugo iste de sanguine regio descendit." "Karolus magnificus filius eius, qui fuit imperator." "Et ceteri usque ad Hugonem comitem parisiensem. . . . et ceteri multi usque ad istum philippum qui modo regnat."

109. Bertrand of Tours 1, *Dico vobis*, Linz Stud B 71, 118v.: "30 vero hec eadem terra produxit alia lilia; quorum primum fuit iste Hugo; 2m fuit Robertus cognominato Pius; et ceteri multi usque ad istum Philippum qui modo regnat. Qui quamvis non fuerit filius regis, descendit tamen secundum rectam lineam de sanguine regio. Pater enim suus scilicet dominus karolus comes valesii fuit filius philippi regis filii beati Ludovici. De numero autem istorum ultimorum liliorum fuit iste gloriosus Rex beatus ludovicus cuius hodie festum celebratur." This emphasis on royal lineage was evident in other of Bertrand's sermons. See D'Avray, *Death and the Prince*, 152–153.

110. Cazelles, *Société politique*, 96–98; Anne D. Hedeman, "Valois Legitimacy: Editorial Changes in Charles V's Grandes Chroniques de France," *Art Bulletin* 66 (1984); Christopher Tyerman, "Philip VI and the Recovery of the Holy Land," *English Historical Review* 100 (1985).

111. D'Avray, *Death and the Prince*, 152–153.

112. Bertrand of Tours 1, *Dico vobis*, Linz Stud B 71, 118v.: "Tamen quia arma francie sunt insignita liliorum floribus, tamen etiam quia proprietas lilii convenit eis." The nine traits are (1)

of the golden lily on the blue shield. Bertrand explained that, because the insignia of the arms of France are the lily flowers, the property of the lilies fits the
House of France. A lily flourishes in its roots and is verdant in its stalk, bril-
liant in its leaves, golden in its seeds, and strong in its roots. Each trait of these
lilies Bertrand elucidated with examples, generally historical, that exemplified
the virtue of the lineage. Under the discussion of the first trait, permanence,
Bertrand compared France to Rome in its prosperity: the roots of the lily thrive
and its flowers burst forth, which means that "the House of France and its
kingdom endured longer than any other royal house in the entire world. For it
lasted longer than the Roman Empire, constantly producing lilies as it flourished."[113] The House of Sicily is a "bough" of the House of France, and thus
they are one and the same. For his second point, clemency and piety, Bertrand
held that the "kings of France were most clement, even more so than the kings
of the house of Israel" (a remarkable one-up twist on Old Testament typology)
and that even the pagan kings who were from the House of France were not
ravagers of churches or persecutors of Christians, as the Romans had been.[114]
Because they are true worshippers of God, the "right arm of the Christian
church," and the "defenders of Christendom," they are called "most Christian
kings."[115] Here Bertrand sets up a rhetorical framework for the kings of
France, who as military leaders were defenders of the church against infidels,
pagans, and persecutors, a framework into which he later wove the theme of
crusade. The theme of sanctified lineage recurs in his third point, on cleanliness and honor, in which Bertrand explains that the French house gleams
among all royal houses of the world in integrity, nor was a "shameful illegiti-
macy of offspring found in the French house, which is often found in other
royal houses."[116]

On characteristic four, love and charity, Bertrand expounds on the French
kings' love of the church, which is manifest through crusade. He cites Pepin
who fought Aistulf, the king of the Longobards, for ecclesiastical liberties;
Charlemagne who fought Desiderius; Louis the Pious who fought the Saracens

---

permanence, (2) clemency and piety, (3) cleanliness and honesty, (4) divine love and charity, (5)
probity and courage ("because the sign at the top of the lily has the form of the royal key and
scepter"), (6) sweetness of fragrance, (7) justice and equity, (8) the celestial color of sapphire, and
(9) the red gules of Sicily. For a relevant discussion of the symbolism of the fleurs de lis, see
Gabrielle Spiegel and Sandra Hindman, "The Fleur-de-lis Frontispiece to Guillaume de Nangis'
Chronique abrégée: Political Iconography in Late Fifteenth-Century France," *Viator* 12 (1981).

113. Bertrand of Tours 1, *Dico vobis,* Linz Stud B 71, 118v.: "Sic et domus francie et regnum
eius plus duravit quam aliqua alia domus regia tocius mundi. Plus enim duravit quam imperium
romanorum in prosperitate sua semper lilia producendo."

114. Ibid.: "Reges enim francie fuerunt clementissimi plusquam reges domus Israel, etiam
reges pagani qui fuerunt de domo francie non leguntur fuisse vas[t]atores ecclesiarum nec persecu-
tores Christianorum sicut Romani."

115. Ibid., 118v.–119r.: "Quia fuerunt veri cultores ipsius brachiumque dextrum ecclesie et
defensores Christianitatis. Unde et reges Christianissimi appelantur."

116. Ibid., 119r. "Sicut enim lilium naturale semper candet in foliis, sic et ista domus inter
alias domus mundi regias canduit honestate. Nec ita fuit inventa in illa ignominiosa prolis illegit-
imitas que sepe in aliis domibus regiis invenitur."

in Spain; and, lastly, this very saint-king (Louis IX) who twice crossed the ocean to fight against the enemies of the faith, only to die in Tunis. And not satisfied to leave it there, Bertrand added a word about Philip, "his son," who died "completing the business of the church" (a reference to the crusade against Aragon), and about Charles of Anjou, who fought the enemies of the church in Apulia (a reference to the crusade in Lucera), and about Charles II of Anjou, who captured the kingdom of Aragon, and about Saint Louis of Toulouse and his brother, Robert, now king of Sicily, who remained in captivity in Catalonia for seven years, also for the church.[117] Crusade is linked to sanctified kingship and associated with the defense of the church and ecclesiastical liberties.

Through the probity and courage of the house—the fifth characteristic—the kings of France conquered a great part of the Christian world and subjugated it under their lordship. The probity and courage of the House of France is symbolized by the top of the lily, which takes the form of the royal key and scepter. The sixth characteristic—the sweet fragrance of the lily—is explained by the grace and power of miracles that extend throughout the entire world. Bertrand treats his seventh characteristic—the golden color of the lily, representative of justice and equity—with a reference to Aristotle's *Ethics* on the virtue of justice.[118] Gold is the most noble of the metals as justice is the most noble of the virtues. The eighth point, which takes up the blue background of the shield, relates the royal touch to dynastic, not individual virtue.

> On the eighth point, for the blue or heavenly hue on which the lily of France is found, I understand the grace and power of miracles. Indeed, this is the singular privilege of this house, insofar as all of its anointed kings, whether in France or in Sicily, gleam with miracles, because it [the privilege], by the touch of the royal hand, cures from a certain infirmity of the neck, which is called the royal disease [*morbus regius*]. And this power is not terrestrial but celestial. And thus fittingly the lily of France is found on a blue or heavenly hue, so that it might indicate that this virtue comes from the heavens.[119]

---

117. Ibid.: "Dilexerunt enim Christum, et dilataverunt eius ecclesiam. Inimicos etiam ecclesie debellaverunt et christianitatem promoverunt. Exemplo de Pipino qui contra Astulphum longobardorum regem pro libertatibus ecclesie dimicavit, et in Karolo magno qui pro eodem negotio, Desiderium eorum regem debellavit, et in hispaniis in Sarracenos. Exemplum etiam de Ludovico pio, qui pugnavit cum Saracenis. Exemplum etiam in isto sancto Rege de quo nunc agitur qui bis transfretavit contra inimicos fidei pugnaturus. Et prima vice captus fuit apud Damiatam. Et secunda fuit mortuus apud Thunicium. Exemplum etiam in Philippo ipsius filio qui peragens negotia ecclesie mortuus fuit. Exemplum etiam in karolo primo Rege Sicilie qui inimicos ecclesie in Appulia debellavit. Et in Karolo secundo filio eius qui eisdem negociis ecclesie in regno Arragonum fuit captus. Et in sancto ludovico Episcopo Tholosano quondam et in domino Roberto fratre suo nunc regnante in Sicilia qui pro eisdem negociis ecclesie 7 annis in Cathalonia captivi manserunt."

118. Ibid., 119ra.

119. Ibid., 119r.: "Per 8m licet per colorem saphireum vel celestem in quo iacet lilium francie, intelligo miraculorum gratiam et potestatem. Est enim hoc huius domus singulare privilegium, quod omnes eius reges uncti sive in Francia sive in Sicilia coruscant miraculis, quia tactu manus regie sanat a quadam infirmitate colli, que [em. For qui] morbus regius appellatur. Et quoniam hec virtus non est terrena sed celestis, ideo congrue iacet lilium Francie in colore saphireo seu celesti, ut innuatur quod hec virtus a celo derivatur."

The miraculous here is associated not with the singular saint but with the line. Louis' glory is applicable to the Angevin as well as to the French (Valois) royal house, and Bertrand's ninth point ends by insisting that they are the same.[120] His ninth characteristic concerns the red gules of the Sicilian house, by which he meant the will and desire to die for the Christian faith; and here he cited Charles I of Anjou adding the color red to the shield of France.[121] Indeed, Charles added the red "label gules" to the lilies for his coat of arms.

Only in the third and fourth sections does Bertrand turn from the House of France to a more traditional praise of Louis himself, comparing him favorably to Solomon who eventually reverted to idolatry. Unlike Solomon, Louis despised temporal glory. Bertrand here drew on a few specific examples from Louis' life. The Saracens did not frighten him when they threatened his life, because Louis was not fearful of losing his body (life). He was a generous patron of churches and monasteries. The fourth section of the sermon listed the seven qualities of Solomon's temporal glory despised by Louis (power over secular things, perversion of worship, and so forth). Louis therefore surpassed Solomon in the virtues of the good king. Bertrand returned to the theme of dynastic sanctity. God praised Louis by having other saints emerge from the House of France after him, specifically Louis of Toulouse, his nephew. "Indeed, these two Louis [*Isti enim duo ludovici*] were special among the lilies of the field, that is, those lilies of the House of France."[122]

The sermon boldly wove together all the principal threads of royal ideology and propaganda around 1330. It emphasized the lineage's support and defense of the church and its ecclesiastical privileges (a reversion to the classic trope of the king as upholder and defender of the church). But it extended that role to the "House of France's" history of crusade and its duty to lead the (widely defined) crusade effort. It also praised the entire line for peace, prosperity, military virtue, and saintliness. The idea of the "House of France" was used to elide the different dynasties in favor of an argument for essential saintly unity as one line. For Bertrand, Louis' sanctity was proof of the divine favor, the sacrality of the "House," and evidence that the French kings merited rule and fulfilled divine will. The kings are holy and sanctified because they work repeatedly for the business of the church, against its persecutors, and for its liberties. In Bertrand's vision, piety, crusade, and ideal kingship come together not only in Louis—the mere exemplar here of the royal sanctity that is manifest

120. An interesting point, because the royal touch was not a principal part of Angevin ideology. Charles I seems to have tried to incorporate it into the Angevin setting but without staying power (Bloch, *Royal Touch*, 90).

121. Bertrand of Tours 1, *Dico vobis*, Linz Stud B 71, 119r.: "Unde convenienter Karolus primus rex Sicilie addidit istud rubeum scuto Francie, quia ipse habuit sicut evidenter patuit ad ea que dicta sunt promptissimam voluntatem."

122. Ibid., 119v.: "Vere deus multiplicavit hunc sanctum donis et virtutibus, multiplicavit etiam sanctis imitatoribus qui de domo Francie venerunt post ipsum, quorum precipuus fuit beatus ludovicus nepos suus condam Episcopus Tholosanus. Isti enim duo ludovici fuerunt specialiter inter lilia huius agri, id est, domus francie illa lilia." On the theme of the two Louis (pl), see Bertaux, "Les saints Louis."

throughout the line's history—but in the lineage from which he descended and the lineage which he bore. The lineage was both of blood and of virtue, confirmed in the person of Louis IX but manifest throughout history. It was not Louis who was a saint, but his line.

Louis, Capetians, Valois

Louis was always going to represent a double-edged sword for the Capetians—symbolizing the legitimacy of their claim to being the *rex christianissimus* but also (*pace* Joinville and the Leagues) providing a standard of behavior and piety by which they would thereafter be judged.[123] And so Louis' sanctity could be presented as an instructive model for virtue or as the symbol of dynastic legitimacy and royal authority. The sword more often sliced in favor of the latter, in no small part because the kings themselves so often promoted that interpretation. But these two modes also point to two kinds of representation—devotional and private, on one hand, and public and propagandistic, on the other.

Thus Louis—the example of what type of behavior makes a king most Christian—was evoked in the devotional iconography, directed inwardly toward instructing Louis' royal descendants in the moral demands of Christian kingship. In this context Louis was envisioned as an intercessor, a link to the heavens, and a focus for devotion. Because he portrayed the virtues of saintliness, both in general terms and to royal women in particular, a model of kingship (and queenship) was melded to the priorities of compassion and active devotion so characteristic of lay sanctity in this period. But the opposite could also be true, where Louis was not a model but rather a manifestation of the broader sanctity of the ruling house. Here, Louis was emblematic as a saint of the larger priorities embedded in royal propaganda in general—the French kings as virtuous, as ensurers of peace, as crusaders, as defenders of the church, as "most Christian," as surpassing all other lines of kings. In this guise, it was Louis' sanctity that sanctified royal self-definition and propaganda. Bertrand's sermon exemplified such a "public" presentation of Saint Louis—not as a model to be emulated but as an icon of dynastic legitimacy. Bertrand was not unique in using the sermon form as a mechanism for royal propaganda after 1300 and in presenting a lineage of saint-kings in which Louis was the linchpin. Samantha Kelly, David D'Avray, Jean-Paul Boyer, Darleen Pryds, and Christine Chevalier Boyer have all explored sermon literature that fed the royal and dynastic image. The sermon edited by Leclercq and preached for the Flanders war (probably in 1317, before the dynastic break) spoke of the saint-kings of France (in the plural) who love sanctity and beget sanctity and cited Saint Louis in conjunction with his heirs in virtue. Like Bertrand, the preacher

---

123. For other examples, see Beaune, *Birth*, 104–105, 121; and Elizabeth A. R. Brown and Sanford Zale, "Louis Le Blanc, Estienne Le Blanc, and the Defense of Louis IX's Crusade, 1489–1522," *Traditio* 55 (2000).

emphasized the purity of the French line; recalled the Trojan origins of the lineage; spoke of figures such as Constantine, Clovis, Charlemagne, and Philip Augustus, along with Saint Louis, as exemplary members of French royalty; emphasized the role of the crusades and defending the faith; and praised the French kingdom as peaceful and Christian.[124] In this way, the image of Saint Louis was interwoven into a complex of ideological claims about French kingship that drew on the image of the most Christian, now saintly, king as peacemaker, crusader, defender of the church and faith, good and just king, and manifestation of the virtuous lineage.

That the Capetian line died out in 1328 with the death of Charles IV did not mute the sanctifying authority that Louis brought to the royal image and line because it was descent from Louis himself that mattered. As Bertrand showed, in 1328 Philip VI Valois could not only pick up the image of Louis bequeathed to him by the Capetians, he could use his direct descent as a legitimating attribute, as part of the sanctified line. The Valois would frequently draw on the image of the Capetian saint. As noted, Philip Valois himself made references to Louis, particularly in his first turbulent years as king. At the start of the Hundred Years War (when legitimacy and descent were key arguments in who was the rightful heir to the French throne), Edward III of England (d. 1377), himself a descendant of Saint Louis, wrote a letter to Philip Valois and vouched that as rightful king of France it was he who would return the kingdom to the "good laws and customs that were in place during the time of my ancestor, Saint Louis, king of France."[125] Copies of the *Grandes chroniques* made for John the Good (d. 1364) around this time emphasized Saint Louis as a good king, a crusader, and above all John's holy ancestor.[126] In turn, John cited Louis' reign repeatedly as a model in his own legislation.[127] Charles V (d. 1380) made the model of Saint Louis a hallmark of his own reign, citing Louis in his legislation, holding Louis up to Parlement as the patron of France, and describing him as "notre saint aieul et predecesseur, notre patron, notre defenseur et notre special seigneur."[128] He owned several copies of Louis' *vita*, *miracula*, and Hours, and also Louis' *Enseignements*. Christine de Pizan spoke of Charles V's particular devotion to Saint Louis, and Charles's royal secretary offered Saint Louis as a model to the sovereign in defending the church.[129]

---

124. Leclercq, "Un sermon prononcé," 169–170. On dating, see Brown, "Kings Like Semi-Gods," 10, n. 15.

125. Froissart, *Oeuvres de Froissart, publées avec les variants des divers manuscrits*, ed. Kervyn de Lettenhove (Brussels, 1867–1877, repr. 1967), vol. 18, 108: "les bones loys et custumes, qui furent ou temps nostre ancestre progénitour saint Lowys roy de Fraunce." The letter is dated to 8 February 1389.

126. Hedeman, *Royal Image*, 63–68.

127. Finhaber-Baker, "From God's Peace to the King's Order," 24.

128. Anne D. Hedeman, *Of Counselors and Kings: The Three Versions of Pierre Salmon's Dialogues* (Urbana, Ill., 2001), 106, n. 45.

129. Christine de Pizan, *Le Livre des Faits et Bonnes Moeurs du roi Charles V le Sage; traduction, avec introduction, chronologie et index par Eric Hicks et Thérèse Moreau* (Paris, 1997), 1–3, ch. 33; Hedeman, *Of Counselors and Kings*, 34.

Philip of Mézières then offered Louis as model of Christian kingship to the future Charles VI, and Louis appeared in the company of other saints in royal entries and tableaux vivants throughout the fifteenth century.[130] Charles VII had himself depicted as Saint Louis in an altarpiece that hung in the Parlement.[131] Charles VIII (d. 1498) had a personalized vernacular incunable of saints' lives decorated with an image of Saints Charlemagne and Louis ushering him to heaven.[132] Entrance ceremonies for Charles VIII invariably included images of lily-tree-genealogies that had Louis at the base of a stalk flourishing with Valois kings.[133] Examples could be multiplied, but the key was always descent. Again, with dynastic ruptures in 1498 (with the ascent of Louis XII), in 1515 (with the ascent of Francis I), and then again in 1589 (with the ascent of Henry IV Bourbon),[134] newly enthroned kings looked to their descent from Louis to argue for their own legitimacy. The cult of Louis was officially reestablished in 1618 by Louis XIII with the celebration of a solemn mass and the proclamation of a panegyric, and with this Saint Louis became an emblem for absolutist rule.[135] The Bourbon kings would make a habit of creating images of Louis that bore the features of reigning kings.[136] Louis' virtue, piety, compassion, and devotion would be remembered, but the attribute of his saintly identity that would win out over all others would always be his royalty.

130. Jacques Krynen, *Ideal du prince et pouvoir royal en France a la fin du moyen âge (1380–1440): Étude de la literature polique du temps* (Paris, 1981), 89.
131. Malcomb G. A. Vale, *Charles VII* (Berkeley, Calif., 1974), 197.
132. Christiane Prigent, ed., *Art et société en France au XVe siècle* (Paris, 1999), 298.
133. Spiegel and Hindman, "Fleur-de-lis Frontispiece," 405–406.
134. Elizabeth A. R. Brown, "The Religion of Royalty: From Saint Louis to Henry IV, 1226–1589," in *Creating French Culture: Treasures from the Bibliothèque Nationale de France*, ed. Marie-Hélène Tesnière and Prosser Gifford (New Haven, 1995), 132–133; Brown and Zale, "Louis Le Blanc, Estienne Le Blanc, and the Defense of Louis IX's Crusade, 1489–1522," 236.
135. Boureau, "Enseignements absolutistes," 79.
136. Feuilloy, Jannie Long, and Mulpeou, "Représentations."

9

Conclusion

Louis IX was the last king to be canonized in the Middle Ages. (King Ferdinand of Castile [d. 1272] was canonized in 1671—but that belongs to a different age.) In part, this was because the historical conditions that could make a saint-king were shifting, as the new monarchies of Europe emerged and papal universalism gave up ground to national churches. Almost a century and half after Louis' canonization, in 1438, the prelates and nobility of France gathered at Bourges, at the behest of King Charles VII, a descendant and devotee of Saint Louis. France was embroiled in the Hundred Years War, and the papacy was struggling to emerge from the troubles of the Great Schism, conciliarism, and demands for reform. The French churchmen essentially loyal to the king issued what has come to be known as the "Pragmatic Sanction of Bourges," a document that drew on the constitutional groundwork of conciliarism and was aimed at limiting papal authority in France and establishing the contours of an independent French church—Gallicanism. In support of this an old document was dug up to give these claims their historic legitimacy, the Pragmatic of Saint Louis. Dated to March 1268, the Pragmatic of Saint Louis protested papal exactions and decried the lamentable impoverishment of the kingdom that resulted.[1] Indeed, the Pragmatic laid down all the principles that the French prelates sought to justify in the wake of 1438.

It turns out that the document was a forgery—produced by royal lawyers sometime after that year. And so it is telling, though not at all surprising, that, at a moment when the French church sought to define itself independently from universal papal authority, when the French ecclesiastical establishment was in need of a new historical memory into which to root their current objec-

---

1. Noèl Valois, *Histoire de la Pragmatique Sanction de Bourges sous Charles VII* (Paris, 1906), clxi.

tives and ideals, they turned to Louis.[2] In this way did Louis become the spiritual father of a move for French ecclesiastical independence and the definition of the French national church. A saint of the universal church became a symbol of the French monarchy and ultimately a symbol of French nationhood.

Although the cult of Louis IX at times waned, the image of the royalized saint long remained powerful in the ongoing discourse of the catholic state, because Louis was the very-most Christian of the most Christian kings.[3] Within the context of the Wars of Religion, Henri IV (founder of the new Bourbon line, and a Protestant turned Catholic in order to become king) worked to establish his credentials as a proper Christian monarch by plumbing his descent from Saint Louis. The first Bourbon king then named his son Louis, which became thereafter the given name for all heirs to the throne. Ecclesiastical dedications to Louis increased substantively after 1589.[4] In the seventeenth century, Louis' cult was actively fostered as a symbol for the absolutist cause of divine right by Louis XIII, Richelieu, and Louis XIV.[5] Louis XIII officially renewed the cult of Saint Louis on August 25, 1618, and only then was Louis' cult officially established, by papal decree, throughout the entire kingdom of France. An explosion of laudatory writings produced by courtiers and panegyrists praised Louis for his defense of the French church (Gallicanism), as an absolute monarch, as the founder of rational royal administration, and ultimately as the "embodiment of all the virtues of the royal French dynasty."[6] Almost all royal religious foundations were dedicated to Louis.[7] A new office written for Louis for use at the chapel at Versailles drew on the ideals of Louis as just, virtuous, and an intercessor to the divine.[8] As a symbol of both royalty and catholicity Saint Louis so embodied at once the catholic and the royal identity of the ancient regime that, on October 11, 1793, in Evreux, revolutionaries burned him in effigy.[9] He could then be revived as a symbol of Christian monarchy in the debates over the Restauration following the Napoleonic Wars.[10]

2. Ibid., clix–clxiv; Victor Martin, *Les origines du gallicanisme* (Paris, 1939), 303–324; Beaune, *Birth*, 121–122.

3. For this paragraph, see Lucien Pfleger, "Le Culte de Saint Louis en Alsace," *Revue des Sciences Religieuse* (1921): 222–227; Morel, "Culte"; Michael Tyvaert, "L'image du roi: légitimité et moralité royales dans les histoires de France au XVIIe siècle," *Revue d'histoire moderne et contemporaine* 21 (1974): 521–547; Manfred Tietz, "Saint Louis roi chretien: un mythe de la mission interieure du XVIIe siecle," in *La conversion au XVIIe siècle: actes du XIIe Colloque de Marseille (janvier 1982)* (Marseille, 1983); Pierre Zobermann, "Généalogie d'une image: L'éloge speculaire," *XVIIe siècle* 146 (1985); Boureau, "Enseignements absolutistes"; Bruno Neveu, "Du culte de saint Louis à la glorification de Louis XIV: la maison royale de Saint-Cyr," *Journal des Savants* (1988): 277–290; and Adam Knobler, "Saint Louis in French Political Culture," in *Medievalism in Europe II*, ed. Leslie Workman and Kathleen Verduin (Cambridge, 1996), 156–173.

4. Morel, "Culte," 134–137.

5. Ibid., 137–139.

6. Boureau, "Enseignements absolutistes"; Boureau, "The King," 205–206.

7. Morel, "Culte," 139.

8. BNF Lat 8831.

9. Tietz, "Saint Louis roi chretien," 59–60.

10. Jean-Paul Clément, "L'utilisation du mythe de Saint-Louis par Chateaubriand dans les controverses politiques de l'Empire et de la Restauration," *Revue d'histoire littéraire de la France* 98 (1998): 1059–1072.

This book has, I hope, outlined the early stages of the development of how Louis—canonized for his piety, his crusade, and his just rule—was turned into a figure of legitimate political authority. These three interrelated spheres—piety, crusade, and kingship—offered the common building blocks for different interpretations. Piety was always the sine qua non of sanctity, though the forms Louis' piety took often highlighted other ideals, and certainly different people understood his piety in very different ways. But his kingship and his crusading were potentially more complicated, and the ways in which they were valuated reflected the fact that the monarchy and crusading were both in times of transition and transformation around 1300, both subjects of debate and discord. These aspects of Louis' identity were parsed and reconstructed to specific ends for specific purposes. A common stock of stories was established early on in the canonization process (though some new details and interpretations accrued as well). These were taken up, made reference to, repeated, recopied, and rewritten, again and again. But this was not done consistently or predictably, and these stories, qualities, and attributes bore different force at difference times. So, for instance, Franciscans cared little for Louis' royalty but thought deeply about the passion and devotion he exhibited on crusade. Yet crusading at court was perhaps more appropriately understood as a function of Christian kingship. Louis' great patronage of monastic orders was interpreted by a Dominican who was also a royal client (William of Chartres) as a mark of ideal kingship. A Franciscan sermon understood this same patronage as a mark of piety, and so forth.

In seeking to unpack the different ways in which these ideals of saintly virtue were understood by those who memorialized Louis, I hope this book offers two broader contributions. The first is to reconstruct some of the evolution of Louis' cult, to give a more complete picture of the richness and variation within the early history of devotion to Louis, and to present a sustained treatment of the first two generations or so of devotion to the saint-king. This view reinforces our understanding of the crucial if contested role played by Philip the Fair, both as the monarch in power at the time of Louis' canonization but also because of his own commitment to honoring his sainted grandfather. But the saint-king was not only a saint for kings, and this reconstruction points to other centers of his cult and the competing interpretations of his sainthood among Dominicans, Franciscan, Cistercians, other Benedictines, bishops, aristocrats, and poor devotees looking for miraculous cures. This is by no means a comprehensive account of Louis' cult. It ends, for all intents and purposes, in the first third of the fourteenth century, long before the "discovery" of Joinville's text in the sixteenth century and its exposure to a broad readership in the seventeenth,[11] before the many glazing cycles of the fourteenth and fifteenth centuries,[12] before the rediscovery of Saint Louis by

---

11. Boureau, "Enseignements absolutistes," 88–89.

12. Pierre-Marie Auzas, "Essai d'un répertoire iconographique de saint Louis," in *Septième centenaire de la mort de Saint Louis: Actes des Collogues de Royaumont et de Paris (21–27 mai 1970)* (Paris, 1976), 3–56; Charles Tesseyre, "Le prince chrétien aux XVe et XVIe siècles, à travers les représentation de Charlemagne et de Saint Louis," *Annales de Bretagne* 87 (1980): 409–414.

the absolutist governments of Louis XIII and Louis XIV. But my hope is that this focus on this initial, critical half-century following Louis' death suggests something of the complex politicized, devotional, and representational aspects of Louis' sainthood, not only to the crown but to a variety of devotional constituencies.

Second, a parsing of the sources, and an emphasis on some of the less well-known liturgical and homiletic material, reveals Louis' remarkably multifaceted identity, his memory, and ultimately his meaning to contemporaries—meaning that, because of its richness and its sincerity, offered multivalent possibilities of representation and projection.[13] Louis personified different values to different constituencies, institutions, or individuals, in ways that were motivated by both politics and devotion, even as they reflect broader ideological fissures in the religious and spiritual ideals of the later Middle Ages. The logic for the definition of Louis' sanctity played itself out, with different results, in each case. So, for example, the myriad of devotees who made their way to St.-Denis in hopes of a miracle rooted Louis' sanctity in his thaumatological powers. Cistercians saw in Louis a series of conservative monastic and spiritual ideals that defined themselves and the order. Joinville saw in Louis a chivalric figure and an example of ideal kingship, but one designed not so much to glorify the monarchy as to define a royal comportment that coincided with aristocratic ideals and interests.

None of this is perhaps a priori surprising, but documented in this way, I hope, it shows how dynamic were the early stages of Louis' cult and the construction of his saintly identity, the extent to which he was a potent symbol of religious virtue and political idealism, and, finally, the way in which such a sanctified symbol of virtue could be a mechanism for the discourse of political and religious ideals during the tendentious later Middle Ages. Louis reflected social ideals of Christian perfection, virtuous kingship and ideal rule, and what is perhaps worth noting is that, after 1300, those ideals fractured along the fault lines of various constituencies and competing interests—that once canonized, these ideals were seen through different ideological lenses or colored by broader political agendas. All these arguments point more broadly to the realization that Louis' sanctity—and sanctity generally—was not only the representation of social ideals but also a vehicle for a cultural discussion of ideals, a symbolic focus of competing ideologies and values, and a mechanism of articulating and constructing identity.

13. These are categories of the representation of the king explored by Boureau, "The King."

Appendix 1

Sources for the Liturgical Tradition

Please note that I have listed here only manuscripts whose contents I have verified; there are surely others. Most are breviaries, and I have noted when a manuscript is otherwise. Other pertinent details are noted marginally.

For provenance and dating information, see Leroquais, *Les Bréviaires manuscrits de bibliothèques publiques de France*, 5 vols.

NUNC LAUDARE

Mss:

London BL 30072, 413v.–420r. (OP use, adapted for Poissy in early fourteenth century, notated)

Paris Mazarine 374, 462v.–463v. (OP use, for St.-Jacques, fourteenth century)

Rouen BM Y233, 277v.–278 (Diurnal Psalter, OP use, for Poissy, early fourteenth century, notated)

Ed:

AH: v. 13, 194–197, no. 74 (for office); v. 11, 178–179, nos. 320–322 (for hymns)

LMLO: LV24

Bibl:

Naughton 1995, Gaposchkin 2004

LUDOVICUS DECUS REGNANTIUM

Mss: (selected)

Châteauroux BM 2, 297v.–304r. (Paris use, early fifteenth century, includes octave)

London BL 23935, 7r.–14r. (OP use, Humbert of Romans' consultation copy, added to manuscript mid-fourteenth century, notated)

London BL 30072, 421r.–431v. (OP use, adapted for Poissy in early fourteenth century sometime after *Nunc laudare*, notated)

Lyon BM 524, 323–329 (Langres use, partial witness, ca. 1300)

Melbourne, The State Library at Victoria 096 1.R66A, 310r.–315r. (OP use, made for Poissy, mid-fourteenth century, notated)

Paris Arsenal 133, 433r.–435v. (Paris use, for the Oratory of St. Magloire, fifteenth century)

Paris Arsenal 276, 374v.–377v. (Coutence use, fifteenth century, shortened for use as semi-duplex)

Paris Arsenal 279, 580v.–585r. (Bayeux use, added to manuscript in fourteenth or fifteenth century)

Paris Arsenal 582, 582–589 (Paris use, fifteenth century)

Paris Arsenal 603, 313–320v. (OP use, for Poissy, after 1336, includes readings [not antiphons] for the octave)

Paris BNF Lat 745, 365–372v. (Paris use, after 1366, includes octave)

Paris BNF Lat 910A, 45r.–51v. (Libellus, fifteenth century)

Paris BNF Lat 911, 3r.–35r. (Libellus, probably for Ste.-Chapelle, ca. 1310, includes octave)

Paris BNF Lat 1023, 560r.–562v. ("Breviary of Philip the Fair," use of the Capella regis, ca. 1300)

Paris BNF Lat 1026, 251v.–262 (Paris use, fourteenth century, includes octave)

Paris BNF Lat 1028, 328r.–339v. (Sens use, ca. 1300, notated)

Paris BNF Lat 1029, 429v.–434 (Auxerre use, fourteenth or fifteenth century)

Paris BNF Lat 1032, 395v.–398 (Tours use, fifteenth century)

Paris BNF Lat 1052, 468v.–476v. ("Breviary of Charles V," use of the Capella regis, before 1380)

Paris BNF Lat 1291, 386r.–389v. (Paris use, fifteenth century)

Paris BNF Lat 1324, 193r.–195v. (Diurnal, OP use, fifteenth century)

Paris BNF Lat 10484, 303v.–309r. ("Belleville Breviary," OP use, fourteenth century)

Paris BNF Lat 10485, 429r.–432r. (Paris use, fourteenth century, includes octave)

Paris BNF Lat 10491, 114r.–116v. (Roman use, fifteenth century)

Paris BNF Lat 10872 67v.–72v. (ca. 1310, Meridional)

Paris BNF Lat 13233, 673r.–679r. ("Breviary of Charles V," use of the Capella regis, before 1380, altered by incorporation of items from *Sanctus voluntatem*)

Paris BNF Lat 13238, 290v.–299v. (Ste.-Chapelle use, fifteenth century, includes octave)

Paris BNF nal 388, 310r.–312v. (Evreux use, fourteenth century)

Paris BNF nal 622, 301v.–305v. (Arras use, fourteenth century)

Paris Mazarine 342, 396v.–433v. (Paris use, fourteenth century)

Paris Mazarine 344, 242r.–249v. (Paris use, from the Oratory of Saint Magloire, fourteenth century, notated)

Paris Mazarine 354, fragment: 2v. (Limoges use, fourteenth century)

Paris St. Genevieve 2626, 328r.–343v. (Rouen use, fourteenth century, notated, includes octave)

Provins BM 8, 295v.–298r. (Paris use, adapted to Senlis, fourteenth century)

Rouen BM 197, 329v.–331r. (Diurnal, OP use, early fourteenth century)

Troyes BM 1780, 313r.–316r. (Troyes use, fourteenth century)

Washington DC Library of Congress 15, 553v.–560r. (Royal, added ca. 1300, lections from *Glor. reg.*)

Ed:
AH: v. 13, 185–188, no. 71 (for office); v. 11, 177–178, nos. 317–319 (for hymns).
LMLO: LV21
Heysse 1917
Epstein 1978

Bibl:
Epstein 1978, Naughton 1995, Gaposchkin 2002, Gaposchkin 2004

EXULTEMUS OMNES (THE OFFICE OF THE TRANSLATION)

Mss:

Paris Arsenal 660, 499v.–502r. (Paris use, ca. 1400)

Paris BNF Lat 746A, 296rb.–297va. (Paris use, fifteenth century, with variant third lection)

Paris BNF Lat 911, 35v.–38r. (Libellus, probably for Ste.-Chapelle, added late fourteenth century, notated)

Paris BNF Lat 1024, 415vb.–418ra. (Paris use, fourteenth century)

Paris BNF Lat 1052, 374v.–376r. ("Breviary of Charles V," use of the Capella regis, before 1380)

Paris BNF Lat 1291, 311vb.–313vb. (Paris use, fifteenth century, with variant third lection)

Paris BNF Lat 13233, 589rb.–591va. ("Breviary of Charles V," use of the Capella regis, fourteenth century)

Paris BNF Lat 14511, 179r.–182r. (Compendium from Saint Victor's, fourteenth century, including Translation office with original lections for the Translation office, notated)

Paris Mazarine 342, 556v.–559v. (Paris use, fourteenth century)

Paris Mazarine 345, 503v.–506v. (Paris use, ca. 1410)

Ed:

AH: v. 13, 197–198, no. 75 (for office); v. 11, 180–181, nos. 326–328 (for hymns)

LMLO: LV26

LAUDA CELESTIS 1 (CISTERCIAN)

Mss:

Troyes BM 1973, 224v.–226v.(Cistercian use, ca. 1300)

Troyes BM 2030, 537r.–539 (Cistercian use, office added in fourteenth or fifteenth century, partial witness)

Bibl:

Gaposchkin forthcoming

LAUDA CELESTIS 2 (SECULAR USE)

Ms:

Orleans BM 348, 18–22. (Made for the chapel of Notre-Dame des Miracles, Avignon, fourteenth century)

Bibl:

Gaposchkin forthcoming

LAUDA CELESTIS 3 (ST.-GERMAIN-DES-PRÉS, ST.-DENIS)

Mss:

Oxford Bodleian Canon Liturg 192, 422r.–424r. (St.-Denis use, ca. 1350).

Paris BNF Lat 13239, fols. 383v.–387v. (St.-Germain-des-Prés use, ca 1300)

Ed:

Breviarium iuxta ritum regalis cenobii Christi martyris Ariopagite Dionysii nunc primum accuratissime Parisiis excussum (Paris, 1550).

AH: v. 13, 188–191, no. 72 (for office); v. 11, 178–179, nos. 320–322 (for hymns)
LMLO: LV22

Bibl:
Gaposchkin forthcoming

FRANCORUM REX

Mss:
Cambridge D.d.V. V5, 294v.–299v. (OM use, Breviary of Marie of Saint Pol, Countess of Pembroke, 1330–1342)
Evreux BM 12, 397r. (Evreux use, late fourteenth century)
London BL Harley 2864, 368v.–370v. (OM use, fifteenth century)
New York Pierpont Morgan M.75, 484v.–487v. (OM use, fourteenth century)
New York Pierpont Morgan M.149, 465v.–470v. (OM use, fourteenth century, perhaps made for Blanche of France, daughter of Philip V)
Paris BNF Lat 1288, 491v.–494v. (OM use, 1334–1347)
Padua University of Padua 734, 375r.–377 (OM use, Italian, fifteenth century)
Tours BM 143, 389r. (Roman use, fifteenth century, lacunary)

Ed:
AH: v. 13, 192–194, no. 73 (for office); v. 11, 179–180, nos. 324–326 (for hymns)
LMLO: LV23

SANCTUS VOLUNTATEM (THE HOURS OF LOUIS)

Mss:
New York Public Library Spencer 56 (for Blanche of Burgundy? ca. 1315)
New York Metropolitan Museum of Art 54.1.2 (The Hours of Jeanne d'Evreux, 1324–1328)
Paris BNF nal 592 (ca. 1330–1340)
Paris BNF nal 3145, 85v.–105v. (Hours of Jeanne de Navarre, after 1329)
Savoy Hours (mostly lost, ca. 1335–1340, remnants, not including Hours of Louis, at Yale, Benicke 390)
Venice, Bibl Naz Marc Lat I 104/12640, fols. 178–198v. (Hours of Marie de Navarre, 1339–1340)

Facsimiles:
Libro de horas de la reina Maria de Navarra: cuyo original se conserva en la Biblioteca Nazionale Marciana, Venecia, bajo la referencia Lat. I, 104 (=12640): Officium. 1 + commentary vols (Barcelona: Moleiro, 1996).
Das Stundenbuch der Jeanne D'evreux = The Hours of Jeanne d'Evreux = Le Livre d'heures de Jeanne d'Evreux (Luzern and New York: Faksimile Verlag and the Metropolitan Museum of Art, 1998), p. [426].

Ed:
Longnon, 1882, 53–66 (Jeanne de Navarre)
Delisle 1905, 521–530 (NYPL Spencer 56)
Libro de horas 1996, commentary Volume, 348–362 (Marie de Navarre)
Das Stundenbuch 1998 (Jeanne d'Evreux)

Bibl:
NYPL Spencer 56: Delisle 1905.
Jeanne d'Evreux: Randall 1972, Caviness 1993, Holladay 1994, Guest 1995, Das Studenbuch commentary 1999, Gertsman 2003.

Jeanne de Navarre: Thomas 1976, Mertzman 1994, Louvre 2001, 193, no. 46, Keane 2002, 71–89, 150–155.
Marie de Navarre: Saulnier-Pinsard 1985, Yarza 1999, Keane 2002.
Savoy Hours: Carta 1899 (pl. lvii for surviving reproduction from lost material), Durrieu 1911a, 1911b, De Hamel 1990, Wieck 1991, Manion 1998, 45–50.

BEATUS LUDOVICUS QUONDAM REX FRANCORUM

Mss:
As vita (that is, not subdivided into lections)
  Paris Mazarine 1732, 347r.–349r. ("Sanctilogium")
  Paris BNF Lat 14652, 220r.–231v. ("vitae sanctorum")
  Paris BNF nal 1755 10v.–12v. ("vitae sanctorum," fifteenth century)

As lections, in complete form
  Paris Arsenal 276, 580v.–585r. (fifteenth century)
  Paris BNF Lat 911, 7v.–18v. (ca. 1310)
  Paris BNF Lat 10872, 67v.–72v.

Ed:
  RHF v. 23, 160–167 (taken from Paris BNF Lat 10872, 67v.–72v., ca. 1300–1310)
  Heysse 1917, Epstein 1978 (both taken from Paris BNF Lat 911)

Appendix 2

Liturgical Offices for Saint Louis
of France

Preliminary

This appendix presents the texts for the different office traditions. It has
two purposes: first, to provide the texts that are referenced throughout
the book; and second, to demonstrate the transmission of individual
items from one tradition to the next.

Where possible, the order of the texts as they appear in the manuscript(s)
chosen to represent the tradition has been followed, though in a few cases the
placement of texts has been shifted so as to keep them aligned with the format
of this chart. Equivalency in structure breaks down after lauds, and so from
this point onward the texts are simply listed in the order they appear in the
base sources. Even though SV (the Hours for Louis) follows a different structure entirely, its texts are aligned as best possible to indicate how it adopted
texts from earlier traditions. Here the original order is followed.

Each tradition is represented by either two or three manuscripts, except for
LC2, which has a single known source (G). Epstein's edition from BNF Lat
911 has been used for LDR, though C was consulted for the octave antiphons,
and the text has been compared to Washington Library of Congress ms 15,
which represents another early and royal exemplar of the tradition. Delisle's
1905 edition has been used for SV, the Hours of Louis. For LC1–3, the manuscripts used constitute the known sources for the tradition. Editions from the
other exemplars are listed in Appendix 1.

The base manuscript for each office is marked with an asterisk (*), and the
orthography of that manuscript is followed, except for standardizing *u/v and
i/j*. The base text has been collated with one or two other manuscripts, and on
occasion readings from one of these manuscripts have been adopted when they
are superior to those found in the base. Rubrics have been suppressed in favor
of the system of reference outlined in the Excursus. The last stanzas of the
matins and lauds hymns in all manuscripts have been abbreviated since they

repeat the last stanza from the first vespers hymn, and the repetenda and other standard items (Amen and Alleluya, for instance) that are listed irregularly in the exemplars have been omitted. Common abbreviations have been expanded (Christo for xpo, and so forth), as have liturgical abbreviations that were commonplace in the liturgy (Magnificat for Mag). Capitalization and punctuation have been introduced sparingly, and Psalm incipits included only if they appear in one of the exemplars (though the sequence in all follows the office for nonpontiff confessors). In no case have the lections been included, which in any event vary in length in different exemplars of the same tradition.

The columns are ordered in such a way that a reader might trace the relationship between NL and LDR, the three versions of LC, and NL, LDR, EO, and SV. LC1 was probably composed before LDR (which adopts its Magnificat antiphon), and FR was composed before the octave antiphons were compiled for LDR, which was probably completed *after* the composition of the body of the office. I have noted in brackets when a text is adopted from an existing tradition.

Manuscript sigla are as follows:

A: London BL Add. 30027*
B: Paris Mazarine 374
C and C$_2$: Paris BNF Lat 911 (after Epstein 1971)*
D: Washington DC Library of Congress ms 15
E: Troyes BM 1973*
F: Troyes BM 2030
G: Orleans BM 348*
H: Oxford Canon Liturg. 192
I: Paris BNF Lat 13239*
J: Paris BNF Lat 1024
K: Paris BNF Lat 13233
L: Paris BNF Lat 1288*
M: Cambridge D.d.V.
N. New York Public Library Spencer 56 (after Delisle 1905)*

Notes on the manuscript sources

NL: *B* comes from a manuscript from the Dominican convent in Paris (Rue St. Jacques) which probably served as source book for other copies, and dates to ca. 1300. *A* belonged to Poissy, and is the cleaner copy of the text, though probably postdates *B*.

LDR: *C* is the "shrine book" (*libellus*) probably made for the Ste.-Chapelle ca. 1300–1310 (not a breviary) and possibly to serve as source exemplar. On *C*, see Epstein 1978 and Gaposchkin 2004. Changes in music, notations, and orthography were made in *C* by the same hand that also copied EO to the back of the volume (indicated here by *C$_2$*). *D*, also a royal manuscript, may well

represent an earlier example of the office, since there the version is provisionally paired with lections from *Glor. reg.* On this manuscript, see Baltzer 2000.
Transcriptions reflect existing orthography.

LC1: *E* dates to shortly after 1297. The office is an addition to *F*, with the
first folio of LC1 sliced from the manuscript. In *F* the text begins only with the
Magnificat of 1 vespers. *F* does not include hymns. Psalm incipits were sometimes provided by the edition of 1641.

LC2: *G* is the only known example of the secularized version of the office.
The manuscript itself appears to be mid-fourteenth century, though it must
represent a process of adaption that dated to the early fourteenth century.

LC3: *I* dates to ca. 1300–1325. *H* dates to ca. 1350. The structure differs for
H and *I*, with *I* maintaining more original items. *I* retained more antiphons for
1 vespers and lauds, and the prayers are distributed differently in the two exemplars after lauds. On the manuscript tradition for LC1–3, see Gaposchkin
2008.

EO: No exemplars of EO are found in any manuscript from the beginning of
the century, though the assumption is that it was composed for the translation
of 1306 or shortly thereafter. The office was copied into *C* in a later hand from
LDR, and is identified as C_2. C_2 and *K* are royal or courtly. *J* is likely from
Notre Dame.

FR: *L* and *M* both belong to a family of Franciscan manuscripts illustrated
in Paris in the first half of the fourteenth century.

SV: The transcription for SV follows *N* and is taken from Delisle, 1905,
521–529.

Appendix 2.1. Texts of the Offices for Saint Louis of France

NUNC LAUDARE	LUDOVICUS DECUS	LAUDA CELESTIS 1	LAUDA CELESTIS 2	LAUDA CELESTIS 3	EXULTEMUS OMNES	FRANCORUM REX	SANCTUS VOLUNTATEM
(Dominican)	(Secular/ royal)	(Cistercian)	(Secular)	(St.-Denis, St.-Germain-des-Prés)	(Translation Office)	(Franciscan)	(Hours of Louis)
A. BL 30027, 413v.-420r.* B. Mazarine ms 374, 462v.-463v.	C. BNF Lat 911, 3r.-22r.* (After Epstein 1973) D. D.C. Library of Congress ms 15, 554r.-560r.	E. Troyes BM 1973, 224v.-226v.* F. Troyes BM 2030, 537r.-539r.	G. Orleans BM 348, 18r.-22r.*	H. Oxford Canon Liturgy 192 (St.-Denis) 422r.-425r. I. Paris BNF Lat 13239 (St.-Germain des Prés) 383v.-387v.*	C₂ BNF Lat 911, 35v.-38r.* J. BNF Lat 1024, 415v.-418r. K. BNF Lat 13233, 589r.-591r.	L. BNF Lat 1288, 490v.-494v.* M. Cambridge D.d.V, 294r.-298v.	N. NYPL Spencer 56* (after Delisle 1905)

FIRST VESPERS

NUNC LAUDARE	LUDOVICUS DECUS	LAUDA CELESTIS 1	LAUDA CELESTIS 2	LAUDA CELESTIS 3	EXULTEMUS OMNES	FRANCORUM REX	SANCTUS VOLUNTATEM
[VA1] Nunc laudare Dominum debet plebs fidelis; extirpator criminum regnat rex in celis. P. Laudate pium.	[VA1] Ludovicus decus regnantium transit felix ad celi solium, cuius prece cetus fidelium summi regis intret in gaudium.	[VA1] Lauda celestis regio regem seculorum; tuo dignus collegio adest rex francorum.	[VA1] Lauda celestis regio regem seculorum; tuo dignus collegio adest rex francorum.	[VA1] Lauda celestis regio regem seculorum; tuo dignus collegio adest rex francorum. P. Dixit Dominus.	[VA1] Exultemus omnes et singuli diem festum agentes[a] gratiose; Ludovicus cuius nos servuli translatus est[a] hodie gloriose. [a] est] et J.	[VA1] Francorum rex magnificus, Ludovicus vir celitus, summopere[a] studuit soli Deo placere, a quo tantam meruit gratiam obtinere. P. Dixit Dominus [a] summopere] sumus opere L.	
	[=NL. Bend. A.]		[=LC1 VA1]	[=LC2 VA1]			
[VA2] Gaude regnum Francie, cui dedit rex glorie tam excellens donum[a], quod tu regem proprium habes in subsidium in celis patronum.	[VA2] Collaudent[a] ecclesie humilem, pudicum, pium regem Francie, sanctum Ludovicum.	[VA2] Collaudent ecclesie humilem, pudicum, pium[a] regem Francie, sanctum Ludovicum.	[VA2] Collaudent ecclesie humilem, pudicum, pium[a] regem Francie, sanctum Ludovicum.	[VA2] Collaudent ecclesie humilem, pudicum, pium regem Francie, sanctum Ludovicum. P. Laudate pium.	[VA2] Gloriose prefuit regno seculari; virtuose studuit Christo famulari; pauperibus profuit zelo singulari.	[VA2] Crucis Christi signaculum contra gentilem populum suscepit, primum iunior[a] et post modum provectior, ad meritorum cumulum. P. Confitebor	
[a] donum] domum C.	[a] Collaudent] Collaudant E.		[a] pium] absent in ms.	[=LC2 VA2] J only.		[a] iunior] minor L.	

253

Appendix 2.1-*cont.*

Nunc Laudare	Ludovicus Decus	Lauda Celestis 1	Lauda Celestis 2	Lauda Celestis 3	Exultemus Omnes	Francorum Rex	Sanctus Voluntatem
	[VA3] Te dum ipse viveret ac coronam regeret, tamquam rex deffendit, nunc particeps glorie factus tue venie diligens intendit.	[VA3] Hostem pestis heretice progenitorem habuit, qui fidei catholice fortis athleta claruit.	[VA3] Hostem pestis heretice progenitorem habuit, qui fidei catholice fortis athleta claruit.	[VA3] Hostem pestis heretice progenitorem habuit, qui fidei catholice fortis athleta claruit. P. Credidi.	[VA3] Singulari pollebat gratia pietatis, nec unquam deserebat limam equitatis, sicque[a] regnum regebat virga veritatis.	[VA3] Hic regnum, matrem, liberos,[a] infantes adhuc teneros reliquit, ac sororem, sed post assumptis filiis, herens Christi consiliis, dimisit et uxorem. P. Beatus vir.	
			[=LC1 VA3]	[=LC2 VA3] *J* only:	[a] sicque] *K* sit que.	[a] liberos] om. *L.*	
	[VA4] Plebs ergo francigena, non tanquam gens advena, Christo refer laudes, in cuius palatio tui patrocinio quondam regis gaudes.	[VA4] Pater[a], illustris genere mira, pollens, pericia, docuit eum colere deum a puericia.	[VA4] Mater, illustris genere mira, pollens, pericia, docuit eum colere deum a puericia.	[VA4] Mater, illustris genere mira, pollens, pericia,[a] docuit eum colere deum a puericia. P. In vertendo.	[VA4] Veritatis doctores fervente dilexit, et ad bonos mores se totum erexit, suos successores ad deum direxit.	[VA4] Sanctus hic sprevit omnia quecumque transitoria propter regnum celorum, tam carnales delicias quam fallaces divicias, cum fastu[a] superborum. P. Laudate pueri.	
		[a] *1641 edition retains* Pater.	[=LC1 VA3]	[=LC2 VA3] *J* only: [a] pericia] *overwritten I.*		[a] cum fastu] confastu *M.*	
	[VA5] In terris regimine ac sub eius nomine protecta fuisti modo tibi gratiam impetret ac veniam in conspectu Christi.		[VA5] Laudem in regimine regni sublimatus, virtutum culmine concedit ornatus.		[VA5] Direxit reges Francie sanctus Ludovicus, nitore consciencie Dei factus amicus, ob hoc regnum glorie nunc est sibi vicus.	[VA5] Hic miraculis rutilat qui in celis iam iubilat exultans cum beatis. O Ludovice rex pie memento nostri hodie qui sumus in peccatis. P. Laudate Dominum omnes gentes.	
[Cap] Benedictus Dominus Deus patrum nostrorum qui dedit hanc voluntatem in cor regis clarificare	[Cap] Benedictus Dominus Deus patrum nostrorum qui dedit hanc voluntatem in cor regis clarificare	[Cap] Dilectus[a] a deo.		[Cap] Beatus vir qui inventus est sine macula et qui post aurum non abiit. Nec speravit in pecunie thesauris; quis est hic et	[Cap] Benedictus Dominus Deus patrum nostrorum qui dedit hanc voluntatem in cor regis: clarificare	[Cap] Beatus dives qui inventus est sine macula et qui post aurum non abiit. Nec speravit in peccunie thesauris,	

domum suam que est in Ierusalem. Deo gratias. [Cf. Ezra 7.27; =NL] "Benedicus . . . gratias] om. A.	domum suam que est in Ierusalem. Deo gratias. [Cf. Ezra 7.27; =NL Cap] [Cf. Eccli. 45.1] "Dilectus] corr. from Lilectus E. Appears after VCapRV in ms.		laudabimus eum, fecit enim mirabilia in vita sua. [Cf. Eccli. 31.8-9] "est sine . . . vita sua] om. L.	domum suam que est in Iherusalem. Deo gratias. [Cf. Ezra 7.27; =NL Cap, LDR Cap] "Deus patrum...in iherusalem] quere in primis vesperis alterius: C2. Supplied by K.	quis est hic et laudabimus eum, fecit eius mirabilia in vita sua. [Eccli 31.8-9] "quis] quid M. b sua] tua L.
[VCapRV] Cum esset in accubitu, rex interne dulcedinis, arcens potenti spiritu pestes carnis et sanguinis bonorum septus ambitu, sceptro fulsit regiminis. [v] David regis sedit in solio, Salomonis Utens iudicio [=NL MRV7]	[VCapRV] Miles Christi gloriose, Ludovice sanctissime, tuo pio interventu culpas nostras ablue. [v] Ut celestis regni sedem valeamus scandere.		[VCapRV] Cum esset in accubitu, rex interne dulcedinis, arcens potenti spiritu pestes carnis et sanguinis bonorum sceptus ambitu, sceptro fulsit regiminis. [v] David regis sedit in solio, Salomonis utens iudicio. [=NL MRV7, LDR VCapV, MRV6 Incorporated LC3 also at MRV8] "interne] in eterne L. "sceptro] sceptr L.	[VCapRV] O sparsor divitiarum erogando pauperibus, O spretor deliciarum insudando laboribus, O tutor ecclesiarum eas iuvando viribus, duc nos ad regnum preclarum tuis devotis precibus. [v] Qui tot egris prestitisti curationum gratiam, nobis confer dono Christi transgressionum veniam. [=NL MRV9 altered, EO MRV3] "divitiarum . . . precibus] Supplied by K.	[VCapRV] En regi genti gallice divina providentia prepositum mirifice lustratum sapientia. Eya Dei amice mundo refulgens gratia [v] Nomen Dei Ludovice est pro lucis Domine tam vigili custodia. "en regi . . . custodia] om. M.
[VHymn] Gaude mater ecclesia nove laudis preconio quam Ludovici gloria solempni replet gaudio.	[VHymn] Gaude mater ecclesia nove laudis preconio quam Ludovici gloria solemni replet gaudio.	[VHymn] Pulset celum laus amena, laus cunctorum fidelium, moduletur vox serena Ludovici preconium.	[VHymn] Pulset celum laus amena, laus cunctorum fidelium, moduletur vox serena Ludovici preconium.	[VHymn] Studeamus attollere Ludovicum ex viribus, quem scimus Dei munere dignum devotis laudibus.	[VHymn] Gaude chorus fidelium pro Ludovici, gloria celestium, terrestrium, tota simul ecclesia.
De regno terre vehitur ad regni celi solium, cuius vita dinoscitur forma virtutum omnium.	De regno terre vehitur ad regni celi solium, cuius vita dignoscitur forma virtutum omnium.	Ludovicus infantulus devoto mentis studio cepit vacare sedulus virtutum exercicio.	Ludovicus infantulus devoto mentis studio cepit vacare sedulus virtutum exercicio.	Ab etatis primordiis fecit hunc mater imbui moribus et scientiis et studere profectui.	Hic puer simplex, docilis, adolescens, amabilis, iuvenis, fide ferbuit pro qua se senex posuit.
Fide purus, spe patiens et caritate fervidus, omni petenti largiens, Pius, pudicus, providus.	Fide constans, spe subvectus caritatis operibus, digne vacans est electus ex perfectorum milibus.	Fide constans, spe subvectus caritatis operibus, digne vacans est electus ex perfectorum milibus.	Fide constans, spe subvectus caritatis operibus, digne vacans est electus ex perfectorum milibus.	Bis pro fide christiana Transfretavit, quem graviter captum duxit gens prophana, quod pertulit humiliter.	Regnum sprevit et omnia Christi sequens vestigia, non pepercit diviciis, non uxori, non filiis.

(continued)

Nunc Laudare	Ludovicus Decus	Lauda Celestis 1	Lauda Celestis 2	Lauda Celestis 3	Exultemus Omnes	Francorum Rex	Sanctus Voluntatem
Fraus, furor, violentia relegantur a subditis; signa choruscant varia virtutum eius meritis.	Fraus, furor, violentia relegantur a subditis; signa choruscant varia virtutum eius meritis.	Omnem reatum anime quem contraxit humanitus, pie laverunt lacrime simul et maris transitus.	Omnem reatum anime quem contraxit humanitus, pie laverunt lacrime[b] simul et maris[b] transitus.	Omnem reatum anime quem contraxit humanitus, pie laverunt lacrime simul et maris transitus.	Fidem in reverentia semper habere studuit, nec in hanc indecentia verba proferri voluit.	De navi quam[b] ascenderat, ut transfretaret maria, tres natos quos assumpserat hortatur ad similia.	
Pro corona iusticie iam coronatus gloria; nostre memor miserie celi procuret premia.	Pro corona iusticie iam coronatus gloria; nostre memor miserie celi procuret premia.	Omnis spiritus invocet supernum regem inclitum qui nos in regnum collocet per Ludovici[a] meritum.	Omnis spiritus invocet supernum regem inclitum qui nos in regno collocet per Ludovici meritum.	Omnis spiritus invocet supernum regem inclitum qui nos in regno collocet per Ludovici meritum.	Quesumus actor[b] omnium in tanti festi gaudio; sit nobis in subsidium Ludovici translatio.	Gloria tibi Domine qui simul in hoc homine exemplum das mortalibus, et gaudium celestibus.	
Trino Deo et simplici Laus, honor, virtus, gloria, qui nos regis mirifici coronet per suffragia.	Trino Deo et simplici Laus, honor, virtus, gloria, qui nos regis mirifici coronet per suffragia.						
[a]B certe. [b]B fervidis	[=NL. VHymn]	[a] Ludovici] ludovicum E.	[=LC1 VHymn] [a] vacare] corr. from vaca G. [b]maris] corr. from mari G.	[=LC2 VHymn] [a] perfectorum] profectorum I. [b] inclitum] iudicum I.	[a] pertulit] protulit K. [b] actor] auctor K.	[a] pepercit] perpersit L, perpercit M. [b] quam] qua corr. from quandam L.	
[v] Ora pro nobis beate Ludovice.[a] [a]beate ludovice] beato ludovico B.				[v] Ora pro nobis beate Ludovice.			
[Mag] Rex per quem ecclesia fuit sublimata, per quem tota francia nunc est honorata, cui semper iustitia fuit comitata, nobis Christi gratia da regna beata.	[Mag] Magnificat gesta clarissima sancti Ludovici divino cultui devotum hodie presens collegium, cuius sancta conscendit anima sub fine felici regni perpetui cum sanctis patrie sublime solium.	[Mag] Magnificat[a] gesta clarissima sancti Ludovici divino cultui devotum hodie presens collegium,[b] cuius sancta conscendit anima sub fine felici regni perpetui cum sanctis patrie sublime solium.	[Mag] Magnificat gesta clarissima sancti Ludovici divino cultui devotum hodie presens collegium,[a] cuius sancta conscendit anima sub fine felici regni perpetui[c] cum sanctis patrie sublime solium. P. Magnificat.	[Mag] Magnificat gesta clarissima sancti Ludovici divino cultui devotum hodie presens colegium,[a] cuius sancta conscendit[b] anima sub fine felici, regni perpetui cum sanctis patrie sublime solium. P. Magnificat.	[Mag] O Dei cultor et amice vindex et ultor malorum rex francorum Ludovice fontem ora pietatis ut peccatis nostris det veniam nobisque gloriam[a]. P. Magnificat.	[Mag] Magnificat Dominum et exultat spiritus pauperum et divitum in Deo salutari; qui generi hominum hunc regem divinitus Ludovicum inclitum dedit pro exemplari. P. Magnificat.	

	[^aF starts here. ^bdevotum ... collegium] om F.]	[=LC1 Mag A] [^a solium] solum C.]	[=LC2 Mag] [^aH collegium. ^bI ascendit. ^cI perpetuu.]	[^a gratiam JK, 1024]		[appears in Lauds, below A: Rex sub quo vixit...]
[Oratio] Deus qui beatum Ludovicum confessorem tuum de terreno ac temporali regno ad celestis et eterni gloriam transtulisti; eius quesumus meritis et intercessione regis regum Ihesu Christi, filii tui, nos coheredes efficias esse consortes.	[Oratio] Deus qui beatum Ludovicum confessorem tuum de terreno ac temporali regno ad celestis et eterni regni gloriam transtulisti; eius quesumus meritis et intercessione regis regum Ihesu Christi, filii tui, nos coheredes efficias et eiusdem regni esse consortes.	[Oratio] Deus qui beatum Ludovicum confessorem tuum de terreno ac temporali regno ad celestis et eterni regni gloriam transtulisti; eius quesumus meritis et intercessione regis regum Ihesu Christi, filii tui, nos coheredes efficias et eiusdem regni esse consortes.	[Oratio] Deus qui beatum Ludovicum confessorem tuum de terreno ac temporali regno ad celestis et eterni regni gloriam transtulisti; eius quesumus meritis et intercessione regis regum Ihesu Christi, filii tui, nos coheredes efficias et eiusdem regni tribuas esse consortes.	[Oratio] Deus qui de cura temporalis regiminis beatum Ludovicum confessorem tuum ad celestis regni[a] curiam transtulisti; concede propitius ut qui venerandi capitis ipsius translationem devote agimus eius apud tuam clementiam patrociniis adiuvemur.	[Oratio] Deus qui beatum Ludovicum confessorem[a] de terreno ac temporali regno ad celestis et eterni gloriam transtulisti; eius quesumus meritis[b] et intercessione regis regum Ihesu Christi, filii tui, nos coheredes[c] efficias et eiusdem regni tribuas esse consortes.	[Oratio] Deus qui beatum Ludovicum, confessorem tuum, de terreno ac temporali regno ad celesti et eterni gloriam transtulisti; eius quesumus meritis et intercessione, regis regum Ihesu Christi, filii tui, nos coheredes efficias et ejusdem regni tribuas esse consortes.
[a] Oratio absent in A. B added in upper margin: et eiusdem regni tribuas esse consortes.	[E added in bottom margin of page; absent in F]		[N.B. appears is ms. at Second Vespers]	[a] regni] regis K.	[a] confessorem] tuum add. M. [b] quesumus meritis] meritis quesumus M. [c] eiusdem] eiudem L.	

COMPLINE

[CA1]
Ludovicus[a] Dominum
de celis laudavit,
quando vite terminum
celo dedicavit.
P. Cum invocarem.

[=NL LA5, LDR LA5]

[CA2]
Coronatur gloria
sanctus et honore
quia mundi gaudia
duxit in timore.
P. Nunc dimittis

(continued)

Appendix 2.1-*cont.*

NUNC LAUDARE	LUDOVICUS DECUS	LAUDA CELESTIS 1	LAUDA CELESTIS 2	LAUDA CELESTIS 3	EXULTEMUS OMNES	FRANCORUM REX	SANCTUS VOLUNTATEM
	[=LDR MA6] *a vacat, interlin. C, in later hand.* NB: *Compline are absent in most versions of LDR.*						
			MATINS				
[Invit] Ludovici nova sollempnia leta colat mater ecclesia. P. Venite.	[Invit] Ludovici leta solemnia leta colat mater ecclesia. P. Venite.	[Invit] Adsunt[a] cum gloria christiane legis, sacra sollempnia Ludovici regis. P. Venite.	[Invit] Assunt cum gloria christiane legis, sacra solemnia Ludovici regis. P. Venite.	[Invit] Assunt cum gloria christiane legis, sacra sollempnia Ludovici regis. P. Venite.	[Invit] Regem per quem reges regnant venite adoremus. P. Venite.	[Invit] Laudemus Christum Dominum, qui regem[a] Ludovicum prestat[b] saluti hominum solamen salvificum. P. Venite.	[Invit] Regem per quem reges regnant venite adoremus.
	[=NL Invit (nova *altered to* leta.)]	[a] Adsunt] Adsint *F.*	[=LC1 Invit]	[=LC2 Invit]		[a] regem] regum *L.* [b] prestat] prestrat *L.*	[= EO Invit]
			First Nocturn				
[MHymn] Nova[a] regis preconia sollempni digna cantico devota promat Francia cantu plaudens angelico.	[MHymn] Nova regis preconia solemni digna cantico devota promat Francia, cantu plaudens angelico.	[MHymn] Nocturni cursus tempore devota mens evigilet; casto producta corpore vox indefessa iubilet.	[MHymn] Nocturni[a] cursus tempore devota mens evigilet; casto producta corpore vox indefessa iubilet.	[MHymn] Nocturni cursus tempore devota mens evigilet; casto producta corpore vox indefessa iubilet.	[MHymn] Iocundetur ecclesia dulce producens canticum de cuius orto lilia fructum reddunt mirificum.	[MHymn] In celesti collegio Ludovicus suscipitur, pro cuius natalicio festivitas hec[a] agitur.	[MHymn] Iocundetur ecclesia dulce producens canticum de cuius orto lilia fructum reddunt mirificum.
Regis[a] huius religio et aspectus gracissimus monstrabant quid de premio[b] eius gustaret[c] animus.	Regis[g] huius religio et aspectus gratissimus monstrabant quid de premio eius gustaret animus.	Genti francorum oritur laudis novelle gaudium; Ludovicus assequitur in celo[a] thronum regium[b].	Genti franctorum oritur laudis novella gaudium; Ludovicus assequitur in celo tronum regium.	Genti francorum oritur laudis novelle gaudium; Ludovicus assequitur in celo thronum regium.	Fructu vite iam vescitur Ludovicus in gloria, cuius vite dinoscitur resplenduisse gratia.	Maiestate rex inclitus, honestate compositus, hunc abscondit humilitas quem revelavit caritas.	Fructu vite iam vescitur Ludovicus in gloria, cuius vultus dignoscitur resplenduisse gratia.
Monstrant quoque miracula quantus sit in celestibus, morbos, pestes, pericula suis fugando precibus.	Monstrant quoque miracula quantus sit in celestibus, morbos, pestes, pericula suis fugando precibus.	Post labores exilii, post virtutum congeriem, viam currens compendii[c] ad beatorum requiem.	Post labores[b] exilii, post virtutum congeriem,[c] viam currens compendii ad beatorum requiem.	Post labores exilii, post virtutum congeriem, viam currens compendii ad beatorum requiem.	De quieto regimine, gloriabantur subditi nullo pressi gravamine tutela regis incliti.	Cum ipso ab infantia excrevit miseratio, pro qua potitur gloria in sanctorum consortio.[b]	De quieto regimine, gloriabantur subditi nullo pressi gravamine tutela regis incliti.

Matins Hymn (MH)

1	2	3	4	5	6	7
O quam dulce spectaculum in Ludovico cerneret, qui virtutis signaculum eius vultum inspiceret. Nam vultus eius claritas nunquam in terra corruit, nec affectus benignitas Deo presente caruit. Trino Deo et simplici. *ut supra.* [a]Nova] Ora B. [b]premio] gremio B. [c]gustaret] gustarent B.	Quod[d] videns enigmatice carnis clausus ergastulo, sublato videt obice lucis eterne speculo. Omnis spiritus. *ut supra.* [a]celo] *corr. from* celum in E. [b]regium] *om. in* E, *but necessary for rhyme scheme. The word appears in 1641 edition.* compendii] *corr. from* compendii E. [d]Quod] *corr. from* Quo E. [=NL MHymn] [a]Regis] *corr. from* regi C.	Quod videns enigmatice carnis clauses ergastulo, sublato videt obice lucis eterne speculo. Omnis spiritus. *ut supra.* [=LC1 MH] [a]Nocturni] *corr. from* nocturnum G. [b]labores] *corr. from* laboris G. [c]congeriem] *corr. from* congerie G.	Quod vidit enigmatice carnis clausus ergastulo, sublato videt obice lucis eterne speculo. Omnis spiritus. *ut supra.* [=LC2 MH]	Impendebat obsequium infirmis, non negans beneficium personis indigentibus. Quesumus actor[b] omnium in tanti, *ut supra* [a]reddunt mirificum] *om.* K. [b]actor] auctor JK.	Hic recreator pauperum collatione munerum et informator procerum perfectione operum. Sit laus patri piissime natoque eius unico, sancto simul paraclito qui hec dedit Ludovico. [a]hec] hoc M. [b]consortio] collegio L. [c]ingenito L. ingenito] o *add.* M.	Impendebat obsequium infirmis et debilibus, non negans beneficium personis indigentibus. Presta pater piissime Ludovici suffragiis splendorem lucis intime quo purgemur a vitiis. [=EO MHymm]

Matins Antiphons (MA1–MA3)

1	2	3	4	5	6	7	8
[MA1] Sanctus voluntatem in lege Dei fixit, qui cordis puritatem servavit cum vixit. P. Beatus vir.	**[MA1]** Beatus qui solium, iter et consilium malorum vitavit; sanctus ab infantia Ludovicus hec tria semper declinavit. P. Beatus vir.	**[MA1]** Ex strenuo[a] milite patre procreatus, sensu matris inclite crevit educatus. [a] E Extrenuo	**[MA1]** Ex strenuo[a] milite patre procreatus, sensu matris inclite crevit educatus. [=LC1 MA1] [a] Ex strenuo] *corr. from* Extremo G.	**[MA1]** Ex strenuo milite patre procreatus, sensu matris inclite crevit educatus. P. Beatus vir. [=LC2 MA1]	**[MA1]** Cuius corpore Dyonisius habunde ditatur, huius capite nunc Parisius iocunde[a] dotatur. P. Beatus vir. [a] iocunde] iocinde C₂, letatur *add.* K.	**[MA1]** Puer hic, defuncto patre, nutritus[a] est decenter a religiosa matre, cui paruit libenter. P. Beatus vir. [a] nutritus] nuctritus L.	**[MA1]** Sanctus voluntatem in lege Dei fixit, qui cordis puritatem servavit cum vixit. [=NL MA1]
[MA2] A Deo constitutus rex custos innocencie cum eo consecutus est solium[a] glorie. P. Quare fremuerunt. [a] solium] solum B.	**[MA2]** Regni sedem consequutus humilem se prebuit et in Syon constitutus cultu Dei claruit. P. Quare fremuerunt.	**[MA2]** Oritur in gaudium sacre puer indolis, felix puerperium felix ortus sobolis. P. Quare fremuerunt.	**[MA2]** Oritur in gaudium sacre puer indolis, felix puerperium felix ortus sobol.s. [=LC1 MA2]	**[MA2]** Oritur in gaudium sacre puer indolis, felix puerperium felix ortus sobolis. P. Quare fremuerunt. [=LC2 MA2] *I only.*	**[MA2]** Dotatur in celestibus stola iocunditatis Ludovicus, qui regibus est norma sanctitatis. P. Quare fremuerunt.	**[MA2]** Languoris[a] vehementia a Deo visitatus est in convalescentia cruce Christi signatus. P. Quare fremuerunt. [a] tanguoris] languoris M.	**[MA2]** A Deo constitutus rex custos iustitie cum eo consecutus est solium glorie. [=NL MA2, *altered:* innocencie *to* iustitie]
[MA3] Tu sanctum, Domine, regem suscepisti qui sine crimine cultor fuit Christi.	**[MA3]** Susceptus ad meritum gloria dotatur, capud Deo subditum celo coronatur.	**[MA3]** Ab amore seculi iuvenis abstractus, ea que sunt parvuli vacuat vir factus.	**[MA3]** Ab amore seculi iuvenis abstractus, ea que sunt parvuli vacuat vir factus.	**[MA3]** Ab amore seculi iuvenis abstractus, ea que sunt parvuli vacuat vir factus.	**[MA3]** Sanctitatis culmine divinitus erectus angelorum agmine, iam ad celos est vectus.	**[MA3]** Tres fratres suos comites secum cruce signavit, et regni sui divites[a] ad idem animavit.	**[MA3]** Tu sanctum, Domine, regem suscepisti qui sine crimine cultor fuit Christi.

(continued)

Appendix 2.1.-cont.

Nunc Laudare	Ludovicus Decus	Lauda Celestis 1	Lauda Celestis 2	Lauda Celestis 3	Exultemus Omnes	Francorum Rex	Sanctus Voluntatem
P. Domine quid multiplicati.	P. Domine quid multiplicati.	P. Cum invocarem.	[=LC1 MA3]	P. Cum invocarem.	P. Domine quid multiplici.	P. Domine quid multiplici.	
		abstractus] abstratus EF.		[=LC2 MA3] *J* only.		*a divites] iam exp. L.*	[=NL MA3]
		[MA4] Audiens utiliter summum preceptorem, servavit humiliter parentum honorem. P. Verba mea.		[MA4] Veritas et misericordia ceperunt habitaculum cordis; pax et iusticia convenerunt ad osculum. P. Verba mea.			
				[=LC2 MA4] *J* only.			
		[MA5] Veritas et misericordia ceperunt habitaculum cordis eius; pax et iusticia*a* convenerunt ad osculum. P. Domine Dominus noster. *a pax et iusticia] E* iusticia et pax		[MA5] Evitans mundi strepitum, sedens dogmatis angulo, reficiebat spiritum sacre doctrine pabulo. P. Domine Dominus noster.			
				[=LC2 MA5] *J* only.			
		[MA6] Evitans*a* mundi strepitum sedens domatis angulo, reficiebat spiritum sacre doctrine pabulo. P. In Domino confido. [=LC3 MA5] *a Evitans] Devitans E.*		[MA6] Creatoris iniuriam graviter ferebat; blasphemorum perfidiam dure puniebat. P. In Domino confido.			
				[=LC2 MA6] *J* only.			

[Column 1]

[MRV1]
Rex regum regis^a filio
regales parans nuptias,
post certamen in stadio
celi prebet delicias
glorioso commercio.

[v] Pro regno
temporalium
habet regnum celestium
Ludovicus in premium.^b

[=NL MRV1]
^a regis] regi A.
^a in premium]
impremium C.

[MRV2]
Gloriosus apparuit
non cultu prefuit
sed cum in cultu prefuit
more David ludentis;
nec ex^a hoc sibi defuit
auctoritas regentis.

[v] Virgam virtutis habuit,
in qua malos compescuit
sed sub norma clementis.

[v] Ludocivus sic terris
prefuit,
quod regnando cebos
promeruit.

^a ex] in A.

[MRV3]
Felix regnum cuius rex
providus,
pacificus, pius et pudicus,
in adversis semper
intrepidus;^a
talis fuit sanctus
Ludovicus.^b

[Column 2]

[MRV1]
Ludovicus rex inclitus
regum francorum gloria,
a primevo^a sollicitus
Christi sequi vestigia,
promeruit divinitus
eterni regni premia.

[v] Rex sedens in solio
decernens iusticiam,
contuitu^b premio
dissipans maliciam.

^a a primevo] a premens E.
^b contuitu] cum tuitu F.

[MRV2]
Felix terra cuius rex
sapiens,
iustus, clemens,
modestus, paciens,
cuius vultus est malos
feriens,
bonos alliciens.

[MRV3]
Hunc natura genuit
regno fructuosum,
voluntas exercuit
mundo graciosum,
Deus manus prebuit
celo gloriosum.

[Column 3]

[MRV1]
Ludovicus puer inclitus
regum francorum gloria,
a primevo sollicitus
Christi sequi vestigia,
promeruit divinitus
eterni regni premia.

[v] Rex sedens in solio
decernens iusticiam,
cum tuitu premi.o^a
dissipans maliciam.
P. Promeruit.

[=LC1 MRV1]
^a premio] corr. from
previo G.

[MRV2]
Gratam vite iuventutem^a
sapienter inspiciens
Christi iugo^b supposuit;
de virtute in virtutem
cotidie proficiens;
vite coronam meruit.

[v] Si legis attentus^c
in iosya figuratur
cuius sic iuventus
regi regum famulatur.

[=LC1 MRV2]

^a inspiciens] inspiciens E.
^b iugo] virgo E. ^c legis
attentus] legislator F.

[MRV3]
In fundandis^a ecclesiis,
in relevatione pauperum,
quam devotus exterit,
certis patet indiciis
presens nobis aspectus
operum
indubitanter aperit.^c

[Column 4]

[MRV1]
Ludovicus rex inclitus
regum francorum gloria,
a primevo sollicitus
Christi sequi vestigia,
promeruit divinitus
eterni regni premia.

[v] Rex sedens in solio
decernens iusticiam,
contuitu premio
dissipans maliciam.

[=LC2 MRV1]

[MRV2]
Gratam vite iuventutem
sapienter inspiciens
Christi iugo supposuit;
de virtute in virtutem
cotidie proficiens;
vite coronam meruit.

[v] Si legis attentus
in iosya figuratur
cuius sic iuventus
regi regum famulatur.

[=LC2 MRV2]

[MRV3]
In fundandis ecclesiis,
in relevatione pauperum,
quam devotus exterit,
certis patet indiciis
presens nobis aspectus
operum
indubitanter aperit.

[Column 5]

[MRV1]
Felix regnum cuius rex
providus,
pacificus, pius et
pudicus,
in adversis semper
intrepidus;
talis fuit sanctus
Ludovicus.

[v] Rex sedens in solio
decernens iusticiam,
contuitu premio
dissipans maliciam.

[=LC2 MRV1]

[MRV2]
Gratam vite iuventutem
sapienter inspiciens
Christi iugo supposuit;
de virtute in virtutem
cotidie proficiens;
vite coronam meruit.

[v] Si legis attentus
in iosya figuratur
cuius sic iuventus
regi regum famulatur.

[=LC2 MRV2]

[MRV3]
In fundandis ecclesiis,
in relevatione pauperum,
quam devotus exterit,
certis patet indiciis
presens nobis aspectus
operum
indubitanter aperit.

[Column 6]

[MRV1]
Felix regnum cuius rex
providus,
pacificus, pius et
pudicus,
in adversis semper
intrepidus;
talis fuit sanctus
Ludovicus.

[v] Rex sedens in solio
decernens iusticiam,
contuitu premio
dissipans maliciam.

[=NL MRV3]

[MRV2]
Pauperitatis larga subsidia
veritatis equa^a iudicia,
honestatis certa indicia,
sanctitatis sunt^b
testimonia
pii regis.

[v] O quieta gregis^c
protectio
O discreta recogitatio
summe legis.

[=NL MRV4]
^a equa] equa J. ^b sunt]
summe K. ^c gregis] regis
C.K.

[MRV3]
O sparsor divitiarum^a
erogando pauperibus,
O spretor deliciarum
insudando laboribus,
O tutor ecclesiarum
eas iuvando viribus,
duc nos ad regnum
preclarum
tuis devotis precibus.

[Column 7]

[MRV1]
Felix regnum cuius rex
providus,
pacificus, pius et
pudicus,
in adversis semper
intrepidus;
talis fuit sanctus
Ludovicus.

[v] Rex erexit terram et
patriam,
qui dilexit sequi
iusticiam.

[=NL MRV3]

[MRV2]
Pauperitatis larga subsidia
veritatis equa iudicia,
honestatis certa indicia,
sanctitatis sunt
testimonia
pii regis.

[v] O quieta gregis
protectio
O discreta recogitatio
summe legis.

[=NL MRV4]

[MRV3]
O sparsor divitiarum
erogando pauperibus,
O spretor deliciarum
insudando laboribus,
O tutor ecclesiarum
eas iuvando viribus,
duc nos ad regnum
preclarum
tuis devotis precibus.

[Column 8]

[MRV1]
Francorum iam exercitu
sub rege Ludovico
preparato pro transitu
in conductu nautico,
legato ab ecclesia
dato cum indulgentia.

[v] In pasagio signato
Deo primum invocato
transivit princeps maria.

[MRV2]
In Dei fervens opere
statim ut transfretavit
infideles laccessere
gravi bello temptavit;
et Damiatam propere
vi captam occupavit.

[v] Quam deserente^a
turpiter
populo degenere
ipse potenter intravit.

^a deserent] deserene L.

[MRV3]
Dum pater
clementissimus
suum verberat populum,
vir^a iste devotissimum
ad deum levat oculum,
ut erat ferventissimus
obsequium dans
sedulum.

[Column 9]

[MRV1]
Felix regnum cuius rex
providus,
pacificus, pius et
pudicus,
in adversis semper
intrepidus;
talis fuit sanctus
Ludovicus.

[v] Rex erigit terram et
patriam,
qui diligit sequi
iusticiam.

[=NL MRV3, EO
MRV1]

[MRV2]
Pauperitatis larga subsidia
veritatis equa iudicia,
honestatis certa iudicia,
sanctitatis sunt
testimonia pii regis.

[v] O quieta gregis
protectio
O discreta recogitatio
summe legis sanctitatis
sunt testimonia pii regis

[=NL MRV4, altered]

[MRV3]
O sparsor divitiarum
erogando pauperibus,
O spretor deliciarum
insistendolaboribus,
defensor ecclesiarum
suis favendo.

(continued)

Appendix 2.1-cont.

NUNC LAUDARE	LUDOVICUS DECUS	LAUDA CELESTIS 1	LAUDA CELESTIS 2	LAUDA CELESTIS 3	EXULTEMUS OMNES	FRANCORUM REX	SANCTUS VOLUNTATEM
[v] Rex erigit[c] terram et patriam, qui diligit sequi iustitiam.	[v] Normam vite posuit hunc Deus et tribuit signis virtuosum.[a]	[v] Cum manus instancia, devoto mentis studio, secum ab infancia crevit miseracio.	[v] Cum magna instancia, devoto mentis studio, secum ab infancia crevit miseracio.	[v] Cum manus instancia, devoto mentis studio, secum ab infancia crevit miseracio.	[v] Qui tot egris prestitisti curationum gratiam, nobis confer dono Christi transgressionum veniam.	[v] Hic Thobias notissimus qui mortuos humilimus portabat ad tumulum.	[v] Qui tot egris prestitisti curationum gratiam, nobis confer dono Christi transgressionum veniam.
[a] In adversis semper intrepidus] om. B line. [b] Ludovicus] lodovicus B. [c] erigit] exigit B.	[a] virtuosum] corr. from virtusum C.	[a] fundandis] fundendis F. [b] relevacione] revelacione E. [c] aperit] apperit E.	[=LC1 MRV2]	[=LC2 MRV3] [a] In fundandis] Infundendis I.	[=EO VCapV above] [a] abbreviated KJ. quere super in vesperis.	[a] dominus expunged L.	[=NL MRV9]
		[MRV4] Post genitoris obitum, regni magnificencia de iure promotus, honorem matri debitum sub mira reverencia complevit devotus.		[MRV4] Verborum moderamine mire circumspectus, grata trahens dulcedine hominum affectus, veritatis examine noscitur perfectus.			
		[v] Mater regno prefuit in potioribus bonis; matri thronum posuit more regis Salomonis.		[v] Concepto sermone sobrius, iuramentum cavit, est est, non non, dicens, amplius malum indicavit. [=LC1 MRV7]			

Second Nocturn

NUNC LAUDARE	LUDOVICUS DECUS	LAUDA CELESTIS 1	LAUDA CELESTIS 2	LAUDA CELESTIS 3	EXULTEMUS OMNES	FRANCORUM REX	SANCTUS VOLUNTATEM
[MA4] Mirificavit Dominus sanctum regem francorum, cuius nunc est terminus in regno beatorum. P. Cum invocarem.	[MA4] Invocantem exaudivit Deus regem humilem, et preclaris insignivit signis suum pugilem. P. Cum invocarem.	[MA7] Creatoris iniuriam graviter ferebat; blasphemorum perfidiam dure puniebat. P. Domine quis habitabit.	[MA4] Veritas et misericordia ceperunt habitaculum cordis eius; iusticia et pax fecerunt osculum.	[MA7] Transit mare rex insignis firma fide fultus, multos graves ab indignis paciens insultus. P. Domine quis habitabit.		[MA4] Lassato[a] iam exercitu diuturno langore infideles[b] cum fremitu accurrunt[c] et furore. P. Cum invocarem.	
			[=LC1 MA5]	[=LC2 MA7]		[a] Lassato] laxato M.[b] infideles] infides L.[c] accurrunt] occurrant M.	

[MA5] In misericordie multitudine Deum adorabat, qui consciencie rectitudine celis inhiabat. P. Verba mea	[MA5] Deductus in iusticia clemens subiectis prefuit; leges, penas et premia sapienter instituit. P. Verba mea.	[MA8] Erat in divino cultu vigil assuetus^a, mente cum sereno vultu ubique quietus. P. Domine in virtute. ^a assuetus] F om.	[MA5] Evitans mundi strepitum sedens dogmatis angulo, reficiebat spiritum sacre doctrine pabulo. [=LC1 MA6]	[MA8] I only: Occulto iudicio sub crucis signaculo, captus infortunio, solvitur miraculo. P. Domine in virtute. [=LC2 MA8]	[MA5] Populi princeps furie non cedit^a effrenati, monstrans se voluntarie pro Christo mala pati. P. Verba mea. ^a cedit] sedit L.
[MA6] Gloria et honore regnat rex coronatus, qui semper in amore Dei fuit firmatus. P. Domine Dominus.	[MA6] Coronatur gloria sanctus et honore quia mundi gaudia duxit in timore. P. Domine Dominus.	[MA9] Transit mare rex insignis firma fide fultus^a, multos graves ab indignis patiens insultus. P. Domini est terra. ^a fultus] sultus E.	[MA6] Creatoris^a iniuriam graviter ferebat; blasphemorum perfidiam dure puniebat. [=LC1 MA7] ^a Creatoris] corr. from Eratoris G.	[MA9] Hinc reversus ad patriam ecclesiam dilexit, veram exibens latriam semper bonos evexit. P. Domini est terra. I only. NB: No equivalent in LDR or elsewhere	[MA6] Ductus^a ad locum carceris, mire fert ad tentorium sollicito pro vesperis paganus breviarium. P. Domine Dominus. ^a Ductus] Ducto M, Dutus L.
		[MA10] Occulto iudicio sub crucis signaculo, captus infortunio, solvitur miraculo. P. Exaudi Deus.		[MA10] Deductus in iusticia clemens subiectus prefuit; leges, penas et premia sapienter instituit. P. Exaudi Deus. [=LDR MA5] I only.	
		[MA11] In omni discrimine reputabat gloriam, hic pro Christi nomine pati contumeliam. P. Te decet.		[MA11] Coronatus gloria sanctus et honore quia mundi gaudia duxit in timore. P. Te decet. [=LDR MA6] I only.	

(continued)

Appendix 2.1-*cont.*

Nunc Laudare	Ludovicus Decus	Lauda Celestis 1	Lauda Celestis 2	Lauda Celestis 3	Exultemus Omnes	Francorum Rex	Sanctus Voluntatem
		[MA12] Mente raptus ad divina sub regni dyademate, quasi stella matutina fulsit in omni climate. P. Bonum est confiteri.		[MA12] In omni discrimine reputabat gloriam, hic pro Christi nomine pati contumeliam. P. Bonum est confiteri. [=LC2 MA9] *I* only.			
[MRV4] Paupertatis larga subsidia, veritatis equa iudicia, honestatis certa indicia, sanctitatis sunt testimonia pii regis. [v] O quieta gregis protectio. O discreta[a] recogitatio summe legis. [a] discreta] discreti *B.*	[MRV4] Gloriosus apparuit, non cultu presidentis sed cum incultus prefuit more David ludentis; nec ex hoc sibi defuit auctoritas regentis. [v] Virgam virtutis habuit, in qua malos compescuit sed sub norma clementis. [=NL MRV2]	[MRV5] Pro catholice fidei promotione sedula mare transiturus, subit ad honorem Dei terre maris periculo de Deo securus. [v] Ut angelus Domini cum David immobilis, non cedit discrimini vir in fide stabilis.	[MRV4] Pro catholice fidei promotione sedula mare transiturus, subit ad honorem Dei terre maris periculo de Deo securus. [v] Ut angelus Domini cum[a] David immobilis, non cedit discrimini vir in fide stabilis. [=LC1 MRV5] [a] domini cum] dominicum *in ms.*	[MRV5] Pro catholice fidei promotione sedula mare transiturus,[a] subit ad honorem Dei terre maris periculo. de Deo securus. [v] Ut angelus Domini cum David immobilis, non cedit[b] discrimini vir[c] in fide stabilis. [=LC2 MRV4] [a] transiturus] transitus *I.* [b] cedit] credit *I.* [c] vir] vix *I.*		[MRV4] Laus tibi per secula patri nato paraclito quod rex sine macula per te liberetur[a], dum in soldani subito illa gens incredula tuo beneplacito morte effrenatur. [v] En Dei virtus sedula pro suis que tam cito pellendo[b] pericula mira operatur. [a] liberetur] liberatur *M.* [b] pellendo] pellando *M.*	
[MRV5] Fulget signis rex insignis, nam egrotis eius votis prestantur remedia. [v] Dati neci liberantur, Claudi, ceci reparantur, fugantur demonia.	[MRV5] Coram rege conspicitur liber in preda[a] perditus, miraculose solvitur rex sarracenis traditus, et hostibus expositus. [v] Ionas undis eripitur, Ioseph detentus solvitur et David antro positus.	[MRV6] Prorsus iactans in Dominum cogitatus sui curam mundanorum discriminum nullam meruit pressuram sperans a patre luminum opem semper affuturam.[a] [v] Confidens ut leo iustus imperterritus,	[MRV5] Prorsus iactans in Dominum cogitatus sui curam mundanorum discriminum opem semper affuturam. [v] Confidens ut leo iustus imperterritus, constanter a deo prestolatur celitus.	[MRV6] Prorsus iactans in Dominum cogitatus sui curam mundanorum discriminum nullam metuit pressuram sperans a patre luminum opem semper affuturam.[a] [v] Confidens ut leo iustus imperterritus,		[MRV5] Bissenis cum baronibus firmus rex in fide vera de pactis iuraturus Sarracenis furentibus respondet[a] voce libera, "Nunquam sum hoc facturus." [v] "Si non stas hiis sermonibus",	

(continued)

			constanter a deo prestolatur celitus.		constanter a deo prestolatur celitus.	ait illi gens effera, "Christum es negaturus."
	[a] in preda] C impreda.		[a] affuturam] ad futurum E.	[=LC1 MRV5]	[=LC2 MRV5] [a] affuturam] adfuturam H.	[a] respondet] respondit M.
[MRV6] Regnum mundi supergressus et eius ornatum, regnum celi iam ingressus sibi preparatum, nostros ad se regat gressus post hunc incolatum.	[MRV6] Cum esset in accubitu, rex interne dulcedinis, arcens[a] potenti spiritu pestes carnis et sanguinis bonorum septus ambitu, sceptro fulsit regiminis.	[MRV8] Nomen Dei non in vanum digne sumens in honore[a] pio fervens[b] iudicio blasphemantis os prophanum, ferri iussit in ardore consignari cauterio.	[MRV7] Verborum moderamine mire circumspectus, grata trahens dulcedine hominum affectus, veritatis examine noscitur perfectus.	[MRV6] Verborum mcderamine mire circumspectus, grata trahens dulcedine hominum affectus, veritatis exam.ne noscitur perfectus.	[MRV7] Coram rege conspicitur liber in preda[a] perditus, miraculose solvitur rex sarracenis traditus, et hostibus expositus.	[MRV6] Regressus rex ad propria non destitit insistere operi virtuso; se mactat penitentia egenos levat munere et ministrat leproso[a].
[v] Peregre Iacob egressus patris ad mandatum, Deum[a] vidit sic professus vite celibatum.	[v] David regis sedit in solio, Salomonis utens iudicio.[b]	[v] Ut que non veretur verba proferens indecencia, penam mereretur cauteriata consciencia.	[v] Concepto sermone sobrius, iuramentum[a] cavit, est est, non non, dicens, amplius malum iudicavit.	[v] Concepto sermone sobrius iuramentum cavit, est est, non nor, dicens, amplius malum iudicavit.	[v] Ionas undis eripitur Ioseph detentus solvitur et David antro positus.[b]	[v] Visitat monasteria, domos Dei ex opere construxit sumptuoso.
[=NL MRV7, LDR VCapV] [a] arcens] ardens D. [b] Rex eterne . . . iudicio] [a] Deum] dei B.	Require supra ad vesperas C.	[a] in honore] F om. [b] fervens] fruens F.	[=LC3 MRV4] [a] iuramentum] om F.	[=LC1 MRV7]	[=LDR MRV5] [a] I pre dei. [b]H ponitus. [MRV8] Cum esset in accubitu[a] . . . ut secundum ad vesperas.[b] Ad capitula. [A] Beatus est iste dives inventus sine macula de quo paradisi[c] cives deum laudant in secula. [Cf: Eccli. 31:8] [=NL MRV7, LDR MRV6 and VV] [a]Iacubitu. [b] ut secundum ad vesperas] om, add etc. [c]H paradysi.	[a] leproso] leprosos L.

Appendix 2.1.-cont.

Third Nocturn

NUNC LAUDARE	LUDOVICUS DECUS	LAUDA CELESTIS 1	LAUDA CELESTIS 2	LAUDA CELESTIS 3	EXULTEMUS OMNES	FRANCORUM REX	SANCTUS VOLUNTATEM
[MA7] Habitabit in tabernaculo Domini gloriose quia vixit in isto seculo rex noster virtuose. P. Domine quis habitabit.	[MA7] Habitabit confidenter rex in monte Domini, quia vixit innocenter omni gratus homini. P. Domine quis habitabit.		[MA7] Transit mare rex insignis firma fide fultus, multos graves ab indignis patiens insultus.			[MA7] Cor verbis sacre scripture sollicitus apponit omnique regali curie[a] verbum Dei proponit[b]. P. Domine quis habitabit. [a]curie] cure *L.* [b]proponit] apponit *M.*	
[MA8] In virtute Domini rex sanctus letabitur[a] nunc sanctorum agmini iunctus gloriatur. P. Domine in virtute. [a]letabitur] letatur *B.*	[MA8] Rex virtutis in virtute divina letatur, quia sibi de salute spes firma donatur. P. Domine in virtute.		[MA8] Occulto iudicio sub crucis signaculo, captus infortunio, solvitur miraculo. [=LC1 MA10]			[MA8] Bonis semper operibus sanctus rex intendebat, simile facientibus devotus inherebat. P. Domine in virtute.	
[MA9] Rex, innocens manibus atque corde mundo, regnat cum celestibus[a] in regno iocundo. P. Domini est terra. [a]celestibus] celesti *B.*	[MA9] Innocens manus prebuit cordis quoque mundicia Ludovico, quod meruit regni celestis premia. P. Domini est terra.		[MA9] In omni discrimine reputabat gloriam, hic pro Christi nomine pati contumeliam. [=LC1 MA11]			[MA9] Ut regis sancti merita remunerentur[a], natis, hiis pia tradit monita semitas equitatis. P. Domini est terra. [a]remunerentur] remunerantur *L.*	
[MRV7] Cum esset in accubitu, rex interne dulcedinis, arcens potenti spiritu pestes carnis et sanguinis bonorum septus ambitu,	[MRV7] Fulget signis rex insignis, nam egrotis eius votis prestantur remedia.	[MRV9] Corpus eius confectum macie, subiugatum suo spiritui, monstravere[a] crebra ieiunia,	[MRV7] Corpus eius confectum macie,[a] subiugatum suo spiritui, monstravere crebra ieiunia,	[MRV9] Corpus eius confectum macie, subiugatum suo spiritui, monstravere crebra ieiunia,		[MRV7] Toto corde cum rege[a] Iosia quesivit Deum ab infancia, David alter misericordia et Salomon[b] est sapientia.	

sceptro fulsit regiminis.	[v] Dati neci liberantur, Claudi, ceci reparantur, fugantur demonia.	discipline, fletus, vigilie*b*, pallor, livor vultus emortui cilicium lecti duricia.	discipline, fletus, vigilie, pallor, livor vultus emortui cilicium lecti duricia.	discipline, fletus, vigilie, pallor, livor vultus emortui cilicium lecti duricia.	[v] Joseph est providentia et Gedeon constantia.
[v] David regis sedit in solio, Salomonis utens iudicio.		[v] Statum penalem et asperum rex pius*c* elegit, se velut Manassem alterum penitens subegit.	[v] Se sui iudiceret se verum rex pius elegit, se velut Manassem alterum penitens subegit.	[v] Statum penalem et asperum rex pius elegit, se velut Manassem alterum penitens*a* subegit.	*a*L regem. *b*LM salmon.
[=NL MRV5]	[=NL MRV5]	*a*monstravere] monstravero E. *b* vigilie] vigilit E. *c* pius] piis E.	[=LC1 MRV9] *a*macie] *corr. from* in acie G.	[=LC2 MRV7] *a* penitens] penitus H.	[MRV8] De largitatis horreo rex misericors tribuit plena manu pauperibus quos*a* visitando circuit; cibos ori intromittit et pedes suplex abluit.
[MRV8] Pro se suisque*a* subiectis orans deum et cum rectis rectum iter faciens, domum Dei rex intravit et ad templum adoravit, ut predixit moriens,	[MRV8] Pro se suisque subiectis orans deum et cum rectis rectum iter faciens domum Dei rex intravit et ad templum adoravit, ut predixit moriens.	[MRV10] De quinque cathenis ferreis occulte suscepta*a* verbera manu confessoris benigne ferebat in eis, devote recolens vulnera nostri redemptoris.	[MRV8] De quinque cathenis ferreis occulte suscepta*a* verbera manu confessoris benigne ferebat in eis, devote recolens vulnera nostri redemptoris.	[MRV10] De quinque cathenis ferreis occulte suscepta verbera manu confessoris benigne ferebat in eis, devote recolens vulnera nostri redemptoris.	[v] O quantus et qualis fuit qui tam pium cor habuit, quod egenis compatiens servicium hoc prebuit.
[v] Felix cursus sic*b* viventis, felix finis sic currentis Deo semper uniens.	[v] Felix cursus sic viventis, felix finis sic currentis Deo semper serviens.	[v] Erutus*a* a penis carcere solvitur, libera cathenis regnum ingreditur.	[v] Erutus a penis carcere solvitur, liber a cathenis regnum ingreditur.	[v] Erutus a penis, carcere solvitur, liber a cathenis regnum ingreditur.	*a* quos] quod L.
a suisque] suique B. *b* sic] si A.	[=NL MRV8]	*a* occulte] occulte *add in* F. *b*Erutus] Crutus E, Eructus F.	[=LC1 MRV10] *a*suscepta] *corr. from* susceptis G	[=LC2 MRV8]	
[MRV9] O*a* sparsor diviciarum erogando pauperibus; O spretor deliciarum insistendo laboribus; defensor ecclesiarum tuis favendo*b* viribus, duc nos ad regnum preclarum, tuis*c* iuvando precibus.	[MRV9] Regnum mundi supergressus et eius ornatum, regnum celi iam ingressus sibi preparatum, nostros ad se regat gressus post hunc incolatum.	[MRV11] Imminente mortis articulo, diem vite clausurus ultimum morbo pressus decumbens*a* lectulo testamentum condidit optimum memorie dignum spectaculo.	[MRV9] Imminente*a* mortis articulo, diem vite clausurus ultimum morbo pressus decumbens lectulo testamentum condidit optimum memorie dignum spectaculo.	[MRV11] Imminente mortis articulo, diem vite clausurus ultimum morbo pressus decumbens lectulo testamentum condidit optimum memorie dignum spectaculo.	*NB: Most manuscripts do not include a proper item for MRV9, which follows Franciscan use, although NY Pierpont Morgan M149 and M75 employ VCapRV* [En regi genti...custodia] *as MRV9.*

(continued)

Appendix 2.1-*cont.*

Nunc Laudare	Ludovicus Decus	Lauda Celestis 1	Lauda Celestis 2	Lauda Celestis 3	Exultemus Omnes	Francorum Rex	Sanctus Voluntatem
[v] Qui tot egris prestitisti curationum gratiam, nobis confer dono Christi transgressionum veniam.	[v] Peregre Iacob egressus patris*a* ad mandatum, Deum vidit sic professus vite celibatum.	[v] More Iacob liberis, thesaurum doctrine profuturum posteris ligavit in fine.	[v] More Iacob liberis, thesaurum doctrine profuturum posteris ligavit in fine.*b*	[v] More Iacob liberis, thesaurum doctrine profuturum posteris legavit in fine.			
*a*O] *abs. B.* *b*favendo] tuendo *B.* *c*tuis] piis *B.*	[=NL MRV6.] *a*patris] *overwritten as* matris *in C.*	*a*decumbens] decumbena *E.*	[=LC1 MRV11] *a*Imminente] *corr. from* iminente G. *b* fine] *corr. from* fune G.	[=LC2 MRV9]			
		[MRV12] Regie tribus gemine spiritus sincerus Ludovicus origine cultor Dei verus celesti regnat agmine factus Assuerus.		[MRV12] Regnum mundi supergressus et eius ornatum, regnum celi iam ingressus sibi preparatum, nostros ad se regat gressus post hunc incolatum.			
		[v] Assumptus in illa superna requie de regum mamilla lactatur hodie.		[v] Peregre Iacob egressus patris ad mandatum, Deum vidit sic professus vite celibatum.			
				[=NL MRV6, LDR MRV9]			
	Ad cantica an. Operibus misericordie die laborabat in canticis ecclesie nocte perorabat.			*H:* Evang. Ecce nos reliquimus omnia . . . [Matt 19:27]			
	Evangl: Dixit Symon petrus ad Ihesum. [Matt. 19:27]			*I:* In illo tempore respondens Dominus Ihesu dixit Confitebor tibi pater Domine . . . Iugum enim meum suave est et onus*a*			

Omelia: Grandis fiducia.^b

meum leve. [Matt 11:25-30]^b

^a onus] corr. from bonus I. ^b text elided.

^b Cf. PL v. 28, col. 138 (Jerome's Commentary on Matthew)

LAUDS

[LA1] Ludovicus hodie decorem indutus est celestis patrie regnum consecutus.	[LA1] Ludovicus hodie decorem indutus est celestis patrie regnum consecutus.^a P. Dominus regnavit. [=NL LA1] ^a consequtus] consecutus D.	[LA1] Adest dies leticie, quo transit ex mundo, flos dignitatis regie cum fructu iocundo. [=LC1 LA1]	[LA1] Adest dies leticie, quo transit ex mundo, flos dignitatis regie cum fructu iocundo. P. Dominus regnavit. [=LC2 LA1]	[LA1] Dominus regnavit Ludovicus in mundo, qui peccatum cavit et vixit corde mundo.	[LA1] Magnus^a rex gentis francorum, divine legis zelator ac promotor^b bonorum religionis amator, fuit et extirpator viciorum.^c P. Dominus regnavit. ^a est add M. ^b promotor] premoter M ^c fuit et extirpator viciorum] viciorum fuit extirpator M.	[LA] Nunc laudare Dominum debet plebs fidelis persecutor criminum rex regnat in celis. [=NL VA1. "extirpator" altered to "persecutor"]
[LA2] Omnis terra iubilet Deo leta serviens, laudibus invigilet^a novum festum faciens. ^a invigilet] vigilet B.	[LA2] Omnis terra iubilet Deo leta serviens, laudibus invigilet novum festum faciens. P. Iubilate Deo. [=NL LA2]	[LA2] Angelorum choris^a defertur in iubilo de valle meroris sol egressus nubilo. [=LC1 Prime] ^a choris] corr. from chorus G.	[LA2] Angelorum choris defertur in iubilo de valle meroris sol egressus nubilo.^a P. Iubilate Deo. [=LC2 LA2] ^a H: text used at Terce, no text for LA2	[LA2] Iubilate creatori tota gens christiana, sed voce iocundiori^a psalle plebs gallicana. ^a iocundiori] iocundari K.	[LA2] Iustus in iudiciis, prudens in consiliis, bonis semper favit; stetit pro ecclesia, cui, ne iniuria inferretur, cavit.	[Cap] Dedit Dominus illi fortitudinem et usque in senectutem permansit illi virtus ut ascenderet in excelsum terre locum et semen ipsius obtinuit hereditatem [=NL Sext, LDR, EO LCap]
[LA3] Ad te, Deus meus, semper vigilavit, sicque numquam reus celos penetravit.	[LA3] Ad te, Deus meus, semper vigilavit, sicque numquam reus celos penetravit. P. Deus Deus.	[LA3] Luce vigil^a ad Dominum prudens et fidelis servus cum patre luminum iungitur in celis.	[LA3] Luce vigil^a ad Dominum prudens et fidelis servus cum patre luminum iungitur in celis.^a P. Deus Deus.	[LA3] Deus Deus salutis nostro sancto regi viam dedit virtutis obedire legi.	[LA3] In vestitu humilimo atque victu parcissimo fit cunctis in stuporem; virtutis factis predicat et operibus indicat se perfectum doctorem.	

(continued)

Appendix 2.1-*cont.*

Nunc Laudare	Ludovicus Decus	Lauda Celestis 1	Lauda Celestis 2	Lauda Celestis 3	Exultemus Omnes	Francorum Rex	Sanctus Voluntatem
	[=NL LA3]		[=LC1 Terce] *a* vigil] *corr. from* vigili *G.*	[=LC LA3] *aH: text used at Sext, no text for LA3.*			
[LA4] Benedixit creatorem in suis operibus, Ludovicus gerens morem datum celi civibus.	[LA4] Benedixit creatorem in suis operibus, Ludovicus gerens morem datum celi civibus. P. Benedicite.		[LA4] Benedicant opera cuncta creatorem, qui dat supra sydera regnum post laborem.	[LA4] Benedicant opera cuncta creatorem, qui dat supra sydera regnum post laborem.*a* P. Benedicite.	[LA4] Benedicite populi Dominum angelorum, collaudate seduli sanctum regem francorum.	[LA4] Patris natum unicum benedicant Dominum cuncte creature, qui tot per Ludovicum signis auget hominum vite spem future.	
	[=NL LA4]		[=LC1 Sext]	[=LC2 LA4] *aH: text used at None, no text for LA4.*			
[LA5] Ludovicus Dominum de celis laudavit quando vite terminum celo dedicavit.	[LA5] Ludovicus Dominum de celis laudavit quando vite terminum celo dedicavit. P. Laudate Dominum.		[LA5] Laudes*a* Deo concinit egressus exilium; pressure non meminit translatus in gaudium.	[LA5] Laudes Deo concinit egressus exilium; pressure non meminit translatus in gaudium.*a* P. Laudate Dominum.	[LA5] Laudate Dominum et patrem luminum in translatione, cuius vitam scimus ductam et finitam cum devotione.	[LA5] Laudet iam felix Francia, tota laudet ecclesia opera Salvatoris, et pro*a* tot beneficiis quod potest surgat gratis ad laudem largitoris.	
	[=NL LA5]		[=LC1 None] *aLaudes] corr. from* Saudes *G.*	[=LC2 LA5] *aLaudes...gaudium] H: used for 2Vespers, no text for LA5*		*a* pro] per *L.*	
	[Cap] Dedit Dominus illi fortitudinem et usque ad senectutem permansit illi virtus, ut ascenderet in excelsum terre locum, semen ipsius obtinebit hereditatem.			[Cap] Beatus vir qui inventus est. R. Sancte Ludovice confessor Christi .	[Cap] Dedit Dominus illi fortitudinem et usque in senectutem permansit illi virtus ut ascenderet in excelsum terre locum et semen ipsius obtinebit hereditatem.*a*	[Cap] Beatus dives. . . .	

(continued)

[Cf: Eccli 46:11; =NL None]			H only.	[Cf: Eccli 46:11; =NL None, LDR LCap] [a]illi fortitudinem . . . hereditatem] *om. C₂J.* *Add.* Quere in laudibus alterius solennitatis. *Text supplied in K.*		
[LHymn] Ympnum nove leticie regi canamus omnium, qui sancto regi Francie novi dat regni solium.[a]	[LHymn] Hymnum nove letitie Regi canamus omnium, qui sancto regi Francie novi dat regni solium.[a]	[LHymn] Laus matutina suscitet sompnolente de cantica; psallencium vox recitet[a] gesta regis magnifica.	[LHymn] Laus matutina suscitet sompnolentos ad cantica; psallentium vox recitet gesta regis magnifica.	[LHymn] Hymmum dicant cum gaudio cuncti cetus ecclesie sedet in celi solio Ludovicus rex Francie.	[LHymn] Beata nobis gaudia nostri regis dant merita, pro cuius tanta gloria[a] laudum solvamus debita.	[LHymn] Ymmpnum dicant cum gaudio cuncti celus ecclesie sedet in celi solio Ludovicus rex Francie.
Ludovicus ex nomine lucis dator exprimitur, et custos in certamine presentis vite ponitur.	Ludovicus ex nomine lucis dator exprimitur, et custos in certamine presentis vite ponitur.	Principibus pre ceteris magnificat humilitas in adversis et prosperis mira mentis equalitas.	Principibus pre ceteris magnificat humilitas in adversis et prosperis mira mentis equalitas.	In preceptis dominicis apponens diligentiam sedensque sede iudicis dissipabat maliciam.	Ad sacrum eius tumulum ubi fiunt miracula a struma super oculum liberatur iuvencula.	Rex preceptis dominicis apponens diligentiam sedens in sede iudicis dissipabat malitiam.
Crucis hostes concuciens, concussus egritudine, vitam invenit moriens tali felix certamine.	Crucis hostes concuciens, concussus egritudine, vitam invenit moriens tali felix certamine.	Mentis monstrat modestiam vultus eius angelicus moderatam iusticiam status regni pacificus.	Mentis monstrat modestiam vultus eius angelicus moderatam iusticiam[a] status regni pacificus.	Sumpto crucis signaculo captus ab infidelibus cultu colebat sedulo deum verbis et actibus.	Anus[b] annis quadraginta tremula toto corpore, annorum iam sexaginta, redit resumpto robore.	Sumpto crucis signaculo captus ab infidelibus cultu colebat sedulo deum verbis et actibus.
Nam sic in vita viguit ut[b] paciendo vinceret, et hoc in morte meruit ut moriendo viveret.	Nam sic in vita viguit ut paciendo vinceret, et hoc in morte meruit ut moriendo viveret.	Sectatorem modestie collaudant viri simplices; zelatorem iusticie commendant veri iudices.	Sectatorem modestie collaudent viri simplices; zelatorem iusticie commendant veri[b] iudices.	Mors timetur ab omnibus nave collisa subito sed liberantur precibus pii regis et merito.	Mutus surdus recuperat verbum simul et auditum, et qui visum amiserat lumen recipit[c] perditum.	Mors timetur ab omnibus nave collisa subito sed liberantur precibus pii regis et merito.
Vivit ergo feliciter rex francorum in gloria, quem Christus singulariter sua replevit gratia.	Vivit ergo feliciter rex francorum in gloria, quem Christus singulariter sua replevit gratia.	Omnis spiritus invocet. *ut supra.*	Omnis spiritus invocet. *ut supra.*	Mors timetur ab omnibus nave collisa subito sed liberantur precibus pii regis et merito.	Illic plene sanitati redduntur[d] epilentici, contracti et fistulati, multique paralitici.	Presta, pater piissime Ludovici suffragiis splendorem lucis intime quo purgemur a vitiis.
Trino Deo et simplici. *ut supra.*	Trino Deo et simplici. *ut supra.*			Quesumus actor[a]. *ut supra.*	Patri nato paraclito decus, honor et gloria qui Ludovici merito tanta fecit magnalia.	
[a]"solium] solidum *B.* [b]ut] *om. B.*	[=NL, LHymn] [a]E retiget.	[=LC1 LH]	[=LC2 LH] [a]iusticiam] molestiam *I.* [b]commandant veri] commendent viri *I.*	[a]K auctor.	[a]"gloria] merita *M.* [b]anus] agnus *M.* [c]recipit] recepit *M.* [d]redduntur] reddantur *L.*	

Appendix 2.1-_cont._

	NUNC LAUDARE	LUDOVICUS DECUS	LAUDA CELESTIS 1	LAUDA CELESTIS 2	LAUDA CELESTIS 3	EXULTEMUS OMNES	FRANCORUM REX	SANCTUS VOLUNTATEM
	[Ben] Ludovicus decus regnantium transit felix ad regni[a] solium, cuius prece cetus fidelium summi regis intret in gaudium. P. Benedictus.	[Ben] Benedictus Dominus qui nobis erexit cornu, quod paulominus a David dilexit; hic virtute geminus rex in pace rexit, quem regendi terminus ad celos direxit. P. Benedictus.	[Ben] Benedictus spiritus sancti regis hodie post carnis divortium tunicii castris[a] evocatus celitus ad bravium patrie transit emisperium sublimatus astris.	[Ben] Sancti regis hodie post carnis divorcium Tunicii castris evocatus celitus ad bravium patrie transit emisperium sublimatus astris.	[Ben] Benedictus Dominus qui nobis erexit cornu quod paulominus a David dilexit hic virtute geminus rex in pace rexit quem regendi terminus ad celos direxit. P. Dominus regnavit.	[Ben] Benedictus Dominus virtutum digne debet modo benedici pro meritis sancti Ludovici, quem novimus celos assecutum cuius translatio facta cum gaudio reddat ab hostibus et malis omnibus regnum tutum.[a]	[Ben] Iam sanctus post laborem recepturus premium regnaturum maiorem exhortatur filium ad matris honorem, de fide et moribus testamentum condidit et bonis operibus commentum[a] addidit divinum amorem.	[A] Rex sub quo vixit Francia pacifice in te thronum fixit iustitia, Ludovice deprecantes et laudantes veridice pietatis aspectu nos respice.
	"regni] celi _B._	_D repeats Oratio here._	[a]tunicii castris] _E castum._ _A space is open for a word in the ms._	[=LC1 Ben (_altered_)]	[LDR Ben]	[a]_C₂ ends here, and sends the celebrant for the texts below to Little Hours in LDR._	[a] commentum] complementum _M._	

PRIME

Adest dies. . . . [as in LA1]

| | | [A]
Angelorum choris[a]
defertur in iubilo
de valle meroris
sol egressus nubilo.

[a]choris] chorus _E._ | | | | | [Hymn]
Iam lucis orto sydere
Ludovicum ex viribus studeamus attollere
dignum devotis laudibus.

Ab etatis primordiis fecit hunc mater imbui virtutibus sciencis et studere profectui.

[A]
In misericordie multitudine
deum adorabat, qui conscientie rectitudine celis |

inhabitabat.
[=NL MA5]

[Cap]
Regi autem seculorum immortali invisibili soli deo honor et Gloria in secula seculorum.

[Oratio]
In hac hora huius diei tua nos, Domine, reple misericordia, ut beati Ludovici laudibus insistentes a cunctis ejus intercessione periculis exuamur. Per Dominum

[Hymn]
Nunc sancte nobis spiritus laudis prebes materiam, nam Ludovicus inclitus iam celis tenet gloriam.

Dum hic adhuc adolescens studeret consciencie semper in virtute crescens rex est confectus Francie.

[A]
Gloria et honore regnat rex coronatus,[a] qui semper in amore Dei fuit firmatus.

[a] coronatum in *ms*.
[=NL MA6]

(continued)

TERCE

Beatus dives . . . .
[Eccli 31.10]

[Cap]
K: In gentibus multis non est rex similis ei et dilectus a Deo suo erat et posuit eum Deus regem super Israel.

[Cf: 2 Ez 13.26; =LDR Terce]

[A]
H: Angelorum choris defertur in iubilo de valle meroris sol egressus nubilo.

[=LC2, *I:* LA2]

I: Ludovice rex francorum in felici beatorum regno gaudens gloria de hac valle miserorum recto calle nos iustorum duc ad celi gaudia.

[=LDR WA, NL Ben]

[Cap]
In gentibus multis non erat rex similis ei et dilectus Deo suo erat et posuit eum Deus regem super Israel.[a]

[Cf: 2 Ez 13:26]
[a]*D* om. *D* add: *ad horas antiphona de laudibus ad terciam capitulum*

[A]
Luce[a] vigil ad Dominum prudens et fidelis servus cum patre luminum iungitur in celis.

[a] Luce] Lux *E*.

Appendix 2.1-*cont.*

NUNC LAUDARE	LUDOVICUS DECUS	LAUDA CELESTIS 1	LAUDA CELESTIS 2	LAUDA CELESTIS 3	EXULTEMUS OMNES	FRANCORUM REX	SANCTUS VOLUNTATEM
							[Cap] In omnibus gentibus non erat rex similis ei et dilectus Deo suo erat. Et posuit eum Dominus regem super Israel. [Cf: 2 Ez 13.26; = LDR Terce] [Oratio] Deus per quem reges regnare noscuntur, concede propicius ut qui beati Ludovici merita gloriosa recolimus, eius apud te suffragiis adiuvemur. Per Dominum.
					SEXT		
[Cap] Dedit illi Dominus fortitudinem et usque ad senectutem[a] permansit illi virtus ut ascenderet in excelsum terre locum et semen ipsius optinuit hereditatem. [Cf: Eccli 46:11] *B only. Absent in A.* [a] *sectutem in B.*	[Cap] In vinculis non dereliquit eum Dominus, donec afferret illi sceptrum regni et potentiam adversus eos qui eum deprimebant. [Cf: Wis 10:14; =NL None]	[A] Benedicant opera cuncta creatorem, qui dat supra sydera regnum post laborem.		[A] H: Luce vigil ad Dominum prudens et fidelis servus cum patre luminum iungitur in celis. [=LC2, I LA3] I: Deductus in iustitia [*as in MA10*]	[Cap] In vinculis multis non derelinquit eum Dominus donec afferret illi sceptrum regni et potenciam adversus eos qui eum deprimebant. [Cf: Wis 10:14; =NL None, LDR Sext] *K only:*	[Cap] Qui probatus est in illo et perfectus[a] inventus est et erit illi gloria eterna. [Cf: Eccli 31.10] [a]*L profectus.*	[Hymn] Rector potens, verax Deus amore tui nominis dimisit rex spontaneus terram sui regiminis. Bis[a] pro fide christiana transfretavit quem graviter captum duxit gens prophana quod portavit humiliter. [a]Bis] Uis *in ms.*

[Cap]
In vinculis non dereliquit eum Dominus, donec afferret illi septrum regni et potentiam adversus eos qui eum deprimebant.
[Cf: Wis 10:14]
B only. Absent in A.

[Cap]
Magnificavit eum Dominus super omnem Israel et dedit illi gloriam regni qualem nullus habuit ante eum rex.
[Cf: 2 Chr 19:25]
R. Iustus ut palma.

[A]
Laudes Deo concinit egressus exilium; pressure non meminit translatus in gaudium.

[Cap]
Qui potuit transgredi et non est transgressus et facere mala[a] et non fecit. Ideo stabilita sunt bona illius in Domino et elemosinas illius enarrabit omnis[b] ecclesia sanctorum.
[Cf: Eccli 31.10]
[a]L magna. [b]L omnia

[Cap]
K: Magnificavit eum Dominus super omnem israel et dedit illi gloriam regni qualem nullus habuit ante eum rex.
[Cf: 2 Chr 19:25; =LDR None]

[A]
H: Benedicant opera cuncta creatorem, qui dat supra sydera, regnum post laborem.
[=LC2, I LA4]

I: Coronatur gloria [as in MA11]

[A] Habitabit in tabernaculo Domini gloriose quia vixit in isto seculo rex noster virtuose.
[=NL MA7]

[Cap] In vinculis non reliquit eum Dominus donec afferret illi sceptrum regni et potentiam adversus eos qui eum deprimebant.
[Cf: Wis 10:14; =NL None, LDR Sext, EO Sext]
[=LDR Sext]

[Oratio] Annue nobis Domine quesumus ut sicut beatus Ludovicus confessor tuus in terris digne famulari meruit ita nos facias eius apud te precibus adiuvari.

[Hymn]
Rerum Deus tenax vigor Ludovicum iusticie semper sociavit rigor cum virtute clemencie.

Fidem in reverencia semper habere studuit nec in hanc indecencia verba proferre voluit.

(continued)

NUNC LAUDARE	LUDOVICUS DECUS	LAUDA CELESTIS 1	LAUDA CELESTIS 2	LAUDA CELESTIS 3	EXULTEMUS OMNES	FRANCORUM REX	SANCTUS VOLUNTATEM
[Mag] O decus ecclesie, pie rex francorum, exemplar iustitie lex et norma morum, Ludovice requie fruens beatorum, tue dono gratie, da regna celorum. [Ben] Ludovice rex francorum in felice[d] beatorum regno gaudens gloria, de hac valle miserorum recto calle nos iustorum duc ad celi gaudia. [d] felice] felici B. [A] O lumen ecclesie doctor veritatis rosa patientie ebur castitatis aquam sapientie propinasti gratis predicator gracie nos iunge beatis. [found in A. Absent in B. = Magnificat for office of Saint Dominic, =LMO DO21, WE]				[Oratio] *H only* Potuit vir iste transgredi et non est transgressus facere mala et non fecit ideo stabilita sunt bona illius in Domino et elemosinas illius enarrabit omnis ecclesia sanctorum. [Cf: Eccli. 31:10-11] [Oratio] *I only:* Presta quas omnipotens Deus ut sicut beatus Ludovicus confessor tuus per habundanciam gracie tue oblectamentis mundialibus spretis soli regi Christo placere studuit; ita eius oratio nos tibi reddat acceptos. [=*mass secretum*] [Oratio] *I. only:* Deus qui almum confessorem tuum Ludovicum mirificasti in terris; quos ut iam in celis gloriosum effectum ecclesie tue constituas defensorem eamque eius meritis et precibus ab omni adversitate liberare digneris. [= *mass postcommunio*]			[A] In virtute Domini rex sanctus locabitur; nunc sanctorum agmini iunctus gloriatur. [=NL MA8] [Cap] Magnificavit eum Dominus regem super israel et dedit illi gloriam regni qualem nullus habuit ante eum rex. [Cf: 2 Chr 19:25; =LDR None Cap.] [Oratio] Beati Ludovici, confessoris tui quesumus Domine nobis preces gloriose subveniant quem de cura terreni regiminis ad celestis regni curiam perduxisti. [A] Rex, innocens manibus atque corde mundo, regnat cum celestibus in regno iocundo.

H only: Corona aurea super caput iusti, expressa signo sanctitatis gloria honoris et opus fortitudinis.

[Cap]
Benedictus Dominus
deus partum nostrorum
qui dedit hanc
voluntatem in cor regis
clarificare domum suam
que est in Ierusalem.
Deo gratias.

[Hymn]
Lucis creator optime
Ludovicus dum regeret
subiecit corpus anime
ut virtuose viveret.

Ludos vincens Ludovicus
secularis lascivie
cuncte fuit inimicus
et destructor malicie.

Dum mancipatur carceri
liber amissus cernitur
et petens miles fieri
digne repulsam patitur.

Virtuosum se reddidit
verbo signis et gratia
cum successori tradidit
documenta salubria.[a]

[a]NB: This hymn appears
in Rouen Y 233, a
diurnal that contains a
version of *Nunc
laudare*. It does not
appear in BL 30072 (*A*)
or Mazarine 374 (*B*)

(continued)

Appendix 2.1-*cont.*

Nunc Laudare	Ludovicus Decus	Lauda Celestis 1	Lauda Celestis 2	Lauda Celestis 3	Exultemus Omnes	Francorum Rex	Sanctus Voluntatem
							[A] Rex per quem ecclesia fuit sublimata, per quem tota Francia, nunc est honorata, cui semper iustitia fuit comitata,[a] nobis[b] Christi gratia da regna beata.
							[=NL Mag] [a] comutata *in ms.* [b] om. *in ms.*
							[Oratio] Concede quesumus omnipotens deus ut beati Ludovici confessoris tui merita gloriosa nos ad celestia regna promoveant, quem de regno francie ad regnum glorie transtulisti.
							COMPLINE
							[A] Mirificavit Dominus sanctum regem francorum, cujus nunc est terminus in regno beatorum.
							[Cap] Consummatus in brevi, explevit multa tempora, placita enim erat deo anima illius. Deo gratias.

[Hymn]
Te lucis ante terminum
christi sacramentaliter
recepit rex et Dominum
confessus est humiliter.

Quod finito certamine,
vivat nunc rex in secula
beatorum agmine
probant plura miracula.

[A]
Salva nos Domine
    vigilantes
Ludovicum venerantes
ut precibus ipsius adjuti
quiescamus in hac nocte
    tuti. Domine exaudi
    orationem meam
et clamor meus ad te
    veniat.

[Oratio]
Accepta sint tibi,
    Domine, nostra servitia
que nos, interveniente
beato Ludovico
confessore tuo, ad
    premia perducant
eterna. Per Dominum
    nostrum jhesum
Christum, filium tuum,
qui tecum vivit et
regnat in unitate spiritus
sancti deus. Per omnia
    secula seculorum.
Domine exaudi
    orationem meam. Et
clamor meus ad te
veniat benedicamus
Domino. Deo gratias.

(continued)

Appendix 2.1-*cont.*

NUNC LAUDARE	LUDOVICUS DECUS	LAUDA CELESTIS 1	LAUDA CELESTIS 2	LAUDA CELESTIS 3	EXULTEMUS OMNES	FRANCORUM REX	SANCTUS VOLUNTATEM
				2 VESPERS			
				H only: Laudes Deo concinit [as in / LA5] [=LC2, / LA5]			
		[WA1] Extrenuo. . . . [WA2] Oritur in gaudium. . . . [WA3] Ab amore. . . . . [WA4] Audiens . . . . . [WCap] Dilectus a Deo . . . [WCapR] Amavit eum. . . . . [WCapV] Iustus. . . .					
	[Mag] Magnificat miraculis Ludovicum divinitas, in quo cunctorum oculis David fulsit humilitas, Salomonis serenitas et Ezechie veritas, quem gratiarum titulis sollempnem fecit populis Iosye par benignitas.[a] P. Magnificat. Capitulum et hymnus sicut in primis vesperis, supra.	[Mag] Magnum magnatum speculum, Ludovice rex Francie cunctis relinquens, titulum sanctitatis eximie, prece iuvans in seculum, commenda regi glorie devotum tibi populum.	[Mag] Magnum magnatum speculum, Ludovice rex Francie cunctis relinquens, titulum sanctitatis eximie, prece iuvans in seculum, commenda regi glorie devotum tibi populum. [=LC1 Mag.]	[Mag] *I only:* Magnum magnatum speculum, Ludovice rex Francie cunctis relinquens, titulum sanctitatis eximie, prece iuvans in seculum, commenda regi glorie devotum tibi populum. P. Dixit Dominus. [=LC2 Mag] [Mag] *HI:* Magnificat miraculis Ludovicum divinitas, in quo cunctorum oculis David fulsit humilitas, Salomonis serenitas et Ezechie veritas, quem gratiarum titulis sollempnem[a] fecit populis Iosie[b] par benignitas. P. Magnificat [a]H solemnem. [b]H iosye. [=LDR 2 Vespers Mag A]	[Mag] *KJ:* Magnificat gesta clarissima sancti Ludovici divino cultu devotum hodie presens collegium, cuius sancti conscendit anima sub fine felici regni perpetui cum sanctis patrie sublime solium. [=LC3 VMag, LDR VMag]	[Mag] O martyr desiderio, quam pie mentis studio crucifixo compateris, cuius crucem in humeris tuis bis affixisti,[a] passio tibi deficit sed martyrem te effecit fervor et zelus Christi.[b] [a]L afflixisti. [b]M zelus et amor christi	

[OA1]
Ludovice rex francorum,
in felice beatorum
regno gaudes gloria
de hac valle miserorum
recto calle nos iustorum
duc ad celi gaudia.

[=NL Ben]
C only, throughout octave

[OA2]
Magnificat Dominum
et exultat spiritus
pauperum et divitum
in Deo salutari,
qui generi hominum
hunc regem divinitus
Ludovicum inclitum
dedit pro exemplari.

[=FR VMag.]

[OA3]
Iam sanctus post laborem
recepturus premium,
regnaturum maiorem
exhortatur filium
ad matris honorem,
de fide et moribus
testamentum condidit,
et bonis operibus
complementum addidit
divinum amorem.

[=FR LBen]

[OA4]
O martyr desiderio,
quem pie mentis studio
crucifixo compateris,

(continued)

Appendix 2.1—*cont.*

Nunc Laudare	Ludovicus Decus	Lauda Celestis 1	Lauda Celestis 2	Lauda Celestis 3	Exultemus Omnes	Francorum Rex	Sanctus Voluntatem
	cuius crucem in humeris tuis bis affixisti; passio tibi defecit sed martyrem te effecit fervor et zelus Christi.						
	[=FR Mag]						
	[OA5] Tu, cecorum oculus, debilium baculus, oppressorum clipeus, perversorum malleus, nutritor minorum, miserere populi te laudare seduli, nobilis rex Francie, Ludovice, glorie consors beatorum.						
	[OA6] O decus ecclesie, pie rex francorum, exemplar iusticie, lex et norma morum, post finem angustie, mortis et laborum presta dono gratie regnum beatorum.						
	[=NL Ben (*altered*), EO]						
	[OA7] Magnum magnatum speculum, Ludovice rex Francie, cunctis relinquens titulum sanctitatis eximie, prece iuvans in seculum,						

commenda regi glorie
devotum tibi populum.

[=LC1 Mag. Ant.]

[OA8]
O patriarcha procerum,
piorum sator munerum,
curam gerendo pauperum,
Ludovice, rex beate,
efficaces sint oblate
tibi preces impetrate
pacis nobis indilate
fructum reportantes a te.

[O Mag]
Ora, pater Ludovice,
hac pro gente peccatrice
sui reatus conscia,
ut pax, Dei genitrice
tecum nobis adiutrice,
detur et indulgentia,
adiuva nos[a] clementia,
que relicta cicatrice
carnis palma cum victrice
coronavit te gloria.
P. Magnificat.

[a]nos] add interl C.

Appendix 3

Sermons in Honor of Saint Louis (IX)

"Schneyer" numbers refer either to the hard-copy *Repertorium* (published 1969–1971), which covers the period from 1100 to 1350, or the CD-ROM *Repertorium* (issued 2001), which covers the period from 1350 to 1500.

The bibliographic entries consist only of particularly pertinent entries. For a full bibliography, refer to Schneyer, or Schneyer CD.

Anon 1.
(1) *Ipse fuit ornatus quoad Dominum, se et proximum.*
Schneyer, Jacob of Lausanne 608 (vol. 3, 104)
Ms: Vat Lat 1259, 281r.–v.
N.B. This sermon appears in a collection of sermons by Jacob of Lausanne, added in a later hand to the last folio of the volume.

Anon 2. O. Cist.
(1) *Honoratus—commendatur a nomine, fuerat a rege.* (cf. Tob. 1:16)
Schneyer 608 (vol. 6, 391)
Ms: Charleville BM 31, 238r.–v.

Anon 3. OFM.
(1) *Misericordia et veritas custodiunt regem.* (Prov. 20:28)
Schneyer: Not listed
Ms: Paris BNF Lat 3303, 183–193v.

Anon 4. OFM.
(1) *Perfectus inventus est et erit illi gloria eterna.* (cf. Eccli. 31:10)
Schneyer 14 (vol. 9, 244)
Ms: Paris BNF Lat 16512, 52rb.–57ra.

Anon 5.
(1) *Uigilate quia nescitis.* (Matt. 24:42) *Congrue possumus dicere ad laudem beati lodwici regis francie.*

Schneyer: Not listed
Ms: Uppsala C383, 175v.–176r.

Anon 6.

(1) *Rex sapiens stabilimentum populi est.* (Wis. 6:26) *Naturaliter quondam truncus arboris plenus est pinguedine et humore quam attrahit a terra rami eius persistunt in suo decore et virore.*
Schneyer: not listed
Ms: Paris BNF Lat 14969, 254v.–257r.
N.B. Appears in a collection of sermons by Jacob of Lausanne, but is a different sermon than his *Rex Sapiens* (no. 3 below)

Anon 7. University Preacher, Heidelberg.

(1) *Misericordia et veritas custodiunt regem.* (Prov. 20:28)
Schneyer CD 58
Ms: Heidelberg, Palat. Lat. 454, 230r.–233v.
(2) *Justus ex fide vivit.* (Gal. 3:11)
Schneyer CD 59
Ms: Heidelberg, Palat. Lat. 454, 233v.–241r.

Arnaud Royard. OFM. Archbishop of Salerno. d. 1334.

(1) *Rex justus erigit terram.* (Prov. 29:4)
Schneyer: Bertrand of Tours 1228 (vol. 1, 589)
Ms: Padua, Anton. 208, 337v.
(2) *Hic est ut Melchisedech rex Salem.* (Heb. 7:1)
Schneyer: Bertrand of Tours 1225 (vol. 1, 589)
Ms: Padua, Anton. 208, 335r.

N.B. Schneyer thought these were by Bertrand of Tours. But see Nold 2001, XI.

Bertrand of Tours (Bertrandus de Turre), OFM, Archbishop of Salerno, Cardinal, Vicar Minister General, d. 1332/33

(1) *Dico vobis, quod nec Salomon in omni gloria sua.* (Matt. 6:29)
Schneyer 711 (vol. 1, 558)
Mss: Vat. Burg. 31, 143–145v.; Linz Stud. B71, 118va.–120rb.; Graz UB 717, 188rb.–189vb.; Toulouse BM 328, 187r.–189v.
(2) *Beatus dives qui inventus est sine macula.* (Eccli. 31:8)
Expositio epistole que legitur in festo beati Ludovici quondam regis francorum
Schneyer: not listed. See Nold, 2002, 632.12
Ms: Toulouse BM 325, 249r.–250v.
(3) *Beatus dives qui inventus est sine macula.* (Eccli. 31:8)
Schneyer: not listed. See Nold 2002, 632.13
Ms: Toulouse BM 325, 250v.–253r.
(4) *Probatus est in illo et perfectus inventus est.* (Eccli. 31:10)
Schneyer: not listed. See Nold 2002, 632.16
Ms: Toulouse BM 325, 253r.–254r.
N.B. Schneyer nos. 1225 and 1128 are in fact sermons by a contemporary Franciscan Arnaud Royard. See entry above on Arnaud Royard.

Bibl: Nold 2001; Nold 2002.

Boniface VIII (Benedict Gaetani), Pope. d. 1303.

(1) *Reddite que sunt Cesaris Cesari, et que sunt Dei Deo.* (Matt. 22:21)
Schneyer: not listed.
Ed: *RHF*, vol. 23, 148–152; French translation in Carolus-Barré 1994.

(2) *Rex pacificus magnificatus est.*
Schneyer: not listed
Ed: *RHF,* vol. 23, 152–153; French translation in Carolus-Barré 1994.
Bibl: Carolus Barré 1994; Gaposchkin 2003.

Jacob of Lausanne (Jacobus Losanna), OP, d. 1322

(1) *Videte regem Salomonem* (Cant. 3:11)
Schneyer 609 (vol. 3, 104–105)
Mss: Avignon BM 304, 68rb.–70ra.; Paris BNF Lat 14962, 63ra.–64rb.; BNF Lat
    14963, Part 2, 39v.–40r.; BNF Lat 15962, 25vb.–28rb.; BNF Lat 18181,
    273r.–274r.; Vat. Lat 1250, 102ra.–104ra.; Vat. Lat 1259, 164vb.–167ra.; Vat. Lat
    1260, 62vb.–64va.
(2) *Bene omnia fecit.* (Mark 7:37)
Schneyer 610 (vol. 3, 105)
Mss: Troyes BM 1787, 216v.–217v.; Avignon BM 304, 303va.–304rb.; Paris BNF Lat
    14964.
N.B. This is the same sermon as Schneyer listed under Michael Forno, where he gives
    the Troyes BM 1787 as a citation.
(3) *Rex sapiens stabilimentum populi est.* (Wis. 6:26)
Schneyer 611 (vol. 3, 105)
Mss: Paris BNF Lat 14799 92v.–93v, BNF Lat 14966, Pt II. 25r.–26r.; Vat. Lat 1259,
    162va.–164vb.
(4) *Bene omnia fecit.* (Mark 7:37) *Sicut dicit Gregorius: Miracula Domini et Salvatoris
nostri sic intelligenda sunt.*
Schneyer 360 (vol. 3, 83)
Mss: Vat. Lat 1259, 169rb.–173ra., Paris BNF Lat 14966, 10v.–11r., BNF nal 1475,
    157vb.–160rb.
5) *Salomon filium meum elegit Deus.* (1 Chr. 29:1)
Schneyer: Not listed
Ms: Vat. Lat 1259, 167rb.–169rb.

James (Jacobus) of Viterbo, OESA. Bishop of Naples, d. 1308.

(1) *David in sua misericordia consecutus est sedem regni in secula.* (I Mach. 2:57)
Schneyer: Not listed
Ms: Vat. Capit San Pietro, D 213, cols. 17–18.
(2) *Rex in eternum vive.* (Dan. 3:9)
Schneyer: Not listed
Ms: Vat. Capit San Pietro, D 213, cols. 114–119.
(3) *Fecit Ezechias quod placuit deo.* (Eccli. 48:25)
Schneyer: Not listed
Ms: Vat. Capit San Pietro, D 213, cols. 247–251.
(4) *Magnificans salutes regis eius.* (Ps. 17:51)
Schneyer: Not listed
Ms: Vat. Capit San Pietro, D 213, cols. 377–382.
(5) *Tronus eius sicut sol in conspectu meo.* (Ps. 88:38)
Schneyer: Not listed
Ms: Vat. Capit San Pietro, D 213, cols. 487–492.

Bibl: Anderson 1995; Ferzoco 1999; Morello and Piazzoni 1998, no. 20.

Jean Courtecuisse (Johannes Brevicoxa). Bishop of Paris. d. 1423.

(1) *Tu, domine, mi rex, sicut Angelus Dei est.* (2 Sam. 19:27)
Schneyer: not listed
Mss: Paris BNF Lat 3546, 90–99v. BNF Lat 14969, 83–90.
Ed: Ellies de Pin's 1702 edition of Gerson's work. Volume 3, c. 1440–1449.

(2) *Que multi prophete et reges voluerunt videre.* (Luke 10:24)
   Schneyer: not listed
   Ms: Paris BNF Lat 3546, 112–117.
(3) *Considerate lilia agri.* (Matt. 6:28)
   Schneyer: not listed
   Ms: Paris BNF Lat 3546, 104–110.

   Bibl: Coville 1904; Omont 1919; Gorochov 1999.

Jean Gerson (Johannes Gerson). Chancellor of the University of Paris, d. 1429.
(1) *Dedit illi gloriam regni.* (1 Chr. 29:25)
   Schneyer CD 14
   Ed: Gerson 1960, vol. 5, no. 219, 179–190.
(2) *Dominus regnavit, decorem indutus est.* (Ps. 91:1)
   Schneyer CD 18
   Ed: Gerson 1960, vol. 5, no. 233, 229–243.
(3) *Considerate lilia agri quomodo crescunt.* (Matt. 6:28)
   Schneyer CD 12
   Ms: Paris BNF Lat 14969, 254v.–257r.
   Ed: Gerson 1960, vol. 5, no. 217, 151–168.

   Bibl: Gorochov 1999; Hinkle 1991, 52–53.

John of Aragon. Bishop of Toledo, son of King James II, d. 1334.
(1) *Inveni David servum meum oleo sanco meo unxi eum.* (Ps. 88:21)
   Schneyer 406 (vol. 3, 324)
   Ms: Valencia Cat. 182, 207ra.–207va.
(2) *Rex qui sedet in solio iudicii.* (Prov. 20:8)
   Schneyer 407 (vol. 3, 324)
   Ms: Valencia Cat. 182, 207va.–208va.
(3) *Rex qui sedet in solio iudicii.* (Prov. 20:8)
   Schneyer 408 (vol. 3, 324)
   Ms: Valencia. Cat. 182, 208va.–209rb.
(4) *Inveni David servum meum [in] oleo sancto meo unxi eum.* (Ps. 88:21)
   Schneyer 409 (vol. 3, 324)
   Ms: Valencia Cat. 182, 209rb.–209va.
(5) *Beatus vir, qui non abiit.* (Ps. 1:1)
   Schneyer 410 (vol. 3, 324)
   Ms: Valencia Cat. 182, 209va.–210ra.

   Bibl: Avezou 1930.

John of Capestrano (Johannes de Capestrano), OM, d. 1456
(1) *Nolite nocere terrae et mari.* (Rev. 7:3)
   Schneyer CD 20
   Ms: Capistrani, Bibl. OFM XXIX, 8v.–9r.

John of Naples (Johannes de Napoli, Giovanni Regina di Napoli), OP, d. after 1347.
(1) *Bene omnia fecit.* (Mark 7:37)
   Schneyer: not listed

   Ms: Paris BNF Lat. 14799, 161r.–163r.
   Bibl: Kapelli 1962; Kelly 2003, 121, n. 172.

John of San Gimigniano, OP, d. after 1333.
(1) *Domine, in virtute tua letabitur rex.* (Ps. 20:2)
   Schneyer 398 (vol. 3, 754)

Mss: Florenz, Naz. I.I.41; G.1.516; G.9.1477; Nurenburg, St. B. Cent.III, 48; Tours 481 297r.–299r.; Troyes 913; Troyes 966 174r.–175v.; Vat Barb.513, 132vb.–133vb.

Bibl.: Dondaine 1939.

Michael de Forno.

(1) *Bene omnia fecit.* (Mark 7:37)
Schneyer 43 (vol. 4, 181)
See entry for Jacob of Lausanne (2)

Peter Berengar (Petrus Berengarius), OP.

(1) *Justum deduxit Dominus.* (Wis. 10:10)
Schneyer 242 (vol. 4, 617)
Ms: Bordeaux BM 297, 182rb.–v.
(2) *Dilectus Deo et hominibus.* (Eccli. 45:1)
Schneyer 243 (vol. 4, 617)
Ms: Bordeaux BM 297, 182vb.–183ra.

Pierre d'Ailly (Petrus de Alliaco). Bishop of Cambrai, Cardinal, d. ca. 1420.

(1) *Fide reliquit egiptum.* (Heb. 11:27)
Schneyer CD15
Mss: Angers 324, 54v.–60r.; Cambrai 531, 169rb.–169vb.
Ed. Pierre d'Ailly (Petrus de Ailliaco) 1490. The 1490 edition does include original pagination. Counting from the first page, the sermon appears on 300–305.
N.B. The sermon was preached at the Council of Constance (1414–1418). In the printed version of 1490 the rubric erroneously lists the sermon as dedicated to Saint Louis of Toulouse.

Remegius of Florence (Remigius Gioralami Florentinus), OP, d. ca. 1319.

(1) *Ludam et vilior fiam.* (2 Sam. 6:22)
Schneyer 859 (vol. 5, 118)
Ms: Florenz, Naz. D. 1.937, 271r.–v.

Bibl: Panella 1990.

Robert of Anjou (Robert the Wise). King of Sicily, d. 1343.

(1) *Considerate lilia agri.* (Matt. 6:28)
Schneyer 235 (vol. 5, 216)
Ms: Cod. Venet. Marc. Cl. III. nr. 76, pp. 97–98
(2) *Adeamus cum fiducia ad thronum gratie.* (Heb. 4:16).
Schneyer 122 (vol. 5, 206–207)
Ms: Rome Angel 151, 193v.–202r.
Bibl: Pryds 2000; Kelly 2003, 123–124.
N.B. The rubric in 2, *Adeamus cum fiducia,* indicates that the sermon can be preached to Louis of France and Louis of Toulouse. "*In festo Ludovici regis Francie et posset esse de sancto ludovico episcopo, fratre suo paucis dictionibus commutatis.*"

Sigerius of Courtrai, Deacon at Notre Dame of Courtrai. d. 1341.

(1) *Preposui illam regnis et sedibus.* (Wis. 7:8)
Schneyer 47 (vol. 5, 437)
Ms: Troyes BM 759, 95vb.–97ra.
(2) *Regnum meum non est de hoc mundo.* (John 18:36)
Schneyer 48 (vol. 5, 437)
Ms: Troyes BM 759, 97ra.–97vb.

William (Guillaume) of Saint-Pathus, OFM. d. after 1315.

(1) *Princeps clarissimus et magnus es* (1 Mach. 2:17)
   Schneyer: Not listed
   Ms: Chartes BM 226. The manuscript was destroyed during World War II.
   Ed. and bibl.: Delaborde 1902.

William (Guillaume) of Sauqueville, OP, d. ca. 1330.

(1) *Rex sapiens populi stabilimentum est* (Wis. 6:26)
   Schneyer 70 (vol. 2, 593), not identified as honoring Saint Louis
   Mss: Paris BNF Lat 16495, 161v.–162r.
   Ed: Coester 1935/36; Chevalier Boyer 2007, 557–559. Sermon no. 70.

   Bibl: Coester 1935/1936; Chevalier Boyer 2007; Brown 1988, 60–61.

Appendix 4

Sermons Misidentified as in Honor of Louis IX in Schneyer's Repertorium

S ermons in honor of Saint Louis of Toulouse listed by Schneyer as being in honor of Saint Louis of France, and other sermons misattributed. The following list does *not* comprise all sermons to Saint Louis of Toulouse, only those attributed by Schneyer to Louis IX. For manuscripts and editions, refer to Schneyer and Schneyer CD.

Anon.
(1) *Quoniam partem elegit.* (Luke 10:42)
   Schneyer 13 (vol. 9, 244)

Anon Franciscan.
(1) *Assimilatus filio Dei.* (Heb. 7:3)
   Schneyer 16 (vol. 7, 409)
(2) *Rex Israel mutavit habitum* (1 Kings 22:30)
   Schneyer 17 (vol. 7, 409)

Anon Franciscan.
(1) *Totonderunt Joseph.* (Gen. 41:14)
   Schneyer 45 (vol. 7, 412)

Anon Franciscan.
(1) *Loquebatur recte.* (Mark 7:35)
   Schneyer 63 (vol. 7, 443)

Anon Franciscan.
(1) *Humiliavit semetipsum.* (Phil. 2:8)
   Schneyer 11 (vol. 7, 461)
(2) *Tertius angelus tuba cecinit.* (Rev. 8:10)
   Schneyer 21 (vol. 7, 462)
(3) *Perduxit filium regis et posuit super eum diademate.* (2 Kings 11:12)
   Schneyer 22 (vol. 7, 462)

Arnaud Royard, OFM. Archbishop of Salerno. d. 1334.

(1) *Benedictio Domini super caput justi.* (Prov. 10:6)
Schneyer: Bertrand of Tours 1230 (v. 1, 589)

Conrad (Johannes) Gritsch. Lector at Strasburg. d. 1475.

(1) *Rex Israel mutavit habitum suum.* (1 Kings 22:30)
Schneyer CD 191
(2) *Rex Israel mutavit habitum suum.* (1 Kings 22:30)
Schneyer CD 219

Francis Meyronis (Franciscus de Mayronis, François de Meyronnes), OFM. d. ca. 1328.

(1) *Humiliavit semetipsum.* (Phil. 2:8) *sicut Dei Filius, qui cum in forma Dei esset.*
Schneyer 136 (vol. 2, 75)
(2) *Luce [splendida] fulgebis.* (Tob. 13:13)
Schneyer 171 (vol. 2, 78)

John of Aragon. Bishop of Toledo, son of King James II, d. 1334.

(1) *Dedi te in lucem gentium.* (Isa. 49:6) *Per quam viam spargitur lux.* (Job 38:24)
Schneyer 398 (vol. 3, 323)
(2) *Joseph filius accrescens.* (Gen. 49:22)
Schneyer 399 (vol. 3, 323)
(3) *Vir Dei venit ad me.* (Jdgs. 13:6)
Schneyer 400 (vol. 3, 323–324)
(4) *Cum cognovisset, quia venturi essent.* (John 6:15)
Schneyer 401 (vol. 3, 324)
(5) *Dedi te in lucem gentium.* (Isa. 49:6)
Schneyer 402 (vol. 3, 324)
(6) *Vir Dei venit ad me.* (Jdgs. 13:6)
Schneyer 403 (vol. 3, 324)
(7) *Dedi te in lucem gentium.* (Isa. 49:6)
Schneyer 404 (vol. 3, 324)

John of Capestrano (Johannes de Capestrano), OFM, d. 1456.

(1) *Regnabit rex et sapiens erit.* (Jer. 23:5)
Schneyer CD 18
(2) *Vovete et reddite Domino Deo vestro omnes, qui in circuitu.* (Ps. 75:12)
Schneyer CD 429
(3) *Glorificavit eum in conspectu regum* (Eccli. 45:3)
Schneyer CD 465

John of Cardalhaco. Archbishop of Toulouse.

(1) *Sermo in festo beati Ludovici pontificis in romana curia, per eundem dominum reverendissimum factus in curia Romana. Bene omnia fecit surdos fecit audire et mutos loqui. marci vii* (Mark 7:37)
Schneyer CD 50

Landulphus Caracioli of Naples, OM. Bishop of Castellamare, archbishop of Amalfi, d. 1355.

(1) *Produxit filium regis et posuit super eum diadema.* (2 Kings 11:12)
Schneyer 90 (vol. 4, 7)
(2) *Collat. Produxit filium regis.* (2 Kings 11:12)
Schneyer 91 (vol. 4, 7)

Oswald of Lasko, OFM, d. 1511.

(1) *Vade et vende omnia quae habes.* (Matt. 19:21)
Schneyer CD 75

(2) *Rex Israel mutavit habitum suum.* (1 Kings 22:30)
    Schneyer CD 464

Pelbart Ladislav of Temesvar, OFM, d. 1490.
(1) *Rex mutavit habitum suum.* (1 Kings 22:30)
    Schneyer CD 464

Petrus Aureoli, OFM, d. 1322.
(1) *Humiliavit semetipsum.* (Phil. 2:8)
    Schneyer 155 (vol. 4, 594)
    NB: This sermon is also listed by Schneyer under the listings of an Anonymous
    Franciscan. See above.

Pierre d'Ailly (Petrus de Alliaco). Bishop of Cambrai, Cardinal, d. 1420.
(1) *Euge serve bone et fidelis.* (Matt. 25:21)
    Schneyer CD 14

Robert Caracciolo (de Licio), OFM, d. 1495.
(1) *Quasi sol refulgens.* (Eccli. 50:7)
    Schneyer CD 252

Thomas Brinton, OSB. Bishop of Rochester, d. 1389.
(1) *Erat docens cotidie.* (Luke 19:47)
    Schneyer CD 80

Wilkinus (William of Büschen), OM. Bishop of Minden, d. 1402.
(1) *Humiliavit semetipsum factus obediens.* (Phil. 2:8)
    Schneyer CD 9

To Saint Landericus (Saint Landry)
John of Essone (Jean d'Essomes). Secular master. d. before 1310.
(1) *Exaltavi electum de plebe mea.* (Ps. 88:20)
    Schneyer 41 (vol. 3, 470)

To Saint Augustine
John of Aragon. Bishop of Toledo, son of King James II, d. 1334.
(1) *Ecce intelliget servus meus.* (Isa. 52:13)
    Schneyer 411 (vol. 3, 324)

Bibliography

BIBLIOGRAPHY OF MANUSCRIPTS CITED

N.B. This includes only those manuscripts cited in the text. More information about sources is found in Appendices 1 and 3.

AUSTRIA

Vienna ÖNB 1921, 12807, 12706

BELGIUM

Brussels Bibliothèque royale 197

ENGLAND

Cambridge D.d. V
London, British Library Harley 2864, Add 30027, Add 23935, Add 40154
Oxford, Bodleian Canon Liturg 192

FRANCE

Chantilly, Musée Condé ms 1887.
Orleans Médiathèque (previously Orleans BM) 348
Paris Bibliothèque de l'Arsenal 114, 603, 660,
Paris BNF Fr 5716, 13568; Lat 746A, 750, 911, 1023, 1024, 1028, 1052, 1107, 1288, 1291, 1332, 1435, 1475, 3303, 5406, 6784, 8828, 8831, 8890, 1291, 10485, 12043, 12085, 13233, 13238, 13239, 13568, 14511, 14562, 14799, 14811, 14969, 15962, 16512, 16622; nal 592, nal 1755
Paris Bibliothèque Mazarine 342, 345, 347, 374, 1732
Paris Bibliothèque Sainte Geneviève 2628
Rouen BM Y233
Toulouse BM 325, 328
Troyes, Médiathèque de l'agglomération (previously Troyes BM) 1973, 2030

GERMANY

Graz UB 717
Linz Stud B 71

ITALY

Padua Anton 208
Padua Univ 734

UNITED STATES

New York Pierpont Morgan Library M75, M149
New York Public Library Spencer 56
Washington DC Library of Congress 15

VATICAN

Biblioteca Apostolica Vaticana Burg 31; Capit San Petri D 213; Ottob Lat 221; Reg Lat 534, Reg Lat 1259.

BIBLIOGRAPHY OF PRINTED SOURCES

Acta sanctorum. Edited by Jean Bolland et al. 70 vols. Paris, 1863.

d'Ailly, Pierre (Petrus de Ailliaco). *Tractatus et sermons.* Strasbourg, 1490; reprint Frankfurt, 1971.

Allirot, Anne-Hélène. "*Filiae regis Francorum*: princesses royales, mémoire de saint Louis en conscience dynastique (de 1270 à la fin du XIVe siècle)" (Ph.D. Thesis, Université Paris X-Nanterre, 2007).

Analecta Franciscana 10 (1895–1946): 375–405.

Anderson, David. " 'Dominus Ludovicus' in the Sermons of Jacobus of Viterbo (Arch. S. Pietro D. 213)." In *Literature and Religion in the Later Middle Ages: Philological Studies in Honor of Siegfried Wenzel.* Edited by Richard Newhauser and John Alford. Binghamton, N.Y., 1995, 275–295.

Andersson-Schmitt, Margarete, and Monica Hedlund. *Mittelalterliche Handschriften der Universitätsbibliothek Uppsala: Katalog über die C-Sammlung.* Stockholm, 1988.

Anton, Hans H. *Fürstenspiegel und Herrscherethos in der Karolingerzeit.* Bonn, 1968.

Apel, Willi. *Gregorian Chant.* Bloomington, Ind., 1958.

Archambault, Paul. "Joinville: History as Chivalric Code." In *Seven French Chroniclers: Witnesses to History.* Syracuse, N.Y., 1974, 41–57.

——. "The Silences of Joinville." *Papers on Language and Literature* 7 (1971): 115–132.

Armstrong, Regis J., J. A. Wayne Hellmann, and William J. Short, eds., *Francis of Assisi: Early Documents* 3 vols. New York, 1999–2001.

Artonne, André. *Le mouvement de 1314 et les chartres provinciales de 1315.* Paris, 1912.

Auzas, Pierre-Marie. "Essai d'un répertoire iconographique de saint Louis." In *Septième centenaire de la mort de Saint Louis: Actes des Colloques de Royaumont et de Paris (21–27 mai 1970).* Paris, 1976, 3–56.

Avezou, Robert. "Un prince aragonais—archevêque de Tolède au XIVe siècle." *Bulletin Hispanique* 32 (1930): 326–71.

Avril, François. *Manuscript Painting at the Court of France: The Fourteenth Century, 1310–1380.* New York, 1978.

Avril, François, Louisa Dunlop, and Brunsdon Yapp. *Les Petites Heures de Jean, duc de Berry: Introduction au manuscrits lat. 18014 de la Bibliothèque Nationale, Paris.* Luzern, 1989.

Baldwin, John W. *The Government of Philip Augustus: Foundations of French Royal Power in the Middle Ages.* Berkeley, Calif., 1986.

Baltzer, Rebecca A. "A Royal French Breviary from the Reign of Saint Louis." In *The Varieties of Musicology: Essays in Honor of Murray Lefkowitz.* Edited by John Daverior and John Ogasapian. Warren, Mich., 2000, 3–25.

Baluze, Étienne, and Guillaume Mollat, eds., *Vitae paparum avenionensium; hoc est Historia pontificum romanorum qui in Gallia sederunt ab anno Christi MCCCV usque ad annum MCCCXCIV.* New ed., 4 vols. Paris, 1914–1927.

Barbero, Alessandro. "La propaganda di Roberto d'Angiò re di Napoli (1309–1343)." In *Le forme della propaganda politica nel Due e nel Trecento: relazioni tenute al convegno internazionale organizzato dal Comitato di studi storici di Trieste, dall'École française de Rome, e dal Dipartimento di storia dell'Universitá degli studi di Trieste, Trieste, 2–5 marzo 1993.* Rome, 1994, 111–131.

Barth, Medard. "Zum Kult des h. Königs Ludwig im deutschen Sprachgebiet unde in Skandinavien." *Festschrift J. Vincke, Frieburger Diözesan-Archiv,* 3rd ser. 14/15 (1962/1963), 127–226.

Bartholomew of Lucca and Thomas Aquinas. *On the Government of Rulers: De regimine principum.* Edited by James M. Blythe. Philadelphia, 1997.

Beaumont-Maillet, Laure. *Le Grand couvent des Cordeliers de Paris: étude historique et archéologique du XIIIe siècle à nos jours.* Paris, 1975.

Beaune, Colette. *The Birth of an Ideology: Myths and Symbols of Nation in Late-Medieval France.* Translated by Susan Ross Huston. Berkeley, 1991.

———. *Naissance de la nation France.* Paris, 1985.

Beer, Jean de. *Saint Louis: Louis IX, un roi de justice.* Paris, 1984.

Beer, Jeanette M. A. "The Notion of Temporality in Early Vernacular History." *New Zealand Journal of French Studies* 8 (1987): 5–15.

Bell, Dora M. *L'idéal éthique de la royauté en France au Moyen Âge, d'après quelques moralistes de ce temps.* Geneva, 1962.

Berger, Anna Maria Busse. *Medieval Music and the Art of Memory.* Berkeley, 2005.

Berges, Wilhelm. *Die Fürstenspiegel des hohen und späten Mittelalters.* Leipzig, 1938.

Bériou, Nicole. *L'avènement des maîtres de la Parole: la prédication à Paris au XIIIe siècle.* 2 vols. Paris, 1998.

———. "Les sermons latins après 1200." In *The Sermon.* Edited by Beverly Mayne Kienzle. Turnhout, Belgium, 2000, 363–448.

Bernard Gui. *De fundatione et prioribus conventuum provinciarum Tolosanae et provinciae ordinis praedicatorum.* Edited by Paul A. Amargier. *Monumenta Ordinis fratrum praedicatorum,* Vol. 24. Rome, 1961.

Bernard of Clairvaux. *On the Song of Songs.* Translated by Kilian Walsh. 4 vols. Spencer, Mass., 1971–1980.

Bertaux, Émile. "Les saints Louis dans l'art italien." *Revue des deux mondes* 158 (1900): 616–644.

Bibliotheca hagiographica latina antiquae et mediae antiquae. 2 vols. Brussels, 1898–1901. *Novum supplementum,* Brussels, 1986.

Billson III, Marcus K. "Joinville's Histoire de Saint Louis: Hagiography, History and Memoir." *The American Benedictine Review* 31 (1980): 418–442.

Binski, Paul, and Stella Panayotova, eds., *The Cambridge Illuminations: Ten Centuries of Book Production in the Medieval West,* London, 2005.

Blanchard, P. *Les Heures de Savoie: Facsimiles of Fifty-Two Pages from the Hours Executed for Blanche of Burgundy, Being All That Is Known to Survive of a Famous Fourteenth-Century Ms, Which Was Burnt at Turin in 1904.* London, 1910.

Blezzard, Judith, Stephen Ryle, and Jonathan Alexander. "New Perspectives on the Feast of the Crown of Thorns." *Journal of the Plainsong and Medieval Music Society* 10 (1987): 23–47.

Bloch, Marc. *The Royal Touch.* Translated by J. E. Anderson. New York, 1989.

Boase, Thomas Sherrer Ross. *Boniface VIII*. London, 1933.

Bordonove, Georges. *Saint Louis*. Paris, 2006.

Born, Lester Kruger. "The Perfect Prince: A Study in Thirteenth- and Fourteenth-Century Ideals." *Speculum* 3 (1928): 470–504.

Bougerol, Jacques-Guy. "Saint Bonaventure et le roi Saint Louis." In *Sanctus Bonaventurea 1274–1974*. Rome, 1973, 469–493.

Bouman, Cornelius A. *Sacring and Crowning: The Development of the Latin Ritual for the Anointing of Kings and the Coronation of an Emperor before the Eleventh Century*. Groningen, 1957.

Bouquet, Martin, ed., *Recueil des historiens des Gaules et de la France* 24 vols. Paris, 1738.

Boureau, Alain. "How Christian Was the Sacralization of Monarchy in Western Europe (Twelfth–Fifteenth Centuries)?" In *Mystifying the Monarchy: Studies on Discourse, Power, and History*. Edited by Jeroen Deploige and Gita Deneckere. Amsterdam, 2006, 25–34.

——. "The King." In *Rethinking France = Les lieux de mémoire*. Edited by Pierre Nora. Translated by Mary Trouille. 2 vols. Chicago, 2001–, 181–216. Translated version of "Le roi." In *Lieux de Mémoire*. Edited by Pierre Nora. 3 vols. in 8. Paris, 1986, 785–817.

——. *La religion de l'état: La construction de la République étatique dans le discours théologique de l'Occident médiéval (1250–1350)*. Paris, 2006.

——. "Les Enseignements absolutistes de Saint Louis 1610–1630." In *La monarchie absolutiste et l'histoire en France: Théories du pouvoir, propagandes monarchiques et mythologies nationales*. Paris, 1987, 79–97.

Boutet, Dominique. "Hagiographie et historiographie: la Vie de saint Thomas Becket de Guernes de Pont-Sainte-Maxence et la Vie de saint Louis de Joinville." *Le moyen âge* 106 (2000): 277–293.

——. "La méthode historique de Joinville et la réécriture des *Grandes chroniques de France*." In *Jean de Joinville: de la Champagne aux royaumes d'outre-mer*. Langres, 1998, 93–108.

——. "Ordre, désordre et paradoxe dans le prologue et l'épilogue de la *Vie de Saint Louis* de Joinville." In *"Si a parlé par moult ruiste vertu": mélanges de littérature médiévale offerts à Jean Subrenat*. Paris, 2000, 73–81.

——. "Y a-t-il une idéologie royale dans la Vie de saint Louis de Joinville?" In *Le prince et son historien: la vie de Saint Louis de Joinville*. Paris, 1997, 71–99.

Boyer, Jean-Paul. "*Ecce Rex Tuus*: Le roi et le royaume dans les sermons de Robert de Naples." *Revue Mabillon*, n.s. 6 (= 67) (1995): 101–136.

——. "La 'foi monarchique': royaume de Sicile et Provence (mi-XIIe–mi-XIVe siècle)." In *Le forme della propaganda politica nel Due e nel Trecento: relazioni tenute al convegno internazionale organizzato dal Comitato di studi storici di Trieste, dall'École française de Rome, e dal Dipartimento di storia dell'Università degli studi di Trieste (Trieste, 2–5 marzo 1993)*. Rome, 1994, 85–110.

——. "Prédication et état napolitain dans la première moitié du XIVe siècle." In *L'état angevin: pouvoir, culture et société entre XIIIe et XIVe siècle: Actes du colloque international organisé par l'American Academy in Rome, l'École française de Rome, l'Istituto storico italiano per il Medio Evo, l'U.M.R. Telemme et l'Université de Provence, l'Università degli studi di Napli "Federico II" (Rome-Naples, 7–11 november 1995)*. Rome, 1998, 127–157.

——. "Sacre et théocratie: le cas des rois de Sicile Charles II (1289) et Robert (1309)." *Revue des sciences philosophiques et théologiques* 81 (1997): 561–607.

Boyle, Leonard. "Dominican Lectionaries and Leo of Ostia's *Translatio S. Clementis*." *Archivum Fratrum Praedicatorum* 28 (1958): 362–394.

Boyle, Leonard, and Pierre-Marie Gy, eds., *Aux origines de la liturgie dominicaine: le manuscrits santa sabina XIV L 1*, Rome, 2004.

Bozóky, Edina. *La politique des reliques de Constantine à Saint Louis*. Paris, 2006.

Branner, Robert. "The Painted Medallions in the Sainte-Chapelle in Paris." *Transactions of the American Philosophical Society*, n.s. 58 (1968): 5–42.

——. "The Sainte-Chapelle and the *Capella Regis* in the Thirteenth Century." *Gesta* 10 (1971): 19–22.

Bray, Jennifer R. "Concepts of Sainthood in Fourteenth-Century England." *Bulletin of the John Rylands University Library of Manchester* 66 (1984): 40–77.

Brenet, Michel. *Les musiciens de la Sainte-Chapelle du palais*. Paris, 1910.

Breviarii monastice congregationis casalis benedicti, pars estivalis. Paris, 1586.

Breviarium Bituricense. Bourges, 1587.

Breviarium cluniacense. Paris, 1546.

Breviarium Parisiense: Ad Formam Sacrosancti Concilii Tridentini Restitutum. Illustrissimi et Reverendissimi In Christo Patris D.D. Ioannis Francisci de Gondy, Parisiensis Archipiscopi auctoritate, ac eiusdem Ecclesia capituli consensu editum. Parisiis. Paris, 1640.

Breviarium sancti dominici ad unque curatissime castigatum iuxta correctorium totius ordinis predicatorum quod in conventus Parisiensi habetur. Paris, 1519.

Brooke, Rosalind B. *The Image of St. Francis: Responses to Sainthood in the Thirteenth Century*. Cambridge, 2006.

Brown, Elizabeth A. R. "Burying and Unburying the Kings of France." In *Persons in Groups: Social Behavior as Identity Formation in Medieval and Renaissance Europe: Papers of the Sixteenth Annual Conference of the Center for Medieval and Early - Renaissance Studies*. Edited by Richard Trexler. Binghamton, N.Y., 1985, 241–266.

——. "The Ceremonial of Royal Succession in Capetian France: The Funeral of Philip V." *Speculum* 55 (1980): 266–293.

——. "*Cessante Causa* and the Taxes of the Last Capetians: The Political Applications of a Philosophical Maxim." *Studia Gratiana* 15 (Post Scripta) (1972): 567–587.

——. "The Chapel of St. Louis at Saint-Denis." *Gesta* 17 (1978): 76.

——. "The Chapels and Cult of Saint Louis at Saint-Denis." *Mediaevalia* 10 (1984): 279–331.

——. "Death and the Human Body in the Later Middle Ages: The Legislation of Boniface VIII on the Division of the Corpse." *Viator* 12 (1981): 221–270.

——. "Kings Like Semi-Gods: The Case of Louis X of France." *Majestas* 1 (1993): 5–37.

——. "La généalogie capétienne dans l'historiographie du Moyen Age: Philippe le Bel, le reniement du *reditus* et la création d'une ascendance carolingienne pour Hugues Capet." In *Religion et culture autour de l'an Mil: royaume capétien et Lotharingie. Actes du colloque Hugues Capet 987–1987. La France de l'an Mil. Auxerre, 26 et 27 juin 1987—Metz, 11 et 23 septembre 1987*. Edited by Dominique Iogna-Prat and Jean-Charles Picard. Paris, 1990, 199–214.

——. "La notion de la légitimité et la prophétie à la cour de Philippe Auguste." In *La France de Philippe Auguste: le temps de mutations. Actes du Colloque international organisé par le C.N.R.S. (Paris, 29 septembre–4 octobre 1980)*. Edited by Robert-Henri Bautier. Paris, 1982, 77–111.

——. "Paris and Paradise: The View from Saint-Denis." In *The Four Modes of Seeing*. Edited by Evelyn Staudinger Lane et al. Aldershot, UK, 2007.

——. "Persona et Gesta: The Images and Deeds of the Thirteenth-Century Capetians. The Case of Philip the Fair." *Viator* 19 (1988): 219–246.

——. "Philippe le Bel and the Remains of Saint Louis." *Gazette des Beaux-Arts* 97 (1980): 175–182.

——. *Politics and Institutions in Capetian France*. Hampshire, UK, 1991.

——. "The Prince Is the Father of the King: The Character and Childhood of Philip the Fair of France." *Mediaeval Studies* 49 (1987): 282–334.

——. "Reform and Resistance to Royal Authority in Fourteenth-Century France: The Leagues of 1314–1315." *Parliaments, Estates, and Representation* 1 (1981): 109–137.

——. "The Religion of Royalty: From Saint Louis to Henry IV, 1226–1589." In *Creating French Culture: Treasures from the Bibliothèque nationale de France*. Edited by Marie-Hélène Tesnière and Prosser Gifford. New Haven, 1995, 131–148.

——. "*Rex ioians, ionnes, iolis*: Louis X, Philip V, and the Livres de Fauvel." In *Fauvel's Studies: Allegory, Chronicle, Music and Images in Paris, BNF fr. 146*. Edited by Margaret Bent and Andrew Wathey. Oxford, 1988, 53–72.

——. "Royal Salvation and the Needs of State in Late Capetian France." In *Order and Innovation in the Middle Ages: Essays in Honor of Joseph R. Strayer*. Edited by William C. Jordan et al. Princeton, N.J., 1976, 365–379.

——. *Saint-Denis: La basilique*. Paris, 2001.

——. "The Trojan Origins of the French and the Brothers Jean du Tillet." In *After Rome's Fall: Narrators and Sources of Early Medieval History. Essays Presented to Walter Goffart*. Edited by Alexander Calladar Murray. Toronto, 1998, 348–384.

Brown, Elizabeth A. R., and Sanford Zale. "Louis Le Blanc, Estienne Le Blanc, and the Defense of Louis IX's Crusade, 1489–1522." *Traditio* 55 (2000): 235–292.

Bruning, Eliseus. "Giuliano da Spira e l'Officio ritmico di S. Francesco: osservazioni critico-estetiche sulla musica et sulla sua restaurazione attuale." *Note d'Archivio per la Storia Musicale*, ser. 1 (1927): 129–202.

Buc, Philippe. *L'ambiguïté du livre: prince, pouvoir, et peuple dans les commentaires de la Bible au Moyen Âge*. Paris, 1994.

——. "Pouvoir royal et commentaires de la Bible (1150–1350)." *Annales ESC* (1989): 619–713.

Burr, David. *Olivi and Franciscan Poverty: The Origins of Usus Pauper Controversy*. Philadelphia, 1989.

——. *The Spiritual Franciscans: From Protest to Persecution in the Century after Saint Francis*. University Park, Pa., 2001.

Callebaut, André. "Les provinciaux de la province de France au XIIIe siècle." *Archivum Franciscanum Historicum* 10 (1917): 289–356.

Canivez, Joseph. *Statuta Capitulorum Generalium Ordinis Cisterciensis ab anno 1116 ad annum 1786*. 8 vols. Louvain, 1935.

Cantimpré, Thomas de. *Les exemples du "Livre des abeilles": une vision médiévale*. Edited by Henri Platelle. Paris, 1997.

Carns, Paula Mae. "The Cult of Saint Louis and Capetian Interests in the Hours of Jeanne d'Evreux," July 2, 2006 [cited 1 2]. Available from http://peregrinations.kenyon.edu/vol2–1/FeaturedSection/Jeanne_d_Evreux_Peregrinations_1.pdf.

Carolus-Barré, Louis. "Guillaume de Chartres clerc du roi, frère prêcheur, ami et historien de saint Louis." *Collection de l'École française de Rome* 204 (1995): 51–57.

——. "Guillaume de Saint-Pathus, confesseur de la reine Marguerite et biographe de saint Louis." *Archivum Franciscanum Historicum* 79 (1986): 142–152.

——. "La Grande ordonnance de 1254 sur la réforme de l'administration et la police du Royaume." In *Septième centenaire de la mort de Saint Louis: Actes des Colloques de Royaumont et de Paris (21–27 mai 1970)*. Paris, 1976, 85–96.

——. *Le procès de canonisation de Saint Louis (1272–1297): Essai de reconstitution*. Edited by Henri Platelle. Rome, 1994.

——. "Les enquêtes pour la canonisation de Saint Louis de Grégoire X à Boniface VIII et la bulle *Gloria Laus*, du 11 août 1297." *Revue d'histoire de l'Église de France* 57 (1971): 19–31.

——. "Les franciscains et le procès de canonisation de saint Louis." *Les amis de St François*, n.s. 12 (1971): 3–6.

Carruthers, Mary. *The Book of Memory: A Study of Memory in Medieval Culture*. Cambridge, 1990.

Carta, Francesco, Carlo Cipolla, and Carlo Frati. *Monumenta palaeographica sacra. Atlante paleografico-artistico compilato sui manoscritti esposti in Torino alla Mostra d'arte sacra nel 1898, e pubbl. dalla R. Deputazione di storia patria delle antiche provincie e della Lombardia*. Turin, 1899.

Caviness, Madeleine. "Patron or Matron? A Capetian Bride and a Vade Mecum for Her Marriage Bed." *Speculum* 68 (1993): 333–362.

Cazelles, Raymond. *La société politique et la crise de la royauté sous Philippe de Valois.* Paris, 1958.

———. "Une exigence de l'opinion depuis saint Louis: la réformation du royaume." *Annuaire bulletin de la société de l'histoire de France* (1962–1963): 91–99.

Chaney, William A. *The Cult of Kingship in Anglo-Saxon England: The Transition from Paganism to Christianity.* Berkeley, Calif., 1970.

Chapotin, Marie-Dominique. *Histoire des dominicains de la province de France. Le siècle des fondations.* Rouen, 1898.

Chareyron, Nicole. "Représentation du corps souffrant dans la Vie et les Miracles de Saint Louis" *Cahiers de recherches médiévales (XIIe–XVe s.)* 4 (1997): 175–187.

Charvin, G, ed., *Statuts, chapitre généraux et visites de l'ordre de Cluny.* Vol 2: 1290–1324. 9 vols. Paris, 1965–.

Chennaf, Sharah, and Odile Redon. "Les Miracles de Saint Louis." In *Les Miracles Miroirs des Corps.* Paris, 1983, 53–85.

Chevalier Boyer, Christine. "Les sermons de Guillaume de Sauqueville: l'activité d'un prédicateur dominicain à la fin du règne de Philippe le Bel." Université Lumière Lyon 2, 2007.

Chung-Apley, Jane Geein. "The Illustrated *Vie et Miracles de Saint Louis* of Guillaume de Saint-Pathus (Paris, B.N., ms. fr. 5716)." Ph.D. diss., University of Michigan, 1998.

Clément, Jean-Paul. "L'utilisation du mythe de Saint-Louis par Chateaubriand dans les controverses politiques de l'Empire et de la Restauration." *Revue d'histoire littéraire de la France* 98 (1998): 1059–1072.

Coester, Hildegard. "Der Königskult in Frankreich um 1300 in Spiegel von Kominkaner predigten." Ph.D. diss. University of Frankfurt, 1935/36.

Cohen, Meredith. "An Indulgence for the Visitor: the Public at the Sainte-Chapelle of Paris." *Speculum* 83 (2008).

———. "The Sainte-Chapelle of Paris: Image of Authority and Locus of Identity." Ph.D. diss., Columbia University, 2004.

Cole, Penny. *The Preaching of the Crusades to the Holy Land, 1095–1270.* Cambridge, Mass., 1991.

Congar, Yves. "Aspects ecclésiologiques de la querelle entre mendiants et séculiers dans la seconde moitié du XIIIe siècle et le début du XIVe." *Archives d'histoire doctrinale et littéraire du Moyen Âge* 28 (1961): 35–161.

Constable, Giles. "Cluny and the First Crusade." *Collection de l'École française de Rome* 236 (1997): 179–193.

———. "The Ideal of the Imitation of Christ." In *Three Studies in Medieval Religious and Social Thought.* Cambridge, 1995, 143–248.

———. "Nudus Nudum Christum Sequi and Parallel Formulas in the Twelfth Century." In *Continuity and Discontinuity in Church History: Essays Presented to George Hunston Williams.* Leiden, 1979, 83–91.

Contamine, Philip. "L'oriflamme de Saint-Denis au XIVe et XVe siècles." *Annales de l'Est* 25 (1973): 179–244.

Corbet, Patrick. *Les saint ottoniens: Sainteté dynastique, sainteté royale et sainteté féminine autour de l'an Mil.* Sigmaringen, 1986.

Coste, Jean. *Boniface VIII en procès: articles d'accusation et dépositions des témoins (1303–1311).* Rome, 1995.

Courtenay, William. "The Parisian Franciscan Community in 1303." *Franciscan Studies* 53 (1993): 155–173.

Courtenay, William J. "Between Pope and King: The Parisian Letters of Adhesions of 1303." *Speculum* 71 (1996): 577–605.

Coville, A. "Recherches sur jean Courtecuisse et ses Oeuvres Oratoires." *Bibliothèque de l'École des Chartes* 65 (1904): 469–529.

Cowdrey, H. E. J. "Anglo-Norman Laudes Regiae." *Viator* 12 (1981): 37–78.

———. *The Cluniacs and the Gregorian Reform.* Oxford, 1970.

Cremascoli, Giuseppe. "Iuliani de Spira: Vita Sancti Francisci. Introduzione." In *Fontes Franciscani*. Edited by Enrico Menestò and Stefano Brufani. Assisi, 1995, 1015–1023.

Crist, Larry S. "The Breviary of Saint Louis: The Development of a Legendary Miracle." *Journal of the Warburg and Courtauld Institutes* 28 (1965): 319–323.

Cubitt, Catherine. "Memory and Narrative in the Cult of Early Anglo-Saxon Saints." In *The Uses of the Past in the Early Middle Ages*. Edited by Yitzhak Hen and Matthew Innes. Cambridge, 2000, 29–66.

D'Avray, David L. *Death and the Prince: Memorial Preaching before 1350*. Oxford, 1994.

——. *The Preaching of the Friars: Sermons Diffused from Paris before 1300*. Oxford, 1985.

Dalarun, Jacques. *The Misadventure of Francis of Assisi: Towards a Historical Use of the Franciscan Legends*. St. Bonaventure, N.Y., 2002.

Daniel, E. Randolph. "The Desire for Martyrdom: A *Leitmotiv* of St. Bonaventure." *Franciscan Studies* 32 (1972): 74–87.

Daniel, E. Randolph. *The Franciscan Concept of Mission in the High Middle Ages*. Lexington, Ky., 1975.

David, Marcel. "Le Serment du Sacre du IXe au XVe siècle: contribution à l'étude des limites juridiques de la souveraineté." *Revue du moyen âge latin* 6 (1950): 5–272.

Davis, Adam. *The Holy Bureaucrat: Eudes Rigaud and Religious Reform in Thirteenth-Century Normandy*. Ithaca, N.Y., 2006.

De Hamel, Christopher. "Les Heures de Blanche de Bourgogne, comtesse de Savoie." In *Le manuscrits enluminés des comtes et ducs de Savoie*. Edited by Agostino Paravicini Bagliani and Enrico Castelnuovo. Turin, 1990, 89–91.

Delaborde, H.-François. "Une oeuvre nouvelle de Guillaume de Saint-Pathus." *Bibliothèque de l'École des Chartes* 63 (1902): 261–288.

Delaborde, Henri-François. *Jean de Joinville et les seigneurs de Joinville, suivi d'un catalogue de leurs actes*. Paris, 1894.

Delaruelle, Etienne. "The Crusading Idea in Cluniac Literature of the Eleventh Century." In *Cluniac Monasticism in the Central Middle Ages*. Edited by Noreen Hunt. Hamden, Conn., 1971, 191–216.

De la Selle, Xavier. *Le service des âmes à la cour: confesseurs et aumôniers des rois de France du XIIIe au XVe siècle*. Paris, 1995.

Delehaye, Hippolyte. *The Legends of the Saints*. Translated by V. M. Crawford. Notre Dame, Ind., 1961.

Delisle, Léopold. "Anonyme: Auteur du *Liber de informatione principium*." In *Histoire littéraire de la France*, vol. 31 (1893): 35–47.

——. "Durand de Champagne." In *Histoire littéraire de la France*, vol. 30 (1888): 302–333.

——. *Inventiarie des manuscripts de la bibliotheque nationale fonds de cluny*. Paris, 1884.

——. "Les Heures de Blanche de France, duchesse d'Orléans." *Bibliothèque de l'École des Chartes* 66 (1905): 489–539.

——. *Recherches sur la librarie de Charles V*. 2 and Atlas vols. Paris, 1907.

Delooz, Pierre. "Politiques et canonisations." In *Les églises comme institutions politiques / Churches as Political Institutions*. 1970, 203–213.

——. *Sociologie et canonisations*. Liège, 1969.

Deschamps, Paul. "À propos de la statue de Saint Louis à Mainneville." *Bulletin monumental* 127 (1969): 35–40.

Dickinson, John. "The Medieval Conception of Kingship and Some of Its Limitations, as Developed in the *Policraticus* of John of Salisbury." *Speculum* 1 (1926): 308–337.

Digard, Georges Alfred Laurent. *Philippe le Bel et le Saint-siège de 1285 à 1304*. 2 vols. Paris, 1936.

Digard, Georges, Robert Fawtier, and Maurice Faucon, eds. *Les registres de Boniface VIII: recueil des bulles de ce pape publiées ou analysées d'après les manuscrits originaux des archives du Vatican*, Paris, 1884.

Dimier, Anselme, OCR. *Saint Louis et Cîteaux*. Paris, 1954.

Direction des archives de France and Sainte-Chapelle (Paris France). *Saint Louis: Sainte-Chapelle: mai–août 1960.* Paris, 1960.

Dondaine, Antoine. "La vie et les oeuvres de Jean de San Gimignano," *Archivum Fratrum Praedicatorum* 9 (1939): 128–183.

Douais, Celestin. *Les frères prêcheurs en Gascogne au XIIIème et au XIVème siècle: chapitres, couvents et notices: documents inédits.* Paris, 1885.

——. *Statuts de Cluny édictés par Bertrand, Abbé de Cluny, le 3 Avril 1301.* Paris, 1893.

Dreves, Guido Maria, and Clemens Blume, eds., *Analecta hymnica medii aevi.* 55 vols. Leipzig, 1886–1922.

DuBois, Gérard. *Historia Ecclesiae Parisiensis.* Paris, 1690.

Du Cange, Charles Du Fresne. *Glossarium ad scriptores mediae et infimae latinitatis.* 7 vols. Basel, 1762.

Duchesne, André. *Historiae Francorum scriptores coaetanei . . . Quorum plurimi nunc primum ex variis codicibus mss. in lucem prodeunt: alij vero auctiores & emendatiores. Cvm epistolis regvm, reginarvm, pontificvm . . . et aliis veteribus rerum francicarum monumentis.* 5 vols. Paris, 1636–1649.

Duclos, Henri Louis. *Histoire de Royaumont, sa foundation par saint Louis et son influence sur la France.* 2 vols. Paris, 1867.

Dufeil, Michel-Marie. "Le roi Louis dans la querelle des mendiants et des séculiers." In *Septième centenaire de la mort de Saint-Louis: Actes des Colloques de Royaumont et de Paris (21–27 mai 1970).* Paris, 1976, 281–289.

Dufournet, J. "Rutebeuf et les moines mendiants." *Neuphilologische Mitteilungen* 85 (1984): 152–168.

Dupuy, Pierre. *Histoire dv différend d'entre le pape Boniface VIII et Philippes le Bel, roy de France.* 2d ed. Paris, 1655.

Durrieu, Paul. "Les aventures de deux splendides livres d'heures ayant appartenu au duc Jean de Berry." *Revue de l'art ancien et moderne* 30 (1911): 5–16.

——. "Notice d'un des plus importants livres de prières du roi Charles V, Les Heures de Savoie ou 'Très belles grandes heures' du roi." *Bibliothèque de l'École des Chartes* 72 (1911): 500–555.

Edwards, Owain Tudor. "Chant Transference in Rhymed Offices." In *Cantus Planus: Papers Read at the Fourth Meetings, Pecs, Hungary, September 1990.* Budapest, 1992, 503–519.

Ehrle, Franz. "Die ältesten Redactionen der Generalconstitutionen des Franziskanerordens." *Archiv für Literatur- un Kirchen-Geschichte des Mittelalters* 6 (1892): 1–138.

Epstein, Marcy. "*Ludovicus Decus Regnantium:* Perspectives on the Rhymed Office." *Speculum* 53 (1978): 283–334.

Erickson, Norma. "A Dispute between a Priest and a Knight." *Proceedings of the American Philosophical Society* 111 (1967): 288–309.

Erlande-Brandenburg, Alain. "Art et politique sous Philippe le Bel. La priorale Saint-Louis de Poissy." *Comptes rendus de l'Académie des Inscriptions et Belles Lettres* (1987): 507–518.

——. "La Priorale Saint-Louis de Poissy." *Bulletin monumental* 129 (1971): 85–112.

——. *Le roi est mort: étude sur les funérailles, les sépultures et les tombeaux des rois de France jusqu'à la fin du XIIIe siècle.* Geneva, 1975.

——. "Le tombeau de Saint Louis." *Bulletin Monumental* 126 (1968): 7–36.

Étienne de Bourbon (Stephanus de Borbone). *Anecdotes historiques, légendes et apologues, tirés du recueil inédit d'Étienne de Bourbon, dominicain de XIIIe siècle.* Edited by Albert Lecoy de La Marche. Paris, 1877.

Farmer, Sharon. *Communities of Saint Martin.* Ithaca, N.Y., 1991.

——. "Down and Out and Female in Thirteenth-Century Paris." *American Historical Review* 103 (1998): 345–372.

——. *Surviving Poverty in Medieval Paris: Gender, Ideology, and the Daily Lives of the Poor.* Ithaca, N.Y., 2002.

Fassler, Margot Elsbeth, and Rebecca A. Baltzer, eds. *The Divine Office in the Latin Middle Ages: Methodology and Source Studies, Regional Developments, Hagiography: Written in Honor of Professor Ruth Steiner.* Oxford, 2000.

Favier, Jean. *Philippe le Bel.* New rev. ed. Paris, 1998.

Fawtier, Robert. *Comptes royaux (1285–1314).* 3 vols. Paris, 1953.

———. *Les Capétiens et la France; leur rôle dans sa construction.* Paris, 1942.

Fay, Percival B., ed., *Guillaume de Saint-Pathus: Les miracles de saint Louis*, Paris, 1932.

Felder, Hilaren. *Die liturgischen Reimofficien auf die heiligen Franciscus und Antonius gedichtet und componiert durch Fr. Julian von Speier (+1250).* Freiburg, Schweiz, 1901.

Fentress, James, and Chris Wickham. *Social Memory.* Oxford, 1992.

Ferlampin-Acher, Christine. "Joinville, de l'hagiographe à l'autobiographe: approche de *La Vie de saint Louis.*" In *Jean de Joinville: de la Champagne aux royaumes d'outre-mer.* Edited by Danielle Quéruel. Langres, 1998, 73–91.

Ferzoco, George. "The Context of Medieval Sermon Collections on Saints." In *Preacher, Sermon, and Audience in the Middle Ages.* Edited by Carolyn Muessig. Leiden, 2002, 279–291.

———. "Sermon Literature concerning Late Medieval Saints." In *Models of Holiness in Medieval Sermons.* Louvain-la-Neuve, 1996, 103–125.

Feuilloy, Cotilde, Jannie Long, and Catherine de Mulpeou. "Représentations de Saint Louis sous l'aspect des roi de France." *Les monuments historiques de la France,* n.s. 16 (1970): 47–54.

Field, Sean L. *Isabelle of France: Capetian Sanctity and Franciscan Identity in the Thirteenth Century.* Notre Dame, Ind., 2006.

———. "The Missing Sister: Sébastien Le Nain de Tillemont's Life of Isabelle of France." *Revue Mabillon,* n.s. 18 (2008).

———. "New Evidence for the Life of Isabelle of France." *Revue Mabillon,* n.s. 13 (2002): 117–131.

———. *The Writings of Agnes of Harcourt: The Life of Isabelle of France and the Letter on Louis IX and Longchamp.* Notre Dame, Ind., 2003.

Firnhaber-Baker, Justine. "From God's Peace to the King's Order: late medieval Limitations on Non-Royal Warfare." *Essays in Medieval Studies* 23 (2006): 19–30.

Fleming, John. *An Introduction to the Franciscan Literature of the Middle Ages.* Chicago, 1977.

Folz, Robert. *Études sur le culte liturgique de Charlemagne dans les églises de l'Empire.* Paris, 1951.

———. "La chancellerie de Frédéric Ier et la canonisation de Charlemagne." *Le Moyen Âge* 70 (1964): 13–31.

———. "La sainteté de Louis IX d'àpres les textes liturgiques de sa fête." *Revue d'histoire de l'Église de France* 57 (1971): 31–45.

———. *Le souvenir et la légende de Charlemagne dans l'Empire germanique médiéval.* Geneva, 1973.

———. *Les saintes reines du Moyen Âge en Occident: Vie–XIIIe siècles.* Brussels, 1992.

———. *Les saints rois du Moyen Âge en occident (Vie–XIIIe siècles).* Brussels, 1984.

Foulet, Alfred. "When Did Joinville Write His 'Vie de saint Louis'?" *Romanic Review* 32 (1941): 233–243.

Fournée, Jean. "Le culte et l'iconographie de saint Louis en Normandi." *Art de Basse Normandie* 61 (1971): 35–46.

Friedman, Lionel J. "Text and Iconography for Joinville's *Credo.*" Cambridge, Mass., 1958.

Froissart. *Oeuvres de Froissart, publiées avec les variants des divers manuscrits.* Edited by Kervyn de Lettenhove. 25 vols. Brussels, 1867–1877; reprint 1967.

Frugoni, Chiara. *Francesco e l'invenzione delle stimmate: una storia per parole e immagini fino a Bonaventura e Giotto.* Turin, 1993.

———. "Saint Francis, a Saint in Progress." In *Saints: Studies in Hagiography.* Edited by Sandro Sticca. Binghamton, N.Y., 1996, 161–190.

——. "Saint Louis et Saint François." *Medievales* 34 (1998): 35–38.

Galbraith, G. R. *The Constitution of the Dominican Order 1216 to 1360.* Manchester, UK, 1925.

Gaposchkin, M. Cecilia. "Boniface VIII, Philip the Fair, and the Sanctity of of Louis IX." *Journal of Medieval History* 28 (2003): 1–26.

——."*Ludovicus Decus Regnantium*: The Liturgical Office for Saint Louis and the Ideological Program of Philip the Fair." *Majestas* 10 (2002): 27–90.

——. "The Monastic Office for Louis IX of France: *Lauda Celestis Regio*." *Revue Mabillon* (forthcoming).

——. "Philip the Fair, the Dominicans, and the Liturgical Office for Louis IX: New Perspectives on *Ludovicus Decus Regnantium*." *Plainsong and Medieval Music* 13 (2004): 33–61.

——. "The Role of the Crusades in the Sanctification of Louis IX of France." In *Crusades: Medieval Worlds in Conflict*. Burlington Vt., forthcoming

Gardner, Julian. "The Cult of a Fourteenth-Century Saint: The Iconography for Louis of Toulouse." In *I francescani nel Trecento: Atti del XIV convegno internazionale, Assisi, 16–17–18 ottobre 1986*. Perugia, 1988, 167–193.

Gastoué, Amédée. *Les primitifs de la musique française.* Paris, 1922.

Gaucher, Elisabeth. "Joinville et l'écriture biographique." In *Le prince et son historien: la vie de Saint Louis de Joinville*. Paris, 1997, 101–122.

Genet, Jean-Philippe, ed., *Four English Political Tracts of the Late Middle Ages*, London, 1977.

Géraud, Hercule. *Paris sous Philippe-le-Bel, d'après des documents originaux et notamment d'après un manuscrit contenant "le rôle de de taille" imposée sur les habitants de Paris en 1292*. Paris, 1837.

Gerson, Jean. *Oeuvres completes.* Edited by Palèmon Glorieux. 10 vols. Paris, 1960.

Gertsman, Elina. "Vir Iustus Atque Perfectus: St. Louis as Noah in the Miraculous Recovery of the Breviary Miniature from the Hours of Jeanne d'Evreux." *Source: Notes in the History of Art* 23 (2003): 1–8.

Giles of Rome. *De regimine principum.* Rome, 1482.

Goodich, Michael. "The Judicial Foundations of Hagiography in the Central Middles Ages." In *"Scribere sanctorum gesta": Recueil d'études d'hagiographie médiévale offert à Guy Philippart*. Turnhout, Belgium, 2006, 627–644.

——. "The Politics of Canonization in the Thirteenth Century: Lay and Mendicant Saints." *Church History* 44 (1975): 294–307.

——. "A Profile of Thirteenth-Century Sainthood." *Comparative Studies in Society and History* 18 (1976): 429–37.

——. *Vita Perfecta: The Ideal of Sainthood in the Thirteenth Century.* Stuttgart, 1982.

Gorochov, Nathalie. "Entre théologie, humanisme et politique. Les sermons universitaires de la fête de Saint Louis sous le regne de Charles VI (1380–1422)." In *Saint-Denis et la Royauté: Études offertes à Bernard Guenée*. Paris, 1999, 51–64.

Górski, Karol. "La naissance des états et le 'roi-saint'." In *L'Europe du IXe au XIe siècles*. Edited by T. Manteuffel and A. Gieysztor. Warsaw, 1968, 425–432.

——. "Le roi-saint: un problème d'idéologie féodale." *Annales ESC* 24 (1969): 370–376.

Goudesenne, J.-F. *Les offices historiques ou "historiae" composés pour les fête des saints dans la province ecclésiastique de Reims (775–1030).* Turnhout, Belgium, 2002.

Gouttebroze, Jean-Guy. "Deux modèles de sainteté royale. Édouard le Confesseur et saint Louis." *Cahiers de civilisation médiévale* 42 (1999): 243–258.

Graus, Frantisek. "La sanctification du souverain dans l'Europe centrale des Xe et XIe siècles." In *Hagiographie, cultures et societes, Ixe–XIIe siècles*. Paris, 1981, 559–572.

——. *Völk, Herrscher und Heiliger im Reich der Merowinger.* Prague, 1965.

Gres, de Combarieu du. "La chanson du roi Louis (de Joinville et de la chanson de geste)." In *Jean de Joinville: de la Champagne aux royaumes d'outre-mer*. Edited by Danielle Quéruel. Langres, 1998, 109–129.

Grodecki, Louis. "Saint Louis et le vitrail." *Les monuments historiques de la France*, n.s. 16 (1970): 22–30.

Grossel, Marie-Geneviève. "La sainteté à l'épreuve de la croisade: *La Vie de saint Louis* de Jehan de Joinville." *Cahiers de recherches médiévales (XIIe–XVe s.)* 1 (1996): 129–146.

Grundmann, Herbert. *Religious Movements in the Middle Ages: the Historical Links between Heresy, the Mendicant Orders, and the Women's Religious Movement in the Twelfth and Thirteenth Century, with the Historical Foundations of German Mysticism.* Translated by Steven Rowan. Notre Dame, Ind., 1995.

Guenée, Bernard. "État et nation en France au moyen âge." *Revue historique* 237 (1967): 17–30.

Guérard, Benjamin, ed., *Cartulaire de l'église Notre-Dame de Paris.* 4 vols. Paris, 1850.

Guest, Gerald. "A Discourse on the Poor: The Hours of Jeanne d'Evreux." *Viator* 26 (1995): 153–180.

———. "The People Demand a King: Visualizing Monarchy in the Psalter of Louis IX." *Studies in Iconography* 23 (2002): 1–27.

———. "Queens, Kings, and Clergy: Figures of Authority in the 13th-Century Moralized Bibles." Ph.D. diss., New York University, 1998.

Guibert de Tournai. *Le traité Eruditio regum et principum de Guibert de Tournai, O.F.M. (étude et texte inédit).* Edited by Alphonse de Poorter. Louvain, 1914.

Haggh, Barbara. "An Ordinal of Ockeghem's Time from the Sainte-Chapelle of Paris: Paris, Bibliothèque de l'Arsenal, ms 114." *Tijdschrift van de Koninklijke Vereniging voor Nederlandse Muziekgeschiedenis* (1997): 33–71.

———. *Two Offices for St Elizabeth of Hungary: Gaudeat Hungaria and Letare Germania. Introduction and Edition.* Edited by László Dobszay et al. Ottawa, 1995.

Hallam, Elizabeth M. "Philip the Fair and the Cult of Saint Louis." In *Studies in Church History 18 (Religion and National Identity).* Oxford, 1982, 201–214.

Hamesses, Jacqueline, Beverly Mayne Kienzle, Debra L. Stoudt, and Anne T. Thayer, eds. *Medieval Sermons and Society: Cloister, City, University (Proceedings of International Symposia at Kalamazoo and New York).* Louvain-la-Neuve, 1998.

Harper, John. *The Forms and Orders of Western Liturgy from the Tenth to the Eighteenth Century: A Historical Introduction and Guide for Students and Musicians.* Oxford, 1991.

Hauck, Karl. " 'Geblütsheiligkeit'." In *Liber Floridus. Mittellateinische Studien. Paul Lehmann zum 65. Geburtstag gewidmet.* Edited by Bernard Bischoff and Suso Brechter. St. Ottilien, 1950, 187–240.

Head, Thomas. *Hagiography and the Cult of Saints: The Diocese of Orléans, 800–1200.* Cambridge, 1990.

Hedeman, Anne D. *Of Counselors and Kings: The Three Versions of Pierre Salmon's Dialogues.* Urbana, Ill., 2001.

———. *The Royal Image: Illustrations of the Grandes Chroniques de France, 1274–1422.* Berkeley, Calif., 1991.

———. "Valois Legitimacy: Editorial Changes in Charles V's Grandes Chroniques de France." *Art Bulletin* 66 (1984): 97–117.

Heffernan, Thomas J. *Sacred Biography: Saints and Their Biographers in the Middle Ages.* New York, 1988.

Heinlen, James Michael. "The Ideology of Reform in the French Moralized Bible." Ph.D. diss., Northwestern University, 1991.

Henriet, Patrick. "Les paroles de la mort dans l'hagiographie monastique des XIème et XIIème siècles." *Histoire médiévale et archéologie* 6 (1993): 75–86.

———. " 'Silentium usque ad mortem servaret': La scène de la mort chez les ermites italiens du XIe siècle." *Mélanges d'archéologie et d'histoire publiés par l'École française de Rome: Moyen Âge* 105 (1993): 265–298.

Hesbert, René Jean, and Renatus Prévost. *Corpus antiphonalium officii.* 6 vols. Rome, 1963.

Heysse, P. Albanus. "Antiquissimum officium liturgicum S. Ludovici regis." *Archivum Franciscanum Historicum* 10 (1917): 559–575.

Hiley, David. *Western Plainchant: A Handbook.* Oxford, 1993.

Hinkle, William. *The Fleurs de Lis of the Kings of France, 1285–1488.* Carbondale, 1991.

Histoire littéraire de la France. 41 vols. Paris, 1832–1974.

Hoch, Adrian. "Pictures of Penitence from a Trecento Neapolitan Nunnery." *Zeitschrift fur Kunstgeschichte* 61 (1998): 206–226.

——. "St. Martin of Tours: His Transformation into a Chivalric Hero and Franciscan Ideal." *Zeitschrift für Kunstgeschichte* 50 (1987): 471–482.

Hoffeld, James. "An Image of Saint Louis and the Structuring of Devotion." *Bulletin of the Metropolitan Museum of Art* 29 (1971): 216–66.

Holladay, Joan. "The Education of Jeanne d'Evreux: Personal Piety and Dynastic Salvation in Her Book of Hours at the Cloisters." *Art History* 17 (1994): 585–611.

——. "Fourteenth-Century French Queens as Collectors and Readers of Books: Jeanne d'Evreux and Her Contemporaries." *Journal of Medieval History* 32 (2006): 69–100.

Housley, Norman. *The Later Crusades, 1274–1580: From Lyons to Alcazar.* Oxford, 1992.

Hughes, Andrew. "Antiphons and Acclamations: The Politics of Music in the Coronation Service of Edward II, 1308." *Journal of Musicology* 6 (1988): 150–168.

——. *Late Medieval Liturgical Offices: Resources for Electronic Research: Sources and Chants.* Toronto, 1996.

——. *Late Medieval Liturgical Offices: Texts.* Toronto, 1994.

——. "Late Medieval Plainchant for the Divine Office." In *Music as Concept and Practice in the Late Middle Ages.* Edited by Reinhard Strohm and Bonnie Blackburn. Oxford, 2001, 31–96.

——. "Memory and the Composition of Late Medieval Office Chant: Antiphons." In *L'Enseignements de la musique au Moyen Âge et à la Renaissance. Colloque organisé par la Fondation Royaumont en coproduction ave l'A.R.I.M.M.* Asnière-sur-Oise, 1987, 53–72.

——. "Modal Order and Disorder in the Rhymed Office." *Musica Disciplina* 37 (1983): 29–51.

——. "The Monarch as the Object of Liturgical Veneration." In *Kings and Kingship in Medieval Europe.* Edited by Anne J. Duggan. London, 1993, 375–424.

——. "*Rex sub deo et lege: Sanctus sub ecclesia.*" In *Political Plainchant? Music, Text and Historical Context of Medieval Saints' Offices.* Edited by Roman Hankeln. Ottawa, forthcoming in 2008.

——. "Rhymed Offices." In *Dictionary of the Middle Ages.* Edited by Joseph R. Strayer. New York, 1988, 366–377.

Huglo, Michel. "Notated Performance Practices in Parisian Chant Manuscripts of the Thirteenth Century." In *Plainsong in the Age of Polyphony.* Edited by Thomas Forrest Kelley. Cambridge, 1992, 32–44.

Jackson, Richard A., ed. *Ordines Coronationis Franciae: Texts and Ordines for the Coronation of Frankish and French Kings and Queens in the Middle Ages.* 2 vols. Philadelphia, 1995–2000.

Jacob of Voragine. *The Golden Legend, or, Lives of the Saints as Englished by William Caxton.* London, 1900.

James of Viterbo. *Le plus ancien traité de l'église: Jacques de Viterbe, De regimine christiano (1301–1302).* Edited by Henri Xavier Arquillière. Paris, 1926.

——. *On Christian government = De regimine Christiano.* Translated by R. W. Dyson. Woodbridge, UK, 1995.

John of Paris. *On Royal and Papal Power.* Edited by John A. Watt. Toronto, 1971.

John of Salisbury. *Policraticus.* Translated by Cary J. Nederman. Cambridge, 1990.

Johnson, Elizabeth A. *Truly Our Sister: a Theology of Mary in the Communion of Saints.* New York, 2003.

Johnson, Glenn Pierr. "Aspects of Late Medieval Music at the Cathedral of Amiens." Ph.D. diss., Yale University, 1991.

Johnson, James R. "The Tree of Jesse Window of Chartres: 'Laudes regiae.'" *Speculum* 36 (1961): 1–22.

Joinville, Jean de. *The Life of St. Louis*. Translated by René Hague from the text edited by Natalis de Wailly. New York, 1955.

Joinville, Jean de. *Vie de Saint Louis*. Edited by Jacques Monfrin. Paris, 1995.

Jones, Chris. "The Role of Frederick II in the Works of Guillaume de Nangis." In *Representations of Power in Medieval Germany, 800–1500*. Edited by Björn Weiler and Simon MacLean. Turnhout, Belgium, 2006, 273–294.

Jones, Michael. "The Last Capetians and Early Valois Kings, 1314–1364." In *The New Cambridge Medieval History*, Vol. 6 *c. 1300–c. 1415*. Edited by Michael Jones. Cambridge, 2000, 388–421.

Jonsson, Ritva. *Historia. Études sur la genèse des offices versifiés*. Stockholm, 1968.

Jordan, Alyce. "Stained Glass and the Liturgy: Performing Sacral Kingship in Capetian France." In *Objects, Images, and the Word: Art in the Service of the Liturgy*. Edited by Colum Hourihane. Princeton, N.J., 2003, 274–297.

———. *Visualizing Kingship in the Windows of the Ste.-Chapelle*. Turnhout, Belgium, 2002.

Jordan, William Chester. "Honoring Saint Louis in a Small Town." *Journal of Medieval History* 30 (2004): 263–277.

———. "Liturgical and Ceremonial Cloths: Neglected Evidence of Medieval Political Theology." *Revue des archéologues et histories d'art de Louvain* 12 (1979): 104–119.

———. *Louis IX and the Challenge of the Crusade: A Study in Rulership*. Princeton, N.J., 1979.

———. "The 'People' in the Psalter of Saint Louis and the Leadership of Moses." In *Medieval Paradigms: Essays in Honor of Jeremy Duquesnay Adams*. Edited by Stephanie Hayes-Healy. New York, 2005, 13–28.

———. "The Psalter of Saint-Louis (BN Ms. Lat. 10525): The Program of the Seventy-Eight Full-Page Illustrations." In *The High Middle Ages: Acta*. Edited by Penelope Mayo. Binghamton, N.Y., 1983, 65–91.

———. "The Representation of Monastic-Lay Relations in the Canonization Records for Louis IX." In *Religious and Laity in Western Europe, 1000–1400: Interaction, Negotiation, and Power*. Edited by Emilia Jamroziak and Janet Burton. Turnhout, Belgium, 2006, 225–239.

———. *Unceasing Strife, Unending Fear: Jacques de Thérines and the Freedom of the Church in the Age of the Last Capetians*. Princeton, N.J., 2005.

Kaeppeli, Thomas. "Note sugli scrittori dominicani di nome Giovanni di Napoli." *Archivum Fratrum Praedicatorum* 32 (1940): 48–71.

Kaeppeli, Thomas, and Emilio Panella. *Scriptores Ordinis Praedicatorum Medii Aevi*. 4 vols. Rome, 1970–1993.

Kantorowicz, Ernst H. *The King's Two Bodies: A Study in Mediaeval Political Theology*. Princeton, N.J., 1957.

———. *Laudes Regiae: A Study in Liturgical Acclamations and Mediaeval Ruler Worship*. Edited by G. H. Guttridge R. J. Kerner, and F. L. Paxson. Berkeley, Calif., 1946.

Kauffmann, Martin. "The Image of Saint Louis." In *Kings and Kingship in Medieval Europe*. Edited by Janet Bately. London, 1993, 265–288.

Keane, Marguerite A. "Remembering Louis IX as a Family Saint: A Study of the Images of Saint Louis Created for Jeanne, Blanche, and Marie of Navarre." Ph.D. diss., University of California at Santa Barbara, 2002.

Kedar, Benjamin Z. *Crusade and Mission: European Approaches towards the Muslims*. Princeton, N.J., 1984.

Kelly, Samantha. *The New Solomon: Robert of Naples (1309–1343) and Fourteenth-Century Kingship*. Leiden, 2003.

———. "Religious Patronage and Royal Propaganda in Angevin Naples: Santa Maria Donna Regina in Context." In *The Church of Santa Maria Donna Regina: Art, Iconography, and Patronage in Fourteenth-Century Naples*. Edited by Janis Elliott and Cordelia Warr. Burlington, Vt., 2004, 27–43.

Kemp, Eric Waldram. *Canonization and Authority in the Western Church*. London, 1948.

Kienzle, Beverly Mayne. "Introduction." In *The Sermons*. Edited by Beverly Mayne Kienzle. Turnhout, Belgium, 2000, 143–174.

——, ed. *The Sermon*, Turnhout, Belgium, 2000.

King, Archdale Arthur. *Liturgies of the Religious Orders*. London, 1955.

Klaniczay, Gábor. *Holy Rulers and Blessed Princesses: Dynastic Cults in Medieval Central Europe*. Edited by Lyndal Roper and Chris Wickham. Cambridge, 2002.

——. "Le culte des saints dynastiques en Europe Centrale (Angevins et Luxembourg au XIVe siècle)." In *L'église et le peuple chrétien dans les pays de l'Europe du centre-est et du nord (XIVe–XVe siècles): Actes du colloque organisé par l'École française de Rome avec la participation de l'Istituto polacco di cultura cristiana (Rome) et du Centre européen de recherches sur les congrégations et ordres religieux (CERCOR), Rome 27–29 janvier 1986*. Rome, 1990, 221–247.

——. "The Paradoxes of Royal Sainthood as Illustrated by Central European Examples." In *Kings and Kingship in Medieval Europe*. London, 1993, 351–375.

——. *The Uses of Supernatural Power: The Transformation of Popular Religion in Medieval and Early-Modern Europe*. Translated by Susan Singerman. Edited by Karen Margolis. Princeton, N.J., 1990.

Klauser, Theodor. "Die Liturgie der Heiligsprechung." In *Heilige Uberlieferung, Festschrift I. Herwegen*. Münster, 1938, 212–233.

Knobler, Adam. "Saint Louis in French Political Culture." In *Medievalism in Europe II*. Edited by Leslie Workman and Kathleen Verduin. Cambridge, 1996, 156–173.

Koziol, Geoffrey. *Begging Pardon and Favor: Ritual and Political Order in Early Medieval France*. Ithaca, N.Y., 1992.

——. "Is Robert I in Hell? The Diploma for Saint-Denis and the Mind of a Rebel King (Jan. 25, 923)." *Early Medieval Europe* 14 (2006): 233–267.

Krynen, Jacques. *L'empire du roi: Idées et croyances politiques en France XIIIe–XVe siècle*. Paris, 1993.

——. *Idéal du prince et pouvoir royal en France a la fin du moyen âge (1380–1440). Étude de la literature politique du temps*. Paris, 1981.

Kuttner, Stephen. "La reserve papale du droit de canonisation." *Revue historique du droit français et étranger*, 4th ser. 17 (1938): 172–228.

L'art au temps des rois maudits: Philippe le Bel et ses fils, 1285–1328. Paris, 1998.

Labarge, Margaret Wade. *Saint Louis: Louis IX, Most Christian King of France*. Boston, 1968.

LaFond, Jean. "Les vitraux de l'abbaye de la Trinité de Fécamp." In *L'Abbaye Bénédictine de Fécamp: ouvrage scientifique du XIIIe centenaire, 658–1958*. Fécamp, France, 1961, 97–120, 253–264.

Lajard, Félix. "Arnaud du Pré (Arnaldus de Prato)." In *Histoire littéraire de la France*. Paris, 1898, 240–244.

Lambert, Malcolm. *Franciscan Poverty: The Doctrine of the Absolute Poverty of Christ and the Apostles in the Franciscan Order, 1210–1323*. Rev. and expanded (original 1961) ed. St. Bonaventure, N.Y., 1998.

Langlois, Charles Victor. *La vie au moyen âge*. Vol. 4, *La vie spirituelle: enseignements, meditations et controverses d'après des écrits en francais à l'usage des laics*. 4 vols. Paris, 1928.

——. *Saint Louis—Philippe le Bel. Les derniers Capétiens directs (1226–1328)*. Edited by Ernest Lavisse. Vol. 3, pt. 2. Paris, 1901.

Laurent, Françoise. "La Vie de saint Louis ou le miroir des saints." In *Le prince et son historien: la vie de Saint Louis de Joinville*. Paris, 1997, 149–182.

Lawrence, C. H. *The Friars: The Impact of the Early Mendicant Movement on Western Society*. London, 1994.

Leclercq, Jean. "Le cloître est-il une prison?" *Revue d'ascétique et de mystique* 47 (1971): 407–420.

——. "Lettres de vocation à la vie monastique." *Analecta Monastica* 3 (Studia Anselmiana, 37: Rome, 1955) (1955): 169–197.

——. *The Love of Learning and the Desire for God: A Study of Monastic Culture.* 3d ed. New York, 1982.

——. "Un sermon prononcé pendant la guerre de Flandre sous Philippe le Bel." *Revue du moyen âge latin* 1 (1945): 165–172.

Lecoy de la Marche, Albert. *La chaire française au Moyen Âge: Spécialement au XIIIe siècle d'après les manuscrits contemporains.* Paris, 1886.

——. "Saint Louis, sa famille et sa cour d'après les anecdotes contemporaines." *Revue des questions historiques* 22 (1877): 465–484.

LeGoff, Jacques. "A Coronation Program for the Age of Saint Louis: The Ordo of 1200." In *Coronations: Medieval and Early Modern Monarchic Ritual.* Edited by János M. Bak. Berkeley, Calif., 1990, 46–57.

——. "La sainteté de Saint Louis: Sa place dans la typologie et l'évolution chronologique des roi saints." In *Fonctions de saints dans le monde occidental (IIIe–XIIIe siècles): actes du colloques.* Rome, 1991, 285–293.

——. "Les gestes de saint Louis: approche d'un modèle et d'une personnalité." In *Melanges Jacques Stiennon.* Liege, 1982, 445–459.

——. "Mon ami le saint roi: Joinville et Saint Louis (réponse)." *Annales: histoire, sciences sociales* 56 (2001): 469–477.

——. "Portrait du roi idéal." *L'histoire* 81 (1985): 71–76.

——. "Royauté biblique et idéal monarchique médiéval: Saint Louis et Josias." In *Les juifs au regard de l'histoire: Mélanges en l'honneur de Bernhard Blumenkranz.* Edited by Gilbert Dahan. Paris, 1985, 157–167.

——. "Saint de l'Eglise et saint du peuple: les miracles officiels de saint Louis entre sa mort et sa canonisation (1270–1297)." In *Histoire sociale, sensibilités collectives et mentalités: Mélanges Robert Mandrou.* Paris, 1985, 169–180.

——. *Saint Louis.* Paris, 1996.

——. "Saint Louis et la Pratique Sacramentelle." *La Maison-Dieu* 197 (1994): 99–124.

LeGoff, Jacques, Éric Palazzo, Jean-Claude Bonne, and Marie-Noel Colette. *Le sacre royal à l'époque de Saint-Louis.* Paris, 2001.

Lekai, Louis J. *The Cistercians: Ideals and Reality.* Kent, Ohio, 1977.

Leniaud, Jean-Michel, and Françoise Perrot. *La Sainte Chapelle.* Paris, 1991.

Leonelli, M.-Cl. "Mémoires pour la vie de saint Louis. Rheims. La Pucelle d'Orléans. Les énergumènes et la sorcellerie . . ." In *L'universel épistolier. Nicolas-Claude Fabri de Peiresc (1580–1637).* Carpentras, France, 1998, 103–108.

Leroquais, Victor. *Les bréviaires manuscrits de bibliothèques publiques de France.* 5 vols. Paris, 1934.

——. *Les livres d'heures manuscrits de la Bibliothèque nationale.* Paris, 1927.

——. *Les sacramentaires et les missels manuscrits des bibliothèques publiques de France.* 3 vols. Paris, 1924.

Lettrone. "Sur l'authenticité d'une lettre de Thibaud, roi de Navarre, relative à la mort de saint Louis." *Bibliothèque de l'École des Chartes* 5 (1843–1844): 105–117.

Levillain, Léon. "L'office divin dans l'abbaye de Saint-Denis." *Revue Mabillon* 1 (1905): 54–72.

Lewis, Andrew. *Royal Succession in Capetian France: Studies on Familial Order and the State.* Cambridge, Mass., 1981.

——. "Suger's Views on Kingship." In *Abbot Suger and Saint-Denis: A Symposium.* Edited by Paula Lieber Gerson. New York, 1986, 49–54.

Lewis, Ewart. *Medieval Political Ideas.* 2 vols. New York, 1954.

Libro de Horas de la reina Maria de Navarra: cuyo original se conserva en la Biblioteca Nazionale Marciana, Venecia, bajo la referencia Lat. I, 104 (=12640): Officium. 1 + commentary vols. Barcelona, 1996.

Linehan, Peter, and Francisco J. Hernández. "'Animadverto': A Recently Discovered *Consilium* concerning the Sanctity of King Louis IX." *Revue Mabillon* 66 (1994): 83–105.

Little, Lester K. "Saint Louis' Involvement with the Friars." *Church History* 33 (1963): 125–147.

Livre de Guillaume le Maire. Edited by Célestin Port. Paris, 1877.

Lombard-Jourdan, Anne. *Fleur de lis et oriflamme: signes célestes du royaume de France.* Paris, 1991.

Longère, Jean. *La prédication médiévale.* Paris, 1983.

Longnon, Auguste. *Documents parisiens sur l'iconographie de S. Louis.* Paris, 1882.

Louvre, Musée du. *Le trésor de la Sainte-Chapelle.* Paris, 2001.

Lower, Michael. "Conversion and Saint Louis's Last Crusade." *Journal of Ecclesiastical History* 58 (2007): 211–231.

Lucken, Christopher. "L'Évangile du Roi: Joinville, témoin et auteur de la *Vie de Saint Louis.*" *Annales: histoire, sciences sociales* 56 (2001): 445–467.

Lütolf, Max. *Analecta hymnica medii aevi: Register.* Bern, 1978.

Maier, Christoph T. *Crusade Propaganda and Ideology: Model Sermons for the Preaching of the Cross.* Cambridge, 2000.

——. "Mass, the Eucharist, and the Cross: Innocent III and the Relocation of the Crusade." In *Pope Innocent III and His World.* Edited by John Moore. Brookfield, Vt., 1999, 351–360.

Mâle, Emile. "La vie de Saint Louis dans l'art français au commencement du XIVe siècle." In *Mélanges Bertaux: recueil de travaux, dédié a la mémoire d'Émile Bertaux.* Paris, 1924, 193–204.

Manion, Margaret M. "Women, Art, and Devotion: Three French Fourteenth-Century Royal Prayer Books." In *The Art of the Book: Its Place in Medieval Worship.* Edited by Margaret M. Manion and Bernard J. Muir. Exeter, 1998, 21–67.

Marlot, Guillaume. *Histoire de la ville, cité et université de Reims, métropolitaine de la Gaule Belgique.* 4 vols. Reims, 1843–1846.

Marrone, John, and Charles Zuckerman. "Cardinal Simon-of-Beaulieu and Relations between Philip-the-Fair and Boniface VIII." *Traditio* 31 (1975): 195–222.

Martin, Hervé. *Le métier de prédicateur à la fin du moyen âge, 1350–1520.* Paris, 1988.

Martin, Victor. *Les origines du gallicanisme.* Paris, 1939.

McGinn, Bernard. *The Presence of God: A History of Western Christian Mysticism.* Vol. 2, *The Growth of Mysticism.* 3 vols. New York, 1991.

McGrade, Michael. "O Rex Mundi Triumphator: Hohenstaufen Politics in a Sequence for Saint Charlemange." *Early Music History* 17 (1998): 183–219.

Menestò, Enrico, and Stefano Brufani, eds. *Fontes Franciscani,* Assisi, 1995.

Mercuri, Chiara. *Corona di Cristo corona di re: la monarchia francese e la corona di spine nel Medioevo.* Rome, 2004.

——. "Les reflets sur l'iconographie de la translation de la couronne d'épines en France." In *Reliques et sainteté dans l'espace médiéval.* Edited by Jean-Luc Deuffic. St.-Denis, 2006, 117–126.

——. "Stat inter spinas lilium: le lys de France et la couronne d'épines." *Moyen âge* 110 (2004): 497–512.

Mertzman, Tania. "An Examination of Miniatures of the Office of St. Louis in Jeanne de Navarre's Book of Hours." *Athanor* 12 (1994): 19–25.

Meyer, Paul. "Notice: Daspol (Vers 1270)." *Bibliothèque de l'École des Chartes* 30 (1869): 280–289.

Meyvaert, Paul. "The Medieval Monastic Claustrum." *Gesta* 12 (1973): 53–59.

Migne, J.-P., ed. *Patrologia cursus completus.* 221 vols. Paris, 1844–1891.

Milis, Ludovicus. *Angelic Monks and Earthly Men: Monasticism and Its Meaning to Medieval Society.* Woodbridge, UK, 1992.

Minois, Georges. *Le confesseur du roi: les directeurs de conscience sous la monarchie française.* Paris, 1988.

Miskuly, Jason M. "Julian of Speyer: Life of St. Francis (*Vita Sancti Francisci*)." *Franciscan Studies* 49 (1989): 93–174.

Mlynarcyk, Gertrud. *Ein Franziskanerinnenkloster im 15. Jahrhundert.* Bonn, 1987.

Molinier, Auguste, and Louis M. Polain. *Les sources de l'histoire de France des origines aux guerres d'Italie (1494).* Vol 3, *Les capétiens, 1180–1328.* Paris, 1903.

Mombritius, Boninus. *Sanctuarium seu Vitae Sanctorum*. Milan, 1477.

Monfrin, Jacques. "Introduction." In *Vie de Saint Louis*. Paris, 1995, 11–142.

Montfaucon, Bernard de. *Les monuments de la monarchie françoise, qui comprennent l'histoire de France*. 5 vols. Paris, 1729–1733.

Monumenta Ordinis fratrum praedicatorum historica. 27 vols. Rome, 1896–.

Moorman, John. *A History of the Franciscan Order from Its Origins to the Year 1517*. Chicago, 1968.

Morand, Kathleen. *Jean Pucelle*. Oxford, 1962.

Morand, M. Sauveru-Jérôme. *Histoire de la Sainte-Chapelle royale*. Paris, 1790.

Morel, Pierre. "Le culte de Saint Louis." *Itineraires, documents* (1970): 127–151.

———. *Le culte de saint Louis et les vocables paroissiaux*. Paris, n.d.

Morello, Giovanni, and Ambrogio Piazzoni. *Diventare Santo: Itinerari e riconoscimenti della santità tra libri, documenti e immagini*. Vatican City, 1998.

Muessig, Carolyn, ed. *Preacher, Sermon and Audience in the Middle Ages*. Leiden, 2002.

Murray, Alexander Calladar. "*Post vocantur Merohingii*: Fredegar, Merovech, and 'Sacral Kingship.'" In *After Rome's Fall: Narrators and Sources of Early Medieval History. Essays Presented to Walter Goffart*. Edited by Alexander Calladar Murray. Toronto, 1998, 120–152.

Naughton, Joan. "Books for a Dominican Nuns' Choir: Illustrated Liturgical Manuscripts at Saint-Louis de Poissy, c. 1330–1350." In *The Art of the Book: Its Place in Medieval Worship*. Edited by Margaret M. Manion and Bernard J. Muir. Exeter, 1998, 67–110.

Naughton, Joan M. "Manuscripts from the Dominican Monastery of Saint-Louis de Poissy." Ph.D. diss., University of Melbourne, 1995.

Nelson, Janet. "Royal Saints and Early Medieval Kingship." In *Sanctity and Secularity: The Church and the World*. Edited by Derek Baker. New York, 1973, 39–44.

Neveu, Bruno. "Du culte de saint Louis à la glorification de Louis XIV: la maison royale de Saint-Cyr." *Journal des Savants* (1988): 277–290.

The New Interpreter's Bible: General Articles and Introduction, Commentary, and Reflections for Each Book of the Bible, including the Apocryphal Deuterocanonical Books. 13 vols. Edited by Abingdon Press. Nashville, Tenn., 1994.

Newman, Martha. *The Boundaries of Charity: Cistercian Culture and Ecclesiastical Reform, 1098–1180*. Stanford, Calif., 1996.

Noel, William, and Daniel Weiss, eds. *The Book of Kings: Art, War, and the Morgan Library's Medieval Picture Bible*. London, 2002.

Nold, Patrick. "Bertrand de la Tour: Life and Works." *Archivum Franciscanum Historicum* 94 (2001): 274–323.

———. *Pope John XXII and His Franciscan Cardinal: Bertrand de la Tour and the Apostolic Poverty Controversy*. Oxford, 2003.

Nora, Pierre, ed., *Realms of Memory*. Translated by Arthur Goldhammer. 3 vols. New York, 1996–1998.

Oakley, Francis. *The Western Church in the Later Middle Ages*. Ithaca, N.Y., 1979.

O'Carroll, Maura. "The Friars and the Liturgy in the Thirteenth Century." In *La predicazione dei frati dalla metà del '200 alla fine del '300*. Spoleto, Italy, 1995, 189–227.

O'Connell, David. *The Instructions of Saint Louis: A Critical Text*. Chapel Hill, N.C., 1979.

———. *The Teachings of Saint Louis: A Critical Text*. Chapel Hill, N.C., 1972.

O'Meara, Carra Ferguson. *Monarchy and Consent: The Coronation Book of Charles V of France, British Library MS Cotton Tiberius B. VIII*. London, 2001.

Omont, Henri. "Gui de Châtres, Abbé de Saint-Denys, auteur d'un Sanctilogium." In *Histoire littéraire de la France*, 1927, 627–630.

———. "Inventaire des livres de Jean Courtecuisse, évèque de Paris et de Genève (27 Octobre 1423)." *Bibliothèque de l'École des Chartes* 80 (1919): 109–120.

———. "Le *Sanctilogium* de Gui de Châtres, Abbé de Saint-Denys." *Bibliothèque de l'École des Chartes* 86 (1925): 407–410.

O'Neill, John Philip. *Enamels of Limoges: 1100–1350.* Translated by Joachim Neugroschel, Sophie Hawkes, and Patricia Stirneman. New York, 1996.

Ordonnances des roys de France de la troisième race, recueillies par ordre chronologique. Edited by Eusèbe Laurière et al. 21 vols. Paris, 1723.

Oroux, Abbé. *Histoire ecclésiastique de la cour de France, Où l'on trouve tout ce qui concern l'histoire de la chapelle et des principaux officiers ecclésiastique de nos rois.* Paris, 1776.

Palazzo, Eric. *A History of Liturgical Books from the Beginning to the Thirteenth Century.* Collegeville, Minn., 1998.

Panella, Emilio. "Nuova Cronologia Remigiana," *Archivum Fratrum Praedicatorum* 60 (1990): 201–202.

Paris, Gaston. "Jean, sire de Joinville." In *Histoire littéraire de la France.* Vol. 31 (1898), 291–451.

——. "La composition du livre de Joinville sur saint Louis." *Romania* 23 (1894): 508–524.

Paris, Matthew. *Matthæai Parisiensis, monachi Sancti Albani, Chronica majora.* 7 vols. London, 1872.

Paris, Paulin. "Le confesseur de la reine Marguerite, auteur de la Vie et des Miracles de saint Louis." In *Histoire littéraire de la France.* Vol. 25 (1869): 154–177.

Pelikan, Jaroslav. "Christ—and the second Christ." *The Yale Review* 74 (1985): 321–345.

Penco, Gregorio. "Monasterium—Carcer." *Studia monastica* 8 (1966): 133–143.

Perret, Michèle. "A la fin de sa vie ne fuz je mie." *Revue des sciences humaines* (1981–1983): 17–37.

Perrot, Jean-Pierre. "Le 'péché' de Joinville: Écriture du souvenir et imaginaire hagiographique." In *Le prince et son historien: la vie de Saint Louis de Joinville.* Paris, 1997, 183–207.

Pfleger, Lucien. "Le culte de Saint Louis en Alsace." *Revue des sciences religeuses* (1921).

Picot, Georges. *Documents relatifs aux États généraux et Assemblée: réunis sous Philippe le Bel.* Paris, 1901.

Pinoteau, Hervé. "La main de justice des rois de France: Essai d'explication." *Bulletin de la Société Nationale des Antiquaires de France* (1982): 262–264.

——. *La symbolique royale française: Ve–XVIIIe siècles.* La Roche-Rigault, France, 2003.

——. "La tenue de sacre de Saint Louis IX roi de France son arrière-plan symbolique de la 'renovatio regni juda.'" In *Vingt-cinq ans d'études dynastiques.* Paris, 1982, 447–504.

Pizan, Christine de. *Le Livre des faits et bonnes moeurs du roi Charles V le Sage; traduction, avec introduction, chronologie et index par Eric Hicks et Thérèse Moreau.* Paris, 1997.

Plagnieux, Philippe. "Une foundation de la reine Marie de Brabant: La chapelle Saint-Paul Saint-Louis." In *Mantes médiévale: La collégiale au coeur de la ville.* Paris, 2000, 110–116.

Potthast, Augustus, ed. *Regesta pontificum romanorum inde ab a. post Christum natum MCXCVIII ad A. MCCCIV.* 2 vols. London, 1875.

Prigent, Christiane, ed. *Art et société en France au XVe siècle,* Paris, 1999.

Pryds, Darleen N. *The King Embodies the Word: Robert d'Anjou and the Politics of Preaching.* Leiden, 2000.

Quétif, Jacques, Jacques Échard, and Remi Coulon. *Scriptores ordinis Praedicatorum.* Louvain, 1961.

Randall, Lilian M. C. "Games and the passion in Pucelle's Hours of Jeanne d'Evreux." *Speculum* 47 (1972): 246–257.

Recueil d'anciens inventaires imprimés sous les auspices du Comité des travaux historiques et scientifiques: Section d'archéologie. Vol. 1: *Inventaires de l'abbaye de Notre-Dame la Royale dite Maubuisson de Pontoise.* Paris, 1896.

Reinburg, Virginia. "Remembering the Saints." In *Memory and the Middle Ages.* Edited by Nancy Netzer and Virginia Reinburg. Boston, 1995, 17–33.

Renna, Thomas. "Kingship in the *Disputatio Inter Clericum et Militem.*" *Speculum* 48 (1973): 675–693.

Riant, Paul Edouard Didier. "Déposition de Charles d'Anjou pour la canonisation de saint Louis." In Notices et documents publiés pour la Société de l'histoire de France à l'occasion du cinquantième anniversaire de sa fondation. Paris, 1884, 155–176.

——. Exuviae sacrae constantinopolitanae fasciculus documentorum minorum, ad exuvias sacras constantinopolitanas in occidentem saeculo XIII translatas, spectantium, & historiam quarti belli sacri imperijo: gallo-graeci illustrantium. Geneva, 1876.

Ribadeau-Dumas, François. Histoire de St. Germain des Prés, abbaye royale. Paris, 1958.

Richard, Jean. Saint Louis: Crusader King of France. Translated by Jean Birrell. Edited by Simon Lloyd. Cambridge, 1992.

Richard, Jules-Marie. Une petite nièce de Saint Louis: Mahaut, comtesse d'Artois et de Bourgogne (1302–1329). Etude sur la vie privée, les arts et l'industrie, en Artois et à Paris au commencement du XIVe siècle. Paris, 1887.

Ridyard, Susan J. The Royal Saints of Anglo-Saxon England: A Study of West Saxon and East Anglian Cults. Cambridge, 1988.

Ripoll, Thomás, and Antonin Brémond. Bullarium Ordinis FF. [i.e. Fratrum] Præadicatorum: sub auspiciis SS. D.N.D. Benedicti XIII, pontificis maximi, ejusdem Ordinis. Rome, 1729.

Robertson, Anne Walters. The Service-Books of the Royal Abbey of Saint-Denis: Images of Ritual and Music in the Middle Ages. Oxford, 1991.

Roisin, Simone. L'hagiographie cistercienne dans le diocèse de Liège au XIIIe siècle. Louvain, 1947.

Rollason, D. W. "The Cult of Murdered Royal Saints in Anglo-Saxon England." Anglo-Saxon England 11 (1983): 1–22.

Rouse, Richard. "Mahiet, the Illuminator of Cambridge University Library, MS Dd.5.5." In The Cambridge Illuminations: the Conference Papers. Edited by Stella Panayotova. New York, 2007, 173–186.

Rouse, Richard, and Mary Rouse. "Mary de St.-Pol and Cambridge University Library Ms Dd.5.5." In The Cambridge Illuminations: the Conference Papers. Edited by Stella Panayotova. New York, 2007, 187–191.

Rubin, Miri. "Choosing Death? Experiences of Martydom in Late Medieval Europe." In Martyrs and Martyrologies. Papers Read at the 1992 Summer Meeting and the 1993 Winter Meeting of the Ecclesiastical History Society. Oxford, 1993, 153–183.

Salimbene. The Chronicle of Salimbene de Adam. Binghamton, N.Y., 1986.

Salmon, Pierre. L'Office divin au Moyen âge, histoire de la formation du bréviaire du IXe au XVIe siècle. Paris, 1967.

Saulnier-Pinsard, Alix. "Une nouvelle oeuvre du Maitre de San Marcos: le Livre d'Heures de Marie de Navarre." In La Miniatura Italiana tra Gotico e Rinascimento. I: Atti del II Congresso di Storia della Minatura Italiana, Cortona 24–26 Settembre 1982. Edited by Emanuela Sesti. Florence, 1985, 35–50.

Sbaralea, J.-H., ed. Bullarium Franciscanum. 4 vols. Rome, 1759–1768.

Scandaletti, Tiziana. "Una ricognizione sull'ufficio ritmico per S. Francesco." Musica et storia 4 (1996): 67–101.

Schein, Sylvia. "Philip IV and the Crusade: A Reconsideration." In Crusade and Settlement. Edited by Peter W. Edbury. Cardiff, 1985, 121–126.

Schneyer, Jean-Baptist. Repertorium der lateinischen Sermones des Mittelalters für die Zeit von 1150–1350. 11 vols. Münster, 1969–1973.

Schneyer, Jean-Baptist. Repertorium der lateinischen Sermones des Mittelalters für die Zeit von 1150–1350. CD-ROM. Münster, 2001.

Scholz, Bernhard. "The Canonization of Edward the Confessor." Speculum 36 (1961): 38–60.

Schrade, Leo. "Political Compositions in French Music of the 12th and 13th Centuries." Annales musicologiques 1 (1953): 9–63.

Schramm, Percy Ernst. Der König von Frankreich: das Wesen der Monarchie vom 9. zum 16. Jahrhundert, ein Kapitel aus der Geschichte des abendländischen Staates. 2 vols. Weimar, 1960.

Schwarzenberg, Erkinger. "Der Hl. Ludwig von Frankreich in Anbetung der Reliquien der Sainte Chapelle auf einer toskanischen Schüssel des späten Trecento." *Mitteilungen des Kunsthistorischen Institutes in Florenz* (1985): 159–173.

Sedulius Scottus. *On Christian Rulers, and the Poems.* Translated by Edward G. Doyle. Binghamton, N.Y., 1983.

Serper, Arié. "Le roi Saint Louis et le poete Rutebeuf." *Romance Notes* 9 (1967): 134–140.

Simons, Walter. "Aantekeningen bij de XIVde-eeuwse geschiedenis van de timmerliedenbroederschap in de Brugse franciscanenkerk." *Het Brugs Ommeland* (1985): 155–160.

Sivéry, Gérard. *Louis IX: le roi saint.* Paris, 2002.

———. *Saint Louis et son siècle.* Paris, 1983.

Slattery, Maureen. *Myth, Man, and Sovereign Saint: King Louis IX in Jean de Joinville's Sources.* New York, 1985.

Slocum, Kay Brainerd. *Liturgies in Honour of Thomas Becket.* Toronto, 2004.

Smalley, Beryl. *English Friars and Antiquity in the Early Fourteenth Century.* New York, 1960.

Smith, Caroline. *Crusading in the Age of Joinville.* Burlington, Vt., 2006.

———. "Martyrdom and Crusading in the Thirteenth Century: Remembering the Dead of Louis IX's Crusades." *Al-Masaq: Islam and the Medieval Mediterranean* 15 (2003): 189–196.

Spiegel, Gabrielle. "Memory and History: Liturgical Time and Hisstorical Time." *History and Theory* 41 (2002): 149–162.

———. *The Chronicle Tradition of Saint-Denis: A Survey.* Brookline, Mass., 1978.

———. "The Cult of Saint Denis and Capetian Kingship." *Journal of Medieval History* 1 (1975): 43–69.

———. "Political Utility in Medieval Historiography: A Sketch." *History and Theory* 14 (1975): 314–325.

———. "The reditus regni ad stirpem Karoli Magni: A New Look." *French Historical Studies* 7 (1971): 145–174.

Spiegel, Gabrielle, and Sandra Hindman. "The Fleur-de-lis Frontispiece to Guillaume de Nangis' *Chronique abrégée*: Political Iconography in Late Fifteenth-Century France." *Viator* 12 (1981): 381–407.

Stahl, Harvey. "Old Testament Illustration during the Reign of St. Louis: The Morgan Picture Book and the New Biblical Cycles." *Il Medio Oriente e l'Occidente nell'arte del XIII secolo* (1982): 79–93.

———. *Picturing Kingship: History and Painting in the Psalter of Saint Louis.* University Park, Pa., 2008.

Starbuck, Scott R. A. *Court Oracles in the Psalms: The So-Called Royal Psalms in Their Ancient Near Eastern Context.* Atlanta, Ga., 1999.

Sterling, Charles. *La peinture médiévale à Paris: 1300–1500.* 2 vols. Paris, 1987.

Stock, Brian. *The Implications of Literacy: Written Language and Models of Interpretation in the Eleventh and Twelfth Centuries.* Princeton, N.J., 1983.

Strayer, Joseph R. "The Crusade against Aragon." *Speculum* 28 (1953): 102–113.

———. "France: The Holy Land, the Chosen People, and the Most Christian King." In *Action and Conviction in Early Modern Europe: Essays in Memory of E. H. Harbison.* Edited by Theodore K. Rabb and Jerrold E. Seigel. Princeton, N.J., 1969, 3–16.

———. *On the Medieval Origins of the Modern State.* Princeton, N.J., 1970.

———. *The Reign of Philip the Fair.* Princeton, N.J., 1980.

Suger. *The Deeds of Louis the Fat.* Edited by Richard Cusimano and John Moorhead. Washington, D.C., 1992.

Szövérffy, Josef. *Die Annalen der lateinischen Hymnendichtung: Ein Handbuch.* 2 vols. Vol. 2: *Die lateinischen Hymnen vom Ende des 11. Jahrhunderts bis zum Ausgang des Mittelalters.* Berlin, 1965.

Szövérffy, Joseph. *Latin Hymns.* Turnhout, Belgium, 1989.

Taylor, Judy. "Rhymed Offices at the Sainte-Chapelle in the Thirteenth Century: Historical, Political, and Liturgical Contexts." Ph.D. diss., University of Texas at Austin, 1994.

Taylor, Larissa. *Soldiers of Christ: Preaching in Late Medieval and Reformation France.* New York, 1992.

Tesseyre, Charles. "Le prince chrétien aux XVe et XVIe siècles, à travers les représentations de Charlemagne et de Saint Louis." *Annales de Bretagne* 87 (1980): 409–414.

Thomas Aquinas. *On Kingship, to the King of Cyprus.* Edited by G. B. Phelan. 2d ed. Toronto, 1982.

——. *Summa Theologiae. Latin Text and English Translation, Introductions, Notes, Appendices, and Glossaries.* 60 vols. Cambridge, 1964–1976.

Thomas, Marcel. "L'iconographie de Saint Louis, dans les *Heures de Jeanne de Navarre.*" In *Septième centenaire de la mort de Saint Louis: Actes des colloques de Royaumont et de Paris (21–27 mai 1970).* Paris, 1976, 209–231.

Thompson, Nancy. "Cooperation and Conflict: Stained Glass in the Bardi Chapel of Santa Croce." In *The Art of the Franciscan Order in Italy.* Edited by William R. Cook. Leiden, 2005, 257–277.

Thomson, Williell. *Friars in the Cathedral: The First Franciscan Bishops, 1226–1261.* Toronto, 1975.

Tietz, Manfred. "Saint Louis roi chretien: un mythe de la mission interieure du XVIIe siecle." In *La conversion au XVIIe siècle: actes du XIIe Colloque de Marseille (janvier 1982).* Marseille, 1983, 59–69.

Tillemont, Sébastien Le Nain de. *Vie de Saint Louis, roi de France.* 6 vols. Paris, 1847–1851.

Toynbee, Margaret. *Saint Louis of Toulouse and the Process of Canonisation in the Fourteenth Century.* Manchester, 1929.

Treitler, Leo. "Oral, written, and literate process in the transmission of medieval music." *Speculum* 56 (1981): 471–491.

Trexler, Richard. *Naked before the Father: The Renunciation of Francis of Assisi.* Edited by Peter Lang. New York, 1989.

Tyerman, Christopher. "Philip VI and the Recovery of the Holy Land." *English Historical Review* 100 (1985): 25–52.

Tyvaert, Michael. "L'image du roi: légitimité et moralité royales dans les histoires de France au XVIIe siècle." *Revue d'histoire moderne et contemporaine* 21 (1974): 521–547.

Uitti, Karl. "Novelle et structure hagiographique: Le recit historiographique nouveau de Jean de Joinville." In *Mittelalterbilder aus neuer Perspektive* 1985, 380–391.

Ullmann, Walter. "A Medieval Document on Papal Theories of Government." *English Historical Review* 61 (1946): 180–201.

Vale, Malcomb G. A. *Charles VII.* Berkeley, Calif., 1974.

——. *The Princely Court: Medieval Courts and Culture in North-west Europe, 1270–1380.* Oxford, 2001.

Valois, Noël. *Histoire de la Pragmatique Sanction de Bourges sous Charles VII.* Paris, 1906.

Van den Wyngaert, A. "Querelles du clergé séculier et des ordres mendiants à Paris au XIIIe siècle." *France Franciscaine* 5 and 6 (1922–1923): 5: 257–281; 6: 46–70.

Van Dijk, Stephen Joseph Peter. *Sources of the Modern Roman Liturgy; The Ordinals by Haymo of Faversham and Related Documents (1243–1307).* Leiden, 1963.

Van Os, H. W. "St. Francis of Assisi as a Second Christ in Early Italian Painting." *Simiolus* 7 (1974): 115–132.

Vauchez, André. "*Beata stirps:* sainteté et lignage en occident aux XIIIe et XIVe siècles." In *Famille et parenté dans l'Occident médiéval.* Rome, 1977, 397–406.

——. "Lay People's Sanctity in Western Europe: Evolution of a Pattern (Twelfth and Thirteenth Centuries)." In *Images of Sainthood in Medieval Europe.* Edited by Renate Blumenfeld-Kosinski and Timea Szell. Ithaca, N.Y., 1991, 21–32.

——. *Sainthood in the Later Middle Ages.* Translated by Jean Birrell. Cambridge, 1997.

——. "The Stigmata of St. Francis and Its Medieval Detractors." *Greyfriars Review* 13 (1999): 61–89.

Viard, Jules Marie Édouard, ed.. *Les Grandes chroniques de France.* 10 vols. Paris, 1920.

——. *Les journaux du trésor de Philippe IV le Bel.* Paris, 1940.

Vidier, Alexandre. *Extraits de comptes royaux concernant Paris: I. Journal du tresor (1298–1301)*. Paris, 1912.
——. *Le trésor de La Sainte-Chapelle: inventaires et documents*. Paris, 1911.
Villeneuve, Marquis de. *Histoire de saint Louis, roi de France*. 3 vols. Paris, 1839.
Vincent of Beauvais. *De morali principis institutione*. Edited by Robert J. Schneider. Turnhout, Belgium, 1995.
Viollet, Paul. "Les Enseignements de saint Louis à son fils." *Bibliothéque de l'École des Chartes* 35 (1874): 1–56.
Vogel, Cyrille, and Reinhard Elze, eds., *Le Pontifical romano-germanique du dixième siècle*. 2 vols. Rome, Vatican City, 1963.
Von Campehausen, Hans. "The Ascetic Idea of Exile in Ancient and Early Medieval Monasticism." In *Tradition and Life in the Early Church: Essays and Lectures in Church History*. Philadelphia, 1968, 231–251.
Wailly, Natalis de, ed. *Histoire de Saint Louis, par Jean sire de Joinville, suivie du Credo et de la letter à Louis X*. Paris, 1868.
——. "Mémoire sur le 'roman' ou chronique en langue vulgaire dont Joinville a reproduit plusieurs passages." *Bibliotheque de l'École des Chartes* 35 (1874): 217–248.
Wallace-Hadrill, J. M. *Early Germanic Kingship in England and on the Continent*. Oxford, 1971.
——. "The *Via Regia* of the Carolingian Age." In *Trends in Medieval Political Thought*. Edited by Beryl Smalley. Oxford, 1965, 22–41.
Weinstein, Donald, and Rudolph Bell. *Saints and Society: The Two Worlds of Western Christendom, 1100–1700*. Chicago, 1982.
Weiss, Daniel. "Architectural Symbolism and the Decoration of the Ste.-Chapelle." *Art Bulletin* 77 (1995): 308–320.
——. *Art and Crusade in the Age of Saint Louis*. Cambridge, 1998.
Wieck, Roger S. *Painted Prayers: The Book of Hours in Medieval and Renaissance Art*. New York, 1997.
——. "Savoy Hours and Its Impact on Jean, Duc de Berry." *Yale University Library Gazette* 66 (1991): 159–180.
——. *Time Sanctified: The Book of Hours in Medieval Art and Life*. New York, 1988.
Wood, Charles T. *Philip the Fair and Boniface VIII: State vs. Papacy*. 2d ed. New York, 1971.
Wright, Craig M. *Music and Ceremony at Notre Dame of Paris, 500–1550*. Cambridge, 1989.
Wright, Georgia Sommers. "The Royal Tomb Program in the Reign of St. Louis." *Art Bulletin* 56 (1974): 224–243.
——. "The Tomb of Saint Louis." *Journal of the Warburg and Courtauld Institutes* 34 (1971): 65–82.
Yarza, Joaquin. "Ferrer Bassa revisado." In *Arte d'Occidente: temi e metodi: studi in onore di Angiola Maria Romanini*. Rome, 1999, 715–725.
Zink, Michel. *The Invention of Literary Subjectivity*. Translated by David Sices. Baltimore, 1999.
Ziolkowski, Jan. "The Highest Form of Compliment: *Imitatio* in Medieval Latin Culture." In *Poetry and Philosophy in the Middle Ages: A Festschrift for Peter Dronke*. Edited by John Marenbon. Leiden, 2001, 293–305.
Zobermann, Pierre. "Généalogie d'une image: L'éloge speculaire." *XVIIe Siècle* 146 (1985): 79–92.

Index

In this index, the page number suffixes, *t, d,* and *m* indicate a table, diagram, or map on that page. An *n* indicates a note; thus 162n35 refers to note 35 on page 162. Page numbers in full *italics* indicate photographs.